The Intellectual Roots
of the Italian Enlightenment

Originally published as *Scienza natura religione: Mondo newtoniano e cultura italiana nel primo Sottecento*, © 1982 by Casa Editrice Jovene—Napoli.

Published by Humanity Books, an imprint of Prometheus Books

Inquiries should be addressed to
Humanity Books
59 John Glenn Drive
Amherst, New York 14228–2197
VOICE: 716–691–0133, ext. 207
FAX: 716–564–2711

04 03 02 01 00   6 5 4 3 2

Library of Congress Cataloging-in-Publication Data

Ferrone, Vincenzo.
   [Scienza natura religione. English]
   The intellectual roots of the Italian Enlightenment : Newtonian science, religion, and politics in the early eighteenth century / Vincenzo Ferrone ; translated by Sue Brotherton.
      p. cm.
   This translation originally published: Atlantic Highlands, N.J. : Humanities Press International, 1995.
   Includes bibliographical references and index.
   ISBN 1–57392–452–0
   1. Religion and science—Italy—History—18th century. 2. Natural theology—History of doctrines—18th century. 3. Newton, Isaac, Sir, 1642–1727—Influence. 4. Enlightenment—Italy. 5. Italy—Intellectual life—1559—1789. I. Title.

BL240.2.F45713 1994
261.5'5'094509033—dc20
                                           93–34485
                                            CIP

Printed in the United States of America on acid-free paper

The Intellectual Roots of the Italian Enlightenment

Newtonian Science, Religion, and Politics in the Early Eighteenth Century

VINCENZO FERRONE

Translated by
SUE BROTHERTON

This publication was made possible
through the cooperation of
Biblioteca Italia, a Giovanni Agnelli Foundation
programme for the
diffusion of Italian culture.

Humanity
Books

an imprint of Prometheus Books
59 John Glenn Drive, Amherst, New York 14228-2197

Originally published as *Scienza natura religione:
Mondo newtoniano e cultura italiana nel primo Sottecento*,
© 1982 by Casa Editrice Jovene—Napoli.

Published by Humanity Books, an imprint of Prometheus Books

Inquiries should be addressed to
Humanity Books
59 John Glenn Drive
Amherst, New York 14228–2197
VOICE: 716–691–0133, ext. 207
FAX: 716–564–2711

04 03 02 01 00   6 5 4 3 2

Library of Congress Cataloging-in-Publication Data

Ferrone, Vincenzo.
    [Scienza natura religione. English]
    The intellectual roots of the Italian Enlightenment : Newtonian sci-
ence, religion, and politics in the early eighteenth century / Vincenzo
Ferrone ; translated by Sue Brotherton.
        p. cm.
    This translation originally published: Atlantic Highlands, N.J. :
Humanities Press International, 1995.
    Includes bibliographical references and index.
    ISBN 1–57392–452–0
    1. Religion and science—Italy—History—18th century. 2. Natural
theology—History of doctrines—18th century. 3. Newton, Isaac, Sir,
1642–1727—Influence. 4. Enlightenment—Italy. 5. Italy—Intellectual
life—1559—1789. I. Title.
BL240.2.F45713 1994
261.5'5'094509033—dc20   93–34485
                                                                CIP

Printed in the United States of America on acid-free paper

Contents

Foreword

The postwar generation of American and British scholars who have interpreted the Enlightenment have done so with a vision that has been biased towards the Atlantic. By contrast with the Continental European historiography that begins with Cassirer and culminates with Peter Gay and Franco Venturi, our writings have been dominated by events in Paris, London, Edinburgh, sometimes Berlin, and, occasionally, The Hague and Amsterdam. The publication of Vincenzo Ferrone's important book on Italian intellectual life from the 1680s to the 1750s, coming as it does from one of the leaders of the generation that matriculated through the Italian universities in the 1970s, should have the effect of turning our attention south. This is a magisterial work from a senior colleague, now Professor of Modern History in Venice, from whom we have a great deal to learn and who, with this translation, can finally be known more widely and deeply.

Some of the themes present in Ferrone's study of the early Enlightenment in Italy are already known from the translated writings of Giuseppe Ricuperati and Franco Venturi: the central role of Newtonianism, the vitality of Italian materialism, the influence of Toland's writings in those circles, and, most especially, the ideological, practical, and reformist nature of enlightened and progressive thought in the heartland of the Inquisition. But the originality of Ferrone's massive study lies in the depth that he brings to each of these themes, the richness of his archival discoveries, his sense of regional and local diversity, and, most originally, his articulation of a moderate Enlightenment, rooted in a Catholic milieu but deeply indebted to the writings of Newton, Samuel Clarke, Derham, Cheyne, and the Boyle lecturers in general. At the center of this extraordinary search for a middle way between the extremes of the Inquisition and the temptations of materialism stands the figure of Celestino Galiani.

Ferrone's fascinating exposition of Galiani and of intellectual life in Naples, Rome, and Venice should nip in the bud any attempt to approach eighteenth-century Italian intellectual life that downplays the power and danger posed by the Inquisitional clergy. As a devout Catholic priest, eventually a bishop, dedicated to reforming the Church from within and hence to a lifelong struggle with his clerical colleagues, Galiani decided to publish virtually nothing. Thus uncommitted in print, he was immune to censure. As a result of this self-imposed public silence, Galiani's entire life and its passionate search for moderation and enlightenment had to be pieced together by Ferrone and others largely from his unpublished writings.

While most students of Newtonianism know the Abbé Conti, Galiani turns out to be by far the more important figure in the Italian milieu that Ferrone patiently reconstructs. He brought to Italy the mathematical form of Newtonianism pioneered by the Dutch Newtonians. This he learned from direct contact with 'sGravesande, Marchand, and the semi-clandestine circle that produced the *Journal littéraire* for which Galiani was a collaborator. In a stroke, Galiani set Newtonian science into an Italian framework that was essentially phenomenological and empirical, sliding out from under the materialist implications of Newtonian matter theory and, in the process, robbing the Inquisition of its most valuable polemical strategy. In 1734 it had placed even Locke on the *Index of Forbidden Books*, having arrived at the view that he, too, had dangerously materialistic tendencies. Such was the atmosphere within which Galiani and the other moderate Catholic proponents of the Enlightenment had to operate. With tools provided them by Clarke and by other English as well as Dutch Newtonians, the reformist elements within the Italian Church used their own immense erudition to build an edifice of science-inspired religiosity, a shell that en-cased the eighteenth-century renewal of Italian science. By the 1730s Newtonianism had made inroads in Italian elite culture as deep as those to be found in France.

For those who like their Enlightenment less moderate, Ferrone's study will, however, be equally fascinating. Libertines, deists, materialists, Spinozists—and their many detractors—populate *The Intellectual Roots of the Italian Enlightenment*. In the 1690s the Neapolitan Inquisition put them on trial and thereby opened the first round in the struggle that Ferrone rightly sees not simply as another instance of repression but as the opening phase in Italy of Hazard's crisis, the turning point from which emerged a new secular culture. In Naples De Cristoforo recanted his atomism in 1697—at precisely the moment when the Boyle lecturers were preaching it from the London pulpits—but his school lived on there to influence the materialist Giannone and, possibly, Vico. Clandestine print shops, like that run by Lorenzo Ciccarelli, rivaled the ingenuity of their Dutch and French Huguenot counterparts. The Enlightenment, both moderate and radical, was woven into the fabric of Neapolitan political life as secularists, Newtonians, and Lockians vied for influence and power with Inquisitors and Aristotelians. Anyone familiar with the ideological role of science, religion, and philosophy in the political struggles of Whigs and Tories will understand the kind of contextual analysis that Ferrone has provided for Naples and the other major Italian intellectual centers. When in 1730 Count Radicati arrived in London preaching materialism, those were the ideological wars from which he had been forced to flee. Because of his habit of saying the outrageous in print, now in English translation, Radicati was again to be imprisoned, eventually to flee to the final resting place of refugees and clandestine publishers, the Dutch Republic.

By the 1730s the new secular culture, aggressive and mature, moved in jagged lines from Edinburgh to Naples, and everywhere the battle lines had emerged, with the devout, traditional, and orthodox in one corner, the materialists in the extreme opposite corner, and the moderates from Clarke through Galiani, and later to Kant, trying to mediate and refine centrist positions that in some quarters remain to this day the source of deep controversy and polemic. Ferrone has now placed Italian intellectual life within the framework of these triangulated cultural wars and has once again demonstrated the deeply international character of eighteenth-century European high culture.

In welcoming this American translation into print, I am also saluting its publisher and the Agnelli Foundation that made this translation possible. Keith Ashfield of Humanities Press should be congratulated for having the courage to undertake a highly technical work, dense in places (just take a look at those footnotes!), but one that all scholars will be immensely grateful for having in translation. The publisher's tenacity is comparable only to the vitality of Enzo Ferrone. In person as well as in print, he offers probably one of the most vital, engaging, and memorable experiences that any colleague and scholar can have. Professor Ferrone is passionate about ideas, indefatigable in the way one can only imagine Radicati or Galiani to have been. There is no cynicism or relativism in his approach to the secular and the enlightened, no coy retreat from modernity. Ferrone does not imagine that because Galileans or Newtonians could be courtiers and politicians with the best of their adversaries, we should remain indifferent to the outcome of the power struggle between those who drew up the *Index* and those who published in the backrooms of print shops, using phony imprints and selling under the counter to local clergymen.

Vincenzo Ferrone now belongs in the first tier of Italian scholars of his generation, deeply indebted to the Turin school, yet a scholar with his own voice. This is his first book in translation; there are many others of his now in Italian that should have a similar good fortune. As a friend and admirer of Enzo Ferrone—who made me think less provincially—I especially and gratefully recommend him to his now larger audience.

MARGARET C. JACOB
NEW SCHOOL FOR SOCIAL RESEARCH

Translator's Note

In the interests of space, the American translation of *Scienza Natura Religione* has substantially reduced the volume of information in the notes accompanying the text. No notes have been eliminated, and readers are urged to consult the corresponding notes in the Italian edition in order to take advantage of the wealth of archival material and in-depth observations offered by Professor Ferrone. The text is completely unabridged.

The bibliography is new to this edition of the work, and every effort has been made to locate English-language versions of the works cited.

I would like to thank Professor Ferrone for his courteous and good-humored assistance in the preparation of this translation. I am also in debt to the support and flexibility of the people at Humanities Press.

SUE BROTHERTON

Preface

This book intends not only to examine the dissemination of Newtonianism in Italy but also to comprehend its fundamental meaning in the culture of the early eighteenth century. From the very first phases of research, it was clear that in Italy, knowledge about and interest in the new cosmology were not engulfed in strictly scientific debates; rather, they presented extraordinary and complex aspects and a great richness of implications. Philosophy, politics, religion: all seemed to bear on the discussion of the new horizons that were opened and unexplored. One sign of the disquieting problems posed by the Newtonian world, before they were progressively reabsorbed and incorporated in a reassuring version, was that the entire Continent experienced what Paul Hazard has called "the crisis of European mind." Since this crisis everywhere assumed the characteristics of a revolution, not limited to the scientific realm but, rather, a harbinger of profound philosophical, religious, and more generally ideological innovations, the study of Newtonianism offers a privileged point of view that allows one to become acquainted with and understand one of the main conduits through which European culture was able to make its way to the Enlightenment. Just as in the rest of Europe, this occurred in Italy as well, where many powerful forces, as well as the limits and contradictions of Enlightenment thought, confronted their roots in the great debates of the first decades of the 1700s, disputes that certainly cannot be reduced to the tired literary debates in the Academy of Arcadia. In addition to Newton, Spinoza, Bayle, Le Clerc, Toland, Collins, and Locke, many other great intellectuals were also read and passionately discussed at the time, held aloft as standards of courageous battles or made the subject of fierce arguments. Their works finally brought Italy back into the heart of a very lively debate from which it had been marginalized for too long. Simultaneously, these readings, these texts, and these thoughts interwove with specific Italian cultural traditions, foremost among these being the great Galilean heritage, finding new meaning and significance in a reality different from the reality it had emerged from, a reality profoundly shaped by the ancient hegemony of Catholicism and the Roman Church.

As I bring this work to its fruition, it is not only for professional courtesy but with sincere gratitude that I wish to thank all those who have made possible the research here presented and who over the years offered me the indispensable support of their experience and friendship. To the "Fondazione Luigi Einaudi" of Turin I owe thanks not only for indispensable financial

xi

support but also for the opportunity that the foundation provided for encouragement and suggestions from Mario Einaudi and Franco Venturi. I am in debt to Raffaele Ajello for his welcome reception of my book in the Italian series where it first appeared, and for the help that he gave along with the valuable collaboration of his pupil Anna Casella, and above all for the affection that he has so often shown me. I am convinced that this work (for which, obviously, I assume complete responsibility) would have been very different without his advice, his stimulating suggestions, and the attention with which he was able to discuss entire chapters with me and reread the entire typescript. I wish to thank Salvatore Rotta for the extraordinary generosity with which he made available to me his inexhaustible knowledge of the eighteenth century and the fruits of his personal research, in particular some important unedited documents regarding Francesco Bianchini, his journey to England, and his relations with Newton. I am most grateful to Elvira Chiosi for her constructive suggestions, for intelligent and joint collaboration in my efforts, and for her constant friendship, on which I have always been able to rely. Finally, I gained insights from frequent conversations with Dino Carpanetto, Marisa Perna, and, especially, Giuseppe Ricuperati, who followed the entire course of my research with spirited criticism and shared concern. My greatest debt of gratitude goes to my dearest friends Massimo Firpo and Luciano Guerci for everything they taught me over many years of intense intellectual and scientific comradery, for their complete and continued willingness to offer me encouragement and help, and for the patient affection demonstrated by accepting the egocentric arrogance with which I sought to learn.

The second and fifth chapters (here revised) had appeared in *Rivista storica italiana* and in *Archivio storico per le province napoletane*. I would like to thank the editors and directors of these journals, Franco Venturi and Giuseppe Galasso, for having agreed to the new edition.

This book is dedicated to my wife Tiziana; without her and her help none of this would have been even conceivable.

Abbreviations

B.C.R.	*Biblioteca Corsiniana*, Rome.
B.C.V.	*Biblioteca Capitolare*, Verona.
B.V.R.	*Biblioteca Vallicelliana*, Rome.
B.U.P.	*Biblioteca Universitaria*, Pisa.
D.B.I.	*Dizionario biografico degli italiani*, Rome: Istituto dell'enciclopedia, 1960–.
B.N.N.	*Biblioteca Nazionale*, Naples.
D.N.B.	*Dictionary of National Biography*, Oxford: Oxford University Press, 1953–.
S.N.S.P.	*Biblioteca della Società napoletana di storia patria.*

ONE

The First Debates on Newtonian Science

1. THE DAWN OF THE EIGHTEENTH CENTURY

After Galileo's death and the subsequent intensification of ecclesiastical repression against those of his disciples who persisted in venerating his memory and in following his teachings, their task of proselytism became increasingly difficult during the seventeenth century. Rejected by the universities and compelled by the threat of the Inquisition and by the suffocating conformity of Counter-Reformation culture to a sort of preventive self-censure, the pupils of the Pisan scientist nevertheless succeeded—even if through compromise and mediation—in disseminating the "new science" in broad areas of Italian intellectual life.[1] At the hands of the faithful Viviani, Torricelli, Cavalieri, Castelli, and others, the vitalizing leaven of Galilean thought was spread through many cities, penetrating particularly deeply in Rome, where in the 1730s there was a strong and lively "Galilean colony."[2] It was in Rome that the "new science" was fruitfully interwoven with the modern currents of thought that stemmed from Gassendi and Descartes, creating a new framework within which to reopen ancient debates.

Even if we do not yet know the outlines of the Roman intellectual environment of the 1730s well enough, we can indeed form a rich and nuanced picture. It is not surprising that it was precisely in Rome during this period that Tommaso Cornelio, one of the founders of the Accademia degli Investiganti, found the ideas necessary to bring together the teachings of Telesian naturalism, Galilean experimentalism, and Cartesian metaphysics into a more advanced philosophical-scientific synthesis.[3] But the most interesting aspect of the Roman culture of the time was the underground presence of a strong Libertine current that, along with the progressive success of the "new science," was bound to alarm ecclesiastical authorities considerably. In fact, a large group of scholars tied to the French Libertine circles of Bourdelot and of Naudé formed around Cassiano Dal Pozzo.[4] Throughout the latter half of the seventeenth century, intellectual groups activated by the creation of academies such as those of the Cimento, the Investiganti, and Ciampini's Fisicomatematica made possible the circulation not only of scientific ideas but

1

also, in a number of cases, of the more disquieting results of modern thought.

While it is very difficult to define precisely the outlines of seventeenth-century Italian Libertinism, there is no doubt that it was interwoven with Lucretian and Gassendian atomism, which was quite widespread at the end of the century.[5] The appearance of Catholic apologists, led by the fulminating priests Father Frugoni and Father Segneri, indicates that the apologists perceived the widespread presence of Libertine theories in Italy.[6] Lorenzo Magalotti, author of the splendid *Lettere familiari* [Domestic letters] (1680–1684), in which he traced a comprehensive account of the ideas held by the atheists of the period, also testifies to the uneasy existence of large pockets of incredulity and Libertinism among scientists and intellectuals.[7] Eugenio Garin's research on Italian culture from Campanella to Galileo and Vico has brought to light this renewed interest in modern thought in late-seventeenth-century Italy. Besides the forging of the "new science" at the hands of the academics of the Cimento, the Investiganti, and, later, the scholars grouped around Ciampini, there was an increasingly intense and quite significant circulation of the prohibited books by Bruno, Vanini, and Campanella.[8] At the end of the century, Italy, too, was overwhlmed by the so-called crisis of the European mind, if less directly than other, neighboring countries. Basic texts of this profound cultural transformation— such as Spinoza's *Tractatus theologico-politicus* [Theological-political treatise], the works of Richard Simon and Isaac de Lapeyrère, the anti-Spinozan polemics of Huet, the vast literature on non-European countries, and the numerous works on sacred chronology and biblical exegesis—were read in Rome, Florence, Naples, and Venice, creating serious problems for the Holy See.[9] A great deal of turmoil was caused throughout Italy by the dissemination of Libertine literature, Spinozism, and atomism and its disturbing, anti-Christian consequences. Thus, aside from any local context, we can consider the trial of the Neapolitan atheists at the end of the century as a kind of preventive response from the Church to the alarming effects of the crisis.

This trial, begun in Naples in 1688, certainly represented one of the darkest moments not only for southern-Italian culture but for the entire peninsula. Even if it aimed its harshest blows at secondary figures, such as Basilio Giannelli, Filippo Belli, Francesco Paolo Manuzzi, and Giacinto de Cristoforo, the repression set in motion by the Neapolitan clergy immediately assumed the form of an attack against the entire group of Investiganti. Above all, the explicit declarations of Giovan Battista De Benedictis, prefect of the Jesuit schools, were an even more general censure of the very principle of *libertas philosophandi* [freedom of philosophizing].[10] In his *Lettere apologetiche in difesa della teologia scolastica e della filosofia peripatetica* [Apologetic letters in defense of scholastic theology and Aristotelian philosophy] (1694), deliberately published at the conclusion of the trial, De Benedictis bitterly challenged all of modern science, atomism, Cartesian physics (which he accused of being a vehicle for atheism), and, above all, the excessive freedom allowed scholars. It was this freedom, the Jesuit wrote, that gave "to the good arts much worry and fright, as these [arts] can never be safe as long as this [freedom]—I know not whether to call it Siren or Fury—is the arbiter of talent and rules over academies."[11] The *novatores* [innovators] re-acted swiftly against such an explicit attack. Valletta, D'Andrea, Porzio, and Grimaldi responded with great fervor to De Benedictis's threats and categorically denied any direct confrontation between Christianity and modern science. With great originality, Neapolitan intellectuals reworked the Investiganti's scientific theses within a reassuring philosophical framework consistent with Christian orthodoxy, seeking to re-create the conditions necessary for exercising their *libertas philosophandi*.[12] The trial ran its course, interweaving with political maneuvering over the competing jurisdictions of Naples, Madrid, and Rome.[13] The charges leveled by the Inquisitors against the presumed atheists confirmed the presence in Naples of ideas then at the center of the European debate: sacred chronology, atomism, and the pre-Adamitic theories of Lapeyrère.[14] Dangerous statements, such as the affirmation that "the world was not created by God, but produced by chance by atoms" and that "atoms are the principles of all things," were attributed to De Magistris.[15] De Cristoforo was accused of having said,

> with his other companions [who were] skilled in law, that there had been men before Adam composed of atoms equal to those of other animals, that all was taken care of by nature, that there was no God, that there was no Hell, Purgatory, or Paradise, that the soul was mortal, that Christ should not be called the son of God but a seducer, that the sacraments should not be recognized, and even that the authority of the pope was not real.[16]

The result of the nine-year trial was to limit throughout Italy the condi-tions necessary for free scientific research open to the European debate. The Neapolitans had to take part in a public ceremony of retraction that seemed to bring to life an already distant past.[17] The news of the Neapoli-tan events, filtered throughout Italian intellectual circles, left few hopes for those who had until then fought for *libertas philosophandi*. In the preced-ing years warning signs of the harsh crackdown desired by Rome had al-ready appeared in many places. In 1671 the Congregation of Holy Inquisition had sent the archbishop of Naples a sharp warning about the dangers stem-ming from men and books spreading new atomist and Cartesian theories. Intervention was necessary, wrote Cardinal Barberini, because there were sound reasons for

> supposing that in [Naples] there would be found some who, in order to prove their ingenuity, might promote some philosophical opinions of a certain René Descartes, who years ago had published a new philosophical system, reawakening the ancient opinions of the Greeks regarding atoms, and that from this doctrine some theologians might claim to prove how

the accidents of the bread and wine remain after the consecration, [while] the substance of the said bread and wine changed into that of the body and blood of our lord Jesus Christ.[18]

In Tuscany between 1669 and 1670, the philo-Galilean proponents of materialism and atomism had been harshly repressed and expelled from the Pisan university, causing great consternation among those who nurtured the hope of finally seeing the principle of *libertas philosophandi* affirmed.[19] In 1689 Michelangelo Fardella was denounced to the Venetian Inquisitor for having wished to teach the doctrines of "a certain Peter [*sic*] Descartes."[20] During the trial of the atheists, some of the greatest Italian intellectuals came to appreciate fully the Roman Church's intention to reaffirm its hegemonic role through the repressive tool of the Inquisition. Marcello Malpighi, who in those years resided in Rome, when questioned by Viviani about the rumors circulating about the Neapolitan affairs, did not hesitate to emphasize that the trial was part of a design both long contemplated and meticulously prepared: "In the Sacred Congregation there are learned cardinals with whose efforts the preparations developed. Regarding this matter I have no precise information, but I know that it has been schemed for quite some time."[21] All hope of obtaining Galileo's rehabilitation, regardless of the efforts of Viviani and the Galileans throughout Italy, was destroyed by the rapid conclusion of the Neapolitan affair. The Jesuit Antonio Baldigiani, the Inquisitorial Tribunal's consultant and a person well informed about what was happening in Rome regarding the trial of the atheists, was compelled to point out the changing climate and the difficult times ahead for all Italian intellectuals. He wrote to Viviani:

> All Rome is in arms against the mathematicians and physico-mathematicians. The cardinals have staged and are staging unscheduled meetings before the pope, and there is talk of making general prohibitions against all authors of modern physics. They are drawing up very long lists, and among those at the top of them are Galileo, Gassendi, [and] Descartes, as those most pernicious to the literary republic and to the sincerity of religion. The principal ones judging this are the religious, who at other times have tried to issue such prohibitions. At the present they well know how to seize the opportunity offered to them by the legal case against some doctors and legists at Naples, there and here imprisoned by the Inquisition, who are said to have availed themselves of such doctrines and books in order to clear the way for their errors.[22]

2. The Opticks, the Principia mathematica, and Roman Scientists

The Roman cultural situation at the close of the seventeenth century has elicited particular interest among scholars. Once the most harshly repressive phases of the Counter-Reformation had run their course, the Holy See

was quick to perceive the need to come to terms with the new ideas circulating in Europe in order to avoid a dangerous impoverishment of its own
intelligentsia—intellectually or culturally. Opening to these new ideas, even
if effected in a Machiavellian fashion with the intent of neutralizing and
transforming modern thought for the *maiorem Dei gloriam* [greater glory of
God],[1] soon proved to be a difficult operation to control, even dangerous
in some ways. Francesco Nazari's *Giornale de' Letterati* and the Accademia
Fisico-matematica created by Giovanni Giustino Ciampini are two typical
examples of this interesting renewal at the end of the century. The *Giornale
de' Letterati* (1668–1683)—the first Italian periodical explicitly inspired by
the French *Journal des savants*—finally gave Italian scholars the possibility
of learning relatively easily about the greatest scientific research that was
then being carried out throughout Europe.

The magazine announced and reviewed articles in the *Philosophical Transactions* and books by French, English, and Dutch scholars. The *Giornale*,
while tightly controlled by an editorial committee utterly submissive to the
Roman Curia, during its brief and troubled existence publicized the names
not only of Tommaso Cornelio and Leonardo Di Capua, but also of William
Harvey, Robert Boyle, and Pierre Gassendi. Above all the *Giornale* sought
to present once again—in terms quite different than those of the years that
had seen his trial and recantation—the name and ideas of Galileo; his partial rehabilitation was a goal that some Roman scientists had worked towards
for quite some time with prudent but dogged determination. Science, philosophy, travel reports, and agrarian techniques were themes frequently treated
in the *Giornale*, which dedicated only one-tenth of the 1,010 articles published to theology.[2]

The dangers implicit in similar initiatives, though for the most part these
initiatives were aimed at neutralizing the most insidious aspects of modern
thought, were plainly evident, especially in the Accademia Fisico-matematica
founded in 1677 by Cardinal Ciampini, a prominent personality among Roman
intellectuals who had been able to rely on the continued support of Queen
Christina of Sweden.[3] Among other things, Ciampini was responsible for
the creation in 1671 of the Accademia dei Concili, in which many of the
teachings of the new Maurist historiography were developed.[4] Ciampini's
academy rapidly became the most important and informed center of scientific
research in Italy in the late seventeenth century. Comprehensively furnished
with sophisticated equipment, including some of the best telescopes in the
world,[5] the academy's membership included scientists of great prestige such
as Alfonso Borelli, who within the academy completed the *De motu animalium*
[On the motion of animals] and continued research on celestial mechanics
begun in Florence with the *Theoricae Mediceorum planetarum* [Theories of
the Medicean planets]. During these years Francesco Bianchini wrote the
still-unpublished treatise *De methodo philosophandi in rebus physicis* [On the
method of philosophizing regarding matters of physics], and in 1685 he

demonstrated to his associates at the academy Cassini's new method for measuring the parallax of the planets from a single position. Lucantonio Porzio, by repeating Boylian experiments in the academy, explained the Investiganti's theories of physics based on the reality of ether and on Cartesian concepts of physics. Giorgio Baglivi, Vitale Giordani, Giovanni Maria Lancisi, Gianvincenzo Gravina, Francesco Eschinardi, Giuseppe Campani, and Domenico Quartieroni were also renowed members of the Accademia dei Concili. In 1708 Ciampini's biographer wrote to the academy: "Here all the eclipses and the comets of those times were observed. Here mathematical problems were solved. . . . In short, no new celestial phenomenon was discovered, no new object on earth appeared . . . that was not submitted to a most diligent examination here."[6]

Although situated in the heart of the Catholic Church, the academy rapidly became a sort of open port in which all scientific hypotheses could be discussed, even those most dangerous to orthodoxy.[7] It was in those rooms at the end of 1689 that Leibniz expounded his philosophical theories and particularly his Copernican convictions, seeking to engage privately such a prestigious associate as Francesco Bianchini in the fight to rehabilitate the heliocentric system.[8] And yet internal tensions must have been very strong if in 1683 a not-entirely-orthodox scientist such as Porzio decided to leave Rome, thoroughly angered by the directives that Ciampini attempted to impose on the academy.[9] Only the very high scientific level of the experiments and the continued and fruitful contacts with the Royal Society and the Académie des Sciences, favored by the international ties of the Holy See, could in part make possible the partnership between men like Borelli and Baglivi—openly Galilean and sensitive to new scientific theories—and implacable anti-Galileans like Francesco Eschinardi and Tommaso Vanni.[10]

The most significant and long-lasting result that the academy achieved, despite long disputes and internal rifts, was to bring the impious Democritean and Epicurean atomism to the attention of Catholic scientists in the reassuring—at least superficially—Christian version fashioned by Pierre Gassendi and Robert Boyle.[11] And it was in Ciampini's academy, in fact, that the most recent Boylian experiments and Torricelli's barometric experiment (which, depending how one interpreted it, could confirm or deny the *horror vacui* [fear of the void]) were repeated with extreme rigor, using instruments impossible to find anywhere in Italy.[12] The positions taken by Robert Boyle in *The Christian Virtuoso: Shewing That by Being Addicted to Experimental Philosophy a Man Is Rather Assisted Than Indisposed to Be a Good Christian* (1690), not to mention a series of other works aimed at reconciling corpuscular mechanism with the Christian religion, were decisive for the acceptance of a "Christian corpuscularism" in the early 1700s by scholars such as Bianchini, Galiani, Bottari, and Averani. For Boyle, a familiar figure in contemporary Rome,[13] the principle of matter divided into particles and the principle of movement were the only explanatory principles to which one had recourse. According to Boyle, at the origins of the universe was not Lucretian "chance" but divine will that (contrary to what Descartes maintained) even after the initial phase continued to oversee the movements of matter.[14] Boyle's "practical atomism" aimed at making corpuscularism the basic theory of physics for a mechanistic description of the universe and allowed no concessions to animistic explanations of the nature of matter. In fact his atomism was interpreted faithfully only in some Italian scientific circles; more often it became confused, and dangerously so, with the traditional Lucretian interpretation.

Within the academy, the problem of the structure of matter and the epistemological models related to it brought out the incompatibility of two profoundly diverse theses: the Cartesian view of matter-extension as explained in the three principal elements (a theory adopted as their own by the Neapolitan Investiganti, who elaborated it within an original synthesis laced with naturalism),[15] and the atomistic-Boylian interpretation, suitably reassuring as far as faith was concerned. These opposing viewpoints—which continued to characterize profoundly the successive philosophical-scientific debates in Italian culture—contributed to the beginning of the repression at the end of the century and to the trial of the Neapolitan atheists. In Rome, too, the effects of the trial were soon felt, and with the death of Ciampini in 1698, research conditions rapidly deteriorated. The Accademia Fisico-matematica, which had become a valuable point of reference for Italian scientists, ceased to exist. The great experimental tradition renewed by the academy, although it continued to characterize Roman scientific culture, no longer had room to develop, nor could it maintain contact with the European academic environment. For many years in Rome, too, it became dangerous to address publicly the great issues surrounding the structure of matter, atomism, and celestial dynamics. In 1714, uncomfortable at the Inquisition's continued attention, Celestino Galiani commented on the Roman intellectuals' plight, venting his anger to Camaldolese monk Guido Grandi: "Here the *belles artes*, and especially philosophy, are held in horror; they hate them more than the plague, and if it were up to them they would annihilate even the name, in order to allow the foolish chattering of the Arabs to rule."[16] The increased activity of the Inquisitorial Tribunal notwithstanding ("the prisons of that tribunal"—wrote Francesco Valesio in 1703—"are full of men to be questioned; their number is always growing"),[17] the Roman cultural ambience was rapidly able to recover its noteworthy late-seventeenth-century vitality, albeit with greater circumspection and clearcut limitations.

In the 1710s the end of Spanish hegemony over Italy inaugurated a period of political instability and helped to make Rome "the only international city in Italian society"[18] at a cultural level as well. Ludovico Antonio Muratori evaluated the contemporary political situation and the presence of scholars of the calibre of Francesco Bianchini, Biagio Garofalo, Gianvincenzo

Gravina, Giovanni Maria Lancisi, and Giusto Fontanini, and he suggested Rome as the focal point about which Italian intellectuals ought to reorganize their activity. This plan was soon rejected by Bianchini, who thought it opposed to the traditional Catholic model of a universal culture.[19] The resumption of humanist studies in Rome was stimulated by the affirmation of the Maurist method and the actions of the Arcadia (to which Clement XI himself belonged, under the name of Alnano Meleo), whose importance in the work of reorganizing eighteenth-century culture should not be underestimated. Such a resumption did not, however, seem immediately capable of extending to scientific studies.[20] Officially neglected, they remained the exclusive prerogative of a small and well-trained group of scholars headed by the young Celestino Galiani and Francesco Bianchini.[21] Given Bianchini's reluctance to undertake initiatives involving cultural policy, Galiani would soon propose that he should be the true driving force behind Roman science.

In his small room at the monastery of Sant'Eusebio in the years between 1708 and 1720, Galiani customarily gathered together a large group of scholars, among them Father Joseph Roma, Cardinal Lorenzo Imperiali, Abbot Francesco Landi (future archbishop of Benevento), Bernardo Andrea Lama, Francesco Antonio Gimezzi, Gaspare Cerati, Francesco Bianchini, and, during his Roman visits, Antonio Niccolini.[22] During these meetings they conducted experiments of the highest calibre, commented on Newtonian and Cartesian texts and on the various hypotheses on the nature of light, and, above all, laid the foundations for future coordinated action for the renewal of Italian science. Celestino Galiani's "Roman colony"—as Bernardo Andrea Lama loved to call it[23]—intelligently utilized the Holy See's international contacts to keep up-to-date on the results of new scientific research conducted in every corner of Europe. It was through these channels that Catholic intellectuals learned of Newtonian science.

In the years following the Glorious Revolution of 1688–1689, the relations between the papacy and England intensified, mainly through Rome's initiatives, which explicitly intended to obtain English authorities' greater tolerance for England's small Catholic presence. The actions of Roman emissaries—amply documented by the reports preserved in the Vatican Secret Archives—were not limited to normal diplomatic pressures; they assumed a genuinely missionary character. In those years there were a number of conversions to Catholicism among the English nobility and secret (or at times widely publicized) crises of conscience, such as that of the wealthy Wriothesley Russell, duke of Bedford, which occurred 16 April 1699.[24] The close relationship that existed between the Holy See and the exiled court of James II explains the growing number of English who traveled to or resided in Italy, and in particular Rome. Among these, a very active minority of Protestants, court officials, and personal friends of the fugitive sovereign created no small embarrassment for the papal authorities by their actions aimed at discrediting Catholicism.[25] In general, however, the presence of a large English colony in Italy contributed to improved relations between England and the Holy See, thus favoring a climate of mutual tolerance. In fact, the Anglican Sir Henry Newton, envoy extraordinary of the United Kingdom to the Tuscan court of Cosimo III de' Medici, personally inspired cultural exchanges between Great Britain and Italy.

Sir Henry Newton,[26] together with Thomas Dereham and William Burnet (to whom we will return later), was one of the central figures through whom we can reconstruct the dissemination of Newtonian science in Italy. Newton was the heir of a well-to-do family of Staffordshire with a degree in law from Oxford. After a brilliant career as a government official, he was sent in 1704 by the English government to the court of the grand duke of Tuscany. His task was to monitor the evolution of the Italian political situation during the War of the Spanish Succession, and he carried it out with great success, among other things personally conducting the secret negotiations for the neutralization of the Genoan republic. His brilliant political maneuverings took ready advantage of the friendship of Clement XI, whom he met on a trip to Rome in 1708. But it is particularly interesting to follow the cultural relationships that he had with many Italian scholars. He was a man gifted with a good humanist education—indeed, harboring poetic pretensions. Immediately after his arrival in Florence, he contacted the greatest Tuscan intellectuals, gathered at the Accademia della Crusca (where Newton became a member in 1710), bringing about an increase in their already frequent contacts with some of the greatest English literati.[27] In 1709, at the end of his stay in Italy, the diplomat collected into a booklet entitled *Epistolae, orationes et carmina* [Letters, orations, and poems] roughly eighty letters that he had exchanged with various Italian cultural personalities, among them Anton Maria Salvini, a prominent figure at the Accademia della Crusca, Benedetto and Giuseppe Averani, Guido Grandi, Piergerolamo Bargellini, Lorenzo Magalotti, Antonio Magliabechi, Domenico Passionei, and many others. Beyond the ritualized conventions and the usual protestations of esteem, Newton's letters clearly reveal his desire to support the majority of the Italian literati in their bitter dispute against the aesthetic-literary Cartesianism of the French. One example of his support was the admiration he expressed for Giuseppe Orsi, who had been harshly attacked in this vein by the French Jesuit Dominique Bouhours in the *Mémoires de Trévoux* [Memoirs of Trévoux].[28] Newton skillfully widened the discourse of aesthetic-literary anti-Cartesianism, comparing metaphysics and Cartesian science with the Galilean experimentalism that had, so he said, its natural heirs in Isaac Newton (no relative of the ambassador), Robert Boyle, and John Locke.[29] For the duration of his Italian sojourn, the English diplomat earnestly and skillfully mediated between Italian scientists, particularly Tuscans and Romans, and the Royal Society. From a series of his unedited letters, preserved among Grandi's manuscripts at Pisa, it is possible to reconstruct this intense activity of providing information and stimulation. He was re-

sponsible for coordinating research on the speed of sound, completed in the
1710s, between the Royal Society in England and the Pisan scientists Guido
Grandi, Giuseppe Averani, and Lorenzo Magnolsi in Italy.[30] The direct contact
between the most prestigious Italian mathematician of those years, Guido
Grandi, and Isaac Newton was also a product of Sir Henry Newton's continual work as liaison.[31]

From the time of his arrival in Italy, Henry Newton strengthened ties of
friendship with Roman cultural circles as well, in particular with the *pastori*
[pastors] of the Arcadia, in which in 1705 he became an academic, under
the name of Argeste Melichio;[32] it was thanks to his intercession that Roman scientists learned of Isaac Newton's works. In an important letter from
December 1707, he informed Newton of the warm reception extended to
his works in Rome. Men within the Holy See had requested the *Principia
mathematica* [Mathematical principles] from him in 1706,[33] but the bookseller to whom he had turned sent to Rome, instead, the recent Latin edition of the *Opticks*, translated by Samuel Clarke.[34] Catholic scholars were
quick to comment, for the ambassador wrote to Isaac Newton:

> Rome is but grateful for the favours shee has received on this head from
> Brittain, when upon my sending thither some time since, ye books of
> Opticks, one of their learned men in this answer thence, was pleasd thus
> to express his own thoughts thereon, and those of ye virtuosi there: and
> now turning to your most pleasant letter, I must first thank you greatly
> for sending Newton's precious work the *Optices*, which you sent here from
> England, in order to please all my friends and me. Now the book is in
> the hands of Galiani, who knows these disciplines extremely well. It will
> then go to Fontanini, Vignolio, Gravina, Garofalo, and the rest of the
> finest literati in this city of exquisite culture. And how great will my
> honor be, for because of your gift I first had the fortune of presenting to
> Rome this new treasure, the fruit of the heroic genius of Sir Newton, so
> famous throughout Europe. One must regret the fault of the bookseller
> who sent this work instead of the *Principiorum philosophiae mathematicorum*;
> in fact, as Galiani told me, in it he found theses so new, and propositions
> and reflections on light and colors so disturbing, that not even René
> Descartes, prince and creator of a new philosophy, arrived at these con-
> clusions. Again, unceasing and eternal thanks to you, my most kind lord.[35]

The *Optice sive de reflexionibus, refractionibus, inflexionibus et coloribus
lucis* [The optics, or on the reflection, refraction, inflection, and colors of
light] was thus introduced to Rome.[36] The text was read and commented
on by scholars of the calibre of Giovanni Vignolio, Giusto Fontanini,
Gianvincenzo Gravina, Biagio Garofalo, Francesco Bianchini, and, especially,
Celestino Galiani, who was entrusted with the difficult task of repeating
some of the experiments and explaining Newtonian theories to his colleagues. Galiani performed the most important experiments between 1707
and 1708[37] in the small Accademia degli Antiquari Alessandrini, which

met in the rooms of the Quirinale palace under the direct control of Francesco Bianchini and with the valuable protection of Alessandro Albani, nephew of Clement XI.[38] These experiments were certainly among the first, if not the very first, performed by Continental scientists to verify Newtonian optical theories. Their importance for the renewal of a high level of Italian scientific activity after the trauma of the trial of the atheists should not be underestimated, even if we must remember the limits within which the Catholic hierarchy wished to confine this revival of interest in modern science. Indeed, it is not surprising that we can study the dissemination of modern scientific ideas in Italy only through unedited texts or letters, nearly always censored by their authors and ambiguous regarding the most controversial scientific issues, such as the structure of matter, Copernicanism, and the relationship between science and faith. With the disbanding of Ciampini's Accademia Fisico-matematica on the occasion of its founder's death and with the events in Naples, the greatest challenges to Italian science became indifference, lack of initiative, and, above all, a sort of resignation and antiscientific conformity that caused the best Italian scholars to grapple with less dangerous and more gratifying disciplines. In a letter addressed to Guido Grandi in 1705, Celestino Galiani clearly depicted the situation of Italian scientists, writing bitterly: "What is to be feared is not so much the Inquisitor as the beliefs of men who hold [scientific experiments] to be little more than the tricks of acrobats . . .; it is necessary to make them understand that if one devotes some time to the sciences . . ., not for this is he any less than others with respect to the divine sciences and to erudition."[39]

In 1707 Galiani had subjected the *Optice* to a very accurate analysis, discussing many details with the students of the small coterie at Sant'Eusebio. His conclusions, admirable for the lucidity with which he was able to understand the importance of the Newtonian work, are synthesized in two manuscripts preserved among his papers. The *Optice* is divided into three books: the first studies the phenomena of the reflection, refraction, dispersion, and decomposition of white light; the second deals with the interference of light in thin, transparent plates, the permanence of colors in natural bodies, and the periodicity of light's properties; the third reports the celebrated *quaestiones* and some observations on diffraction.[40] Galiani directed his attention almost entirely to the first book, in which he rightly saw the most scientifically interesting fruit of the entire work. The results of the second book, even though essential for the mathematicization of optical phenomena, acquire meaning only in relation to the experiments on prism light carried out in the first book. The third book, especially with regard to *quaestiones* XVII through XXIII, is quite important for a complete understanding of the metaphysics of absolute space and time, as well as the atomistic conception of matter and the apologetic meaning that universal gravitation assumed in Newton's cosmology; it does not seem that Galiani had grasped its entire meaning, at least on his first reading of the work. As Galiani had not yet read the *Principia mathematica*, Newton's harsh arguments against the Cartesian concept of matter-extension and the hypothesis of vortices must have seemed quite incomprehensible to him, and his *Animadversiones nonnullae circa opticem Isaaci Neutoni* [Some remarks about Isaac Newton's Optics] confirm such an impression. Here he returns to and examines nearly all of the Newtonian propositions from a strictly scientific viewpoint.[41]

Surpassing the geometricization of optics achieved by Grimaldi and Descartes, Newton had opened the road to understanding light's phenomena in physical terms. In his theories, through the notion of the corpuscle, the luminous ray had become "a sort of cylinder of infinitely small diameter, divisible into infinitely small parts,"[42] that was propagated rectilinearly. He had analyzed the nature of this luminous ray in the numerous experiments that had so excited Bianchini and Galiani. Galiani transcribed the famous Newtonian definition of colors thus:

> The homogeneal light or those rays which appear red, or rather make objects appear so, I call rubrific or red; those which make objects appear yellow, green, blue, and violet, I call yellow, green, blue, violet.... For the rays, to speak properly, are not colored. In them there is nothing other than a certain power and disposition to stir up a sensation of this or that color.[43]

In the second manuscript, a report on the *Optice* probably meant to be read to Roman scientists, Galiani synthesized the background for the definition:

> By the experiments that he expounded in the first part, clearly one recognizes that the lights that are of different color also have different refractability. Newton hence believes from his experiments that he clearly knows that the solar light is an agglomeration of rays of diverse type or manner and, as they say, heterogeneous, that are varied, that is to say in refractability and reflectability.... In addition, he observes that each type of ray is of a specific color, for example those that are most refractable are of cerulean color, those barely [refractable] are of red color, those moderately [refractable] of green color, etc. And thus all the others have a specific color corresponding to their precise refractability.[44]

Galiani's comfortable acceptance of Newtonian experimentalism and empiricism becomes evident from the report. Nor did other Roman scholars, at least those most sensitive to the Galilean heritage and the recent traditions of experimentalism at Ciampini's Accademia Fisico-matematica, seem to have experienced any epistemological impediment in the face of the *Optice*'s revolutionary theories. (In fact the Galileans viewed favorably the crisis of Cartesian science, which sometimes had been subjected to Libertine and materialistic interpretations; this attitude encourages reflection on the latent antagonism between some followers of Galileo and of Descartes in Italy.) Galiani's report opens with the explicit declaration of his desire "to expound in few words the difference between the new discoveries about light of the learned and ingenious English duke Isaac Newton, and the Cartesian hypothesis about the same matter." Cartesian apriorism is here firmly contrasted to Newton's "sound experiences." According to Galiani,

> first it is necessary to point out that the new things Newton puts forward regarding the nature of light and of colors, he claims to know either directly, through experiments he made in such a subject, or at least from what can be deduced from those [experiments] by means of sound and clear reasoning. Nor has he in any way fabricated new hypotheses to make sense of the phenomena that were observed regarding such a matter.[45]

For Descartes light was nothing other than a very rapid pressure that the sun and other sources of light exercised with practically infinite velocity on the tiniest spheres of light-bearing material.[46] Newtonian emissionist theory, on the other hand, gave corporeality to light, opposing an atomistic conception of the world to that of Cartesian matter-extension. Post-Galilean mechanics could, however, "very well accept the atomist hypothesis and could simultaneously show it remained consistent with Galileo's own teaching regarding the limits and duties of science."[47] The "tiniest particles of solar light" (as Galiani expressed it) did not in fact create any embarrassment to Catholic Galilean scholars more attuned to the demands of modern science. The tone of Galiani's dispute with Cartesian hypotheses became sharper when analyzing color theory: "Descartes supposed that light [was] entirely homogeneous, . . . and the diversity of colors came from none other than the varied modifications that the rays received from the surfaces of the reflective and refractive bodies." Galiani, however, did not fail to observe that Descartes "advanced all that for mere hypothesis, while Newton inferred his findings from experiments," and his conclusion was, therefore, drastic: "The Cartesian system regarding light and colors is pronounced false."[48] Even if due to chance, his reading of the *Optice*, full of experimentally measurable results, without a doubt led to Roman scholars' subsequent benevolent reception of the *Principia*'s celestial mechanics. Just how much this early positive judgment of Newton's work might have influenced the Holy See's later attitude towards Newtonian science appears evident from the fact that, unlike the Cartesian works that were placed on the *Index librorum prohibitorum* [Index of prohibited books] in 1663, those of Newton and of the Newtonians Clarke, Whiston, Derham, and Cheyne did not suffer the same fate. In Italy, only Francesco Algarotti's *Newtonianesimo per le dame* [Newtonianism for ladies] was in 1739 added to the *Index*, and that primarily for its explicit acceptance of Copernicanism and because of the wide audience at which the book was aimed.[49] This does not mean that the struggle for the dissemination of Newtonianism was any less arduous, for there was clear-cut and relentless hostility towards modern culture within a great part of the ecclesiastical hierarchy.

In 1706 Roman scientists had asked Henry Newton for a copy of the

Principia, and their request was not a sign of isolated and spontaneous interest. Even ecclesiastical circles had pointed to the urgent necessity of definitively evaluating the original text containing the cosmology that, at the Royal Society meeting of 28 April 1686, had been hailed as a "mathematical demonstration of the Copernican hypothesis such as Kepler had presented."[50] The Galilean drama, far from having definitively shut down the broad scientific debate on Copernicus's theories, had simply narrowed the discussion to a few courageous scholars. Despite the Inquisitorial Tribunal's repression, the cosmological issue had remained one of the subjects debated by Roman scientists. The condemned hypothesis again became the focus of covert discussion on two occasions, the first during Leibniz's stay in Rome in 1689, and the second while the debates on the thorny problem of the reform of the Gregorian calendar raged in the 1710s. With the revival of Catholic scientific interest, thanks to Bianchini and Galiani, it was inevitable that the *Principia mathematica* would be taken into account.

In 1688 Christian Pfaultz's long review of the *Principia*—appearing in Leipzig's *Acta eruditorum*[51]—brought the Italian and European scientific world up-to-date on new Newtonian theories. The importance of this review was considerable, for the *Acta* was then the most prestigious European journal, the only one that could boast a widespread international circulation. It was in the *Acta*'s favor that it used Latin, allowing scholars of all countries to read it, and as it was always full of valuable reviews of books in all disciplines, from mathematics to sacred history, from medicine to law, the *Acta* was essential for transmitting cultural information and trends. From an ideological viewpoint, the journal could count on a large consensus, permeated as it was by free and open Christian universalism, especially under the editorial direction of Johann Burckard Mencken between 1707 and 1732.[52] It has already been demonstrated elsewhere that the *Acta* lay at the origins of Neapolitan juridical, philosophical, and scientific culture,[53] and this was also true for the remaining regions of Italy, in particular for Rome. The periodical published dozens of reviews of Italians' works. From the earliest issues we find commentaries, nearly always favorable, on the works of Gianvincenzo Gravina, Giusto Fontanini, Lucantonio Porzio, Bernardo Trevisan, Giovanni Maria Lancisi, and others.[54] In light of the journal's noteworthy circulation, its review of Newtonian work can be considered the first true contact between Newton and Italian scientists. While very precise and analytical, Pfaultz's commentary on the *Principia* did not offer readers an explicit judgment of the value of the theories Newton enunciated; Pfaultz limited himself to a very careful presentation of some of the most important passages of the book. The choice of passages and the subjects treated outlined the essential features necessary for an indirect reading of the Newtonian work, and for decades it remained one of the few sources available to Italian scientists. Pfaultz cursorily summarized the entire first book of the *Principia* and a good deal of the second; he delved more into the method of the first and last reasons (in which he rightly perceived some elements of the new infinitesimal calculus), rather than into the basic concepts of classical mechanics such as quantity of motion and the principle of inertia. Pfaultz's attention was actually entirely directed at expounding the revolutionary celestial mechanics. The *Principia*'s Copernicanism, although not explicitly declared (not even Newton had dared to make an open profession in his work),[55] was taken as a matter of fact by the reviewer Pfaultz, whose intent was to outline the irresolvable contradiction between the Cartesian mechanistic conception of planetary motion (which attributed planetary motion to the rotation of vortices of ether) and the Newtonian conception (which was based on gravitational attraction and the vacuum). Citing from Newton (and repeating Newton's erroneous attribution of the hypothesis of elliptical orbits to Copernicus and not to Kepler), Pfaultz wrote: "Further, in the Copernican hypothesis the planets revolve in ellipses around the sun, fixed as their only center, and they describe areas proportional to their [periodic] times." All this, however, openly contradicted Cartesian theories. Therefore it followed that "the parts . . . of the vortex could not revolve with such a motion, since the planets move—more slowly in aphelion, more rapidly in perihelion—according to astronomical laws, when according to the mechanical law of the vortices the contrary ought to occur." Newton, Pfaultz concluded,

> states that the hypothesis of vortices so greatly lauded by the Cartesians is diametrically opposed to celestial phenomena, and it serves not so much to explain as to disturb celestial motions. In the third book, the author demonstrates in many ways through his exposition of the world-system how the said motions are accomplished in vacuums without the vortices.[56]

The fascinating synthesis of the third book, which described the admirable Newtonian universe-machine, was the most significant part of the ample review of the *Acta*. There Pfaultz described the concept of gravity, the inverse square law, the motion of comets, and the results of the most recent research on the earth's dimensions and form. In short, there was enough in the article to make the extraordinary importance of the Newtonian *systema mundi* [world system] understandable.

In Naples Giuseppe Valletta, who attentively followed the commentaries in the *Acta*, read the review and ordered a copy of the *Principia*, which today is one of the most valuable works of his exceptional library.[57] Actually, none of the local scientists read the book, and it remained virtually unknown to astronomers such as Monforte as well as to scholars such as De Cristoforo, Porzio, and Valletta. Only Agostino Ariani, professor of mathematics in the Neapolitan *Studio pubblico*, mentioned Isaac Newton during his lectures at the Accademia Palatina del Medinaceli in 1701.[58] The reference was, however, merely the affectation of a scholar who wished to prove himself up-to-date; one need only read his works to realize the wide gap that separated his antiquated and blighted scientific knowledge from that of Newton. With the arrival of Gottfried Wilhelm Leibniz in Rome in 1689, the review gained quite an interesting following.[59] During his stay the German philosopher contacted nearly all of the greatest Italian intellectuals. His visit to his Roman colleagues was designed to involve the most outstanding personalities of the Catholic world in an ambitious plan—which soon proved to be utopian—directed at reunifying the differing Christian confessions.[60] While in the company of members of Cardinal Ciampini's Accademia Fisico-matematica, Leibniz learned of Newtonian cosmological theories from the commentary in the Acta and came away profoundly impressed. His celebrated response, the Tentamen de motuum coelestium causis [Essay on the causes of celestial motions], was composed in Rome, in the circle of Bianchini, Lancisi, and Quartieroni.[61]

At that time Leibniz had, in a most diplomatic way, desperately attempted to convince the highest Catholic authorities to rescind the condemnation of Copernicanism, given Catholic astronomers' acceptance of the principle of the relativity of the movement of bodies, according to which the systems of Tycho Brahe, Ptolemy, and Copernicus were equivalent. He therefore wished to add a lengthy introduction to the Tentamen in which, developing the argument of the relativity of the movement of bodies, he asked for a public retraction of the condemnation. But his Catholic astronomer friends, who certainly knew better than he the obstinate rigidity of the Inquisitorial Tribunal, firmly advised, after they read the new introduction, that he not publish it.[62] The dangerous proposition therefore remained in manuscript form, but the Tentamen nevertheless endures as an important document in the history of modern cosmology. Leibniz made it understood that he considered the Copernican–Keplerian hypothesis of the elliptical planetary motion around the sun to be a physical reality, just as Newton had stated in the Principia. His profound divergence from the latter rested, instead, in his identification of the princple of planetary motion. Leibniz would not forsake the hypothesis based on a universal plenum, and at the time such an affirmation encountered no opposition in Rome. Francesco Bianchini, who would later become one of the greatest Catholic astronomers, in 1687 subscribed to the theory of the plenum and of Cartesian vortices in his long treatise De gravitate [On gravity], as yet unedited.[63] Only Alfonso Borelli, one of the most prestigious followers of the Galilean school and the author of the Theoricae Mediceorum planetarum ex causis physicis deductae [Theories of the Medicean planets deduced from physical causes] (1666), described a celestial dynamics that dismissed Cartesian ether and attributed planetary motion to solar energy and gravity (understood as the planets' natural tendency towards the sun). However, his theory, which harked back to Keplerian discoveries and represented the sole example of Galilean celestial mechanics produced by contemporaries, lacked the following in Italy that it deserved.[64]

The fluid ether that Leibniz thoerized was nevertheless profoundly different from that of Descartes. The author of the *Tentamen* attributed to Kepler, rather than to Descartes, the authorship of the hypothesis that the ether encircled and moved the planets (according to Leibniz, Galileo and Torricelli had shared such a theory as well). He also explained that the motion of the fluid ether obeyed a particular "circulatio harmonica"—the velocity of a body's revolution was inversely proportional to its radius, or its distance from the point around which it revolved. Along with the harmonic circulation of the ether, which drew along with it the planets at rest, Leibniz examined the paracentric motion of the planets, following patterns that were not so far from those of Newton. He correlated the thrust of expulsion acting on the planets (centrifugal force), due to the harmonic circulation of the ether, to a rather mysterious solar "attraction," actually quite similar to that of Newton. After lengthy calculations obtained through infinitesimal analysis and Huygens's formula for centrifugal force, the "law of attraction," which brought about an elliptical orbit of the planets under the sway of such forces, proved to be the celebrated inverse square law that Newton had derived from completely different hypotheses. Leibniz's work was actually aimed at reconciling the needs of a mechanistic explanation (hence his acceptance of the plenum) with the Keplerian laws of motion, utilizing in part the Newtonian concept of attraction.[65] The *Tentamen* was a text of great interest whose importance must be understood not only in terms of its high scientific quality, but above all in terms of the decisive Copernican stance it maintained, bound to raise a considerable response among the scholars of the Roman world, with whom the author must have discussed the subjects he examined. The relationships between Leibniz and Catholic intellectuals nevertheless remained quite intense and inclined towards extreme frankness. Still, in 1690, in a particularly prudent and self-censored letter (the Copernican system, for example, was called "*astronomia melior* [the better astronomy]"), addressed to Bianchini, Leibniz worried about the fate of Vincenzo Viviani ("alone in whom Galileo still lives and breathes") and the Roman resistance to the retraction of the Copernican condemnation:

> We have a most learned pope who, if he had the time to listen, would set free the better astronomy, certainly oppressed by the preposterous judgments of some men not so well versed in those branches of knowledge. If you and other friends understanding these matters would be of some assistance on this occasion, indeed you would bind the Roman church to you with a substantial benefice. In fact it is of no little consequence to unmask the slanderous opinions of those who maintain that the truth is being oppressed, which causes no little damage to Roman authority among the most learned and the scholars of other lands.[66]

The sinister warning that came from Naples in the wake of the atheists' trial certainly dampened the spirits of those who were to have "set free" scientific truths. Despite the prestige of some Catholic Galileans, the struggle for the rehabilitation of Copernicanism in fact still remained clandestine and lacking in open support.

With Bianchini's construction of the sundial in the Roman church of Santa Maria degli Angeli,[67] and the creation of a congregation for the reform of the Gregorian calendar presided over by Cardinal Enrico Noris (whose secretary was Bianchini himself), the contacts between Roman scholars and the greatest European mathematicians and astronomers intensified.[68] The letters exchanged among Leibniz, Bianchini, and Noris were particularly significant, and they elicited harsh reactions from the Jesuits and some scholars of Rome's La Sapienza University, who were opposed to such close collaboration with a Lutheran.[69] Bianchini had established a profitable contact with the famous English astronomer John Flamsteed and with the Académie des Sciences of Paris, to which, beginning in 1702, he had regularly sent his own astronomical observations.[70] Plainly the time for a useful analysis of the Principia was at hand, whether for the high level of astronomical studies in Rome or for the considerable dynamism imparted to scientific research by Bianchini himself and the young Galiani. We do not know if the request for the Principia that Galiani made to Ambassador Henry Newton in 1706 was complied with after the Optice was sent; since only about three hundred copies of Principia had been printed, it had certainly already become very rare.[71] Despite this fact, beginning in 1708 Galiani studied the work extremely attentively, in collaboration with Bianchini, whom he considered a "brother," and his pupils of the "Roman colony," who continued to follow with growing admiration his most updated scientific lectures in the monastery of Sant'Eusebio.

It is difficult to say through which channels in this period Galiani might have obtained a copy of the book. One person to whom he could have turned in order to look over the Principia was the learned Neapolitan Giuseppe Valletta. He had met Valletta, along with other local intellectuals such as Costantino Grimaldi, Lucantonio Porzio, and Giacinto De Cristoforo, during the course of a fruitful trip to Naples in 1708.[72] It is most probable, however, that Roman scholars utilized the Holy See's very effective international channels.[73] Galiani's work regarding the Principia, his Osservazioni sopra il libro del Newton intitolato "Principia mathematica" [Remarks about Newton's book entitled Principia mathematica], was a good deal more than a plentiful series of notes. The organic way in which he treated subjects and expounded on some parts of the book seems to indicate clearly Galiani's desire eventually to write a handbook synthesizing and popularizing the most momentous results of the Principia. The work remained unpublished, however (as did a great deal of Galiani's writings), and it probably served only as a basic text to illustrate the fundamental theorems of the Principia to his friends of the "Roman colony."

The Osservazioni sopra il libro del Newton, remarks made with extreme scientific precision, dealt to a great extent with celestial mechanics and universal gravitation. Newton, in his introduction to the third book on the *systema mundi*, had affirmed that one only needed to study some initial sections of the first book in order to understand the characteristic elements of the new cosmology well.[74] Accepting Newton's suggestion, Galiani concentrated his attention on the theory of centripetal forces; basic for successfully investigating planetary motion. The result was a brief compendium of the most important propositions about centripetal forces; with examples and sharp observations, Galiani explained in detail their meaning and relative demonstrations and, in addition, the use that Newton had made of them in the *systema mundi*.[75] The *Principia* was a difficult book, both for the objective complexity of its subject and for its subtle epistemological choices, and Galiani's perplexities and the effort he expended in the book's thorough evaluation emerge plainly from his own text. He advanced important and profound criticisms in his *Osservazioni intorno alla quarta proposizione del primo libro di Newton* [Remarks regarding the fourth proposition of Newton's first book], a fundamental stage in the construction of a new celestial mechanics. The fourth proposition affirms that "the centripetal forces of bodies, which by uniform motion describe different circles, tend to the centers of the same circles, and are to each other as the squares of the arcs described in equal times divided respectively by the radii of the circles."[76] Galiani's questioning of the scientific validity of this affirmation was quite harsh and circumstantial, and it was articulated around two principal elements of the *Principia*'s mathematical-deductive system: the concept of mass and the method of the first and last reasons. In an early paragraph of his *Osservazioni*, Galiani had specially studied the two concepts of the quantity of matter and of the quantity of motion.[77] The first definition finally brought to light the clear-cut difference between mass, a concept linked to inertia and the atomic structure of matter, and weight. The second definition established the value of the motive power in a body in motion. Both concepts, but especially that of mass, were instrumental in achieving a fundamental process of revising traditional scientific methodology, based on the notion of *substance* and on the analysis of qualitative causes.[78] Newtonian mass, qualitatively indifferent to the type of matter in a body, was an essential element in the physico-mathematical treatment in the *Principia*. Through the mathematical concept of punctiform mass, which was beyond any immediate reality, Newton was able for the purposes of his study to represent "both an extremely small part of a body, as well as a planet or a star."[79] Even though Galiani gave a positive judgment of the definitions and laws of motion, he does not seem to have fully understood their profound epistemological meaning. In the preface to his *Osservazioni intorno alla quarta proposizione*, in which he dealt with the problem of the relationship between the motive powers of different bodies, he denounced the abstract geometrical character of the fourth proposition, which apparently contradicted the very definition of the quantity of motion:

Therefore from a consideration only of the spaces covered by several bodies, without considering their quantity as well, he cannot know what relationship the motive powers from which they are produced might have between them. And therefore one sees how fallacious the above fourth proposition of Newton's first book is. . . . He errs because he does not consider the size or quantity of mobiles; that would be true when B, G [the bodies in question] were supposed to be equal, which is not the case. This is so much the more [a problem] because this proposition is applied by him to celestial bodies, that is to say to the planets, which are not equal in size.[80]

Although Galiani's affirmations were revised and corrected in the continuation of the *Osservazioni*,[81] they demonstrate how difficult it was for an Italian scientist to free himself of the complex and at times contradictory Cartesian-naturalist scientific heritage that in the latter seventeenth century had been capable of competing with the Neoplatonic mathematicism of one element of the Galilean school in Italy. Galiani's doubts of a geometrical nature hence confirm the difficulties that he encountered, at least in the 1710s, in fully grasping the possibilities offered by the *Principia*'s physicomathematics. Newton had used the method of the first and last reasons in the geometrical proof of the fourth proposition, thus avoiding the lengthy and boring reasoning *ad absurdum* necessary in similar cases. At the time Galiani was himself at the center of a great debate on the foundations of infinitesimal calculus involving scientists of the calibre of Guido Grandi, Jakob Hermann, and Giacinto De Cristoforo. He disagreed with the correct Newtonian demonstration, affirming that by using the method of the first and last reasons, there was "nothing geometrical" and that all was conducted "by approximation."[82]

Despite his harsh criticisms of the fourth proposition, his judgment of Newton's work was nevertheless positive overall. Each proposition of the *Osservazioni*'s chapter that was designed to explain the important theory of the centripetal forces concluded with an effective explanation of the use of such forces to illustrate planetary motion. Hence the conclusion of the fourth proposition affirmed:

Therefore it was thus demonstrated that the forces by which the various planets are attracted by the sun (and it is the same regarding Jupiter's moons) are reciprocally like the squares of the reciprocal distances. But the force that acts on the same planet, for example on the moon in various places, on the apogee and the perigee, is known as the square of the reciprocal distances. That cannot be demonstrated through the fourth [proposition], but it seems that Newton infers it from the motion of the apsides through proposition XLV of the first book. Once that is postulated, one deduces through the eleventh [proposition] that the planets move in ellipses, and that the sun is the focus, etc. Having demonstrated the force by which the planets are attracted and the curves which they describe, one wonders how all other phenomena observed in the heavens can be inferred and explained.[83]

Following the pattern of the *Principia*, Galiani treated the problem of universal gravitation through a detailed analysis of lunar motion as a particular instance of centripetal forces. The source he utilized to illustrate the mathematical theory of gravitation was no longer the *Principia* itself but, rather, the celebrated work of the Scottish mathematician and astronomer David Gregory, *Astronomiae physicae et geometricae elementa* [Elements of physics, astronomy, and geometry], which appeared in 1702 at Oxford.[84] The choice was due to the simplicity and didactic purpose with which Gregory had broached the arduous task of explaining Newtonian celestial mechanics. With great scientific integrity, he added to these explanations an interesting attempt to historicize the cosmological theories that had appeared since antiquity, thus making the very genesis of the *Principia* more fascinating. In the preface, repeating the theses of the *Prisca theologia* [Ancient theology], Gregory attributed the discovery of universal gravitation to the most ancient Greek philosophers. According to Gregory, the Ionic school (in particular Anaximenes, Anaxagoras, and his pupil Archelaus) had not only already asserted the igneous nature of the stars, but it had also maintained that celestial bodies gravitated reciprocally and that such forces of gravity served to keep the planets within their orbits. Democritus, Metrodorus, Diogenes, and Thales had also affirmed the nonmechanical nature of the celestial planets' gravity.[85] Gregory pursued his historical excursus, focusing on the scientific theories passed from the Ionic school to the Italian school, "whose followers teach that a star is just like a world, and that it contains the earth and the stars and is placed in infinite ether, and that not only is the moon similar to our earth, but also a habitat for the most beautiful animals." He asserted that men such as Epicurus, Lucretius, and Democritus had emphasized the identification between the earth's matter and that from which the planets were composed. In addition, they had already perceived that gravity worked on each body according to precise mathematical laws.[86]

Galiani, who noted how recklessly Gregory had moved modern gravitational theory towards subjects dear to the Hermetics and the Libertines, carefully refrained from repeating in the *Osservazioni* the theses from this admittedly provocative preface. Instead, he exploited the brilliant scientific explanations that Gregory offered regarding the most difficult topics Newton confronted, including the fundamental study of lunar motion. Applying the theory of centripetal forces to lunar motion, Newton had written in the *Principia*: "The force through whose effect the moon is kept in its own orbit tends towards the earth, and it is inversely proportional to the square of the distance of the loci from the center of the earth."[87] Having established that the force operating on the moon was centripetal in nature, all that was left was to verify whether such a force was the same one that regulated the fall of weights on the earth. This fundamental demonstration of the *Principia*—analytically illustrated by Galiani in his *Osservazioni* and taken from Gregory's *Elementa*—concluded Galiani's painstaking examination of the great Newtonian book.[88] Thanks to Galiani's *Osservazioni*, the basic elements of Newtonian theories gradually became known to Roman scientists. Finally the slow and oft-thwarted work of disseminating the *Principia* throughout Italy could be said to have started.

3. FRANCESCO BIANCHINI'S TRIP TO ENGLAND AND CARDINAL GUALTIERI'S ROMAN ACADEMY

With Francesco Bianchini's trip to England in the early months of 1713, a new phase in the dissemination of Newtonian science in Italy opened for Catholic scientists living in Rome. A pupil of the Galilean astronomer Montanari, not only was Bianchini famous as a brilliant astronomer and scholar attuned to modern scientific theories, but he also enjoyed a very solid reputation as a historian and antiquarian; this induced Muratori to make him head of the new "literary republic" of Italy.[1] His journey across the channel was just another stop during a long trip across all of Europe, including stays in France, Belgium, and Holland, during which he encountered scholars such as Flamsteed, Hartsoecker, Le Clerc, Fontenelle, and Newton. The official motivation behind the journey was to present the cardinal's cap to Prince Armand de Rohan in France; the real reason was that Bianchini had to carry out a delicate diplomatic mission for the Holy See: to sound out Louis XIV's position on the European political situation, in particular the fate of James II. Bianchini then had to reestablish contacts between Rome and Catholic minorities in England and the Protestant countries, looking ahead to the soon-anticipated end of the War of the Spanish Succession. These were predominantly political tasks that confirmed the trust and esteem that the Roman Curia and Clement XI harbored for Bianchini.[2] With the aid of the valuable journals he diligently kept throughout the lengthy trip (from May 1712 until May of the following year), we are able to reconstruct his many contacts with political personalities and eminent scholars and, particularly, to document his extraordinary interest in the most recent scientific experiments.[3] This interest profoundly influenced his entire visit to England.

Having arrived in London on 16 February 1713, accompanied by Count Giovanni Antonio Baldini (a diplomat of the duke of Parma), Bianchini had the opportunity to meet the greatest political and cultural figures in all England. He sent the upper echelons of the Roman hierarchy his impressions of the English political and economic situation, as well as of the research of local scholars, and, equally important, he reassured the Holy See about the less-than-dramatic fate of the Catholic minority. His notes are full of admiration and appreciation for the extraordinary welcome he received both on an official level and during informal friendly contacts with prestigious scholars such as Newton, Keill, Arbuthnot, and Flamsteed.[4] Bianchini wrote to Cardinal de Rohan:

> Certainly I count among the best fruits of my trip my having been taken to see this flowering kingdom. The preconception that I had of its magnificence was great, and great as well [the preconception] of its courtesy towards foreigners. But in actuality I found it much greater in both areas. The initial entrance into London in an uninterrupted parade of vessels to the right and to the left for a six-mile journey, in my opinion, has no equal spectacle in the whole world. This court seemed even more splendid in the crowded gathering of ladies and knights at the queen's court in the evening when she inaugurated the festivities. Except for the king's [court], I do not know if I have ever seen one more abundant, particularly for the ladies, who numbered more than two hundred.[5]

A few days after his arrival in London, Bianchini was accompanied by John Inghilis (a scholar he had met in Rome) and the famous mathematician and astronomer John Keill[6] to greet Isaac Newton in his residence. The especially warm encounter gave him an opportunity to report to Newton the experiments from the *Opticks* that had been duplicated in Rome at the Accademia degli Antiquari Alessandrini and the favorable reception that his theories had received in Roman scientific circles.[7] On 2 February, immediately after the initial meeting between Newton and Bianchini, Bianchini participated in an important meeting of the Royal Society. Newton was present and proposed that both Bianchini and Count Baldini become members of the academy,[8] and Francis Hauksbee, the official experimenter of the Royal Society, demonstrated an important and spectacular experiment from his recent research on electricity.[9] From this first meeting—which had quite an impact on Bianchini because of the level and organizational capacity exhibited by official English science—a second followed, again presided over by Newton himself, at which they discussed a number of problems of optics and hydrodynamics.[10] This was enough to convince Bianchini of the superiority of the research sponsored by the prestigious English institution over that conducted at the Académie des sciences in Paris, or in any of the other analogous centers of Continental study.

Bianchini wasted no time during his stay in Great Britain; he visited Greenwich Observatory, where he took notes on the features of its most modern instruments and discussed his recent observations regarding comets and fixed stars with his friend Flamsteed.[11] Then he toured Oxford University and its scientific laboratories, paying close attention and gathering information about the celebrated university's internal regulations and the scholars' research programs there.[12] Afterward he did not miss the chance to consult prestigious scholars such as Needham and Arbuthnot about their research and the results of the latest historical and scientific studies in England.[13] He received a warm reception everywhere:

Then here in London every day I was favored by dilettantes of antiquity, and My Lord Pembrok and other lords of quality had me look at the most exceptional collections of Raphael's sketches and of antique medals. And other literati had me inspect all the most noteworthy things for the sciences, as happened yesterday at the Greenwich Observatory with the celebrated mathematician Flamsteed and today with Lord Newton, perhaps the most distinguished [person] there is in Europe in this profession. I see that this is a very much friendlier nation than we believe in Italy, hence it is worthy of particularly zealous cultivation.[14]

The encounters with Newton proved to be particularly fruitful, both for the deep reciprocal admiration that grew between the two and for the special interest that Newton showed in his Catholic guest. He entrusted Bianchini with two copies of the Optice, one as a personal gift, the other for the Vatican Library.[15] Bianchini had frank discussions with him about astronomical problems and described the state of Italian science and the work of his friends Galiani, Manfredi, and Grandi. It is not surprising that these very three were to be the recipients of the Commercium epistolicum [Epistolary correspondence], responsible for intensifying the rancor of the bitter dispute between Leibniz and Newton over who had discovered infinitesimal calculus.[16]

After Bianchini returned to Rome, the first truly cultural undertaking aimed at disseminating Newton's theories in Italy took shape at the hands of Celestino Galiani. Galiani's action—which was finalized in a brief treatise extremely critical of Cartesian theses on gravity and planetary motion, the Epistola de gravitate et cartesianis vorticibus [Letter on gravity and Cartesian vortices]—was clearly related to the success of Bianchini's journey to England and the protection that Bianchini was able to guarantee through both his prestige and his close ties with the Curia. The Epistola, which remained unpublished but was originally planned for inclusion in the Giornale de' Letterati d'Italia,[17] took its inspiration from the widespread and heated Italian and European debate on Cartesian vortices and the Newtonian concept of gravity. Even if not always explicitly, the work echoed the arguments raised in France by Huygens's Discours sur la cause de la pesanteur [Discourse on the cause of gravity] (1690), Villemot's Nouveau système ou nouvelle explication du mouvement des planets [A new system or new explanation of the movement of the planets] (Lyons, 1707), and Saurin's Examen d'une difficulté considérable proposée par M. Huygens contre le système cartésien sur la cause de la pesanteur [Examination of a considerable difficulty proposed by M. Huygens against the Cartesian system regarding the cause of gravity] (1709). All of these works attest to the difficulties that Newtonian theories encountered in gaining acceptance in France.[18] Galiani's Epistola, addressed publicly to one of the most authoritative Italian Cartesians, Gregorio Caloprese,[19] thus represented a distinctive stance within Neapolitan culture in favor of Newton.[20] It was also a response, albeit an indirect one, to the theses of the

Cartesian Giovanni Poleni, author of *De vorticibus coelestibus dialogus* [Dialogue on celestial vortices] (1712), which appeared in Padua and was the object of considerable discussion and commentary in the following years.

In the early eighteenth century the marked lack of interest in Newtonian theories within Neapolitan culture (which was in a state of disarray since there were no men and no epistemological consciousness which could revitalize the now-bankrupt heritage of the Investiganti) contrased sharply with the traditional vivacity of Paduan scientific circles and those of the Veneto in general. Through the works of men such as Antonio Vallisnieri, Bernardino Zendrini, Jacopo Riccati, Antonio Conti, and Giovanni Rizzetti, the Veneto cultural region rapidly became engaged in a heated confrontation over the new Newtonian scientific theories. The first reflection on the *Principia* appeared in the only periodical worthy of such a name then existing in Italy, the Venetian *Giornale de' Letterati d'Italia*, which first appeared in 1710.[21] The Swiss mathematician Jakob Hermann, then teaching in the Paduan university, opened the discussion with his *Metodo d'investigare le orbite de' pianeti nell'ipotesi che le forze centrali o pure la gravità degli stessi pianeti sono in ragione reciproca de' quadrati delle distanze, che i medesimi tengono dal centro* [A method of investigating the orbits of the planets using the hypothesis that the central forces or rather the gravity of the same planets are inversely proportional to the squares of the distances that they maintain from the center]. At Antonio Vallisnieri's request, Hermann brilliantly confronted the difficult issue of mathematically evaluating the central forces— a much debated theme in France as well[22]—providing Italian readers with a lengthy presentation of Newtonian gravitational theory and attributing the discovery of the inverse square law simultaneously to Leibniz and to Newton:

> From the time that Misters Newton and Leibniz began to consider the laws of celestial motion by using the proofs of the most abstruse geometry, astronomy—once deformed by many fictions—was reduced to the simplicity that nature affects in any of its actions. . . . [The theorems of Kepler] are demonstrated by Mr. Newton in the first book of his illustrious work of the *Mathematical principles of natural philosophy*, and also by Mr. Leibniz in his most elegant dissertation on the causes of celestial motion that appeared in the *Acta* of Leipzig in February 1689. These incomparable literati claim that the action of gravity is exercised not only on the bodies that crowd our earth but equally on all the planets, both primary and secondary.[23]

It is quite evident in Hermann's article that he attempted to minimize Newton's real merits, for the piece emphasizes the incompleteness of the theory of central forces from a mathematical viewpoint. In the *Continuazione dell'articolo XV del tomo II di questo giornale ovvero soluzione generale del problema inverso delle forze centrali* [Continuation of Article XV of Volume II of this journal, or the general solution of the inverse problem of central forces], which appeared the following year, Hermann seemed aware that he had exaggerated his assessment of the limits of the Newtonian work. Backpedaling somewhat, he was, in fact, compelled to write:

> The famous Mr. Newton has certainly given a solution to the inverse problem in general, but, as we have said in the second issue of this journal, without taking care to apply his general solution to that particular hypothesis of the forces in duplicate inverse proportion to the distances of the mobile from the center (which produces the unique sections of the cone), despite the fact that nearly his entire world system depends on this hypothesis. Since I was curious to know if the three unique conical sections result from that particular hypothesis, I have tried to explain the problem only for this case.[24]

In the same issue of the *Giornale de' Letterati*, there was a harsh reaction to the Swiss scholar's writings from mathematician Giuseppe Verzaglia of Cesena, who published his *Considerazioni sopra l'articolo XVI del tomo V nel quale si tratta del problema inverso delle forze centrali* [Considerations regarding Article XVI of Volume V in which is treated the inverse problem of the central forces] (1711). Defending "the incomparable Newton," he expressed his doubts about the possibility of working out a general mathematical theory of the central forces using the recently discovered differential and integral calculus. Verzaglia maintained that Hermann had not understood the spirit of the Newtonian physico-mathematical method. Each problem of celestial mechanics had to be treated without omitting considerations of physical nature, "as did the grand master of this art, Mr. Newton, who by keeping to the first hypothesis taught us how to handle this subject without ambiguity."[25] The dispute on the problem of central forces was far from exhausted, and it continued in the *Giornale de' Letterati* until the 1720s, eliciting comment, of the highest scientific calibre, from Hermann himself and, most notably, from Jacopo Riccati, one of the greatest Italian mathematicians of the eighteenth century.[26] But the nature of the controversy and the difficulties related to the very comprehension of the new infinitesimal calculus certainly did not favor a broader participation of scholars in the debate. The disputes over the basic themes of Newtonian and Cartesian cosmologies were simpler to evaluate. While formally preserving a middle position between the litigants, the *Giornale de' Letterati* in the end betrayed its preference, and in certain cases it revealed a staunch acceptance by scholars in the Veneto of the classic arguments of Cartesian mechanicism. The articles written by Zendrini and Poleni, as well as the reviews of the works of Giambattista Mazini and Domenico Guglielmini,[27] documented the peculiarity of the Veneto's scientific culture; it interwove (and confused) the Galilean experimental heritage, the naturalist tradition of the Paduan university, and Cartesian metaphysics. This peculiarity is particularly evident from the critical and somewhat instrumental approach taken by scholars like Antonio Conti and Jacopo Riccati, who wrote on the *Principia*'s theories. From the earliest years of Newtonianism's dissemination in Italy, the

Veneto thus represented a very real dialectic counterweight to the Catholic intellectuals headed by Celestino Galiani, first opposing Newton's theories on a scientific level, and then (particularly Conti) reinterpreting them within a complex and original ideological framework.[28]

Again in the pages of the *Giornale de' Letterati*, Bernardino Zendrini[29] opened the debate on cosmological issues in 1710 by rejecting Giovanni Ceva's vaguely Newtonian gravitational theory. Zendrini accused Ceva, who proposed the bizarre (to say the least) concept of a gravity inherent in bodies, of having misunderstood Newton himself. In Zendrini's opinion, only Cartesian ether and the plenum could adequately explain how the "great machine of the world" functioned.[30] The *Giornale de' Letterati* attested to the escalation of the debate in the Veneto when in 1712 it announced an important work by Marquis Giovanni Poleni:

> About to appear . . . is the following work of Giovanni Poleni, professor of meteors and astronomy in this university: *De vorticibus coelestibus dialogus* [Dialogue on celestial vortices]. Since the controversies over the explanations until now given for many celestial phenomena in the system of vortices are serious, and as there are, in addition to those [phenomena], yet others that merit no less consideration, the author has proposed to treat them all. This is not [done] however with the goal of establishing the hypothesis of the vortices as true or discrediting it as false, but with the sole object of opening the path to research the truth, leaving judgment to the learned.[31]

This brilliant, Galilean-type dialogue between Publius, Laelius, and Marius, three astronomers gathered together with Poleni in a villa, succinctly illustrates Poleni's preference for the arguments of the Cartesian Marius. With his work bound to meet with success (particularly in France),[32] Poleni intervened in the European dispute over Cartesian vortices with great authority and clarity, first presenting the cosmological systems of Kepler, Descartes, Newton, and Leibniz, and then expounding his personal reflections on the most recent scientific endeavors of European Cartesians.

The entire defensive strategy of the European Cartesians against the dissemination of Newtonian theories was founded on progressive work updating the original idea of Descartes's vortices. In response to the particular problems raised by Newton,[33] Cartesian scientists countered with some theories that, leaving aside the mechanistic hypothesis, strove principally to reconcile the vortices with Keplerian laws of planetary motion. Huygens, Villemot, Saurin, and, last but not least, Poleni all moved in this direction. Unlike his French colleagues, however, Poleni insisted on an experimental approach to the entire problem. How could one reconcile Keplerian laws with the vortices? How could one refute Huygens's precise calculations stating that the earthly vortex had to spin seventeen times more rapidly than the earth itself in order for the gravity on the planet to equal the centrifugal force produced by the vortex's motion? These are questions to which Poleni responded by rejecting the hypotheses of Villemot, who attributed the same velocity both to ether and to the planets. He proposed, instead, a return to Descartes's original theories positing the planets' delay with respect to the velocity of the vortex, and he then hypothesized a different density for ether in order to explain the delay necessary to reconcile the vortices' motion with Kepler's laws. Through a series of ingenious experiments, Poleni insisted on demonstrating the existence of earthly phenomena analogous to celestial ones. The overarching purpose of his work was to show how the mechanistic hypothesis was by far the most scientifically correct, since it was founded on exacting experimental verification.

After having read Poleni's work (which he deprecatingly labeled "very superficial"),[34] Galiani set out to compose his *Epistola*, and the anti-Newtonian offensive that the scientific circles in the Veneto were preparing was evidently very much on his mind. He was motivated to request the support of Guido Grandi, who had contact with the editors of the *Giornale de' Letterati*, to get the *Epistola* published in the periodical; however, the project was never realized—most likely for lack of support by Grandi himself, who was not interested in fully sharing Galiani's harsh anti-Cartesian criticisms. Completed in March 1714, the *Epistola* represented a true abstract of Newtonian theories, neatly set forth and explained through lemmas, theorems, and corollaries, based not only on the *Principia* but also on the works of John Keill and David Gregory.[35] The work's tone is noticeably confrontational when dealing with the Cartesian system, and the presentation seems almost like a calculated attack intent on breaking down not only the cosmology of the vortices but also the very aprioristic logic on which that cosmology was founded. Addressing the man who was reputed to be one of the leaders of Italian Cartesianism, Gregorio Caloprese, Galiani wrote without mincing words:

> In the first place, I wish you to know that in Cartesian philosophy there are many things I do not approve of at all, and while I reflected on it or read others' commentaries, these things seemed to me entirely uncertain, and even false. If I wished to expose all those things as they deserve, I would write a book rather than a letter. Thus in order not to go too far beyond the limits of a letter in this examination of Cartesian philosophy, I broach only two issues (i.e., that of the vortices spinning around the sun and the fixed stars, and that of gravity, which Descartes based on ether's pressure).[36]

Galiani constructed a painstaking demonstration of the famous fortieth theorem (the fifty-second proposition) of the *Principia*'s second book, which had established that the periodic times of the vortices' motion around a sphere were proportional to their distances from the center of the motion. Hence he countered point for point the arguments of Descartes's *Principia philosophiae* [Principles of philosophy] and the theories of the French Cartesians who imitated them.

Based on Descartes's opinion (*Princip.*, p. 3, num. XXVIII and elsewhere), when the planets are relatively at rest in the celestial region in which they orbit, at the same time they follow their orbits, and the nearby small spheres are carried around by them. From this it stands that the periodic times of the planets are respective to the periodic times of the small spheres, this is to say (as in the theorem) as the squares of the distances from the center. And because Saturn's distance from the sun is more than ninety times the earth's distance from the sun, [the ratio] of the earth's periodic time to Saturn's periodic time would therefore be nearly 1 to 90. And when the earth completes its orbit in one year, Saturn ought to complete its about ninety times, while it makes only just thirty. Hence the Cartesian hypothesis is false to whomever reasonably finds such a consequence false.[37]

The work of demolishing the Cartesian cosmology developed through a precise concatenation of axioms, lemmas, theorems, and scientific considerations on the dynamics of fluids that made no concessions to the reader. In 1715, after having read the *Epistola*, Giovambattista Pignatelli, prince of Marsiconovo, wrote to Galiani in Naples, with the not unexpected observation: "[These are] truly insurmountable objections, since they are deduced by reliable geometrical principles."[38] Galiani thoroughly dismantled the very Cartesian thesis stating that the quantity of motion would be constant.

Therefore a new motion from the sun's rotation on its own axis is added to the small spheres near the sun. With that posited, it seems necessary that their motion accelerates without stopping. If in fact we suppose that the sun ceases to draw the nearby small spheres into its orbit, because of the laws of nature established by Descartes, they would nevertheless continue in their uniform rotation with the very same velocity. For based on Descartes's opinion, what once is set in motion continues to move, and what moves without communicating anything to another mobile body loses none of its motion. . . . But you, intelligent man, can already see what an absurdity this is: if Descartes's hypothesis were true, all the planets would have to follow their orbits in the approximately twenty-seven days in which the sun rotates on its axis, and there is nothing more false than this.[39]

Even on the subject of gravity Galiani did not hesitate to engage in a long, exacting scientific discussion in order to refute the Cartesian theses, employing a compact series of calculations that took into account the most recent measurements of the earth's diameter and the Huygensian theories about centrifugal forces.[40]

In order to evaluate fully the meaning and the importance of Galiani's *Epistola*, it is necessary to re-create the environment in which the work developed. We know that the suggestion to address the letter to Caloprese came from the latter's cousin, Gianvincenzo Gravina,[41] after one of the frequent discussions that occurred in Rome among the greatest local scholars. Nothing more has survived for us, however, regarding the names of the participants at these meetings. While Galiani's little treatise was certainly the personal contribution of a sharp and informed militant intellectual, the work's real import comes to light only if one considers the foundation of a scientific academy in Rome in April 1714, an effort headed by Bianchini and Galiani himself. Named Accademia Gualtieri (after its inspiration and patron Cardinal Filippo Antonio Gualtieri),[42] it was an important element for the history of eighteenth-century scientific culture in Italy. We know little of the lectures held at the weekly gatherings in the cardinal's palace, but that little safely permits us to judge how free and of what high calibre the scientific debate that developed there was. From its inception the academy flourished under the auspices of modern science, and of Newtonian science in particular. In April 1714 Bianchini wrote a long letter to Newton full of attestations of esteem, assuring him of Catholic scientists' interest in his works and promising a close collaboration with the Royal Society. Among other things, he conveyed the impatience with which Roman scholars awaited the appearance of the second edition of the *Principia*, as well as his personal and substantial propaganda favoring Newtonian theories directed at curial circles:

> Your Excellence [Newton], I notified His Most Excellent Lord Alessandro Albani, the pope's nephew, that as soon as possible he would receive a copy of the new edition of your works, which ever since they went to press as I was leaving, I intended to have them sent as soon as the typographer had published them. [Albani] says he is most obliged by your benevolence and generosity, which for quite some time he admired for the reputation that all scholars agree in expressing. Just recently it has been learned that this wonderful edition has been completed, and some friends have said they saw the additions added, summarized by their headings in the brief, published list. I anxiously await this collection that all covet.[43]

The academy's scientific program plainly reflects the desire of Bianchini and Galiani to take advantage of the practical protection from the Curia extended by that unique personality, Cardinal Gualtieri. They did so in order to finally come to terms with modern science, although they maintained a firm commitment to bring to light the complete compatibility of modern science with the truths of Christian faith. Referring to Gualtieri's initiative, Galiani wrote to his friend Bottari:

> We then arrived at the subject to be treated in the first gatherings, and His Excellency commanded that we continue discussions about the things of nature in the same order in which God created them, and therefore that we should begin with light; thus it was done. . . . Monsignor Bianchini explained Gassendi's opinions about light, Mr. Resta those of Christian Huygens, and I those of Descartes and Newton. And we determined to continue in order, generating the experiments referred to by Newton himself in his book *De luce et coloribus* [On light and colors].[44]

The problem of the structure of light was particularly discussed at the academy's meetings in the forum of a frank debate in which the cardinal himself participated.[45] What distinguished this academy from the others that had appeared earlier in various Italian cities was its abundant financial means, which permitted the acquisition of numerous and select scientific instruments. Referring to the cardinal, Galiani wrote to Guido Grandi, "He has built a prodigious collection of instruments and gadgets, and he is ready to spend all that one might ever desire."[46] There was no lack of results: Roman engineer Giovambattista Resta's construction of a modern version of the Boylian pneumatic machine built in London permitted the execution of the first Italian experiments on electricity. The prisms of very high quality that Bianchini brought from England allowed Galiani to repeat Newtonian experiments under optimal conditions and to evaluate the complex question of the rainbow in mathematical terms.[47] But the importance of this small academy even went beyond conspicuous scientific merits: it embodied the first serious attempt on the part of a group of Catholic intellectuals to reconnect the threads of a dialogue between modern science and Catholic culture that had been brusquely interrupted by the clamorous trial of the atheists. Just as in Cardinal Ciampini's earlier academy, there were, in this complex operation, men differing not only in temperament but also in ideological and cultural convictions; we should not get a false impression from their common Catholic background. Even while working within the academy with Bianchini and Gualtieri, Galiani did not seem to share wholly in the cardinal's plan, aimed, above all, at uniting—and thus placing under certain conditions—the various Italian centers in a common program of scientific research. This would advance the more general work of cultural renewal to a second stage, one that the future *cappellano maggiore** of the Kingdom of Naples believed was indispensable. It was also the start of the interweaving and overlapping of Gualtieri's personal initiatives, more problematic and more open to modern thought than the more cautious ambitions of other scholars present in the academy.

In a letter to Guido Grandi, Galiani clarified Cardinal Gualtieri's plan to coordinate Italian research centers, and he asked expressly, in Gualtieri's name, for close collaboration in verifying the experiments completed at Rome.[48] Galiani was concluding an analogous task of organizing and coordinating information, both for the scientific academy founded in Rimini by Cardinal Giannantonio Davia and directed by his personal doctor Antonio Leprotti, and for Florentine (through Giovanni Bottari) and Neapolitan scholars. Galiani was aided by Giovambattista Pignatelli and his longtime friend Giacomo Grazini, who wrote to him: "I read with infinite pleasure of the experiments on light and electricity, and the friends to whom I read the letter

---

*The *cappellano maggiore* was a secular office equivalent to Secretary of Education—Trans. note.

enjoyed them as well. We now wish to hear about other experiments that might be performed, since in Rome they are fortunate enough to hear the conversations of men of such good taste."[49] Galiani's interest in Naples reached the point where he proposed that local scholars form a new scientific academy in which they would repeat Newtonian experiments on light. But the difficulties proved to be beyond all expectations. Grazini's negative response to Galiani's urging was in fact quite explicit and detailed.

> With regard to the academy, which you say you proposed to the lord prince of Marsiconovo, the subject between us here is a sore point. The whims of these literati are not so easily united, and one sees through experience that all the authority of the duke of Medinaceli could not help but cause a thousand quarrels and difficulties among his academics that finally ended in a mockery. And then the professors of the sciences here for the most part must find another job to make a living (or to live better), and this makes it difficult for them to accept the time wasted in enterprises from which they enjoy no profit. Until the prince (who commits his authority, money, and rewards) resolves to found a society fashioned after the other celebrated ones of Europe, we cannot hope to start anything good—or that anything begun might last.[50]

Bianchini, too, contributed personally to forging a network of relationships with Pisan circles and, especially, the Istituto di Scienze of Bologna directed by Eustachio Manfredi.[51] But it remained Galiani's task to coordinate the sending of reports about the experiments run in the new academy. Under the protection of the important Roman research center, he could thus set in motion his plan: to propagate Newtonian science and to present it as the prestigious result of a rigorous application of the Lockean epistemological model. As we shall see, thanks to Galiani's elaboration in succeeding years, Locke would acquire a politico-cultural association that was extremely fascinating and meaningful to many areas of early-eighteenth-century Italian culture. Hence the *Epistola de gravitate et cartesianis vorticibus* [Letter on gravity and Cartesian vortices] remains primarily Galiani's own personal initiative devoted to introducing his thought to Italian scholars. Yet, to this end, Galiani capably used the favorable atmosphere created by the propagation of Newtonian scientific interests in Rome, officially consecrated by the Accademia Gualtieri. The little treatise had vast repercussions, even though it remained in manuscript form. Traces of its passage—with very different reactions—are found in Naples, Florence, Pisa, and Rimini,[52] and it is easy to hypothesize that it was also read elsewhere. The importance of this *Epistola* is further confirmed by the fact that Pietro Giannone, and, especially, Bernardo Andrea Lama and Joseph Roma (both pupils of Celestino Galiani's "Roman colony"), would imitate its arguments to promote the dissemination of Newtonianism in Piedmont during the 1730s.[53] The *Epistola* is an incomplete document, however, for in it there is merely a strong criticism of Cartesian vortices and gravitational theory without any hint of the *Principia*'s alternative theses. Actually Galiani envisioned, as part of his project, the future publication (in the *Giornale de' Letterati*, as always) of another open letter, addressed this time to Guido Grandi, in which he would furnish a clear-cut version of Newtonian gravitation, following the conclusions of the *quaestiones* and the apologetic interpretation present in the *Scholium generale*. Nevertheless, this second part was never more than an intention, and it is possible to reconstruct only some of its features through allusions in letters sent to friends in those years.[54]

Having been introduced to the *Epistola* through Bargellini,[55] Guido Grandi dealt his friend Galiani's project a cruel blow, for he was not able to hide his disappointment over the strongly confrontational character of Galiani's criticism of Cartesian philosophy. Referring to one of his earlier letters commenting on the *Epistola*, he wrote Galiani:

> I did not raise that objection to Your Reverence in order to confirm the Cartesian hypothesis or to distract you from your praiseworthy plan to dispute its validity. My only goal was to give you a means for anticipating the objections that could be given to your calculation from whomever might wish to defend the said hypothesis—not entirely, but in that part which one could [defend] and which conforms to mechanical laws. While I wish to stand firmly behind all that Descartes said and hold to the fine points of his opinions, I am nevertheless aware that one could not come out honorably, as there are many contradictions in his manner of philosophizing. But in the end—and in essence—there are very lovely passages that for many satisfy better than the other hypotheses do.[56]

Grandi possessed a penetrating and concerned understanding of the danger that a frontal attack against Cartesianism might pose by favoring the forces most hostile to modern culture in Italy, already locked in a death struggle to defend a thoroughly bankrupt Aristotelian philosophy. For at the time Aristotelianism and Cartesianism represented the great metaphysical systems subscribed to, on the one hand hand, by conservative Italian circles and, on the other, by those who fought for the affirmation of *libertas philosophandi*, albeit in a less organic and direct manner. The reluctance of Tuscan mathematician Grandi to support Galiani's avowedly anti-Cartesian work is therefore understandable.[57] Another interesting discussion between the two on the philosophical and scientific meaning of gravity can be understood to some extent against the background of those tensions. Grandi wrote to Galiani:

> Certainly it agrees more with mechanical principles to say that a body is pushed by other bodies until one goes back to any matter placed in motion first by God Himself, than to say that there are those attracting forces of which Mr. Newton speaks in matter's parts. And there are some who strongly lament that Newton might little by little bring to life Aristotelian qualities and let us fall back into the darkness of Aristotelianism—God help us. . . . It seems to me that recourse to certain ideal

laws of nature's author, and the claim that one can explain all phenomena through these laws, is equivalent to shirking any exertion and failing
to explain anything through its specific reason.[58]

In the preceding barbs of this exchange of letters, Galiani was forced to
illustrate the exact meaning of his *Epistola*, and he revealed to Grandi some
of his doubts regarding an important aspect of gravitational theory. He wrote
in July 1714: "One thing I do not understand in the Newtonians: they say
that all bodies gravitate towards all things; . . . the assertion seems to me
completely arbitrary."[59] However the gravitational theory of reciprocity was
not so complex[60] that it prevented him from insisting on the scientific
foundations of Newtonian theories and on the need to expose them to the
greater public.

> It seems to me it would not be difficult for me to demonstrate that all
> the best hypotheses on gravity are at least quite tentative, in order to
> prove the Newtonian opinion quite probable. For it is no more than a
> constant law of nature's author, which is to say of God's will, that all
> bodies move towards certain points with forces proportional to their size,
> and that these forces diminish in proportion to the increase of the squares
> of the distances. This is precisely the manner in which the other virtues
> spread themselves. And with regard to this, to my satisfaction some days
> ago an experiment on light was run in Cardinal Gualtieri's academy, and
> it came out exactly: that is, at various distances from the body, the light's
> efficacy becomes inversely proportional to the squares of the distances.[61]

But the most interesting aspect revealed in the letters Galiani addressed to
various friends is his constant preoccupation, dating from the very early
eighteenth century, with frustrating an erroneous and dangerous materialist
interpretation of universal gravitation.

All scholars of Newtonian issues are well aware that the Latin translation of Jacques Rohault's *Traité de physique* [Treatise on physics], edited and
annotated by Samuel Clarke, was fundamental to the European dissemination of Newton's theories. The work has been called a double-headed mon-
ster, for Clarke, commenting adeptly in Newtonian language on the basic
concepts of Cartesian physics, helped in his notes to denounce Cartesianism's
errors and hasten their renunciation in European universities.[62] The Latin
translation of Rohault's *Traité*, universally thought to have been published
in 1713 in Cologne,[63] was actually printed in a clandestine Neapolitan
typeshop. Published in honor of the Neapolitan patrician Don Filippo Colonna,
son of the prince of Sonnino, the work bears no indication of the publisher. At the end of the dedication, however, it carries the mysterious signature of Cellenio Zacclori, the anagram of Lorenzo Ciccarelli, a Neapolitan
lawyer who had transformed his house into a well-equipped typeshop.[64]
Although Ciccarelli's shop has yet to be the focus of further study, we know
that one of its principal tasks was the printing of prohibited books. For
example, the edition of Galileo's *Dialogo intorno ai due massimi sistemi* [Dia-

logue about the two greatest systems], to which we will return, appeared with the false attribution of Florence, 1710; the typeshop produced books particularly difficult to find on the Italian market. Galiani knew personally of the secret typeshop's existence, and he knew that the group of scholars to which Ciccarelli belonged had taken the initiative in publishing Clarke's edition of Rohault's *Traité*. In fact Galiani redirected Giovanni Bottari's attention to the need to protect that fundamental work from possible censure by the Inquisitorial Tribunal, preparing the ground in Rome within curial circles. This was why he wrote to his friend in Florence on 25 August 1714:

> I do not know if you remember what I once told you about Rohault's *Physics*, namely that because of the new reprint produced in Naples, it would become available to a wider audience. It might easily have fallen into the hands of some rogue zealot, who would have arranged for its prohibition in the *Index*. You wisely told me that it would never be like those [prints] that deal with matters of faith and morality. Now despite all that, my prophecy is coming true: the book is already under censure and I am told that it will doubtless be prohibited.[65]

We do not know how Galiani and his Roman friends intervened to prevent the imposition of a catastrophic condemnation. The episode nevertheless confirms his agonizing preoccupation with avoiding any possible clash with Catholic authorities. Such confrontations would certainly have created obstacles for his plan to renew Italian science through the dissemination of Newtonian theories, without giving in to rifts and traumatic fractures. Galiani's fears concerning a possible misunderstanding of the concept of gravity in a materialist sense probably evolved from his own convictions about philosophical connections. More important, he possessed a lucid vision of the insurmountable difficulties of a political nature that such an interpretation would have meant for the fate of the entire Italian scientific movement, especially after what had happened with the trial of the atheists. Not even Clarke's definition of gravity in the *Tractatus physicus* [Treatise on Physics]—"the primary and general law of the universe of matter imprinted by God"[66]—seems to have reassured Galiani entirely. In an important letter to the apostolic nuncio at Brussels, Monsignor Vincenzo Santini, he plainly stated his sincere desire to clarify the entire matter as soon as possible:

> Presently I have in my hands a dissertation in which I use mathematical reasoning to reject all that is most sound and said to sustain the Cartesian hypothesis. And as I find it suitable, [I] speak of the Newtonians' opinion on the same subject—they who would have it that gravity is a primary quality of matter, just as its extension and divisibility are. For I believe [this opinion] is falser than the Cartesian one, and I can only reject it. And it is my opinion that we do not yet know what the true reason is why, for example, an unsupported stone falls down.[67]

The lengthy account offered by Jean Le Clerc in his *Bibliothèque choisie* [A select library] of the disputes between Dodwell and Clarke—an account containing clear allusions to the dangers of a materialist interpretation of gravity—was in all probability related to his heightened attention to the matter.[68] But as we shall see, at the time Galiani was already quite well acquainted with the bitter controversy that had developed in England between the Free-Thinkers and the Boyle lecturers, who were favorable to an apologetic reading of the new Newtonian science. His letters are especially geared towards quelling any possible materialist interpretation of the *Principia's* universe-machine, and they coherently develop Isaac Newton's thoughts on the divine nature of gravitation's cause.[69]

4. THE *PRINCIPIA* AND COPERNICANISM

The concept of gravity was not the only issue to demand the consideration of Galiani and his friends in this first general evaluation of Newtonian cosmology. Even leaving aside the problems raised by the *Principia*, Galiani courageously renewed the analysis of the Copernican system's physical reality, an old war horse for all those who fought for the affirmation of *libertas philosophandi*. On first analysis, reopening the Copernican question to discussion might seem a delaying tactic in a losing battle. But, as other scholars have emphasized, at that time research on the proofs of the earth's diurnal motion was still an entirely topical scientific argument.[1] In Italy, after the harsh dispute between the Jesuit Giovambattista Riccioli and the Copernicans Alfonso Borelli and Stefano Degli Angeli that occurred in the mid-seventeenth century, the fire long continued to smolder under the ashes.[2] In 1688 the *Philosophical Transactions* had published a detailed account, edited by James Gregory, of the debate between Borelli and Riccioli over the proofs of the earth's diurnal motion. A discussion, whose protagonists were Hooke and Newton, on the problem was thus opened in the Royal Society.[3] We have already noted the efforts of Bianchini and Leibniz in the 1710s to solicit a retraction of the Inquisitorial Tribunal's condemnation. The struggle of Galiani and his friends was far from a lingering over ancient and obsolete disputes. Certainly a majority of Italian scientists were resigned to the well-known salutary edict of 1616 condemning Copernicanism. Some of them, in fact, had accommodated the edict by proclaiming the falsity of the Copernican system and then presenting their own true, Copernican convictions clearly within their text (a good example is Poleni's treatise *De vorticibus* [On vortices]).[4] Ascertaining the reality of the Copernican system could finally reopen the debate on such vital questions as the function and autonomy of modern science: this was the result that Galiani sought, soliciting his friends to give their opinions on the thorny question.

To help impede ecclesiastical assertions about the primacy of theology in all disciplines, including science, an underground clique of partisans of

Copernicanism and Galileism had taken shape among Italian scientific circles immediately after the death of Galileo, a group that, however small, had infiltrated even the religious orders themselves.[5] In contrast to this fragile but stubborn opposition, the overwhelming majority of Italian scholars stood united, having caved in without great fanfare to what Romeo De Maio in an effective image has called the "reason of the Church" of Counter-Reformation ideology.[6] These two groups were clearly antithetical and destined to spark an intense and lacerating conflict within the Catholic community itself—we should never forget, as Arnaldo Momigliano has written, that Italian culture of that time remained essentially a culture of "self-taught men in ecclesiastical dress."[7] It was not long before a different position formed between the two extremes, a viewpoint held, although with different nuances, by many Catholic scientists, especially astronomers. This viewpoint greatly respected scientific research while simultaneously refusing to recognize its full autonomy or its distinct function in the wholly secular and earthly development of humanity. One of the greatest Italian astronomers of the early eighteenth century with close ties to the Roman Curia, Eustachio Manfredi, offers a representative example of such a view.[8] In his works he demonstrated that he kept up-to-date on scientific research from all corners of Europe. He knew the *Principia* well, and in his astronomical manuals he paid tribute to Newtonian cosmology, maintaining its superiority over that of Descartes. His ideas on the autonomy and truth of science were nevertheless different from those of many European and Italian researchers. Manfredi took his lead from new theories critical of the Cartesian system, and he declared his utter disbelief in the physical reality of the various cosmological models. All scientific theories, he maintained, were necessarily commensurate with historical ages and their corresponding levels of human knowledge, and they could never presume to be of any use for the entire truth.[9] Consequently it was useless to discuss the physical reality of the Copernican, Ptolemaic, or Tychian systems or to derive from each a new image of nature, humans, and the God–nature relationship, each different from the teachings of ecclesiastical tradition. His was plainly what Popper today would define as an "instrumentalist" conception of science: a legitimate conception that, since it deprived all scientific research of ontological capacity, nevertheless resulted in its impoverishment and depotentialization from a cultural and ideological standpoint.[10] In fact, concepts such as an accurate evaluation of science and its function in the context of contemporary society, and the desire (let alone the capacity) to seize its innovative impulse, to trust one's self to it in order to open long-accepted truths to discussion, and then to accept entirely and without compromise profound philosophical and ideological implications, were completely foreign to Manfredi's mentality. Solely on the basis of the astronomer's writings, it is difficult to evaluate the extent to which Manfredi's limitations were the fruit of an epistemological choice, not without its own cultural integrity, and how much they should be attributed to the harsh conditions of the contemporary Italian historical reality that imposed precise limitations on scholars. Certainly Galiani's position in the early eighteenth century appeared completely different, careful as he was to identify and to combat a tendency emerging among the ranks of Catholic intellectuals: the complete disengagement from any possible political or cultural implications of the scientific movement. In his letters Galiani pointed out the epistemological difficulties inherent in the theory of vortices as a proof of how much the Church had helped to increase Descartes's errors by frightening him with Galileo's trial.

> But certainly what I say is that I cannot agree with what Descartes says— that is, that ether spins with the same velocity as the earth, and the fall of bodies that we call weights depends on nothing less than the pressure of ether moved with such a velocity. Perhaps the great Descartes himself saw this slight difficulty and for no other reason wrote that the velocity of ether closest to earth spins with the same velocity as [the earth] in order to keep on maintaining that the earth rests. . . . And in order to determine if a body moves or not, he would have it that one should have special regard for those bodies that touch things immediately. Therefore in order to say that the earth rests, he was compelled to assert that the earth rests in its vortex and that it rotates with the same velocity as the ether that immediately surrounds it. In his first treatise entitled *The World* (which according to his biographer Baillet he later burned, frightened by Galileo's condemnation), I would perhaps have summarized it otherwise.[11]

Galiani's thought provides evidence for the vindication of the Galilean concept of modern science's complete autonomy from theology. The clear mathematical demonstration that the *Principia* provided for the heliocentric system, far from suggesting to him greater caution in disseminating Newton's theories, spurred him instead to reopen the Copernican issue unhesitatingly, giving it a precise ideological and cultural meaning in the context of Italian intellectuals' struggle for *libertas philosophandi*. In the *Discours de la pesanteur* [Discourse on gravity], Huygens had explicitly linked his observations about the pendulum's movements at various latitudes to the problem of the proofs for terrestrial motion. Now, discussing recent gravitational theories, Galiani once again frankly proposed the entire problem to his colleagues.[12] He wrote to Guido Grandi, "And if the earth does not move, how would we explain that other phenomenon of the pendulum which slows down at the equator? But leave that unsaid, because here the Inquisition wishes that the earth be at rest, without anyone writing otherwise."[13] He also addressed a detailed letter to Giovanni Bottari, who was personally interested in Huygens's theses and the European debate on Copernicanism. Even in this instance his conclusion was simultaneously full of bitterness and irony:

There are some who believe that by now the motion of the earth ought
not be deemed as a simple hypothesis, but as something entirely certain.
But those so-called reasons ought not be of any consequence for us, because the Inquisition's decree is itself enough to dispel any doubt from
our minds.[14]

In his response to Galiani's suggestions on the Copernican problem, Leprotti,
director of Cardinal Davia's scientific academy at Rimini, privileged the
scientific side of the matter from the beginning. He widened the discourse
at the Istituto di Scienze of Bologna with his request that it complete the
measurements with pendulums and collect as much data as possible on the
subject from abroad.[15] The discussion between the two, about which Cardinal Davia undoubtedly was also kept informed, cannot be reconstructed from
contemporary evidence because Leprotti burned the numerous letters Galiani
sent him on his express order, for Galiani was always particularly careful
not to leave too many traces of his aversion for the Inquisition.[16]

The renewed initiative within Catholic scientific circles obtained a preliminary result with the translation and publication in 1716 of Francis
Hauksbee's physical and mechanical experiments in Florence. Once again
Galiani, Bianchini, and Grandi directed the entire operation. The book
had been brought from England by Francesco Bianchini, who had overseen
a partial translation in Rome in order to facilitate the repetition of the
most important experiments in the Accademia Gualtieri. In collaboration
with Rome, these experiments were carried out in Pisa as well by Grandi,
who confirmed Hauksbee's deductions.[17] The idea of having the book translated and published in Florence evolved from contacts between Roman,
Florentine, and Pisan scholars.[18] Among them, the academics of the Crusca
distinguished themselves, in particular the censor Giuseppe Averani, whose
interesting work transposed Newtonian optical theories within a metaphysics of light clearly Galilean in origin, and Tommaso Buonaventuri, one
of the principal organizers of Tuscan culture.[19]

Hauksbee's work marked an important moment in the history of Italian
scientific culture, because it presented the best of what the Royal Society
had produced in its recent activity. Right from its anonymous introduction,
the book revealed its relationship to Newtonian science, unequivocally linking
the experimentalism of Galilean origin with Newton's theories:

The literary world is already quite generally convinced that, instead of
losing time in empty hypotheses that are little different from fiction,
there is no other method of illustrating natural philosophy than by means
of demonstration and conclusions based on judiciously and diligently performed experiments. . . . With the same method, the most learned and
incomparable Mr. Isaac Newton has invented and established the theory
of light and colors.[20]

By publishing Hauksbee's book, its remarkable translator, Sir Thomas Dereham,[21] commenced his collaboration with Catholic scientific circles, in particular with the group of Bottari, Grandi, and Galiani. Dereham, whose activity as translator was decisive for the Italian dissemination of an apologetic version of the Newtonian universe-machine, was then in the service of the Medicean government. A Catholic and an ardent Jacobite, during the course of his long stay in Italy (interrupted by brief trips to England) the English baronet maintained contacts with Royal Society circles and in particular with William Derham and George Cheyne, contacts whose importance was vital for the group of enlightened Catholics in the 1720s and 1730s.

TWO

Galileo, Newton, and
Libertas Philosophandi

1. THE GALILEAN HERITAGE

In an article entitled "Saggio sul Galileo" ["Essay on Galileo"] which appeared in *Caffé* in 1765, the Enlightenment scientist Paolo Frisi wrote:

> Galileo and Newton were bound to follow each other: both were free enough, enterprising, and active as to give a new form to science; both had vast and precise ideas, a fervid imagination, a slow and mature judgment. . . . Both were equipped with all the necessary talents, the former to begin the scientific revolution, the latter to give it the form that they must keep stable.[1]

The connection between Galileo and Newton, so explicitly illustrated by Frisi, is mentioned again and again in the best works of Italian Enlightenment literature; in fact it became a sort of archetype that allowed the unfolding of the most varied and stimulating subjects.[2] Here Frisi found an exact confirmation of the idea, which matured during the Enlightenment, of humanity's indefinite progress, at least in the vast field of scientific knowledge.[3] Others such as Algarotti insisted on the nearly analogous breakthrough effect caused by Galileo and by Newton within European culture, the former with his attack on Aristotelian philosophy, the latter by calling into doubt the results attained by the new Cartesian scholasticism.[4] Furthermore, through a penetrating analysis of the attitude that English society assumed towards Newton and the different view of Italian society towards Galileo, Frisi broached the knotty issue of the relationship between Galileo and the Catholic Church.[5] This is a matter that, at the end of the century, Giovambattista Nelli's ironic pen treated in a strident attack on the Catholic Church, which he deemed responsible for Galileo's "martyrdom" and, because of the infamous trial, guilty of having constrained Italian culture to a perennial state of inferiority in comparison to European science.[6] Certainly the connection between Galileo and Newton was nourished in Italy in the latter eighteenth century by various factors that range from the renewal of national pride (offended by foreign slights to the great Pisan scientist) to

41

Nelli's anticlericalism, tinged by Jacobinism. However, something in the preceding years had contributed to the consolidation of a connection that all believed was natural. A problem as vast and complex as that of eighteenth-century Galileism,[7] embracing a broad time span and factors unique to Italian culture, certainly cannot be exhausted in the confines of this research. Nevertheless, we may focus on a number of points that illustrate the background of the connection between Galileo and Newton and the establishment of this link in Italian scientific circles during the first half of the eighteenth century.

The Galilean heritage has justly been defined as a "difficult bequest." Throughout Italy the efficient ecclesiastical organization decisively hindered knowledge about and dissemination in universities of the scientist's works. In addition to neutralizing the most destructive aspects of Galilean thought (from the cosmological and philosophical viewpoint), some ecclesiastical circles engaged in relatively subtle activity against its most prestigious scientific results. The long and virulent dispute over the problem of the evaluation of momentum in falling bodies is but one typical example. Between the latter seventeenth and early eighteenth centuries, the disagreement was played out in the Jesuits' campaign to discredit the new science and the impassioned reaction of Galilean intellectuals. Above and beyond the struggle for the survival of this great intellectual heritage, the development of the dispute makes it possible to comprehend the transformations that this inheritance had to undergo in the sometimes disparate interpretations found even among Galileo's followers.[8]

In his *Discorsi e dimostrazioni intorno a due nuove scienze* [Discourses and demonstrations regarding the two new sciences], Galileo articulated a postulate that would in the following years become a formidable bone of contention: "I accept that the degrees of velocity of the same body acquired above different inclinations of planes are then equal, when the elevations of their planes are equal."[9] The property that Galileo sought to demonstrate by referring to the distance between centers of gravity was studied in depth by Torricelli and Viviani, who were acutely aware of the need to clarify the exact terms of the entire question and hence avoid a dispute about the lack of a true and genuine demonstration. It was in fact Viviani who gave the first coherent systemization to the entire statics of the inclined plane as theorized by Galileo, introducing a distinction between the "gravitative momentum" and the "descensive momentum." This distinction allowed a glimpse of the concept that resolved the entire matter, namely the parallelogram of forces.[10] Alessandro Marchetti, a teacher at the Pisan university and famous for his translation of Lucretius's *De Rerum Natura* [On the nature of things], confronted the problem of the demonstration in his treatise *De resistentia solidorum* [On the resistence of solids] (1669) where he vindicated the soundness of Galileo's postulate. The work spared no criticism of Viviani and Torricelli, or even of Galileo on specific points, and it denounced the poor solidarity of the Galilean party and the difficulty of reaching a definitive conclusion on the matter.

This makes Jesuit Giovanni Francesco Vanni's *Specimen de momentis graviorum* [Model of the momenta of weights] (which appeared in the *Acta eruditorum* of 1684) an understandable addition to the debate. Without any reverential awe for the great Pisan Galileo, in his little treatise Vanni denied the validity of the postulate in question, enlarging on his incisive task of destroying Galilean statics entirely. On the basis of fundamental concepts that were, in short, erroneous, but arguing with strict logic and not without a certain charm, he indicated some presumed aprioriae in Galileo's reasoning on the motion of weights along an inclined plane.[11] In Italian cultural circles, his work was taken as a further maneuver by the Church (and in particular by the Jesuits) aimed at discrediting Galilean scientific work in its entirety.

The Neapolitan mathematician Antonio Monforte, responding to Antonio Magliabechi's invitation to reply to Vanni, indicated that the Jesuit's intervention had made him uneasy: "I ask that you rest assured that this judgment, whatever it may be, remains between us, because I would not wish to quarrel with [the Jesuits], for although they are fruitless friends, they are nevertheless efficient enemies."[12] The initial fear of having to take on the Jesuits' organic, anti-Galilean enterprise did not restrain Italian intellectuals for long.[13] Magliabechi took upon himself the task of sowing discord between the two parties, and at his behest Domenico Guglielmini, Antonio Monforte, Francesco Spoleti, Vincenzo Viviani, and Giuseppe Averani vigorously contested Vanni's affirmations. And from abroad, the Polish Jesuit Adamand Kochański and, especially, Leibniz used the *Acta* to highlight the paralogisms of this "implacable" enemy of Galileo, as Vanni called himself.[14]

2. EPISTEMOLOGICAL MODELS IN COMPARISON

During the 1710s the bitter dispute that Galilean circles had conducted in the latter seventeenth century to defend the foundations of the new science assumed a rather more complex significance. In the seventeenth century the "moderns" had demonstrated a certain solidarity in rebuffing Vanni's insidious activities, denouncing the Jesuit's errors and extolling the validity of the Galilean corpus. In the eighteenth century the specific attacks, and the defenses that followed, came from the most disparate sectors of Italian culture, and they brought to light the existence of an even wider division between groups that had made quite contrasting epistemological choices.[1]

In February 1704 the Florentine mathematician Bartolomeo Intieri, who was to become one of the key figures in Neapolitan culture,[2] briefly advised Antonio Magliabechi of the fact that someone in Naples was contemplating the resumption of the ancient diatribe: "I believe that very soon something will be published against Mr. Galileo's doctrine regarding mechanics; for the moment I know nothing certain or new."[3] In April of the same year, Intieri confirmed: "Mr. Lucantonio Porzio has impugned the doctrine of Mr. Galileo and all the other mechanists who said that the absolute gravity of the weight on a plane inclined at the horizon of the relative gravity had the same proportion as the inclination to the perpendicular."[4]

The work to which Intieri referred was the treatise *De motu corporum* [On the motion of bodies], which Porzio had long contemplated before actually publishing in 1704. It contains the most significant elements of a gnosiology—that of the Investiganti—that had played an extremely important role in breaking Aristotle's hegemony in southern Italian culture. In the Investiganti group, Porzio had represented the faction most attentive to the results of Cartesian mechanicism as an alternative to Leonardo Di Capua's vitalistic naturalism, which had instead privileged the chemical analysis of matter. The *De motu corporum* was a proper attack against Galilean statics, and in addition to denying its most prestigious results, it also denied its epistemological foundations, proposing a number of theses from the Investiganti's scientific tradition as alternatives.[5] Through the famous "sensate experiments," Galileo had arrived at general laws, hypothesizing a rational and mathematical world, while Porzio maintained a naturalistic monism whose *mechanical order* could never be revealed by universally valid laws, capable of gathering all the aspects of a nature rich in phenomena that were uniquely diverse among themselves. In the treatise of 1704 Porzio also affirmed the provisional nature of every scientific theory, showing that he shared a concept common to all the Investiganti: the probabilistic limit of natural laws.[6] Galilean experimentalism was also rather different from what the Investiganti and Porzio theorized. In his famous little treatise *Del sorgimento de' licori* [On the rise of the liquids], Porzio had addressed his academic colleagues:

> It is not difficult for me to understand how philosophy might draw its origin from marvels; it happens that man can acquire the notion of things only by that [marvel] of the senses, with which he sees and touches. . . . But I see clearly that marveling continually about this universe-machine and its parts, you are advanced in the science of natural things only by experiments on things about which you have marveled. And I see as well that you are not inspired to make progress, except with the guide and accompaniment of observations.[7]

The experience to which Porzio alludes did not envision in any way Galileo's celebrated imaginary experiments, whose foundation lay in extreme geometrization. His was an experience understood in a Baconian way as activity directed at observing the phenomena and then distilling the elements common to them all, which afterward had to lead inductively to provisional conclusions that were always perfectible on the basis of subsequent experiments.[8] The Investiganti's science, even while accepting many of the physical theories of Descartes as well as Galileo, had actually worked out its own rather complex synthesis based on the theory of ether-mind and the rejection of Cartesian dualism between res cogitans and res extensa. Besides the need to create a true alternative to Aristotelianism in every field of knowledge, the homogeneity and organic quality of such a plan (which received its most coherent and complete expression in Tommaso Cornelio's works)[9] came from the desire to reconcile research in quite diverse fields of the new science—mechanics, astronomy, biology, medicine, and chemistry. The Investiganti's admirable efforts at synthesis and their impassioned research into a science that took into account the need for an effective relationship between mens [mind] and corpus [body] and between humans and nature could not help but lead to necessarily qualitative, Baconian physics, in which mathematics was relegated to a secondary position. Probabilism, which gave distinguished service protecting the new science from the attentions of the Inquisition, proved to be a not very effective tool.

The De motu corporum published by Porzio in 1704 is a sort of swan song of Investiganti science, whose qualities and limits were all present and became evident in the scientist's apparently anachronistic criticism of Galileo. Among the most disconcerting elements of the analysis that the author made of falling weights, we find confirmation of the statement (foreshadowed by Descartes) that a sphere descending along an inclined plane will stop at the point where the line perpendicular to the plane from the earth's center drops.[10] Complicating his reasoning even more, Porzio introduced the problem of the substance through which the body passes in the course of its motion. On the basis of such premises, his analysis concluded by calling into doubt the very universality of the Galilean postulate. The motion of falling weights along an inclined plane (except for the case of equilibrium), he affirmed, should be studied case by case, moment by moment. There was a good deal of reaction to Porzio's work. Intieri wrote to Magliabechi in November 1704:

> The most illustrious Don Paolo Doria has already begun to submit to the presses the response to Mr. Porzio, who had—as you will already know—impugned Mr. Galileo's doctrine. Let us hope that from these [responses] it will be made known how much the same Mr. Porzio has strayed from the truth, and if this should not happen, there will be some Florentine who takes it upon himself to show the world how much reverence there ought to be for the venerable memory and profound doctrine of that great man.[11]

The ensuing dispute would last for a number of years, and its principal protagonists were Paolo Mattia Doria, Bartolomeo Intieri, Vitale Giordani, and Guido Grandi. In all their participation, their attention to the epistemological problems so explicitly treated by the Investigante scientist was constant. From this standpoint Bartolomeo Intieri and Paolo Mattia Doria revealed an extraordinary sharpness in their writings. Doria wrote two books, the Considerazioni sopra il moto e la meccanica de' corpi sensibili, e de' corpi insensibili [Considerations of the motion and the mechanics of sensible and insensible bodies] (1711) and the *Giunta di P. M. Doria al suo libro del moto e della meccanica in cui si risponde a varie obiezioni, che al medesimo potrebbon farsi per avventura* [Additions of P. M. Doria to his book on the motion and mechanics in which he responds to various objections which might by chance be made to the book] (1712).[12] In addition to a precise response to Porzio's doubts, they provided an articulated epistemological proposal based on Doria's metaphysical conceptions.[13] In his first work, Doria began an intense dialogue with modern science that in the following years would bring him to a sort of disconcerting scientific counterrevolution and the repudiation of all modern theories, from infinitesimal calculus to universal Newtonian gravitation. Doria set Porzio's antimathematicism and naturalism against a mechanistic science lacking any ties to experimental reality. It was a genuinely Pythagorean-Platonic reading of Galileism, in which geometry became the keystone for understanding all natural phenomena. "I believe I have reduced mechanics to a geometrical demonstration," Doria affirmed with pride, adding:

> I suppose that motion is a property of the body, without demonstrating that the mobile body exists. Then in the very way in which the geometers, who suppose that the body exists, abstract its motion from gravity, I form the definitions of absolute and relative motion. And with that, from motion I draw out momentum and gravity with its properties.[14]

And the promise was maintained with a series of rather disputable geometric demonstrations that nevertheless had the merit of representing an organic epistemological model, even comprising some cosmological considerations based on the Cartesian theory of ether—or rather Platonic circumpulsion, as Doria loved to emphasize—integrated with the erroneous Galilean affirmations on the circularity of the planets' orbits.[15]

In a lengthy review, the *Giornale de' Letterati* defined Doria's work as "a summary of sound and mature doctrine,"[16] yet it elicited the harsh reaction of the scientists tied to the Investiganti's tradition. Antonio Monforte, Giacinto De Cristoforo, and Porzio himself, along with his pupil Nicola Cacciapuoto, advanced bitter criticisms of Doria in the Neapolitan salons, obliging him to react publicly with his *Giunta di P. M. Doria al suo libro del moto*. The reply, presented through some letters addressed to his adversaries, remains one of the most interesting documents of the epistemological crisis that Neapolitan culture (and, more generally, Italian culture) underwent in that period.[17] Deliberately leaving aside any comment about the specific criticisms aimed at his demonstration of the Galilean postulate, Doria explained anew his own method, "the sole, true, and pure geometrical one . . . that demonstrates a priori and that deduces consequences from demonstrated principles."[18] His unique "mechanical geometry," which studied the motion of bodies entirely apart from their experimental reality, unfolded in a continual parallel to the traditional model of "linear geometry" that was fundamental to the entire architecture of Dorian metaphysics. If "the subject of linear geometry is naked quantity," he affirmed, "the subject of our mechanics is motion and gravity, which it states are properties of the body." Whereas "Euclid determines the axioms . . . , we in the general supposition assign a well-known property of motion obvious to the senses." He continues: "Having made his definitions and axioms, Euclid determines the properties of lines, planes, and bodies in the theorems and problems. . . . And we, having made the definitions and axioms, make the propositions, and in them we determine the properties of motion and of gravity."[19] In sum, his work proved to be a systematic geometricization vaguely inspired by analogous Cartesian mechanism but far from Galilean dynamics, which gives due consideration to a factor such as time, without which a modern mathematical analysis of motion is meaningless.[20]

Doria's science, whose implications were subsequently made clearer within a rather complex cultural project, repudiates the fundamentals of Galilean dynamics, although it does not fail to utilize some of its results. There is no room for physico-mathematical concepts such as time, velocity, acceleration, and the like in Doria's mechanics. Nevertheless, despite certain inadequacies that keep him from a modern vision of science, he sharply perceives the twilight of the Investiganti's naturalistic tradition and denounces its disconcerting aprioriae in a harsh letter to Giacinto De Cristoforo. "The ancients considered mechanics as a physical and sensate science, restricted to our sphere and our horizon," and, with their lack of capacity for abstracting from natural reality, they blocked the distillation of the universal mathematical laws that are the foundations of modern science. "This is the very reason why Mr. Lucantonio, wishing to deal with mechanics, cannot even do what he does in the tenth proposition of his book: divide a horizontal plane into various regions in order to see in which of these a weight will remain still."[21]

The dispute over the Galilean postulate was enriched in 1710 by the participation of Guido Grandi and Bartolomeo Intieri. In order to understand the importance of this discussion, we ought to recall that behind each, to a different degree, we find the group of enlightened Catholics, friends of Celestino Galiani. In 1705 a long, handwritten *Epistola* by Vitale Giordani (mathematician of the Roman Sapienza university) to Giacinto De Cristoforo was circulated; it repeated in substance Porzio's theses with yet another version of the problem of weights falling along an inclined plane.[22] Bartolomeo Intieri, who had relationships with Grandi in Florence and Galiani in Rome, asked the former for an immediate response, which appeared in 1710, following vicissitudes that even today remain quite obscure. In the *Considerazioni del P. D. Guidone Grando e del Sig. N. N. sopra le scritture del signor Luc'Antonio Porzio circa il moto de' gravi per il piano inclinato* [Remarks of P. D. Guidone Grando and Mr. N. N. on the writings of Mr. Luc'Antonio Porzio regarding the motion of weights on an inclined plane], a little volume published in Naples (but indicating Rome on its

title page), we finally find a ray of light pointing to the correct interpretation of Galileo's postulate.[23] By clearly demonstrating Porzio's errors, Grandi
wholly vindicated the Galilean physico-mathematical tradition against the
naturalism of much Italian culture, which however linked its own modern-
izing action to Galileo's name. In a long note to Grandi's letter in Latin,
Bartolomeo Intieri, who hid behind the initials "N. N."[24] and who had
favored the publication of the little volume, denounced Investiganti science's profound separation from the true Galilean tradition. With biting
irony, coupled with a certain irreverence for the old and prestigious Porzio,
Intieri attested that he could not believe "that such a great literatus could
fall into such errors." Porzio's disconcerting affirmation—that the weight
in its motion along the inclined plane ought to have stopped at a specific
point—induced Intieri to exclaim severely: "I regret wasting time clarifying
this mistake."[25] And yet it was by beginning with this problem that Intieri
developed his criticism of the Investiganti's followers' strange manner of
conceiving the experiment. Intieri emphasized that the Galilean "sensate
experiments" were something quite different from Porzio's purely qualitative
reconstruction. Galileo's experiments confirmed a vision of reality whose
goal was the search for universal mathematical laws, limiting the analytical-
inductive phase only to the collection of facts, in order to reach a mathematical synthesis that would be verified with the final experiment.[26] The
bodies Galileo considered, Intieri wrote, do not "slide or fall headlong" on
the inclined plane because "the plane is not hard and smooth, as the mathematician posits."[27] The reference to the experiment that Porzio theorized
was almost useless in a mechanistic science that strove to privilege physico-
mathematical language even more. Intieri maliciously invited his antago-
nist Porzio to demonstrate, through his concept of the experiment, the thesis
that a sphere could come to a full stop along an inclined plane: "He says
that the sphere on an inclined plane does not fall down. Well then, let
him kindly demonstrate this to me."[28]

In truth Intieri could not emphasize more strenuously or passionately the
profound diversity in epistemological choices.[29] While each echoed Galileo,
Doria, Porzio, and Intieri represented three different ways of vindicating his
difficult heritage, not only through the ideological and cultural import that
it had assumed in the intricate relationship between intellectuals and ecclesiastical power, but, above all, through the various methodological interpretations that each in various measure followed in Galileo's prestigious
name. A disconcerting mathematicization, based on metaphysics and Paolo
Mattia Doria's elementary geometry, was set up against the anachronistic
Investiganti gnosiology, whose naturalistic monism was in various circles
accused of Spinozism.[30] In light of the methodological fidelity that Grandi,
Intieri, and Galiani maintained to Galileo's "sensate experiments," making
them the most correct interpreters of Galilean thought, it is not at all coincidental that the trio, joined by Bottari, Niccolini, and Cerati, became

the most impassioned defenders of the Pisan scientist's cultural patrimony in the following years.

3. THE EIGHTEENTH-CENTURY EDITIONS OF GALILEO'S WORKS

It is easy to imagine the difficulties encountered by those who wished to introduce Galileo's works to Italian intellectuals after his death—provided we remember the harshness of the Roman Inquisition's decrees. Antonio Favaro and other scholars have more recently remarked on the tenacious persecution directed at Galilean works throughout the seventeenth century.[1] Extremely useful were the efforts of intellectuals like Vincenzo Viviani, who, having inherited their master's papers, dedicated their lives to an attempt to rehabilitate him and make his genius known. An early, partial publication of Galileo's works occurred in Bologna in the latter seventeenth century. With the support of Cardinal Leopoldo de' Medici, Viviani delivered part of the Galilean manuscripts to scholar Carlo Manolesi of Bologna with the intent of undertaking Galileo's rehabilitation. But the initial optimism that surrounded the entire enterprise was soon transformed into impotent rage because of the obstacles and continual prohibitions that ecclesiastical authorities imposed, even on merely scientific writings. The edition that appeared from Bologna's Del Dozza press did not contain the *Dialogo* and other important works, and it proved to be, as Viviani wrote bitterly, "quite lacking and defective" in everyone's eyes.[2] For more than half a century the genuine *odium theologicum* of a greater part of the Jesuits towards Galileo and the counterreformatory zeal of ecclesiastical institutions impeded any Italian reprint of the great Pisan's works. And yet Viviani's patience and stubbornness, supported by the underground but vital influence of Galilean circles in Rome, appeared to produce the miraculous possibility of Galileo's rehabilitation by the end of the century, if the Inquisition retracted its "salutary decree" regarding the *Dialogo*. The protagonists of this rather complex affair included Cardinal Leopoldo de' Medici, the Jesuit Antonio Baldigiani, Vincenzo Viviani, and Lorenzo Magalotti. But their attempt fell short, both because of the cardinal's death[3] and, especially, because of the unexpected turn of the Inquisitorial screw in the last decades of the century, to the detriment of all Italian culture. As we have said earlier, the so-called trial of the atheists in Naples was merely the most visible manifestation of this repression. Viviani died in 1703, having abandoned all hope of seeing his mission realized, leaving an important *Vita di Galileo* and the precious collection of the scientist's unpublished manuscripts.

The thorny problem of reprinting Galileo's works, necessary for reopening the dialogue about the most modern and revolutionary aspects of his thought, was resolutely confronted from the beginning of the eighteenth century by men such as Guido Grandi, Giovanni Bottari, Tommaso

Buonaventuri, Benedetto Bresciani, Giuseppe Averani, and others. The edition of the *Opere di Galileo Galilei*, begun shortly before 1710, appeared in Florence in 1718 after a lengthy and difficult gestation. This reprint was certainly highly open to criticism because the text was collected "at random, without editorial criteria,"[4] and it lacked some of the most important texts of the Galilean corpus, such as the *Dialogo* and the *Letter alla Granduchessa di Toscana* [Letter to the grand duchess of Tuscany]. The circumstances leading to its production have been systematically ignored by Italian historiography, but from the correspondence of Guido Grandi, Giovanni Bottari, and, especially, Tommaso Buonaventuri (director of the Florentine grand ducal press), it is possible to reconstruct the intermittent course of the enterprise that, during the time that it dragged on amidst myriad difficulties for more than a decade, served as the focal point for consolidating some intellectuals' resolve to impose Galileo's rehabilitation on the Catholic Church. The history of this publication is in many ways symbolic of the difficulties encountered by Italian scholars who tried to cast a ray of light into an environment hindered by and under the hegemony of ecclesiastical power. Buonaventuri and, especially, Bottari, who as superintendent of the grand ducal press was the real editorial brain of this and other significant cultural undertakings, mobilized themselves in the active solicitation of specialists such as Grandi and Averani to collaborate on the book's preparation.[5] Guido Grandi and Giovanni Bottari even made long and fruitful journeys to Rome to smooth over difficulties created by the Inquisition.[6] The solidarity among Celestino Galiani, Gaspare Cerati, and the Roman scholars tied to them was continually invoked in the most difficult moments, with positive results. Despite the editors' passion, the outcome was not what they had hoped for at the outset. Conditioning, as well as a sort of self-censorship (certainly not the only instance of such in contemporary culture), had prevailed, robbing the edition of Galileo's most stimulating and provocative works. Traces of this underground struggle remain in Grandi's correspondence in a batch of anonymous, undated letters, periodically sent by an important, unnamed Roman figure, informing him about the Holy See's mood. Grandi had asked his anonymous source to test the waters in Rome with an eye to the publication of Galileo's valuable letters found in Parma, which Benedetto Bacchini took an active interest in having inserted in the new anonymous edition. The anonymous source responded discouragingly, without mincing words:

> I do not believe that it makes sense to print those letters of the most learned Galileo that Your Excellency has favored to show me, because in them he reasons in favor of the earth's motion according to the Copernican system, an assertion prohibited by the holy Congregation and only permitted to be discussed as a hypothesis.[7]

Despite the obvious limitations of this reprint, the positive signs that it contained should not be underestimated. With its publication, the great

Pisan's scientific mastery was in fact vindicated, and his works became newly accessible to a public that for more than half a century had not been able to procure them. Most important, the influence that mathematics and experiments had had on the Galilean epistemological design was emphasized and correctly interpreted. In his ample *Prefazione universale* [General preface], Tommaso Buonaventuri exalted the *libertas philosophandi*, and, referring to the *querelle* between the ancients and the moderns, he supported Galileo's decisive place in leading the moderns to victory over the ancients: "The celebrated Lionardo Di Capua spoke well [when he said that] Galileo alone was enough to obscure and completely bury the glory of all antiquity."[8]

A comprehensive evaluation of the reprint must include a few brief considerations about the incisive editorial service performed by the Medicean grand ducal press of Florence. Together with typograhers Gaetano Tartini and Santino Franchi, Giovanni Bottari and Tommaso Buonaventuri set in motion a series of publications that give us a sense of what kind of cultural renewal the Tuscan group and their Roman friends under Galiani's leadership had as their goal. In 1716 the important translation of Hauksbee's *Esperienze fisico-meccaniche* [Physico-mechanical experiments] appeared, which explicitly confirmed the experimental nature of modern science and established a preliminary, ideal link between the Galilean tradition and Newtonian thought. The preceding year the publishing house had licensed the *Lezioni accademiche di Evangelista Torricelli mattematico e filosofo del serenissimo Ferdinando II granduca di Toscana* [The academic lessons of Evangelista Torricelli, mathematician and philosopher of the Most Serene Ferdinand II, grand duke of Tuscany]. This splendid book, which opened with a portrait of Torricelli and a long exposition of the scientist's life, was yet another profession of the impassioned fidelity that Bottari's group demonstrated towards the Galilean school and the "divine Galileo," in whom "death extinguished the greatest [person] conceded to mortals by God, to show them marvelous novelties and outlandish truths in the heavens and on earth, hidden and obscured to all of antiquity."[9]

In light of the activities of Florentine and Roman scholars, the clandestine èdition of Galileo's *Dialogo intorno ai due massimi sistemi* published in Naples in 1710 assumes a rather different political and cultural meaning.[10] Remarkably similar in its layout to Torricelli's *Lezioni Accademiche* (both bore the logo and motto of the Crusca on the title page), the work enjoyed a wide dissemination in every region of Italy. The mystery surrounding the editor and place of publication was then a sort of open secret, for if we read the chronicle of Neapolitan events in the *Giornale de' Letterati* from 1710, we find a genuine publicity announcement:

> Having been advised by letter from Naples that Galileo's *Dialogo* on the two greatest systems of the world, the Ptolemaic and the Copernican, a work justly condemned by ecclesiastical censure, has been reprinted, at this point of [our] literary news we inform the public about it as well.

Nevertheless, we are not certain either of the place or the person who has produced it. We hear, however, that the edition is correct and clean, with the addition of a letter of Galileo himself never before printed, in which—as they write to us—he defends his system. Moreover there is a letter from Father Paolo Antonio Foscarini the Venetian in defense of his opinion; another letter of Kepler on the moons of Mars; and finally, the *Abiura* [Recantation] that Galileo made of his system.[11]

Dedicated to the duke of Maddaloni, Don Carlo Carafa-Pacecco, the edition was the work of Cellenio Zacclori, alias Lorenzo Ciccarelli, an extraordinary character who—as we have seen—had also been the editor of one of the reprints of Rohault's renowned *Tractatus physicus* containing Samuel Clarke's notes. The lawyer Ciccarelli, who is proving to be an increasingly significant figure, was certainly not an unknown person as one might imagine when considering his dangerous activities as a publisher of works from the *Index*. He had many contacts throughout the Neapolitan cultural world and Italy in general. His work was familiar to Ludovico Antonio Muratori, Giambattista Vico, Matteo Egizio, Niccolò Cirillo, Giacinto De Cristoforo, and many others.[12] But, most important, Ciccarelli had rather intense relations with Bartolomeo Intieri and Giovanni Bottari, who took advantage of his secret typeshop to publish texts believed dangerous for the grand ducal press of Florence.[13] The director of the Tuscan press himself, Tommaso Buonaventuri, explicitly referred in a number of letters to the close ties established between Florence and Naples. Our documentation regarding these relationships dates, however, from the 1720s, while this edition of Galileo's works is from 1710. But that does not deny the approval, or even the genuine participation, of the Roman group, since among Bottari's friends contacts with Naples were entrusted especially to Celestino Galiani. In 1708 he was staying in Naples, where he had encountered the most famous local intellectuals and made friends with Giacinto De Cristoforo, Costantino Grimaldi, Giacomo Grazini, and, in all probability, Ciccarelli himself.[14] In an anonymous letter dated 1709 (which we know was from De Cristoforo), he thanked Galiani for having sent him Galileo's by-then rare work on sunspots, and he confirmed his admiration for the Pisan's theories and his own willingness to take on the battle to vindicate Galileo's great merits.[15] In the same period, Galiani agreed to sound out people in Rome regarding a future reprint of Rohault's work with Samuel Clarke's notes, a work that, significantly, opened with Ciccarelli's words, as a sign of continuity with the preceding publication of the *Dialogo*.[16] Hence Galiani was aware of the Neapolitans' intention to publish an Italian edition of Alessandro Marchetti's "impious Lucretius in translation," using the usual secret press. Giacomo Grazini, himself the author (under the pseudonym of Francesco Noja) of a pamphlet against religious superstition that was named in the *Index*,[17] kept Galiani continually updated about what was developing in Valletta's clique and in the group of scholars that patronized the press.[18] There is much support for the hypothesis that Galiani's friends intervened directly to guarantee that the clandestine typeshop's activities received minimal attention. We see the logic of such backing if we evaluate some noncoincidental connections between the Roman and Tuscan circles' cultural plans and Ciccarelli's reprinting of specific works, such as those of Galileo.

Above and beyond the intrinsic value that the *Dialogo*'s publication had in Italy nearly a century after the first edition, this first reprinting in Italy of what we might call the Pisan scientist's ideological manifesto brought a novel element to the framework of the contemporary political and cultural debate. The manifesto bore the ungainly title of *Lettera del signor Galileo Galilei scritta alla granducessa di Toscana, in cui teologicamente e con ragioni saldissime cavate da Padri più sentiti si risponde alle calunnie di coloro, i quali a tutto potere si sforzarono non solo di sbandirne la sua opinione intorno alla costituzione delle parti dell'universo, ma altresí di addurne una perpetua infamia alla sua persona* [Letter of Mr. Galileo Galilei written to the grand duchess of Tuscany, in which he responds—theologically and with most authoritative reasons extrapolated from the Fathers—to the slander of those who with all their might strive not only to banish his opinion about the constitution of the parts of the universe, but also to connect perpetual infamy to his person]. The letter, also published by Ciccarelli in a separate edition dated Florence, 1710, was taken from a manuscript codex that we have not been able to identify. Once we discard the hypothesis that the letter was transcribed from the single edition in print made abroad in 1636,[19] a transcription from a manuscript codex that does not exist in any Neapolitan library points once again to participation from outside the Neapolitan realm, probably at the hands of Galiani's group, which would have been able to furnish a copy from the numerous codices existing in Rome or Florence.

In his *Lettera* Galileo brought into focus the fundamental problems inherent in the troubled relationship between modern science and Catholic ideology. Aware of the total identification between theology and Aristotelian science that had matured in the course of centuries-long struggles, and cognizant of the need (vital for modern science) to break away from such a scenario, he had taken on the job of reconciling the *libertas philosophandi*, necessary for the progress of natural research, with the fetter imposed by traditional biblical exegesis. Though there is undoubtedly only one truth, Galileo stoutly maintained, there are, however, two languages for understanding it: one scientific and one ordinary. The first, rigorous and mathematical, goes back to the natural order, whose laws are ironclad and immutable. Through this language one approaches scientific truth, which human power has no capacity to interpret to its liking, as, on the other hand, one can who cultivates moral and philosophical disciplines.

I would like to ask that these most prudent and wise fathers consider seriously the difference between debatable and demonstrative doctrines;

so that, bearing in mind with what force the necessary inferences hold up, they might furthermore ascertain that it is not in the power of professors of demonstrative science to change opinions at their will, applying themselves to this and then to that, and that there is a great difference between commanding a mathematician and a philosopher and directing a merchant or a jurist, and that demonstrated conclusions regarding things of nature and heaven cannot be changed as easily.[20]

The ontological basis of modern science cannot be vindicated better than this. The Church, Galileo insisted, cannot suppress science's truths. In order to eliminate the Copernican theory from modern thought, "it would be necessary to prohibit not only Copernicus's book and the writings of other authors who follow the same doctrine, but to ban all science and astronomy on earth, and, furthermore, to forbid men to look towards the heavens."[21] According to Galileo, the ordinary language that we find in other disciplines and in the Holy Scripture itself is quite another thing: "the Holy Spirit dictated those propositions that were used accordingly by sacred writers to accommodate the capacity of the rather crude and undisciplined common people." Where such propositions are not in accord with scientific demonstrations, theologians can therefore legitimately interpret them to achieve complete agreement with scientific reality. The scientist can clearly surmount eventual conflicts between scientific truths and articles of faith by maintaining a precise separation between theology and science. "With things as they stand, it seems to me that in the disputes of natural problems, one should not begin with the authority of passages in Scripture but with sensate experiments and the necessary demonstrations."[22] In matters of faith, on the other hand, the authority of Holy Scripture was beyond discussion.

In reality, things were not as simple and schematic as the scientist thought, and Cardinal Roberto Bellarmino, one of the ideologues of the Counter-Reformation who had no difficulty grasping the disruptive nature of such a theory, understood this well. Destroying the framework of Aristotelian theology-science, accepting the hypothesis that a scientific truth was on the same level as an article of faith, even though in separate realms, and agreeing to the complete freedom to philosophize would have meant for the Catholic Church setting in motion quite a dangerous process. No one could guarantee that scholars would hold to Galileo's conceptualization of a careful distinction between scientific truth and the truth of faith. The future would demonstrate that obstacles even more thorny would rise for Christianity, precisely from the utilization of a rational, scientific method in ecclesiastical and moral historiography.

On first reflection, publishing such a work in Naples in 1710 might seem to have been an anachronistic act of little merit. That assessment would be true for the rest of Europe; in England and in Holland, and in part in France as well, scholars had gone a long way towards resolving the problems pointed out by Galileo. The Italian cultural situation, however, was quite different. The same themes reappear, variously articulated yet always vibrantly topical, in the thought of the best Italian intellectuals. The works of D'Andrea, Valletta, and Porzio, too, all echo, to varying degrees, the arduous struggle to impose a minimal freedom to philosophize.[23] Some of Muratori's most interesting works echoing Galilean themes date from roughly the same years in which the *Lettera* appeared. The celebrated and much-discussed treatise *De ingeniorum moderatione in religionis negotio* [On the moderation of minds in matters of religion], over which Muratori had a brush with an Inquisitorial condemnation, faithfully transmits sentences and entire sections of the *Lettera alla granduchessa di Toscana*.[24] In Naples appeared the second part of Muratori's treatise *Delle riflessioni sopra il buon gusto nelle scienze e nelle arti* [Reflections on good taste in the sciences and the arts] (1715), in which criticism of Aristotelians' apriorism blended with an early Enlightenment faith in the progress of knowledge. Exalting Galileo, Muratori employed an original synthesis to reintroduce themes of paramount interest, such as the relationships between authority and reason and experimentalism and apriorism.[25] Another confirmation of the topical relevance of some salient aspects of Galilean thought lies in the works of Costantino Grimaldi, a Catholic philo-Jansenist with cordial and friendly ties to Galiani and Bottari. A number of penetrating studies have revealed the problems this militant intellectual faced while searching for new solutions capable of reconciling his profound religiosity with an affirmation of modern scientific theories. Grimaldi's attempts to test the limits and possibilities of rationalism in exegetical and learned historical research of sacred texts have been analyzed carefully. Under Muratori's influence, Grimaldi pondered his personal plan for religious reform, in which methodical Cartesian doubt and Galilean *libertas philosophandi* represented two essential starting points for beginning a new era in Catholic thinking.[26] The redefinition of the possibilities and limits of human reason in relation to the truths of faith was the key theme that the most open Catholic intellectuals had to face in the early eighteenth century, if they did not wish to lose the political room necessary for free research.[27] Men like Pietro Giannone and Alberto Radicati di Passerano carried to extreme consequences their examination of the complex relationships between human reason and the truth of faith, finally denying any limitation imposed on human nature by Catholicism and other positive religions, even at the cost of paying dearly for their courage.[28] Leaving aside such clamorous examples, all those who operated in the harsh Italian cultural reality of the early eighteenth century had to compromise continually in order to see the rights of reason prevail, at least partially, over those of faith and authority.

4. A MANIFESTO FOR THE RENEWAL
OF ITALIAN CULTURE

The matter of the Galilean corpus's significance for the history of Italian culture has recently seen renewed interest, especially with regard to the seventeenth century. Accurate research has confirmed the remarkable character of seventeenth-century Italian Galileism, its scientific results, and, above all, its philosophical limitations. Eugenio Garin is certainly correct to caution historians wishing to study Galileism as if it were a precise doctrinal corpus with its own dogmas and all-encompassing schemes, as Cartesianism and Gassendism, in contrast, appear to be.[1] The force of Galileo's new science lies in its corrosive capacity to assault interpretive schemes of reality already surpassed by research, in the need to re-create a language capable of reading and understanding what surrounds us, and, above all, in its revolutionary ontological redefinition of a science with fairly defined limits and possibilities. Galileo has not "in clear conscience understood all the implications of his own science," and throughout the course of the seventeenth century his followers avoided drawing from his theories a philosophical corpus designed to oppose squarely the Aristotelian system. Extremely capable experiments and valuable physical, biological, and mathematical research form a fragmentary and unconnected picture of the results obtained by the greatest Italian scholars, although they all took inspiration from Galileo's principles. Even today historians heatedly discuss to what extent this reluctance was the fruit of the natural evolution of Galilean scientific thought, which shied away from seeking an all-encompassing vision of reality, or to what extent it was due to a conscious defensive tactic, a genuine, preventive self-censure necessary to guarantee the survival in Italian culture of some aspects of the new science, recently besieged by ecclesiastical obscurantism.[2] There are many possible analyses of the how and why that lay behind the failure to utilize the Pisan scientist's theories and principles during the seventeenth century.[3] The only certain factor is the frequent prevalence in Italian culture of a strong tendency towards philosophical syncretism and the incorporation of various fragments of diverse intellectual traditions within the heterogeneous front of moderns, in which we find Epicurus, Lucretius, Gassendi, Descartes, Galileo, and even Locke and Newton side by side. In this context, Galilean mechanistic-Cartesian literature is a significant example of the need Italian intellectuals perceived to set up a new *Weltanschauung* in opposition to the Aristotelian one.

For decades Cartesianism represented the philosophical doctrine adopted by the most advanced segment of the party of the moderns in Italy.[4] However, Cartesianism was certainly not embraced in its orthodox version, which was never considered in its organic whole but either subtly mediated by naturalism (as is the case for the Neapolitan region) or in its Malebranchian version, that of spiritualizing philosophers and Neoplatonists such as

Michelangelo Fardella, Gregorio Caloprese, and the young Paolo Mattia Doria. For entire generations of intellectuals from Valletta to Muratori, the more or less direct reference to Descartes meant clear and distinct ideas, methodical doubt, and an exultant and convincing picture of modern science that could be contrasted to Aristotelianism.[5] On the other hand, it was much less simple to articulate the relation between Cartesian apriorism and Galilean experimentalism. In Italy the variegated and complex party of the moderns in the 1710s divided internally yet again over the thorny issue of an organic reformulation of Galileism and its utilization for opening new research prospects and political breathing room for modern thought.[6] As we have already seen, at the start of the 1720s Galiani's friends had again brought almost all of Galileo's work to the attention of Italian scholars through an arduous editorial campaign. Under the aegis of renewed Galileism, the time was ripe for confronting the complex problem of a reform of Catholicism that would finally take into account the extraordinary successes of modern science and the disquieting discoveries that a critical and rational method had made possible in the studies of sacred history and moral philosophy.[7]

Historically many of Galileo's followers turned to the doctrinal corpus of Epicurean atomism and Gassendism to find a philosophical foundation that bound and explained the fragmentary experimental results of the era. In fact, corpuscular mechanics (with its extremely minute particles, the void, and the laws of movement) freed them from discredited forms and scholastic qualities. The entire latter seventeenth century was marked by the publication of works of Epicurean atomism. Ludovico Sergardi, Ottavio Scarlatini, Crisostomo Magneno, Isaac Cardoso, and Alessandro Marchetti are but a few of the many scholars who took it upon themselves to vindicate atomism as a valid and, above all, Christian philosophical-scientific doctrine. The greatest obstacle that they had to confront lay in the difficulty of neutralizing the irreligious component of Epicurean thought. Philosophical-scientific Epicureanism could not always be entirely separated from the atheism implicit in its theories. Harsh ecclesiastical repression at the end of the century evinces the dangerous diffusion that those doctrines had achieved in some areas of Italy. Since many among the Catholics might have held atomist theories in their hearts, it became vitally necessary to construct a convincing Epicurean apologetics capable of reassuring the Holy See.[8]

The Florentine edition of Pierre Gassendi's *Opera omnia* (1727)[9] is incomprehensible and anachronistic unless it is placed in the wider framework of an organic cultural proposal centered on the figure of Galileo. Far from "concluding a direction" (as has been written),[10] the work instead represented a preliminary, concrete outline for the vast program of some Italian intellectuals who aimed to establish a different relationship between Catholicism and modern thought. All of Galiani's friends, including Intieri, Bottari, Cerati, Niccolini, Buonaventuri, and Leprotti, were involved in the edition in various ways. An edition of six splendid, hefty tomes continuing and correcting the celebrated *Lugdunensis* [Lyons] edition of 1658, publication was a very costly enterprise in the end, plagued with all sorts of difficulties.

The first problem, that of high costs, was in part resolved by a subscription campaign, ably promoted by Niccolini and Galiani in Rome[11] and Bartolomeo Intieri in Naples. The latter risked being "pummeled" by his buyers for the extreme slowness with which the printing and delivery of the volumes proceeded.[12] But the key problem once again was the attitude of the Inquisition. At the urging of prominent figures close to the Medicean government itself,[13] the Florentine Inquisition demanded only a few corrections in the introductory section, nevertheless requiring the supervision of curial authorities.[14] Bottari was in Rome in 1725 to reassure those prelates who feared a large-scale renewal in Italy of the dangerous debate on atomism. An intense debate had developed within Galiani's circle regarding the aims of the new edition and the Inquisition's possible reactions.[15] Again on the completion of the works and during the sale of the volumes, fears about the Inquisition's unexpected reconsideration of its approval for the edition continued to trouble the group of friends. In 1726 Intieri wrote to Bottari, revealing that the Neapolitans were surprised by the Inquisition's unusual behavior: "Here Gassendi's edition, which is being printed there [in Florence], is known everywhere, and all marvel that it was permitted. And I suppose that it had to be bowdlerized."[16] The long introductory essay entitled *Typographus philosophiae studiosis* [The typographer to the scholars of philosophy], presented as a sort of programmatic manifesto and presumably written with the consent of the entire group, shows the very explicit significance of the group's commitment and tenacity in its desire to conclude the enterprise at all costs.[17]

The dense essay directly confronts the serious problem of identifying the major obstacles that had to be removed in order to restore energy to Italian culture, justifiably believed to be in a deep crisis. In its organic quality and clarity of intent in the pursuit of a true reform of Catholicism, the manifesto of Galiani's group is comparable to Muratori's analogous project, begun with an invitation to Italian intellectuals to construct a literary republic and later articulated in the treatises *De ingeniorum moderatione* and *Riflessioni sopra il buon gusto*. For Galiani and for his friends, the lack of freedom to philosophize was a determining factor in Italian cultural decadence. Their continued and impassioned appeal for liberation from sectarian spirit and all prejudice radiates through and unites a great deal of the essay, imbuing it with the feel of a genuine call to arms. Arguments common to the Catholic tradition supported the thesis that there was a need for a variety of ideas to give new energy to a univocal debate, culturally impoverished as the Italian one was. In fact we find the customary harkening to the Fathers of the Church, who had favored philosophical syncretism, and the naive nominalist interpretation of the profound differences among Plato, Aristotle, Xenophon, and others in the field of ethics.[18] The exaltation of philosophical eclecticism, which appears frequently in this essay, is certainly indispensable to the search for cultural breathing room, and it allows the authors to confirm their condemnation of sectarianism. However, it becomes more corrosive to the prevailing cultural schemes through the continual and potent reminder of the typically Enlightenment idea, ever present in Galilean writings, of human knowledge's inexorable progress:

> Indeed the mental capacity of humans is not confined by certain gates such that it cannot progress farther. All reason and experience opposes, which teaches us how much we have progressed in the arts and disciplines, and from what small principles any art is started. Indeed what is more lowly or unworthy to the philosopher than to hold in contempt that which he does not know, and not to confute whatever new men's studies bring with reason, but to satirize it, repeating loud laughter with a curled lip, and to attack youth with curses if they carry on their discoveries with a certain zeal?[19]

One must, therefore, invite the young to study all disciplines without fear and with an open mind. History has demonstrated how much evil the enslavement of thought has produced. The author or authors do not hesitate to drag in the Inquisition and its culpable actions.[20] They rather explicitly accuse some sectors of Catholicism of having bound a tool like the Inquisition, created to defend religion against heretics, to the cause of a philosophical sect: Aristotelianism.

Having determined the mental attitude needed to inspire intellectuals interested in a concrete program of renewal, the essay finally confronts the issue of the lessons to be drawn from every philosophical corpus, with the goal of outlining an organic cultural project open to new discoveries but at the same time capable of responding to Italian scholars' needs. Yet again the choice made by Galiani's friends is particularly interesting, because their objective lay beyond distilling a gnosiological method able to guarantee the continued growth of human knowledge. They chose Galilean empiricism, updated and revised in the light of Newtonian scientific theories and Gassendist philosophy.

> I believe it is easy to see in this way to what extent those who thought highly of Galileo's principles carried out his philosophy. Indeed they, wisely having left studies of parts as that most wise leader of theirs had done, wished all hypotheses were banished from philosophy. Those hypotheses, as the most illustrious Newton said, are worthless in philosophy, which consists in experiments.[21]

By wisely integrating Galileo's empiricism with a detailed exposition of Newtonian methodology drawn from the *quaestiones* in the *Optice*, the explanation of the new epistemological plan gains penetrating insight.[22]

Cartesian apriorism, the true counterpart of such a project, is never mentioned at all in the essay, but its presence as a dialectical pole is evident.

The atomism of Epicurus and Democritus in Pierre Gassendi's apologetic version is sufficient for the authors to furnish the needed physical interpretation of the new discoveries. But Gassendism, with its naturalism and negative assessment of mathematics, is firmly corrected by an exact understanding of the "*utilitatem geometriae*" [usefulness of geometry] in research activity.[23] The authors sketch the framework for a renewal of Italian science in the smallest particulars; they believe that mathematical empiricism inspired by Galileo and Newton is capable of guaranteeing real scientific progress that can build on itself in every discipline—from astronomy to mechanics and medicine.[24] All this implied new directions in historical research as well, as has been demonstrated by the analysis of the connections among empiricism, philology, and historiography in the eighteenth century.[25]

Galiani's circle did not stop at proposing a new epistemological framework, but in confirmation of their program's extraordinarily organic nature, they took into consideration the need perceived in broad areas of Italian culture for a different attitude within the Church regarding Epicurean morality. Once again the weapon used to introduce the delicate issue was an impartial examination of the breakdown caused by sectarianism and the prohibition of free philosophizing. Taking up classical themes of Epicurus's apologetics[26] without renouncing the condemnation of some ambiguous and unacceptable aspects of the Greek philosopher's theories, the authors criticized Cicero who, blinded by sectarianism, had mired Epicurus's memory in mud. But surely the most interesting part of this dense preface lies not as much in Epicurus's rehabilitation (accurate even if carried out with predictable arguments) as in the .contrast between Stoic morality, which had always been accepted by much of Christianity, and Epicurian morality, considered to be a source of atheism.[27] Galiani's friends solidly demystified the Stoics' heroic virtues, which had shaped entire generations of Catholics, virtues that we find at the base of Muratori's moral philosophy and, as Venturi has demonstrated, at the center of intense debates in Italy around the mid-eighteenth century.[28] In their essay the authors maintain that these virtues are superhuman, above and beyond any reality, and therefore it is not only useless but downright dangerous to attempt to impose them as though they were within everyone's grasp. In order to be genuine and to conform to reality, a moral code cannot forgo an impartial analysis of what happens around us: "Those who pretend men are heroes are indeed wrong; for whether they wish it or not, there will be vices as long as men live." To attack the "voluptuous sect," accusing it of the most horrendous crimes, was, therefore, mistaken and evil. The foundation of moral codes, far from being entrusted to philosophical cages such as Christianized Stoicism, had first to analyze human behavior and then to express itself (as in the jusnaturalist tradition) by establishing human laws more useful than philosophy for eliminating vices.[29] In this important testimonial of the early eighteenth century, the original matrix of Galilean empiricism, wisely updated by Newtonian theory, flows into an organic proposal for the renewal of Italian culture on bases quite different from the Investiganti's naturalistic Cartesianism still alive in Grimaldi, and different from Muratori's Galileism with its Cartesian sympathies. These bases are, moreover, very critical of the Stoic morality dominating the period's entire cultural history. It does not strike us as mistaken to reveal the significance of this document, for it constitutes a genuine index of how complex the cultural programs were that came into conflict in the contemporary moral, political, and epistemological crisis.

Having attested to the importance of such a project, it is necessary to ask who its promoters were. The most careful historiography of pre-1750s culture has long shown the implications of what has rightly been defined as a European "crisis of religious conscience" in those decades, certainly very familiar to Italian Catholic intellectuals.[30] The existence and import of an intensive reformatory action on the part of those sensitive Catholics most open to modern thought has been sufficiently documented by many scholars. Muratori, Maffei, Grimaldi, Cerati, and others were at the center of painstaking investigations that aimed to bolster the elements of a common (if vague) reformatory plan, capable of creating the groundwork of a moderate Enlightenment in Italy similar to the Catholic *Aufklärung*; however, they chose not to examine the profound cultural and ideological differences that, nevertheless, existed between them. Years ago it was shown that a historiographical direction primarily intent on clarifying who was Jansenist, who was Jesuit, or who belonged to a phantom *"tiers parti catholique entre jansénistes et zelanti"* (a party spread across the entire old continent and surviving down through the centuries) is not always useful.[31] Only recently have we finally begun to pose the problem of examining the personalities of the most important Catholic Italians in relation to their specific contributions to civic life, independent of what they thought about divine grace and the papal bull *Unigenitus*.

This was traditionally how one outlined Gaspare Cerati's position and function in Pisan culture (and Italy in general),[32] and that of his Roman friends, the so-called enlightened Catholics. (While this label is too generic and clearly inadequate to embrace figures who were so different among themselves and who held distinct responsibilities in the ecclesiastical hierarchy, it seemed to be the only one capable of identifying, with some precision, the contours of a group of intellectuals that, nevertheless, presented itself as compact and solid and was built on tightly woven, intense bonds of friendship, intellectual interests, scientific research, courageous initiatives and open-minded advances.) Gathered around Celestino Galiani, figures like Giovanni Bottari, Antonio Leprotti, Antonio Niccolini, and Bartolomeo Intieri shared common ideological underpinnings and a common cultural project, permitting us to identify them as a group. As has been neatly written, they were also the ones who tenaciously sought to open their world to culture and to all manifestations of the human spirit, without renouncing their viewpoints at all. They wished to know and were ready to discuss, to criticize, [and] to reject whatever did not coincide with their convictions or revolted their consciences. They were firmly convinced that the discontinuations, the prohibitions, and the ostracisms with which the works or writings of nonorthodox or suspect authors were struck and slandered, merely served the cause of obscurantism.[33]

During the entire first half of the eighteenth century, the political and cultural actions of these "clerics open to rationalism" were of primary importance, as Franco Venturi indicated,[34] and he justly attributed the realization of the indispensable premises of the Neapolitan Enlightenment to Galiani and Intieri. Cerati and Galiani personally oversaw the reform of the Pisan and Neapolitan universities, respectively. Bottari even had the opportunity to condition, to a considerable degree, the Inquisitorial machine itself.[35] In Naples, Intieri linked his name to the foundation of the first European university chair in economics.[36] Leprotti became the papal doctor of Benedict XIV.[37] Niccolini carried out delicate diplomatic duties throughout Europe on behalf of the Holy See.[38] In sum, the solidarity of enlightened Catholics enabled major contributions at every level. However, it would be a mistake to look for absolute homogeneity in their solidarity, in order to have it anachronistically represent a sort of "philosophical party" *ante litteram*. Certainly the group's solidarity operated efficiently, saving Galiani (accused of spreading Lockean philosophy) from Inquisitorial persecution in the 1730s in Naples; but in the following years a different emphasis on the *libertas philosophandi* took over from the common empiricist and Galilean matrix. Through deist reading, Galiani and Niccolini, and Intieri as well, felt the potent effects of the attraction of the by-now enlightened reason. Cerati and Bottari (especially the latter), however, remained well outside of the Enlightenment, fearful as they were of the violent unraveling of the new Enlightenment culture and its vigorously anti-Christian component. Under close scrutiny, the very general plan of these enlightenment Catholics exhibits both light and shadow. From a tactical point of view, their critical function is beyond doubt, for by denouncing philosophical sectarianism, reintroducing Epicurean morality, and diffusing Newtonianism, they opposed the Catholic conformism to which many other celebrated intellectuals of the period adapted themselves. Yet they clearly worked not to break the burdensome Catholic hegemony in Italy but to reform and to renew it, to inject it with new lifeblood, and to make it more subtle, encompassing, and less liable to frontal attack. With extraordinary ability, they created a sort of new frontier of Italian Catholicism, capable of neutralizing the most disruptive aspects of Enlightenment culture.

THREE

Enlightened Catholics and Newtonian Natural Theology

1. A NEW IMAGE OF GOD

Between 1709 and 1716 enlightened Catholics began to take up, in rather general terms, the matter of the relationship between Newtonian scientific theories and Christian orthodoxy. They quickly understood and evaluated the entire significance of the apologetic interpretation that Newton, Clarke, Derham, Cheyne, and Bentley had given to the *Principia*'s theories. In the following years, their action aimed at spreading such an interpretation throughout Italy was to be carried out under capable direction and with rather precise objectives, but it was during the period 1709–1716 that they began to define their attitude. Newton had been driven by the Cartesians' fiery objections and disputes, and had been vexed by the publication of some works that utilized his theories of absolute space and universal gravitation to confirm barely orthodox hypotheses about the relationship between God and nature. Hence he had perceived the need to specify his thought on this latter point in the *Optice*. *Quaestiones* XVII–XXIII were added to the 1704 edition of the *Opticks*, with the specific intent of countering the accusation that he favored atheism.[1] Even though the importance of these *quaestiones* had already been hinted at to Roman scientists in 1706 by the diplomat Henry Newton through Abbot Piergerolamo Bargellini,[2] their actual importance became evident to them only after the 1710s, after Galiani, Bianchini, and the other members of the Accademia Gualtieri had had the opportunity to evaluate thoroughly the exceptional scientific value of Newtonian theories.

Starting with a series of considerations on the rarification of air and the resistance that ether might pose to planetary motion, in *quaestio* XX Newton had maintained the necessity of a vacuum in celestial space. The attack against the Cartesian concept of matter-extension was already amply spelled out in the *Principia*, but in the *Optice* it became an aspect of Newton's most general complaint against a rigidly mechanistic vision of nature that rendered God's constant intervention in the world's activity superfluous.

In order to refute such a medium [ether], we have the authority of the most ancient and celebrated philosophers of Greece and Phoenicia, who made the vacuum, the atoms, and the atom's gravity the first principles of their philosophy, tacitly attributing gravity to some cause other than matter's density. The most recent philosophers eliminate the consideration of such a cause from natural philosophy, formulating hypotheses to explain all causes mechanically, and they leave the other types of causes to metaphysics. The principal duty of natural philosophy, on the contrary, is to infer from the phenomena without formulating hypotheses, and to deduce the causes from the effects, until one arrives at a true first cause, which is certainly not mechanical.[3]

To the questions "Why does nature not act in vain?" and "From what does all the order and beauty that we see in the world derive?," Newton did not hesitate to reply that the divine creative presence became evident from a careful study of natural phenomena. "There is an incorporeal Being—living, intelligent, omnipresent—who, in infinite space, sees inside things as if He were in His own sensorium, and He perceives and understands them entirely from their immediate presence in Him."[4] This final affirmation would raise lively debates on the Continent,[5] and Newton explained it more rigorously in the *Scholium generale* to the *Principia's* second edition, and partially in the final *quaestio* (XXIII), which was undoubtedly especially appreciated by enlightened Catholics because it contained a clear pronouncement in favor of natural theology.

The central theme of *quaestio* XXIV pivoted around gravitational attraction and its correct interpretation in relation to the new image of the universe. Dozens of examples taken from the study of chemistry, physics, hydraulics, and optics permitted the scientist to conclude in favor of a theory in which matter is composed of hard, impenetrable, and mobile "tiny particles" whose cohesion was due not to atoms chained together or to the "converging movements" of ether (as Gassendi and Malebranche respectively thought) but, rather, to an extremely powerful attraction that acted on each single particle according to precise laws. Thus gravitational attraction became the key for explaining all natural phenomena, from those on a microscopic level related to the behavior of particles of light to those on a macroscopic level dealing with orbital planetary motion. Newton specified: "That which I call attraction can be produced by an impulse and by some other means unknown to me. Here I use that word only generally to indicate some force by whose effect bodies tend towards each other, whatever the cause might be."[6] It is from the "active" and "immaterial" nature of that cause that Newton took his lead to illustrate a *systema mundi* based on the total rejection of Cartesian mechanics' fundamental principles. Newton conducted the exposition on two organically linked levels: one scientific, aimed at demonstrating the contradictions and fallacies of Cartesian science; and one theological, where he considered the divine presence central to his universe-machine. In his *Principia philosophiae*, Descartes had maintained the thesis that the quantity of the universe's motion was constant, and according to many theologians, particularly English ones, he thus had made a formidable weapon available for those who presented a deterministic interpretation of nature by affirming its self-sufficiency. Newton completely overturned the Cartesian hypothesis and maintained instead that movement, far from being constant, could wax and wane "because of the tenacity of fluid bodies, from the friction of their parts, and the weak elastic force of solid bodies." Rather, he clarified, "movement has a greater tendency to wane rather than wax, and it is always lessening."[7] In the Newtonian universe, God's direct and, above all, constant intervention through active and immaterial principles therefore became necessary.

> [These principles are] the cause of gravity, by whose effect the planets and the comets keep moving in their orbits, and falling bodies acquire great momentum; the cause of fermentation, by whose effect the heart and blood of animals are kept in continual motion and warmth, the inner parts of the earth are constantly heated and in some places they become very hot, bodies burn and send out light, mountains emit fire, the earth's cavities are torn by explosions, and the sun is always violently hot and luminous, and with its light it warms everything.[8]

By examining the much-discussed problem of the world's origin, the English scientist once again made his apologetic plan explicit, and he argued openly both with Descartes and his followers—who had claimed to reconstruct all the phases of the earth's formation, interpreting the initial disorder through rigid mechanical laws[9]—and with the modern Epicureans, who were still convinced that the world could have been created out of initial chaos. "Blind fate could never move all the planets in the same direction in concentric orbits, with the exception of a few, hardly relevant irregularities."[10] The natural determinism implicit in the Cartesian system was disproven by the continual and necessary divine intervention through the active and immaterial principles mentioned above, but, above all, it was contrary to God's absolute freedom in the face of the laws of nature.

> And seeing that space is infinitely divisible, while matter is not necessarily found in all places, one can even admit that God can create particles of matter of varying sizes and shapes, and in various proportions with respect to the space and, perhaps, of different density and varied forces, and for that very reason He can vary the laws of nature and create worlds of different species in different parts of the universe.[11]

Actually, Newton concluded, the "marvelous uniformity of the planetary system," far from being the fruit of chance or a rigidly predetermined nature, was due to the result of a divine "choice." Echoing the greatest French and English apologists of the late seventeenth century, the scientist linked the complexity and richness of natural manifestations (in particular of the

human body, made with "much skill") to the geometrical and free "wisdom" of a "powerful and eternal agent."[12]

Jean Le Clerc and his well-known Bibliothèques[13] performed a major role
in the history of the European diffusion of what Margaret C. Jacob has
defined synthetically as Newtonian ideology.[14] The versatile Arminian writer
was suspected by his contemporaries of Socinianism because of his impassioned
battle in favor of tolerance and religious rationalism and his sympathy towards
the Unitarians, and he had a considerable following in Italy, particularly
among enlightened Catholics. Galiani, for example, in July 1715 had the
Dutch bookseller Thomas Johnson send him all of Le Clerc's major works,
in addition to the twenty-seven little volumes of the Bibliothèque choisie [A
select library], which appeared between 1703 and 1713 as a sequel to the
prestigious Bibliothèque universelle [A universal library].[15] But it was not only
Galiani who attentively followed Le Clerc's untiring works. The entire Catholic
Roman circle, and part of the Florentine one, established an especially intense relationship with him.[16] In his periodical Le Clerc lamented that the
books that appeared in Italy rarely reached Amsterdam (and then rather
late), which justified his lack of attention to Italian culture.[17] Not coinci-
dentally, the few works that did arrive were all by Tuscan and Roman authors.
In the issues of the Bibliothèque choisie between 1703 and 1713, there is not
a single commentary on the writings of Maffei, Muratori, Vallisnieri, Poleni,
Porzio, Monforte, or other scholars from the Veneto and Naples, no matter
how interesting. In compensation, there were generally favorable reviews of
the works of Abbot Giovanni Vignolio, Giusto Fontanini, Cardinal Enrico
Noris, Benedetto Averani, and Francesco Bianchini.[18]

This privileged bond between the Catholics and Le Clerc in the early
eighteenth century was due in some measure to English diplomat Henry
Newton's efficient mediating work,[19] and it undoubtedly contributed to introducing some of Le Clerc's most interesting cultural positions in Italy.
Several examples include his critical-philological analysis of the Old Testament (in contrast to the traditional orthodox exegesis), his propaganda work
in favor of the empiricist theology of Limborch and Locke, and, especially,
his capable and intelligent defense of English modern science against the
attacks of those who saw in it the seeds of atheism. Le Clerc dedicated
ample room in his Bibliothèques to works of a scientific nature that had
appeared in England. In fact, he had even cultivated those studies, and
unlike his rival Pierre Bayle, he was fluent in English.[20] In a long review in
1706 he broached the problems that Newton had raised with his publication of the Opticks, which had arrived two years earlier. In a clear and
efficient exposition of the most important arguments treated in the work,
the Genevan writer brought to light Newton's great merits. "He has discovered so many things that neither the ancients nor the moderns had ever
seen, that there is no one who does not wish that he had worked similarly
on all the principal parts of physics." As an advocate of an experimental

and empirical method, Le Clerc promised in conclusion to "rectify and enrich" his own "compendium of physics—if it is printed a fourth time—with the discoveries of Mr. Newton, just as I have already used his *Principles of Physics Demonstrated Mathematically* since the first edition."[21] In 1711 his steadfast acceptance of Newtonianism was confirmed in another review of the *Physico-Mechanical Experiments on Various Subjects, Containing an Account of Several Surprising Phaenomena Touching Light and Electricity*, an already familiar work written by the Royal Society's official experimenter, Francis Hauksbee. Commenting on the experiments that confirmed the *Optice's* theories, Le Clerc wrote that all modern physics could reach new, important results only through "demonstrations based on experiments conducted judiciously and exactly."[22] Such impassioned propaganda in favor in Newtonian science also struck Celestino Galiani who, in a letter to Guido Grandi, expressly cited Le Clerc's flattering judgment of Hauksbee's experiments.[23] Alongside the reviews of Newtonian authors (including 'sGravesande), Le Clerc also presented the *Bibliothèque choisie's* audience with books harshly critical of Newton by scientists such as Guillaume Muys, George Berkeley, and, especially, Nicolas Hartsoeker, with whom he engaged in a lively debate when Hartsoeker reacted to his enthusiastic commentary on George Cheyne's Newtonian *Philosophical Principles of Natural Religion*.[24] Le Clerc's acceptance of the *Principia's* theories did not occur just on a merely scientific level, however; it involved the very interpretation that English Newtonian circles, in the works of Richard Bentley and Samuel Clarke, gave to the new image of the universe and its theological consequences.

The problem of how modern science considered itself in relation to the dogmas of Christian faith was always at the center of Le Clerc's preoccupations. In the first issues of the *Bibliothèque choisie*, he expounded on some of the most interesting chapters of Ralph Cudworth's *True Intellectual System of the Universe* (1678) and dealt with the problem of ancient philosophers' atheism, drawing some clear-cut distinctions between decidedly atheist theories and doctrines that had simply been later misunderstood. Thus was born an interesting premise that informed his decision in favor of Newtonian natural theology. Unlike what Pierre Bayle had maintained in his *Pensées sur la comète* [Thoughts on the comet], Le Clerc was firmly convinced of the incompatibility of atheism and virtue, and he sympathetically presented Cudworth's scheme for possibly reducing the ancient systems of "philosophical" atheism to only four forms: that of Anaximander or the "hylopathists," that of the Stoics, that of the Epicurean atomists, and finally Stratonic hylozoism.[25] He was most interested in the latter two forms of atheism because of the topical nature of their basic scientific hypotheses. Both atomism and hylozoism, in his opinion, assumed different meanings according to how they were variously articulated in the theories of ancient philosophers and modern scientists. Because the atomist thought of Moses and Pythagoras allowed the existence of a God distinct from nature and, above all, of an "intelligent nature" operating in light of a rational, divine design within matter, it could not be accused of atheism in the same way as the more recent doctrines of Democritus and Epicurus, for whom the entire universe was the product of chance.

> [Epicurus] and Democritus made of the world an *egg of the night*, in the worst sense in which one can take this expression: that is, a product not of an intelligent nature but of senseless matter, of Thouhou and Bohou as Moses says, or of chaos, as the pagans say. And they searched for the origin of all the perfections of the universe and all that is in it in the most imperfect and last of all beings.[26]

Even hylozoism, the belief that attributes life and feeling to matter, does not in and of itself lead to atheism. Le Clerc distinguished between a religious and a Stratonic hylozoism. The religious form accepted nature's ability to organize within itself without direct divine intervention but nevertheless allowed for "another type of substance, which is immaterial and immortal," and above all for the supreme being's rational plan. The Stratonic vision of the universe would be founded only on the "matter's life."

> Nature according to the hylozoists is a mysterious absurdity, because they suppose that it is a perfectly wise thing since it is the cause of the admirable disposition of the universe, and nonetheless it has no inner consciousness and no thoughtful knowledge.[27]

Given Cudworth's remarks about the various philosophical atheisms, Le Clerc identified two elements common to all of its forms: materialism and natural determinism. However, not all supporters of materialism were to be considered atheists. Those who confirmed the presence of a divine intelligence along with matter had nothing in common with those who, instead, resolved all forms of life into matter alone, leaving out any kind of "spirit" and immaterial substance. The problem of natural determinism was rather different, for it was indeed a characteristic element of all philosophical atheism. In Le Clerc's wide survey, the concept of an order essential to nature but independent of a precise divine plan became an important criterion for evaluating the components of atheism in modern scientific theories, most notably those of Descartes.

> There can be no doubt that regarding mechanical causes, his physics is at least equal to the best physics of the ancient atomists. Nonetheless one finds several objectionable points in it, of which the principal one is that when describing the origin of the physical world, he has rejected any manner of plastic nature and has claimed that everything has been formed by the necessary movements of matter, which is divided into particles and rotates without guidance from any intelligent nature. He prides himself on explaining all the phenomena of bodies through mechanical movement, without the existence of any being that has set the creation of the universe as its goal. But he does not explain the greatest of all phenomena—the beauty and regularity of the world.[28]

Le Clerc's acceptance of the system of plastic nature came primarily out of a strictly theological assessment, and not from purely scientific considerations about whether vitalist hypotheses were more likely to be reliable than mechanistic ones. In sum, Cudworth's theory posited plastic nature as the mediator between divine will and the natural world, and thus simultaneously eliminated both the danger of atheism implicit in a radically mechanistic vision of reality and the Spinozans' equally dangerous identification of God with nature. All of Le Clerc's successive works in defense of the English science in the pages of the *Bibliothèque choisie* stemmed from the theological and scientific premises outlined above. This explains his keen and enthusiastic review of Nehemiah Grew's *Cosmologia Sacra, or a Discourse of the Universe As It Is the Creature and Kingdom of God,*[29] and, above all, his complete acceptance of Newtonian cosmology, perceived as a new and prestigious bastion against Cartesian mechanism.

In an entire issue of the *Bibliothèque choisie* from 1713 dedicated to "English books" (actually confined only to Samuel Clarke's works), Le Clerc concluded his journey through modern English science by accepting Newtonian physics and theology, quite different from Cudworth's naive and in some ways indefinable world view.[30] The occasion was offered by the fierce debate that flared between Henry Dodwell, who had maintained the natural mortality of the human soul (unless the individual had been baptized by the Anglican rite), and Samuel Clarke, defender of Christian orthodoxy.[31] The broad analysis of their brief treatises on the subject, as well as the argumentative letters between the two authoritative English scholars,[32] was preceded, significantly, by the exposition of Samuel Clarke's most celebrated work: *A Demonstration of the Being and Attributes of God, More Particularly in Answer to Mr. Hobbes, Spinoza, and Their Followers.* This was a genuine manifesto for Newtonians, publicly discussed by the author in the course of his Boyle Lectures of 1704. Le Clerc wholeheartedly shared the ideas expressed in the *Demonstration,* and once he briefly alluded to the Anglican theologian Clarke's subtle criticism of the usual ontological arguments aimed at demonstrating God's existence a priori. He grasped the very foundation of the new natural theology inspired by Lockean empiricism and Newtonian science quite well, emphasizing Clarke's words against the old substantialist conception of God. Though "we have no idea of God's essence, that does not harm in any way the certitude of His existence, because there is no creature whose essence we can grasp, and yet that does not mean that we doubt that the creature exists."[33] Hence there was a need to shift the research field of new theology, in a Lockean fashion, from the substance of the divinity to its attributes—in short, to create a new image of God.

According to Mr. Clarke one cannot prove this attribute of God a priori, but one can easily prove it a posteriori, as he argues in the following: (1) by the different degrees of perfection which one sees in things and between causes and effects; (2) by the intelligence which one sees in created minds which they could not have derived from matter, which is what the author proves against Hobbes and his followers; (3) by the beauty and order of the creatures that surround us and by the final causes for which things were made, about which our author quotes the works of Mr. Boyle and Mr. Ray on this matter; (4) by the first cause of movement, which cannot have a body as Mr. Clarke capably demonstrates, countering Spinoza.[34]

Painstakingly, Le Clerc illustrated to his readers Clarke's sharp and minute analyses of God's attributes: eternity, infinity, omnipresence, unity, intelligence, power, wisdom, goodness, and above all, freedom. According to Le Clerc, the essential value of physico-theology lay in the fact that it allowed an authoritative refutation of the most widespread European atheist tendencies. In essence, the atheists' error was to give matter some attributes belonging to the divine essence, hence confusing two entities that, on the contrary, were quite distinct in Newtonian cosmology. Clarke entrusted the duty of destroying the atheists' theses where they were vulnerable to the modern science of the *Principia* and *Optice*, with their discoveries about the structure of matter. Both his harsh criticism of the Spinozan conception of a necessarily existing matter and the subtle debate with John Toland (whose name, however, does not appear in the *Bibliothèque choisie*) over the problem of motion essential to matter were conducted through the skillful use of Newtonian concepts. Denying the hypothesis of self-propelled matter, Clarke affirmed the need for the presence of active and immaterial causes in the life of the universe, without which movement would have been rapidly exhausted, something fully illustrated by Newton in 1706 in the *Optice*'s *quaestiones*.[35]

> We have great reason to believe that immaterial beings exist, even though we do not know what their simple essence is. Mr. Clarke believes that it can even be proven by the principle of weight in [the case of] inanimate matter. Weight is always proportional not to the surface of bodies or their particles, but only to the solid mass in them. According to Mr. Clarke, it is then clear that weight cannot be caused by a matter that acts on the surface of another substance—which is all it can do—but by something else that penetrates the solid substance.[36]

Again from modern science Clarke drew clues for developing more fully the fundamental problem of divine freedom in the face of nature. "Movement itself and all of its quantities and directions, including the laws of weight, are entirely arbitrary and could have been very different from what they are."[37] Therefore God appeared to be absolutely free with regard to what the theologian defined as the "fatal necessity" of natural laws. In light of a divine law guaranteed by immutable ethical principles, Clarke perceived the need to reconstruct the neat division established in Newton's universe-machine between inert matter, which lacked attributes, and divine omnipotence. But only in relation to the human species, the question of free will, and the need to give a solution to the difficult question of theodicy did he introduce and develop the theme of moral necessity in God's works. "[God] necessarily—not by a fated necessity, but by moral necessity—causes that everything that He makes is the best suited; that is, He always acts in conformity with the most exact rules of his goodness, His justice, His truth, and other moral perfections."[38] After having quoted large sections of Clarke's analysis, Le Clerc drew from his remarks a series of very precise conclusions that gave a sense of the organic nature of Samuel Clarke's new natural theology.

The necessity of God's moral attributes is compatible with perfect freedom, for God always does what is the best and the most appropriate for all. . . . God can place a creature endowed with reason in such a high degree of knowledge and holiness that, despite the natural freedom of creatures, it will not be possible for it to be deprived of sovereign happiness. . . . The foundations of moral obligations are eternal and necessary and depend on no laws.[39]

2. THE NEWTONIANS OF LONDON, THE HAGUE, AND ROME

If Le Clerc's works, particularly the articles contained in the *Bibliothèque choisie*, contributed to the elimination of many doubts from the minds of enlightened Catholics about the apologetic potential of the new cosmology, a decisive acceleration of their plan to disseminate Newtonian natural theology in Italy certainly came from developments during William Burnet's trip to Italy in 1709. The son of the famous bishop of Salisbury, Gilbert Burnet, and Newton's personal friend,[1] the young William was already a leading member of the influential nucleus of Anglican intellectuals tied to Whig circles, which used the apologetical Newtonianism of the Boyle Lectures and their control of the Royal Society to consolidate and legitimize the power of the English establishment that had emerged victorious after the Glorious Revolution of 1688–1689. Newton himself had also suggested a kind of political reading of the new celestial mechanics in his philosophical and religious speculations, explicitly confirming the close interrelationship between the social order and the natural order. He wrote:

The entire natural world composed of the heavens and the earth, or however much of it is considered in prophecy, stands for the entire political world composed of thrones and peoples, and the things in that world stand for analogous things in this. The heavens, with the things present in them, stand for thrones and dignity and those who enjoy them, and the earth with all the things present in it [stands for] the lesser people, and the deepest parts of the earth, called Hades or Hell, [stands for] the most base and miserable section of the people. . . . Great earthquakes and the tremors of the heavens and of the earth [stand for] the tremors and ruinings of kingdoms. The creation of a heaven and of an earth and their decline, or as is the same, the beginning and the end of the world, [stand for] the rise and fall of the body politic.[2]

Burnet was well informed about the bitter philosophical and religious debates underway in England between the Free-Thinkers and orthodox Newtonians, working to establish the image of the new celestial mechanics as an unshakable bastion of Christian faith. He certainly advised his Roman correspondents of what was happening across the Channel, and, among other things, he explained the profound religious spirit that animated Isaac Newton's research. It was nevertheless in Celestino Galiani's tiny cell at the monastery of Sant'Eusebio that he had the most intense and interesting meetings.[3] He engaged in conversations not only on matters of sacred history (in particular about the millenarian thesis, which he believed in fanatically, as, for that matter, many in Newtonian circles did),[4] but also on the Principia's theorems, definitively clarifying for Galiani the revolutionary meaning of Newtonian physico-mathematics. The importance of the bond that the two scholars established thus goes beyond their brief and fruitful Roman meeting. Traveling through Italy and encountering, one after the other, Giuseppe Valletta in Naples, Eustachio Manfredi in Bologna, Jakob Hermann and Giovanni Poleni in Padua, and Bernardino Zendrini in Venice, Burnet became aware firsthand of how precocious and isolated was the acceptance by Galiani's "Roman colony" of Newtonian theories, compared to the Cartesian convictions of the majority of Italian scholars. Hence he chose the Roman group as the English Newtonians' privileged correspondent. Thanks to Burnet, by the end of 1711 some of the best scientific writings yet produced by the Newtonian circle had already arrived in Rome. In this context, Galiani wrote to Abbot Antonio Conti:

> From England I received four books: two by Mr. Whiston, Praelectiones physico-mathematicae and Praelectiones physico-astronomicae. The author wrote them to interpret Newton's book Principia philosophiae mathematica, hence they are optimal for this purpose, but they contain nothing new. Of the other two, one is a good algebraic primer, the other a collection of schediasma and fragments of geometrical things also by Mr. Newton.[5]

Again through Burnet in November 1713 a very valuable package of documents arrived regarding the new edition of the Principia (which had appeared a few months earlier). Among these texts were a copy of the brief author's preface to the second edition and a diligent and complete reproduction of the Scholium generale, a genuine theological manifesto of Newton's entire work.[6] What was hidden behind the London Newtonians' extraordinary interest in the Roman scientists can be understood only by looking at the intermediary Burnet used to transport the package of documents to Rome: the Dutch scientist Willem 'sGravesande, director of the

Journal littéraire and later head of a mysterious literary society in which Free-Thinkers and orthodox Newtonians came together.

The international contacts activated throughout the Continent by the London group are among the most interesting and least studied aspects of Newtonianism's European dissemination. Through a careful investigation into European Libertine circles, Margaret Jacob has come to some surprising conclusions about the unique overlapping of channels of communication that were established between the inventors of Newtonian ideology and those who preached a pantheistic reading of the *Principia*.[8] The fascinating world made up of functionaries, adventurers, spies, and art dealers that animated the European salons during the War of the Spanish Succession formed the common ground between the two groups. Through the Huguenot refugees in Holland, the adventurer journalists who would wield their pens in the service of any cause, and the embassy functionaries always moving from one capital to another, there was an increase in the Free-Thinkers' underground exchange of manuscripts and prohibited books sold at exorbitant prices. In addition there was an increase in the complex and ambitious political and cultural operations favored by the unstable political climate. Within its borders the English government battled vigorously against the Free-Thinkers, but it did not hesitate to unabashedly use them abroad, for example by weaving diplomatic plots against Louis XIV. With its strategic position, Rome could not help but be interested in these clandestine circuits. Figures like Baron Philip von Stosch—an antiquarian, but also an adventurer, Libertine, spy, and open homosexual—had free access to the pontifical suites, despite the fact that all knew of his contacts with the Free-Thinkers and with the Dutch Spinozans,[9] and he and others could lose themselves in the populous colony of foreigners who resided in or passed through the eternal city. Cardinal Alessandro Albani himself, nephew of the pope and patron of Bianchini and Galiani, did not hesitate either to sell information to the house of Hanover or to market archaeological finds through the most disreputable merchants.[10]

The fundamental nucleus of this web of relationships (and often more or less obscure plots) did not, however, lie in Vienna at the court of Prince Eugene of Savoy, a great collector of prohibited works, which were read in his entourage.[11] Nor was it in Paris, where the aristocrats opposing Bourbon absolutism gathered around Count Henri de Boulainvilliers, exploring Spinozan themes,[12] or in Rome, where erudite Libertinism dug in its roots, especially in the Curia's immorality and sordid affairs. It was, instead, in Holland that the strings of European philosophical and political radicalism were pulled, among the Huguenot refugees and the numerous adventurers and diplomats gathered there from every corner of Europe. In 1710 John Toland, Anthony Collins, Jean Rousset de Missy, Prosper Marchand, and others may have founded the Knights of Jubilation, a Masonic-like society in The Hague.[13] Within it took shape an intense drive to disseminate prohibited books that addressed numerous areas of European culture, creating the foundations for what has been called the radical Enlightenment of d'Holbach and Diderot. Some of the Knights publicized a new civic religion—made of Hermetical, Druidic, pantheistic, and Brunian echoes—through Toland's writings and the publication of works from the magical and Libertine tradition of the Renaissance that could no longer be found.[14] Their philosophical and religious radicalism came together with the anti-absolute and libertarian republicanism of the neo-Harrington tradition, and it found much sympathy and complicity among a few Huguenot refugees. Some support may have come from the English government, at least for the anti-French elements of their attack.

Along with the Knights of Jubilation, there were also other Newtonians working in Holland who were interested in spreading the *Principia*'s theories according to their moderate and apologetic interpretation. Better organized than the Knights, they were able to transform the Royal Society, and especially official English Masonry, into an efficient means of propaganda for their theories. The Great Lodge of London, inaugurated in 1717, from its inception carried out this task quite well under the direction of Jean-Théophile Désaguliers.[15]

In the preceding years, the presence of the ideas from the Boyle Lectures in Holland was guaranteed by the work of Willem 'sGravesande and by the publications of the *Journal littéraire*, rightly defined by Margaret Jacob as a powerful instrument "for the dissemination of Newtonian science on the Continent."[16] The journal started in 1713 in The Hague immediately after the signing of the Peace of Utrecht as an expression of the enigmatic literary society in which moderate Newtonians and radical Libertines (among them a few of the Knights of Jubilation) came together.[17] Participants included Willem 'sGravesande (recognized as a leader), Justus van Effen, Themiseul de Saint-Hyacinthe, Prosper Marchand, possibly Thomas Johnson, Pierre Des Maizeaux, and others. In the political arena, the journal aligned itself in favor of the house of Hanover's diplomatic action in Europe, while on the cultural level it aimed at the blanket dissemination of the new Newtonian science as presented in the Boyle Lectures. That, nevertheless, did not prevent the editors from dedicating ample space to the examination of Libertine and heterodox literature. Authors such as Bayle (Marchand was one of the editors of his *Dictionnaire*) and Montesquieu (the Libertine of the *Lettres persanes* [Persian letters]) were singled out. Favorable commentaries accompanied the works of Mandeville, Shaftesbury, Defoe, Voltaire, Toland, and Collins, as well as the implacable anti-Spinozan accusations of Fénelon, Clarke, and Berkeley. However, they devoted most of their attention to the works of the Boyle lecturers, especially to those of Derham and Clarke,[18] and to the scientific exposition of the *Principia*, on which 'sGravesande himself worked. Confirming the close ties between the *Journal littéraire* and Royal Society circles, Newton personally intervened in the journal to attack Leibniz during the debate over infinitesimal calculus.[19]

Through William Burnet's graces, in 1713 Celestino Galiani was plugged into this circuit of moderate Newtonians who planned to conquer all European culture, beginning with London and The Hague. That year, at Burnet's request, 'sGravesande officially asked Galiani to collaborate on the *Journal littéraire*, something that he did without hesitation; four years later Thomas Johnson (publisher for Toland, Collins, and Radicati di Passerano) thanked Galiani in the name of the entire editorial body.[20] Through this unique network of contacts, both the *Scholium generale* and the most disconcerting works of Toland and Collins reached Rome.[21] Burnet sent the *Scholium* first to the Dutch Newtonians of the *Journal littéraire* so that they might publish it, and then it was sent from Holland to Rome. The *Scholium* was accompanied by a long letter from Burnet asking Galiani to have the precious document circulated in his group, so that everyone might be convinced of the apologetic intentions of the London group of Boyle lecturers.[22] Among other things, Burnet informed Galiani of the "preface added to that edition by Mr. Cotes, professor of mathematics and philosophy at Cambridge," a long introduction to the work "to explain Mr. Newton's sentiments regarding philosophy more amply." In his writing, Cotes demonstrated "the impossibility of the doctrine of vortices" and emphasized "the temerity of those who want to penetrate the first cause of things, because on account of the nature of our faculties it is impossible to go beyond experiences, and God's wisdom must necessarily be beyond our research." While praising Cotes's preface, Burnet nevertheless put enlightened Italian Catholics on guard against the ambiguous definition of gravity as a primary quality of matter, for according to Burnet, Cotes's definition did not favor the original plan of Newton and "Doctor Bentley," which was aimed at employing the concept of gravitation "in order to refute the atheists' ideas." In the following months, that copy of the *Scholium generale* circulated throughout Italy, where the implacable attack against Cartesian mechanicism that it contained was widely known and, along with it, Newton's sincere desire to demonstrate that the "most elegant structure of the sun, the planets, and the comets cannot come into being without the plan and power of an intelligent and powerful being."[23]

There are traces of this exchange in the letters between Galiani and the future custodian of the Vatican Library, Giovanni Bottari,[24] who would become one of the most powerful men in the Roman Curia. Bottari received the manuscript and certainly made it known to other Florentine friends as well, and in his letters he enthusiastically confirmed his interest in the dissemination of the new celestial mechanics in Italy. Antonio Leprotti, Cardinal Giannantonio Davia's personal doctor and a scholar well versed in Newtonian theories, sent an equally significant response from Rimini:

> Regarding your second, rather curious letter about the *Scholium*, added to the new edition of Newton's philosophy, in order to see how the author draws from his principles the consequence of God's existence, if it is not too difficult for you, I ask that you send me some clues about it (since

your friend has sent it to you word for word), if it is separated from the letter, favor me at your least inconvenience with the original itself, which I will faithfully send back immediately.[25]

It is fairly safe to hypothesize an early, concrete consensus among enlightened Catholics regarding "Newtonian orthodoxy,"[26] based on the *Principia*'s theories and the reworking of the relationship between science and faith contained in Samuel Clarke's new Christian apologetic.

3. THE ITALIAN EDITIONS OF THE BOYLE LECTURES

The reassuring *quaestiones* of the *Optice*, and above all the *Scholium generale* of the *Principia*'s second edition, had for the moment sufficiently calmed those who feared new reasons for friction between scientists and the ecclesiastical hierarchy. In the following years, the delineation of a genuine natural theology in England based on the *Principia mathematica*, not to mention the accentuation of an intense debate on burning questions about the relationships between God and nature, human reason and divine revelation, and sacred history and profane history, had reawakened in Italian Catholic circles ancient feelings of hostility towards and an unappeased mistrust for English scientific theories. It therefore became necessary for enlightened Catholics to confront determinedly the thorny matter of natural theology in order to avoid letting the dangerous interpretations of some English deists become known in Italy, which would compromise the increasingly complex project of intellectual renewal towards which they were working, largely through the dissemination of Newtonianism.

With the brilliant success of modern science in the study of nature, natural religion had assumed increasing importance throughout Christian Europe from the mid-seventeenth century. Christianity based its dogmas and its very raison d'être exclusively on divine revelation, but from the dawn of the eighteenth century, nature—with its complexity and biological and mechanical order—came for many scholars to be the most immediate testimony of God's existence and of a divine plan. In eighteenth-century culture various interpretations grew out of common premises about the centrality of the concept of nature, thus making references to natural theology dangerously ambiguous.[1] The intense debates on the foundations of Christian religion, bitterly contested in the years of the so-called crisis of the European mind, were concerned, above all, with the different interpretations given to the function of nature, the limits of human reason, and the value of sacred texts and revelation. In accordance with theological rationalism and animated by the desire to reduce Christ's message to a few truths of an essentially ethical-moral nature, some made impassioned requests for reform that conflicted with the irreducible, critical voices of other scholars who departed from commonly accepted premises about human reason and nature and came instead to contradict Christian dogmas drastically and deny any meaning in revelation and the message of sacred texts.

In England at the turn of the eighteenth century, the clash grew particularly heated between those who wished to utilize the growing interest in natural reality as an apologetic and those who, instead, took their lead from the marvelous complexity and self-sufficiency of nature itself, calling into doubt the very foundations of the positive religions. Inevitably, the new image of the universe depicted by Isaac Newton also became involved. We are now sufficiently familiar with the fundamental lines of the harsh collision between the Free-Thinkers and the rationalist theologians of the Anglican Low Church.[2] While these two groups shared the appeal to reason as an essential instrument of critical exegesis in every facet of reality, they were profoundly divided between different cultural traditions and contingent political interests. But, above all, they sought opposite objectives with respect to truth and the historical function of Christianity in modern society. Moving from Herbert of Cherbury's deist tradition and passing through Hobbes's anti-Christian materialism, Libertine naturalism, Spinozan biblical exegesis, and even the corrosive conclusions of Richard Simon's anti-Protestant polemics, men such as Charles Blount, John Toland, Anthony Collins, Matthew Tindal, and others joined to create an ideological framework capable of confronting what has been defined as Newtonian ideology. Their attack on Newtonian apologetics, as it had been intelligently worked out by Richard Bentley, Samuel Clarke, William Derham, and Isaac Newton in the *Scholium generale*, was designed to crack the very foundations of the formidable alliance between Royal Society scientists, Anglican Low Church Latitudinarians, and members of the new postrevolutionary establishment that had guaranteed order and political stability in England in the years of the Restoration. It also sought to break out from a cultural atmosphere ever sensitive to the theological debate surrounding the Anglican Church.[3]

From the 1720s on, the essential outlines of this tough confrontation, and the varied and articulated positions of the major protagonists of this wide debate, became the object of an attentive examination by enlightened Italian Catholics. Distinguishing themselves from the majority of intellectuals, early on they grasped the significance of the themes dealt with in England and their importance for Continental scholars' goals—a new universal culture that overcame the most disquieting aspects of the crisis of the European mind.

As we have seen, Jean Le Clerc's French-language periodicals had quite a following in Italy, and from them enlightened Catholics had learned to distinguish the positions of rationalist theologians (such as Philippe van Limborch, Samuel Clarke, and Le Clerc himself) from the violent attacks against Christianity unleashed by the Free-Thinkers in the name of human reason. The hearty appreciation with which Le Clerc had commented on John Locke's works, from the *Essay Concerning Human Understanding* to the much-discussed *Reasonableness of Christianity*,[4] had, to their minds, forever clarified the possibility of bringing back within the orthodox fold the English philosopher's thought and his work's truly apologetic meaning, which in the realm of traditional Anglican theological rationalism sought to reduce Christianity to a few fundamental truths, giving precedence to ethical and moral values.[5] However vaguely, these elements, with differences and nuances due to their various positions within the Christian community, were known to the most sensitive of the enlightened Catholics, who were already primed to confront European culture and draw from it the vital lifeblood for their ambitious project of reforming Catholicism and its bankrupt intellectual structures. Such a program went far beyond the sterile and provincial theological discussions on divine grace, by now irreparably entangled in ancient and controversial conundrums. Even when the Inquisition put Locke's works on the *Index* in 1734, Bottari, Galiani, Cerati, and Niccolini continued to think of him as one of the fathers of modern culture.

The basic texts of Newtonian natural theology drew strength both from the author's discoveries in the *Principia* and from Anglican theologians' desire to demonstrate Christianity's own rationality, through an analysis of natural reality with its mathematical laws. These texts were first known in Italy through Jean Le Clerc's *Bibliothèques* and subsequently through the *Journal litéraire*'s lengthy extracts, on which Celestino Galiani collaborated as a correspondent from Italy. The Boyle Lectures of the Reverend William Derham, a Royal Society scientist and Newton's personal friend, had first appeared in 1712 in London under the title *Physico-Theology: Or a Demonstration of the Being and Attributes of God, from His Works of Creation*. In 1715 the Jacobite Sir Thomas Dereham[6] brought them to Italy, and there they circulated among the enlightened Catholics. Discussions between Galiani, Bottari, Niccolini, and those in charge at the Florentine grand ducal press led to the decision to translate this fundamental work and present it to the Italian public. Bearing the title *Dimostrazione dell'essenza ed attributi di Dio dall'opere della sua creazione*, the book appeared in 1719 in Florence. This was only after various problems from the hostility of the local Inquisition, which maintained that the archbishop's ordinary approval was insufficient and based their judgment on the opinion of the monk Virginio Valsechi, a reader of Holy Scripture at the University of Pisa. Senator Filippo Buonarroti,[7] who proved to be decisive for the completion of their difficult task, had to undersign the definitive authorization himself in the name of the Medicean government. Indeed, the book's complete lack of even a merely formal reference to divine revelation as the essential cornerstone of Christian religion raised a great deal of suspicion among the Florentine clergy, and in certain curial circles of the Inquisition as well.

In this book Derham had entrusted the demonstration of God's existence solely to what has been called the "physico-theological" proof. Using a fairly faithful translation of the English original opportunely annotated with the editor's personal notes (designed for an audience ignorant of what the Boyle

Lectures were),[8] the editor presented a genuine manifesto of the new English rationalist theology to Italian readers. The impassioned, scientific examination of the chain of beings, running from inorganic matter to humans, allowed Derham to perceive everywhere God's presence and the precise and marvelous plan that governed the organization of the universe.[9] Through scientific research, human reason could independently find the laws and natural mechanisms offering solid, common foundations for all positive religions. The true protagonist of Derham's book was nature and its vital mechanisms, the complex but rational anatomical structures of insects and mammals, and the problems of generation of plants and animals.[10] There thus emerged a theology profoundly different from what Italian Catholics were accustomed to, a theology that did not concede any ground to traditional Christological or exegetical problems. The metahistorical God who resulted, with His universality and open estrangement from any eschatological design, drew dangerously near to "the disembodied and abstract God of deism, similar to a mathematical equation."[11]

Enlightened Catholics were quite aware of such dangers, but they deliberately chose to confront them, as is shown by the decision to suppress only the book's final chapter, dedicated to the *Practical Inferences from the Foregoing Survey*. In this chapter Derham vindicated the efficacy of his apologetic proposal against the atheists and disputed modern Epicureans—Spinozans and Libertines—who, though they had also taken their lead from the examination of nature, nevertheless reached disturbing atheistic conclusions.[12] The translation was disseminated and read throughout Italy, and the *Giornale de' Letterati* greeted its arrival with a favorable commentary.[13] In the Veneto, the close ties that Thomas Dereham had established with Antonio Vallisnieri, Giovambattista Morgagni, and Giovanni Poleni guaranteed a considerable local distribution.[14] A similar situation occurred in Bologna, where Dereham personally knew Eustachio Manfredi and the scholars who surrounded him at the Istituto delle Scienze. And Galiani and Bottari took pains to see that some copies of the book reached Naples and Rome.

But the most significant translation that the enlightened Catholics effected with their shrewd editorial policy was certainly the *Astro-Theology: Or a Demonstration of the Being and Attributes of God from a Survey of the Heavens*, which appeared in London in 1714 and reiterated the other eight lectures given by William Derham and inserted in the Boyle Lectures. This translation condensed some of the Newtonian universe-machine's most provocative themes, which would become rather common in Enlightenment culture. They included heliocentrism and the *Principia's* Copernicanism, and then a detailed examination of the mathematical laws that regulated life in the world, and an apologetic interpretation of universal gravitation, not to mention the anthropomorphic figure of God the watchmaker, bound by His rationality (quite similar to human rationality), who animated the eighteenth-century eudaemonism found in Leibniz's writings and in Alexander

Pope's *Essay on Man*. Starting with the astonished marveling of King David, "The heavens explain God's glory," in his *Astro-Theology* Derham had opened an impassioned vindication of Copernicanism, explicitly pointing "the reader to Galileo's world system"[15] to counter all scientific opposition. The authoritative Anglican pastor Derham referred again to Galileo (this time, however, to the *Lettera alla granduchessa di Toscana*) when he replied to the accusations of those who denied heliocentrism on the basis of some passages in Sacred Scripture, writing: "One might say in general that the plan of Sacred Scripture is to instruct us in theological and not philosophical matters."[16] The new image of the universe, in which the fixed stars were no more than many small solar systems with inhabited planets, unequivocally pointed to a divine plan, the author concluded.[17] The Fontenellian and Libertine hypothesis of the universe's infinite nature and the plurality of worlds (which Derham appropriated from Huygens's *Cosmotheoros*) was resolved in the *Astro-Theology* by considering a further positive widening of divine activity, in God's greater glory.[18]

Though it stayed within the realm of the apologetic, rationalist Anglican tradition that was in opposition to the radical Cartesian mechanism expounded by Boyle, More, and Ray, the *Astro-Theology* nevertheless represented a remarkable leap in quality. Having discarded the plastic natures of Cudworth and More and gone beyond Ray's semivitalistic naturalism, the new Newtonian *Weltanschauung* drew strength and vigor from the painstaking illustration of the harmony reigning in the universe and its rigorous mathematical laws. The work's overall thrust lay in making explicit the reversal that had occurred in the prospects for the relationship between faith and reason in the wake of Galileo's trial. By condemning the Pisan scientist, the judges had affirmed the centrality of sacred texts and ecclesiastical tradition in every field of investigation. Derham's work, on the other hand, under the seal of the greatest scientist of the century, definitively ratified the original role that human reason and the study of natural reality had already conquered, and it came to base the very idea of God on radically different foundations.

It is redundant to underline the novelty and danger of such a work in Italian culture; not surprisingly, the difficulties in publishing the translation proved to be greater than originally foreseen. Early on, the grand ducal press in Florence refused, for there had already been some problems with the publication of the *Physico-Theology*. Having decided against other Italian cities, Dereham, Niccolini, Galiani, and Bottari turned their attention to Naples. Galiani and Bottari contacted their longtime friend Costantino Grimaldi, who in 1728 convinced the publisher Felice Mosca to issue the translation in Naples.[19] In order to avoid trouble from the Inquisition, Mosca was careful to declare the book's absolute orthodoxy in the beginning of the text, although he referred as well to the work's Copernicanism.

In complete submission to the decrees of the Holy Roman Apostolic See, I declare that I did not set out to publish this work, but in view of the great objective undertaken by he who wrote the work, to demonstrate the existence of God also by contemplating the heavenly world, without establishing as doctrine that which is proposed only as a system.[20]

The choice of Naples proved to be particularly felicitous, marking a turn in the editorial policy of the enlightened Catholics. Once the privileged relationship with the grand ducal press had concluded, Giovanni Bottari's departure from Florence made Naples the center of their editorial operations. In the southern capital of Naples, at Mosca's press and under the direct control of Celestino Galiani and Costantino Grimaldi, the five volumes of the *Philosophical Transactions* appeared between 1729 and 1734, translated into Italian by Thomas Dereham. In order to understand the importance and the significance of the publication—one of the numerous, increasingly organic and effective initiatives of Galiani's circle—it is necessary to recall that while Dereham enjoyed a privileged and especially profitable rapport with the Roman group, in the first half of the eighteenth century he became the official intermediary between Italian scholars and the Royal Society. Through his epistolary contacts with the London scientific academy's directors, nearly all scientific works written in Italy were sent to England. Dereham had established a close relationship with the Milanese group patronized by Countess Clelia Borromeo, to whom he dedicated the first volume of his translation of the *Philosophical Transactions*. He had an analogous relationship with the Istituto di Scienze in Bologna, in particular with the physicist Jacopo Bartolomeo Beccari and Eustachio Manfredi, and in Pisa he knew Giuseppe Averani and Guido Grandi. In the Veneto he corresponded with Poleni, Vallisnieri, Morgagni, and Conti, while in Naples his contacts were Niccolò Cirillo and other local scholars. In short, the English baronet Dereham had a veritable network of acquaintances whom he did not hesitate to put at the disposal of his Roman friends. Because of these ties and his capacity as the Royal Society's correspondent for Italy, the translations were widely disseminated in every region, contributing to the success of the enlightened Catholics' program.[21]

Even with its limitations—there were some linguistic uncertainties and some confusion in the memoirs' order of presentation—the Italian edition of the *Philosophical Transactions* finally allowed a wide audience of scholars to become acquainted with the progress modern science had made. With these five volumes, to which Celestino Galiani himself had personally contributed,[22] Dereham brought the enlightened Catholics' editorial program to an ideal conclusion. Their efforts to reinstate the epistemology of Galilean empiricism began with the reprinting of the great Pisan scientist's works and reached an important milestone with the publication of those of Gassendi. Through the translation of the *Philosophical Transactions*, they finally brought to everyone's eyes the sweetest fruits of modern science. Acoustics, astronomy, metallurgy, hydrostatics, agriculture, technology, and botany filled the arguments of those precious memoirs, rich in current information and equipped with clear tables that illustrated anatomical details, sketches of winches and scales, the shapes of fossils that had been found, and seeds with peculiar details. Some of the memoirs translated in their entirety deserve to be singled out for their importance. That of Doctor John Arbuthnot, *Della costante regolarità delle nascite di ambo i sessi* [Regarding the constant regularity of the births of both sexes], was one of the first studies of demographic statistics.[23] The *Relazione di un libro intitolato Statica dei vegetali* [Report on a book entitled the statics of vegetable matter], which Buffon would translate in France in 1735, introduced to Italy the most significant results of Stephen Hales's fundamental book of vegetable physiology.[24] Finally, there were those of Jean-Théophile Désaguliers and Francis Hauksbee, true masters of experimental physics. The fifth volume also carried the famous *Lettera del signor Giacomo Bradley dante relazione di un movimento delle stelle fisse di fresco discoperto* [James Bradley's letter reporting a recently discovered movement of the fixed stars], dealing with the most important astronomical discovery of the century, the aberration of the fixed stars.[25] In Rome, Galiani and Bottari decided to present the text to Italian scholars. Eustachio Manfredi, confirming the Roman control of the edition, wrote in 1729 to Dereham:

> I heard with infinite pleasure that Your Most Illustrious Lordship already has in hand the much renowned discovery of Mr. Bradley, and that you were about to communicate it to Mr. Leprotti, Father Cerati, Abbot Antonio Niccolini and Father General Galiani, in order to have the long-awaited news then pass to me.[26]

In 1729 another important Thomas Dereham translation appeared from Mosca's press in Naples, George Cheyne's *Principi filosofici di teologia naturale* [Philosophical principles of natural theology], which had appeared for the first time in London in 1705. It was a part of the English deist debates and was an articulate response to John Toland's *Letters to Serena*, written in defense of orthodox Newtonianism, and especially against Toland's fifth letter, *Motion Essential to Matter; in Answer to Some Remarks by a Noble Friend on the Confutation of Spinoza*. The significance of this translation, highly desired by Galiani's circle, lies entirely in Cheyne's bitter disputes with the materialists, as if to emphasize the need to eliminate unhesitatingly any possible Tolandist reading of the *Principia* among Italian intellectuals. The translation was based on the second edition, the *Philosophical Principles of Religion, Natural and Revealed, in Two Parts*, which appeared in London in 1715. Like the first edition of 1705, it was only the first part of the work, which focused on the primacy of natural religion and carried on a bitter controversy with the deists.[27] In the opening of the Neapolitan edition, the publisher admitted the complete absence of any reference to revelation in the book, noting:

Therefore publishing these principles of natural religion before those of a science, which in the opinion of the English author does not go further than sensible appearances, I have no other object than to show you how much the principles of revealed religion comply with those of natural [religion], which I suppose is not an antecedent but a consequence of the former. For whatever in these matters can be found less agreeable to Catholic truths will always be alien to my mind and my heart.[28]

The desire to reiterate Newtonian orthodoxy in all its force against any materialistic interpretation was one factor behind the decision not to translate the second, very short part; another was the verification of the profound regression in Cheyne's Hermetical and occultist thought, demonstrated in the second part's mystical affirmations. Enlightened Catholics, occupied with publicizing English theological rationalism in Italy, presumably found Cheyne's final switch to a Hermetical tone disconcerting and contradictory; hence the decision to translate only one part of the work.[29]

In the *Spiegazione del senso nel qual vien presa la natura e le sue leggi* [Explanation of the sense in which nature and her laws are taken], Cheyne presented the already classic archetype of the universe-machine: "By nature I mean that vast if not infinite machine of the universe, the perfect and wise production of omnipotent God, that is made of an infinite number of lesser machines, each of which is adjusted according to weight and measure."[30] The five dense chapters of the work organically examined important arguments, arguments that were much discussed throughout Europe. In the first chapter, "Delle leggi fisiche della natura" [On the physical laws of nature], Cheyne immediately clarified the purely scientific bases of his analysis of the cosmos, affirming that there was no "universal soul created that animated that vast system according to Plato, or substantial forms according to Aristotle, or a radical omniscient heat according to Hippocrates, or a plastic virtue according to Scaligero, or any hylarchic principle according to Henry More,"[31] but merely simple natural laws of mathematical character. He conducted the analysis of these laws on the basis of a painstaking examination of the laws of motion in the *Principia mathematica*, starting with the principle of inertia. In the second chapter he broached the issue of universal gravitation, rejected the Cartesian and Leibnizian system of vortices, and began his angry dispute against Toland's interpretations of the *Principia*. In the opening of the treatise, Cheyne had indicated the need to separate the laws governing creation, with their extraordinary nature, from ordinary and natural laws. "Here we must distinguish between the laws of creation and those of nature, because not only the great bodies of this universe but also the lesser machines of the universe were formed according to a law different from that by which they are presently governed."[32] This is an important distinction, directly contradicting the Cartesian school's attempts (such as Thomas Burnet's famous *Telluris theoria sacra* [Sacred theories of the earth]) to reconstruct the genesis of the universe mechanistically, without recourse

to God's extraordinary intervention, and trusting only in nature's autonomous laws.[33] Divine action in the initial phase of the world's existence
therefore proved to be one of the cornerstones of Newtonian natural theology.
Universal gravitation justly became one of the laws of creation, for it was
not possible to explain it in mechanistic terms. Rejecting Toland's observations that gravitation was an essential property of matter, Cheyne affirmed:

> The attraction by which there is universal gravitation between bodies
> cannot be explained mechanically and, since it was demonstrated that
> the planets cannot continue their motion within their orbits without the
> supposition of a similar attraction or gravitation, it becomes plain that
> this necessarily is a principle imprinted in the matter by the world's cre-
> ator, and that it is a principle in no way essential to matter, since it is
> the source and origin of celestial motion, as Lord Isaac Newton has dem-
> onstrated. And according to the first law of matter and its corollaries,
> no type of motion is essential to matter, and therefore attraction or gravi-
> tation cannot be essential.[34]

In the third chapter, Cheyne disputed the theses of the fifth of the *Letters
to Serena* and furnished a careful rejection of the materialistic reading of
Newtonian works made by the Free-Thinkers, Spinozans, and Hobbesians,
all falling under the generic rubric of modern Epicureans.[35]

Using Newton's own text, Toland had capably overturned the apologetic
background within which the English scientist and his circle of friends operated. An attentive reader of the *Principia mathematica* capable of exploit-
ing any hint of ambiguity present in Newtonian affirmations, Toland had
drawn a picture of the universe entirely unconstrained by a God in the
traditional role—envisioned by Bentley and Clarke—of life's maker and
protagonist in the cosmos.[36] In Toland's design, infinite matter endowed
with motion became the only true actor of life's world. In sum, any form of
organic or inorganic matter found a simple (but troublesome) explanation
in the continual and incessant movement inherent in matter itself. Animals, plants, humans, planets—according to Toland all moved in an incessant, flowing motion: "All the parts of the universe are in this constant
motion of destroying and begetting, of begetting and destroying."[37] Important moments for humans such as life and death were nothing other than
changes of state that certainly did not scratch the most intimate essence of
our being, matter: "But the species still continues by propagation, notwithstanding the decay of the individuals and the death of our bodys, is but
matter going to be drest in some new form . . ., and indeed death is in
effect the very same thing with our birth."[38] Unveiling the theological foundations with which the Newtonians had explained difficult and ambiguous
concepts such as absolute space and absolute time, Toland called into doubt
the very foundations of Newtonian apologetics. According to him, universal gravitation, if considered correctly as essential to matter, would have
confirmed the movement of the latter. To complete the picture of his bitter

dispute with rationalist theologians of the Anglican Low Church, he capably attacked Newtonian theses on the vacuum and absolute space, conceived of as a sort of divine receptacle for intrinsically passive bodies, on the bases of considerations on the motion inherent to matter and of the relational interpretation of space.[39] Utilizing such diverse sources as Bruno, Hobbes, Leibniz, and Descartes (from whom he drew the hypothesis of the ether vortices), Toland overturned the usual reading of the *Principia* made by his contemporaries. The movement of matter, the plenum, the rejection of any finality, and the fierce criticism of the mathematical positivism implicit in the *Principia*'s laws of motion were all elements that seriously alarmed Newton, Clarke, Cheyne, Derham, and others.[40]

Cheyne's response appeared in 1715 and is incomprehensible if one does not take into consideration the context within which it came to assume a precise significance. Cheyne had passionately denounced the thesis of matter mobile of its own accord, taking recourse in scientific principles and in particular in a correct interpretation of the principle of inertia that saw the parity between the rest and motion of bodies. Thus he sought to demonstrate the existence of rest in nature, both experimentally and theoretically, in order to confirm the true basis of Newtonian metaphysics: the total passivity of matter incapable of moving itself in a vacuum without God's direct intervention. This is not the place to review Cheyne's ample refutation,[41] but it is the place to point out the organic nature of his response to modern Epicureans. In the fourth chapter, "Della eterna durezza e durevolezza del presente stato di cose" [On the eternal length and durability of the present state of things], his attack is focused on Libertine theses of the world's eternity (correctly attributed to Aristotle),[42] and it broaches the issues of creation, the Hobbesians' cosmic determinism, and the continually diminishing quantity of motion in the universe. Finally, the fifth and sixth chapters, respectively entitled "Della esistenza di una deità" [On the existence of a deity] and "Prove delle essenza di un Iddio derivanti dalla contemplazione della struttura umana" [Proofs of the essence of a God derived from the contemplation of human structure], reiterated the image of the Newtonian cosmos made of "marvelous" mechanisms, above all endowed with a genuine "beauty" in its geometric perfection. In essence, only God would have been able to make it so.

Given enlightened Catholics' interest in these translations, at this point it is necessary to ask what their objective was and what significance the dissemination of these works had for Italian culture. Certainly in a complex reality lacking European depth, the initiatives of Galiani's circle at least had the value of animating the surrounding debate through entirely topical cultural proposals. Hence, the popularization of natural theology revealed Italian intellectuals' vital need to reopen the political breathing room necessary to launch a serious project of renewal. The old Galilean program of linking new science with the fortunes of the Church, removing Aristotelianism and Scholasticism from the privileged positions that the Council of Trent had conferred upon and guaranteed them, failed miserably with the great Pisan's trial and condemnation.

Nearly a century later, enlightened Catholics planned to accomplish a similar program and readmit prestigious scientists such as Galileo and Newton in a process of general renewal for Catholic culture. Although it had previously faltered during the stifling Counter-Reformation repression, the effort could perhaps be resumed and proposed anew, now with some hope of success in a moment of general crisis for Christianity. This meant an attempt to lay similar foundations in Italy for that fruitful accord between Anglicans and the Royal Society's scholars, a relationship that allowed England to position itself in the vanguard of European science. The principal merit of Galiani's circle lay precisely in having understood from the start that this was the only path politically possible in Italy for opening a season of renewal. The new theology, the rationalism that pervaded it, and the continual reference to the ethical-moral content common to all Christian confessions thus furnished the freest and most open consciences with the evidence necessary to grasp the need for a reform in the Church's customs and pastoral procedures, and to erect a barrier against its interference in the state's problems, an issue that was especially close to the hearts of enlightened Catholics.[43]

The Italian situation is too fragmentary and complex to attempt a synthetic assessment of the part played by Newtonian natural theology. A comparison with France is, nevertheless, useful to understand better the peculiarities and significance of these groups' intellectual choices. In France the anti-Newtonian front remained close-knit until 1730, but even after that one certainly cannot speak of a complete victory of the new science.[44] Heterogeneous in composition and intent, the anti-Newton party combined Jesuits, Jansenists, Malebranchians, mechanistic Cartesians with Libertine roots such as Fontenelle, physicists from the Parisian Académie des Sciences, and others. The entire French ecclesiastical world, for example, was obstinately tardy in defending narrow Aristotelianism and rife with anti-mathematicism, and it wholeheartedly fought against the avalanche of Cartesianism in society and the great universities. The French clergy succeeded in performing an acrobatic about-face, adapting to accept—or, more accurately, to suffer—Cartesian influence.[45] From the 1730s on the Jesuit fathers, in fact, preferred to aim their slings at a new enemy—Newton's universe-machine. This attitude of French Catholics, so different from the one assumed by Galiani's group in Rome, probably found its explanation in the French clergy's deep marginalization from the mainstream of modern thought.

The unspoken hegemony that the ecclesiastical institution still exercised in Italy at the beginning of the eighteenth century was such that it became a privileged vehicle for ambitious projects of cultural renewal; the French scenario was quite different. With the exception of some isolated cases, such as Malebranche and a few others, the sharpest scholars were able to find the road to a different and autonomous intellectual effort in their political and ideological struggles.[46] Paradoxically, in this way Italian culture's historical lag became a point of modernity for the Church, which proved it was still capable of internally accommodating a debate like the one launched by the new Newtonian science, since this naturally implied the possibility of orienting, directing, and controlling the debate. Even in their Machiavellian capacity for utilizing whatever novelty modern thought produced for the greater glory of God, French Jesuits never succeeded in imposing their cultural hegemony in the French context, which was otherwise quite animated and lively. Newtonian cosmology's metaphysical background, philosophical empiricism, and Locke's utilitarian morality in an Epicurean matrix, all of which enlightened Catholics in Italy wisely utilized to open new spaces in an environment hardened by the Church, in France were to become instead the cornerstones of the thought of one of the great fathers of the Enlightenment, Voltaire.[47] In fact there are more than a few points of similarity between Voltaire, the brilliant propagandist of Newton's thought, and Galiani's group. They are alike in their apologetic reading of Newton via Clarke, their tenacious antimaterialism, and their search for ethical-moral values in Christianity. It would certainly be absurd to compare Voltaire's showy deism and his anticlericalism, and the difficult battle for civil rights in favor of enlightened thought, to the theses of Roman clerics, even if they were rationalists and "enlightened," as we have so often labeled them. But they covered the first leg of the journey together, and it was not a coincidence that in the first half of the eighteenth century Voltaire's most widely disseminated works in Italy were his *Métaphysique de Newton* and *Eléments de la philosophie de Newton*, translated and printed in Florence (1742) and in Venice (1741) respectively.[48] However, it is well known that the Church did not become hostile towards Voltaire until after mid-century. In the preceding years Galiani and Niccolini, who had read some of his great historical works and the *Lettres philosophiques*, unhesitatingly spoke enthusiastically of them to each other.[49]

With the popularization of Newtonian natural theology, Voltaire strove futilely to involve the French Jesuits in a campaign against Cartesian mechanism, which he accused of having favored the birth of Spinozism. An entire faction of the philosophes shared a similar theological and metaphysical background; even Rousseau, in his famous *Profession de foi du vicaire savoyard* [The vicar of Savoy's profession of faith], sought to resolve—albeit with different emphasis—the grave problems posed by his restless religiosity.[50] Both Voltaire and the enlightened Italian Catholics resolutely attacked Cartesian thought under the banner of Locke and Newton. Voltaire had to counter a richer and more lively culture, in which Descartes's teachings assumed various meanings, such as the Malebranchians' spiritualizing interpretation, which was radically opposed to the Libertines' materialist interpretation. In the eyes of Italian Catholics, on the other hand, Cartesianism represented the bastion of the party of the moderns who, while huddled in a sterile defense to the bitter end of a mechanism long since outdated, operated within the context of a culture still tenaciously tied to the scholastic tradition that rigidly hegemonized it. This meant there was a profound difference in the meaning assumed by operations that were similar in appearance but that were carried out against backdrops of very different historical realities. With the dissemination of natural theology, enlightened Italian Catholics aimed to bring the most active forces in Italian culture back to the foreground and into a European context, even as they took pains not to cross the threshold of the moderate prudence that appeared indispensable for making such a project compatible with the Catholic Church's position in Italy. In this light we can understand their attempt to realize a sort of shift of Italian intellectuals from the Cartesian frontier, no longer productive for a profound cultural renewal and ever threatened by dangerous Libertine developments, to the reassuring apologetic empiricism that had originated in England.

FOUR

Newton and Scientific Traditions in the Veneto

1. ANTI-NEWTONIAN POLEMICS

The enlightened Catholics' project to disseminate a reading of Newtonian science compatible with religious orthodoxy faced a concrete alternative in a cultural region traditionally hostile to Roman Counter-Reformation hegemony: the Veneto, the hinterlands around Venice. In Italy this city, known as the Republic of San Marco, had always represented a pole dialectically opposite papal Rome, not only in political terms (the most telling example being the interdict Paul V pronounced against Venice, and Paolo Sarpi's lively response) but, above all, as a valid cultural alternative to the Catholic model produced by the Council of Trent. For Italian intellectuals of the sixteenth and seventeenth centuries experiencing a loss of identity, Venice constituted a real "harbor against the crisis,"[1] and it would continue to remain such until the dawn of the eighteenth century.

Even more than local scholars' original studies, the presence of a flourishing publishing sector and its contribution of a largely free and open debate on modern thought nourished Venetian culture, which was opposed to Counter-Reformation political culture. Nevertheless, there were established tools of censure and repression directly controlled by the state, which allowed the republic to exercise watchful supervision over the internal political dialectic and prevented any evolution of the traditional form of aristocratic power. At the same time, no obstacles existed to hinder the free circulation of printed works of all sorts; in fact, Venetian publishers endured no periods of serious crisis, and Venice always remained among the most important publishing centers in Continental Europe.[2] In the Venetian academies, Libertine thought rested securely on the very consensus and protection of the nobility in power. Paduan academic tradition, built on extensive international ties and animated by a free and lively debate (vainly opposed by the Jesuits), long remained a strong element in a lay culture extremely attuned to the ideological problems that arose from the defense of the republic and its jurisdictional prerogatives.[3]

The enduring cultural tradition of the Veneto certainly influenced

Muratori's great project of the literary republic. It has been noted that *I primi disegni della Repubblica letteraria d'Italia* [The first outlines of the literary republic of Italy], edited by Muratori between 1702 and 1703, coincided with the French occupation of the duchy of Modena during the turbulent phases of the War of the Spanish Succession.[4] It is no coincidence that the literary republic's five official protectors were the same Italian princes who had opted for cautious neutrality. The harsh conditions brought on by invasions and military occupations (which, despite their neutrality, some of these princes had to suffer) pushed Muratori to work out a broad cultural and political plan that, along with Italian intellectuals' newly assumed civil consciousness, foreshadowed concrete political support structures by establishing a confederation of neutral states.[5] First of all, the project envisaged an institutional structure with the election of the Arconte, Consiglieri, and censors for each of the five provinces into which the Italian peninsula had been divided. They were the "Provincia Reale" (Naples and Sicily), the "Pontificia" (the papal state), the "Etrusca" (the Grand Duchy of Tuscany, the Republic of Genoa, and Lucca), the "Veneta" (the Republic of San Marco), and the "Lombarda" (the duchies of Mantua, Modena, and Parma). A detailed, discipline-by-discipline program of cultural renewal, with clear-cut methodological directions, rounded out the project. In virtue of its importance and prestige, not to mention its real political strength within the new confederation, Rome was to become the governing center and driving force of the newborn literary republic. It was a brilliant undertaking, demonstrating a sagacious evaluation of the Italian situation; it was certainly not a joke between literati, as Muratori later made clear. Nothing more came of it, however. Even today the reasons behind its failure are rather unclear. On a merely political plane, the ambitious plan of a neutral league of Italian princes, along the lines of a reborn neo-Guelfism made palatable by Clement XI's advances, fell apart quickly because of the imperialist predilections of some princes and the escalation in warfare. After 1708 and the Comacchio affair, during which Duke Rinaldo d'Este and papal Rome had a head-on confrontation, any further hope for a confederation vanished. Among its many problems, the entire project was internally flawed by the attempt of philosopher Bernardo Trevisan (another promoter of the undertaking) to make Venice the driving force behind the novel literary republic, thus accentuating the city's ancient antagonism with Rome. Despite enormous political difficulties and a series of setbacks, uncertainties, and even sabotage on the part of some intellectuals, Italian scholars retained their sense of renewed determination to be a critical presence in social life.[6]

While in this context Muratori's project failed on the level of practical realization, it was bound to influence more than a generation of Italian culture, since it expressed a widely perceived need that could no longer be suppressed. After the *Primi disegni*, in his subsequent works Muratori reinforced the necessity for reform, which could not be delayed. His *Lettera esortatoria ai capi, maestri, lettori ed altri ministri degli ordini religiosi d'Italia* [An encouraging letter to all leaders, teaching masters, readers, and other ministers of the religious orders of Italy] circulated in manuscript form in 1706 and 1707. Then came the two volumes of the *Riflessioni sopra il buon gusto intorno le scienze e le arti* [Reflections on good taste in regards to the sciences and the arts], the first of which appeared in Venice in 1708, and the second in Naples in 1715. Finally, his important *De ingeniorum moderatione in religionis negotio* [On the moderation of minds in matters of religion] followed in 1714. Rome had officially had the honor and the responsibility of directing the new republic, but anyone should have been able to comprehend the meaning of the harsh accusations contained in the *Primi disegni* against the escapist culture that ruled in Italy and against the *"bagatelle canore"* [melodious bagatelles] and the bucolic pastorals. These charges were actually meant to strike a blow at the effective instrument of control that the intellectuals had created in Rome, namely the Arcadia, with its rites and formulas that subtly and internally sabotaged any commitment to renewal possessed by the most sensitive scholars.[7] This was the root of Rome's inevitable opposition to and lack of enthusiasm for the literary republic of Italy, despite the favorable attitude of Fontanini and Passionei, in all probability dictated by the desire to control the initiative from Rome.[8]

Muratori's program holds considerable importance for many of the problems confronted in this book. It encompassed the trends of a culture that in many ways was an alternative to that of the enlightened Catholics. And while it grew out of common needs for renewal, its response to some problems stems from entirely different suppositions. The great Galilean experimental tradition, so widespread throughout northern Italy, provided Muratori with one of his most fundamental gnosiological inheritances, for in his *Primi disegni* he had solemnly affirmed the need to place "our greatest hopes for glory in the philosophy that we call experimental."[9] But he placed the entire efficacy of this inheritance within the Cartesian mechanicism refuted by Galiani's circle. The Cartesian philosophical method percolates through a great deal of the *Riflessioni sopra il buon gusto*, but it would be erroneous to speak simplistically of Muratori's Cartesianism.[10] Just like other great scholars of Italy, Muratori attributed to Descartes the honor of having broken the oppressive Aristotelian hegemony by opening new horizons: "Until Descartes, for many centuries all philosophers had been enclosed in a large room or gallery, or prison."[11] But this realization did not bring about the tranquil acceptance of every aspect of Cartesian physics. Defending Descartes from the accusation of being a heretic, Muratori addressed an Italian ecclesiastical audience when he wrote in his *Lettera esortatoria*:

Perhaps it appears that I wrote this because of some bond or obligation that I might have with Descartes's school. But solely for love of truth and good taste, I believed that I should not remain silent here. Because

I appreciate nothing in Descartes, I embrace nothing, except what he persuades me of with strong reasoning.[12]

Actually, all Muratori's works echoed Cartesian philosophical methods. Despite continually distancing himself from Cartesian scientific errors, in his mature works he still made use of such fundamental components as the criterion of rational evidence, methodical doubt, and the dualism between matter and spirit.[13] The *Giornale de' Letterati*, which appeared in Venice in 1710, presented a great many of these themes, emphasizing that they were the common patrimony of intellectuals throughout the entire Veneto. In the journal's first issue, Italian scholars learned of the program for the literary republic through a long article entitled *Progetto della nuova repubblica letteraria d'Italia e scritture uscite su tal proposito* [The project of the new literary republic of Italy and the writings produced regarding that proposition]. The *Giornale* defended and appropriated the initiative, publishing a lengthy extract from the *Riflessioni sopra il buon gusto* with Bernardo Trevisan's introduction.[14] This articulate exposition of Muratori's enterprise brought to light its characteristics and goals, not to mention the gnosiological environment within which its promoters intended to operate. The two axes of the journal's epistemological framework were Galileo's experimental philosophy, seen as the authentic interpretation of Italian philosophical traditions, and Descartes's method, understood as a rigorous application of methodical doubt. To these axes we must add the significant role attributed to mechanicism as a bastion against any attempt to resolve the problems posed by modern science through solutions of a finalist nature.

We have already seen how from its first issues the *Giornale* engaged its best men in disproving some of the features of the *Principia mathematica*. Antonio Vallisnieri personally solicited Jakob Hermann to intervene in the acerbic dispute over Newtonian central forces. Bernardino Zendrini, another of the periodical's writers responsible for the scientific section, confirmed the validity of mechanism and the theory of ether in a number of articles. Giovanni Poleni, teacher of astronomy and meteors at Padua and the *Giornale*'s editor of physics and astronomy, wrote his *De vorticibus* [On vortices] in 1712 to entreat European scientists to resolve issues regarding gravity by utilizing mechanicism and the theory of ether.[15] In the following years, well after Isaac Newton's fame had been recognized throughout Europe, scientists in the Veneto maintained an attitude of critical acceptance, if not open aversion. There remain many traces of this attitude, which attracted some celebrated scholars and addressed scientific problems of enormous importance: in particular, two destructive *querelles*, one on Leibniz's live forces (whose protagonist was Giovanni Poleni), and the other on the truth of Newton's optical theories, led by the scientist Giovanni Rizzetti of Treviso.

Leibniz had posed the thorny problem of how to evaluate motor force in the pages of the *Acta eruditorum* in 1686, with his *Brevis demonstratio erroris* memorabilis Cartesii et aliorum [A brief demonstration of the error of the memorable Descartes and others]. The German philosopher had maintained that the Cartesian quantity of motion (the product of mass times velocity) did not represent the general measure of force, which was instead tied to the square of the velocity. The dispute that ensued, in which all the greatest European scientists participated, reached its culmination in 1715 with the famous epistolary dialogue between Leibniz and Samuel Clarke, who defended the Cartesian thesis that Newton had appropriated in the Principia. It is not our aim here to reexamine the technical aspects and essential points of the querelle; it has already been amply studied.[16] Nevertheless we must make clear that, above and beyond mathematical formalism and a certain terminological confusion, the disputants had substantially different approaches to natural reality, and a different way of understanding matter. The energetic conception typical of Leibniz's monadology was set against the theory of total passivity that Newton and Descartes shared, though they articulated it differently. For Descartes, motion was something external, imposed on matter by divine action. Both, however, accepted what is the linchpin of modern dynamics: the principle of inertia. As Alexandre Koyré has perceptively noted, Leibniz quite willfully misunderstood this principle, or at the very least he always refused to accept it fully.[17] The German philosopher strongly criticized Newton's vis inertiae [inertial force], interpreted as a passive force, which he countered with a sort of paradoxical dynamic inertia, justifying this in view of the relational theory of space. In order to underscore the strictly dynamic nature of his conception of force, Leibniz defined force as a vis viva [live force], different from a vis mortua [dead force], conceived of as any force (for example, pressure) not linked closely with motion.

That which we could define as an energetic conception of force found many supporters in the Veneto, and it was long discussed favorably. In 1718 Giovanni Poleni's book De castellis per quae derivantur fluviorum aquae habentibus latera convergentia [Regarding castles having converging sides through which the waters of rivers are derived] introduced European scholars to the results of a well-conceived experiment, carried out at the University of Padua, which in his opinion definitively supported Leibniz in the dispute with Newtonians about vital forces.[18] Actually there was nothing particularly new in Poleni's experiment, and Leibniz had already given some insights for completing it in 1686. In Venice the Cartesians who congregated in Luigi Pavini's bookstore, headed by Bernardino Zendrini, had been performing experiments quite similar to Poleni's since 1706.[19] The reverberation across Europe was quite widespread, given the considerable fame of the Venetian scientist who in 1712, with the De vorticibus, had already disproved Newton's interpretation of gravitational theory. In England, Henry Pemberton, who was tied to the Newtonian circle and was to become the editor of the Principia's third edition, responded with a long letter to Richard Mead of the Royal

Society, which appeared in the *Philosophical Transactions*. Poleni's response opened a diatribe that would involve scientists such as 'sGravesande, Bernoulli, Riccati, and others.[20] In the Veneto, Poleni had the support of the greatest local scholars, including Antonio Conti (to whom he addressed a short treatise in the form of a letter reinforcing his own theses), Vallisnieri, Jacopo Riccati, Vincenzo Riccati, Bernardino Zendrini, and Giovanni Rizzetti.[21] Among those in Italy who reacted negatively were the enlightened Catholics. Celestino Galiani had Poleni's experiment repeated in his Accademia delle Scienze in Naples in 1733 on behalf of Bottari, obtaining results that wholly confirmed the exactness of Newton's theories.[22]

Rizzetti's *querelle* on the correct interpretation to give to the *Opticks's* celebrated experiments was equally significant for (and in certain ways representative of) a certain opposition that arose between Galiani's circle and scientists from the Veneto. As we have already seen for Rome, from 1707 on at the Accademia degli Antiquari Alessandrini and then successively at Cardinal Filippo Antonio Gualtieri's academy, Francesco Bianchini (back from his trip to England in 1714) and Celestino Galiani had repeated Newton's experiments, finding them perfectly explained by the theories expounded in the *Opticks*.[23] In 1721 a "Lettera scritta al sig. Cristino Martinelli nobile veneziano dal signor Giovanni Rizzetti sopr'alcune nuove scoperte diottriche" [Letter written to Mr. Cristino Martinelli, noble Venetian, from Mr. Giovanni Rizzetti, on some new dioptric discoveries] appeared in the *Supplementi al Giornale de' Letterati* [Supplements to the *Giornale de' Letterati*] edited by Abbot Girolamo Lioni, who had taken the place of the troubled *Giornale's* original editorial group.[24] From the first remarks, it was easy to see that Rizzetti's new dioptric discoveries were nothing more than a different interpretation of some Newtonian experiments. The article stirred up a hornet's nest. Several times Rizzetti repeated the experiments with prisms in his possession before noble Venetian scholars, provoking a growing interest in the scientific circles at the University of Padua as well, and primarily in Poleni and Vallisnieri. Scipione Maffei, who was not even a scientist, also wished to perform the experiments in question. His considerations of Newtonian optics illustrate well the perplexed attitude in the Veneto region regarding the *Principia's* author. He wrote to Poleni on 22 November 1727:

> Here are all the prisms of Abbot Conti; I do not need them anymore. I ask that you advise him that they are in your hands. . . . Regarding Newton's opinion on colors, I am thinking of putting a discussion in the Observations; I will not do it, however, without first asking him to review it and advise me frankly. In truth I think it is a false and bizarre opinion, and perhaps many others should treat it so, if we were not carried away by the current idolatry of that philosopher's name and by the passion that we have for anything which is foreign.[25]

Abroad, the *Journal des savants* and the *Acta eruditorum* commented very respectfully on Rizzetti's theories. In the *Acta* a lively dispute developed between Rizzetti and German scientist Friedrich Richter, who defended Newton.[26] From Treviso in 1728, Rizzetti issued his *De luminis affectionibus specimen physico-mathematicum* [Physico-mathematical model of the affections of Light], dedicated to Cardinal de Polignac, in which he condensed all of his optical experiments, working out a system that was in many ways an alternative to the Newtonian one. In the preceding years the dispute had involved Isaac Newton himself, along with the Royal Society.[27] The secretary of the academy, James Jurin, had written directly to Thomas Dereham in Florence, asking him to buy Rizzetti's recently released book and send it to him in London for a careful examination.[28] Rizzetti had not hesitated to write to the London academy to advertise his thoughts. The entire English scientific community had nevertheless been up in arms since 1722—as can be seen from the account of the matter published by Celestino Galiani and Thomas Dereham in the Italian translation of the *Philosophical Transactions*— openly disputing Rizzetti. Newton had heard of the Trevisan scholar's experiments through Gislanzoni, a noble from the Veneto, and he had entrusted Désaguliers with officially repeating some of the proofs at a meeting of the Royal Society. Just after the appearance of the *De luminis affectionibus specimen* in 1728, following the lively debates in the *Acta eruditorum* in 1724 between Richter and Rizzetti, enlightened Catholics quickly sent the book to London, where in August 1728 it was discussed publicly. The long report that resulted was translated and printed at the express request of Dereham and Galiani, bearing the title *Sperienze ottiche fatte al principio del mese di agosto 1728 avanti il presidente e a diversi membri della Società Regia e ad altri signori di varie nazioni e a motivo dell'ottica del sig. Rizzetti con una relazione del suo libro da T. Désaguliers* [Optical experiments conducted at the beginning of the month of August 1728 before the president and various members of the Royal Society and other men of various nations, on account of Mr. Rizzetti's optics, with a report of T. Désaguliers's book]. One by one, Désaguliers had repeated the most-discussed experiments, confirming the exactitude of Newton's theories on all points and concluding with the affirmation that "the optics of Sir Isaac have no need for explanation or defense. And when the author [Rizzetti] is in the mood to be convinced, ten months well spent rereading the book of Sir Isaac will reassure him after his useless examination of the last ten years."[29] The overall tone of the report was quite harsh when dealing with the Italian scholar: "The author in his preface and throughout the body of the book has insulted in a most arrogant manner the greatest of philosophers that this or any other century has ever produced."[30]

The issue cannot, however, be reduced (as Désaguliers maliciously attempted) to a sterile dispute between a giant and an envious dwarf. It was ascertained very quickly that Rizzetti's theories were mistaken. The Trevisan scholar had, nevertheless, raised a rather serious issue: were experiments liable to a single interpretation, as Newton claimed, or could they sometimes offer disconcerting alternative interpretations, as Robert Hooke, Christian Huygens, Willem 'sGravesande, and others objected at different times? This was a complex problem that divided entire generations of scientists during the eighteenth century. As Rupert Hall has indicated, some profound non sequiturs of Newton's epistemological design, containing internal methodological contradictions, encouraged many European scholars to disagree with and dispute his views, in particular on matters concerning optics.[31]

Count Jacopo Riccati of Treviso, Rizzetti's friend and a scientist of some merit, quickly became aware of the underlying motives behind the sparks between Rizzetti and Newton. In defense of his friend, Riccati emphasized ironically that an experiment was in reality always "cheated" by anyone who appealed to and organized it. Therefore it would be difficult for that person not to find whatever he wished to discover from the beginning:

> If I look at the color spectrum extended in the distance, standing in the room across from another prism with the angle turned upwards, it lowers, and at a certain distance it constricts into an entirely white circle whose diameter is only two inches. Mr. Newton attributed this phenomenon to the varied refrangibility of colors; Rizzetti credited it to the different direction of the rays.[32]

The dispute continued at length, and in 1741 the discredited Rizzetti issued his *Saggio dell'antineutonianismo sopra le leggi del moto e dei colori* [Anti-Newtonian essay regarding the laws of motion and colors], in which he still rejected the great English scientist's interpretations.[33] This *querelle* also provided the background for Francesco Algarotti's celebrated work *Il newtonianesimo per le dame, ovvero dialoghi sopra la luce e i colori* [Newtonianism for ladies, or dialogues on light and colors] (1737), which appeared for the first time in Milan (incorrectly credited as Naples). The occasion for Algarotti's work came as a result of the reaction that the *De luminis affectionibus specimen* caused in Galiani's circle. The Istituto di Scienze in Bologna directed by Eustachio Manfredi, tied as it was to the group of enlightened Catholics, formally had the Newtonian experiments repeated using the prisms bought in England at the request of Galiani and Dereham.[34] Francesco Algarotti, then a fellow at the Istituto and a pupil of Francesco Maria Zanotti, was entrusted with conducting the experiment. He also promised to respond publicly to Rizzetti soon, but things dragged on for some time. Algarotti's voyages abroad and his contact with the philosophes, the Parisian environment, and Maupertuis contributed significantly to his modification of his original idea.[35] Because the dialogues were first laid out in Bologna in 1734 and then completed during Algarotti's Parisian stay, the cold and rigorous scientific response anticipated by Manfredi and Zanotti in 1728 became, instead, a lively and brilliant manifesto of Newtonian science and its empirical, antimetaphysical, and Copernican foundations, which linked it uninterruptedly with Galileo's work.[36] Taking up a dispute central to the enlightened Catholics' plan, Algarotti brilliantly underlined the limitations and backwardness of the Cartesian system, whch in his opinion was irreconcilable with Galilean empiricism.

The Swiss periodical *Bibliothèque italique ou histoire littéraire de l'Italie,* published in Geneva between 1728 and 1731 by bookseller Marc-Michel Bousquet, was tied to the cultural experience of the Veneto and its greatest proponents, in particular Antonio Vallisnieri. The *Bibliothèque,* whose noteworthy significance for Italian culture has been highlighted in a recent study,[37] also fitted into a substantially mechanistic-Cartesian scientific framework, where the theological finalism of the *Principia mathematica* and Newtonian commentators was rejected. We should not be fooled by the existence of men within the *Bibliothèque*'s editorial group like Bousquet and Jean-Louis Calandrini, who were attuned to the new celestial mechanics from across the channel. Actually the journal's overall attitude was not alien to a Muratorian-type project for reforming Italian culture, made more seamless and explicit by a deep-rooted acceptance of the Cartesian method and the *Giornale de' Letterati*'s Galilean experimentalism. The "Estrait d'une lettre sur les objections que font les newtoniens contre le système des tourbillons de Descartes" [Extract of a letter on the objections that the Newtonians make against Descartes's system of the vortices], which appeared in the *Bibliothèque* in 1731, confirmed the journal's Cartesian orthodoxy. Taking inspiration from a treatise by some Piedmontese Newtonians—almost certainly Bernardo Andrea Lama and Joseph Roma, both pupils of Celestino Galiani[38]—that circulated in the University of Turin, the journal wholly restated the classic themes of post-Cartesian mechanicism outlined by the scientists from the Parisian Académie des Sciences and, in Italy, by Giovanni Poleni's *De vorticibus.* There is nothing new in the article's arguments; on the contrary, in some specific points concerning the motion of fluids, its steady refusal (never marred by a hint of doubt) to consider any interpretation of gravitational theory not in the Cartesian-vorticist vein is surprising. In the arena of cosmological problems, the entire document quite significantly represented a new restatement meant to confirm the basic assumptions of Poleni's *De vorticibus* and Vallisnieri's entire group.

In the Veneto, the noticeably reserved attitude towards Newton's theories was widespread; only his incontrovertible scientific results were accepted, while the underlying premises were rejected. This attitude is reflected in the Somascan father Giovanni Crivelli's *Elementi di fisica* [Elements of physics] (1731) produced by the Orlandini typographers. The manual was much appreciated throughout the Veneto, and it was known in other parts of Italy as well. Adopted as a textbook in the episcopal seminary of the Somaschi of Murano, it was widely dispersed, as attested by the second edition that was released by Simone Occhi in Venice a year after Crivelli's death. Crivelli, who became director of the seminary and had important responsibilities within this religious order as well, was friendly with Vallisnieri, Riccati, and Conti, to whom he wrote a letter on the "motor forces." He was also a member of the Royal Society and Bologna's Istituto di Scienze. Most important, he was tutor to the youth of some of Venice's most prestigious families.[39] His book was thus a meaningful record of the attitude of a large segment of society in the Veneto with regard to Newton's works.

The *Elementi* opens with a learned and interesting history of scientific thought, from the Greek philosophers through Cartesian and Newtonian works. Crivelli devoted much space to the "Italic sect" begun by Pythagoras and perpetuated through the centuries, until the renewal of the ancient glories in men like Telesio, Campanella, and the heretic Giordano Bruno; "but no one promoted the doctrines of physics more than Galileo Galilei."[40] When analyzed attentively, the two volumes reveal a disconcerting text, contradictory and fleeting, offering different, yet all legitimate, levels of reading. After having noted that the "voice of Nature is an ambiguous one" because of the varied interpretations that men give to the relationship between God and nature, Crivelli laid the final foundations for understanding natural reality. Not through brief hints but concretely with intelligent, firsthand readings, he produced an essentially Aristotelian science in which there was a place for the greatest scientists of the age: Newton, 'sGravesande, Keill, Leibniz, Bernoulli, Vallisnieri, and many others. He wrote: "Therefore I say that all bodies that comprise the universe can be adduced from two universal principles, and they are matter and form."[41] Following Aristotle, Crivelli disagreed with Newton's concept of the vacuum, associating Aristotelian principles with Leibniz's theses on relational space, and he cited a lengthy portion of Leibniz's fourth letter to Samuel Clarke published in the famous *Recueil des diverses pièces sur la philosophie* [A selection of various writings on philosophy] edited by Des Maizeaux.[42] The singular task of reinterpreting modern science within a renewed Aristotelianism continued then with the acceptance of the Cartesian and Leibnizian theory of ether, correlated to a rejection of any energetic conception of matter. Crivelli strongly denied the hypothesis that motion was essential to matter, disagreeing with the "modern Epicureans" (whom he never explicitly named). The first volume offers the most complete exposition of Newton's gravitational theory ever to have appeared in Italy, replete with quotations from the *Principia* commented on in a learned fashion. He devoted considerable space to the theories of the *Opticks* as well, in the framework of a presentation that nevertheless seemed to suggest a further level of reading of the entire manual. After the broad introduction in which all modern physics were brought back into the field of scholastics, in the later chapters he limited his extremely complete exposition to the most up-to-date scientific theories, comparing them to earlier ones. For example, in the section concerning optics, one finds both the *Spiegazioni dei Cartesiani* [Explanations of the Cartesians] and the *Spiegazioni dei Newtoniani* [Explanations of the Newtonians]. The *Esposizione delle dottrine del sig. Newton circa i colori* [The exposition of the doctrines of Mr. Newton about colors] is followed by the *Obiezioni del sig. Rizzetti* [The objections of Mr. Rizzetti], as if he subtly desired to neutralize every scientific truth, hence bankrupting them and making them illusory. Similarly he compared Copernican, Tychian, and Ptolemaic cosmological hypotheses.[43] From reading the manual, one gets the impression that beginning in the 1730s there was wide-ranging knowledge of Newtonian theories, no longer reserved for the few intellectuals in the vanguard but extended to a wider public. One also clearly gets an image of local scholars rejecting what we might define as Newtonian orthodoxy. This rebuff was made concrete by a complex use of the *Principia* directed at reviving gnosiological traditions (such as the Aristotelian) long on the defensive, or at updating the purely mechanistic and naturalistic conception of reality still dominating large areas of culture in the Veneto.

2. GALILEAN REASON IN CONTI AND MURATORI

The reasons why intellectuals of the Veneto gave Newton's works a different reading than that of enlightened Catholics go beyond specific matters of science. Their motives were steeped in the entire apologetic interpretation of celestial mechanics as it is expounded in the *Principia*; they had to do with the relationships between God and nature and science and theology, and the solutions that Galiani's fraternity had outlined following the seamless plan proposed by the Anglican Latitudinarians. In light of these considerations, the dispute between Antonio Conti and Francesco Maria Nigrisoli, a doctor from Ferrara, is a very great help to us in focusing on the distinctive nature of the Venetian intellectuals' reservations.

In 1710 the *Giornale de' Letterati* announced the preparation of Nigrisoli's "noble and laborious" work on "the generation of living things."[1] The book appeared in Ferrara under the title *Considerazioni intorno alla generazione de' viventi e particolarmente de' mostri* [Considerations about the generation of living things and particularly monsters] (1712). It presented Cudworth's theory of plastic forces (disseminated throughout Europe by Jean Le Clerc's *Bibliothèque choisie*), and it vigorously attacked any mechanistic interpretation of natural reality. Nigrisoli was the first Italian scholar explicitly to use the particular conception of continuous and necessary divine intervention in order to guarantee the existence and life of the cosmos, an idea worked out by the Cambridge Neoplatonists and appropriated by Latitudinarians of the Boyle Lectures.[2] It was a blatant attack against the *Giornale de' Letterati*'s mechanistic epistemological model and those who identified with it.

The response came quickly. Later in 1712, in violation of the periodical's tradition calling for the most neutral review possible of any book recently published, with the sole aim of introducing the content of Nigrisoli's text, Antonio Conti wrote a lively, annotated treatise. His *Lettera sopra le Considerazioni* [Letter about the *Considerations*], addressed to Monsignor Filippo della Torre, bishop of Adria, was a kind of manifesto for what we might term a secular, antitheological conception of modern science, shared by wide sectors of culture in the Veneto. Conti had yet to begin his fruitful travels abroad (during which he would come in direct contact with Malebranche, Newton, and Fontenelle). However, he started reproposing a theme dear to the Venetian periodical's writers, that of a great philosophical tradition that was entirely Italian, founded on Galilean sensate experiments and a rejection of all finalism. The review rapidly assumed a violently confrontational, sarcastic tone, eventually becoming ferocious and nearly villainous when dealing with Nigrisoli. Conti accepted next to nothing from Nigrisoli's book, "a book at once botanical, anatomical, physical, metaphysical, and cabalistic, and adorned with Sacred Scripture and the most holy fathers, and, if please God, with who knows what theology—certainly not His."[3] Nigrisoli's defense of the moderns was for Conti not only inadequate but profoundly erroneous in its basic outline. Citing Galileo from Ciccarelli's Neapolitan edition of the Dialogo, he maintained that in "matters of philosophy one argues with reasons and experiments, and not with authorities."[4] Inspired by Boyle and Fontenelle, Conti energetically corroborated the plan for a completely lay science, defended the great merits of the moderns, and vindicated human intellectual autonomy. The "final causes" that Nigrisoli liked so much were censured without any concessions: "The immediate goal of the Holy Spirit has not been to reveal the secrets of nature in order to make philosophers, but [to reveal] the mysteries of grace and glory in order to make Christians."[5] Taking up the teachings of the Cartesian tradition, Conti delivered a rebuke to Nigrisoli, affirming that "the Arte del pensare [Art of thought] has already demonstrated that the truth of axioms does not depend on the details of induction, but on clarity and distinction of ideas."[6] The merciless analysis, particularly of biological themes, and the meticulous argument on the nature of worms in the human body reveal the influence of Antonio Vallisnieri. According to Conti, Nigrisoli was above all a great bungler: "He wished to mix together seeds and eggs and structures and means and costumes and transformations and developments, so that it seems we see the animals in that ark he has described in his annotations, almost with his own kind of theology."[7] Conti keenly comprehended the close connection between Hermetists and theorizers of natural theology in some sectors of modern science, vindication at their expense of the "true genius of Italian philosophy." Attacking plastic natures and the concept of seminal light, Conti wrote: "With no regard either for our curiosity or for the title of his work, [Nigrisoli] enters into long, wandering, and cabalistic digressions, and intellects and the soul of the world appear suddenly and frighten just like figures from magic lamps."[8] Conti's writing was almost the periodical's official response to those who wished for a Le Clercian and apologetic interpretation of modern science. The key point behind Conti's work was that he had perceptively identified the importance that the Principia's celestial mechanics was assuming as a strong nucleus of the English natural theology propagated in Europe by Le Clerc. Conti was quite familiar with Newton's works, for he cited them directly in notes, and he had attentively followed Le Clerc's cultural activities through the *Bibliothèques*. In consequence, his harsh and public attack on Newtonian science acquires greater importance.

Galileo, Malpighi, Borrelli, and Bellini have given a start to this judicious philosophy, which (either for inconsistency of genius or for lust of novelty) it appears that many English heartily oppose, bringing to life again qualities, attractions, and plastic forces adorned with geometrical figures, algebraic characters, and experiences and physical syllogisms. But let these great geniuses and Aristotelians be quiet: their theorems about geometry and algebra prove nothing, nor do experiments prove anything when they are completed not in an absolute vacuum, but in a non-vacuum, in which the intermediate and invisible bodies can produce the phenomena that they attribute to the attractions; [if it is not so], it is up to them to demonstrate it.[9]

The debate over plastic forces also continued at length in the pages of the periodical and drew in other scholars.[10] Later in 1716 the *Risposta del signor abate Antonio Conti nobile veneziano alla difesa del libro delle Considerazioni intorno alla generazione de' viventi indirizzata al signor marchese Scipione Maffei* [Response of Abbot Antonio Conti, noble Venetian, in defense of the book *Considerations* about the generation of living things addressed to Marquis Scipione Maffei] appeared, at Vallisnieri's behest. This time, however, the tone was different from the review in the *Giornale*. The steadfast defense of preformism and the mechanistic hypothesis was in fact more studied and problematic. Frequently exchanging opinions with Malebranche and Newton had somewhat mitigated Conti's long-standing security and had made his anxiety for knowledge more mature and conscious of the difficulty of definitive explanations. Commenting on the *Risposta* to Vallisnieri, he wrote that in this response he weighed "the opinions according to their degree of probability and decided nothing."[11] Nevertheless, the *Risposta* contains a rejection of natural theology and any providential interpretation of modern science. This rejection became even more cognizant of and tied to precise ideological assumptions, and it led, in the context of the *Risposta* itself, to an explicit reference to Ludovico Antonio Muratori, for he had shared in the attack against Nigrisoli and was in his day involved in a bitter dispute over Le Clerc's conceptions of human reason's cognitive possibilities.[12] Conti willingly recognized that Nigrisoli was nothing but a pretext "not to have to give a particular name to such a general critique," a critique that was all the more necessary for enlightened Catholics' entire program aimed at imposing an edifying reading of modern science throughout Italy in the following years.

As close as he was to the *Giornale de' Letterati*'s editorial group, Muratori, too, experienced firsthand the complex vicissitudes that the interpretation of Newton's *Principia* endured among scholars from the Veneto. His thought was less conditioned than that of Antonio Conti by a direct knowledge of the English scientist's works, for he was not competent to read and evaluate them fully. Nevertheless, to a remarkable degree his ideas echo the problems posed by the dissemination of the new Newtonian *Weltanschauung* in Italian culture,[13] and in those years both Conti and Muratori seemed to operate within a common cultural framework. By virtue of his greater scientific and philosophical knowledge, Conti had decisively curbed Nigrisoli's vitalist and apologetic hypothesis of plastic forces, viewing them as a prelude to an edifying interpretation of gravitational attraction. Muratori, on the other hand, concluded an analogous and subtle work, demystifying Newtonian natural theology along less scientific lines, more sensitive to the function of science in society and in contemporary culture in general. Along with many other Italian scholars lacking the necessary mathematical preparation, the great Muratori was acquainted with Newtonianism not in its original scientific essence—deprived of sociopolitical implications—but in the successive clarifications presented in the Boyle Lectures or by Jean Le Clerc. Muratori, and intellectuals from the Veneto in general, originally referred to Le Clerc's interpretation, which in Italy preceded those of Derham and Cheyne that were promoted by enlightened Catholics.

As we have already seen,[14] in the *Bibliothèques* Le Clerc had ably united the Boyle Lectures' natural theology with a more general and ambitious program of gnosiological refoundation centered on John Locke's works. Le Clerc closely linked the reasonableness of Christianity, theological empiricism, the critical-philological method in biblical exegesis, and the exaltation of religious tolerance (with its political implications) to Locke's critique of the concept of substance, Newton's universe-machine, and the *Optice*'s theories about light. The *Essay Concerning Human Understanding* and the *Principia mathematica*, with all their implications on theological, political, and moral levels, appeared in Le Clerc's periodicals as two sides of the same coin.[15] Conti himself wrote to Muratori from France in 1716, and he confirmed the dissemination of a similar interpretation in Europe, made evident by Voltaire's Newtonianism in the following years. "Sir Newton has an astounding grasp of the ancient history of the Egyptians and Greeks, [and] has corrected many things from Sir Marsham's chronology. And there is no doubt that everything that is most sound and original in Locke's essays on the human intellect comes from him."[16] We shall see later how Le Clerc's interpretation had produced its best fruits precisely in Italy, leaving traces in Celestino Galiani's moral, political, and economic thought, and in the thought of enlightened Catholics, who took inspiration from such theses. For now, we are content to emphasize how the current of thought from England (whose most prestigious proponents were Newton and Locke), popularized by Le Clerc, was already evaluated in its systematic complexity in Italy.

In 1714 the *De ingeniorum moderatione in religionis negotio* appeared in

Paris; here Muratori responded vigorously to Jean Le Clerc's charges against Saint Augustine regarding the issues of grace and predestination. Muratori embraced the occasion to advance a new and particularly stimulating chapter of his program for reforming Italian culture, straightforwardly confronting the knotty problem of the relationship between reason and religion. The result was one of the most interesting and explicit writings that he ever published. In the chapter devoted to the Socinians, who, following a stereotype popular in the early eighteenth century, were summarily identified with those who gave precedence to rationalist solutions to religious problems,[17] Muratori clarified his disagreement with Le Clerc's theological empiricism and the consequent research into Christianity's intrinsic rationality, accusing the Genevan of semi-Pelagianism. Religious truth, Muratori affirmed, ought to be sought primarily in faith and revelation, and not through the continual use of human reason. Therefore, far from having its basis in nature understood as a product of divine workings, theology depended entirely on revelation. Muratori insistently pointed to human reason as something relative, bound to individual conscience, and as such incapable of testifying to absolute truth. "True religion," he vehemently claimed, "must not depend on man's intellect. In fact not we but God made it; God revealed it. In physics one should be permitted to create some sort of system. The desire to do likewise in the field of religion is temerity, or rather folly."[18] The key element of Muratori's religious thought lay entirely in the neat separation between, on the one hand, religion and faith, and, on the other, theology and scientific speculation.[19] In the second volume of the *Riflessioni sopra il buon gusto nelle scienze e nelle arti* (1715), Muratori reexamined the theme and clarified the relationship that ought to be established between authority and reason. To believe in authority meant to trust others; to listen to reason was instead "to believe in our mind, our fantasy, and our own senses, if we know that they evidently lead us to the truth."[20] Reason must always be used in the analysis of political, scientific, and philosophical propositions, "because the reputation, the name, and the mere words of famous authors are not reasons; but on the contrary solid and true arguments are what force us to subscribe to their opinions." Within the confines of faith and religious matters, however, reason was totally excluded from and subordinate to authority. "Even if one deals with many things in which reason could claim the right, listening to authority is sufficient, and it is necessary to yield to authority without wishing to turn to the most intrinsic reasons."[21] Galilean ideology could not be vindicated with greater zeal. On the scientific methodological level, enlightened Catholics could boast of having understood the value of mathematical language and an experimentation that was not merely qualitative much better than intellectuals in the Veneto had. On the ideological level, the Galileism of the *Giornale de' Letterati* and Muratori could forcefully proclaim its absolute congruity with the Pisan scientist's original plan, aimed at a clear-cut separation between science and faith. Muratori always remained faithful to this separation, which subjected the very foundations of Newtonian natural theology to discussion.

On the religious level, by neutralizing the moderate deism of Locke and Le Clerc, Muratori's thought remained the prisoner of a logic that seemed to foreshadow positive developments for modern thought but that was in reality narrow and already outdated. A sincere Catholic obedient to Roman authority, Muratori always refused to use reason to cast doubt on the bases of traditional religion, thus denying himself the very possibility of going beyond marginal adjustments, showing an affable and paternalistic good sense that left intact old modes of thought and moral assumptions inadequate for modern society. The very concept of "good taste" elaborated by Muratori to stimulate and guide Italian scholars' research echoed his desire to neutralize the divisive effects of reason in religious themes. "Good taste" was presented as a sort of middle ground between the old and the new, between the need to present an up-to-date version of the importance of human reason and the need to guarantee the authority of Catholic faith and the moral supremacy of the Holy See. The clear-cut rejection of Newton's natural theology and Locke's reasonableness of Christianity connected to it does not mean, however, that Muratori was hostile to Sir Isaac Newton's science. Muratori's ability to supersede historical Pyrrhonism and Pierre-Daniel Huet's skepticism was the result of Locke's and Newton's influence. Muratori confined himself to using empiricism's epistemological dimension as a necessary complement to a correct interpretation of Cartesian methodical doubt, in direct contrast to the skepticism within some areas of European culture.[22] But he did not wish to go beyond this point.

Antonio Conti (on the scientific level) and Muratori (examining the correct relationship between reason and religion) had very clearly delineated the foundations of a national philosophy anchored in the Galilean empiricist tradition and opposed to the scientific providentialism of the English Newtonians' new natural theology. However, their common appeals to the most rigid Galilean orthodoxy and the precise separation between scientific problems and religious matters allowed for different developments and emphases. The exaltation of mechanism and the rejection of natural theology led Conti to an obstinate search for truth in a wholly human, entirely earthly science, in virtue of which the negation of providentialism was tinged with a materialist flavor. Muratori, on the other hand, separated science and faith and was thus able to avoid posing disquieting problems about the relationship between God and nature. He also reevaluated revelation and the Catholic tradition within the framework of an empirical science directed at resolving social problems, and he refrained from entering into a conflict with the foundations of faith. They were, in sum, two different ways of utilizing the precious Galilean heritage: the first fully coherent with the very preconceptions of modern science; the second more prudently inclined to remove from reason's jurisdiction religious matters pertaining to the legitimacy of the Catholic Church's moral authority. United by their acceptance of Galilean mechanism, these two tendencies (in particular Muratori's) found many followers among Italian scholars. The interpretive direction articulated by Antonio Conti, while less popular, was not entirely without a following among intellectuals in the Veneto. His views confirmed the preference for a naturalistic reading of reality already present in some segments of local culture. And it is necessary to turn our attention to these segments in order to identify further reasons for dissent from the natural theology touted by enlightened Catholics.

3. THE LIBERTINE AND NATURALIST HERITAGES: VALLISNIERI AND RICCATI

Even without entering into a detailed analysis of Libertine circles in the Veneto, for whose existence there is more than a hint of evidence,[1] it is necessary to outline the cultural vehicles and content through which these new representatives of currents of thought—quite active during the seventeenth century—expressed themselves.[2] In the first place, it should be made clear that attempting a typology of Libertinism in the Veneto (and Europe in general) would be a useless undertaking, if one accepts at all the hypothesis that a genuine eighteenth-century Libertinism indeed existed. Certainly it is not necessary to confuse the learned, classic Libertinism of Naudé, La Mothe, and Vanini with that of the early decades of the eighteenth century, which made the crisis of the European mind even more profound and tormented. The former was a phenomenon confined to a narrow group of esoteric elites, tied to an absolutist political vision and a self-conscious, religious Nicodemism. For the latter, which, according to some, saw John Toland as its leader, the cultural climate was already different, and at least in Catholic countries, eighteenth-century Libertinism was in direct confrontation not only with the Counter-Reformation hegemony but also with a much wider culture whose dynamic elements were modern science, experimentalism in the European academies, and the unbiased use of human reason in biblical exegesis.[3] Hence the framework within which Libertinism must be understood widens considerably, and its boundaries become blurred. Despite difficulties in arriving at a cut-and-dried definition of the concept, we are always left with the sensation that a Libertine attitude was regarded as heresy by the dominant culture, or at least seen as a determination to raise issues in a different and open-minded way, regardless of traditional interpretive schemes. In light of these considerations, the Counter-Reformation conditioning that continued to permeate Italy makes it even more difficult to sketch the eventual characteristics of Italian Libertinism fully.

In the Veneto the new Libertinism had abandoned Cremonini's heterodox Aristotelianism, which had constituted the philosophical ground in the age of Giovan Francesco Loredano and the Accademia Veneziana degli

Incogniti.[4] The early part of the eighteenth century was a particularly stimulating period, filled with open-minded readings, preferences for scientific materialism, and the enthusiastic application of critical, philological analysis to biblical exegesis. Bonaventura Lucchi wrote a polemical oration against Hobbes, Spinoza, and Toland at Padua in 1737 in which he affirmed that one should not sum up these men's ideas just because they were "well known in the area."[5] Important people in the Veneto were accused of Spinozism.[6] But above and beyond genuine forms of Libertinism and heterodoxy, which would eventually become isolated, lies the naturalist vision typical of the old seventeenth-century Libertine tradition, deeply rooted at the University of Padua and common in various forms to the majority of intellectuals in the Veneto. This way of thinking was inevitably on a collision course with Newtonian natural theology.

Antonio Vallisnieri and Jacopo Riccati (but especially the former) are two of the most prestigious proponents of this culture in the Veneto, which aimed to reinterpret what remained of the old Libertine naturalism in a single, new, mechanistic, and Galilean scientific dimension. Born in 1661 in a castle in the Garfagnana (then under the jurisdiction of the duchy of Modena), Vallisnieri considered himself—with good cause—a disciple of the great Galileo. He had studied at Modena and Reggio, and he had then been a pupil of the famous Galilean Marcello Malpighi at Bologna, where he graduated in 1685.[7] His successful activity as a researcher had begun with a series of observations on the generation of insects, which introduced him to Italian scholars through the *Galleria di Minerva* [Minerva's gallery], a periodical published irregularly in Venice. After this early work his fame as a capable scientist began to spread abroad as well. In the following years his publications, which were particularly delightful for their ironic and biting style, were accompanied by honoraria bestowed on him by all the European academies.

In 1710, by now a professor of theoretical medicine at Padua, Vallisnieri started writing for the *Giornale de' Letterati* (of which he was one of the founders and driving forces), and thus he initiated his active work as an intellectual militant in favor of modern, secular, Galilean science based on the hypothesis of mechanism. His most important book, which would provide an alternative to the world image that emerged from Newtonian natural theology, was the *Istoria della generazione dell'uomo e degli animali se sia da vermicelli spermatici o dalle uova* [History of the generation of man and animals, whether from worms, spermatozoa, or eggs]. Vallisnieri outlined a comprehensive framework of all the scientific hypotheses ever formulated about the generation of living things. While faithfully illustrating contrary opinions, between ovism and spermatism, the scientist for the first time inclined towards the hypothesis inspired by Augustine's preformist theory (later taken up by Malebranche) of the development of "little human machines" in infinite Chinese boxes.[8] This theory held, in contrast to Newton's view of God intervening directly in earthly life to reconstitute the active forces already dissipated, that at the beginning of time, God had once and for all impressed into matter both the motion and the form of the "little machines," one inside the other, leaving to matter the task of unfolding itself. For Vallisnieri, every point of matter contained "an infinity of organized bodies, each of which is more marvelous than the stars and the sun."[9] The infinite divisibility of matter allowed for the theoretical possibility of infinite Chinese boxes, whose temporal unfolding was entrusted to the mechanist hypothesis of the Galilean infinite impact. Malebranche said, "It is not impossible that an organic body may be formed while still in marble by using motion." Because of God's initial impact, which impressed matter and is amplified over time, the unfolding of natural reality is guaranteed. Vallisnieri asked himself, "In order that [the little machines] develop sequentially, is it not enough that the motion imprint itself in the infinite turns of the glands of the brain, and that there it acquire an infinity of impetuses that finally, as a result of multiplying, will terminate in a perceptible impetus?"[10]

But Vallisnieri's image of the universe, which reverberated widely through the Veneto and throughout Italy, would become blurred and imprecise if we were to forget his vision of a great chain of beings. His was far from a hypothesis with origins in abstract Platonic philosophical speculations, as has been claimed,[11] in the context of the development of such ideas among European intellectuals of the eighteenth century. In Vallisnieri's mind, the hypothesis was born from a Galilean tradition, from an experimental and scientific way of thinking, and from an entirely worldly analysis of natural reality, and it differed notably from the usual interpretive archetype then in circulation throughout Europe. In this articulation of natural continuity, first made privately by Antonio Conti in 1715 and then made publicly in 1721, there was no Platonic or Christian reference to the great chain as *ascensio mentis ad Deum per scalas creaturarum* [the ascent of the mind to God through the chain of beings]. The imperceptible passage from inorganic nature, such as rocks and stones, to "rocky plants [corals, madrepores . . .], the link of this chain between the stones and vegetables," to the "zoophytes, who are part animal and part plant," to the "hermaphrodites," until reaching, through insects, fish, quadrupeds, and the apes, to humans, is in fact singularly lacking in any reference to divine presence.[12] All this is the work of the "great mother nature" that marvelously unfolds its being, already programmed and organized from the beginning of time. One ought to note that it is at least a dubious beginning, if one recalls that, according to some, the infiniteness of the impact predicted the world's eternity as a logical consequence.

William Derham's *Fisico-teologia* [Physico-Theology] and George Cheyne's *Principi filosofici di teologia naturale* [Philosophical principles of natural theology] at every juncture correlated the marvels of nature with God's continual and necessary presence in the world. Vallisnieri, on the other hand, called on God in only one case, and there only to confirm his own theses and to guarantee that they had a veneer of orthodoxy. In his chain of beings, there is no place for hierarchy, a concept present in many of the eighteenth-century interpretations. On a higher level, humans also live in the entirely worldly nature of the "fierce and most lustful apes that in the Indies even marry women."[13] Origen's and Plotinus's interpretations of the chain envision that beyond humans, who live in a material and spiritual dimension, there is a further unfolding of incorporeal entities, reaching to the pure spirit, or God. Vallisnieri's chain, instead, stops with humans, and it contains no explicit reference to a divine, providential plan or to angelic beings. In a century in which many scientists carried out their research with a Bible in hand, Vallisnieri, from his earliest work, rejected the tutelage of Sacred Scripture. His famous hypothesis of "ordinary worms" in the human body, which he believed were present because of mechanical developments already present in Adam and Eve, did not fail to elicit the troubled comments of Roman theologians. They saw this thesis as a contradiction to Sacred Scripture, which referred to a marvelous world before the Fall, uncontaminated by any ugliness such as worms.

In 1711 Father Antonio Maria Borromeo wrote to Vallisnieri from Rome, disagreeing with him and arguing that, if he considered Adam to be "in a state of innocence, it seems to me unlikely that God had planted the first worm in his body."[14] Far from being intimidated by such questions, Vallisnieri squarely confronted the entire problem of animal nature before the Fall, stoutly casting doubt on the biblical thesis depicting the existence of an Eden where all was serene and peaceful. What emerged was a recurring theme in Vallisnieri's worldview, which made rather more explicit the naturalist dimension of his chain of beings and the position humans occupied in the world. If the sordid and repugnant worms created theological problems for those who refused to consider their existence before the Fall, how could one then resolve the thorny matter of animals' ferocity? Were they already ferocious in the period before the Original Sin, or had they become so after the fateful taste of the apple? For Vallisnieri, "the issue is not so easily established." As Galileo had taught, Sacred Scripture had no jurisdiction to decide such questions. Why were animals "armed" in such a way, the scientist maliciously asked, if there was only innocence in Eden? "We see all too well the difference between the beaks and the claws, the teeth and nails, and the internal organs of the animals that must be either predators or prey."[15] In reality God Himself wished all of this, placing his imprint on the Hobbesian world that emerged in all its dramatic ferocity and permanent confrontation in Paduan naturalist Vallisnieri's crude but fascinating pages. In response to Borromeo, Vallisnieri explained his thoughts completely:

Your Reverend Excellence sees that so many kinds of offensive and defensive arms were not placed by that divine maker in so many animals
just to go unused and grow rusted, if they would always live in harmony
and in tranquil peace, and they would never spill innocent blood. . . .
The instinct always present in living beings acts in such a way that the
wolf willingly feeds on the sheep, [and] the fox on hens. . . . God wished
to use this rather than royal grandeur; in other words, in this world one
should live off of the other, and the animals ought to kill each other
continually without ever losing a species, otherwise such a portentous
number of them might grow that the economic order of this world would
be ruined.[16]

Not even humans escaped this terrible logic of nature's economy: "Man,
the lord and tyrant of all, kills all and lives off of all, with a thousand tricks
and in a thousand ways."[17]

The open-minded detachment from all natural theology was yet more
explicit in another famous book by Vallisnieri, the *De' corpi marini che su
monti si trovano, della loro origine e dello stato del mondo avanti il diluvio, nel
diluvio, dopo il diluvio* [Of marine bodies found on mountains, of their origin
and their status in the world before, during and after the Flood]. The Galilean
spirit filtered through these witty, ironic pages, frankly desanctifying what
Vallisnieri defined as "romances" constructed out of the need to reconcile
the biblical Flood to modern science, whether Newtonian or Cartesian. The
underlying thesis that emerged between the lines was a complete denial of
the Flood's historical truth independent from the testimony of Genesis.[18]
Responding to the question about the cause of marine animals on mountains, with subtle irony Vallisnieri demolished "the most lauded opinion of
the universal Flood." None of the veiled hypotheses alluded to convinced
him. Thomas Burnet and John Woodward were the victims of his penetrating analysis: "I hear Your Most Illustrious Excellence has called me impossible to please, difficult and very hard to understand,"[19] he wrote to his
correspondent. The hypotheses in the *Telluris theoria sacra* [Sacred theories
of the earth] merely made him smile for their candid ingenuity and inad-
missible mixing of the sacred and the profane.

Vallisnieri hinted at two solutions to the problem. One answer, cautiously
advanced against eventual accusations of heterodoxy, posited a completely
miraculous Flood, inexplicable through natural laws. The other (which he
truly believed) was that the earth had undergone a natural evolution without traumas or floods, according to the unfolding of an intrinsic plan. This
was how "great mother nature" was presented to the reader; its mechanical
development and the "eternal mutations" lay outside any providential conditioning. The continents rose and sank imperceptibly, without causing
catastrophes, such that creation could be said to be still in progress: islands
rose and sank in the seas, while the mountains slowly rose and crested.[20] If
some wished to believe in the Flood, it was even acceptable, as long as

they bore in mind that it had barely influenced the structure of the world. "God wished to chastise men then, not to turn the entire world upside down; it is the illusion of a bizarre and ingenious invention to pretend that before the Flood the earth was entirely flat, more beautiful, more friendly, and richer than what we see now."[21] In these pages, laced with biting irony, Vallisnieri concluded that the world "has always been roughly the same as it is today." Miracles were, therefore, not able to alter "nature's always uniform laws."[22]

Vallisnieri's Libertine sympathies appeared clearer in the scientist's reflection on the matter of the soul's immortality. This kind of reflection is a common element throughout Vallisnieri's circle of friends. His great Roman friend Giovanni Maria Lancisi, Clement XI's pontifical doctor and a man for whom there is some evidence of Libertine sympathies, delved intensively into the subject of the soul's immortality, and he kept Vallisnieri informed.[23] Giacinto Gimma, tied to the Neapolitan world and a longtime friend of the scientist, was similarly occupied.[24] While showing a certain degree of sympathy for Tertullian's materialist hypothesis about the creation within Adam of all the souls of posterity, in his *Istoria della generazione dell'uomo* [A history of the generation of man], Vallisnieri wound up sharing Saint Augustine's more orthodox hypothesis of a single creation of each soul, which violated the coherence of his mechanist hypothesis about the chain of beings. In private, however, without the risk of Inquisitorial interference, he disowned this Nicodemian repeal of his world image with an explicit resumption of the Libertine theme of the soul's mortality. Writing to Antonio Conti in 1727, Vallisnieri did not hesitate to affirm with great clarity: "Here is a confession that not even my charitable Jesuit confessor has heard." And, returning to the theme of the soul's position in his naturalistic interpretation of the chain of beings, from the devil he drew (or better, was forced to draw) the consequent logic implicit in his world system:

My forte was in meditation and, when one day I began to meditate about our spiritual soul's immortality, that black devil which frightens us and always whispers the most eccentric things into our ears made me think about the souls' progression. This devil wished me to believe that all [souls] were of one kind, and that they merely differed in a more or less polished operation of better or more poorly well-worked organs. We see, the devil said, that God did not want to leave gaps in all things created, but He passed from one genus to another, and from one species to another imperceptibly and through degrees, with an ever admirable uniformity of forms. If it happened thus, farewell to Descartes's machines, farewell to those watches that deceive our eyes! All organic bodies that have senses, that are born, that grow, that develop, and that give birth to like creatures, have a soul, as we do, and it would not be such a dangerous and mortal sin in philosophy to believe that all plants have one. We see that from a plant we progress to the plant-animal, and to the most sluggish animal, such as oysters and the like, and from these sluggish and rather insentient life-forms we climb to the more sentient. And thus degree by degree we reach dogs, monkeys, and other animals that in their actions often display more judgment than we, and finally we reach humans, the animal that is tyrant over all, the most arrogant and often the craziest of all. Therefore if we consider this chain and the progression of souls, and we see that God did not wish to leave gaps between sentient things, it seems that a legitimate consequence is that all the souls are of the same nature; if this were not so, otherwise there would be a great somersault from the material soul of brutes to the immaterial one of man, which would be the same as the leap from a watch to a living thing.[25]

Count Jacopo Riccati's work belongs on a different level from Vallisnieri's explicitly naturalist-Libertine material.[26] Even though it is the fruit of the same environment and founded on mechanist and Galilean suppositions, Riccati's thought operates in a substantially apologetic framework and is hence foreign, as we have seen, both to Conti and to Vallisnieri. The importance of Riccati's apologetics, however, lies in its sharp difference from that of the enlightened Italian Catholics and the Latitudinarians of the Boyle Lectures. A great mathematician, Riccati rethought all modern Newtonian science and some key ideas of naturalism popular in the Veneto, such as the hypothesis of force-matter and the Cartesian thesis of the constancy of the quantity of motion in the world, in one great cosmological work, the *Saggio intorno il sistema dell'universo* [Essay about the system of the universe]. His book confirms the image of a culture in the Veneto particularly receptive to the *Principia* while at the same time driven to produce concrete alternatives to Newtonian natural theology. But before entering into an analysis of this work, it is worthwhile to sketch a profile of this interesting intellectual, unjustly forgotten.

Born in Venice in May 1676 to Count Martino and Giustina Colonna, both members of the noblest and richest families of Castelfranco Veneto, Jacopo Riccati studied in Brescia under the Jesuits and at the University of Padua, in accordance with aristocratic tradition in the Veneto. In 1695 he already had in his hands a copy of Newton's *Principia mathematica*, a work that would influence all of his activities as a scientist and an intellectual.[27] When he was barely twenty, he returned to Castelfranco Veneto, which he rarely left (and never to travel abroad); he married the heiress of the Count of Onigo, with whom he had eight children, nearly all of whom would eventually hold important posts as teachers in the best Italian universities. By virtue of his considerable talent, Riccati soon became the greatest Italian mathematician of the first half of the eighteenth century.[28] A member of various European academies, he had the honor of being offered the presidency of the newly founded Imperial Academy of Saint Petersburg, an honor he refused, just as he refused every university post in Italy and abroad. Hermann, Leibniz, and Bernoulli justifiably considered Riccati one of the greatest European experts on infinitesimal calculus.

But here we are concerned not as much with his qualities as a scientist revered and esteemed in every European circle as with his reputation as a solitary intellectual who influenced contemporary culture in the Veneto. Whether or not his vast scientific production still preserves any objective relevance for some issues, the historian finds his forays into the fields of biology, philosophy, history, theology, morals, and economics (not to mention his poetical compositions culminating in the tragedy *Il Baldassare*) of noteworthy interest.[29] His ties with Conti and Vallisnieri were particularly close. Together with Abbot Girolamo Lioni, Riccati directed the *Giornale de' Letterati* after the crisis of Vallisnieri's early editorial work. On the question of the origins of fountains, Riccati defended Vallisnieri from the contemporary attacks of Johann Bernoulli and the *Acta eruditorum*, for which Vallisnieri gave him carte blanche: "Let my hero do what pleases him most."[30] We can hazard one hypothesis about the relationship between Conti and Riccati, which was particularly intense and profitable for both. Beyond the openly materialist outcomes that Conti expected from their shared conception of force-matter as the foundation of reality, Riccati served as a kind of scientific advisor whom Conti especially appreciated and followed.[31]

Jacopo Riccati's importance to culture in the Veneto, and in particular for the field of architecture (to which he dedicated valuable treatises on the structure of arches), has been recently reconfirmed, and there has even been discussion of a "Riccatian school," emphasizing the following that the count's ideas gained among intellectuals of the Republic of San Marco.[32] At the time, Riccati was certainly the Italian scholar who best understood, on a purely technical and scientific level, Newton's works. All of his writings—from the important works on the analytical determination of central forces (which appeared in the *Giornale de' Letterati*) to the studies in defense of some corollaries worked out by Newton in the *Principia* and attacked by Bernoulli and other famous scholars—show a lucid awareness of the scientific value of Newton's work. At the same time, they also reveal the clear-cut distance he maintained from the ideological interpretations advanced in the Boyle Lectures.[33]

Riccati made it his stated objective to read the *Principia* differently from the view popularized by the enlightened Catholics, in a way that took into account the mechanism of force-matter and the uniform laws of nature. In the end, despite the author's continued declarations of orthodoxy, Riccati's entire work was an ambiguous compromise between a "revealed system" and a "natural system" that, by Christianizing the naturalism of the Veneto in some instances, shows the limits of a concrete and articulate alternative to Newtonian natural theology.

The *Saggio intorno il sistema dell'universo* [Essay about the system of the universe], written by Riccati shortly before his death at the end of the 1740s, was a synthesis of numerous brief treatises and of letters addressed to Rizzetti, Conti, Vallisnieri, Manfredi, Poleni, and others, beginning in 1710. Hence in many aspects it should be considered a work contemporary with the writings of Vallisnieri and Conti. Riccati lavished all of his immense culture on what was something of an intellectual testament, confronting every aspect of natural reality. His Galilean training was explicitly and openly declared:

> The laudable Galileo has admonished us all that we futilely attempt to fathom the ultimate essence of objects; . . . [he] has unfolded no banner as if it were the head of a faction, and he never dreamed of organizing a general system. Would that God wanted the Italians to have adopted his principles and his cautious ways of discourse. But around here no one values anything but those fashions that are brought from foreign countries.[34]

Riccati based his cosmological system on three fundamental hypotheses, in a large part alien to Newtonian celestial mechanics. The first of these hypotheses referred to an energetic conception of matter; the second was that of the universe "tempering," or more simply, its finiteness; the third maintained the validity of the mechanist conception, in the form of a chain of beings and the constancy of the quantity of motion within the universe. The thesis of the world's tempering occupied an essential place in these mechanist-Galilean apologetics. Riccati developed this part of his system with particular care, because he saw it as the way to clarify a vital element of atheist cosmologies. Beginning with complex philosophical-mathematical arguments about the nature of mathematical infinity and its potential, Riccati used geometrical demonstrations *ab absurdo* to illustrate the conviction that "it is quite impossible for inert matter to raise itself to the highest degree of the infinite, or to lower itself to the lowest of the infinitesimal."[35] Hence the universe was "tempered"—it had natural boundaries. This allowed Riccati to confront the thorny matter of the relationship between God and nature and to ground it in the debate over the infiniteness of space. In his opinion, to presume that space is infinite was to open the gate to those who as a logical consequence envisioned a God congruent with it and concluded that space must therefore be uncreated. Pliny the Elder had begun to spread such a conviction in antiquity, and then the Ionic school appropriated the belief, and eventually the idea had been "renewed by Giordano Bruno in his treatise on the infinite and on the immense, [which] nowadays is making great strides throughout Europe." In Riccati's opinion, Newtonian cosmology proved to be ambiguous on this point: "Without prejudice against his sublime discoveries, it seems to me Sir Newton could avoid the daring expression that space is God's sensorium."[36]

But Riccati's true reference remained Spinozan pantheism. Demonstrating a thorough knowledge of the *Ethica* [Ethics], he sought to disprove the *Deus sive natura* [God as nature] of the great Dutch philosopher. These pages reveal Riccati's complex attitude towards the great Spinozan works. Despite the usual controversial attitude (verging on insult) against the impious Jew Spinoza, and beyond ritual rebuttals, Riccati was in fact unable to extricate himself completely from the allure of a most subtle work that was to be either rejected or accepted as a whole, since it was practically impossible to isolate any of its parts or to destroy them on a logical level. Indeed, at the end of his analysis, all that remained was for the scientist resolutely to propose the problem: "I wish I were told with sincerity whether it is more convenient to righteous reason to rest the divinity on conscience or on extension. A stupid God, who exists and does not know He exists, is less than a man gifted with that prerogative."[37] Riccati was quite familiar with the subsequent developments of Spinozan thought in Europe and the disquieting connection John Toland made between Spinozism and Newton's *Principia* in his *Letters to Serena*. In fact, Riccati reserved his parting shots for these theses: "I remember the epitaph of the famous Toland, mired with this tar [Spinozism], who left his body to mother earth; the spirit to rise again forever to the eternal father, but not under Toland's form."[38]

The most interesting hypothesis of Riccati's rich and meaningful system was that of force-matter, which demonstrated the enduring naturalism of his thought, totally foreign to the interpretation of enlightened Catholics and outside any apologetic framework. In chapter 2 of the *Saggio*, entitled "Se per formare un sistema corporeo alla materia debbe accoppiarsi la forza" [Whether, in order to form a corporeal system, matter must be joined by force], Riccati clarified that God in his wisdom, power, and freedom had created at the beginning of time "a quantity of force to match to matter."[39] Hence all life in the universe is worked out through force-matter, and the unfolding of the chain of beings, with its vitality in all levels, acquires meaning only by imagining the presence of this vivifying force in the cosmos. This vivifying force is an energy that is continually transformed without ever diminishing. Jacopo Riccati did not at all like the Newtonian God, the watchmaker who continuously rewound the world, as Leibniz ironically labeled Him in his epistolary dialogue with Clarke.

> I always found most strange the statement in which it is professed that at the first origin of things, an infinite mind either did not know how or did not wish to provide beforehand for the periods of chaos that would come with the passage of time, and that this inexpert creator would perpetually remain with his hand on his work.[40]

The writings of Whiston, Derham, and all the natural theology of the Newtonians, founded on the hypothesis of a continual and necessary divine intervention in the world, lacked any scientific foundation. For Conti, force-matter acquired a Stratonian philosophical dimension and would fully reveal its materialist potential, which in Riccati's work had already appeared in ambiguous clothes, liable to heterodox readings. One could not otherwise explain the continuous assurances about Riccati's attachment to the values of Catholic tradition that his heirs zealously advanced at different points of his *Opera omnia*, rejecting a presumed accusation of deism that had been leveled against him during his lifetime.[41]

In the *Riflessioni fisiche intorno l'anima unita al corpo* [Physical reflections about the soul united to the body], whose conclusions were substantially repeated in the *Saggio intorno il sistema dell'universo*, Riccati resolved the problem of the relationship between soul and body in relation to the force-matter, confirming that such a hypothesis was central to his thought. The body-soul connection in humans was an incontrovertible fact for him. Besides, if God had not wanted such interaction between spirit and matter, He would have created two different worlds, "one material, and the other spiritual," without any contact between them.[42] The real problem lay in the soul's nature and in the mechanicism of its relationship with bodies. The soul was certainly spiritual, but matter continually revealed hidden qualities, thus inducing the scientist to suspend judgment on future thrilling discoveries that could even attribute thought to matter.[43] As for the modalities of the soul-body relationship, after having examined and rejected Malebranche's theory of occasionalism and Leibniz's theory of preestablished harmony because they placed too many conditions on God's absolute liberty, Riccati returned to the unique parallelism between the soul and the force that vivifies matter, in the final analysis assimilating the soul into a true and genuine level of the force-matter present in the universe. He wrote:

> I ask license to allow myself a daring and appropriate expression: if the reciprocal give-and-take between the soul and the body is not maintained from what is more spiritual in matter (that is, force), and from what is less spiritual in the soul (that is, virtue), which possesses some analogy with force. I do not know what to say, and I leave the matter undecided.[44]

4. THE MATERIALIST READING OF THE *PRINCIPIA*

Count Riccati's apologetic compromise between the Veneto's deeply rooted tradition of Galilean mechanicism open to naturalistic applications and the conditioning of Catholic culture is noticeably ambiguous. If only in the initial common apologetic intentions, Riccati's attempt recalls the Christianizing reading of Spinozism predicted in those same years by Gaspard Cuenz in his *Essai d'un système nouveau concernant la nature des êtres* [Essay on a new system concerning the nature of beings] (1742), which appeared in Neuchâtel and yet professed a frank materialism.[1] Compared to analogous systems that appeared during this same period, Riccati's system retains a more purely scientific interest. The *Saggio*'s critical adherence to Newtonianism, which it accepted only in its scientific results and which it reinterpreted in a different cosmological framework from the one advanced by the Boyle lecturers, makes this work confused and contradictory but illuminating regarding the *Principia*'s intrinsic capability of lending itself to various levels of reading, independent from the discoveries it contained.

In reality, as with every scientific theory, Newtonian celestial mechanics in itself was neutral, prone to ideological interpretations varying according to the outcome of the conflicts between partisans of different readings.[2] Toland's attempt to bring to the fore any ambiguity in Isaac Newton's thought in order to use the *Principia* as an explicit confirmation of materialism, if perhaps the most alarming example of ideological interpretation, was certainly not the only one, and at least in Italy it was not the most stimulating example to refer to for analogous works. A materialist reading of the *Principia* could leave out Toland's authoritative landmark and find nourishment either from the internal workings of Newtonian celestial mechanics itself or from the vital Libertine and mechanistic tradition that, through hidden paths, permeated both the most open scientific environments and the intellectual circles most hostile to Christianity's centuries-old tutelage. Although it had illustrious precursors in Epicurus, Bruno, and Hobbes, Toland's vitalistic thesis of "motion essential to matter" indeed found other reference points in significant segments of contemporary European scientific culture, as opposed to the hypothesis of matter's complete passivity that was theorized first by Descartes and then by the Newtonians. The problem of the affinity between Toland's theory of matter's activity and Leibniz's energetic conception has been discussed at length. But these theories were part of comprehensive philosophical frameworks that were profoundly different, if not diametrically opposed. Toland's was Lockean, empiricist, fascinated by Bruno's pantheism, and directed not so much at a correct scientific and philosophical definition of the hypotheses on matter as at their immediate and unbiased ideological use, both political and, above all, anti-Christian. Leibniz's, on the other hand, was linked to a metaphysical and apologetic vision in which dynamic matter represented no more than a small part of a much vaster philosophical plan.[3]

Historically, the notable European dissemination of an activist conception of matter was connected to the crisis of Cartesian mechanicism, which was increasingly less capable of explaining the phenomena of biological life. The materialism of Diderot and the Holbachian coterie was remarkably influenced by the latter-eighteenth-century success of what Cassirer referred to as Leibniz's "organicism."[4] In the Veneto the dispute over live forces, in which Riccati, Rizzetti, Poleni, Vallisnieri, Crivelli, and Conti participated, sufficiently demonstrates how very widespread was the hypothesis of a somehow active matter, beyond Toland's reexhumation, which was inspired by an explicitly Brunian materialism. For Riccati, who shared the opinion held by Leibniz and others, force-matter in no way opposed the decisive impulse of the divine creator. For Vallisnieri, and especially for Conti, once force-matter was interpreted correctly, correlated with a principle of order and various levels of reality, it could resolve within itself every aspect of life in the universe without needing to resort to the divine hypothesis.

The famous *Collection of Papers, Which Passed between the Late Learned Mr. Leibniz and Dr. Clarke in the Years 1715 and 1716, Relating to the Prin-*

ciples of Natural Philosophy and Religion certainly made clear to all what problems and dangers were connected to the *Principia's* interpretation. The *Collection of Papers*—the work of Pierre Des Maizeaux with the collaboration of Antonio Conti,[5]—appeared in London in 1717 and had a remarkable dissemination. In the French translation prepared by Des Maizeaux, which appeared in Amsterdam in 1720, the book caused a stir everywhere, and the work was known and discussed throughout Italy. Enlightened Catholics were among the first to comment on it among themselves. Only a few months after its appearance in Amsterdam, Giuseppe Rathegel wrote to Galiani from Florence, announcing that it had been brought to Italy by Dereham, who was returning from England.[6] Another letter from Rathegel confirms the outcry and interest that the *Recueil* (the French edition) elicited in Rome: "I would like to hear of the discussions that you have with your friends over Samuel Clarke's book, especially since the material is worthy and it contains things that merit reflection." In his letter, Rathegel substantiated the increasingly favorable position that Galiani assumed among enlightened Catholics in the treatment of these problems, and he referred explicitly to one of Galiani's works on the subject, almost certainly the unedited *Scienza morale* [Moral science], which we will analyze more fully later:

> Your Most Reverend Father will produce a work worthy of your genius if you undertake to bring light to the obscure way with which the English and the Dutch usually explain the world system using Newtonian principles. And I wish you the perseverance, for you are not lacking the skill. And if by chance you were hindered by your most serious occupations from conducting to the end this enterprise, I beg that you communicate to me whatever little you have finished.[7]

The *Recueil's* contents have been well studied, particularly in light of the behind-the-scenes activity that led to its publication, and it is notably significant for Italian culture, for it was able to draw on meticulous and broad information about the complex problems central to the discussion between Clarke and Leibniz. Leibniz opened the correspondence with a fiercely argumentative letter regarding the materialist seeds implicit in the *Principia* and made explicit by Toland's work.[8] The German philosopher's critique comprised four considerations, which are worth repeating here:

1. It seems that natural religion also is losing much strength in England. Many make souls corporeal; others make God Himself corporeal.
2. Mr. Locke and his followers doubt that souls are material and naturally perishable.
3. Mr. Newton says that space is the organ by which God feels things. But, if He needs some means to perceive them, they therefore do not depend entirely on Him and they are not His production.
4. Mr. Newton and his followers still have a rather funny opinion of God's work. According to them, from time to time God needs to rewind His watch, otherwise it stops working.[9]

This is not the time to examine in detail Clarke's responses and Leibniz's replies, which only confirm how far apart their positions were. Rather, it is necessary to underline the clarity with which both Leibniz and Samuel Clarke expounded their viewpoints, initiating what was without a doubt the most important philosophical-scientific debate of the early eighteenth century.[10] The prestige of the protagonists and the *Recueil*'s wide dissemination in Italy caused the Inquisition to add the book to its *Index*,[11] displaying an unusual severity in the treatment it accorded this work as compared to others substantially more dangerous, such as the *Letters to Serena*.

Roman ecclesiastical authorities, on the other hand, seemed increasingly to aim their arrows not so much at especially impious works as at those for which they were able to identify some consistent circulation in Italy, such as was the case for the *Adeisidaemon* [Without superstition] (dangerously written in Latin), condemned on 4 December 1726. Nevertheless, leaving aside the more or less efficient interventions of the congregations of the *Index*, Toland's works could be known in Italy.[12] In 1729 the *Acta eruditorum* had published a bibliographical essay on the Irish author, on the occasion of the publication of the important collection of some of his writings, edited by Des Maizeaux, entitled *A Collection of Several Pieces of Mr. J. Toland with Some Memoirs of His Life and Writings* (London, 1726). The lengthy essay, free from censorship, clearly illustrated the gist of Toland's greatest works, from the *Letters to Nazarenus* to *Pantheisticon*, insisting in particular on Toland's determinist conception and on his corrosive Old Testament exegesis.[13] Toland's interpretation of the *Principia*, owing to its character, more ideologically and politically than scientifically based, nevertheless did not constitute a model frequently discussed in Italy, aside from individual examples that we will have cause to examine in the next chapter.

It is not by chance that, among Italian intellectuals, only the Piedmontese exile Alberto Radicati di Passerano, who suffered the same political tensions as the Free-Thinkers, seemed fully to embrace Toland's thesis of an organically self-sufficient nature. Both, in fact, courageously disputed the conception of a hierarchical universe ruled by mathematical laws that deferred to God's necessarily active duty, a constant presence that in the end guaranteed that the ecclesiastical institution was the sole earthly representative of such a cosmic order. Radicati and Toland were interested not so much in producing a true scientific analysis as in definitively demystifying a certain image of the universe worked out by modern science, which had provided positive religions (and in particular Christianity) with further, extremely refined legitimization of an effective power structure that in reality had been established through complex historical events built on usurpations and lies.[14]

The celebrated Italian intellectual Pietro Giannone exemplified a more complex and problematic approach to Newtonian science.[15] While he knew Toland's thought in depth, he did not seem at all influenced by the Irish philosopher's reading of the *Principia*. In fact, his Newtonianism, as condensed in the brief treatise *L'ape ingegnosa* [The ingenious bee], seems entirely original and autonomous. Giannone had had an essentially Cartesian and Gassendist philosophical training, especially attuned to the influence of the Investiganti's naturalism and theories of the soul's corporeality. The authors seminal to his thought—Spinoza, Hobbes, Toland, Descartes, Gassendi, Aulisio, and others—had led this historian to a cosmological synthesis particularly explicit in the *Regno terreno* [The earthly realm] of the *Triregno* [The papal crown]. Giannone had already solidly established a framework of scientific thought that combined Cartesian dualism (recomposed in a vitalistic monism of clearly Renaissance origin), the qualitative experimentalism of the Galilean naturalists, and the profoundly ideological and political meaning he attributed to a wholly earthly conception of natural reality, lacking providential intervention. In this framework, Newtonian celestial mechanics, along with the epistemological and ideological revolution that it brought, seemed to be a body entirely extraneous and difficult to assimilate, except at the cost of concessions to ambiguity. Giannone had learned of the errors in Descartes's system of vortices from his friend Bernardo Andrea Lama in Vienna in the 1730s. Lama had acquainted him with a series of scientific considerations, drawn mostly from the *Epistola de gravitate et cartesianis vorticibus* [Letter on gravity and Cartesian vortices] by his teacher Celestino Galiani, which mathematically documented Descartes's serious errors.[16] In the *Triregno*, Giannone had already completely superseded Cartesian cosmological theories, but even more explicit was his acceptance of Newtonianism in the *Ape ingegnosa*. It is nonetheless a Newtonianism sui generis, which merits brief consideration.

Analyzing this work in minute detail, Giuseppe Ricuperati has remarked that it contained "the human and intellectual experience of a deluded old man who, in the new conditions in which he finds himself imprisoned, desperately defends the sense of what he experienced and organized in his own works."[17] Ricuperati first showed that the *Ape ingegnosa* contains a remarkable transposition of classic themes of Newton's apologetics exemplified in the *Scholium generale*, including the universe-machine, the moderately deistic natural theology of Pope and Clarke, and an exaltation of experimentalism and empiricism over Cartesian metaphysics. He then posed the wholly legitimate question of whether Giannone's interpretation of the *Principia* was an apologetic reading tied to schemes widely disseminated in Europe by the Boyle Lectures, or whether it was instead a materialist vision with points in common with Toland's archetype or with the view of force-matter found in the Veneto. His answer is that Giannone did not choose, that, instead, he placed one interpretation alongside the other, since he was driven above all to reinforce the direct rapport existing between nature and morality, without the necessary mediation of positive religions.[18] In reality, Giannone did not choose because he did not understand. His was a

Newtonianism that we might say was conceived through images. The need to guarantee a coherence to his earthly conception of the universe at all costs, keeping in mind that Newtonian science was by now (1743) prevailing, pushed him to overcome, with aplomb, the evident contradictions in his work, composed by restructuring different and heterogeneous elements. Giannone lacked a scientifically correct comprehension of the epistemological foundations of the *Principia*, but we should not fault him, for he had other merits. Besides, such comprehension implied intellectual assumptions foreign to his cultural frame of reference, such as the rejection of antimathematical naturalism and the acceptance of a phenomenalism tied to the Lockean critique of the concept of substance.

Moreover, Giannone's was not an isolated case, and it offers a useful example for understanding the precise limits within which materialist interpretations of the great Newtonian work were placed. Even recently, many scholars have asked why a materialist culture that took its cue from French and English examples failed to spread in Italy. Although there are many possible reasons, one answer might be found in the total absence of any valid scientific content in the few materialist views that emerged in the course of Italian cultural history of the early eighteenth century. The malice towards modern science already borne by some Libertines and materialists in the seventeenth century is well known. An entirely naturalist vision of reality was soon on a collision course with the emergence of modern science, mathematicized and opposed to any esoteric animism.[19] The success both in France and in England (unlike in Italy) of some materialist gnosiologies, more often than not naive and scientifically inadequate, was, nevertheless, guaranteed by the essentially political connotations that they assumed. In a number of European countries, in fact, materialism was historically almost always associated with a political project functioning as an alternative to the existing regime, whether it was Louis XIV's absolutism or Whig power in Augustan England, where political debate could be attached to a more lively social and economic dynamic. All of this was missing in Italy, which was still lazily immobile and trapped in the framework of a Catholic hegemony closed to discussion. Hence it was not possible to launch a materialist hypothesis; painfully insufficient on a scientific level, a materialist hypothesis could be nourished only in a self-conscious political environment.

Paradoxically, in a static culture like that of Italy, the only serious alternative to the enlightened Catholics' proposal for scientific renewal (under the aegis of Newtonian natural theology and under the suffocating solidarity between science and religion) was expressed by Ludovico Antonio Muratori's literary republic and the secular science of the Veneto, which, mindful of Galilean teachings, always attempted to discourage any undue mixing of theology and free scientific research. Elsewhere in Europe, lacerating controversies over what interpretation to give the new Newtonian *Weltanschauung* marked a great part of cultural history in those years. In

Italy, on the contrary, these efforts were muffled within a Catholic conformism careful to avoid any disturbance and to bring any new idea back into the ambit of the flexible but static structure of reassuring doctrinal teachings and the immobile equilibria they guaranteed. On the other hand, as Giannone had bitterly written in reference to the excessive power of the *Regno papale* [The Papal kingdom], the Catholic Church had over the centuries created an empire capable of dominating not only bodies, but also (and above all) souls and spirits.[20] It was this, rather than any kind of censure and repression, that prevented contemporary Italian intellectuals from imposing a radical reading on the *Principia*.

FIVE

Celestino Galiani:
Religious Uneasiness and
Crises of the European Mind

1. His Early Training

Newtonianism's affirmation and dissemination was a phenomenon that had a multifaceted, ambiguous, and profound influence even in Italy. Celestino Galiani, together with Antonio Conti,[1] was certainly a key figure in this process. There is still no real biography of Galiani that brings into focus his ideas and, above all, his daring cultural projects. And yet one still gathers the impression that he had a substantial, even if not always evident, importance within the Italian intellectual world of the early eighteenth century. Fausto Nicolini's valuable work *Un grande educatore italiano: Celestino Galiani* [A great Italian educator] offers information that invites a reconstruction of his thought. Nevertheless, the fragmentary nature of Galiani's unedited writings and the complete absence of his printed publications, in addition to the myriad interests of this mathematician, philosopher, or, rather, "encyclopedist," as Benedetto Croce called him,[2] have always discouraged any attempt to outline the unifying and comprehensive significance of his presence in Italian civic life. I therefore undertake this enterprise in the hope of shedding light on an important period of early-eighteenth-century history.

In the preceding chapters I have already brought to the fore how Celestino Galiani was closely tied to the reform activities of enlightened Catholics. Their love for science, the intensive efforts to see Galileo rehabilitated, the dissemination of Newtonian natural theology, the publication of Gassendi's works, and the reaffirmed need to participate in the dialogue with modern thought are all essential elements of a program that Galiani shared and carried out firsthand. It would, however, be a serious mistake to bring out his unique, militant intellectual work, extremely receptive to any new experience, only in the context of the enlightened Catholics' activities. Certainly the "Roman colony" at Sant'Eusebio, which later became the nucleus of the association that joined enlightened Catholics, had profound impact during the difficult moments of Galiani's life. For him, the "Roman colony" was above all a point of reference and a providential screen against the dangers connected to a life of study open to dialogue with all currents of European thought. If we were to express Galiani's position within the group in schematic terms, we would say that he and Antonio Niccolini were special representatives of a radical wing. A scion of one of the richest Tuscan patrician families, Niccolini was Galiani's closest political and cultural associate.

Possessed of a lively, irreverent spirit and gifted with vast erudition, Niccolini traveled at length throughout Europe and in particular in England, where he made many friends. His reputation as a liberal intellectual of deist and Libertine sympathies followed him throughout his life. There are reports— however unlikely—that after he returned from his first trip to England in 1721, he waited for nearly a year before he was permitted to set foot in Tuscany; the Grand Duke Cosimo III supposedly refused to allow him, "under suspicion that his subject was a Libertine innovator."[3] As if to confirm his restless nature, Niccolini became one of the principal members of the new Florentine Masonic lodge, only distancing himself from the group (at least officially) in 1738 after Clement XII's bull *In eminenti*.[4] In the letters of Niccolini and Galiani (which we will examine later) commenting on the great works of Voltaire and Montesquieu, as well as the writings of Tindal, Clarke, and Wollaston, we find they shared an interest in everything new emerging in European culture, especially regarding the theme of redefining Christianity in rationalist terms. Niccolini and Galiani were the two figures from within the group of enlightened Catholics who participated in the dialogue with the most heterodox currents in European thought.

Among enlightened Catholics, Galiani was certainly the most brilliant scholar and the most receptive to new developments. His in-depth philosophical and scientific studies played a significant role in outlining a reform program for Italian science that centered on the dissemination of Newtonianism. But above and beyond this complex cultural experiment, Galiani's importance lies particularly in his great ability on the political and cultural level. Galiani was among the few Italian intellectuals of the period who were keenly aware of the close relationship between political power and cultural reform. Unlike many other scholars, Galiani had long understood the importance of renewing from within traditions still linked to old Counter-Reformation schemes, for he had occupied positions of great prestige at the heart of church and state institutions, positions which allowed him to encourage and support cultural renewal. His fame as a political man and a capable mediator had begun to take shape in 1725 during his direct participation in the negotiations between the Holy Roman Empire and the Holy See over the thorny problem of the Sicilian monarchy's tribunals. His reputation was definitively established with the positive conclusion of the extremely laborious negotiations over the concordat between the Kingdom of Naples and the Holy See in 1741.[5] His brilliant ecclesiastical career began with his nomination as abbot in 1718, continued when he became procurator of the Celestines in 1722 and abbot-general of that congregation in 1728, and concluded with his consecration as bishop of Taranto in 1731. That same year Galiani was also appointed *cappellano maggiore* for the Kingdom of Naples, an office to which he had always aspired and that finally allowed him to coordinate single-handedly the threads of Neapolitan culture through the direction of the university and direct control over private schools. For Galiani it was a crucial period in his life. His cultural project and reform appeals finally came together in his energetic activities as a militant intellectual, eager to open the political breathing room necessary to attempt renewal.

In 1711 Galiani had made a decision that was especially difficult for a scholar such as he was: never to publish his own ideas. It was a very sad moment in his life, at the culmination of his first difficult clash with the Inquisition over an innocuous pamphlet that Giacomo Laderchi, "the fearsome bloodhound of heresies," accused of containing elements of Jansenism and serious errors in biblical exegesis.[6] Now that he had become *cappellano maggiore*, the position that he had adopted of fighting for reform in Italian culture from within the Church (thus avoiding any conflict with the Inquisition) began to yield results, and it allowed him to carry out his work of renewal without any special restrictions. When he wrote to his fellow Celestine Piergerolamo Bargellini in Florence to comment on his brush with the Inquisition, he said that his own ideas had to be revealed to a few very trustworthy friends, "taking care not to expose them to the masses," otherwise he would be forced to resign himself to the "censure of such vulgar people."[7] Galiani held to this principle for his entire life, avoiding the publication of his writings, exchanging thousands of letters in Italy and abroad, organizing academies, dedicating enormous time to the instruction of men destined for brilliant ecclesiastical careers and positions in the institutions of the various Italian states,[8] and soliciting philosophical and scientific debates, shaping the fates of Neapolitan culture extraordinarily forcefully through the office of *cappellano maggiore*. It is not true that Galiani did not write anything; he simply did not permit the uncontrolled dissemination of his writings in print, and he guaranteed his works considerable freedom of movement through anonymous manuscript editions judiciously shared with experts. In the end, his was a legitimate decision, no less fruitful in results than those of many other scholars who preferred public debate to underground political action conducted from within institutions.

Before he became a monk, Celestino Galiani's given name was Nicola Simone Agostino. He was born 8 October 1681 in San Giovanni Rotondo, a small village near Foggia. When he was seven his father died, and his mother, who later remarried, entrusted him to the care of a relative. At sixteen the young Galiani, lacking any economic support, entered into the congregation of the Celestines. He completed his earliest studies first in the monastery of Sansevero and then in that of Lecce, soon demonstrating his extraordinary intellectual gifts. In 1701 his superiors decided to send him to the monastery of Sant'Eusebio in Rome with the title of "student." There began his true scholarly training, which to a large extent reflected the presence of some of the great intellectuals in the city, men like Gianvincenzo Gravina, Biagio Garofalo, Giusto Fontanini, Francesco Bianchini, Giovanni Maria Lancisi, and others. Galiani's first decade in Rome was a period of intense study, including the traditional readings on Saint Thomas Aquinas and Saint Augustine, classical Greek and Latin texts, and the first rudiments of Hebrew, a language in which he eventually became well grounded. Among his educational interests, modern scientific theories occupied a prominent position. He rapidly passed from the simple elements of Euclidean geometry to the first complex notions of infinitesimal calculus. Galileo Galilei, Pierre Gassendi, Isaac Barrow, and Bernard Lamy were the first authors with whom he grappled.[9] But the turning point in his intellectual training came with his passionate study of René Descartes's writings. In his unpublished *Ristretto della vita di Celestino Galiani* [Abstract of Celestino Galiani's life], the mature monsignor described this event in the third person, particularly his reading of the *Diottrica*, which occurred in 1703:

He found especially pleasing that way of explaining light, and accustomed as he was to the Aristotelians' meaningless words and occult qualities, it seemed as if he had exited from a dark prison and had begun to enjoy the sun's light.... He felt the need to scour Descartes's other works. Therefore he read the *Principia philosophiae* and afterwards the *Meditationes*, which he understood quite well, with greatest pleasure. He wished to read the treatise *De homine*, but he needed some lessons in anatomy.[10]

For Galiani, as had already happened for many Italian intellectuals, Cartesianism played an essential role in the breakdown of an Aristotelian mentality. Through the clear and distinct ideas theorized in the *Discours de la méthode* [Discourse on method], Muratori, Giannone, Grimaldi, Doria, and many others sampled the fundamentals of modern thought. Faced with the oppressive Aristotelian hegemony, Galiani came under the disruptive fascination of Cartesian theories. But though the philosophical rigor and clarity of the *Discours* marked the first step in Galiani's maturation, only a few years later Cartesian apriorism, the *Principia philosophiae*'s fantastic vortices, and the French philosopher's optical theories and metaphysical system itself became the object of the young monk's criticism. The *Ristretto della vita di Celestino Galiani*, which presents the image of a Cartesian Galiani, is not sufficiently trustworthy on this point. The man who in the *Ristretto* recounts that he taught Descartes's ideas in Rome in 1714, as if to vindicate an unquestionable merit, is the same person who is completely silent on his Newtonian optical experiments, his study of the *Principia mathematica*, his crucial role within Cardinal Filippo Gualtieri's important academy,[11] and his preparation of a harsh reprimand of Cartesian cosmology contained in the *Epistola de gravitate et cartesianis vorticibus* [A letter on gravity and Cartesian vortices], not to mention his dogged work of proselytism in favor of Newtonianism in the Naples area. In his manuscript autobiography, Galiani provides a willfully distorted and reticent image of the many other moments of his life. There is no mention of his campaign in favor of Galileo, and nothing on his activity as a promoter of the publishing initiatives undertaken by the association of enlightened Catholics, including the reprinting of the works of Gassendi, Derham, and Cheyne. The reasons behind this reticence lie perhaps in the fact that the *Ristretto* is among the few works by Galiani originally destined for publication.[12]

Galiani certainly attained a prominent position quickly in the community of Roman scholars. His friendships with Bianchini, Cerati, Niccolini, Gravina, Garofalo, Giordani, and many others placed him at the center of the initiatives for cultural promotion apparently favored by Clement XI's pontificate. During his trip to Naples in 1708, Galiani had an opportunity to meet the greatest proponents of local science, including Valletta, Grimaldi, Vico, De Cristoforo, and Matteo Egizio.[13] From that point on, the naturalist tradition of the Investiganti, Cartesian readings, Spinozan suggestions, and jurisdictionalist appeals were the elements of Neapolitan culture that became the patrimony of Galiani's thought. It was in this period, and not (as is generally thought) with his nomination as *cappellano maggiore*, that Galiani's fruitful activities of renewal began in Naples.

In addition to his reports to Roman scholars regarding Newton's works and his correspondence with Giovanni Bottari, Giacomo Grazini, Guido Grandi, and Giacinto De Cristoforo, his lectures about philosophical and scientific issues delivered at Sant'Eusebio and during gatherings of the Accademia Gualtieri provide precious documentation of his intellectual training. The importance of these yellowed pages, collected in a little notebook entitled *Animadversiones physis* [Musings on physics], lies primarily in the sense of disorientation and uncertainty that emerges from these notes. At the same time, they show a rigid determination to sketch a new referential framework, in order to leave behind the great epistemological crisis that Italian thought (and European thought in general) underwent in those years. Once the Cartesian synthesis had overcome seventeenth-century naturalism and abstract Neoplatonic mathematics, the emergence of the new Newtonian science again provided room in the most receptive and informed circles of Italian culture for the still-living Galilean traditions, reopening an intense debate. This epistemological confrontation, closely tied to profound ideological preferences and conditioned by political and religious problems, reached its culmination precisely in the early decades of the eighteenth century.

Galiani was the driving force in the Roman environment. His ambitious but philosophically fragile "collection of arguments" opened with the stated objective of finally tracing the parameters within which modern science would have to operate. He first considered the gnosiological issue. Through what tools, he asked, can humans know reality? "The things that we know are only in our minds through concepts. . . . Someone born blind does not know what light is because he does not possess the concept, but once his eyes are opened and he sees it, even if he becomes blind again, he knows what light is."[14] Firmly rejecting Cartesian apriorism and innatism, Galiani decided entirely in favor of an empirical dimension to human knowledge. The evocative example of the statue, which through the progressive acquisition of senses and the understanding of empirical data arrives at the correct identification of objects that surround it, allowed him to illustrate the crucial role of the senses, without which humans "could never come to find anything certain."[15] However, the theory of ideas that followed from this revealed the theoretical fragility of his arguments. What endured were elements of a naturalist reading of Galileo (common to many Roman scholars) and a good dose of skepticism and Gassendi's anti-mathematicism; most important, his first reading of John Locke's *Essay Concerning Human Understanding* appeared.

Galiani had read the *Essay* in Pierre Coste's French tradition shortly before 1710. Responding to Antonio Conti in 1712, he made plain his acceptance of Locke's gnosiology, clearly preferring it to Malebranche's rationalism. Referring to the latter's theory of ideas, he wrote:

> One encounters great difficulty explaining how we understand concepts that are in us, but much greater is the difficulty we find when we imagine that we understand them in God. What are we to do in these situations? I would much rather suspend judgment and confess candidly that we know nothing and that our information is much more limited than we sometimes believe. For that reason it seems to me that Mr. Locke has done a great service for men who wish to make good use of their minds.[16]

In the first chapter, devoted to empiricist gnosiology, Galiani aimed to "become acquainted with the nature, origin, and use" of concepts. The first explanation regarded the empirical nature of pain. "Pain [is] something I cannot explain, that is produced by a pin in the arm."[17] He followed with a critical examination of Cartesian innatism, largely drawing his lines of argument from Pierre Gassendi's work, nevertheless always creating the suspicion that he did not know the parameters of the issue very clearly. A reading of his considerations on the theory of ideas in the second chapter, entitled "Della natura della sensazioni" [On the nature of sensations] and in the third chapter, "Della causa efficiente delle sensazioni" [On the efficient cause of sensations] gives a similar impression. The most important part of this brief collection of arguments, however, was the scientist's attitude towards defining the operational fields for mathematics and physics. Accepting Gassendi's classic distinction between the mathematical point and the physical point (which Isaac Newton had finally identified in the *Principia's* celestial mechanics), Galiani denied the real cognitive power of mathematics.[18] In a

critique of the fourth proposition of the second book of the *Principia*, he
contested the absolute and privileged role that Newton assigned to it.[19]
Such an attitude was later widely reassessed in the light of the debate waged
in Italy over the foundations of infinitesimal calculus and, above all, over
the lectures of Dutch scientists Musschenbroek and 'sGravesande on the
fundamentals of mathematical empiricism. In the *Animadversiones physis*,
Galiani wrote:

> One clearly sees that pure mathematics is quite certain in the manner
> now said, because such science only consists of the clear information of
> what is proper to quantity and its ways and parts, and that is to say to
> the concept of numbers and figures (such as the circle, triangle, etc.),
> without even checking whether such things exist, or can be or not, and
> that is why one usually says that such sciences lie outside of existence.[20]

In those years Galiani's thought was still rather far from grasping the subtle
Lockean distinction between truth of reason and truth of fact, and above
all the phenomenal approach of Newtonian science. The road was, however, the right one; there was nothing left to do but to follow it coherently
and wait for a more auspicious moment. His very definition of "physical
analysis" went in this direction: "It seems to me that one generally views
physics as the science of perceptible things, that is to say a science that
teaches all the causes of the effects and the phenomena that we perceive
through the senses."[21] The opposition between Gassendi's empirical reason
and Cartesian metaphysical reason is evident here. The limitations of a
science that must give precedence to sensory perceptions, without imposing
questions about the intrinsic nature of bodies impossible to solve, were continually recalled by Galiani, who sketched the confines within which the
scientist's research had to operate. "According to the things presumed to
exist in natural entities, only extension, form, and motion are found. Therefore
one could find no other difference between them except in the size of the
corpuscles out of which they were composed, in motion and form." Galilean
experimentalism was still an essential tool.

> After having diligently examined the effects we know (which are noth-
> ing other than perceptible appearances, or sensations), one infers the cause,
> which is merely the size, form, and motion of the component corpuscles
> in material things. If that is not possible, the only thing left is to at-
> tempt to formulate a hypothesis about the nature of the thing that one
> usually does know,

and then to verify it experimentally and ascertain whether "the hypothesis
could be likely."[22]

Some solid points from Galiani's collection of arguments merit illustration. First is his decisive aversion to any vitalist hypothesis of matter: "It
has elsewhere been demonstrated that the principal cause of motion cannot
be matter itself but something of another sort, which I believe is God."[23]

Second is the rationality of the laws, guaranteed by God, who permits humans to study nature scientifically. Third is the rejection of Cartesian mechanism found on the constancy of the quantity of motion in the universe: "I do not think it is good to infer from God's universality that the same quantity of motion is always found in matter."[24] These are features that in later developments would allow Galiani and Roman scholars who came together at Sant'Eusebio or in Cardinal Gualtieri's academy to easily accept Newton's model of the universe-machine.

The overall significance of Galiani's first philosophical-scientific synthesis, although immature and still strongly dominated by Gassendian and Galilean naturalism, lies in its rejection of Cartesian science, whose apriorism, once its innovative phase was exhausted confronting Aristotelian scholastics, later became a restraint on progress in the sciences. Although the work of Galiani alone, the *Animadversiones physis* reflect to a great extent the convictions of the entire group of Roman scholars who surrounded him. In order to identify in the *Animadversiones* the expression of this group of Italian scholars' ideas in the early eighteenth century, one need only review the Accademia Gualtieri's program, recounted in the letters of Galiani, Grandi, and Bottari, for there all Newton's experiments on optics were performed, and the scientific theories of Descartes and Gassendi were discussed.[25] In a letter to Giovanni Bianchi of Rimini, Galiani's close friend Antonio Leprotti carefully assessed the exact meaning of the epistemological assumptions made by enlightened Catholics against the great philosophical-scientific systems and in favor of an empirical analysis of nature.

> To me, Newtonian philosophy's forte has always seemed to lie entirely in Galileo's way of philosophizing. As you know, he did not produce a general system of physics, for he did not believe there was sufficient data on which to fabricate one. But he furnished some particular treatises, reducing a series of observations that he found had a common principle to a system. Newton did this in his physics, whereas Descartes made a general system. . . . One ought confess that this universe is too vast to wish to put it under a system manufactured by our minds.[26]

In the 1710s, the new algorithm of infinitesimal calculus rapidly spread in Italy, eliciting varied reactions. Among those who demonstrated their own bafflement about the philosophical foundations of the recent mathematical tool was Celestino Galiani. The image contained in his *Ristretto della vita* [taken up later by Nicolini] of a Galiani who was an early advocate of the new calculus does not correspond to reality at all. He, along with Vitale Giordani and Giacinto de Cristoforo, was among the Italian scientists most critical of the new calculus. Letters exchanged between Galiani and De Cristoforo starting in 1708 reveal the particular perplexity that the two harbored towards that strange algorithm that compared infinite quantities, or drew finite quantities from complicated relationships between infinitesimals of a different order.[27] The use of the concept of infinity in mathematics had already triggered interminable discussions. The new analysis, which introduced actual operations between infinite quantities as well, was understandably and justifiably bound to cause arguments. As long as mathematics had confined its operative realm to finite quantities, its logical rigor and solid philosophical foundations had permitted it to develop without any particular problems. The study of infinite quantities, however, while extraordinarily fertile, necessarily led to a weakening of its logical bases.[28] For many scholars, the image of eighteenth-century infinitesimal mathematics is one of a giant with feet of clay. It would be the end of the eighteenth century before the theoretical foundations were finally discussed again and the bases of modern infinitesimal calculus laid. The bafflement of men like Galiani and De Cristoforo (as well as many other European scholars) must be evaluated in light of this tumultuous but confused development.

An initial, important step in the painful dissemination of infinitesimal calculus in Italy was William Burnet's arrival in Rome. He helped Galiani to clarify many obscure points of the new algorithm, among other things allowing him to have contact with Bernardino Zendrini, Antonio Conti, and the great Swiss mathematician Jakob Hermann, who was then teaching at Padua.[29] In 1710, during his stay in Padua, Hermann (to whom Burnet had referred Roman scientists' perplexities regarding the new calculus) sent Galiani a brief autograph on the problems of integration and differentiation, with the intention of dispelling residual doubts.[30] In the same year Antonio Conti also wrote Galiani about these problems. Conti, who had studied infinitesimal calculus at the school of Hermann and Guido Grandi, addressed the complex problem of operations between infinite quantities, seeking to make preliminary clarifications about the concept of the infinitesimal. His explanations, however interesting, confirm his lack of clarity (common to all scholars of the period) in defining such concepts rigorously.[31] Symptomatic was his uncertainty between an actualizing conception of the infinitesimal and a merely potential one.

> The English have wisely given the name of fluxion to the infinitely small particle, for it in a sense always flows, and in itself and in our minds, always converging on zero or on nothing beyond given limits, and never getting there. If finally it became zero or nothing by resolving itself, it would no longer be an element of quantity, but its terminus, which, strictly speaking, is merely the negation of a greater extension. And hence [we have] the difference between zero and the infinitesimally small particle. The former is absolutely nothing; but the latter is absolutely something positive, and it only becomes nothing in relation to some greatness infinitely greater than itself.[32]

As long as he was dealing with an infinitesimal of the first degree, Conti seemed to accept the hypothesis of its immediate reality when speaking of "little particles." When it was necessary to clarify logically operations with infinitesimals of a higher degree, however, his discussion became rather vague, until he finally reached the uncomfortable affirmation that "it is true that here imagination betrays us, but imagination is not the yardstick of science."[33] His advice on a practical level about the methods with which to deal with infinitely "small things" was not, however, entirely useless to Galiani, for spurred on by others' questions he rapidly became one of the greatest experts on infinitesimal calculus in Italy. In 1712 Galiani could proudly write in response to Conti: "For quite some time now I no longer have difficulties with the new calculus; I understand the certainty of its principles."[34]

The encounter with the complex problem of infinitesimal calculus elicited different results in Galiani's and Conti's thought. The latter took his lead from a presumed reality of the infinite and from its application to the chain of beings, and he fully shared Malebranche's genetic theory of infinite Chinese boxes, but interpreted it materialistically as a genuine structure of nature.[35] Galiani, on the other hand, was hostile to any metaphysics dealing with the infinite, such as the one worked out by the fantasies of Guido Grandi or others;[36] he grasped only the instrumental side of the new algorithm, reevaluating its scientific function and thus freeing himself from Gassendi's primitive naturalist framework. The mathematical infinite, which had so worried Pascal and caused him to proclaim the superiority of faith over a proud human science impotent to comprehend the world's reality,[37] provides the proper occasion to evaluate the two different methods of approaching the new scientific discoveries. Antonio Conti was determined to understand nature, and he did not hesitate in the least to use the new algorithm open-mindedly in order to outline the new theory of the infinite Chinese boxes better in a philosophical way. The perennially cautious Celestino Galiani, on the other hand, was strongly attached to an experimental reality and hostile to any metaphysics that might privilege the use of the new algorithm, rejecting a priori any attempt to uncover its philosophical foundations.

As he himself wrote, Galiani's acceptance of infinitesimal calculus was in fact born "from the argument—to avail myself of a term from the schools—a posteriori, that is, from seeing that through [calculus about the infinite], used in various guises, one arrives at the truth."[38] The distance existing between Conti and Galiani in philosophical and scientific terms became even more evident in the following years, however, until it became a genuine ideological battle that influenced the dissemination of Newtonianism in Italy.

2. THE EPISTEMOLOGICAL DEBATE WITH ANTONIO CONTI

Abbot Conti's complex philosophical experiences had matured during his long stays abroad, in particular in Paris and London, and from his personal contacts with great scholars such as Newton, Malebranche, Le Clerc, and others. Together with Francesco Bianchini, Conti was one of the first Italians to meet the author of the *Principia*, and he certainly was among the first lucidly to pose the problem of correctly interpreting the new Newtonian celestial dynamics in relation to contemporary philosophical culture. As we have already noted, in the first great Italian periodical *Giornale de' Letterati*, a genuine lay, mechanistic, Galilean culture took shape in the Veneto, providing an alternative to the enlightened Catholics' natural theology.[1] Before his departure from Italy in 1713 (to which he would not return until 1726), Conti identified himself completely with Galilean culture. After the meetings he had in 1715 with Isaac Newton, Conti rapidly underwent an early and profound crisis regarding Malebranche's mechanism, which he and a great number of intellectuals in the Veneto had once accepted. In Conti's eyes, the limits of Cartesian cosmology and the *Meditationes*'s metaphysical apriorism, elaborated by Descartes's followers, soon became evident and insurmountable. Newtonian science's allure, its empiricism, its rejection of metaphysics, and the very philosophical interpretation that Newton gave to his discoveries—the denial of the world's eternity, the rejection of preformism, and the active presence of the divinity—all received Conti's attentive consideration.

His *Risposta* to Nigrisoli (1716) was strongly marked by his positive encounter with Newton. The anti-Newtonianism of the *Considerazioni* (which had appeared in 1712 in the *Giornale de' Letterati*) was in fact toned down in favor of a balanced exposition of all the great philosophical hypotheses then in circulation: Leibniz's preestablished harmony, Malebranche's mechanism, Le Clerc's theory of plastic forces, and the *Principia*'s celestial mechanics. One element, however, that Conti found important to emphasize in his exposition of Newtonianism for Italian scientists was the role Newton assigned to the "universal spirit," which Conti, repeating the words of the *Scholium generale*, described as follows:

> It is a most subtle spirit that passes through the largest bodies and is hidden in them. It attracts and joins the particles of the bodies lying closely together, and it allows electrical bodies to move at greater distances, either attracting or repelling neighboring bodies. It pushes, directs, reflects, refracts, and bends the rays of light.[2]

This is a dense conglomeration of meanings, which revealed Conti's interest in all those scientific theories that attributed new and interesting properties to matter. In sum, from the beginning his Newtonianism echoed his desire to reinterpret the most important results of the *Principia* in an original and comprehensive philosophical synthesis capable of resolving all the various levels in the chain of being within a mechanistic scheme and without resorting to finalist hypotheses. His stay in Paris and his contact with Libertine circles, in particular with the marquis of Liancourt, the count of Plélo, and Nicolas Fréret, caused a reversal in Conti's thought. Nicola

Badaloni had rightly focused his attention on these French scholars, who, starting with a unique, materialist overthrowing of Malebranche's theories, came to reinterpret Newtonian celestial mechanics in terms not unlike those of Toland.[3] In particular Nicolas Fréret,[4] the anonymous author of the *Lettre de Thrasibule à Leucippe* [Thrasibulus's letter to Leucippus], contributed measurably to the maturation of some of Conti's ideas (and became his intimate friend), especially in clarifying for him the ancient doctrine of Stratonism that Bayle had introduced: a vision of the universe worked out dualistically as a force-matter with an intrinsic principle of order.

Tackling the thorny issue of analyzing religion as a historical phenomenon, in the *Lettre*[5] Fréret had focused on evocative, materialist Egyptian doctrines, rejecting euhemerism and linking the ultimate significance of ancient religions to a sort of religious naturalism. In these materialist doctrines, movement and matter comprised the key to understanding the mysteries of the universe. Conti undoubtedly had the merit of elucidating the possible connection between these ancient cosmologies founded on force-matter and the interpretation of the ultimate cause in Newtonian universal gravitation. The Venetian scholar found that Giordano Bruno's works and some recent writings of Anthony Collins and John Toland entirely illuminated the great questions that vied in the debate over Newtonianism. On the one hand, the Boyle lecturers' providential and apologetic interpretation, supported by Newton himself, aimed to bring the results of modern science back into a great divine plan. On the other hand, the secular interpretation of those who posited a logic intrinsic to nature, without final causes, envisioned Newton's universal spirit and universal gravitation as two of the many manifestations of force-matter. These two contrasting models affected not only philosophical dilemmas, but also actual world images, which had grave ideological effects in every facet of culture. Conti accepted the second interpretation, and once he had returned to Italy he made himself the bearer of a complex philosophical synthesis in which Newton's universal spirit and the *Principia*'s doctrines were skillfully presented (and in a certain sense exploited). His goal was to provide a materialist analysis of the universe centered on the concept of force-matter and the immediate reality of Newtonian ether, considered as one of the many possible levels of matter's structure.[6]

In the Veneto Conti had the opportunity to study in depth the themes surrounding force-matter, enjoying the unanimity of opinion among great scientists such as Riccati, Poleni, and Vallisnieri. Conti's originality, however, lies in his lack of hesitation in accepting that order was intrinsic to matter's structure; this acceptance permitted him (unlike Riccati) to free himself completely from any providentialist debt and to widen his analysis to questions of a historical, political, and aesthetic-literary nature.

Among his most authoritative correspondents Conti chose Celestino Galiani, whose fame as a scholar receptive to the themes of modern science had

already begun to circulate throughout Italy in the 1710s.[7] The fact that
Galiani was at Rome, in the heart of Catholicism, was of special interest to
Conti. In 1712 he sent a long letter to Galiani through his study companion, the Oratorian Giovambattista Baroni, in which he opened an interesting long-distance dialogue that would continue for quite some time. After
the standard professions of admiration, the scholar from the Veneto immediately cut to the heart of the matter:

> Since we are discussing mechanics, may Your Reverence permit me to
> explain to you the great question that concerns the nature of force to-
> day. . . . The Germans, following Mr. Leibniz, who has renewed and civi-
> lized the substantial forms, claim that force is something impressed on
> matter and produced by the power of divine command, which in doing
> so left an impression of something of itself. Therefore they would have it
> that, since God can communicate existence to things without the exist-
> ence communicated being divine, He can thus communicate force with-
> out the communicative force being divine.[8]

Conti, who in 1712 still maintained his distance from a conception of
the universe centered on force-matter, did not hesitate (at least in words
and in this letter) to underline the ambiguous elements of such a conception:

> [Leibniz] speaks obscurely, and in substance he means that it is necessary
> to admit something else beyond matter in a given moment in order to
> distinguish the status—momentary, present, and future—and to remove
> the perfect uniformity of places and times and to assign the difference of
> the parts of matter and bodies. And this thing beyond matter can only
> be motor force, an intrinsic force, since the formal difference of things
> must lie in the things themselves, if one does not wish to change God
> into things and maintain that the particles of divinity are spread through
> matter. This would be tantamount to introducing Spinoza's God, that is
> to say, a God immersed in bodies. In addition he claims that without
> admitting this force in bodies, there would be nothing of substance in
> them, but all [would be] in a continual flux, as the ancient Platonists
> held, and consequently all [would be] merely modifications and appear-
> ances, which again makes things merely forms of substance.

While formally keeping his distance from these ideas, Conti did not hesitate to illustrate every aspect of them, and he insistently asked Galiani to
express an opinion on this complex question. Among the themes he treated,
Conti explicitly referred to the apparent contradiction between Newton's
gravitational force (significantly compared to the "Aristotelian qualities")
and Leibniz's force-matter:

> It is necessary, however, to note that Mr. Leibniz's impressed force is not
> the same as the attracting force of Newton and the English. Leibniz would
> have it that gravity, attraction, magnetism, etc. are nothing but the effects
> of the limitations and modifications of the impressed force, and not ab-

solute forces similar to the Aristotelian qualities. Thus all laws of motion are derived from the limitation of forces, and consequently all order and harmony of nature.[9]

Galiani's lengthy response came quickly. In an important, unedited letter to Conti that was sent through Baroni, Galiani firmly distanced himself from Leibniz's theories and anyone who accepted the thesis of energetic matter. After having purposefully suggested to Conti a series of William Whiston's texts aimed at the apologetic popularization of Newtonian mechanics, Galiani squarely confronted the "question of force": "In order to inform you openly of my humble opinion from the beginning, as far as I could judge from what you have favored to write to me, this opinion does not please me at all."[10] He supported his assessment with a rapid historical excursus, which conveys to us the interest that there was in dealing with the theme of matter's structure at that time. "What is the cause of motion?" Galiani asked.

> Likewise they (and especially Malebranche and Cordemoy) deduce that there are no true principal causes in nature, but only occasional ones, and that the only principal cause is the Author of nature. In other words, they would have it that when a body in motion encounters another—A encounters B—the cause that puts A in motion can only be God's will on the occasion of the encounter, according to the laws He imposed on nature.

Leibniz's hypothesis of a force intrinsic to bodies was unacceptable on a merely scientific level. From the experimental study of matter's properties, nothing in favor of Leibniz's thesis emerged: "Then one may ask Mr. Leibniz what this force is, substance or form of substance. . . . He could say that it is a form and that it is merely a tendency towards motion."

In reality, "nothing good" for modern science could come from accepting Leibniz's force. "The sciences could find" no advantage "in such occult qualities when, lacking a concept, they cannot determine their effects and properties that must and can only be known through sound experiments or good reasoning founded on those experiments."[11]

In the following years Galiani attentively followed the developments of Antonio Conti's studies as their mutual friend Baroni informed him of them. Baroni wrote to Galiani in 1716:

> It has now been nearly two months since I received some letters from Abbot Conti from London. He declares that he is very satisfied by the frequent conversations that he has had and continues to have with Mr. Newton, from which he says he has profited greatly. . . . Newton customarily does not wish to deal with anyone, according to what the abbot has written. . . . He adds that [Conti] has little love for metaphysics, and moreover he is entirely opposed to Malebranche. In this area, he says that he has principles similar to those of Locke, who in this field is a good transmitter of Newton.

Some other interesting information on English culture follows:

> All this is already known; from the time I was in Rome, I was informed . . .
> that there was a pamphlet produced in English by Locke in which he
> contested the doctrine of Malebranche's ideas. For that reason I wrote to
> the abbot in order to be informed of the contents, since he understands
> the language sufficiently well. In addition, he then advised me of many
> things that we already know about the variety of religions and myriad
> Socinians and deists who reign everywhere in those climes.[12]

On his return to Italy, Conti soon noticed that his erstwhile Roman correspondent Galiani had become the recognized head of an apologetic interpretation of Newtonianism because of the reputation he had acquired as a
scientist throughout Italy and his skillful editorial initiatives favoring
Newtonian natural theology. Even though he had avoided publishing his
ideas, Galiani had made long trips to study closely the "regulation" of fluvial
waters, coming into contact with Antonio Vallisnieri, Giovanni Crivelli,
Benedetto Bacchini, Giovanni Poleni, and Eustachio Manfredi, not to mention
the Florentine and Neapolitan scholars whom he had met years ago.[13] The
circulation of ideas, even if slow, guaranteed that nearly all Italian circles
were familiar with what Galiani and enlightened Catholics were publicizing. Galiani's friend Thomas Dereham, because of his close ties with the
Royal Society, was (among other things) a valuable point of contact for all
scholars. It is not at all coincidental that in 1734–1735, after the appearance of the works of Derham and Cheyne in Italian translations, Conti
again turned to Galiani, presenting him with a long essay containing his
conclusions about matter's structure and the exact interpretation of Newtonian
celestial mechanics. During this same period, Conti also looked to another
great intellectual tied to the enlightened Catholics, Gaspare Cerati, to whom
he dedicated a proper cosmological treatise entitled *Il globo di Venere* [Venus's
globe], prefaced by a letter to Cerati, then director of the University of
Pisa. In both writings, Conti's fundamental thesis was one of energetic matter
in its Stratonic and antifinalist interpretation.[14]

Because it was private, the long *Lettera a mons. Galiani* [Letter to Monsignor Galiani]—a commentary on the *Dissertazione su l'egizia poesia* [A dissertation on Egyptian poetry]—contained notably open-minded features and
hence serves as an important testimonial to the ideological confrontation
between the two. Recently it has been read, and rightly so, as further proof
of Conti's Stratonic interpretation of the universe.[15] In light of what we
have reconstructed of the initiatives taken by enlightened Catholics (and
in particular of the specific position that Galiani had assumed in Italian
culture), the brief treatise actually lends itself to another interpretation:
Far from being a simple reconfirmation of his own ideas, the ultimate intent of Conti's writing was to launch an honest and straightforward attack
against Galiani's daring editorial operations and his favoring of Newtonian

natural theology. Conti was aware of the importance that Galiani had assumed with his new duty as *cappellano maggiore* of the Kingdom of Naples.[16] With Galiani as *cappellano maggiore*, with Gaspare Cerati as director of the University of Pisa, and with Bottari and Leprotti very active in Rome, enlightened Catholics already controlled some of the most lively and influential cultural centers in the country.[17] Conti placed all that in the context of the rapid dissemination of the apologetic interpretation of Newtonianism in Italy through translations of Cheyne's and Derham's works.

The official goal of Conti's brief treatise was to request an opinion about the *Dissertazione sull'egizia poesia*, which Conti evidently had sent Galiani in manuscript form. The work's preface clearly indicated, however, the desire to confine the discussion to the matter of the profound historical significance of natural theologies. Referring explicitly to Cheyne's and Derham's works, Conti began by tackling the theme of modern natural theology, "cultivated and enlarged in this century more than in any other for the happy discovery of final causes." The new visions of the world, the astronomical as with any other—

> anatomical, botanical, chemical . . .—conspire to demonstrate that where one discovers order in the parts and in the whole, there is a single intelligence and not many, if the whole and the parts are in accord in a harmonious system. . . . From these attributes of the divinity, it was easy to deduce many others, and there was no dearth of wise authors who observed that the kinds of things could multiply in number and vary in form and location, and that the laws of motion that continually unravel and restabilize the mixtures are more suitable to the present system, but not absolutely necessary, and they concluded that there was a vestige of divine freedom in things.

Conti did not share these opinions. The providential model of the Boyle lecturers and many European scholars was unacceptable in his eyes. Absolute divine freedom as presumed in natural finalism was a conclusion not yet demonstrated by the proponents of modern natural theologies.

> The conclusion is only probable, as long as it does not demonstrate that the contingency of things is real and not imaginary, that is to say, more founded on the nature of the same things than on the ignorance in which we are about their status and their causes. There, Monsignor, are the limits of natural theology; I do not add the metaphysical arguments introduced in Descartes's *Meditationes* and followed by Malebranche, Leibniz, Clarke, and Wolff. If such arguments prove the ingenuity of their authors more than the issue, I do not examine it here, but certainly they gain neither the certainty nor clarity of conclusions immediately from physical phenomena.[18]

In the course of the *Lettera*, the Galilean distinction between faith and reason came to the foreground with the rejection of any implicit finalism of natural theologies. But Conti's discussion in this brief treatise was much more subtle and unbiased than it might seem at first reading. Mindful of Fréret's lesson, he compared modern Newtonian providential theology to an interesting examination of the great Egyptian and Greek cosmologies, bringing to light their materialist, antifinalist, and, in a certain sense, secular origins in which the religious phenomenon was a historical event that came after the philosophical schematization of the world's reality. We are dealing with a paradoxical inversion of modern natural theology. Whereas this modern theology, even though scientifically advanced, had inevitably undergone a precise conditioning at the hands of positive religions with their historical institutionalization, the ancient theologies first analyzed reality and only later posed the problem of their own religious interpretations, and they came to cloak in poetic forms a true physical history of the world in which the function of divinity and the religious phenomenon in general was tightly interwoven with the overall materiality and factualness of the universe.

> Now I claim that this Egyptian system does not contain a natural theology that serves to clarify the revealed, while in fact [this system] is nothing but a travestied physics under a poetic cocoon, whose only utility was to confirm within souls polytheism and belief in the world's eternity, two principles diametrically opposed to Mosaic tradition.[19]

In this context, the detailed exposition that followed of the ancient philosophies from the Egyptian tradition, the Ionic school, the Pythagoreans, and Plato confirms the impression that Conti was sensitive and receptive to the search for an image of the universe completely resolved in an integrated philosophical explanation of nature, entirely separate from Newtonian providentialism.

Conti focused his attention on the cosmologies of Thales, Pythagoras, and Plato, in that order. Reiterating an opinion shared by an entire branch of European culture, from Marsham to Toland and Giannone, Conti traced the origins of these philosophies to the great Egyptian tradition. They all went back to a materialist conception of the world, variously articulated and hidden in poetic symbolism. For Thales, "everything was animate; there were no gods but the spirits distributed in all things." "The opinion of the Egyptians, as Plutarch affirms without enigma where he speaks the word Love in Isis and Osirus," was that "the world is God." Pythagoras, whose philosophy had Egyptian origins,

> according to Cicero understood God as nothing more than a spirit dispersed in all beings of nature, from which human souls are drawn. Hence we have the dogma of the soul of the world and the metempsychosis. . . . From this it is not difficult to infer that Pythagoras's system is no different from Spinoza's recent one, masked in geometry.[20]

Conti particularly emphasized Cicero's philosophical hypothesis of a universal Stratonism revised and corrected through the concept of matter's substantial order, which he presented to Galiani as a genuine alternative to Newtonian providentialism. In his opinion, this cosmogony was capable of resolving many of modern science's interpretive problems.

> In dividing nature into two things—matter and force—it seems that Cicero introduces two substances. But by saying that one cannot exist without the other, he shows us that these two things are nothing other than a single thing with two branches, the one based on that which acts, the other on that which is passive. We can only explain [this] through circumlocution—that compendious *utrumque in utroque*—by which we mean that matter's cohesion depends on force and that, on the other hand, force itself would have no cohesion if it were not supported by matter.[21]

This theory of force-matter had elicited hostility and perplexity among moderns, because whether one admitted the hypothesis of motion inherent in matter, for example, or imagined instead a force external to bodies, the assumption was always conditioned by the concept "of a God creator." The ancients, who were ignorant of such a concept, unhesitatingly accepted "intrinsic force" and the concept of order and progression "in the smallest parts" of matter. In light of these considerations, Conti brought to the fore the merely instrumental nature of the vacuum, preferring to it the reality of the plenum. "One must admit the idea of the vacuum, for which there is no sufficient reason but in the order of ideas." But above all, following Fréret's *Lettre de Thrasibule à Leucippe*, he resolved the religious phenomenon in the realm of Cicero's cosmogony through an allusive interpretation:

> Given the plenum and the transformation of matter through the continual action of force, the invariability of the status of matter and force in everything is reconciled with the perpetual variety of the parts. Force, referring to the equilibrium and the proportions that it maintains within the system, was called God by the ancients. They had as many [gods] as degrees of the particular forces distributed in matter, and they were the basis of their polytheism. . . . Thus the idea of God Cicero presented in the ancient system embraces both materialism and idealism, about which the moderns have said so much nonsense. The impious Spinoza vainly attempted to make believe that by his geometrical method he could say something more than the idolaters, among whom we must number the Egyptians and their disciples Thales, Pythagoras, and Plato.[22]

The recognition of the universe's overall materiality was a cause particularly dear to Conti's heart, for he saw in it the possibility of shaking Galiani from his obstinate acceptance of Newton's apologetics. Reprising a theme common to European materialists (and present in Giannone), Conti broached the matter of the soul's corporeality. Even the Fathers of the Church, and most of all Tertullian, had not been "so chastened in their expressions" when they referred to God's corporeal nature. For Conti, pure spirit was nearly inconceivable.[23] His assimilation of the soul into force came very

near to Jacopo Riccati's theses.[24] In the light of his exposition of these
matters to Galiani, Conti's Newtonianism seems like a scientific-philosophical
choice taken in a very critical and instrumental way. Beyond their different
views on the relation between religion and science and the universe's
materiality, the interpretations of Conti and Galiani of the new image of
the universe offered by the *Principia* were in complete conflict over
gnosiological problems and the very concept of science.

Galiani's unedited treatise *Della scienza morale: Richerche intorno alle prime
origini della scienza moral* [On moral science: Research about the early origins of moral science] is a very valuable document only recently discovered
by scholars.[25] The work permits us to appreciate fully the different method
of confronting themes which emerged from intellectuals like Conti and Galiani
in the wake of the dissemination of Newtonian cosmology. Perhaps the
only work Galiani prepared with the intention of producing a genuine treatise, beyond its specific objective of refounding morals it represents a complete reflection on the questions raised by Newtonian celestial dynamics,
contemporary philosophy, and the broad themes of matter's structure and
the God–nature relationship. Here Galiani decisively faced the gnosiological
issue, and we must broadly outline the value of this work for an understanding of Italian culture in the early eighteenth century. Galiani's acceptance of Locke's empiricism was already complete and mature. As he
wrote in the paragraph dedicated to *Varie riflessioni intorno alle nostre idee*
[Several remarks on our ideas], "Whoever might reflect as much as one can
about one's self will easily be persuaded that all ideas that we find in ourselves came by two paths, and these are sensation and reflection."[26] With
remarkable neatness, and using examples drawn from Locke's *Essay*, Galiani
synthesized and appropriated the most important results achieved by the
English philosopher in his study of the human intellect. After explaining
simple ideas, Galiani passed on to complex ideas:

> We cannot form any simple idea that has not come to us by those paths
> destined by nature; hence in the acquisition of the ideas themselves, our
> mind *mere passive se habeat* [remains utterly passive], and that equally
> applies to the ideas that come to us by means of the senses as well as to
> others that come from the perception of our activities and internal mo-
> tions, but not to composed ideas. And though many of these come to us
> through the very paths by which we have acquired simple ideas, we can
> nevertheless form other ideas at our discretion, since we can combine as
> we like the ideas acquired through different senses, either among them-
> selves or with those that came to us through reflection as well.[27]

Nevertheless, the most interesting aspect of this lucid exposition of the
Essay's second book, for it allows us to evaluate the distance separating
Galiani's science from Antonio Conti's, is the part on the analysis of the
concept of substance. The critique of this concept is in fact illuminating
for understanding the passage from an Aristotelian science, still aimed at

seeking essences and final causes, to a new empirical, phenomenological science, centered on the analysis of the perceptible fact and the properties of bodies. All modern phenomenological mechanisms, based on the description of the motion of bodies and the analysis of primary and secondary properties or qualities of bodies, start in fact with the rejection of the traditional substantialist, Aristotelian physics that was still viable in different forms in the early eighteenth century.[28] Galiani, shaped by the Galilean and Gassendian schools, did not hesitate to accept Locke's critique of the concept of substance down to the last detail. Arguing over complex ideas and in particular harking back to the abstraction that humans can perform on these ideas, Galiani clearly introduced the "abstract" concept of substance.

> If someone were to ask, "When we say the word 'substance,' what concept do we intend to express?", the response would be that it is not as easy as some believe to answer such a question; not least for this reason we will attempt to trace the meaning of this word according to the common language of men.[29]

His analysis was conducted in the footsteps of the *Essay*, but was meaningfully integrated with examples taken from Gassendi, in particular the classic example of wax and its transformations.[30]

> We have no concept of substance; thus when we say that wax *sit res extensa et solida* [is an extended and solid thing], we have no idea what is meant by that *res* [thing], which is to say we have no clear and distinct idea what is being expressed by that *res*. What we have said about the wax is true of every other thing, either extended or thinking. Therefore, as we have a clear idea of extension and solidity, but not of the *res* that is the subject and the support of extension, then however clear a concept we have of thought, we are ignorant, or we have no distinct or clear idea of the thing that thinks; that is to say, of the mind's substance.[31]

On the basis of such conclusions, the only possible science must necessarily be phenomenological and must aim to resolve scientific fact through an empirical analysis of reality. In the *Principia's Scholium generale*, Newton made clear to all his acceptance of Locke's theses, writing that with "bodies we see only the forms and colors, we hear only the sounds, we touch only the exterior surfaces, we smell only the smells, and we taste only the tastes, but we do not know the intimate substances through any sense, through any act of reflection."[32] Galiani went beyond the *Essay*'s scientific gnosiology, strongly critical of mathematics as a privileged language, and through personal contacts with the great Dutch scientist Willem 'sGravesande, he came to accept completely the Dutch mathematical empiricism that in the mid-eighteenth century was the real heir to the Newtonian scientific tradition.[33]

It is clear from what we have said that Galiani's hostility towards Conti's force-matter stemmed not just from the materialist seeds it contained but from a concept of science profoundly different from that of Antonio Conti.

Galiani's phenomenalism and empirical reduction of substance utterly excluded the search for an ultimate structure of matter. However authoritatively one might have insisted on the "factualness" of Conti's Newtonianism, it is undeniable that in Conti's philosophical elaboration there is a systematic spirit tending towards metaphysics and quite unlike Galiani's Lockean empiricism. Solicited (as we have seen) by Galiani himself, Conti had also read the Essay attentively, but his complex theory of ideas, while harkening in part to Lockean teachings rejecting the Platonic separation between ideas and reality, was in the final analysis profoundly different from the theory in the Essay, especially regarding the "internal sense" common to all humans that strongly conditions the very objectivity of Locke's simple ideas.[34]

Bearing in mind that Della scienza morale was probably written in Rome between 1720 and 1730, while Galiani was chair of Church history at the Sapienza University, his thoughts on matter's structure and on some large issues debated in Europe are of considerable interest. First Galiani had to overcome the difficulties inherent in Locke's ambiguous and resounding attribution of thought to matter, which had so horrified religious authorities of every confession.[35] Galiani's work to neutralize this crucial obstacle is even more interesting if we consider that in those very years he fearlessly discussed these themes with enlightened Catholics in Rome, as Niccolini's 1729 letter to Bottari attests.[36]

Although he had appropriated the Cartesian dualist conception of a world divided between spiritual and material substances, Locke had nevertheless finally nourished a materialist interpretation of his theories, hypothesizing that thought was one of matter's properties. In reality, in the economy of Locke's philosophy, the empirical reduction of the intellectual world and the interrelated critique of the concept of substance quelled a great deal of interest in the analysis of thought's ultimate nature. Locke made it understood that thought's operation is based on ideas, and that there is no point in ascertaining whether thought is accomplished by a spiritual substance rather than a material one.[37] His later affirmations confirmed that thought is only an objective operation of the body, and that it made no difference whether it was ultimately considered a material or spiritual substance, precisely because it was unknowable. That the resulting ambiguity nevertheless left room for opposing interpretations is demonstrated by the fact that, without any particular difficulty, both materialists (such as Anthony Collins and John Toland) and authors opposed to materialism (such as Jean Le Clerc and Samuel Clarke) could refer to the Essay. Voltaire made famous in European culture the image of a Locke who attributed thought to matter through his Lettres philosophiques [Philosophical letters], which Galiani and Niccolini read a few years after its appearance.[38] Muratori, along with the majority of Italian intellectuals, saw in Locke and his materialism new dangers for faith. This was one of the reasons why in 1734 the English philosopher's works were placed on the Index.[39]

Galiani was not intimidated by Locke's growing reputation as a materialist, and in chapter 5, Proposizione I, of his *Scienza morale*, he rejected the materialist reading and sought to demonstrate, through the "method used by the geometers," that "matter in our opinion cannot think." Analyzing one of the *Essay*'s most disturbing results, Galiani wrote:

> One might object that experience itself teaches us that the thinking principle of man is not different from the organized body. . . . So too [can] the thinking faculty alter itself, and as the body grows, it also grows. It can sicken and languish along with the body, and in the end it even dies with that same body.

This, however, proves nothing, or at least it proves only that the thinking substance "needs the body in order to exercise its functions."[40] If we were to accept the hypothesis of thinking matter, it would be necessary to consider that matter's every infinitesimal part was gifted with such a property, but by

> maintaining that every particle of matter thinks, one asserts in the first place a thing which is not known, and that is entirely contrary to our notions. We all believe that one of the differences between a man and a cadaver is that one thinks and the other does not; now according to this opinion that is contested, the latter would think no less than the former.[41]

Matter could, however, think "*ratione motus et figurae*" [by reason of motion and form]; this was the hypothesis of Libertines and those such as Radicati, Giannone, and Toland, who saw in matter's continual movement the source of all aspects of reality. Galiani emphatically rejected this opinion as well, resorting instead to an image of the human body singularly similar to the *homme-machine* of Julien Offroy de Lamettrie:

> Let us pretend for a moment that man is nothing but a complex of matter alone, composed of parts of different form and consistency, some solid and some liquid, just as we see our body is made of. Now if man was nothing more than a pure machine, as those who do not wish to recognize substance of another type must pretend, all the motions which that machine would make—both in the solid and in the liquid parts—would be made according to mechanical and necessary laws. And the motion especially of the animal spirits would be more rapid or slow, or would have some determination or another according to the special structure of our body, and the quality of the foods, and the bodies that surround us. In this hypothesis thought either would consist in the very motion of the parts thus formed and moved, or it would result as a necessary effect from motion and form. Whichever the two thoughts one might profess, everyone must allow that in this hypothesis there could be no freedom, and we could not recall, any time we want, whatever idea we had already acquired.[42]

Beasts' power of thought was another traditional aspect of the thought-matter issue that Galiani did not hesitate to confront, for he clearly understood the terms of the argument from reading the famous article "Rorarius" in Pierre Bayle's *Dictionnaire*. Rejecting the automatism of beasts held by the Cartesians, Galiani accepted instead Montaigne's and Charron's thesis (which Locke had appropriated in the *Essay*) positing the presence of a thinking substance in the bodies of animals.

> One should not immediately jump to the conclusion that we give beasts a spiritual mind entirely similar to and of the same perfection as man's, for we are of the opinion that there is a great diversity and gradation in thinking substances.... [The beasts] are still, like man, a composite of two kinds of substance, that is of matter and of thinking substance, but nevertheless this [substance] of the thinking type, however also unextended, is of a condition rather inferior to that of man's [substance].[43]

Seeking to clarify once and for all his aversion to materialism, Galiani dedicated much space in his *Scienza morale* to the problem of motion inherent in matter, a hypothesis then at the center of European debate. The chapter entitled "Ab aeterno non ha potuto esistere la sola materia col moto secondo la sentenza di Epicuro" [Matter alone with motion, according to Epicurus's opinion, cannot have existed from the beginning] illuminates the image of the universe that Galiani appropriated, in opposition to the Tolandists' "motion essential to matter" and Conti's force-matter. In order to eliminate any possible doubt about the issue, it should be said that Galiani's intransigent antimaterialism stemmed not only from apologetic concerns, or from political and cultural considerations about the risks that accepting materialism could bring in Italy, but from a precise philosophical conception of the world's reality. Galiani's God and the morals that ensued from his ideas would in the end prove to be significantly more dangerous for Catholic cultural hegemony in Italy than the crude materialism of some of the heirs of the Libertine tradition. Isaac Newton's universe-machine was the frame of reference for the entire chapter, in which Galiani presented inert matter and spiritualizing, active substance as fundamental elements of the universe.

Early in the *Scienza morale*, where he took up a key aspect of the Boyle lecturers' theology, he had written: "In order to prove the existence of God, one must make it understood that all other things would return to nothing in the absurd and impossible hypothesis that He ceased to exist."[44] The theory that motion was inherent to matter was refuted with the same arguments that Samuel Clarke had used against Toland in the *Demonstration of the Being and Attributes of God*:

> The argument comes down to this: we find in the concept of matter nothing but a pure capacity to be moved according to this direction or determination and according to whatever degree of velocity, and thus equally a purely passive capacity to receive whatever might be the form. And we see through experience that in matter itself, we find movement with certain fixed and constant determinations: for bodies which we call heavy, motion is downwards, and for planets motion is circular along

elliptical paths from certain determined centers, and also various and very diverse determined forms. Of necessity one needs an efficient cause by which matter has received motion, as well as all those many and so diverse forms and combinations.[45]

Galiani rejected the chain of beings, the unfolding of the Chinese boxes present in it, and the naturalist mechanism of Vallisnieri and Conti and other scholars in the Veneto, all of which he accused of leading to the hypothesis of the world's eternity and the repudiation of the initial efficient cause.

Imagine men without number, as many as you will, and let them be full of endless ovaries without limit; nonetheless one such combination of various parts with various shapes and motions is not in any way connected with the concept of matter; there has always been need for an efficient cause.[46]

Galiani's assent to a creation of souls *in tempore* [throughout time] was wholly orthodox and of Augustinian origin, as opposed to the theories of Vallisnieri and Leibniz (who followed Tertullian), with their original encasing in the Chinese boxes.[47]

3. FROM THE *TRACTATUS THEOLOGICO-POLITICUS* TO THE *REASONABLENESS OF CHRISTIANITY*

It would not be entirely possible to grasp Celestino Galiani's experience in its complexity and relationships with European culture if we overlooked a decisive element of his education—his studies of biblical exegesis and Church history conducted in Rome during the 1710s and 1720s. For Galiani, as for other contemporary Italian and European intellectuals, the clash with new interpretive schemes of reality occurred on numerous fronts, without particular emphasis on any one area of research. Rather, it involved an in-depth examination of the ties between the renewed image of the universe and the gnosiology advanced in the *Principia*, the devastating effects of Spinozan biblical critique, the crisis of a Eurocentric culture momentarily incapable of profiting from the confrontation with modes of thought foreign to Western civilization, and the radicalization of the struggle between the Christian tradition and the emerging, substantially lay ideologies.

Just after his arrival in Rome in 1701, Galiani industriously began to study sacred history, learning Hebrew and perfecting his knowledge of Latin and Greek. These were years of intense work, during which he availed himself of the friendship of Domenico Bencini, Gherardo Capassi, Francesco Bianchini, Giusto Fontanini, and Biagio Garofalo in order to refine his preparation. The Roman environment at that time was very stimulating. While the papal state continued to regress on a political and economic level,[1] Catholic culture during those years, under the pontificate of Clement XI, experienced a renewed commitment to reform.[2]

Even abroad, the Holy See sought to relaunch a new image of itself. Muratori's project for a league of neutral Italian states under the pope's insignia rested on this overambitious papal initiative,[3] which lacked genuine political force and did not yield tangible results. But in Rome some trace remained. On an official level, two initiatives prevailed because of their importance. The first was the splitting of the Arcadia in 1711, with the harsh confrontation between those who wished to continue the work of destroying from within any attempt to reform the Arcadia itself, and the Gravinian faction, which proposed greater ideological and political efforts.[4] The second initiative was the relaunching of the Accademia dei Concili in 1708. It is worthwhile to remark here on the direct influence that this initiative had on Galiani.

Formed by Cardinal Ciampini in 1671, the academy endured vicissitudes in the pursuit of its work, with brief interruptions, for the entire eighteenth century. Initially it met in the monastery of San Nicola da Tolentino, then it moved and found a stable location in the college De Propaganda Fide.[5] After years of decadence, the academy's organization was reformed in 1708 at the express desire of Clement XI, and it received new motivation, particularly in the formation of ecclesiastical cadres designed to combat the heresies of modern thought. Lorenzo Zaccagni, Giusto Fontanini, and Domenico Bencini were entrusted with the reorganization, but Bencini was the real architect of the entire operation. He drafted new regulations, and his lectures largely delineated the academy's overall direction.[6] To evaluate fully the importance of this initiative, one must consider not only the academy's programs and lectures but also the fact that the directorial group was linked to most of the prominent members of the Circolo del Tamburo [Circle of the Drum], which met at Passionei's home. Figures such as Capassi, Bianchini, Bencini, Passionei, Galiani, Fontanini, and others "beat the drum" in Rome (according to the felicitous image of their contemporaries) in order to reawaken Catholic culture—although from rather varied perspectives—and they were the protagonists of the meetings held at De Propaganda Fide.[7] It is no coincidence that some of the ideals characterizing the circle, including the desire for an authentic reform of Catholic culture, the opening to modern thought, anti-Jesuit sentiment, and, above all, acceptance of Maurist historiography, were shared by the leaders of the rejuvenated academy.

Bencini's "suggestions" to Clement XI for the reorganization and renewal of the academy clearly identify the spirit and methodology that ought to inspire historical research on the ecumenical councils, and "sacred and ecclesiastical learning" in general. "The way to narrate a subject is first to see briefly how much is needed to trace the time, cause, and conditions" of every historical event, but, above all, there should be no ritualism of an Arcadian type, no "pomp, ostentation, and florid style"; rather, absolute precedence should be given to historical and philological analysis, as in the Maurist tradition, always aimed "at the truth."[8] The hierarchical, strongly centralized organization desired by Clement XI demonstrates the Curia's direct control over the academy, whose president, the young Cardinal Annibale Albani (the pope's nephew), also imposed rigid requirements for entrance, which was guaranteed only to those who had completed at least two years of theological studies and had passed a preliminary exam given by the committee of the Twenty-Four Elders.[9]

Among the studies we know about, those of Abbot Domenico Bencini, secretary of the academy, teacher of Polemical Theology in the college De Propaganda Fide, and friend and teacher of Celestino Galiani, are certainly among the most significant for understanding the interests and problems handled by the members.[10] His traditional learned research on the history of the ecumenical councils is important for studying the Church in its institutional and ideological formation, especially as it examines the gripping debates over the primacy of the bishop of Rome and the ever difficult relationship between temporal and ecclesiastical power. Moreover, Bencini conducted splendid and novel comparative analyses of cultures different from the Judeo-Christian one, following the examples of Marsham's and Spencer's research. In his dense argumentation, he discussed the question of religion in the history of humanity. Bencini did not flinch from evocatively sketching primitive pagan religions from a euhemerist point of view and emphasizing the political significance that religions had acquired in ancient societies. He wrote, "it is a very common opinion that in all things that adorn the universe one finds a correspondence and order among the highest, lowest, and middle parts. In the intellectual order, the highest is God, the lowest is man, and the middle is the angel." The ancients invented the hero and placed him between God and man, "almost as a deified man or a human God."[11] This is all evident in Mediterranean cultures, and in particular in that of ancient Egypt, "once justly compared to heaven."[12] Citing the works of Marsham, Spencer, and Bochart, he found traces of an invariable deification of men gifted with "heroic virtues" in Persia, Phoenicia, and Greece. But it was in ancient Rome that the political significance of this deification of heroes was fully revealed: "Raising first a sumptuous temple to Romulus, then to the Gracchi, and finally to the Caesars," the politicians of Rome had attempted to indicate the path of virtue and social order for Romans.[13]

In other argumentations, Bencini returned broadly to the myths of pagan religions, rituality, and the origin of idolatry in the people of "the crude early centuries," making a broad analysis of themes then much debated by European intellectuals through his up-to-date and open-minded lectures.[14] Alongside the study of the religious phenomenon (taken as an essentially historical fact) and the attentive analysis of the controversial issues of chronology, within the academy Bencini played the role of expert in training ecclesiastics who would combat modern heresies. Some of his lectures were meant to address this exacting task, and they are surprising for the nonchalance—within an official institution such as the academy—with which they expounded the doctrines of Spinoza, Herbert of Cherbury, and Hobbes, even if with the stated intention of preparing Catholic scholars to refute them. Bencini's long lecture, published almost in its entirety in the *Tractatio historico-polemica chronologicis tabulis illustrata* [Historical-polemical treatise illustrated with chronological tables] in 1720, analyzed the doctrines of the Libertines and European deists in depth.[15]

While underscoring the danger of impious Socinian doctrines on the Trinity, in the eyes of the learned abbot the true enemy that the Catholic church had to defeat was the Libertine theory of the fraudulence of religions, from which every modern heresy had derived. Bencini paradoxically took the accusation of imposture against Moses, Mohammed, and Christ contained in the *De tribus impostoribus* [On three impostors] and shifted it onto three modern apostles of heresy: Spinoza, Herbert of Cherbury, and Hobbes.

> In Vanini's blasphemous writings, the existence of God is placed in doubt; in a highly impious book he casts ridicule on the holiest mystery of the Trinity. Everywhere the most sacred secrets of the Christian religion are derided as if they were the laughingstock of the world. And finally, after the mid-eighteenth century, there came from the depths of hell three impostors of Christianity truly more deadly than can be said or imagined, who did not hesitate to tear out by the roots not only this but any other supernatural religion through their impious debates.[16]

Bencini, who demonstrated an extraordinary familiarity with Libertine literature and all the works of the three impious seventeenth-century philosophers, perceptively synthesized the operative role that the thesis of fraudulence had played in undermining Christian religion at its foundations:

> Understand, O listeners, that I am speaking primarily of Baruch Spinoza, who derides the divine voice of the sacred Bible, with his mouth and blasphemous work, mockingly, as if these sacred instruments meant to procure happiness were fraudulent, and he binds every prophecy among the parties of a somewhat too lively intellect. I am speaking of Edward Herbert, who has invented a single universal religion formed by five articles, which he explains, and at which one can arrive through the force of nature alone. And he maintains without any shame that all the rest of divine revelation is not at all necessary for salvation. Last, I speak of Thomas Hobbes, who has introduced a territorial religion, dependent solely on the judgment of each prince and secular power.[17]

To understand the extent to which the abbot was familiar with the works of the three "impostors," and to evaluate the consequent exceptionalness of his lecture, one need only consult the long footnotes in his *Tractatio*, which synthesize what was expounded and discussed in the Roman academy. We find three veritable biographies of Spinoza, Herbert of Cherbury, and Hobbes, along with a detailed list of their works and a careful synthesis of the most famous ones.

Bencini examined entire chapters of Spinoza's *Tractatus theologico-politicus*, citing the philosopher's harsh judgment against the divine meaning of prophecies and commenting negatively on Spinoza's refusal to attribute the *Pentateuch* to Moses. He had no doubt about the ultimate meaning to give the *Tractatus*, and he saw it entirely as human reduction of the Bible's sacrality: "Everywhere this impostor mocks the divinity of the sacred books."[18] As for Herbert of Cherbury, justly considered one of the fathers of deism, Bencini thoroughly grasped the essential features of his universal religion based on a *consensus gentium* [consensus of peoples] and a few articles of faith without any need for revelation. He intelligently cited passages from the English scholar's two greatest works, the *De veritate prout distinguitur a revelatione* [On truth as distinguished from revelation] and the *De religione gentilium* [On the religion of the gentiles].[19] He performed an analogous feat for Thomas Hobbes, discussing his thesis of a state religion and principle *cuius est regio, eius est religio*.[20] According to Bencini, all three authors accepted the Libertine thesis of the imposture of religions, even though this thesis was articulated in various ways and found different solutions in Spinoza's pantheism, Herbert of Cherbury's deism, and Hobbes's state religion. We should not be deceived by the biting if formulaic invectives that the abbot hurled at these "impious authors." His esteem for Spinoza is indicated by his continual citations of Spinoza in the *Tractatio*, a sign of his unconfessed admiration.[21]

The open-minded nature of Bencini's interests and his considerable knowledge of Libertine and deist literature did not pass unobserved among his contemporaries. A German traveler who had spoken with the abbot in Turin during the years when he taught in the city's university described him thus in his diary: "He had such scant faith in Roman religion and such an exact knowledge of archaeology that one might say of him that his religion was based solely on the fact that in antiquity an altar to the goddess *Fides* [faith] had been erected in Rome."[22]

Among the protagonists behind the resumption of the confrontation between Catholic culture and modern thought in Rome, Bencini was not the only one disposed to tackle the works of dangerous authors such as Spinoza and Hobbes. Other intellectuals tied to Celestino Galiani's circle proved particularly active in the debate. Two scholars in particular, Francesco Bianchini of Verona and Biagio Garofalo of Naples, formulated different and interesting responses to a key problem, that of theorizing a scientifically valid historical research. Bianchini had entered the argument on the Catholic side. In his famous *Storia universale provata con monumenti e figurata con simboli degli antichi* [Universal history proven with monuments and illustrated with symbols of the ancients] (1697), he had criticized Isaac de Lapeyrère's heretical theses on pre-Adamites from the *Systema theologicum ex praeadamitarum hypothesi* [Theological system from the hypothesis of the Pre-Adamites] (1655), confirming the accuracy of the chronology advanced in Sacred Scripture.[23]

Beyond its profound erudition and the importance of the themes that Bianchini's work treated, themes that were at the center of the interests of all European scholars, an attentive reading clearly reveals the sense of Catholic historiography's comprehensive response to the disquieting comparative method of John Marsham and John Spencer and, above all, to corrosive Spinozan biblical exegesis, aimed at dangerously confounding sacred and profane history. Bianchini's proposal unfolded on an essentially methodological level, and it constituted a wise compromise between the rights of science and those of erudition. To the immense antiquity that modern chronologers attributed to peoples like the Chinese and the Egyptians, Bianchini countered by asking for proofs and concrete facts, not fables. Objectivity was the cornerstone of his method, clearly of Galilean inspiration. Bianchini believed all human events were bound to the time factor: "Chronology without history is a plan composed of many parts that do not demonstrate the union and the proportion of the entire body . . .; history without chronology is music without a beat."[24] The fundamental feature of Bianchini's investigation, which utterly rejected the opposition of reason and faith and Spinoza's choice in favor of the former, was clearly a conscious transposition of the Galilean double truth in the world of history:

> One plainly sees the necessity of dividing history into two types: that is, into *profane* and *ecclesiastical*. The first leads to a goal of natural knowledge through examples and human means; the second guides its means towards a much greater wisdom. . . . Hence one sees within history that separation which is observed in the laws.[25]

Separating sacred history from profane, almost as if the two were different disciplines with different rules and goals, allowed Bianchini to avoid putting sacred theses to a critical-philological analysis and thereby arriving at embarrassing results. The historian's real and true field of research was profane history, in which it was licit to resort to reason in order to interrogate facts, reconstruct events, and discover the truth. No longer suffering the inhibiting fear of an earthly reduction of sacred history with catastrophic consequences for faith, Bianchini's methodological proposal acquired extraordinary freshness and truly genial features. To Bianchini, philological documents and the proofs were "the soul of history." "The rites, the people, and the ages engraved in metals and in marbles seem the most authoritative and real testimonials, in the opinion of this century."[26] Along with a wise, historical-semantic analysis of names used in antiquity and their variations in meaning over time and in society, Bianchini's comments on the iconographic analysis of archaeological finds, reproduced in splendid plates collected in the *Storia universale*, were the backbone of his historiographical proposal. In good Galilean fashion, Bianchini never tired of insisting on the importance of facts and empirical proofs, and in the *Storia* he underlined the need for in-depth study of what we today would call the "material civilization" of the past, through an analysis of customs, way of dress, eating habits, and counting. Regarding chronology, Bianchini was opposed to the "vainglory" of nations, and years before the Newtonian theses, he called for the correlation of astronomy to chronology, studying the epochs in which eclipses and other astronomical phenomena had occurred by examining their traces in historical documents.

Completely foreign to the spirit of empirical and Galilean historiography that Bianchini wished to propose to scholars in his *Storia universale* was the work of another great friend of Celestino Galiani, Abbot Biagio Garofalo. In 1707 he published his *Considerazioni intorno alla poesia degli ebrei e dei greci* [Remarks about the poetry of the Hebrews and Greeks], which in the early years of the eighteenth century was the Italian work most inspired by the theories and results of Spinoza's *Tractatus*.[27]

Dedicated to Clement XI, the book was part of the renewal of biblical studies in Rome masterminded by Domenico Bencini, Vincenzo Santini, Francesco Bianchini, and Celestino Galiani. In the foreword addressed to Clement XI, Garofalo declared his intent to discover the profound philosophical, political, and religious truths that the verses hid. Referring to the Greek poets, he wrote: "I am investigating the origin and the effects of the passions, civil regulation, and religion of the Gentiles, and how their poets spoke according to the various sects that they professed."[28] One need only advance into the first part, dedicated to Hebrew poetry, in order to comprehend the unbiased and dangerous nature of this book. Ultimately, after many disputes, it was placed on the *Index* in 1718, even though the imprimatur had been signed by Giusto Fontanini and the author enjoyed the protection of the participants of the Circolo del Tamburo.[29] A highly esteemed scholar of Hebrew, Garofalo wholly adopted the suggestions in the seventh chapter of the *Tractatus theologico-politicus* for his analysis of the psalms. He affirmed that if poetry hid profound philosophical messages, careful study of every part of the language in which the verses were expressed was necessary to reconstruct the semantic value of the terms and, above all, the historical sense that they had in the era in which they had been used. Hebrew, gifted with exceptional expressive possibilities since it was "pure," "ordered," and well capable of expressing the "variety of action," therefore ought to be studied with semantic criteria that were historically relative.[30] A correct interpretation of the Hebrew in the sacred text was in this sense an exemplary application of those principles.

Boldly reiterating the theses of Spinoza and Richard Simon, Garofalo affirmed that all the most careful exegetes were convinced that "in many places the Bible [had] been corrupted by Hebrew copiers."[31] Saint Jerome's Vulgate is blatantly gap-ridden and full of errors because, in addition to his ignorance of the Talmud, Jerome did not have the necessary knowledge of ancient Hebrew and of the real vicissitudes of the people of Israel, who over the centuries had abandoned the use of the original language, adopting many Chaldean words. "To that it must be added that their best study was in the knowledge of the law, traditional ceremonies, and allegories, gaining little knowledge from criticism. It was such that at the time of Saint Jerome they did not even have an exact grammar."[32] The most refined analysis of the Book of Psalms in Hebrew and the ample corrections contributed by Garofalo confirm how profoundly Spinoza's *Tractatus* and Richard Simon's *Histoire critique du Vieux Testament* [Critical history of the Old Testament] influenced him. The abbot was quick to admit that in some biblical verses, the very concept of God came out distorted because of successive human "corruptions" in the text. In one entire psalm, he affirmed, "one perceives the meaning is confused and upset" because of the "blunder that they have made putting points [diacritical vowel marks] on Hebrew words."[33]

In the second part of the book, dedicated to Greek poetry, Garofalo's Libertine sympathies became evident in the pleasure with which he (well before Vico) unveiled "the seeds of profound wisdom" hidden in ancient fables. Commenting on the political significance that religious rites had held for the peoples of Greece, he asserted that Plato had "banished Homer from his republic" not because he was an atheist but because the poet had ridiculed the ceremonies in honor of the gods. All the great legislators, from Solon to Licurgus, had, on the other hand, believed the ceremonies essential "for their capacity to lead the ignorant people incapable of knowing God, to honor Him, and to observe the laws, from which peace comes."[34] Analyzing Hebrew and Greek cosmogonies, Garofalo sketched a picture of comparative history and an analysis of myths that is very important for understanding the ardor with which some Roman scholars interpreted the impulses for reform caused by Clement XI's election. The critical-philological analysis of the sacred text, the unbiased use of typical research tools in the field of profane history in order to reconstruct the entire development of human affairs, and the examination of the Bible as an important (but always human) document—these are all important features at play in Garofalo's work, and they testify to the presence in Rome of serious attempts at profitable comparisons with the disquieting but vital historiography of Spinoza, Simon, Le Clerc, and many others.

Celestino Galiani, living in contact with these illustrious masters,[35] soon had to face these same problems. Shortly after his acceptance of the duty of teacher of Sacred Scripture for the monks of the monastery of Sant'Eusebio in 1708, his *Conclusiones selectae ex historia Veteris Testamenti* [Select conclusions from the history of the Old Testament], the central nucleus of his lectures, appeared in Rome. Discussed in a public debate by Galiani, Bencini, Bianchini, and Don Bonifacio Pepe (one of the Celestines of the monastery), the work essentially revolved around the serious problems of biblical chronology and Isaac de Lapeyrère's impious texts. It was an official dispute, and Galiani demonstrated the strictest orthodoxy. In the *Dissertatio de vera aetate mundi* [Dissertation on the true age of the world] (1659),

Isaac Voss had maintained the need to adopt the Septuagint version of the Old Testament, which shifted the beginning of the world backwards by 1,400 years. Thus he hoped to slow the Libertine offensive that posited the immense antiquities of the Egyptians, Chinese, and Persians. Georg Horn had defended the Vulgate and traditional biblical chronology against this thesis. Galiani firmly took Horn's side, resorting to the classic quotation from Augustine's *De civitate Dei* [The city of God] denouncing the fabled antiquities claimed by Gentile peoples.[36] The *Conclusiones's* argumentative responses to all Lapeyrère's theses always centered around the most rigid orthodoxy: Adam, Galiani taught, was certainly the first man who appeared on earth. The existence of the pre-Adamites was a fable entirely without historical reality; sacred history embraced all human events within it and not only the Jewish people, as Lapeyrère would have. The Flood had not struck only a few areas of the earth but had been universal. The Bible must be accorded the dignity of a sacred and incorrupt work in which is condensed the entire history of humanity until Jesus Christ.[37] As if to confirm the high level attained in studies at the monastery, citations of some important works then at the center of European scholars' attention appeared in Galiani's writings, including such works as Pierre-Daniel Huet's *Demonstratio evangelica* [Evangelical Demonstration],[38] with its harsh rebuttal of Spinoza's theses, and John Selden's *De Diis Syris syntagmata* [Treatise on the Syrian gods].

But if we shift our attention from the official debates on sacred history held before prelates and students to Celestino Galiani's private studies in the small cell at Sant'Eusebio, the young monk's vaunted conformism and obedience to the Inquisition's directives are rapidly discredited. For example, in a series of notes entitled *De Aegyptiorum origine et antiquitate* [On the origin and antiquity of the Egyptians], he carefully discussed John Marsham's celebrated *Canon chronicus aegyptiacus, hebraicus, graecus* [Egyptian, Hebrew and Greek chronological model], whose theses stated the superiority of ancient Egyptian culture over Hebrew culture. It represented one of the most common and effective weapons in the hands of the Libertines and Free-Thinkers for the entire early eighteenth century. Galiani's interest, however, was not so much focused on carefully evaluating the different hypotheses on chronology (to which, however, he dedicated a careful illustration of Paul Pezron's book *L'antiquité des temps rétablie et defendue contre les Juifs et les nouveaux chronologistes* [The antiquity of time, reestablished and defended against the Jews and the new chronologers]).[39] Galiani seemed more attracted by the broad analyses of Hebrew, Phoenician, Assyrian, Egyptian, and Greek culture by Spencer, Bochart, Huet, Spanheim, Garofalo, and others. From the early stages it appears that his program of work was to be the respectful and meticulous evaluation of historical events and human affairs without attributing any privileged part to the Jewish nation as compared to the history of other peoples and without recognizing absolute truths in sacred text. He accordingly relegated to the background both the paradoxical reduction of all the great figures of Egyptian, Phoenician, or Persian tradition to Moses, *vir archetipus* (which Huet, Bochart, and Gherard Voss made to combat the dangerous myth of Egyptian or Chinese antiquity) and the obstinate and myopic Catholic and Protestant apologetics that denied any reality to histories different from the sacred and that had used the term "fabled" for the immense antiquities claimed by the Libertines.[40] In truth, what Galiani wanted to privilege in his notes was the pure historical data, as well as the study and examination of events beyond any sort of apologetic conditioning. He focused his interest on the historical reconstruction of such usages transmitted over the centuries among different peoples and on the analysis of sacred rites that harkened to a unique but indicative presence of devotions and cults similar to each other in all nations since antiquity. In short, in these early studies he found confirmation of the thesis of a natural religiosity common to all· peoples, an idea that would accompany him in his subsequent experiences.

His biblical studies are the most interesting documents from this Roman period, whose pinnacle was his appointment to the chair of Church History at the Sapienza University in 1718. Although his writings are rather fragmentary, they serve as a useful window for understanding his intellectual evolution. In Galiani's *Excerpta ex Hugoni Grotii et aliorum eruditorum notis in Vetus Testamentum* [Excerpts from Hugo Grotius and other erudite men's notes on the Old Testament], we find something of a dictionary of sacred history modeled after Grotius's *Adnotationes ad Vetus Testamentum* [Annotations on the Old Testament]. From Grotius, Galiani drew above all the practical outline for a synthetic illustration of his own ideas.[41] The real model of analysis that he followed in his notes was Spinoza's critical-philological model in the *Tractatus*, made even more persuasive by the methodological suggestions taken from the works of Jean Le Clerc and Richard Simon, whom Galiani knew well and cited with the greatest respect.[42] In fact he accepted Spinoza's theses of the successive manipulations of the sacred text without reservation, adding under the entry *Simulatio* that the Fathers of the Church themselves had accused the "Jews of having corrupted their writings."[43] Far from having always remained constant, Hebrew had undergone numerous variations, until it was confused with other languages of the region. He affirmed that all of the Jews who "wrote either grammatical or scriptural books later than 260, after the Hegira, wrote them in Arabic."[44]

His semantic study of Hebrew, which enabled him to compare later translations with original texts, was clearly useful in the analysis of the Book of Isaiah and the parallel translations of Saint Jerome and the Septuagint.[45] The comments under the entries for *Urim et Thummin* and *Serpens*, as well as the examination of the rite of circumcision in Genesis or the sacrifices for the purification in the Book of Numbers, were solid examples of biblical exegesis conducted according to a critical-philological method using comparative research. To understand the meaning of the Hebrew words "*Urim*" and "*Thummin*" (the two stones that Aaron placed on his chest to communicate with God, Exod. 28:30), Galiani reconstructed the Egyptian ancestry of such rites from the works of Le Clerc, Noël d'Alexandre, and, above all, through John Spencer's *Dissertatio de Urim et Thummin* [Dissertation on Urim and Thummin].[46] He performed a similar task in order to explain the point of Saint Jerome's translation where he had written about flaming serpents (Num. 21:6). Using the work of the learned Protestant Samuel Bochart, *Hierozoicon sive historia animalium sacrae Scripturae* [Hierozoicon or the history of animals of the Sacred Scriptures], which explored the historical reality of biblical fauna and explained its symbolic nature in the frame of Jewish culture and early Christianity, Galiani returned once again to the Egyptian origins of Jewish rites. He cited Spencer's famous *De legibus Hebraeorum ritualibus et earum rationibus* [On the ritual laws of the Hebrews and their reasons],[47] and he also identified the elements common to ancient pagan religions according to Herbert of Cherbury's *De religione gentilium* [On the religion of the Gentiles].[48]

Other examples of the comparative arrangement used in his analysis of sacred text can be found under the entries for *Gigantes, Deuteronomi varia loca, Demones,* and *Job,* in which Galiani often referred to Selden's *De iure naturali et gentium iuxta disciplinam Hebraeorum* [On natural law and according to the discipline of the Jewish peoples] and Spanheim's *Historia Jobi* [History of Job]. Along with his demystifying analysis of the purification rites in the nineteenth chapter of the Book of Numbers, his unconditional acceptance of Spencer's thesis that the historical practise of circumcision, as a historical event, was inherited from Egyptian religious tradition and therefore foreign to a primitive origin arising from the pact between God and Abraham, was yet another confirmation of the open-minded attitude with which Galiani addressed sacred text.[49]

In his most well-rounded work, composed on the Pentateuch, the *Observationes in Genesim et alias quatuor Moysis libros* [Observations on Genesis and the other four books of Moses], Galiani started addressing the matter of a possible pantheistic interpretation of Genesis. We know with certainty that when he wrote these observations, he knew firsthand Toland's thesis of a pantheist Moses, which was contained in the *Origines Iudaicae* [Jewish origins] and which would later be reprised in Giannone's *Triregno*.[50] This accounts for the common elements in the analyses of the Free-Thinker and the Catholic scholar. For the Catholic, the key question was the correct interpretation of the Hebrew verb *bārā*, 'to create'. Citing the Spanish biblical exegete Abraham Ibn Ezra (one of the authors whom Baruch Spinoza followed most), he wrote: "In his commentary on the first chapter of Genesis, Ben Ezra refutes those who interpret *bārā* as 'producing from nothing', and he proves with many examples that this meaning is not suitable, but rather [it means] 'to make and to form' *ex re praeesistente* [from a preexisting thing]."[51] According to Galiani, there were many opinions about the meaning of the word because the verb *bārā* seemed to acquire different meanings in other passages of the Bible. Strabo and Diodorus Siculus, Toland's sources, had given Moses a pantheist image; Marsham and Le Clerc appeared to share this interpretation, for they stated arguments for it based on the analysis of the Jewish people's modes of thought, as well as those of the Chaldeans, Phoenicians, and Egyptians.[52] Galiani, too, preferred Toland's thesis, confirming the need he now clearly perceived to read sacred text critically, just like every human document conditioned by different historical, linguistic, and cultural realities. Unbiased analyses of this type are found throughout Galiani's commentary on Genesis, but it is necessary to leave them aside and underline yet again the frequent influence of Baruch Spinoza in the works that Galiani dedicated to sacred exegesis, in particular where he discusses the authentic Mosaic nature of the Pentateuch.

Although supported in different ways by Abraham Ibn Ezra, Hobbes, and Lapeyrère, the thesis that the books of the Pentateuch were written not by Moses but at a later date was only fully and effectively illustrated in the *Tractatus*. Such a declaration elicited clamorous and extremely violent disputes in the learned world. Scholars have widely examined both the harsh reaction of a large part of official Catholic and Protestant historiography and Richard Simon's and Jean Le Clerc's trusting acceptance of the methods (if not the results) expounded in the *Tractatus*.[53]

Celestino Galiani accepted with conviction the Spinozan arguments and analyses of Le Clerc, on whose lead he recognized the essential attribution of the Pentateuch to Moses, without, however, silencing his doubts about the author's divine inspiration in the historical books or about the human corruptibility of the texts. According to Galiani, one key argument for evaluating the authentic Mosaic nature of the Pentateuch stemmed from the very history of the Jewish people before Moses. While no one seemed to doubt that the history of humanity from the beginning of the world until Moses could have been written by his hand, Galiani observed that many scholars "ask . . . whether he was the first to write what he committed to his works, or whether he drew what he wrote from older sources that afterwards disappeared."[54] Though he rejected Spinoza's radical solution of attributing the Pentateuch to Esra, in his analysis Galiani nevertheless confirmed the image of a Bible whose interpolations, textual corruption, and semantic transformations gave evidence increasingly against the hypothesis of direct divine inspiration.[55]

Accepting the critical-philological method used by Spinoza and Richard Simon and the results of the comparative analyses of Spencer, Marsham, and Bochart, Galiani was certainly aware that he distanced himself forever from the safe harbor of Catholic orthodoxy in order to confront worrisome and difficult-to-resolve problems, such as reconstituting Christianity on solid, rational bases. For some time, the most enlightened and receptive scholars in Italy and abroad had understood that one of the most dramatic aspects of the intellectual crisis that shook Europe lay precisely in the systematic destruction of long-standing certainties, a destruction effected by men like Spinoza, Marsham, Bayle, and Toland. Their examples of demystifying the sacrality of the Jewish people in ancient times, doubting biblical veracity, maintaining the existence of populations before Adam, and reconstructing the historical reality of the early Christians, all resulted in undermining the very foundations of the great edifice on which all Western society was built. Providing an outlet for the crisis of Christianity had, therefore, become a vital problem. Certainly one could respond by carrying matters to extremes, that is to say, by attempting to de-Christianize European culture, as the Free-Thinkers or various proponents of Continental Libertinism did (and both these groups later joined together with other currents in the great stream of the Enlightenment).[56] Men such as Jean Le Clerc, Samuel Clarke, John Locke, Malebranche, Leibniz, and others preferred, instead, to tackle the problem of internally reworking Christianity in light of the new discoveries and the spirit of the times. From the very start, Galiani, too, wished to pursue this path of renewal and reconstruction. In the second quarter of the eighteenth century, during his stay in Rome, he chose Newtonian natural theology with great conviction, and he weighed John Locke's "reasonableness of Christianity" with interest. It is necessary, however, to present a careful reconstruction of the stages in his complex evolution in order to verify how profound and well considered his decision in favor of a response to the crisis of Christianity was, a choice that was among the most advanced and receptive to the culture of Enlightenment thinkers.

4. The Socinian Tradition: Reason and Tolerance

Many of Galiani's writings contain a rationalist Socinian component, gained indirectly by reading Jean Le Clerc's works.[1] This tendency was expressed, however, more by adopting general interpretive schemes that privileged the active role of human reason in religious experience and paid greater attention to the problem of tolerance than by specifically tackling Socinian doctrines regarding the Trinity and Christology.[2] Galiani quite precociously appropriated Le Clerc's theses about the essential role that human reason could play in outlining a renewed Christianity capable of withstanding the offensives of the Free-Thinkers and Libertines. "Reason and revelation are just like two sons of the heavens who never fight with each other," Le Clerc wrote.[3] Nevertheless, the reason to which Le Clerc referred was no longer Cartesian reason, understood as a complex of principles or a rigorous system of truths; it was shaped methodologically as a type of procedure used in the search for certain or probable proofs allowing the identification of correlations between different ideas in all disciplines. Whereas Muratori followed the Galilean theory of the double truth and recoiled from Le Clerc in disdain, vehemently accusing him of Socinianism because of his dangerous

injection of human rationality into the world of faith,[4] Galiani proved receptive to gathering the modern features of Le Clerc's work, surely useful
for resolving his own doubts and disquieting thoughts.

There are many such examples of Le Clerc's moral influence over Galiani.
In the *querelle* that set Richard Simon and Le Clerc at odds over the issue
of correctly interpreting sacred texts, in the light of new facts revealed by
Spinoza and the critical-philological analysis that they themselves conducted,
Galiani's decision to favor Le Clerc's theses appears highly significant.[5] In
his *Sentiments de quelques théologiens de Hollande* [Thoughts of some Dutch
theologians], Le Clerc had set the rights of reason and individual conscience
against Richard Simon's Catholic authoritarianism. Simon, with his theory
of inspired scribes and the legitimizing power of the Church, had in fact
defended sacred text from Spinoza's accusation that it was only a human
document. He affirmed that all biblical books must be considered divinely
inspired, for Scripture's authority and substantially divine origin was guaranteed by the Church in its ancient and modern institutional forms—from
the first councils to the contemporary magistrate of the pope—all institutions whose existence and power had been conferred by God.[6] As we shall
see, this thesis was unacceptable to a scholar such as Le Clerc, who, in the
manner of reformed (and especially Socinian) tradition, saw in it a
confirmation of Catholic authoritarianism. Distinguishing between prophet-
ically inspired and historical books, Le Clerc, in his response to Richard
Simon, intended to vindicate the prerogative of reason for analyzing (with
fitting, critical-philological support) the religious myths and historical-so-
cial reality stated in contradictory terms in some parts of the Old Testament. In his *Ars critica* [Critical art] and in the part assigned to logic in his
Opera philosophica [Philosophical works], Le Clerc clarified the importance
that history, understood as human testimony, acquired in virtue of its evidence for confirming the values of faith.[7] Precisely because of its ontological connection to historical events, Le Clerc placed empirical reason in a
framework outlined in support of faith.

All this was quite clear to Galiani when he read the introductory lecture
to his courses on Church History at Sapienza University. The very title of
the broad and learned report, *Oratio de usu et praestantia ecclesiasticae historiae
in studiis theologicis* [An oration on the use and prominence of ecclesiastical
history in theological studies], leaves no doubt of the importance he assigned
to history. In front of an audience of prelates and students, he vigorously
and passionately identified a rationality within human deeds that he could
illuminate and confirm both through faith and through the analysis of the
transcendent. He affirmed that grasping the overall plan of historical events
allowed the clarification of the task that God had assigned to humans.[8] In
the final analysis, Galiani's plan to make theology rational, looking at it
through the historical evolution of the Church and the peoples of the earth,
was in a sense an initiative parallel to Locke's reduction of reality to expe-

rience. And in the realm of his intellectual itinerary, it steadily approached the "reasonableness of Christianity." Beyond his faithful acceptance of Le Clerc's themes, Galiani entertained contradictory ideas, which showed the considerable intellectual tension in the efforts he made to introduce novel ideas into a traditional context. On the one hand, his commentaries on the great works of Francesco Guicciardini and Carlo Sigonio[9] revealed particular sensitivity to the search for the internal logic of historical deeds, far from any geometricizing method. On the other hand, among his papers he left a draft of a work entitled *Chronologiae elementa* [Elements of chronology], in which erudition and rigid scientific mentality coexisted, if laboriously so.[10]

Galiani drew the most disquieting motifs from his confrontation with deism and some texts of European Libertine literature. We know that he was perhaps among the few Italian intellectuals who in 1717 had received the Free-Thinkers' "manifesto"—the French translation of Anthony Collins's *Discours sur la liberté de penser* [Discourse on the freedom of thought]— directly from its publisher Thomas Johnson.[11] With its irreverent and vehemently anticlerical spirit, the *Discours* would leave an indelible mark on Galiani, considering the vigor with which he always defended his and others' freedom of thought, despite myriad difficulties and clashes with the Inquisition. Collins passionately theorized about the right of all men to think freely, and in his brief writings he illustrated the key points of the Free-Thinkers' position: First was the dispute with the Fathers of the Church, whom he accused of having interpreted evangelical truth poorly, thus biasing subsequent debate. Second was the fraudulence of religions, a genuine obstacle to any freedom of thought. Demystifying the "stratagems of the priests," Collins placed pagans and Christians on the same level insofar as they shared the cult of superstition and the mysterious. "All these different frauds"—in his eyes the most ridiculous modern example being the "liquification of Saint Gennaro's blood"* in Naples—really aimed at conditioning the senses and enslaving the spirit, impeding free debate over ideas.[12] The deist thesis of a single natural religion common to all peoples and based on reason, in contrast to the myriad positive religions with their rites and superstitions, emerged clearly from the ironic words Collins used to outline the variegated panorama of beliefs existing on the earth:

> Brahmins who hold sacred the book that they call Shater; among the Persians who have their Zoroaster; among the Bonzes of China who govern their faith according to books written by the disciples of Fohé, whom they call the god and the savior of the world . . . the Talapoins of Siam who recognize for their Scripture the book of a certain Sommonokhon, who the Siamese say was born of a virgin and is the god the universe had hoped for.[13]

---

*If Neapolitan patron saint Gennaro's powdered blood turned to liquid inside its crystal reliquary on the occasion of his saint's day (19 Sept.), all Naples hailed the prospect of a year's good fortune—Trans.

No priests—"Romans, Mohammedans, Lutherans, Jews, Siamese, Presbyterians"—had an interest in seeking truth; instead, they had always been a source of fanaticism and superstition, and, above all, they embodied a sort of determination to prevaricate where freedom of thought was concerned. Ecclesiastical history was nothing more than a continual chain "of the dominant clergy's infamies." According to Collins, social disorders were not born from the debate over ideas but from their brutal repression at the hands of "the devout zealots" ready to partake in great massacres "manufactured for religious reasons." Atheism "has never troubled the states."[14] The virtuous atheist whom Pierre Bayle had described did not jeopardize the social peace of the state at all; on the contrary, the ideological and political confrontation unavoidably primed by his presence provided an incentive for free debate, the only guarantee of and motor force behind all human progress. Collins's intelligent pamphlet, which linked freedom of thought and social progress, clearly brought to light some salient points of the Free-Thinkers' proposal, ideas that came together in the deist hypothesis of a natural religion.

Galiani had the opportunity to ponder these theses in depth, through important readings of works by Herbert of Cherbury, Tindal, Wollaston, and others. Beyond the specific role that Christianity assigned to revelation, enlightened Catholics more open to the appeals of modern thought widely discussed the critical idea of a natural religion common to all peoples. Antonio Niccolini, a trusted friend of Galiani during his tenure as cappellano maggiore of the Kingdom of Naples, wrote to him in 1733:

> I have not seen the work of the bishop of London in response to Tindal and Wollaston; I am very happy that you believe it is good, because I am determined to read it, though I am persuaded that the need for a revealed religion is an argument far from being easy to prove.[15]

In another letter to an unknown person, Niccolini confirmed the sympathy that some deist motifs had evoked in him, and he affirmed:

> Let them think what they will about that, for their thoughts mean little to the world, since Catholics learned only revealed religion and its dogmas, and not reason, which must be applied more widely. In fact, reason must be used by all men, while revealed religion is of no use except for whomever seeks revealed religion and the believers, quite a small number in the vast sum of the human race.[16]

On the evidence of Galiani's manuscripts, the knowledge of deist and Libertine sources appears to have been quite a bit more significant than the buildup of Inquisitorial control in Italy would lead one to believe.[17] Fundamental themes in clandestine European literature, such as that of the materialism in the Pentateuch and the mortality of the soul (illustrated by Toland in the Letters to Serena and the Origines Iudaicae [Jewish origins] and repeated by Collins, Giannone, and others), were in fact at the center of Galiani's attention from his early years of study in Rome. Accepting Spinoza's and, above all, Spencer's conclusions about the absence of any reference in Mosaic laws or in the early customs of the Jewish people to a life different from the earthly one (not to mention rewards and punishments beyond the grave), Galiani appropriated some fundamental theses from the irreverent analyses of the Free-Thinkers, Radicati di Passerano, and Pietro Giannone. In his notes on sacred history, under the entry dedicated to the analysis of the Book of Leviticus, in which were mentioned the promises God made to those who observed His laws (Lev. 26), Galiani commented with exemplary clarity: "Read this verse and observe that as a reward for observing the laws, the Jews are only promised temporal things; and equally transgressors [are promised] temporal punishments."[18] Galiani's notes also contained the entirely historical and human sense of the internecine struggles between the various Jewish sects of the Karaites, Rabbinites, Pharisees, and Sadducees, who all sought to impose differing interpretations of Mosaic law. He identified the Sadducees as those who had most forcefully opposed any innovation in Jewish tradition, particularly regarding two very controversial theses: the soul's immortality and the angelical hierarchies.[19] His analysis went far beyond the results of Spencer's *De legibus Hebraeorum* [On the laws of the Hebrews] and of those who used this text as a source. Under the entry "The Resurrection of the Dead" in his notes on sacred history, in which he integrated Grotius's observations on the Pentateuch[20] with Spencer's comparative analysis, Galiani accepted the thesis that the doctrines on the resurrection of the dead and on immortality originated outside Jewish culture. He lucidly indicated the critical moment—in the apocalyptic literature of the years 198–129 B.C., and in particular in the second Book of Maccabees and in Daniel—when theories claiming that there is an afterlife were introduced into Jewish tradition.[21] In essence, he had a first-rate, comprehensive understanding of the ideas that in those years shook the European debate. For this reason, his decision to pursue a rational renewal of Christianity acquires greater value.

Giannone is another example of a great Italian intellectual who experienced similar problems, undergoing considerable influence from deist and Libertine literature. He proved, however, to be incapable—and willfully so, according to recent interpretations—of concretely approaching the problem of seeking a positive solution to the crisis in Christianity. Galiani, on the other hand, drew precisely on these results of Spinozan and deist analysis for the courage to attempt an arduous and painful rethinking. Both men were scholars of sacred history, although Galiani was perhaps less conditioned by any reliance on the great European commentators' works, since he knew Hebrew very well. Both were masters of Continental literature on Church history and the relations between Church and state, whether Protestant or Catholic in origin.

Nevertheless, Giannone and Galiani held profoundly different attitudes when dealing with definitively overcoming the crisis of the European mind. Giannone, intent on calling the very foundations of the papal state into doubt, threw himself into the impassioned search for the Mosaic origins of and the teachings of primitive Christianity, subsequently distorted by Hellenistic Pauline interpretations. In the end he was left a prisoner of an entirely political and religious analysis of the history of Western society; hence he neglected crucial turning points for modern culture, such as the emergence of new scientific realities, gnosiologies open to the spirit of the times, and moral and economic problems less conditioned by the oppressive presence of the Church. While Galiani shared many of Giannone's jurisdictionalist theses, as well as an aversion to religious intolerance and ecclesiastical hierarchies, because of his solid scientific and philosophical preparation, in the long run he proved more receptive to the need for renewal in broad sectors of European culture, a renewal that aimed to reconstruct a Christianity based on reason, in which the interweaving of moral appeals and firm principles of tolerance guaranteed real progress for society. It would be pointless to pronounce judgment on the value of either proposal. Rather, it is useful to underscore how Galiani and Giannone drew different conclusions from a common intellectual heritage, in a way analogous to what happened in England between the Free-Thinkers and the rationalist theologians of the Low Church, and in France between the followers of moderate and antimaterialist deism (such as Voltaire) and representatives of radical Enlightenment on a philosophical and political level, such as d'Holbach and Diderot.[22]

Grotius's *De veritate religionis christianae* [On the truth of Christian religion] (1622), republished by Le Clerc in the early eighteenth century, was certainly a fundamental reading for Galiani, concerned as he was with the reasonableness of Christianity.[23] In this brief text, Grotius traced the essential coordinates of a new way of conceiving of Christianity, privileging its moral contents to the detriment of theological problems. Starting from the *consensus gentium*, which guaranteed God's existence as an innate idea, Grotius affirmed that among the positive confessions, Christianity was the closest to the ideal and natural religiosity of peoples. Confirming the deist framework that was sharply criticized by contemporaries[24] and leaving aside any consideration of Christological and Trinitarian dogmas or of revelation's divine content, he focused his attention on the moral superiority of Christianity as compared to the Moslem and Jewish religions. He compared the laws of the Gospels to the crude and warlike morals of Islam and the insufficient ethical doctrines of the ancients, shedding light on Christianity's positive and innovative values, as compared to those reigning in the past.[25] The relationship between Jewish and Gospel moral systems was more complex. Even in this case, however, he affirmed the superiority of the Gospels, even if hesitantly and somewhat contradictorily, in order not to create too great a rupture between the Old and New Testaments. Without any apparent contradiction, Christ's new law of life rested on Jewish law, which, following Spencer's correct analysis of sacred text, he believed was blood-thirsty and entirely material.[26] The tendency to exalt the coming of the Messiah and the doctrines of the New Testament over the ancient Mosaic tradition, which was reduced to playing a legitimizing function through its prophecies, was linked in the *De veritate* with the reduction of Christianity to a simple moral doctrine that was the common heritage of deists and rationalist theologians.

As notes on sacred history in the *De veritate* prove, very early during his stay in Rome Galiani demonstrated his appreciation for this reduction of Christianity, and his ideas truly anticipated the *Reasonableness of Christianity*. Though stemming from different philosophical foundations—for in fact Locke had repudiated the thesis of the *consensus gentium*—Locke's reduction of Christianity to evangelical morals, which coincide in the final analysis with the natural law given by God to all peoples, nevertheless remains the *Reasonableness of Christianity*'s most evident result.[27] In comparison with the *De veritate*, Locke's work is rather more articulate in theological issues and is severely constrained by harsh disputes with deists, Socinians, and Libertines;[28] however, it marks the most advanced point reached in achieving a middle ground between the rights of reason and those of Christian tradition. Locke was quite familiar with the results of Le Clerc's bibilical exegesis and the teachings of the Socinian school, which numbered Le Clerc and Limborch among its followers in Holland.[29] He hoped to attribute new tasks and possibilities to reason where issues inherent in faith were concerned, emphasizing the decisive importance of Christ's coming and the evangelical message about the Mosaic "law of works."[30] According to Locke, the Messiah not only restored immortality to humans after the Fall, but, above all, he stood for the complete refurbishing of human rationality, definitively opening the path to salvation. In the final analysis, in Locke's work reasonable Christianity acquired the positive value of a liberating force whose historical significance had been to open, via revelation, the age of an entirely rational acceptance of evangelical morals, which would coincide (in contrast to what the *Essay* affirmed) with natural law itself.

Galiani appreciated above all the *Reasonableness*'s rationalist framework and the emphasis on the renewal of Christianity; he was less fond of some of its contradictory (if successful) conclusions, such as the new and in some ways instrumental role of revelation,[31] or the total identification between natural and evangelical morals.[32] In the *Reasonableness* he found confirmation of that empirical theology that he had learned (as had Locke himself) from Pierre Gassendi and, especially, from Philippe van Limborch's *Theologia christiana* [Christian theology].[33] In the chapter of the *Scienza morale* [Moral science] devoted to the problem "Of Natural Religion" and the one entitled "Of the Idea of God and His Existence," Galiani confirmed his acceptance of the new theology, maintaining (as had Locke) that the concept of God, far from being innate, was formed as a series of "simple ideas united together" and passed to us through "sensation and reflection."[34]

In reality, while Galiani recognized a great deal of the theology of Limborch, Le Clerc, Locke, and Clarke, he preferred an entirely philosophical and rationalist approach to the examination of religious problems. Locke keenly perceived the need to insert revelation into Christianity's intrinsic reasonableness, guaranteeing the evangelical message's continuity and legitimacy in a historical sense. Galiani did not particularly appreciate this need, and in the *Scienza morale* he mentioned revelation fleetingly in order to affirm that it was the only basis for the soul's immortality, which otherwise was not demonstrable rationally.[35] For him, knowledge of God was a gnosiological and scientific fact. The guarantee of divine existence lay in the universe's rationality, the laws of celestial mechanics, and the fascinating precision of Isaac Newton's universe-machine. This kind of Spinozan, intellectual knowledge of God, which could be reached independently of historical tradition, is particularly evident in the passages of the *Scienza morale* dedicated to the acquisition of the concept of God. According to Galiani, this concept was actually born in response to our desires and real needs regarding nature: "In short, picture all we like most, and you will find it included in the concept that we have formed of the most perfect Being."[36]

In the manner of the deists, Galiani privileged the hypothesis of a metahistorical God common to all peoples, thereby reducing Christianity to a universal morality. In his *Rappresentazione per la causa delle controversie cinesi* [A presentation of the case of Chinese controversies], he synthesized the entire case of the Chinese rites that had so shaken seventeenth- and eighteenth-century Europe, opening the door to the Enlightenment.[37] In this undated manuscript, presumably compiled during the 1720s at the request of some Roman prelate involved in the dispute, Galiani provided a meticulously detailed narration of the burning controversy that had pitted Jesuits against Dominicans since the sixteenth century. The former closed ranks in defense of the right of the Chinese to adore the biblical God with local rites and traditions; the latter, instead, were tenacious custodians of orthodoxy and, in the name of the purity of the Catholic religion, were opposed to any concessions to Chinese customs.

The dispute had involved even more complex problems capable of eliciting bold reflections on the examination of a reality such as that of the Chinese. There, a secular culture had developed much earlier based on justice and Confucian morality, capable of guaranteeing progress and social stability equal, if not superior, to what was enjoyed in Western nations, long supported by the foundations of Mosaic law and Christianity.[38] In the *Rappresentazione*, Galiani synthesized in three points the arguments that he would handle: (1) how the Church regulated itself in similar cases, (2) how the two parties behaved in this case, and (3) the actual state of the debate.

On the matter of tolerating other cultures, Galiani said that the Church had proved far more tolerant in its early centuries than in modern times. Citing Baronio and other illustrious scholars, he affirmed that Saint Paul had tolerated a number of Jewish features in early Christian rites. The first apostles behaved extremely cautiously when preaching to the Gentiles: "After Christ's ascension, when Saint Peter was left the head of the Church, he did not depart from the rules his divine master gave him not to impose all precepts to be observed to the new Christians at once, but to introduce them little by little."[39] Even though tolerance towards pagan traditions had often been a source of heresy, nevertheless it was a good thing, Galiani affirmed, which had been maintained until the time of Saint Ambrose, who "still continued the custom of offering food in the church as the Gentiles were seen to do."[40] Galiani cited and examined in great detail many examples of this notable tolerance, whose political roots also claimed his attention. In reality, what mattered to Galiani was faith's substance and its moral content beyond the rites and theological problems.

According to Galiani, risking social conflicts that might raise (among other things) serious repercussions for the relationship between the Holy See and the emperor, solely because the Chinese wished to worship the God of Abraham and Moses with the name of Tien, would have been a grave error. Cutting to the heart of the dispute, he recalled an important precedent: the first Christian preachers among the Gentiles had found disparate names to refer to the divinity, without, however, "causing the Catholic missionaries to raise too many objections."[41] Criticizing the theses both of the rigorists and of many of his own philo-Jansenist Roman friends,[42] Galiani exposed the risks of a rupture between Rome and Chinese authorities, provoked by the Catholic insistence that the Chinese use the European name for God. Certainly "utter and dangerous confusion, particularly among professors of the literary sect," would occur in China. He was quite familiar with the pantheist meaning that the term "Tien" held for Confucians, and he claimed to prefer an ambiguous definition of God to social disorder. Thus we glimpse his intimate conception of Christianity.[43]

Another example of Galiani's particular attitudes towards political and religious issues, an example that reveals his keen awareness of the importance of action within the Catholic community in order to attain an effective renewal of society, is the position he took in 1740 (at the behest of King Charles's government) in favor of introducing a colony of Jews into the Kingdom of Naples.[44] In the *Parere teologico sopra alcuni punti appartenenti all'introduzione degli ebrei ne' due Regni di Napoli e Sicilia* [Theological opinion about some points pertaining to the introduction of the Jews into the two kingdoms of Naples and Sicily], requested by José Joaquin Montealegre and Pietro Contegna in 1739, he forcefully confirmed his conception of a Church whose jurisdiction had to be limited to the conscience and spiritual field. In response to the first question, whether a prince had to ask the pope's approval in order to introduce heretics into his own realm, he responded negatively, and he insisted on the sovereign's complete authority in his own territories.[45] For Galiani the issue of the Jews was not a religious problem, "because, as has been said many times, the power and jurisdiction of the Church and the pope its head have nothing to do with [the Jews];"[46] the issue was only a matter of political choice and economic convenience. Not only could the Jews have free access to the territories of Catholic princes, but they had the right to construct their synagogues and to practice their own ceremonies, even if within strict limitations. Presenting a dark and gloomy sketch of the Sicilian Inquisition, Galiani invited the young sovereign to prevent its unwarranted assumption of jurisdiction over the Jews, because otherwise "they would be troubled with calumnies and false accusations and compelled to leave."[47]

In a difficult moment for the faith in the Kingdom of Naples in 1742, the blood of Saint Gennaro once again was maliciously late in liquefying because (according to some preachers) of the Jews' presence. This stoked ecclesiastical and popular reaction. When he asked in his *Parere teologico* that no distinctive sign be imposed on the Jews, Galiani had shown that he foresaw that the Neapolitan masses, "rude, ignorant, and full of childish superstition," would sooner or later be unleashed against them.[48] With the expulsion of the Jewish colony from the Kingdom of Naples in 1747, the party representing Catholic and noble fanaticism definitively triumphed over the initiatives of Montealegre, Contegna, and Galiani himself. Despite the negative outcome in this case, the *Parere teologico* remains an effective testimony of the determination to fight concretely for a different Church and society.

The religious crisis in the early eighteenth century, his deist and Spinozan readings, and his in-depth study of the history of the Church in its early centuries had sharpened Galiani's need to take into account all the currents of modern thought. The result was a doubt-ridden conception of culture that was so different from the post-Tridentine model constructed of certainties and absolute truths. The illustrious Francesco d'Aguirre, the greatest architect of the reform of the University of Turin, certainly guessed right when in 1718 he invited Galiani to flee Rome and come to teach in Turin: "I encourage you, Father Galiani, to come to enjoy our chicken, wines, and delights, and above all the philosophical and literary freedom that you hold so dear to your heart."[49] Total dedication to the cause of *libertas philosophandi* was, in fact, the most significant fruit of the collapse of Counter-Reformation Christianity's great certainties, a crisis that had involved Celestino Galiani during his stay in Rome during the 1710s and 1720s. His impassioned action as a reformer of Italian culture through the organization of academies, the dangerous trafficking in prohibited books on behalf of his friends and pupils,[50] and the protection of suspected and persecuted intellectuals (who included such prestigious figures as Antonio Genovesi), not to mention the courage with which he faced the Inquisition's multifaceted interest in him, could not be explained adequately if we did not remember those early Roman years that he spent investigating a Bible already irremediably desacralized by Baruch Spinoza, and intensely rethinking a Christianity renewed from its foundations.

Galiani's passion for studying Gassendi, Descartes, Galileo, and, above all, Newton was just another aspect of that anxiety to recapture ancient certainties. He set his faith in reason, science, and the wonderful mechanisms of the Newtonian universe-machine against the crisis of Catholic faith in its most orthodox and authoritative expressions. Galiani preferred an unlimited, rational analysis of all reality to the Galilean double truth, a source of hypocritical inhibitions on the impulses of reason in the field—nevertheless human—of divine knowledge. His studies of moral philosophy and economics, as well as his later receptiveness during the Neapolitan period to enlightened thought, were born in some manner in Rome, in his small cell in Sant'Eusebio, from reading Le Clerc, Locke, Collins, and, especially, Newton.

5. DELLA SCIENZA MORALE

One of the greatest needs the most receptive and sensitive Italian intellectuals were aware of in the first decades of the eighteenth century was the rethinking and formulation of ethical doctrines *ex novo*. With the crisis of Counter-Reformation values, which for years in Italy had represented a barrier against the flood of new problems and new solutions in this field, a season of political and cultural initiatives finally opened, culminating in the publication of Muratori's *Filosofia morale* [Moral philosophy] (1735). This work, published in Verona, was certainly the most advanced synthesis in the direction of modern thought produced in that period by a great Catholic intellectual. Celestino Galiani and enlightened Catholics fully perceived the need to redefine morals. In 1727, through the preface to Pierre Gassendi's *Opera*, they had reintroduced into Italian culture the problem of the Holy See's new attitude towards Epicurean morality, Christianized and presented under a new guise by Descartes. This manifesto contrasted Epicureanism to Stoicism, or the empirical analysis of human reality (with the interrelated reevaluation of passions) to the aprioristic philosophical premises of a heroic morality.[1] Their attempt lay within the general climate of the first half of the eighteenth century in European Catholic culture, a climate in favor of reconciling "worldly good and Christian life," as Robert Mauzi has expressed it. In fact, an entire branch of European Catholicism dedicated considerable effort in those years to "reconciling God and pleasures, [and] religion and the world," rejecting the radical Jansenist decision to "condemn the world." Even enlightened Catholics willingly fought in favor of the new "spiritual hedonism,"[2] always remaining, however, within an entirely orthodox frame of reference.

Though starting from these premises, Celestino Galiani's ideas widened to quite diverse experiences and perspectives, which were yet again stamped by his extraordinary intellectual vigor. His *Scienza morale* [Moral science], though written in the Roman period while he was in contact with Niccolini and Cerati, presents the reader with an Italian scholar's unique attempt to lay the foundations of a new ethical doctrine, unfettered by Catholic tradition and wholeheartedly open to the teachings of European culture. This work represents an important stage in Celestino Galiani's experiences: without it, we would find incomprehensible his later contribution to what has recently been called the maturation of an ideology in eighteenth-century Neapolitan culture receptive to the great debates of economic policy and dealing with Enlightenment themes.[3]

The work's structure, the themes treated, and the spirit in which Galiani comprehensively broached the problem of a new morality all reveal the author's jusnaturalist framework. The very title—*Scienza morale*, rather than *Filosofia morale*, as Muratori chose to call his famous work written a few years later—emphasizes his careful reading of authors like Grotius, Pufendorf, Spinoza, and Locke. From the complex movement of thought known as jusnaturalism, Galiani drew teachings particularly from the empiricist wing, ready to affirm the clear-cut separation between morals and theology, between law and religion. Headed by Pufendorf and Locke, its theses had been corroborated by Jean Barbeyrac's introductory manifesto to the French edition of the *De iure naturae et gentium* [On the law of nature and peoples] (1706),[4] with which Galiani was quite familiar. Here Barbeyrac illustrated the need for a "moral science" unfettered by any religious debt and carried out "through demonstrations," by borrowing methods and results from modern science.[5] Certainly Galiani's acceptance of jusnaturalism (or rather, as has been said, of the jusnaturalists' "method" aimed at identifying the great laws of universal human morality by trusting only in reason) would not have occurred without Spinoza's critical-philosophical reading and his conviction in accepting Newton's universe-machine.

Galiani clarified the overall design of his work from the very first page:

I have always believed that in order to understand what in moral science derives from nature, and in order to distinguish it from what recognizes its origin in the institution of men, it was quite useful to resort to imagination and consider man in his original state, which he was in during that first rude age when he began to exist, and then go on to understand his origin and progress, both with regard to his ideas and thoughts as well as his customs and moral science. In these pages I will demonstrate the thoughts that come to my mind just as they appear before me, without worrying about politeness of style or eloquence in explaining myself, since it is my intention to write only for my own use.[6]

The very plan of his research led Galiani inevitably to confront the central questions of the European debate: the meaning of the law of nature, the conception of the natural state or the "primeval state"—as he defined it, the relationship between religion and morals—and the great problem of the savages' customs and morals compared to European traditions. Taking sides in a clear-cut and definitive way, he firmly rejected moral innatism, and he wholly and unconditionally accepted the theses of large parts of jusnaturalism that were opposed to the *consensus gentium* and attuned to what has been called the "experience of diversity."[7] Galiani repeated Samuel Pufendorf's archetype of the first man, who fell from the clouds, slowly acquired cognizance of his senses and, through experience, was able to process data useful for reconstructing every aspect of the world's reality, including moral elements. "We shall see how this first man who came into the world deprived of any ideas and all information will behave, how he will put his faculties to use, and how he will advance in knowledge of things."[8] This scheme came to be applied rigidly throughout the work, without any concession to innatist tradition.

The tight connection between civil society and religion had to be relaxed immediately and completely. This was an essential premise if one wished to pursue the quest for a universal morality. The Libertines had maintained that the savages were atheists, extrapolating proofs favorable to such a thesis from travelers' testimony. But the dispute over the existence of atheist societies had become virulent only after Pierre Bayle had vindicated such a possibility through subtle arguments. As it circulated rapidly through Europe, the idea of atheist and virtuous men—and entire peoples—had served to reinforce the image of diverse moral behaviors among nations, causing all European apologetics to come to the defense of the hypothesis that all peoples of the earth shared a universal consensus and an innate concept of God.[9] In reality, the problem of societies of atheists was linked to two great themes continually at the center of discussion in Europe: the interpretation of the religious phenomenon and the theoretical possibility of entirely secular morals.

Galiani was perfectly aware of the vastness and the significance of the debate. In 1725 he was among the few Italian intellectuals to receive Giambattista Vico's *Scienza nuova prima* [First new science] with a dedication from the author.[10] As the most recent studies have demonstrated, Bayle's theses of the virtuous atheist and atheist nations formed the nucleus of Vico's arguments.[11] Rejecting Pufendorf's line of thinking (so dear to Galiani) regarding a secular history of humans "thrown into this world without care or divine help," the Neapolitan Vico had ingeniously reinterpreted the phenomenon of religion, presenting it as the driving force behind human history.[12] According to Vico, atheist nations had never existed historically, since the very formation of human society had stemmed from religious ceremonies and the first rough altars. In fact, passage from the feral state to the familial state had come about following the formation of a collective psychology of the divine, demonstrated by the fear of sin, modesty, and other signs that ultimately deferred to the religious phenomenon. In the familial state, significantly defined as the "age of the gods," Vico had found signs of a profound religiosity everywhere, even if expressed in forms so terrible that they induced him to write about the ferocious aspects of "most inhuman humanity" in the last edition of *Scienza nuova*.[13] Unlike what Bayle, Locke, and Gassendi had maintained, Vico had perceived traces of an intense religiosity among savage Americans, too; in the framework of the evolution of the single nations, they lived in a period preceding civil society that had nothing in common with the age of feral vagrancy. Galiani, who in precisely those years was pondering problems analogous to those treated by Vico in the *Scienza nuova*, must have read the latter's harsh accusations against Bayle's hypothesis and in favor of universal consensus; nevertheless, the conclusions he reached were totally opposite to those of Vico.

Galiani, in fact, shared Pierre Bayle's confidence in virtuous atheists, and he did not hesitate to paraphrase a passage of the *Dictionnaire* in his *Scienza morale*: "The true principle of our behavior lies so little in the speculative judgments that we form out of the nature of things, that there is nothing more common than seeing orthodox Christians who live badly and Libertines of conscience who live well."[14] The concept of God is by no means common to all peoples, as Christian apologists stated and as at different times Muratori, Vico, and Genovesi were to maintain.

> We understand from the ancient stories and the reports of the travels made by our contemporaries, above all to America, Africa, and Asia, that there were once and still today are entire peoples—almost all those who call themselves savages: in America particularly the Iroquois and the Illinois, in Africa the Kaffirs, the Monotrosapi and other peoples, and in Asia many of the Indians—who do not have in any form that concept of a most perfect being which we express with the name of God. Instead, some of them have no religion at all, and no concept of something superior of which one could hope for or fear anything.[15]

The atheist nations were, therefore, a reality. According to Galiani, the history of the world contradicts Vico's thesis, which attributes an essential role to religion. The two thinkers reconstructed very differently the ways in which men came to acquire the concept of God, and the divergence hinges on the different importance each assigned to religion in the evolution of peoples. For Vico, humans had first been "great beasts" and then "philosophers," and his concept of God was psychologically fed by fear and by violent and irrational emotions.[16] On the other hand, for Galiani the phenomenon of religion was essentially bound to human rationality and never to emotions, and, most important, it had nothing to do with the entirely earthly development of humanity.

> The man we suppose fell from the clouds, who alone in the midst of uncultivated and uninhabited jungles goes all day around searching for acorns or apples to eat, would find it difficult in his miserable state to elevate his mind to seek sublime truths. The sciences are the daughters

of reflection, and reflection recognizes as its mother leisure, quiet, and the easy life. When man, not distracted by necessities of the body and life, can turn his thoughts where it pleases him most, then he usually dedicates himself to seeking the hidden causes of the effects evident to him. Therefore, as long as the humankind scattered through the jungles has led a forest life similar to what the Iroquois and the Illinois are said to lead in Louisiana today, one can believe he made little or no progress for himself in knowledge of truth. But once the cities were formed, the ownership of goods introduced, and the skills most necessary for comfortable living found, then many found themselves in the state of not having to think about needs of the body, and therefore they enjoyed tranquil leisure, and quite a few of them were able to apply themselves to reflecting on their own ideas and hence to giving birth to the sciences.[17]

In order to set up a new moral science, Galiani was forced to solve another preliminary problem, the correct definition of the state of nature and natural society. Even on this problem he did not hesitate to align himself with positions similar to those of Locke. His idea of the "primeval state" differed somewhat from Hobbes's conception and from that of all the scholastics regarding the virtual opposition between *societas naturalis* and *status naturalis*. His ethnographic documentations were up to date, for he possessed the important study by the Jesuit Jean Lafitau, *Mœurs des sauvages ameriquains comparées aux mœurs des premiers temps* [The customs of the American savages compared to the customs of the earliest times] (Paris, 1724), which led him to conclude that a natural society had temporally preceded the formation of an institutionally conceived state.

But will our savages form some society among themselves bound by certain laws and with some kind of government? From the description that Father Hennepin gives of Louisiana, it appears that the Iroquois, the Illinois, and many other peoples of North America still live without any form of government, totally independent of one another. What is more, they do not have laws, they do not use iron, there is no ownership of goods, they do not cultivate the countryside, but they live entirely from the fruits and grasses that the land spontaneously produces, and principally from hunting and fishing. From the above-mentioned report, one still finds in the southern part of Louisiana that men go entirely naked, and the women barely cover those parts we call shameful with a strip or two of animal skin. Each [man] takes several wives, and they live together as long as they are both content, but at the pleasure of either the man or woman alone, they can go their separate ways and become wife of another man or husband of another woman. Perhaps just like in North America our savages lived independently from each other, all equal among themselves for thousands and thousands of years, and the only one richer was he who was more skilled at hunting.[18]

Hobbes and many other scholars had not yet considered the patriarchal familial nucleus as the embryo of society, but as a feature of the state of nature dominated by conflicts. For Galiani, who yet again restated Pufendorf, these nuclei were already small "societies" able to open the door to successive evolution towards forms of government.[19] His conception of the state of nature was not the Hobbesian one of a fierce battlefield among individuals but that of a generally peaceful existence led by men who aspired to live in a community and to share the better part of disposable goods equitably. To Galiani, the usefulness that each individual gained from the solidarity of the group seemed to be the true lever that moved the mechanism of human evolution towards social institutions.

> From what has been said so far, one gathers first of all that these men who above were thought to have fallen from the clouds naturally would then shortly begin to form some small societies. Second, man is by nature a social animal, that is, he has been produced to live in society with others of his species so that each may help the other.[20]

In Galiani's view, humans associated out of interest and utility. For Vico, it was the collective psychosis of the fear of God that convinced those who lived "in solitude from fierce beasts" to hide themselves under cover. "Dwelling there with some women out of fear for the perceived divinity, under cover, through religious and modest carnal intercourses, they celebrated matrimonies, and they had some children and thus founded families."[21]

To an attentive reading, though Galiani's *Scienza morale* is completely foreign to Vico's work in spirit and overall assumptions, it nevertheless exhibits traces of the *Scienza nuova prima*. For example, in order to negate the Libertine thesis of the world's eternity, both authors resorted to what Galiani defined as the "suave words of Lucretius." Among other things, Galiani appropriated Vico's idea of diverse evolutionary rhythms in the individual nations, precisely the argument that discredited the common belief in a single historical progression for all humanity.[22]

> We know in what state many of the American peoples were before our Europeans introduced some culture with Christian religion into that vast continent, and they still are today. They were wretches entirely deprived of any science and any art . . ., almost in a state similar to the inhabitants of England when the Roman armies entered for the first time, as Caesar's *Commentaries* and Tacitus's *Life of Agricola* recount. And as Tacitus tells us, the ancient Germans were no different at all from the ancient English in their simplicity and crudeness of lifestyle.[23]

Galiani maintained that the world was young, principally on the basis of the hypothesis (entirely foreign to Vico's thought) that cumulative scientific knowledge was the common patrimony of all humanity. In fact, despite the great successes of science, he held that its overall level would have been much higher if the world of nations was much more ancient than orthodox chronologers affirmed.[24] In order to theorize a moral science based on completely renewed ideas regarding traditional innatist philosophies, and in order to grasp the rational and universal elements of those laws that regulate the ethical behavior of peoples, Galiani resorted to a fundamental concept of jusnaturalism—that of a natural law through which one could define human behavior and the very concepts of virtue and vice. This was how he reached the heart of the moral science that Locke had sketched in his *Essay*. In a Lockean fashion Galiani in fact inverted the meaning that the jusnaturalists customarily attributed to the notion of natural law as an expression of the people's civil rights from below. He configured natural law as a direct emanation from above of the divine legislator, who with His existence guaranteed its binding character for all created things.

> First, he who says "law" presumes a legislator, that is, a superior, [and] subjects under his command, for the law is nothing more than a decree or a command by which a superior imposes on his subjects the obligation to regulate their actions in the manner that he prescribes for them. Therefore by "law of nature" we merely mean a law that can be known through the contemplation of human nature.[25]

One must not be deceived by this preliminary theological definition of natural law. The God that Galiani hypothesized limits Himself to guaranteeing the binding character of those norms, although Galiani gives further details about the relationship between the divinity and natural law itself. Actually, once Galiani eliminated universal consensus and the innatist and intellectualist philosophies as the path for reaching the definition of an objective order, all that remained were the empirical data provided by the historical multiplicity of moral traditions, the denial that religion played an essential role in human affairs, and the comparison between the "positive laws that can change and cancel themselves" and the laws of nature that are "eternal and not subject to any mutation."[26] How, then, does one identify these eternal norms, common to all peoples? From the start Galiani aims to document the stubborn human search for happiness and pleasure in every historical period, everywhere. Man "by nature flees pain and loves pleasure. Thus in all his actions he will flee those things that will cause him unpleasant sensation, and he will embrace those from which he will receive pleasure."[27] The many examples capable of supporting this thesis led Galiani to overcome Gassendi's traditional Epicurean approach, tolerated in enlightened Catholic circles, in favor of what has been called the "philosophical and psychological" doctrine of "pleasure" posited in Locke's *Essay*.[28] Here the simple ideas of pleasure and pain had acquired gnosiological value in the process of constructing a universal moral science unfettered by historical moralities. Considered as two emotions fundamental to human activities, pleasure and pain, precisely in virtue of their positive or negative import (entirely outside any human will), were real points of reference for establishing rules of behavior common to all humanity. Galiani demonstrates his grasp of the broad importance of the *Essay*'s theories when he reaffirms the definitions of good and evil in relation to pleasure and pain:

Pleasure and pain are simple ideas that we receive through the senses and reflection, and as simple ideas they cannot be explained but only known through experience. Some sensations—and it is the same for thoughts—are indifferent, and they are not accompanied either by pleasure or by pain; others on the contrary [are accompanied] by pain or by pleasure, some more, some less.

Things are called good or bad in relation to pleasure and pain. We call good whatever serves to produce and increase pleasure in us, or to diminish and shorten any pain, or to gain or preserve our possession of some other good, or the absence of some evil. And on the contrary we call evil whatever serves to produce or increase pain in us, or to diminish some pleasure, or to cause us some evil or to deprive us of some good.[29]

The definitions of happiness and misery—again in relation to pleasure and pain—followed.

Even though Galiani interrupts himself the very moment he faces the revision of all the usual moral categories in the light of such clear theoretical premises, the *Scienza morale* leaves the reader the impression of a work precociously open to the spirit of the century, considering that in 1750 Italian culture, involved in a dispute that "shook all Italy," still refused to consider the need for an entirely rationalist morality. Franco Venturi reconstructed the entire debate caused in Italy by Maupertuis's *Essai de philosophie morale* [Essay of moral philosophy] (1749), in which was theorized the possibility of a mathematical calculus of pleasures and pains. (Venturi has rightly written that the dispute enables us to identify "the new orientation—in Italy as well—of philosophical and scientific thought towards an entirely economic vision of reality."[30] However, Francesco Maria Zanotti's response in the *Filosofia morale secondo l'opinione dei peripatetici ridotta in compendio* [Moral philosophy according to the Aristotelians reduced to a compendium] (1754), reprinted throughout the nineteenth century, rejects not only the possibility of such a calculus but also any concession to hedonism in the name of Italian humanist tradition. Zanotti's work also allows us to verify the uniqueness and interest of Galiani's experience. In the *Scienza morale*, utilitarianism is conceived as the true driving force of history. Throughout his existence, writes Galiani, man

not only abhors pain but instinctively is of a nature most inclined towards pleasure and the easy life, and consequently he is by nature inclined towards society, that is, towards living in common with other men, where he encounters far greater comforts and joys than in solitude.[31]

In the *Scienza morale*, divine work is limited to guaranteeing the binding character of natural law, whose discovery is, however, an entirely human and earthly occurrence. The suitable criteria for delineating this natural law are utilitarianism and the essential information furnished by pleasures and pains. It would be futile to comb Galiani's rationalist ethics for concessions to the teachings of the Gospels (which are never cited) or the Catholic tradition (whose great moralists are not considered). Galiani's criteria for reaching a universal rule have nothing to do with the morals of the positive religions. How he analyzes the serious problem of the soul's immortality is significant; its existence cannot "be demonstrated by natural reasons," but it has a positive function as a restraint on peoples' intemperances, without any theological implications.[32]

But the most disquieting aspect of the work is Galiani's self-conscious intervention in the European debate on moral determinism begun by Anthony Collins. In 1712 Collins had published in London *A Philosophical Inquiry Concerning Human Liberty*, and the entire work was translated into French in Des Maizeaux's famous *Recueil*, and thus it was read with interest in the circle of enlightened Catholics.[33] James O'Higgins has called this treatise "a formidable synthesis of the arguments in favor of determinism,"[34] for Collins skillfully uses Hobbes, Spinoza, Bayle, and Tindal to support the thesis that moral choices are conditioned by nature. Denying that moral choices were indifferent, Collins cited Locke's *Essay* as the reference text for a complete illustration of his theses. The book caused a hornet's nest of controversy throughout Europe.[35] In England, Samuel Clarke restated his old hypothesis that a clear-cut distinction existed between moral and natural necessity, and he retorted harshly, seeking (among other things) to ward off the Free-Thinkers' blatant use of Locke's prestigious name. If there is one part of the *Essay* that lends itself to a deterministic reading, it is the section dealing with the problem of human freedom. While defining freedom as the ability to make impartial choices, Locke had clearly said

> but yet some ideas to the mind, like some motions to the body, are such as in certain circumstances it cannot avoid, nor obtain their absence by the utmost effort it can use. A man on the rack is not at liberty to lay by the idea of pain, and divert himself with other contemplations.[36]

Contemporaries recognized a further confirmation of determinism in Locke's theory of "will," with which he demonstrated that the root of human behavior lay not only in the search for "greater good" but also in something more profound, a real and genuine uneasiness of the mind always present even in the state of satisfaction because men fear losing this state.[37]

Galiani was quite familiar with the exact terms of the debate. In a series of notes entitled *Ricerche sopra la natura della libertà* [Research into the nature of freedom],[38] he had repeated Clarke's example of the watch to explain "noncognizant agents," without, however, accepting the Low Church theologians' classic distinction between moral and natural necessity. His position on the issue is rather complex. He wrote:

> It is certain that if the only thing in nature was matter, which moved according to certain necessarily determined laws and from absolute and geometric necessity, there would be no virtue. Virtue presumes that there

is a law, [and] that such a law is recognized, and that one is able to operate in conformity or not with this law.[39]

The law in question is natural law, on whose articulation the entire *Scienza morale* rests. The author, however, explicitly connects the rejection of materialism to a profoundly heterodox conception of natural law. On the question of the relationship that exists for Galiani between God and nature, or rather between God and natural law, an attentive reading of the work plainly shows the compelling character of natural law and its inexorably coherent obedience only to itself. Although a divine work, in Galiani's reflections natural law eventually conditions even all of God's actions themselves. No one can escape the dictates of natural law, he affirmed:

> In order to develop this intricate subject matter, it should be noted that God certainly is quite free, as is usually said, in *operibus ad extra* [external works], nor is he subject to any necessity. He could create this world or make another completely different from the present one, with other laws of motion and other moral laws. And that is agreed, but it cannot even be denied that some of God's activities *ad extra* have what is usually called hypothetical and conditioning necessity, based on some free decree of God Himself, that one presupposes. For example God can create a triangle at His leisure. But He cannot decide to create a triangle without simultaneously envisioning a figure of three sides in which two of them are in some way always greater than the third.[40]

Given that pleasures and pains are essential and conditioning elements for evaluating this entirely human, earthly, and rational natural law, to which even God owes obedience, the circle closes, and the dangerous conclusions that Celestino Galiani had reached in his impassioned and open-minded research "into the early origins of moral science" become evident.

6. The Many Faces of Enlightened Catholicism

Ludovico Antonio Muratori's *La filosofia morale esposta e proposta ai giovani* [Moral philosophy explained and proposed to youths] (1735) was published by Angelo Targa in Verona. It had been written in response to the need all Italian intellectuals finally recognized for a new compendium of morality that would replace the old treatises of Aristotelian ethics, which were strongly conditioned by the Catholic Church's Counter-Reformation choices. The work achieved tremendous success: by 1739 six editions had already appeared, followed by many others in the following years.[1] In it, Muratori took the great French Catholic moralists—Nicole, Fénelon, and La Bruyère—as his models when he proposed an ethical model that would remain a true point of reference for the entire field of Catholic reformism and for a great part of Italian culture during the Enlightenment, for their balanced and moderate solutions were always attuned to the problems of the century.

In the *Filosofia morale*, as had also been the case for Galiani's *Scienza morale*, the privileged reference was definitely John Locke and the theories he expounded in the *Essay Concerning Human Understanding*. The two works represented two different methods for dealing with the *Essay*'s results. Galiani ultimately remained fascinated by Locke's empirical reasoning and the foundations of a new ethical doctrine—secular and rationalist—illustrated in the treatise; Muratori, on the other hand, clearly noticed the serious dangers hidden in Locke's hedonism and utilitarianism, and he set up his *Filosofia morale*, solidly anchored in the Gospels and the teachings of the Church, as a deliberate alternative.[2]

Bitterly arguing against the thesis of moral relativism among the peoples that was expounded in the *Essay*, Muratori wrote on behalf of a single, innate morality:

> Here now we wish to respond, it is a shame that great men arrive at the point of wishing to discredit human reason even with the example of barbarians and villains. But if these barbarians do not consult the reason God granted them as well, it is no marvel if they do not distinguish between certain actions badly done and those well done. . . . The most subtle English philosopher Locke, who in his book on human understanding (or rather on human intellect) has also spread a poison about which not everyone has reflected, claims that man's mind does not hold any innate principle or moral rule.[3]

Muratori's rejection of moral relativism accompanied an impassioned vindication of the *consensus gentium* and theological innatism, the true basis of Christian religion. Muratori contrasted the natural and empiricist theology theorized by the Boyle lecturers (and publicized in Italy by enlightened Catholics) with Catholic tradition and Cartesian rationalism.[4] His idea of happiness differed from that of Locke, above all in the role assigned to pleasure and pain. While recognizing the existence of passions and the human will to seek pleasure always and everywhere, he staunchly affirmed that God had "fabricated and prepared" perfect happiness "from the beginning of the world in his heavenly kingdom," but not on earth.[5] Thus Muratori rejected the *Essay*'s thesis of a psychological morality essentially bound to emotional features.

> Locke, the famous but pernicious author of the treatise on understanding, claims that it is not good that determines the desire to want or to long for any object but, rather, uneasiness, the word corresponding to our Italian *disagio*, *scontentezza*, or *inquietudine* [inconvenience, discontent, or anxiety].[6]

For Muratori it was extremely serious and dangerous to customs and the social order to declare humans' incapacity to control their own desires and own emotions completely. "As for me, I confess the truth [when] speaking of happiness suitable for the man on earth; I do not know how to convince myself to base this happiness on pleasure."[7] His solution argued bitterly against what Locke ("false Christian, but also a perverse philosopher,"[8] he wrote without leniency) had affirmed, and it again followed in the tradition of Catholic Stoicism. Passions certainly exist, he affirmed, and they have their weight, but humans can and must control them. A Christian morality, respectful of the Gospels' message and above all aware of the heavenly dimension of human happiness, does not have to shirk from the duty of indicating the path for regulating passions and exalting heroic virtues. "The substantial and true happiness to be hoped for on the earth is not already offered by pleasure but, rather, by the tranquillity of the mind and by possessing a quiet heart."[9]

Muratori depended primarily on reason and revelation to identify the theoretical premises behind a morality consonant with the times. His reason was quite different from Locke's, and from the one that Galiani had unhesitatingly vindicated as the privileged tool for investigating the very foundations of moral science. Muratori insisted on the concept of a reason granted by God in order to "illuminate" good and to distinguish it from evil, listing the ways in which many men had betrayed reason with their attitude. Among these were the "faction of slothful reason," formed by those who limited themselves to mere trifles, and the faction of "reason betrayed," composed of evildoers, thieves, and the lustful. He wrote: "I say nothing of flirtations, nor of the assemblies of both sexes that by now have become the daily and even nightly fare in some cities. And even less do I wish to speak of the fops, tearful invention of these recent days." He constrasted these groups to the men of "well-employed resaon," that is, the good fathers of families, the hard-working and obedient farmers, the honest merchants, the nobles who abandoned a life of waste and luxury to work concretely for the benefit of society, and the intellectuals who taught healthy virtues.[10] In the *Filosofia morale* he formulated the design for a Catholic society attuned to the material necessities of the weakest components, based on ancient virtues of the great humanist tradition and sensitive to the need to promote a harmonious development of peoples, all, however, without social conflicts, firmly excluding the *Essay*'s utilitarianism and, especially, its individualism. For Muratori, Locke was dangerous because he left the field open to hedonism and the individual pursuit of pleasure, in such a way rending that social peacefulness, that model of an integrated, unshakably cohesive community that had to be the first objective of any morality. Muratori concluded that one had "to be content with little," respecting the political order as it had been determined historically in every nation, since one had to expect no definitive improvements from governments run differently from contemporary ones, and the inequality must be accepted in a Christian fashion, mitigated by charity.[11] Only healthily educated minds able to check passions in a Stoic way would guarantee such conditions. These concepts would also be reiterated and expressed more coherently, openly taking account of contemporary needs, in *Della pubblica felicità* [On public happiness] (1748). This work's overall significance, beyond a vigorous call to princes to think more about their subjects' happiness, would again be its rejection of Locke's morality and its utilitarianism, rationalism, and vision of a strongly dynamic secular society open to social conflicts.[12] In the end, for Muratori true happiness always remained the heavenly one.

The disparity between Muratori's and Galiani's moral doctrines lies not only in their results: the very philosophical frame of their research was in fact profoundly different. To see this, one only has to note the meager and delusory pages Muratori dedicated to serious problems debated among European intellectuals, such as the soul's immortality, the God–nature relationship, proofs of God's existence, and, most important, the value of revelation and reason in Christianity. Every doubt and perplexity is formulaically resolved, after a brief debate, in the name of the "infallible authority and revelation of Christ our Lord."[13] In the final analysis, the philosophical and ideological background appears as a sort of triumph for Catholic certainties, on whose very solid bases (and not on others) it would be possible to erect new morals. Galiani applied himself to the "search for the early origins of moral science" in a decidedly different spirit. Rather than discovering new laws, Muratori collected and explained to youths norms of behavior that were illuminated by an authentic determination for reform but that still remained within the realm of Catholic tradition. In contrast, Galiani scientifically sought the foundations of an ethics renewed only with the cognitive tool of reason, without any religious conditioning, with pride and uneasiness of an already enlightened quality. His doubts, perplexities, and open contradictions inevitably came into conflict with Muratori's ancient certainties. Both continually appealed to reason (and Muratori perhaps more so than Galiani himself), but a chasm separated their interpretations. Muratori, as Franco Venturi has written, lacked a true "faith in reason, and the determination to impose it was also absent; and that faith and will would become the force behind the wave of Enlightenment."[14] Muratori conceived of reason as a reassuring tool, a kind of good sense—or rather of "good taste"—that illuminated good and bad without ever coming into conflict with the truth of the faith that was ontologically superior to it. His acceptance of Galilean reason yet again clarifies the eighteenth century's different use for Galileo's double truth. But already, the separation of the operative domain of faith from that of reason no longer guaranteed the room necessary for secular culture's progress, as it had until the end of the seventeenth century. In the end, such a separation reduced reason, confining it to fields easily neutralized by Catholic culture. In short, for some Catholic scholars in the eighteenth century, Galileism appeared to be the lesser evil.[15] Galiani rejected an interpretation, such as Muratori's, that limited the use of reason. With a spirit already attuned to the new, enlightened age, he did not place limits on critical thought, accepting (as Locke had) its use as a fundamental cognitive tool capable of handling empirical data and guaranteeing the in-definite advancement in human knowledge.

The turmoil caused by John Locke's works in the 1730s in Italy can be explained by the significance that those works assumed among Italian in-tellectuals based on their new method of conceiving reason. The arguments of Paolo Mattia Doria, Ludovico Antonio Muratori, and other scholars against the author of the *Essay* stemmed from their perception of the disruptive consequences of a message aimed at rationally explaining all reality. When Locke's *Essay* was placed on the *Index* in 1734, after years during which ecclesiastical authorities had paid scant attention to the English philoso-pher, harsh repressions throughout Italy accompanied that decision, and, as we know, Galiani was one of the hardest hit.[16] In 1722 Cardinal Davia, Galiani's protector and friend, informed Eustachio Manfredi that some en-lightened Catholics in those years read the English scholar's works, which he unhesitatingly characterized rather harshly.

I judge Locke a hundred times more dangerous than Machiavelli, for whom an exception is universally made in all licenses given to read prohibited books, because our Italian is no more than a nut who spoke with the limited vision of a little secretary of a very little and ever tumultuous republic. But the Englishman uses a method taken from the sciences of nobles and knowledge of the laws of nature and society to insinuate certain principles that seem universal, and without applying them he makes them serve as foundations . . . , fabricating a very perfidious atheism upon them.[17]

Far from sharing Davia's opinion, in roughly the same years Galiani began writing the *Scienza morale*, taking his cue from Locke's principles. His choices, radically opposed to a cultural climate in which illustrious representatives of Catholic reformism (such as Muratori) solidly closed ranks against the *Essay*'s rationalism, lead us to question yet again who Celestino Galiani really was, and, most important, what he represented for Italian culture. In light of what has been said, he certainly cannot be placed within historiographical categories such as Jansenism, deism, or the Enlightenment. He was not, as some have written, a first-generation Jansenist.[18] His friendship with Bottari, Cerati, and those who frequented the circle of the Archetto should not deceive us. His interests and research were very far removed from the problems of divine grace. Jansenism and its perennial and often abstruse arguments within the Catholic community seemed, in Galiani's eyes, to be a heavy restraint on the realization of an irenical and universalist Christianity, and he especially felt that Jansenism wasted precious intellec-tual energies that would have been better directed at pursuing objectives more important and useful to society. He affirmed these beliefs in 1715 when he wrote to Vincenzo Santini, then papal nuncio in Brussels, com-menting on the Belgian cultural situation.

It seems to me the scarcity of true learned men there [in Rome] is found everywhere; then again I believe that in those countries [Belgium], that blind and stubborn obstinacy of Jansenism has caused no little damage to culture. They read no books other than those they believe they can use to further their efforts; and the more sublime they are, the more the matters of grace confuse their minds and make them less apt for rigorous erudition.[19]

Galiani's nephew Ferdinando, whom he raised in his home, was very familiar with his tormented and free thought; indeed, he did not hesitate to respond to the archbishop of Palermo, Francesco Sanseverino, who had asked for insights into his uncle's supposed Jansenism. From the orthodox viewpoint, the profile he traced was far from reassuring:

Certainly my uncle was not a Jansenist; Newton was too much in his blood. Just what he was, I do not know. Perhaps even he himself did not know. He contrasted the good soul God had given him with the kind of life to which he devoted himself, the city where he lived, and the worldly life in which he lived. God knows what theories, or what perplexities, were the result![20]

Galiani's interest in deism and theological rationalism was quite a different case. Poorly hidden traces of sympathy for some of the Free-Thinkers' ideas can be found in the *Scienza morale*. Nevertheless, we should guard against the tantalizing temptation to imagine Galiani as a sort of Italian Abbé Meslier, leading a double life totally alien to orthodoxy in private and aligned with the positions of the Church in public. One can find many heterodox elements in Galiani's thought, even if they are fragmentary and at times contradict each other. This image of Galiani the Free-Thinker needs to be balanced against the Galiani who was bishop of Thessalonica and *cappellano maggiore* of the Kingdom of Naples, doubly bound to the Holy See and curial circles, without whose protection many of his cultural activities would not only have failed but would have had a tragic outcome for him.[21] Even if in tense moments he could take advantage of his position within the Church apparatus, he paid for it with the costly and certainly bitter price of silence. His place within the ecclesiastical institution guaranteed him considerable freedom of movement, and even the possibility of transforming its problems and receptivity to the European world through a very advanced political and cultural project, for which he sought to gain space and legitimacy within the immobile body of the Church. It is not possible to know, however, what all this meant to him deep down, or in what way or to what extent he believed he was acting within Catholic institutions and Christian religion. Nor is it our task to rummage in the corners of a conscience that was too complicated to fit rigid categories of orthodoxy and heterodoxy. It is difficult to establish a precise boundary in his thought between acceptance of Christianity and love of science, culture, and human reason. In reality Galiani was simultaneously victim and protagonist of that crisis of the European mind that afflicted the most sensitive and perceptive Italian intellectuals. The responses they formulated were different and at times at odds with each other: Muratori's Catholic reformism, attuned to the needs of the weakest, expressed in the formula of *Pubblica felicità*; the painful and radical theories of Giannone and Radicati di Passerano; the complex framework of the culture of the Veneto, with such figures as Vallisnieri and Conti; and, finally, Paolo Mattia Doria's Catholic populism and scientific counterrevolution. Among all these responses, Galiani's research bears the mark of the uneasiness and faith in human reason understood as trust in human cognitive power reaching beyond any providentialism and any religious impediment. It was this very faith that made him recognizable as a conscious advocate of Enlightenment culture.[22]

SIX

From the Natural Sciences to the Social Sciences: The Origins of the Neapolitan Enlightenment

1. The Twilight of the Investiganti's Heritage

On 16 April 1697, Giacinto De Cristoforo recanted his heretical theses on atomism and the pre-Adamites before Inquisitorial authorities.[1] It was a fitting conclusion to the so-called trial of the atheists, which, during the long course of its unfolding, had sealed the fates of Neapolitan and Italian culture in general. The extremely harsh repression unleashed by the clergy against the *novatores* [innovators] had greatly served to unveil the crisis of the Investiganti group. In fact, to blame their failure on the rabid invectives of Aletino and Inquisitorial efficiency would be at best reductive. In reality, there were other causes behind the progressive withering of that prestigious intellectual tradition. Thanks to the works of scientists like Cornelio, Di Capua, Borelli, Caramuel, and Porzio—to name only a few of the most celebrated—this intellectual tradition, because of its vitality, had guaranteed a renewal of Neapolitan culture during the second half of the seventeenth century. The Investiganti group was able to do more than work out a new scheme of gnosiological and philosophical doctrines that could be integrated into an organic system able to withstand Aristotelianism. Rather, this group had succeeded in cleverly bringing together Galilean experimentalism, Cartesian mechanism, and Epicurean and Gassendian atomism, along with the great heritage of Renaissance naturalism from southern Italy. Some of its greatest proponents advanced quite different proposals—Porzio's thesis of the mechanical order of the world is quite unlike Di Capua's chemical vitalism or Cornelio's metaphysics of an ether-mind attuned to understanding social issues, or even Bishop Caramuel's scientific probabilism. Far from being indicative of weakness in the face of the dominant Aristotelianism, these proposals became the most evident sign of the new culture's vitality and success. Beyond scientific merit, the Investiganti were important for

their peculiar and consistent role in the production of a concrete alternative to Aristotelianism, a doctrine no longer capable of representing the
ideologies of the Neapolitan *ceto civile*.*[2] At the very least, Aristotelianism
did not mirror the needs of those intellectuals who kept current with European (and especially French) culture and who felt that the rigid hierarchy
of the qualities and substantial forms and the logical-formal thinking apparatus—both transmitted by Aristotelian-scholastic and Thomist philosophy—
were inadequate when faced with the developments in society and thought.
Certainly the cultural and scientific renewal had for a long time proceeded
apace with the maturation of a new political consciousness.[3] From Francesco
D'Andrea to Giuseppe Valletta, the reading of Grotius's and Pufendorf's
works had shaped a kind of "Investiganti jusnaturalism" and had permitted
valid intellectual experiences in working out a new project, more or less
explicit, of the state and society.[4]

The group's professed naturalism, so naively disposed towards any dangerous overture—even materialist atomism and Spinozan theories—had become
an embarrassing burden at the very moment when Rome had decided on a
drastic turn of the Inquisitorial screw for Italian culture, obliging the *novatores*
to abandon their cause. But it was not enough. Several factors—new intellectual needs, particularly complex political developments tied to the new
position Spain assumed in the European scene after Charles II's death, and
the strong presence of English and French culture in both of the sides as-
sembled to fight the War of the Spanish Succession—had unavoidably exposed
the limits of a gnosiological doctrine no longer capable of embracing and
interpreting the altered Neapolitan historical and social circumstances.[5] An
examination of the works of Lucantonio Porzio, the last proponent of the
school who worked in Naples during the 1710s and 1720s, has already provided us the opportunity to demonstrate that, compared to earlier days, the
group experienced a scientific lag visible in their thesis of qualitative
experimentalism, which appeared at the same time that Newton's *Principia
mathematica* exalted the physico-mathematical method.[6] Antonio Monforte,
tied to Cornelio's teachings, argued vehemently against the study of history, further proof of the depth of misunderstanding among the most orthodox Investiganti regarding the increasing attention that Neapolitan culture
had begun to dedicate to the examination of human affairs.[7]

Historians have generally treated the Accademia Palatina del Medinaceli,
founded in 1696, as a window on the now visible difficulties that the followers of the Investiganti tradition faced in maintaining their prominent
position—if not outright hegemony—in southern culture. Scholars spoke
of the Neapolitan intellectuals' mentalist-Cartesian change of direction and
of a rapid decline in experimentalism and naturalism during those years,
and they identified Caloprese, Doria, Ariani, and others as the advocates

---

*The urban class between the aristocracy and the common people—Trans.

of this new direction.[8] The political and cultural need they expressed, directed at defining a gnosiological doctrine capable of understanding and giving scientific worth to historical research and the nascent civic sciences, has been interpreted as a further aspect of the problem.[9]

In reality the situation was rather more complex, and that "great engine of ambiguity,"[10] as the Accademia Palatina has justly been labeled, showed no evident signs of an abrupt metaphysical restoration at all. Within the academy, the Investiganti were numerous and wielded considerable influence. Philosophers like Caloprese and Doria clearly demonstrated the need to interrogate history in order to grapple with the most current political themes—the crisis of the Spanish regime in Naples and the task awaiting the *ceto civile*—and jurists such as Valletta were no less important for formulating political hypotheses, consciously starting with the meaning of history in the new civic science.[11] On a purely scientific level, the picture that emerges from the confrontation between the various components of the academy is anything but bright.[12] The old naturalism voiced by Galizia, Santoro, Lucina, and Porzio certainly found no valid alternative in Ariani's inconclusive, Neoplatonic mathematicism, for his isolated quotations from Galileo and Newton ought not deceive us. The Accademia Palatina truly marks the low point of Neapolitan science between the seventeenth and eighteenth centuries. Commenting on the *De syderum intervallis* [On the intervals between the stars] (Naples, 1699), Leibniz remarked that he found its author, Antonio Monforte, who was the greatest Neapolitan astronomer of those years, seriously misinformed about scientific progress throughout Europe, and he pitilessly exposed the isolation and backwardness of local scientists.[13] The hegemony that Cornelio, Di Capua, and Porzio exercised over the *novatores* for nearly half a century was harshly contested, as is evident from an examination of the academic lectures and debates that developed among the members. The Investiganti saw their prestige plummet precipitously within the academy. Echoes and hints of their school still probably influenced Niccolò Cirillo, Giambattista Vico, Pietro Giannone, and Francesco Serao, but a great cultural era had definitively ended. However, the important event of those years was not so much this waning, begun long before, as the rise of new needs that now characterized Neapolitan culture.

In the first twenty years of the eighteenth century, the hypothesis of the hegemony of mentalist-Cartesianism, which supposedly replaced the old tradition of Cornelio and Di Capua, proved to be narrow and reductive, incapable of evaluating the unrest caused by a deep gnosiological crisis that, in any event, brought about intense debates and explanatory confrontations between different philosophical solutions. At the dawn of the eighteenth century, the intellectual Neapolitans had left behind the Investiganti's dangerous and ultimately useless naturalism, and now they faced the arduous task of redefining a gnosiological model, using refined tools in order to develop a civic science that could preserve an open dialogue with modern

European science. There were numerous issues that they had to confront: the crisis of Cartesian physics, Newtonianism, historical Pyhrronism, religious rationalism, deism, the troubling consequences of the trial of the atheists (which had restated the Galilean dilemma of faith-reason), and the concept of the intellectual's new political role.[14] For at least two decades, various questions and solutions rivaled each other. Doria, Vico, Porzio, Grimaldi, De Cristoforo, Intieri, Gimma, and others fought among themselves on scientific, ideological, and political levels, fostering endless disputes and strong personal grudges.

In an earlier chapter we reconstructed the important debate, waged mostly in Naples during the 1710s, over what interpretation to give Galilean scientific theories. The confrontation between Doria and Porzio, attracting the intervention of many other scholars, had starkly revealed the unbridgeable gap between the qualitative experimentalism of the Investiganti tradition and the geometricizing model of Cartesians such as Doria and Ariani. It is now necessary to reconstruct the peculiar intellectual climate of those years, when many southern scholars undertook the study of Cartesian writings more attentively than during the second half of the seventeenth century in the hope of finding a new philosophy. One cannot deny the importance and innovative significance that the victorious dissemination of Cartesianism had had and continued to have in Naples during the early eighteenth century. Even more than the Principia philosophiae, whose scientific limits quickly became evident, the illuminating and persuasive arguments of the Discours de la méthode were for years the banner of the novatores. Those whose objective it was to defeat Aristotelianism and the Catholic Church's official culture in the name of libertas philosophandi felt obligated to refer to Descartes, although they undoubtedly interpreted him in different ways. The French philosopher's mechanism and his scientific doctrines were in fact present both in the theses of Neapolitan physiologists and medical doctors and in the Neoplatonic and Malebranchian readings of Descartes produced by Spinelli and Doria.[15] Though we now know many of the details pertaining to the presence of Cartesians in Neapolitan culture, other groups of scholars who always maintained a certain freedom of judgment regarding what some contemporaries spitefully called the Cartesian "sect," even while they battled alongside the novatores, are less well known.

Lorenzo Ciccarelli's secret printing shop[16] and its numerous clandestine publications, indirectly protected by enlightened Catholics from Rome and Florence and particularly Valletta's circle, were for years a beacon of light for an entire Epicurean, Gassendian, and Galilean sector that, even if in the minority, built up solid roots in the southern culture of the first twenty years of the eighteenth century. This intensive propaganda work favoring modern thought guided the production of a number of volumes: the publication of Leonardo Di Capua's works (1714), Jacques Rohault's Tractatus physicus [Treatise on physics] (1713) with Samuel Clarke's Newtonian notes, Galileo's

Dialogo intorno ai due massimi sistemi [Dialogue on the two greatest systems] and his *Lettera alla Granduchessa di Toscana* [Letter to the grand duchess of Tuscany] (1710), and the celebrated translation of Lucretius's *De rerum natura* [On the nature of things] produced by Alessandro Marchetti and published in Naples, although officially it was listed as having been published in London in 1717.[17] Even without referring to Ciccarelli's admittedly important clandestine publications and the still unknown debates that preceded them, a number of works that did not appear clandestinely point explicitly to a wide intellectual milieu that circulated freely and easily among very open and varied fields of science and contemporary European culture: the *Saggi di naturali esperienze fatti nell'Accademia del Cimento* [Essays on natural experiments conducted at the Accademia del Cimento] (Naples, Raillard, 1714) collected by Magalotti; Bernhard Varen's *Geographia generalis* [General geography] (Naples, Gessari, 1715) annotated by Isaac Newton and James Jurin, who polemically closed with the text of Galileo's recantation; and Muratori's *Riflessioni sopra il buon gusto* [Reflection on good taste] (Naples, Raillard, 1715). The translation of Adrien Baillet's *Vie de M. Descartes* [The life of Mr. Descartes] (Naples, 1713) was more than a symptom of Cartesian hegemony; it was an expression of the lively debate under way. In any event one fact seems certain: far from being suffocated by the severe conditioning that hampered all Italian culture, the Neapolitan environment in those years proved capable of successfully overcoming the chains and controls imposed by the ecclesiastical hierarchy, outmaneuvering them on a practical level, and thus asserting a substantial freedom of thought.

Despite some valuable studies on Giuseppe Valletta,[18] who was a figure central to Neapolitan culture of the seventeenth and eighteenth centuries, we still know little about his circle, the contacts he had with the Royal Society, and those who regularly visited his impressive library. Beginning with specific research on these problems, it should be possible to reconstruct an overall picture of Neapolitan culture in the early eighteenth century. Vico, Gimma, Grimaldi, and Intieri either had direct contacts with Valletta, or, at least, saw him and his ideas as a tangible reference point. In fact, many local scholars shared elements drawn from Valletta's *Istoria filosofica* [Philosophical history], published clandestinely (and incompletely) between 1703 and 1704.[19] The work was quite successful in Naples, where it became an ideological and programmatic manifesto for those tied to several aspects of the Investiganti's culture and erudite European libertinism. In Valletta's historicization of ancient philosophical theories, they were able to find a privileged vehicle for demystifying the "millennial distortion and hiding of the original meaning of certain philosophical messages."[20] The basic themes cleverly developed in the *Istoria* came from Pierre Gassendi's Christian atomism, vindicated within a perceptive reevaluation of Renaissance Neoplatonism, and polemically opposed to the native atheism of Aristotelian theories. The call to experiments, scientific probabilism as theorized by Di Capua, and, especially, the vindication of *libertas philosophandi* for all scholars, are all among the *Istoria*'s fundamental issues.[21] Here Valletta also explained the evocative thesis of an original Italic philosophy both atomist and experimentalist, a thesis that would long endure at the center of the defensive line held by a broad portion of the *novatores'* party. In 1723 Abbot Giacinto Gimma proposed the idea again in his famous *Idea della storia dell'Italia letterata* [Outline of the history of learned Italy], published by the Neapolitan printer Felice Mosca.

Gimma's "middling" social origins[22] had induced his parents to send him to Naples in 1688 to pursue courses in law, and there he came in contact with Vico, Monforte, Porzio, and Doria, developing in his works an original philosophical synthesis that, even if not an example of stunning acumen, was certainly a valuable contribution for the period. We possess a subtle reconstruction of his initial Hermetic and cabalistic studies, and his unedited *Nova encyclopaedia* (released in 1692) contained traces of the most famous works of sixteenth- and seventeenth-century magical Hermetism, including Girolamo Cardano's *De subtilitate* [On subtlety], Athanasius Kircher's *Oedipus Aegyptiacus* [Oedipus the Egyptian], the works in the tradition of Robert Fludd's *magia naturalis* [natural magic], and the Llullian works of Cornelio Agrippa, Pedro Gregoire, and Tommaso Garzoni.[23] These studies would mark the cultural shaping of the young intellectual Gimma to a great extent. No less important for his experience, however, was his contact with the Investiganti's school, whose worthy defender and excellent interpreter he became.

With Gimma named "perpetual promotor" in the Society of the *Spensierati* [light-hearted] from Rossano in Calabria, by 1695 it had become one of the most important among those cultural centers cleaving to the party of the moderns.[24] According to the lists of the members furnished in the *Elogi accademici* [Academic eulogies] (1703), membership included many from the *ceto civile*, functionaries, and university teachers, and, most important, some surviving Investiganti such as Monforte, Porzio, Luca Tozzi, and Tommaso Donzelli; strikingly absent were such prestigious men as Caloprese, Doria, and Ariani.[25] The significance of Gimma's specific choice of field in favor of Tommaso Cornelio's friends must nevertheless be reassessed: in fact, almost none of the prestigious members listed took part in the academic "gatherings" directly. Numerous and influential works appeared in Naples, directly inspired by the debates waged there, eloquent testimony to the network of contacts that radiated from Rossano.[26] The *Nuova staffetta da Parnaso* [The new courier from Parnasus], which appeared in 1700 at the conclusion of a terrible dispute between Galenic doctors and the *novatores* gathered in the Society of the *Spensierati*, is a typical example of the position that the society assumed and the role it played in southern culture.[27] In this fanciful and ironic trial of Galen before Apollo that Gimma and Gaetano Tremigliozzi concocted to defeat traditionalist doctors, Bacon and Boyle were the judges, while Galileo, Redi, and Gassendi were Apollo's advisors, and Van Helmont and Vesalio the implacable prosecutors.[28] In the *Nuova staffetta*, the destruction of the Galenic and Aristotelian system took place alongside and parallel to an illustration of Tommaso Cornelio's philosophy of ether-mind, now integrated with Spinozan themes. But the militant commitment of the *spensierati* in the ranks of the moderns becomes evident especially in Gimma's *Dissertationum academicarum tomus primus* [Volume one of academic dissertations] (1714), dedicated to Giovanni Maria Lancisi. In both the first part (*De hominibus fabulosis* [On fabled men]) and the second part (*De fabulosis animalibus* [On fabled animals]), the author criticized those who abandoned the scientific rigor necessary for any investigation and followed the fable-ridden theories about the generation of living things, demon men, tritons, sirens, and beings like the phoenix, Pegasus, and other legendary marvels without any embarrassment.[29] His extraordinary philosophical and historical leaning permitted Gimma to reconstruct the myths related to the most unusual creatures, unveiling the allegorical value and historical-religious meaning they had held among ancient Mediterranean peoples. In his *Fisica sotterranea* [Underground physics] (1730), certainly one of the most important writings on Neapolitan geology, the abbot demystified the "fantastic" in nature, investigating the mineral world and the "nobility, names, species, places, forms, generation, size, hardness, matrix, use, virtues, and the fables" of gems and stones.[30] It was an imposing work, in which the erudite naturalist and scholar of sacred history put to the test problems of modern geology alongside disconcerting analyses of questions typical of *magia naturalis*. In the *Fisica sotterranea* appeared the contradictory and unique face of this heir to the Investiganti tradition, who in Athanasius Kircher's *Mondus subterraneus* [Underground world] had perceived a frame of reference within which Baconian and Galilean experimentalism could be supported and integrated. Gimma discussed the geological theories of Descartes, Baglivi, Boyle, and Gassendi, but he in no way underestimated the ideas of Pliny, Patrizi, Cardano, and Della Porta. In a plainly Galilean spirit, he spoke ironically of the thesis of the gender of rocks maintained by some,[31] but at the same time he did not hesitate to broach sincerely and on a scientific and historical level a typical Hermetic theme such as the supernatural and demonic power of certain rocks.[32] He also made serious contributions to the European debate on the problem of fossils, discussed along with cabalistic theories and the *Pimander*.[33]

In 1723 Gimma published the *Idea della storia dell'Italia letterata* [Outline of the history of learned Italy] in Naples, in which he expounded his interpretation of modern culture. All new science was proudly and unreservedly exalted in the *Idea*. The Galilean and Copernican works were considered the foundation of modern thought. Atomism, experimentalism, the great discoveries of the compass, the telescope, and analytic geometry, and the works of Gassendi, Cornelio, and Descartes were again evoked as essential conquests for humanity.[34] We ought not be deceived by the author's propaganda favoring Italian culture.[35] In reality, Gimma did not develop Valletta's thesis on the origin of all modern European thought from an ancient Italic philosophy with a merely instrumental intent, but he adhered to a specific plan aimed at inserting the Investiganti's Galilean experimentalism into a wider, solidly grounded frame of reference. The gnosiological crisis of those years dictated a response that was eclectic, totally separate from any dogmatism, and bound to an original development of Valletta's theses. At least formally, what was preserved from the Cartesian cultural climate was its intolerance for anything that seemed magical or even "fantastic."

Nevertheless, the proposed solution was resolved ambiguously, and magic reconquered its own position. In the *Fisica sotterranea*, Abbot Gimma wrote that "Adam received science and perfect knowledge of all things created from God, for which he is hailed as the first inventor of all the arts."[36] The hypothesis that God had revealed all the secrets of nature to Adam "since he had to be the teacher and director of all mankind"[37] was developed in the *Idea della storia dell'Italia letterata*, with continuous references to the Hermetic tradition of the *Prisca theologia* [Early theology]. According to Gimma, the most important accomplishments of modern science were already known— even if in an occult form—by Adam and the great patriarchs of the human race, and the Jewish people had hidden the "secret science" under the mantle of the "cabal." Gimma believed that there were precise references to basic disciplines such as chemistry in the ancients' culture: "They attribute to Ham the academy of the Chaldeans and chemistry, or rather 'hamistry,' which took its name from him."[38] Equally interesting is the history of the dissemination of the scientific patrimony. Criminal "magicians" caused a long, obscurantist, and degenerate phase for the interpretation of the natural magic that God gave to Adam, culminating in its confusion with diabolical magic, a creation of Satan full of errors. In Gimma's opinion, based on a disquieting thesis from Giordano Bruno that he cited many times, this phase was finally interrupted by the appearance of Jesus Christ and Saint Paul.[39] Over the centuries the good magicians, repositories of scientific wisdom, had provided for the transmission of the immense gift of knowledge God had entrusted to the first man. "Science given by God to Adam was propagated among his progeny until the Flood, and then Noah and his sons were the masters of all human wisdom, and the academies derived from them."[40] In this development, Italy had the fortune to receive all science directly from Noah, according to Gimma, harking back to Valletta's thesis of an Italic philosophy among whose most recent followers were Galileo and Tommaso Cornelio.[41]

Abbot Gimma's efforts to give a new ideological frame to the Investiganti's heritage proved to be a retreat to positions antithetical to some of the cornerstones of modern thought. His affirming that "the experiment [is the] true interpreter of nature" or proclamation of the glory of Galileo or Gassendi while simultaneously rejecting the cumulative and unmysterious character of modern science reveals the deep-rooted ambiguity of his plan, a typical expression of the crisis and confusion of the day. Galileo, Bacon, Gassendi, and Descartes had vehemently rejected the esoteric nature of wisdom, democratizing and laicizing the human cognitive process and freeing it from all mystical and religious nature. Gimma's Hermetic experimentalism instead insisted on the science of Adam and Noah as transmitted by the magicians, the authority of the ancients as a guarantee of scientific truth, and diabolical magic as opposed to natural magic.[42] While Galileo, Cornelio, and Di Capua had courageously looked forward, trusting in human capacity alone to increase knowledge, Gimma faced a period of crisis, a period when in Italy the very cultural breathing room necessary to guarantee scientific research was again at risk, and he felt the need to turn to Hermes Trismegistus's *Prisca theologia* and to the past in order to find there his experimentalism's prestigious authorities and historical roots themselves.[43]

Gimma was not the only one to show interest in facing the problems of Neapolitan culture in the early eighteenth century. Figures such as Costantino Grimaldi and Bartolomeo Intieri contributed measurably to the debate on, respectively, ideological and more scientific levels, furnishing stimulating responses and keeping abreast of the times. The vicissitudes of Grimaldi's *Risposte* to Aletino, the Inquisitorial persecutions targeting him, and his commitment to the ranks of the moderns and Neapolitan jurisdictionalists have been amply reconstructed, and there is no point in belaboring these issues further.[44] On the other hand, it might be useful to study Grimaldi's positions in the debate of those years in depth. Connected to enlightened Catholics like Bottari and Cerati,[45] and a loyal Muratorian, Grimaldi was an intimate of Galiani, whom he had met in Naples in 1708. In the ideological confrontation between the various currents of Neapolitan culture, he was part of what remained of the late-Investiganti–Cartesian faction most open and receptive to the need for renewal. The trial of the atheists and Giovanni Battista De Benedictis's very harsh charges against *libertas philosophandi* and all modern thought (which he blamed for undermining Christianity internally) had abruptly restricted the latitude granted to Cornelio and Di Capua. In order to reopen the discussion, it was necessary to mount a coordinated effort to confront both the problem of scientific renewal and the reform of the Catholic Church, ever more entrenched in its defense of Aristotelianism.[46] Grimaldi was among the first in Naples to grasp the extraordinary complexity of the situation. His *Risposte* brought to the center of attention the disruptive effects that the late-seventeenth-century rationalism of Spinoza, Pierre Bayle, and the Libertines had had on European culture. Works such as Mabillon's *Traité des études monastiques* [Treatise of monastic studies] (1691), Muratori's *De ingeniorum moderatione* [On the moderation of the intellect] (1714), and Dupin's *Méthode pour étudier la théologie* [Method for the study of theology] (1716) were among those most greatly pondered and utilized to design a new image for the Church. Grimaldi forcefully illustrated themes dear to Celestino Galiani, such as the need for studies of ecclesiastical history in order to form a modern religious conscience, as if to underscore that "when we identify theology with ecclesiastical history, not only discipline but also doctrine is forced to undergo critical examination."[47]

The pressing request for a reform of liturgy and the continual call for evangelical precepts and tolerance were the essential foundations on which Grimaldi constructed his impassioned defense of *libertas philosophandi*. According to him, the Catholic *renovatio* called for the destruction of the pernicious alliance between scholastics and Christianity. Guaranteeing scientific and philosophical freedom to scholars in the human realm of the truths of reason, leaving the truths of faith to the Church (as Galileo had), was in the final analysis a solid ideological base from which to relaunch a Christian science.[48] However, in his analysis of scientific proposals emerging in Neapolitan culture, the author of the *Risposte* did not exhibit that attention to and knowledge of the European debate that supported his project for an in-depth religious renewal. The usual themes of the latter Investiganti, now purified of any materialist or Spinozan traces, came together in his thought with a reevaluation of Descartes's theories of physics, for he considered the philosopher pious and unjustly persecuted.

Grimaldi's science went no further than seventeenth-century authors; it never arrived at the Newtonian scientific revolution.[49] Even so, the clearcut separation between method and doctrine was already a noteworthy step forward compared to the sectarianism common in the Neapolitan culture of the period. The defense of experimentalism, atomism, and Christian skepticism was crucial to his works for exalting the scientific-experimental method as the guarantee of progress in research.[50] At the root of this was a reading of Descartes's *Discours de la méthode*, suitably contrasted with Descartes's *Principia philosophiae*. As Giannone wrote in his *Autobiografia*, synthesizing the way an entire generation of Neapolitan Cartesians thought: "In philosophy, no one should force himself to fight under a particular commander, but the only escort and guide for investigating the stupendous works of nature ought to be reason alone and the experiment."[51] During the 1730s Grimaldi had contact with enlightened Catholics in Rome, and he supported the Neapolitan publication of George Cheyne's *Principi filosofici di teologia naturale* [Philosophical principles of natural theology] and the Italian translation of the *Philosophical Transactions*, concretely demonstrating how important it had been to confirm the primacy of method over doctrine.[52]

Bartolomeo Intieri, the "Florentine ecclesiastic" destined to play a role in the foreground of Neapolitan culture, was to produce a work much more attentive to scientific data. The 1730s were a crucial period for his activity, but we should not underestimate what he accomplished in behalf of modern thought during the 1710s and 1720s. As we have emphasized in an earlier chapter, in the disagreement between Doria and Porzio over the postulate about the motion of falling bodies along an inclined plane, Intieri belonged to the Galilean wing and was largely loyal to the Pisan scientist's teachings on an ideological and scientific level.[53] In the *Considerazioni del P. D., Guidone Grando e del sig. N. N. sopra le scritture del signor Luc'Antonio Porzio circa il moto de' gravi per il piano inclinato* [The considerations of P(aolo) D(oria), Guido Grandi, and Mr. N. N. regarding Mr. Lucantonio Porzio's writings on the motion of bodies along an inclined plane], Intieri (under the pseudonym N. N.) had explained with extraordinary perceptiveness the importance of Galilean "sensate experiments" and the essential role that physics and mathematics had assumed in modern science, with the goal of identifying general mathematical laws. Though the enterprising Tuscan cannot be said to have possessed genuine mathematical talent, he did acquire a notable reputation and prestige among Neapolitan scientists by publishing some interesting pamphlets on the problems of analytic geometry.[54] His heated scientific arguments with Giacinto De Cristoforo on mathematical questions, the part he played in the Galilean *querelle*, and his candidacy for the chair in mathematics at the Neapolitan University[55] created the prerequisites necessary for his active presence in Naples, viewed favorably by enlightened Catholics in Rome and Florence. One of the first significant letters between Galiani and Intieri on defending Galileo from Porzio's attacks dates to 1711.[56] In the following years, Intieri developed his contacts until he completely accepted the programs of Galiani's circle. In 1731 Intieri wrote to Giovanni Bottari:

> I cordially ask that you give my respects to Reverend Father Galiani, Monsignor Leprotti, Father Cerati, Signor Niccolini, and Abbot Foggini, whom I esteem as much as those who are most respected by common opinion— but what am I saying? Not "as much" do I esteem them, but a thousand times more, and I love them myriad times more than everything else.[57]

There were immediately many philosophical and political-cultural points of common ground between Intieri and Galiani's circle. Just like Bottari in Florence and Galiani in Rome, Intieri identified Gassendi, rather than the Cartesian mentalism of Doria and Caloprese, as the natural complement to Galileo's experimentalism. His reading of Gassendi firmly convinced him of the possibility of a reconciliation between the needs of the scientist and the duties of the priest.[58] Not surprisingly, Lucretius's *De rerum natura*, translated by Alessandro Marchetti (judged by Intieri to be "one of the greatest men of our century"), was one of the foremost and first works that he pondered and used in his research.[59]

With the appearance of the *Nuova invenzione di fabbricar mulini a vento* [New invention for constructing windmills] in 1716, Intieri initiated a new chapter in the gnosiological debate that would prove to be particularly fruitful in the following years. Mathematics, physics, and all natural sciences were finally seen in relation to their immediate utility for the human race. "I judge those who spend all their time reading books dealing with geometry and arithmetic, without taking care to go forward and enjoy the fruits of their labor, worthy of great reproof."[60] The project for a windmill that was perfect in every detail, that moved "in the same way and with the same speed whether the wind is very weak or extremely strong," was the first practical realization of his plan (clearly inspired by Bacon) to conceive of science above all as a useful tool for humanity.[61] Intieri certainly played a role in the clandestine Neapolitan publication of Galileo's works, as well as of Marchetti's *De rerum natura*. In the same years Galiani confirmed the vital confrontation underway and the mobile and open cultural situation by sending his *Epistola de gravitate et cartesianis vorticibus* to Naples and inviting local intellectuals, including Giacomo Grazini and Giovambattista Pignatelli, prince of Marsiconovo, to undertake the Newtonian experiments in the *Opticks*, an initiative that certainly did not escape Intieri's attention.[62]

But the most interesting example of collaboration between the Tuscan mathematician and enlightened Catholics before Galiani's arrival in the Kingdom of Naples certainly remains the work he carried out on the occasion of the Florentine edition of Pierre Gassendi's *Opera omnia*. Intieri personally—and not without difficulty—took care of the subscription in Naples to underwrite the financing of this very costly enterprise. When the *Opera* appeared in 1727 and a number of copies were sent to Naples, it elicited favorable comments. The introductory essay, which was the enlightened Catholics' programmatic manifesto for a concrete renewal of Italian culture, authoritatively served to mark a turning point in the hard-won debate in Naples over the twilight of the Investiganti's inheritance. The courageous theses expressed in the brief introduction—which Intieri certainly shared, since they had been formulated after long discussions among his Roman friends—found fertile ground in which to set solid roots. The majority of the *novatores* began to align themselves with the peculiar and demanding program in the manifesto: Galilean and Gassendian experimentalism gnosiologically refounded on the Newtonian *Regulae* in the *Principia*, a new morality attuned to a consideration of the native force of human passions, the rejection of scholasticism and the Church's Inquisitorial activities, and, above all, the firm conviction that universal progress would occur if science and modern philosophy were placed at the service of humanity.[63]

2. THE PARTY OF THE MODERNS AND IDEOLOGICAL REFOUNDATION

In 1731 a special courier of Viceroy Raimund von Harrach bore Celestino Galiani, the new bishop of Taranto, the imperial nomination as *cappellano maggiore* of the Kingdom of Naples. Galiani's biographies have always stressed his disappointment at being withdrawn from the "care of souls" to which he had aspired on being given such a demanding and delicate "earthly"

political duty.[1] In reality, with his promotion Galiani happily saw the fulfill-
ment of an old project that he had begun to cultivate many years earlier.
In 1728, during a brief stay in Naples, he had made an initial attempt to
become coadjutant of the then *cappellano maggiore* Vincenzo Vidania, who
was more than one hundred years old.[2] In the subsequent years, his prestige
as a great diplomat and man of culture, his personal friendship with the
viceroy, and his support in Rome from Cardinal Neri Corsini and enlightened Catholics—not to mention his Neapolitan ties with Costantino Grimaldi,
Bartolomeo Intieri, Niccolò Cirillo, and Matteo Egizio—had led many to
consider him to be among the most likely candidates to fill the imminent
vacancy of the position. Even so, despite the titles, friendships, and dis-
creet but intensive persuasion he and his supporters organized, the nomination only crowned a harsh clash of uncertain outcome involving various
components of the Neapolitan political world.

The political and institutional crisis of 1726 had exposed the extreme
difficulties that the Austrians encountered in their attempt to govern.[3] The
traditional and fruitful alliance between viceroy and *ceto civile* to limit baronial power, hinging on the Collaterale,* experienced the first signs of
breakdown because of the unbridled politics of "gifts" and "graces" set in
place by the government in the final years of Daun's viceregency. Charles
VI's pressing financial needs were in fact one of the fundamental reasons
for the failure of Austrian reformism in Naples. The weapon of the "gifts"
in the hands of the barons and the severe fiscal pressure in the end internally bankrupted any attempt at reform.[4] Thus important initiatives such as
the *Giunta di commercio* [Committee on Commerce] and, particularly, the
Banco di San Carlo, founded during the second three-year period of Cardinal Michael Friedrich von Althann's government, ran aground.[5] This viceroy's philo-curial politics broke the unity of civic power, weakened the
Collaterale, and provided breathing room for the aristocracy.

Those who paid for von Althann's philo-curial attitude were first Giannone,
who was compelled to flee after the appearance of the *Istoria civile*, and
then the entire *ceto civile* and the urban aristocracy itself. The extremely
bitter struggle between the *ministero togato*** led by Gaetano Argento and
the viceroy created a new situation in the Neapolitan political equilibrium.[6]
Despite the fact that earlier he had been driven by reformatory intentions,
von Althann satisfied no one in the end. In 1726 the July funeral celebra-
tions for Alessandro Riccardi, unanimously considered the most advanced
proponent of Neapolitan anticurialism, clearly exposed the opposing sides.[7]
Bottari and Intieri followed the clash with apprehension, openly aligning
themselves with Grimaldi, Giannone, Rapolla, Pallante, and many others.[8]

---

*The supreme council, which collaborated with the viceroy in governing Naples—Trans.
**Members of the *ceto civile* employed in courts of law and in legal professions, recog-
nized by their professional robes—Trans.

Galiani, who had enjoyed an active friendship with Riccardi, kept in contact with Giannone's group in Vienna[9] and helped to solidify the moderns' front. However, the victory over the viceroy and the reopening of the customary wide political latitude for the entire ceto civile and Neapolitan intellectuals had the effect of renewing the ancient debate between the proponents of radical jurisdictionalism, who sometimes went beyond Giannone's own inspiration (as in the case of Contegna and Riccardi), and those who instead desired greater moderation, at least in tone if not in content, in the debate with the Holy See.[10]

Celestino Galiani was long linked to the latter group. Various claimants presented themselves to succeed the late cappellano maggiore Vidania in the struggle between radicals and moderates within the jurisdictionalist area receptive to modern thought. The original candidates proposed by Viceroy Harrach (Ruffo, Filomarino, and Russo) were followed by a second trio (Positano, Mazzocchi, and Garofalo).[11] The clash was quickly reduced to the philo-curial candidacy of Bartolomeo Positano, supported by the secretary of state Monsignor Antonio Banchieri, and the ultrajurisdictionalist and Giannonian candidacy of Biagio Garofalo, an "extremely close friend" of Costantino Grimaldi and a "cloudy brain . . ., a man of unsound doctrine," as Rainiero Simonetti, the apostolic nuncio in Naples, spitefully described him in a report.[12]

In 1731, while feverish negotiations for the nomination were underway, Gregorio Grimaldi, the son of the famous councillor, produced his Istoria delle leggi e de' magistrati [History of laws and magistrates]. The work represented the thought of a wide segment of Neapolitan culture that, while generally aligned on progressive positions, did not hide its determination to undermine the hegemony that the Giannonian group exercised over the local jurisdictionalists.[13] Matteo Egizio, a great friend of Galiani and a figure in the foreground of the world of southern antiquaries, had actively collaborated on the editing of the Istoria delle leggi e de' magistrati.[14] The appearance of the Istoria marked the formation of a new political and ideological block in Neapolitan social life, an alliance that by linking moderate jurisdictionalism with the antiquaries' cultural vivacity, profoundly sensitive to humanist irenism, advanced an additional, authoritative candidate for the prestigious position of cappellano maggiore.

The nomination of Monsignor Galiani was not without charges that there had been underhanded dealings, for Garofalo accused Galiani of getting Cardinal Davia to intervene on his behalf before Marquis Rialp, a powerful Catalan minister of Charles VI.[15] His candidacy stemmed precisely from the crucial support of moderate jurisdictionalists and antiquaries. Father and son Grimaldi, Intieri, Egizio, Niccolò Cirillo, and many others watched approvingly as Galiani's claim emerged, and in the end Galiani proved to be the only candidate acceptable to all parties involved. Even though in the final analysis Galiani's nomination came as the result of the brokerage among all Neapolitan political components, it quickly assumed the impact of a clear victory for the *novatores*. Bartolomeo Intieri enthusiastically wrote:

> The emperor has acted like an emperor when he gave the duty of *cappellano maggiore* to Monsignor Galiani, and it has been so applauded that one cannot even express it. . . . Under the direction of this great man who enjoys all the esteem of the Viennese court, our University will be purged of certain stains that now soil it. Finally I believe that this provision has arrived at an opportune time, in which the barbarity has begun to become known.[16]

Historians have generally interpreted the arrival of the new *cappellano* as a genuine turning point for Neapolitan culture. The Lockean empiricism and Newtonianism, whose ardent promotor Galiani was, would finally convince the majority of local intellectuals because of his energetic efforts at dissemination.[17] Actually, the role he played was much richer and more complex than hitherto believed, if one takes into account the difficult and adverse conditions that the party of the *novatores* encountered in those years, for they were attacked by many others and profoundly divided internally.

By the completion of Cardinal von Althann's viceregency, Paolo Mattia Doria and Giambattista Vico had already been separated from the moderns for some time. The very bitter dispute between Doria and Spinelli on the latent Spinozism in Descartes's works had exposed the virulence and stubbornness with which the *veteres* [old guard] openly opposed any reading of the French philosopher's works, whether that reading was naturalist or metaphysical. On von Althann's order, Costantino Grimaldi's responses to Aletino had been pitilessly drowned at sea in December 1726, crowning a period of severe repression for the intellectuals most sensitive to the research of the great northern European philosophers.[18] Galiani's uncomfortable exclamations when he learned of the condemnation serve to confirm this barely reassuring situation: "O what happiness or triumphs they are singing now. This is the true manner for winning literary disputes, not wasting away over books!"[19] Beyond the political difficulties of guaranteeing latitude for freedom, the philosophical and ideological confrontation within the *novatores* was by no means reduced to mere formalism. In the 1720s, the late-Investiganti flame had been extinguished (although Porzio taught in the university until 1715); and there was little following for either Gimma's Investiganti Hermetism or the Cartesian metaphysical and Neoplatonic interpretation developed by Spinelli, who had seen Paolo Mattia Doria distance himself from the Cartesianism he had promoted in the early eighteenth century and ally himself with the *veteres*. The scientific and philosophical discussions between the moderns posed, on the one hand, Niccolò Cirillo's Cartesian mechanism, and, on the other, the Galilean and Newtonian empiricism of Niccolò Di Martino and Bartolomeo Intieri. Actually, the articulation of the various groups was much more complex and even confused, and it fostered surprising relationships and unions. One gains the impression of a culture rich in unrest, if divided internally, as Francesco Maria Spinelli's evocation of those years confirms, efficiently delineating the chaotic breakdown of the Cartesian front:

> Arrogance induced all Cartesians to scorn all the ancient philosophers, and particularly Aristotle and Plato. And later the division between them gave birth to those sects that began to admit some principles of Descartes's philosophy, such as the existence of that "ego," the infinite divisibility of matter, its inertia, and a few other things. And because they were not capable of understanding the other principles, they dedicated themselves to blaming innate ideas and not accepting anything but the Epicureans' sensory perceptions, and thus they went so far as to accept the vacuum, and even hidden qualities, which they so faulted in the scholastics.[20]

Particularly noteworthy was Niccolò Cirillo, who, together with Biagio Troise and Gioacchino Castaldo, taught at the university and who for a long time represented Cartesian orthodoxy in Naples.[21] Cirillo was educated at the Investiganti school of Porzio and Monforte, attended the Accademia Palatina, and was a great friend of Giannone. During the first decades of the eighteenth century, he became the most famous doctor in Naples, finally being recognized for his prestige as a scholar open to modern thought, almost the leader of Neapolitan intellectuals. Harvesting Valletta's inheritance, he maintained intensive contacts with the Royal Society, he wrote on the *Philosophical Transactions*, and, from 1727 to 1728, he taught Newtonian theories in the university.[22] Cirillo was never an advocate of the *Principia*'s theories, however; rather, he firmly maintained his devotion to Cartesian mechanicism, despite the long-standing and affectionate discussions with two Newtonians such as Antonio Leprotti and Celestino Galiani.[23]

In the notes commenting on the Neapolitan edition of Michael Ettmüller's *Opera omnia* in 1728, Cirillo made his attitude towards modern culture explicit. Confirming his reputation as a Free-Thinker (some contemporaries spoke openly of his atheist sympathies),[24] he rejected any solution of a teleological or providentialist nature, for reasons similar to those put forward by Vallisnieri, Conti, and Riccati in the Veneto. According to Cirillo, the great Cartesian machine of the universe with its vortices, its laws of motion, the plenum, and ether, integrated with a careful examination of the chemical qualities of matter, permitted the resolution of every aspect of nature without resorting to the explanation of God's constant and active presence in the universe. Animal mechanism, the rejection of the existence of the soul in beasts, and, most important, the aversion for the plastic natures of Cudworth and Le Clerc were the premises of his resolute criticism of Isaac Newton's providentialist celestial dynamics.[25] In the notes on Ettmüller, though he devoted greater space to the senses in his mechanistic vision of a Cartesian type, Cirillo did not hesitate to propose innatism as the basis of human knowledge. Cirillo redirected the Newtonians' accusation that Descartes's followers "faked" hypotheses onto Newton himself, whom he accused of having betrayed his *Regulae philosophandi* [Rules of philosophizing] in the *Opticks*.[26]

Thanks to a large following in all aspects of Neapolitan culture, Cirillo's stand against Hermetism and the disguised occultism of Ettmüller and Van Helmont, in a cloaked dispute over Giacinto Gimma's late-Investiganti developments[27] served to reinforce his reputation as a militant intellectual, unbiased and disposed towards fighting to the end for the *novatores*. The Neapolitan Newtonians considered him simultaneously their friend and enemy. The freedom that he allowed for the confrontation between their theories and Cartesian ones in the university shortly before Galiani's arrival certainly facilitated the diffusion of the "latest and most famous Newtonian sect," as Giovambattista Capasso, teacher at the seminary of Aversa, called it in his *Historiae philosophiae synopsis* [Synopsis of the history of philosophy] (1728).[28] Capasso forcefully emphasized the profound differences between the *Principia*'s theses and Descartes's physical and cosmological theories, confirming the impression of a Neapolitan Newtonianism stemming not from developments of post-Cartesian culture, as Francesco Maria Spinelli had misleadingly suggested, but as an alternative to it, at least in the scientific field.[29] Besides, in 1714 Galiani had already sent the very harsh anti-Cartesian charges contained in his *Epistola de gravitate et cartesianis vorticibus* to Naples, with the stated goal of "illuminating Neapolitan philosophizers, who for the most part have such a blind veneration for Descartes that in his works they admire every apostrophe,"[30] and in the following years as well he insistently continued to entreat local scholars to abandon the French philosopher's scientific theories.

According to Mario Lama, from the 1720s on Niccolò Di Martino, teacher of mathematics and Agostino Ariani's successor at the university, could unquestionably be considered the leader of Neapolitan Newtonianism.[31] Born in 1701 in Faicchio near Benevento, contemporaries universally held him to be the greatest Neapolitan scientist of the early eighteenth century.[32] Well connected to enlightened Catholics—especially Galiani and Intieri—and mentor to entire generations of scholars (including Antonio Genovesi), Di Martino began his official militancy in Newtonian ranks with the publication of the *Elementa staticae* [Elements of statics] in 1727. The work opened with an important letter to the head of Neapolitan Cartesians, Niccolò Cirillo, and in the foreword he broached the problems of modern science in their historical development from the times of Galileo to Borelli, Torricelli, and Isaac Newton.[33] Di Martino wrote many other scientific works, however, developing the examination of Newtonian theories mainly through university lectures, which for the most part remained unedited.[34] Some of the courses on physics Di Martino taught during the late 1720s at the university were collected by his brother Pietro Di Martino in three dense volumes, published in 1738 as a veritable manual founded primarily on the

Principia but also including some original studies by Pietro himself.[35] With extraordinary clarity, the young Pietro synthesized the position of the Neapolitan Newtonians, who now aimed openly at supplanting Cartesian apriorism with the phenomenological investigation of nature that the *Principia* theorized. After illustrating the importance of experiments in scientific research, Pietro Di Martino concluded by demolishing simultaneously the Investiganti's scientific probabilism and Cartesian apriorism:

> Things being what they are, from now on we shall not assume as a principle anything that has not already been deduced from the phenomena and then is validated by reason. Hence if it should happen that the phenomena were very clear and plain, even if there were no probable reason for the event they pertain to, we would nevertheless consider such an event most certain. Either we shall refrain entirely from formulating hypotheses, or, if we accept any hypothesis, we shall hold it the standard of questions whose veracity we shall discuss. In this manner we shall distance ourselves as much as possible from the Cartesian method of philosophizing, which is extraordinarily comfortable with hypotheses and conjecture. Moreover we shall also avoid the occult qualities of the scholastics, through which they attempt to explain the properties of bodies with rather mysterious reasons; in fact, such qualities make us no more learned, nor do they cast greater light on things in nature.[36]

In the following pages, the famous four *Regulae philosophandi* posed by Newton to seal the *Principia* were exposed and commented on through many examples that make the modern reader even more aware of the sophistication attained by Neapolitan Newtonianism.[37] The first volume, dedicated to the laws of motion and matter's structure, followed the scheme of Jacques Rohault's *Tractatus physicus*, which Samuel Clarke had transformed into an insidious weapon for disseminating Newtonian theories. Here Pietro Di Martino compared various scientific theories regarding the concepts of motion, inertia, matter, space, and time, thus opening the road to the fourth and central chapter of his study, *De naturae legibus newtonianis* [On the Newtonian laws of nature].[38] Through this text, the Neapolitan students should have been able to acquire a level of information by no means inferior to what was taught at the European universities most receptive to renewal. In the second volume, *De mundo caelesti* [On the celestial world], the broad historical introduction discussing the development of modern astronomy (later used as a model by Antonio Genovesi himself in the *Disputatio physico-historica* [Physico-historical debate]) made more evident his fascination for Newtonian celestial dynamics, with its perfect mathematical laws originating in the research begun by the great Galileo Galilei, whom Di Martino presented as a true hero of modern thought. In the third volume, *De mundo terrestri* [On the earthly world], the author provided a rapid survey of fossils, seas, plants, and animals, always attentive to the most recent scientific discoveries.

At the end of the 1720s the Neapolitan Newtonians' offensive was not limited merely to an active presence in the university; it was also expressed in the direct intervention of Celestino Galiani, Costantino Grimaldi, and enlightened Catholics, through the publication of Italian translations of William Derham's *Astro-Theology* (1728), George Cheyne's *Philosophical Principles of Natural Religion* (1729), and the *Philosophical Transactions*. We have already indicated the apologetic significance of the first two works and the enlightened Catholics' ambitious plan for their dissemination.[39] If we recall the specific Neapolitan situation, it is difficult to escape the impression of a masterly religious interpretation of Newtonianism, certainly useful in a city where the most dangerous accusation long brought against modern thought had been that of profound irreligiosity.

Celestino Galiani's arrival in Naples ought, therefore, to be placed in the context of the tense confrontation not only between moderate and radical jurisdictionalists but also between Cartesian and Newtonian *novatores*. A few months later, Galiani's first great achievement, the Accademia delle Scienze founded in 1732, was openly conceived as a political and cultural work of great import. One need only examine the names of its members to understand the political plan set in motion by Galiani, who was made archbishop of Thessalonica in 1732 in exchange for renouncing the see of Taranto. Niccolò Cirillo, Cartesian mechanist and undisputed leader of the Neapolitan *novatores*, was elected president of the academy. Among the members we find Francesco Maria Spinelli, a mentalist Cartesian and Neoplatonist (but a vehement defender of the moderns); Niccolò and Pietro Di Martino, Mario Lama, and Giuseppe Orlandi, all diehard Newtonians; Giambattista Lamberti, Cartesian and author of a blunt response to Doria defending Spinelli; Michelangelo Ruberto, Domenico Sanseverino, and Francesco Serao, naturalist Gassendians and direct heirs to the late-Investiganti tradition; Gioacchino Poeta, a Cartesian follower of Cirillo; and Bartolomeo Intieri, a Galilean empiricist open to Newtonian and Lockean theories. Galiani himself was also a member; nevertheless, he did not wish to assume any duty within the academy, although his young friend Francesco Serao was elected secretary. All the components of the party of the moderns found themselves united within the academy at Galiani's explicit wish, and he cleverly mediated among them. The programmatic manifesto identifying all the members spoke clearly about the general philosophical directions that would be given to the meetings: "The discussion of metaphysics and general systems is expressly prohibited." The members were to occupy themselves only with "natural philosophy, anatomy, chemistry, geometry, astronomy, and mechanics."[40] The ideological compromise stemmed, therefore, from their common rejection of metaphysics and the ancient academic and Arcadian rites, useless to society and the development of knowledge. The refusal to discuss general systems meant that the new institution was not formed officially either under the sign of Cartesianism or that of Newtonianism. In first place came scientific research, conducted according to the experimental method and aimed at finally inserting Naples into the European circle of great academies. In his autobiography, Galiani wrote that the academy "had to deal with the same subjects of physics, anatomy, and mathematics to which the royal Académie des Sciences in Paris applies itself," and, above all, study "an exact natural history of this entire kingdom, of its fossils and minerals, its plants, its many mineral waters, and all else that can occur in the natural history of a not-too-modest country."[41]

The political import of Galiani's capable activities was evident to all his contemporaries. From the times of Tommaso Cornelio, Leonardo Di Capua, and Lucantonio Porzio, or rather for nearly the preceding half century, a free association of intellectuals explicitly favorable to modern thought had no longer gathered in Naples. Certainly the Accademia Palatina had been an important feature of Neapolitan culture, and its authority had been further enhanced by the official character given to it by its authoritative promotor and financial backer, the Viceroy Medinaceli. A satire of his last will and testament in circulation in Naples affirmed: "In compensation for their labors, we leave to the most erudite Palatine academics the title to be considered as public and shameless flatterers."[42] The governmental stamp that had significantly conditioned the Accademia Palatina was utterly absent in Galiani's academy. Its members, all free intellectuals bound only by the common militant feeling among the *novatores*, renewed the great Investiganti tradition in Neapolitan culture by professing to be experimentalist scientists and advocates of *libertas philosophandi*. It is easy to glimpse an ideal thread that united the two experiences: both followed a period of crisis, and both stemmed not as much from the hegemony of one particular philosophical conception over another as from the peaceful coexistence of different solutions united only by the determination to ward off the attack of tradition and cultural conformism. Galiani did not impose any sudden Newtonian and Lockean slant on Neapolitan culture, nor would he have been able to do so alone. However, with his extraordinary ability he did succeed in gathering the moderns together in a scientific academy that took on the Investiganti's old experimentalist tradition and that was finally able to inaugurate a period of renewed initiative by the *novatores* in every aspect of Neapolitan social life.

The reactions to this plan were harsh and immediate, and they were directed at the *cappellano maggiore* himself. In May 1732 Neapolitan nuncio Rainiero Simonetti wrote, in response to a request from Monsignor Banchieri, the secretary of state, for information about the situation in Naples. In gloomy tones he described the unrest existing among the intellectuals, and he indicated that the "new *cappellano maggiore* has undertaken the foundation of a new academy with many faculties, particularly philosophy and mathematics, and he intends to present the philosophy of Locke and other similar authors, for he has already nominated the teachers for each faculty."[43] This rather dangerous accusation alarmed the secretary of state in

Rome, and when he requested a supplemental investigation on the overall positions taken by the *cappellano*, he used the disquieting formula: "employ the secrecy of the Inquisition."[44] The news of Galiani's incrimination spread quickly throughout curial circles. As Antonio Leprotti wrote to Giovanni Bianchi a year later, reminding him of the event: "This news even reached Rome, and it caused sinister talk about the Monsignor."[45] The problem of who denounced Galiani to the nuncio Simonetti is still a matter of discussion today. Using some yet unpublished sources, Raffaele Ajello has rightly put aside Spinelli's name, cast doubt on the attribution to Doria, and minimized the importance of the information and ill will transmitted by Abbot Riozzi, auditor at the nunciature; instead, he pointed to Galiani's own fellow Celestines as a more probable origin of the earliest denunciations. This was what Leprotti wrote to Bianchi when he commented on the entire affair:

I am still convincing myself that his own [monastic] brothers had invented or at least went about disseminating [the accusations], because the friars, no matter what sort they are, are always friars as long as they live in their friary. And in fact that friar and secretary who was Monsignor's pupil and who had to defend him from this calumny, since he came fresh from Naples, or had to excuse him at least when he might commit some error, was the first to tell me that gossip, saying that the Monsignor had persuaded the study of Newton in Naples, and therefore he had received the response that they were astonished at him and that they wished to continue to be Catholics.[46]

Beyond the issue of the denunciation, there remains an impression of the compact resistance offered by the Neapolitan clergy and groups of intellectuals strongly hostile to the *cappellano maggiore*'s new cultural policy. After all, on his arrival Galiani had demonstrated what he was made of by firing six hundred supernumerary chaplains suspected of fraud and immorality, closing many private schools run by people with few scruples, introducing greater discipline into the university, protecting intellectuals such as Grimaldi who were notoriously critical of the Roman Church, and, most important, making his projects for in-depth renewal well known. This was more than sufficient for provoking hostility towards Galiani among many groups in Neapolitan culture, even without the denunciation that he was a Lockean , a fact long known in Rome among enlightened Catholics.

Galiani himself commented on his situation, writing: "The task I unwillingly exercise implies by its very nature I might not please everyone." Regarding the private schools,

in order to repair such disorder I have been forced to prohibit all private schools with a strict edict, with the exception of grammar schools. I have only allowed a score to people of recognized learning and probity. Now those roughly two hundred pedants I have sacked, some of whom I also had to imprison—do you know what things they said about me?[47]

Even so, despite his adversaries' focused attacks and the dangerous charges meant to induce him to change tack, Galiani was able to resist their offensive successfully. He accomplished this, however, with the aid of a dense network of friendships that he had been able to cultivate in Rome during the preceding years, silently and with long-sighted vision. Alone, he would certainly have ended in the hands of the Inquisition. Bartolomeo Intieri showered Giovanni Bottari and, particularly, Cardinal Neri Corsini with letters, defending, imploring, and threatening:

> If here one makes any step against this fraternity, innocent of the charges made against it, it would only scandalize and nauseate the entire public, which has demonstrated its approval of these kinds of innocent study which are also useful to civic life.[48]

Scholars have long searched for the lengthy letter that Galiani wrote to Leprotti, Bottari, Cerati, and Niccolini, containing a sort of appeal aimed at his friends, and recently a copy was found and published.[49] Guido Grandi was also informed of the persecution under way.[50] But most important, Galiani turned to Cardinal Davia[51] and his Viennese friends from Giannone's group, wisely enlisting the radical wing of Neapolitan jurisdictionalists. Gianjacopo Marinoni, Pio Garelli, Biagio Garofalo, and Pietro Giannone himself requested imperial protection for the acedemy;[52] the protection was quickly granted, despite terrible "insinuations" from Rome, which directed the apostolic nuncio in Vienna, Domenico Passionei, to denounce the scant concern the new *cappellano maggiore* displayed for repairing the "great disorders that are multiplying in the Kingdom of Naples, to the great detriment to the service of God and souls."[53]

However, the cries of alarm of the *veteres* and the Neapolitan clergy were not unfounded, if Intieri, lying to protect Galiani, could write to Neri Corsini: "I assure Your Excellence that this Locke is known to no one; one can say 'no one' when barely two or three alone distantly know of him. As for me, I can swear that I have never heard him discussed."[54] In reality, the academy members had commented on the French edition of Locke's *Thoughts Concerning Education*, as Intieri let slip in the same letter to Corsini;[55] there was probably also a copy of Galiani's *Scienza Morale* circulating, which, as we discussed earlier at length, was destructive for Catholic morality. With its role of mediation between all branches of the party of *novatores*, the academy finally made possible a kind of ideological refounding of the party itself. The confusion and the philosophical conflicts of the preceding years found in the academy a positive outlet through the free confrontation of ideas. The emergence of a new hegemony of Lockeans s and Newtonians among the *novatores* occurred without traumas or splinterings under the capable direction of the new *cappellano maggiore*.

Founded with limited resources and without any financial assistance from Austrian authorities, the academy had to arrange for and furnish its own scientific instruments, relying only on the patronage of Francesco Maria Spinelli and, starting in 1742, an income from Cardinal Francesco Acquaviva.[56] Its vitality in the early years must, therefore, be attributed essentially to the initiative of a few members who guaranteed its entrance into a scientific circuit not only national (they established contacts with Rome, Rimini, Pisa, Bologna, and Padua) but international (Paris and London) through Cirillo and Galiani, members of the Royal Society. In his autobiographical *Ristretto* [Extract], Galiani carefully explained the academy's experimentalist and Baconian character, comparable with the characters of analogous English and French institutions: "A pamphlet was printed and sent to persons and inhabitants in the cities and in other places in the kingdom, inviting them to perform the experiments written [in the pamphlet] and communicate to the academy with which they ought to have regular correspondence."[57] The problem of equipment for performing experiments was staunchly confronted from the very first days. The four hundred florins Spinelli gave to purchase equipment in Holland were considered negligible by the expert Francesco d'Aguirre, to whom Galiani had turned for advice. The Sicilian reformer's disconsolate conclusion in his response is eloquent testimony to the difficulties the Neapolitan academy faced for lack of funds. Commenting on his and Galiani's actions, d'Aguirre wrote: "We have good will, but we are few, unorganized and without prestige; nevertheless we cannot lose hope, because insisting over and over, we will get something."[58]

The stubbornness of Cirillo, Intieri, and Galiani triumphed over every obstacle. In June 1733 the equipment chosen and purchased personally by "Boharave [sic] and 'sGravesande"[59] at Galiani's behest arrived from Holland. Given the task of caring for the maintenance and eventual upgrading of equipment, in October 1733 Bartolomeo Intieri could finally hold the first "conversation" about a pneumatic machine designed by Willem 'sGravesande.[60] Soon the frequent experiments and weekly meetings began to hearten consistent groups of intellectuals, reopening Neapolitan culture to philosophical and scientific problems that were at the center of European debate. Research into natural reality occupied an absolutely privileged position in these gatherings. Intieri was sent to observe the regions of Capitanata in Apulia hit by earthquakes in 1732 and 1733. His reports fostered a discussion about the problems of the origins of earthquakes involving Lamberti, Intieri, Cirillo, and, especially, Giovanni Bottari, whose *Tre lezioni sopra i tremoti* [Three lectures on earthquakes] was requested directly from Rome.[61] Niccolò Cirillo held lectures that were "greatly applauded" on the chemical composition of the mineral waters in Campania and scientific theories related to magnetism.[62]

With Cirillo's death in 1735, the Cartesian faction in the academy slowly lost prestige until it disappeared. Celestino Galiani's pupil Francesco Serao became his heir, and he would eventually assume the position of chief naturalist within the academy.[63] His academic lectures are a valuable document for understanding the new scientific climate inaugurated in Naples. Serao's *Istoria dell'incendio del Vesuvio accaduto nel mese di maggio dell'anno* MDCCXXXVII, *scritta per l'Accademia delle scienze* [History of the eruption of Vesuvius which occurred in the month of May in the year 1737, written for the Academy of the Sciences] (Naples, 1738) went through numerous editions, including a French translation. In the introduction, he developed the academy's Baconian program, insisting particularly on the cumulative character of modern science: "natural science . . . is nothing more than a cloth woven of thousands of events in time and place, more often than not very dissimilar."[64] In his opinion, this was why it was necessary to unite the forces of scientists the world over, to guarantee the exchange of information among different academies. The work is a top-notch scientific analysis of the Campanian geological situation, pleasantly written and rich in references to the most recent theories, without leaving out the positive contributions of the philosophers from antiquity. The author presented the phenomenon of Vesuvius's eruptions using precise scientific data such as temperature, pressure of the surrounding air, and "quality of the day."

The substantial empiricism that Serao theorized, strongly emphasizing the academicians' abandonment of Cartesian mechanicism, is more evident in his lectures on *Tarantola o vero falangio di Puglia* [The tarantula or wolf spider of Apulia], published in 1742. Of the four lectures originally planned, Serao presented only three; nevertheless these were sufficient to outline the cultural framework in which he intended to operate. He maintained here, erroneously, that "the true reason for tarantism" was attributable to the tarantula's poison. Later, when he became aware that the experimental data on which he based this hypothesis were not reliable, he began to consider Tommaso Cornelio's theory less absurd, for it attributed the convulsions in victims of tarantism [*tarantolati*] to other causes.[65] However, the importance of his work does not lie as much in the theories discussed as in his method of investigation and cultural references. Bitterly opposed to the iatrophysics accepted by Cirillo and Neapolitan Cartesian doctors, Serao interpreted the new experimental and empiricist needs of Neapolitan culture, realigning himself with the theses of Thomas Sydenham's "practical medicine" developed in the famous University of Montpellier and by then accepted by great doctors such as Boerhaave, Tissot, and Tronchin.[66] Careful observation of the human body, semiotics, and the refusal to reduce medicine to a physical and mathematical science were the concretely empirical elements in Serao's thought, whose underpinnings went back primarily to Gassendi and Galileo.[67]

Certainly among the naturalists at the academy, particularly Serao, the Newtonian principle *hypotheses non fingo* [I do not fake hypotheses] was developed in light of the Investiganti experimentalist tradition of Cornelio and Di Capua. The relationship between the two groups, however, must be reappraised if one considers that the Investiganti, aside from their experimental approach, aimed to reconstruct a system of the world totally alien to Serao's, whether it was on the mechanist bases that Porzio theorized or on the chemical-vitalist ones maintained by Di Capua.

Judging from the important lectures on mechanics and astronomy held at the academy, its separation from the Investiganti tradition was even more pronounced on the gnosiological plane. The influence of Newtonianism on these two disciplines was particularly evident. Niccolò Di Martino, Mario Lama, Giuseppe Orlandi, Bartolomeo Intieri, and Celestino Galiani scarcely had worthy opponents in these gatherings. Thanks to a series of lectures that Niccolò Di Martino and Mario Lama held simultaneously in Ciro De Alteriis's Accademia Ecclesiastica,[68] it is possible to reconstruct the discussions that developed in the academy, which reveal new details about Neapolitan Newtonianism in the 1730s.

On 27 October 1733 Intieri advised Bottari that two days hence they would perform "some experiments carried out by 'sGravesande and Marquis Polleni of Padua, and they believe they will reach results that are diametrically opposed to those the gentlemen affirm."[69] The experiments in question were the famous ones on living forces that had roused much discussion among European scientists. The Newtonians from Naples were among those who openly sided with the *Principia*'s theses, according to which the quantity of motion was equal to the product of mass times velocity, and not times the square of the velocity, as Leibniz's followers believed, along with Riccati and Conti in Italy.

One sees the sophistication that Neapolitan Newtonianism had reached not only in the unmistakably widespread and in-depth knowledge of the English scientist's works but, above all, in the violent disputes that erupted within the academy between Mario Lama and Niccolò Di Martino over their opposing interpretations of the fifth and sixth corollaries of the *Principia*'s third law of motion.[70] The entire issue grew out of a memorable academic discussion on the very recent discovery of the aberration in the fixed stars made by James Bradley, the greatest astronomer of the century. "Speaking of the parallaxes that ought to be observed in the stars if the earth moved along an elliptical path,"[71] in January 1733 Mario Lama had illustrated Manfredi's theses on the Newtonian Bradley's discoveries, arguing in a friendly fashion against Di Martino and Manfredi himself, who were not fully convinced by the mathematical demonstrations that Bradley put forward. Thanks to Di Martino's piqued response, during subsequent meetings it became evident that in the final analysis the heart of the issue encompassed problems of celestial mechanics, or, rather, some particularly complex interpretations of Newtonian theories regarding the concept of relative and absolute motion. Mario Lama supported the originally Galilean and Cartesian thesis that there existed a generalized and reciprocal relative motion in nature. As an orthodox Newtonian, Di Martino, on the other hand, preferred to stress the importance of the concept of force in the *Principia*'s celestial dynamics and the related notion of absolute and relative motion. We cannot examine the dispute in detail here, but it developed to a very high level through 1735, involving both Lamberti and Galiani.[72] The spirit in which the discussion between these scientifically mature Newtonians was carried out is captured by Mario Lama's sarcastic sally against Niccolò Di Martino, whom he accused of wishing to distort the *Principia*'s true philosophical teachings and of wishing to create a kind of new Newtonian scholastics in Naples: "But what should we care whether he really said this? Should we, therefore, let ourselves be persuaded more by his authority than by reason? I really believe Newton himself would scornfully disapprove such vile and unworthy slavishness in us."[73] These words, spoken in 1734, could have easily had the subscription of either Voltaire or d'Alembert.

Although he was ready to demolish myths in the name of reason, Mario Lama was not the most interesting personality at the academy; that honor fell to Bartolomeo Intieri, already an experienced mathematician and ever more at home with the intellectual and political ferments of those years. His role was, in fact, fundamental. Once Niccolò Cirillo was dead and the Cartesian influence was extinguished, the scientific renewal and empiricist choice increasingly began to assume a more exact ideological and programmatical content, precisely because of Galiani's and Intieri's requests that scholars pay more attention to the political and social problems that Ludovico Antonio Muratori had synthesized in the formula of "public happiness." Having eliminated philosophical systems and redirected intellectuals to the concrete examination of natural reality, Bartolomeo Intieri then had at his disposal an audience more perceptive than the one that in 1716 had indifferently received his project on the windmill. In 1734 the machines he constructed were discussed and evaluated very carefully within the academy. His scales and the heater for preserving grain, presented at the academy in 1734 to some Sicilian nobles so that it might be introduced in Sicily,[74] ultimately became the most obvious sign of the new spirit in Neapolitan culture.

It is important to clarify that, despite this fervent and courageous restlessness, the new spirit was in a precarious position, entrusted to scattered intellectual energies and still lacking a solid institutional base. If not for Galiani's reform of the university already underway, profoundly rooting this new spirit in Neapolitan culture, once the initial period of enthusiasm had passed, a number of parts of the picture would have faced failure: the research on volcanos and earthquakes, the minute analysis of Newtonian mathematical empiricism, the examination of the greatest astronomical discoveries of the century, and the construction of agricultural machinery. But, perhaps most important, people would never have felt the ever more widespread impression that they were experiencing an era of energetic reawakening in which intellectuals were finally called upon as leaders.

In 1714 a similar enterprise had already been attempted as an important element of the politics of renewal promoted at the beginning of Charles of Habsburg's government by ministers favorable to modern culture, including Biscardi, Argento, Contegna, Riccardi, Filippo Caravita, and many others. Lack of funds and the irresolution of then–*cappellano maggiore* Vincenzo Vidania caused the initiative to fail.[75] Galiani, recently arrived in Naples, at the same time that he started regrouping the party of the *novatores*, staunchly undertook the difficult task of radically transforming the entire Neapolitan teaching system, drastically reducing the number of private schools and religious seminaries in favor of the university. In June 1732 Intieri had already advised Bottari: "The Monsignor has conceived of a wonderful reform for this university . . ., but it is meeting with great difficulties."[76] In August of 1732, before this reform plan was sent to Vienna for the crucial opinion of the Council of Spain, it was discussed at the Collaterale along five points— the problem of the university's seat, the renewal of the chairs, the issue of the serious disparity in salaries paid to teachers of different faculties, the drawback of the competitions to enter the university, and the reformulation of a new internal statute binding teachers to specific rules of conduct.

The discussion among Neapolitan rulers developed in a very lively fashion. There was reference to the "similar reform" held in 1714, and the secretary of the Kingdom of Naples, Niccolò Fraggianni, advised that the chaired professors were "content to change the subjects and . . . quite ready to prepare new lectures." Both he and another of Giannone's friends, Francesco Ventura, were decisively in favor of this. Ventura said that the change could not be deferred "in order not to get stuck alone in the mire of barbarism and ignorance"; he did not wish to enter "into the odious comparison and judgment of preferring modern doctrines to ancient," but he noted that if the university were denied Galiani's reforms, it would ultimately cease to exist, and it would be left without students. According to Ventura, the interventions should be allowed even without the Viennese court's involvement, according to an informal and profitable technique well known to Neapolitan ministers: the chair teaching Scotus, rather than reading that "ridiculous abstract doctrine," would be allowed to teach ecclesiastical history. This very system had been adopted at other times, for example "regarding Aristotle, for whom chairs remain without the doctrine being taught." The other rulers maintained that "the order of His Majesty" was indispensable, but they approved various aspects of the reform, especially of activating the chair in ecclesiastical history, already instituted and then suspended by the sovereign on Grazini's death. In any case, even opponents shared the sentiment on the character of Aristotelian and Scotist teachings; Mazzacara said that they kept "brains busy in a variety of opinions over abstract matters of little importance."[77]

Galiani had formulated his integrated plan by requesting detailed information from all his friends "both in Italy as well as north of the Alps."[78] In reality, the project did not foresee steady increases in expenditures, and, instead, it pointed to substantial changes in the structure of education. The faculty of theology was asked first to replace one of the two chairs in "Scotist theology" with a chair in Church history, the keystone in the program of religious renewal of Catholics and those like Muratori and Grimaldi who were appreciative of the spread of Maurist historiography. Galiani's modifications for the study of law were thought to be too radical by Giannone, who was called upon by the Council of Spain to express his opinion in 1733.[79] Regarding the traditional teachings of "decretals and pandicts," Galiani asked that their number be reduced in favor of new disciplines more in line with the choices offered by the great European universities, such as the institution of a chair in the natural law of peoples and one in *ius regni*, or municipal law, as it was then called. In the projected provisions for the faculties of medicine and philosophy, the orientations prominent in the Accademia delle Scienze found a precise and meaningful implementation. In fact, two of the four chairs in theoretical and practical medicine were to be eliminated, in favor of teaching botany, chemistry, and practical surgery. In the field of philosophy the advancement was even greater: the two prestigious chairs in metaphysics and logic were to be combined, thus demonstrating the loss of these disciplines' importance, while for physics a division into theoretical and experimental physics was projected. Even in the faculty of mathematics, the sole chair (held by Agostino Ariani) was to be split into one teaching geometry and algebra and one teaching the entirely new astronomy, navigation, and mechanics.[80]

The reform was blocked, however, in the Austrian capital, despite the fact that Galiani, with his usual skill, involved influential figures in Rome, Naples, and Vienna. Only after the war, with the arrival of Charles of Bourbon, did his realization take off, and then only partially. We will not investigate here the background of these affairs, though because of their importance, they do merit a close-up study. We ought, however, to pause to consider the concrete results of the difficult battles fought during these years. Galiani and Intieri had collected in the Accademia delle Scienze some of the most promising young men in Neapolitan culture, along with very prestigious figures such as Di Martino and Cirillo. Through the capable conducting of competitions for teaching posts and thanks to developments of Galiani's reform project, in the following years the better part of these academy members came to occupy the most authoritative chairs of the Neapolitan university, guaranteeing a type of cultural hegemony that had been absolutely inconceivable a few years earlier and that not even the Investiganti had ever succeeded in establishing, even in the period of their greatest splendor. In the faculty of medicine, Cirillo and Serao had practically no rivals; in philosophy, the new chair formed by combining metaphysics and logic was assigned to Giambattista Lamberti; theoretical and experimental physics were given respectively to Mario Lama and Giuseppe Orlandi; and in the following years ethics went to Antonio Genovesi, another pupil of the *cappellano maggiore.*[81] The influence of the academicians in the faculty of mathematics was indisputable. The first chair in geometry and algebra was definitively assigned to Niccolò Di Martino, and the newly created astronomy chair to Pietro Di Martino, not to mention a series of new nominations of professors connected to Galiani who were to teach in the faculty of theology.[82] Thus within the span of a decade, the Accademia delle Scienze and the university reform profoundly renewed Neapolitan culture, and, most important, the academy and the reformed university were able to give this Neapolitan culture a solid institutional foundation, establishing professors attuned to new culture in the very core of university teaching. In a letter sent to his enlightened Catholic friends, Galiani illustrated the great possibilities that the office of *cappellano maggiore* offered him, an indispensable prerequisite for the renewal to occur in such an integrated manner:

> Here chairs are given through competitions. Each of the claimants must, within a twenty-four-hour period, give a public lecture on some text chosen by lot, and there is an incredibly competitive emulation among the claimants. After all have presented their lectures, the chair will be conferred on one of them by secret vote. Despite this, when the *cappellano maggiore* is considering someone, whomever he wants shall be provided [the chair], as when during my time three chairs were vacated and all were given to whom I thought was most deserving.[83]

In this way Newtonianism and Lockean empiricism could put down roots in Naples that were very much deeper than has ever been suspected. Rarely in the history of Italian culture has it been possible to document such a clear awareness of what a great role institutions and public authorities could play. The ideological refoundation of the party of the *novatores* found an impassioned advocate in Celestino Galiani and his plans for a militant intelligentsia. However, we should not make the serious error of imagining that Neapolitan cultural life was completely dominated by a wing of scholars gathered about the *cappellano maggiore*; in fact, there was no dearth of philosophical or scientific alternatives in those years. Vico, Doria, Giuseppe Pasquale Cirillo, Carlo Antonio Broggia, and many others met in the academies or within the university itself, or acted as private scholars, and they resolutely opposed the theories of Niccolò and Pietro Di Martino, Bartolomeo Intieri, and Francesco Serao, eventually forming a kind of stimulating scientific counterrevolution in the guise of a grand humanist-Christian synthesis that they opposed to the image of Newton's universe-machine.

3. PAOLO MATTIA DORIA'S SCIENTIFIC COUNTERREVOLUTION

A few months after the opening of the Accademia delle Scienze in 1733, the Collaterale authorized the foundation of a new academy named *"degli*

Oziosi" [of the leisured] in the palace of Niccolò Maria Salerno "of the barons of Lucignano."[1] It was an attempt at organization by a large group of intellectuals who opposed the *cappellano maggiore*'s new direction and who wanted to create an effective, permanent structure. Giuseppe Pasquale Cirillo, then one of the greatest teachers of law at the university, was nominated secretary of the academy.[2] Among the figures who supported the initiative, two men had particularly prominent roles: Giambattista Vico and Paolo Mattia Doria, the latter as a "censor." Little is known about the discussions that enlivened the weekly meetings of the Oziosi. In addition to Doria's participation, published in his *Ragionamenti e poesie varie* [Arguments and various poems] (1737), we have the list of the members, some chronicle entries on the internal life of the academy, and the list of lecture titles from 1733 to 1735.[3] It is slim evidence indeed, but enough to clarify a few important points.

In the first place, the subscribers were predominantly ecclesiastical or aristocratic. University professors included Vico, Cirillo, Aniello Firelli (teacher of metaphysics), and Gennaro Giuliani (teacher of theology). Together with other noble members of the academy such as Antonio Capece Zurlo and Giuseppe Maria Salerno, Doria gave interesting lectures on "ancient and modern warfare"; nor did he miss the opportunity to launch violent attacks against the modern science promoted by Galiani's academy. In three works, the sexagenarian Doria clearly outlined the ideological frame of reference in which the advocates of the *veteres*, the protagonists of the academy, were to work: the *Considerazioni sulla vita di Carlo XII di Svezia, scritta dal signor Voltaire* [Considerations on the life of Charles XII of Sweden, written by Mr. Voltaire]; the *Ragionamento V: Nel quale si fa paragone fra l'antica e moderna sapienza e fra l'antica e moderna virtù* [Fifth argument: In which a comparison is made between ancient and modern science and between ancient and modern virtue]; and the *Misantropo: Dialogo critico diviso in due giornate nel quale l'autore, diffendendo la sapienza degli antichi, critica quella dei moderni* [The misanthrope: A critical dialogue divided into two days in which the author, defending the science of the ancients, criticizes that of the moderns].[4] One need only scan the titles of the lectures to perceive the profound influence that Doria had on the Oziosi. The priest Antonio Spinelli was entrusted with the task of refuting Lockean doctrines with a series of specific lectures on the subject; the first was entitled *Dell'uso della ragione nelle cose della fede contra Giovanni Locke* [On the use of reason in matters of faith against John Locke].[5] Much space was reserved for problems of sacred history, biblical chronology, poetics, and the study of ancient Greek and Roman tragedies.[6] Giuseppe Pasquale Cirillo and Doria himself commented on Roman law. Religious orthodoxy was defended against the Libertines and Epicureans and, particularly, against "the impious Benedetto Spinosa," whose philosophical system was rejected in many gatherings.[7]

A noteworthy counterpoint to the considerable attention the Oziosi dedi-

cated to metaphysics, archaeology, the study of law, and "poetics and ora-
tory" was the limited time allowed for natural sciences, which were entrusted to the Jesuit Giambattista Botti and Aniello Firelli, teacher of
metaphysics. The overall efforts of the Oziosi on such important themes as
history, law, morals, and philosophy should not be underestimated in its
very capacity to bring to the fore, by way of contrast, the very different
choices made by Galiani's academy in favor of the study of science and
technology. Actually there were nearly one hundred Oziosi[8]—demonstrating how false was the image that Doria perpetuated of his complete isolation within Neapolitan culture; thus we can say that there existed a steady
nucleus of intellectuals in those years who were determined to reevaluate
humanist studies in the face of the broadening of technical and scientific
interests. In 1735 the academy's secretary Giuseppe Pasquale Cirillo illustrated the overall importance of the cultural choices made by the Oziosi,
pointing explicitly and perceptively to Doria and Vico as points of reference in the new institution, announcing "the former is the restorer of Platonic philosophy and a renowned author of new mathematical proofs; the
latter is also author of a marvelous system of a new science about the principles of the nature of nations."[9]

Although Doria's and Vico's philosophical and more generally ideological influence on the Oziosi is a certainty, the effort they expended in the
foundation and development of the academy is quite another matter. Doria
was long interested in the project, but Vico, after the first lectures he held
on the role of masks in Greek tragedy (in part disagreeing with Cirillo),[10]
abandoned the initiative little by little, tired of disputes and arguments. In
1732 Celestino Galiani intervened on Vico's behalf, requesting that his Roman
friends seek forty ducats from Cardinal Neri Corsini; and in an unedited
letter written in August, he sketched a pathetic portrait of Vico, in no way
comparable to the proud and tenacious figure of Doria, who in those same
years was even accused of having denounced Galiani to the Inquisition rather
than see his theses prevail. The *cappellano* wrote to Bottari: "I know that
you are acquainted with Giambattista Vico by reputation, a professor of
some eloquence in this university. He is a good old man and very erudite,
but poorer than you could ever believe." Evidently the *cappellano maggiore*
sincerely cared for the author of the *Scienza nuova*, and he passionately
pleaded his cause, imploring for an intervention at least "to let this poor
old man die consoled."[11] Vico, increasingly "melancholy and afflicted," apparently no longer actively battled among the *veteres*, as is confirmed both
by the reflections in the *Autobiografia* and by these comments of Galiani.

Of the two prestigious philosophers, only Doria remained to guide the
Oziosi in their offensive against their young antagonists in Galiani's academy. Beyond the disputes of the 1730s, nevertheless, the gnosiological and
philosophical conflict with Galiani's circle had older precedents, and its
foundations lay both in Doria's criticism of modern science and in Vico's

theory of the essential role played by history in the cognitive process.

In 1711 Paolo Mattia Doria handed publishers his *Considerazioni sopra il moto e la meccanica de' corpi sensibili e de' corpi insensibili* [Considerations on motion and mechanics of sentient bodies and insentient bodies], which appeared in 1712, and the *Nuovo metodo geometrico per trovare fra due linee date infinite medie proporzionali* [A new geometric method for finding infinite mean proportionals between two given lines] (1714), the original nucleus of his scientific thought. From 1711 to 1715 he authoritatively participated in the epistemological debate under way among Neapolitan intellectuals, curbing the criticisms against Galilean works on the motion of falling weights developed by Lucantonio Porzio's Investiganti group. Doria's three pamphlets were generally overlooked by scholars, who preferred to examine his mature philosophical writings or political and economic treatises.

Yet one of the keys to understanding the successive developments in Doria's thought, not to mention the essential features of his impassioned debate against the moderns, lies in these writings, as admired by the author as they were denigrated by his contemporaries.[12] All Doria's works appearing after 1715 defended his mathematical inventions and scientific discoveries. In the years during which he introduced Neapolitan intellectuals to his thought on the evolution of modern science and the direction that research ought to take to overcome the stagnant phase that resulted from the irreparable exhaustion of the Investiganti's inheritance, Doria was unanimously considered one of the most prestigious proponents of the party of the moderns in Naples.[13] His *Vita civile* [Civic life], which appeared in 1709, had raised interest and admiration everywhere. In 1716, Jean Le Clerc did not hesitate to compare it to the great works of Grotius and Pufendorf, and the editors of the *Acta eruditorum* and the *Giornale de' Letterati* declared their approval.[14] These were well-merited approvals, for the *Viva civile* remains the most interesting and perceptive work he wrote. It is a work of great breadth and, in some ways, innovative for its times, with its examination of social and political mechanisms as they were shaped in human history, its keen grasp of the complex problems of distinguishing between judicial, legislative, and executive power in the political equilibrium of modern states, and its opinions on republics and monarchies.[15] One of many themes to take shape in the *Vita civile* is the political hypothesis about the essential role of the *Ministero togato* in leading the government, an idea that made the close tie between the author and the progressive groups of the Neapolitan *ceto civile* even more explicit.[16] Whether on the political or intellectual level, in 1713 Doria still fully deserved the title "head of the Cartesians" (understood in the most general sense, as his contemporaries used it, as head of the *novatores*) which Paolo Francone, the marquis of Salcito, attributed to him in the foreword to the Italian translation of the *Vie de M. Descartes*.[17]

Within a few years, however, the situation was entirely reversed. His defense of Galileo in the *Considerazioni*, discussing motion and mechanics and arguing against Porzio, was immediately preceded by Bartolomeo Intieri's even more effective exposition of the Galilean gnosiological model in 1710, in line with modern mathematical empiricism and opposed to Doria's geometrical and metaphysical abstractions. The following disputes made even more evident the internal breakdown that occurred in the party of the moderns between the Investiganti naturalists linked to Porzio, the Galilean empiricists headed by Galiani and Intieri, and the Galilean Neoplatonists and metaphysicists who considered Doria their greatest proponent. The situation only came to a head after the appearance of Doria's *Nuovo metodo geometrico* in 1714. All the Neapolitan intellectuals reacted violently to the theses put forward in this pamphlet. Galizia, Intieri, Ariani, and De Cristoforo spoke out harshly against Doria, who, annoyed by these arguments, invited other Italian and foreign scholars to declare their positions. To his great disappointment, however, Leibniz, Grandi, Galiani, and the mathematicians of the *Acta eruditorum* rejected—not without irony—his so-called mathematical discoveries.[18] Even more tellingly, Celestino Galiani, generally a respectful man who rarely adopted an aggressive tone, did not hesitate to comment on the complete edition of *Le opere matematiche di P. M. Doria* [The complete mathematical works of P. M. Doria], writing pitilessly to Guido Grandi in 1722: "Doria has republished all his *coglionerie* [bullshit] in one volume."[19] All Doria's later works were irreparably marred by his bitterness over the reception his book received, by his particularly difficult and proud personality, and by his exasperated reactions. His *Discorsi critici filosofici intorno alla filosofia degli antichi* [Critical philosophical discourses on the philosophy of the ancients] from 1724 reveals that his complete separation from the *novatores* was by then a fait accompli.

Scholars studying Doria have generally focused on the defense of his three pamphlets that he presented in the following years and on his fierce attacks against such proponents of modern thought as Descartes, Newton, Locke, and Voltaire. Even so, in those three pamphlets Doria had brought into focus an original epistemological model that was certainly unique and paradoxical, but that nevertheless had undoubted attraction and considerable logical rigor if men such as Vico, Broggia, Pasquale Cirillo, and a majority of the Oziosi remained so strongly impressed.

In the *Considerazioni sopra il moto e la meccanica* [Considerations on motion and mechanics], Doria had already laid down the (somewhat confused) foundations for an epistemological model that showed glimpses of a rudimentary distinction between the science of "sentient bodies," qualitative and based on the experiment, and the science of "insentient bodies," to which he assigned the determination of the mathematical laws of the universe. With the publication of the *Nuovo metodo geometrico* some years later, the features of this model finally acquired an organic form, and they were expounded clearly both in the complete edition of the *Opere matematiche* and the *Discorsi critici filosofici* as well.[20] Doria did not at all deny that some aspects of natural reality needed to be understood through experience, understood in a Baconian, qualitative sense. In fact, he believed that the procedure starting from the evidence was extremely valid and had no substitute in chemistry, botany, medicine, and physics of "sentient bodies." However, he rejected modern iatrophysical theories and the mathematization of physiological processes in the study of the human body and nature in general—in other words, Galileo's physico-mathematical method.[21] In research on perceptible realities, once one accepted the experimental method—as Doria approvingly had—one had to be content with likely, probable knowledge, useful to man but far from any truth of a mathematical sort. According to Doria, the science of "insentient bodies" was quite another thing, and as a whole it ultimately shaped Doria's famous "immaterial extension."[22] The serious break between Doria and the moderns came from working out the cognitive processes of this new science and the examination of its ontological foundations.

Rejecting the Cartesian distinction between extension and thought, Doria came to see the "immaterial One" as the ontological foundation—obviously Platonically inspired—of our knowledge.[23] To accept the thesis that the reality that surrounds us is, in the end, nothing more than "a mode of the divine substance," according to Doria, meant a radical redefinition of the contents and cognitive tools of modern science. Just like Vico, Doria, too, had identified the ontological foundation of motion and extension in Zeno's geometrical point, interpreted as an invisible metaphysical being.[24] In his mind, in order to develop coherently, modern science had to take into account these preliminary considerations. It was necessary to agree with Galileo and the greatest scientists of the era about the possibilities granted to humans to reach absolute truths in the determination of universal mathematical laws. This was why it was so important for Doria strenuously to defend Galileo's formula for the motion of falling bodies against the Investiganti's scientific probabilism. His views on cognitive processes and the tools to be used to discover these mathematical laws formed the background of his break with the moderns. Developing his premises on reality's structure according to Zeno's model, Doria vehemently rejected Cartesian analytic geometry as a cognitive tool. In order to overcome the dangerous shoal of Zeno's paradox on motion, modern mechanism had been forced to resort to an empiricist conception of temporal succession.[25] Doria always avoided this step, which was necessary if one wished to attempt a phenomenalist description of the world. He remained rooted in a geometrical conception of reality, stubbornly maintaining that Cartesian analytic geometry and modern infinitesimal calculus were truly a scientific degeneration.[26]

In the *Opere matematiche*, Doria clearly expressed his ideas on Cartesian thought, accusing it of having ruined the purity of synthetic Euclidean geometry, "a divine science that had its origin in the innate idea that the human soul has of God." According to Doria, Descartes supposedly committed the serious error of considering conic sections as trajectories described by points in motion, thus introducing a time factor extraneous to the Euclidean deductive process and explicable only through an empirical examination of the chronological succession. The conic sections that the French philosopher studies with the new method were no longer geometrical curves but merely "mechanical" ones, and were, therefore, inadequate for comprehending the intimate "essence" of natural laws.[27] Taking as literally true Galileo's famous thesis that the book of nature was written by God in geometrical characters, "triangles, circles, and other figures," Doria reached the troubling conclusion that only Euclidean synthetic geometry, with its logical rigor and the purity it derived from being the divine language, could reveal the mathematical truths of natural laws. The geometrical structure of creation, made up of Zeno's metaphysical points totally extraneous to the temporal concept of motion, could not be resolved definitively through Cartesian analytic geometry nor, with greater reason, through Newtonian and Leibnizian infinitesimal calculus. Far from limiting himself to simple declarations of principle, in Euclidean fashion Doria geometricized an entire science analogous to Galileo's in his mechanics, even working out a complicated cosmological system capable of geometrically explaining gravity and the motion of planets through the thesis of Platonic circumpulsion and the circular orbital motion of the planets.[28]

Given such rigorously argued and applied epistemological premises, a harsh confrontation with all Neapolitan scholars was almost inevitable. While modern scientists have posited the time element as the linchpin of a physico-mathematical language through which natural phenomena can be comprehended,[29] Doria, instead, reacted indignantly, accusing all of having confused the science of "sentient bodies," in which he conceded the use of the experimental method, Cartesian "mechanical" curves, and infinitesimal analysis because they were the "means" of divine substance, with the science of "insentient bodies," in which only a rigorous language of superhuman origin, such as synthetic Euclidean geometry, could attain definitive results. In short, Doria's was a kind of genuine scientific counterrevolution that in a single blow canceled out the very foundations on which Galileo, Descartes, and Newton had unfolded the thesis of a single, great, phenomenological science.

In 1724 Doria identified Descartes as the guilty party behind the wretched "confusion" between the two sciences.[30] Keeping in mind Doria's gnosiological premises, it was almost inevitable that Locke, Newton, 'sGravesande, Musschenbroek, Voltaire, and others also came to be identified as responsible parties. His extremely categorical rejection of the "material and carnal science" in the *Principia* and *Opticks* is a primary example.[31] But Doria denounced the epistemological foundations themselves, rather than the scientific results of these works. After all, could he accept the concepts of velocity, acceleration, and gravitational force, all linked to logical developments of a physico-mathematical algorithm like infinitesimal analysis, in which the derivative was interpreted in its kinematical meaning of movement with respect to time?[32] Euclid, synthetic geometry, and Zeno's metaphysical points were radically different gnosiological choices. The modern reader who examines Doria's writings immediately notices that his fierce criticisms of Newton are a global alternative, a genuinely preconceived rejection that can in no way be bridged. The two positions were thoroughly incompatible. In the eyes of the great English scholar and all modern scientists in general, the universe-machine seemed to be a continuation of spatial-temporal events in which it was necessary to grasp the cause-and-effect links in an adequate physico-mathematical language, even if sometimes less than rigorous on a logical level. For Doria, the natural world, coinciding with "the divine Oneness of God," was essentially constructed of points, lines, and angles, whose immutable mathematical laws could be known only through synthetic Euclidean geometry.

The other philosopher to whom the Oziosi explicitly referred, Giambattista Vico, by right placed himself among those who reevaluated the role of metaphysics, to the detriment of the spreading empiricist phenomenalism of Cartesians and Lockeans such as Niccolò Cirillo and Celestino Galiani. From the very early eighteenth century, Vico contributed in a wholly unique way to the redefinition of an epistemological model that took metaphysics and the traditional humanist type of synthesis fully into account. Vico's thought has been so thoroughly studied that there are few uncertainties about its chronology and how it matured. For our purposes, it is important to review some of the aspects that came together, along with Doria's scientific arguments, in the ideological framework of the Oziosi.[33]

Vico restated many of the arguments that his Genoan colleague and friend used against Cartesian analytic geometry and the novatores, and in particular against their inability to give certain and not merely probable answers in the study of reality. In fact, Doria's theory of the two sciences finds many parallels in Vico's writings.[34] Nevertheless, the criticism of Cartesian mathematicism and rationalism ("we demonstrate geometric things because we make them; if we could demonstrate physical things, we would also make them") led Vico quite far from Doria's paradoxical synthetic theories.[35] Whereas Doria ultimately worked out the not merely abstract possibility of a science of absolutely certain mathematical truths (with interesting implications in the fields of morals, economics, religion, and politics as well), Vico utterly rejected the allure of the "synthetic" and "metaphysical" image of science that Doria had envisioned. His elaboration of an epistemological model adequate for the needs of the times initially brought him to spurn mathematicism and logicism in the Orazioni inaugurali [Inaugural speeches]. His goal in the De antiquissima Italorum sapientia [On the most ancient learning of the Italics] was to distill his metaphysics based on the identification of "doing" and "knowing," and then to move on to the concrete foundation of philosophy based on philology and the historical event, and then to the identification of thought with its own history and the reevaluation of poetry and human imagination as crucial elements of knowledge.[36] Vico held that Cartesian rationalism and the fascination of Galilean and Newtonian mathematical laws were useless for the study of society and human history. Unlike Doria, who envisioned a synthetic and metaphysical image of science, in the end Vico preferred a gnosiology founded on the truth of human "doing" and the examination of the historical process, the sole antidote to the division between man and nature implicit in the phenomenalist objectivity of modern science.[37]

From this stemmed his *Principi di scienze nuova* [Principles of new science]. This work proposed intuitions and thoughts more effective and integrated than those put forth by Doria, and capable of finally providing comprehensive and original responses to troubling questions about the origin and role of humans in the historical process, the birth of society, political mechanisms, and the God–nature relationship. Vico hence confronted the unavoidable need for the study of society on a different level, proposing an alternative to modern scientific rationalism under many aspects. The results could not help but be different and contrasting.

Doria, with his rigid philosophical idealism (of which synthetic science was merely one particular aspect), and Vico, with his ingenious suggestions in the *Principi di scienza nuova*, had ultimately constructed epistemological projects that provided alternatives to the Newtonian "material and carnal science" of Intieri and Galiani. The philosophical and cultural implications of their theses appear to be quite a bit more profound than is generally believed, if such an authoritative figure of the Neapolitan age of reforms as Carlo Antonio Broggia referred explicitly to the two patriarchs in his broad economic works. In fact, he drew from Doria's theory of the two sciences the simultaneous acceptance both of experimentalism in the study of physics and medicine, and also of synthetic geometry, the only science able to resolve the "quiddities of things."[38] As with Vico, Broggia, too, came to abandon the hypothesis, so widespread in contemporary thought, that it was possible to understand rationally social and natural reality through research into mathematical laws, whose universal value would demonstrate the validity of the rational cosmic order. Having discarded an image of nature borne by mathematical laws, as Intieri and Galiani maintained, Vico's theory of the fundamental historicity of all natural processes became an obligatory frame of reference for Broggia. The well-known saying according to which "philosophy thinks of the man as he ought to be," and not as he actually is, was echoed in Broggia's clear-cut rejection of scientific objectivity.[39] Ultimately, this irreparably conditioned all of his political and economic thought.

Nevertheless, any desire to attribute schematically an excessive weight to the gnosiological and scientific doctrines of Doria, Vico, Broggia, Cirillo, and many other Neapolitan scholars who opposed the members of the Accademia delle Scienze would be a serious error, for it would overlook the contributions that these men made towards resolving other great problems. Vico's humanist synthesis and Doria's Neoplatonism actually brought a new epistemological model into focus, not only developing fundamental principles of their metaphysical assumptions, but also reacting to the spread of empiricist theories. They were among the first to perceive and identify with extraordinary perspicuity the aspects strongly destructive to Catholic morals and the social balance brought about by the affirmation of modern science. Their disputes with the *novatores* held consequences for all fields of human activity, finally reaching a particularly intense and interesting peak (especially in the case of Doria and Broggia) in the political, economic, and cultural debates of the so-called heroic period.

4. NEOMERCANTILISM AND THE ENLIGHTENMENT: FROM INTIERI TO VENTURA

With Charles of Bourbon's entrance into a festive and rejoicing Naples on 10 May 1734, many people of the time were firmly convinced in their hearts that they were participating in events of great importance, destined to mark a decisive turning point in the political and social life of the entire south of Italy, with repercussions for the rest of the peninsula as well.[1] The great difficulties that awaited the new administration were nearly forgotten in light of the prospects for renewal and reform that the foundation of a national state promised for territories long subject to a direct and often rapacious foreign domination. The hopes raised by the change in regime and the anxiety in finally inaugurating a new period after the dismal failure of Austrian reformism were not disappointed, if we consider the innovations that the old administrative structure of the state underwent between 1734 and 1742 in the fields of commerce, culture, and justice.

Thanks to recent research on these years—so event-filled that Bernardo Tanucci, a level-headed and keen statesman, gave them the felicitous label, the "heroic period" of the Bourbon dynasty—we have finally begun to learn of the true protagonists of Charles's politics of reform, from Pietro Contegna to Francesco Ventura, Bartolomeo Intieri, Celestino Galiani, and José Joaquin de Montealegre.[2] Of this group, Contegna and Ventura in particular, typical proponents of the *ceto civile* and ministers who inherited the great Neapolitan jurisdictionalist tradition, along with high functionaries such as Giovanni Brancaccio and others of great statute like Montealegre, concretely realized the neomercantile program for renewing the state and developing the economy, getting involved firsthand in designing projects and struggling to implement them despite the obstinate resistance of the clergy and conservative groups. In the alliance that they established with Montealegre and Contegna in order to give greater strength to reform plans, Intieri, Galiani, Niccolò Cirillo, Serào, and the *novatores* of the Accademia delle Scienze played, above all, a supportive and externally bracing role aimed at building a new cultural climate adapted to the economic and political changes, limiting their direct intervention to particular occasions, such as the cases of university reform, the concordat with the Holy See, and the decree granting Jews free access in the Kingdom of Naples—all affairs in which Galiani was the protagonist.

Half a century after the experiments of the Frenchman Colbert and of other great European monarchies, Montealegre, Contegna, and Ventura had clear ideas about imposing their daring and intelligent neomercantile plan in Naples. The plan was founded on the indispensable and now realized premise of the national state, but it had distant origins and ideological-cultural references from outside Neapolitan political life. Part of its background was the dissemination of English and French mercantilistic theories in Barcelona among Charles of Habsburg's functionaries.[3] Another important antecedent was the influence of Rocco Stella, a powerful minister and advisor of Archduke Charles, whom Contegna learned about in 1713. Stella, in fact, believed that a politics for developing commerce was "worthwhile for making all classes and every order of the kingdom rich and successful, as the experience of many other kingdoms, especially England, shows."[4] The Spanish or Italo-Spanish *afrancesados* [pro-French], such as Brancaccio, Giuseppe Patiño, and Montealegre, had completed their political apprenticeship in a noticeably modern environment, even in the Bourbon realm of Philip V. These direct or indirect inspirations for Charles's reform were the ones who, together with Ventura and Contegna, bet all their cards on commerce, the centralization of state administration, and a politics of buying back fiscal incomes and staunch opposition to ecclesiastical claims.[5]

In the new direction, the most interesting figure among the Neapolitan *afrancesados*—who included "cultured" jurists attracted to northern European theories such as Biscardi, Riccardi, Argento, and Lucina—was Pietro Contegna.[6] In 1713 in Vienna, an environment (like that of Charles VI) strongly oriented towards intervening in the financial and economic situation of the Neapolitan kingdom, Contegna had already worked out programs for development based on the creation of "societies of merchants." In 1725 he contributed personally to the politics set in motion by the Austrians of buying back the fiscal yields, focusing on a broad plan of renewal centered on the confiscation of ecclesiastical goods.[7] The clergy's intractable opposition, however, had again done away with a great many of the project's most radical features. Many of the harsh battles he fought to impose economic reforms in the Kingdom of Naples quickly resulted in failed experiments; this was how the daring initiative that brought about the foundation of the Banco di San Carlo ended.

Nevertheless, these episodes are valuable evidence of a neomercantile reformism already present in Naples, in the broadest outlines, in the first decades of the eighteenth century. We can verify the intellectual tension and interest that the reformers' proposals raised in many scholars, often of opposing convictions, through a number of works: the radical *Considerazioni proposte a sua Maestà che Dio guardi sull'espediente che può maggiormente contribuire al ristabilimento dello stato del Regno di Napoli* [Considerations proposed by his majesty that God watches over the expedient that can best contribute to the reestablishment of the state of the Kingdom of Naples], which Contegna had circulated anonymously in 1737;[8] Gregorio Grimaldi's *Considerazioni intorno al commercio del Regno di Napoli* [Considerations about commerce in the Kingdom of Naples];[9] or the affirmations contained in Giovanni Pallante's *Stanfone o sia memoria per la riforma del Regno di Napoli* [Stanfone or memoir for the reform of the Kingdom of Naples].[10] Thanks to the public offices they held, Contegna, Ventura, and Brancaccio were able to carry out their plans. In the field of Church and state relations, Celestino Galiani was instrumental in negotiations for the concordat of 1741 (which finally placed limits on the local, personal, and royal immunities enjoyed by the Neapolitan clergy), relying on Pietro Contegna as a valued and esteemed counselor. His *Considerazioni* was a valid theoretical prop for the *cappellano maggiore*'s vindication of the sovereign's rights.[11] In 1738 Francesco Ventura, whom his contemporaries unanimously held was the greatest proponent of the Neapolitan *Ministero togato* after the death of his uncle Gaetano Argento, set up and personally handled the important legislative project aimed at finally bringing order to jurisdiction within Naples.[12]

The reforms of the heroic period left clear signs in the old administrative, political, and social structures of the Neapolitan region.[13] Great attention was dedicated to fostering commercial development. The year 1742 marked the ambitious project of a giant land register, named the *catasto onciario* after the monetary unit chosen for the calculation of taxes.[14] In October 1739 the government established the Supreme Magistrate of Commerce, whose task was to foster and control the development of mercantile activities, on both juridical and institutional levels. It was an initiative full of innovations, capable of shaking up the social and political equilibrium in the Kingdom of Naples.[15] The new magistracy, presided over by Francesco Ventura, handled important activities, such as negotiations and projects for great commercial companies along the lines of English, Dutch, and French models, and the signing of mercantile agreements with the Ottoman Empire, Venice, and France.[16] The edict of 1740 in favor of introducing a colony of Jews into the Kingdom of Naples in order to increase trade was a sign of the break with the past. Finally, political and economic arguments vigorously and convincingly opposed religious pressures and limits. Galiani and Contegna, the latter nominated "delegate"—a sort of official protector—for the Jews, were yet again in the forefront of a new battle against ecclesiastical claims.[17] Neomercantile politics were perhaps most concretely expressed in the construction of ships meant to protect the maritime traffic of the Kingdom of Naples, which was especially plagued by African, Dalmatian, and Albanian pirates, and in the start-up of great public works.[18]

These initiatives, and the intellectual climate that prepared and accompanied the economic and political reawakening, strongly contributed to the flowering of the extraordinary civilization of the eighteenth century in Naples, which still today is astounding for the intense creativity of its artisans and artists in every field.[19]

Bartolomeo Intieri also actively participated in the renewal of those years, "fully convinced of the happy wealth of the Kingdom" and, most important, of the attitudes of its inhabitants, who (as he wrote to Galiani in 1738) were "capable of everything and extremely talented."[20] At that time a secret counselor to the government, Intieri mainly identified the development of agriculture as the kingdom's strong point. He certainly did not underestimate the role of commerce; in fact he continually plied the sovereign for greater effort in the construction of ships and the acquisition of commercial contracts with the Turks, the French, and the Venetians.[21] In his view, however, the great European powers had made their fortunes once they possessed a solid, national agricultural base. Therefore, the new Bourbon state also had to look at the cultivation and trade of grain as the prerequisite for development. He wrote to Galiani in 1739: "It is truly very deplorable when one considers that the great *Tavoliere* [tableland] of Apulia serves only to sustain a few people, where sowing it would yield an immense crop. If I have the time, I will make a calculation of the difference [in yields] between the agricultural and pastoral industries."[22]

In those very years, along with Galiani, Rinuccini, Orlandi, and a few other friends, Intieri also carefully studied the greatest economic issues facing the Neapolitan region from the perspective of a correct scientific understanding of these sometimes complex problems, problems such as inflation and the consequences of the monetary devaluations ordered by the princes. Nevertheless, Intieri did not merely insist on the necessity of grain cultivation; he also sought, through close debates, particularly with Galiani, to identify the defects in Naples's commercial mechanisms that impeded the gradual development of production and exports. He found the government's mistaken policy of tolls to be a weak point: "In his memoirs, De Witt says that imposing a toll of one cent on top of goods can do millions in damage for the state. We have burdened grains with the extraction of quite a few cents, and many other obligations." The free-trade choice and state aid to commerce proved to be indispensable for giving economic development a boost:

What would ever happen if selling this commodity [grain] was freed from the many obstacles that it has . . .? What would happen if the prince facilitated transportation to the sea by building safe and comfortable roads . . .? It is certain that the Kingdom of Naples is the most fertile region in Italy, and therefore the grain and all the rest of the foodstuffs must come from here, and not from Poland and England.[23]

Intieri's analysis was not far from the truth, as basic studies of southern economics in the eighteenth century confirm. If ever there was a relatively flourishing era during the modern age in which some funds were available to launch a process of development in the Kingdom of Naples, it was certainly the heroic period of the Bourbon dynasty.[24] The politics of reform was not only an abstract project imposed from above, but it corresponded to the deep needs of an economy in expansion, whose actual potential justified, to a great extent, the level of practicality reached in the ideological and cultural debate regarding the choice of neomercantilism. Basic institutions such as the Supreme Magistrate of Commerce not only brought about a crisis in the archaic economic structure, no longer productive and founded on essentially parasitic yields, but also had the merit of contributing to the dissolution of what has been called "the dialectic of the social orders."[25] Bringing middle-class groups like merchants, bankers, lawyers, and university professors together with ministers and aristocrats in one very authoritative institutional organ such as the Supreme Magistrate, giving each equal weight in decisions, proved to be a noteworthy contribution to the social rise of new figures in Neapolitan political life that just a few years earlier had been rigidly opposed by the clergy, the nobility, and the Ministero togato.

Neomercantile politics in the 1730s and 1740s (already formulated in Naples in the 1710s and 1720s) had remarkable consequences in every realm of Neapolitan social life. The failure of Charles's reforms, whose motives have long been a subject of debate,[26] must not allow us to forget the profound influence that the emerging figure of the merchant had, for with values and morals that were so different from the usual Catholic models, the merchant fostered the process whose final outcome would lie in the culture of the Enlightenment.[27] The nascent Neapolitan Enlightenment of Intieri and Galiani certainly took advantage of the interest in economic problems in Neapolitan culture primed by the Habsburgs' neomercantilism, which the Bourbon dynamism exalted in political and social life; this brought into focus a series of questions and basic values such as the leading roles of science and technology in human affairs, the redefinition of a secular and rational morality, and the emergence of new social sciences, in particular economics, whose concrete results were to have guaranteed that progress to which all enlightened thinkers referred.

An important step along this road was the anonymous appearance in Paris of Jean François Melon's Essai politique sur le commerce [Political essay on commerce] in 1734. The essay elicited a great outcry because of the audacity of its theses and the clarity with which it handled some important problems such as usury, luxury, and the attitudes of the state and the Church towards commerce and economic laws. Confirming concepts that were to become the heritage of an entire wing of philosophes (including Voltaire, author of the Apologie de luxe [Apology for luxury]), Melon passionately described the positive role played by trade in determining the peace and development of European peoples: "The spirit of conquest and the spirit of commerce are mutually incompatible in one nation."[28] The *Essai's* importance lay not as much in its proposal of the peace-commerce equation, which ended a troubled process of ideologically rehabilitating the figure of the merchant, traditionally considered by the Church to be a source of spiritual and material ruin for mankind,[29] as in its frank exposition of an "economic" type of morality, already irreversibly freed from evangelical conditioning and Christian tradition. Restating in part some ideas that Mandeville had developed in the famous *Fable of the Bees, or Private Vices, Public Benefits*, which appeared anonymously in 1714,[30] Melon analytically indicated for legislators which initiatives they should take in order to favor the development of commerce. In addition to emphasizing the important role played by the great sea companies, he addressed important problems such as colonialism, slavery, luxury, and usury, and he made clear that the only valid criteria for deciding on such matters must be their utility and their role in the economic life of a nation. In this sense, colonies and slavery (considered contrary "neither to religion nor to morality") were said to be essential for guaranteeing the solid bases for economic expansion.[31] Discussing the importance of luxury in the development of artisan crafts and commerce, Melon restated Mandeville's and Bayle's theses on how the interests and passions of private individuals converged with the overall benefit of the community.[32] He ironically demolished the Church's opposition to the flaunting of wealth and the heated sermon on frugality and austerity of custom that Fénelon had included in the *Aventures de Télémaque* [The adventures of Telemachus][33] a few decades earlier, considering that passions alone truly constituted the driving force behind human actions: "The military is only valorous because of ambition, and business only works because of cupidity."[34] The state, therefore, had to turn to its advantage this tendency towards luxury, which had always existed in humans, making the individual's cupidity congruent with the collective interest. Melon saw religious prejudices against luxury, no small impediment to the emergence of an economic ideology in the modern era, as an interference in matters outside the jurisdiction of the Church, and, therefore, he vehemently repudiated such prejudices: "We have already said that men rarely conduct themselves according to religion; it is up to religion to seek to destroy luxury, and it is up to the state to turn it to its profit."[35]

After the enlarged second edition of the *Essai* (Amsterdam, 1738), several copies of Melon's book reached Bartolomeo Intieri and Celestino Galiani, helping the circle of scholars gathered about them to develop already clearly enlightened ideas about the relationship between man and society and between Christian values and the needs of modern secular society. In letters to Galiani, Intieri could not help but boast of the "never sufficiently praised little book entitled *Saggi politici sopra il commercio* [Political essays on commerce]," as he wrote in October 1738.[36] The enthusiasm raised by Melon's treatise among Galiani's circle in Naples is, therefore, no surprise, if one considers the overall trend in Neapolitan culture: the empirical bent of the Accademia delle Scienze, Intieri's Gassendian Epicureanism, and, most important, the affirmations contained in that precious document of nascent Italian Enlightenment, Celestino Galiani's *Scienza morale*, where one becomes clearly aware of the desacralizing results of Spinozan biblical exegesis and the corrosive analysis of the English Free-Thinkers Toland, Collins, and Tindal.

After a troubled and contradictory search, Galiani ultimately came to prefer a secular ethics based on the examination of human passions, on Lockean utilitarianism, and on the recognition of the intrinsic rationality of human behavior, over the traditional Catholic moral model. Bayle's thesis of the virtuous atheist and the enlightening reflection on the incompatibility of evangelical morality and the needs for the development of modern society—commerce, manufacturing, competitiveness, and individual utilitarianism[37]—had long since convinced him. Melon, therefore, came to corroborate the choice already made years earlier, cementing in Galiani's heart the conviction that he had to abandon all references to traditional Catholic categories, even generally, when examining economic problems.

An example of Galiani's new attitude is particularly evident in his clear stance on the thorny problem of the lawfulness of usury. In the dispute between Scipione Maffei, author of a small book *Dell'impiego del denaro* [On the use of money] (1744) favorable to loans at interest (with some clearly defined limitations), and the Dominican Daniele Concina, who had rabidly repudiated Maffei's arguments in his *Esposizione del dogma che la Chiesa romana propone a credersi intorno all'usura* [An exposition on the dogma the Roman Church proposes should be believed regarding usury] (1746), Galiani did not hesitate to intervene on Maffei's behalf.[38] The analysis that he made of the problem was conducted on the level of factual reality, without any concession to traditional theological categories, and was thus quite separate from Maffei's positions because of its essentially economic-minded character, predisposed to seeing the mechanism of the loan at interest as a useful tool capable of generating wealth and well-being for all, as well as an incentive for commerce and a creator of new entrepreneurial activities. Whereas the point of view that Maffei expressed in favor of usury ultimately remained that of the "landowner, the patrician of the city, the lord who lives off his own incomes,"[39] for it vindicated the nobility's sacrosanct right to the usufruct of loans in order to live in splendor, without moral impediments on the part of the Church, Galiani instead concentrated his attention on the problem of loans as a feature of the new economic reality emerging in Naples. Following on the disputes that arose in Verona and Rome with the publication of Benedict XIV's *Vix pervenit* in 1735, he wrote to Bottari asking him for in-depth information "on this affair."[40] His Roman friend's long and detailed letters allowed Galiani to express his frank assessment shortly thereafter.[41] Referring to the attempt that Concina and Dominican rigorists like Giuseppe Agostino Orsi and Tommaso Maria Mamachi made to interpret the ambiguous papal bull in their favor, Galiani did not withhold his disdain:

It is claimed that the pope says that not even when a case of resulting damage occurs in a loan can one receive more than the capital. What nonsense! And no one would ever have believed one could find a man so ignorant and of such a deceitful and stupid mind capable of finding such a line in that decretal.[42]

The *cappellano maggiore* made it his personal task to convince Concina to revise his position. But the fiery Dominican, the author of an impious and sharp analysis of the harm that the unrestrained concentration of usurious capital in the hands of a few unscrupulous merchants could have for social life,[43] would not let himself be persuaded. Galiani wrote Bottari in 1746:

Concina is here and came to see me yesterday. We spoke of usury and we found we were of rather different opinions. In fact, as far as concerns those reasons we can call metaphysical, [he] claims to have more arguments than the defenders of the contrary belief. . . . He would have it that tradition is on his side, but I rather doubt it. The writings of the Fathers are certainly full of exclamations against usury and usurers; but did the Fathers understand usury as Concina would have it? Herein lies the problem.[44]

In his *Dell'impiego del denaro* Maffei had already perceptively noted the need to historicize a concept such as usury, which had assumed different implications and meanings in the Middle Ages and in the modern era. Galiani's rejection of the Church's ahistorical theology as a clarifying criterion meant a further confirmation of the inadequacy of the Catholic and Counter-Reformation model for understanding and guiding the evolution of a modern society. Shortly before he died, he wrote disapppointedly: "I saw Concina again . . .; I do not know if he adapted to the conditions of his times. The world goes as he wishes, and not as we wish, and it will take a lot more than a prayer to get him to find the way."[45]

Although also a man of the Church and shaped by deep philosophical and humanist studies, Bartolomeo Intieri was perhaps less doubtful than Galiani, and, in a rapid and efficient style, he identified and expressed better than any other the renewal that had been confirmed in Neapolitan culture by the progressive secularization underway in every discipline. For quite some time his scientism, empiricism, and firm conviction that reality had to be examined just as it was and not as one wished it were had led him to reject the traditional Catholic image of society so dear to Muratori in the *Filosofia morale*. Intieri very carefully examined natural law as a law of the physical world, and the complexity of human nature, human creativity, and human passions. "Men run to where there is profit," he repeatedly wrote to his friend Galiani,[46] as if he wished to synthesize the general sense of the works of Melon, Bayle, and Locke, whom he considered the most suitable for interpreting his age. According to Intieri, the true problem did not lie in opposing the Catholic heroic virtues with the destructive force of passions, but in tempering them and directing them towards individual interest, from which, in the final analysis, could only grow a positive evolution of all society.[47] It was now necessary to replace the primacy of politics and Christian morality with the primacy of economics and a scientific rationality certainly more fruitful for the fate of humanity.

The proliferation of studies on commerce and the neomercantile politics of Charles of Bourbon's government, which Intieri secretly supported, opened new research horizons for him, in the wake of the efforts he had lavished on constructing agricultural machinery and in carrying out mathematical research. In a letter to Galiani of November 1738, he argued against the frivolities studied by many intellectuals in Naples, inviting them, finally, to dedicate themselves to concrete things such as the examination of economic problems. "If the learned men attack" research on economics, he insisted in February 1739, "they free themselves from the bad reputation of being useless, as they truly are for the most part."[48] The profound transformation underway in Neapolitan culture did not escape Intieri. Commenting on the astonishing information he received from Paris about Melon's and Charles Dutot's total ignorance of Latin, he drew important conclusions about the uselessness in some disciplines of the knowledge of a dead language, which had been believed to be fundamental in the old cultural model. He wrote to Galiani:

> You know better than I with what wisdom this said book [Melon's *Essai*] was written. And this proves that the Latin language, necessary to whomever wishes to be lettered now, is a great waste of time. A third [of the time] would suffice to learn my mother tongue perfectly, and employing all the rest in studying sciences would profit greatly.[49]

The crisis of the European mind had destroyed old certainties for Galiani, leading him step by step from Bayle's theses on the atheists' virtues, to Lockean utilitarianism and Mandeville's and Melon's economicism, and even to the already-enlightened rationalism of the *Scienza morale*. From the beginning, for Intieri modern scientific thought, with its multifaceted wealth, its fascinating suggestions, and its ever more efficient technological realizations, had, instead, meant a kind of privileged vehicle towards the Enlightenment, the indispensable guide for understanding the changes that had occurred in the intellectual and social life of humanity.

> Who would ever have believed in the time of the barbarous Aristotelian tyranny that a pendulum, two polished crystals, [and] a prism of the same material . . .—considered in that unhappy time to be the most vile tools— would have become the delight of the most noble academies, the ornament

of royal palaces and the most noble bookstores, and—most astounding—with their help men have been able to penetrate into some secluded part of the sacrosanct philosophy that had always hidden from the vain seriousness of those ancient wise men full of ignorance and mere arrogance.[50]

As his contribution to the nascent Neapolitan Enlightenment, Intieri brought a Promethean myth of man's ever greater control over nature through mechanization and the construction of tools for agriculture, industry, and the sciences.[51] Certainly he would have enthusiastically endorsed the grandiose program of technological domination over nature that was one of the most exciting messages of enlightened culture, contained under the entry "Art" written by Diderot for his *Encyclopédie*.[52] Mindful of Bacon's legacy and Galileo's respectful words in the *Discorsi intorno a due nuove scienze* about the craftsmen in the Venetian Arsenal ("most skilled men of extremely refined discourse"), Intieri worked within Neapolitan culture (and in particular in the Accademia delle Scienze) to accelerate that shifting of interests from natural sciences to social sciences that represented a crucial moment in the European Enlightenment. Even if he was its most enthusiastic proponent, Intieri was not the only one in Naples to identify promptly the essential contribution offered by modern science to the developing process of enlightened culture. Celestino Galiani, Giuseppe Orlandi, Niccolò and Pietro Di Martino, Alessandro Rinuccini, and, later, Ferdinando Galiani and Antonio Genovesi were able to evaluate fully the great possibilities opened to scholars by what many throughout the Continent then called the Newtonian revolution.[53]

It is now recognized in general terms that the relationship between science and the Enlightenment in Europe[54] was organic and decisive. The multifaceted expressions of this intimate connection remain less known, as is the original acceptance they received in different cultural contexts, for example as regards the mechanist gnosiological foundations of the *Principia*, destined to become the basis of the scientific Enlightenment.[55] In truth, the theme of science and the Enlightenment, or, rather, the problem of precisely evaluating the role of science in the genesis of Enlightenment culture in Italy, has been broached by Franco Venturi in the chapter "The Value and Calculation of Reason" in the first volume of his *Settecento riformatore* [The reforming eighteenth century], even if the widespread knowledge of Newtonian works in Italy up until the 1730s is underestimated.[56] Nevertheless, he intuitively understands the progressive advance of the scientific model, in whose success we must carefully identify the fruits of the "Newtonian revolution" whose ideas had by then been penetrating Italian culture for years.

In February 1750 Galiani wrote to Bottari, inviting him to visit Naples and, in particular, the villa of Massa Equana, where Intieri lovingly instructed a group of young economists who would, in the future assume prominent responsibilities. Referring to the study of economics, he added: "If you come here for a while as I would like, we will have long discussions with our most honored Marquis Rinuccini and Mr. Intieri, who in such subjects are the Newtons of our day."[57] Although they at first seem relatively trifling, his praises for Intieri and Rinuccini actually reveal (as we shall see through the connection Galiani established between Newtonianism and economics) one of the most interesting cultural processes to occur in Naples in the 1730s within the Accademia delle Scienze, in the wake of the affirmation of the *Principia's Regulae*: that is, the shifting of scientific and cultural interests from natural to social (particularly economic) disciplines. In 1730 the gnosiological prerequisites for this evolution were already clear to Galiani, who wrote:

> In the [prince's] court, the philosopher, when other occupations leave him no time to observe the operations of nature in order to gather knowledge of the principles and causes, he can at least observe those [activities] of men, and then discover their spirit . . . and the motives that move them, a study no less pleasing than physics and much more useful. In the end one finds—I am certain that you will discover it as well in those who would prefer to hide themselves—that the great moving forces are the passions, and that the mothers of these are temperament modified by the habits and prejudices of education. Just as the forces and laws with which they operate are disclosed by Newtonian physics, and known as they are, using these as principles we come to know other phenomena, thus in the study of man from certain of his constant traces, by one who knows well how to observe and think, the forces that are usually one or more passions combined together are deduced, and as these are traced, one forms the character . . ., to such an extent that one can become a soothsayer and a prophet and predict without danger of error what he will do in any posture, or in any combination of circumstances in which he might find himself.[58]

Galiani's work to extend the Newtonian *Regulae* to the study of society, which he certainly had the means to develop in depth among Neapolitan scholars after 1732 and the foundation of the Accademia delle Scienze, was, nevertheless, not the *cappellano's* original idea but, rather, a logical consequence of his acceptance of a particular kind of interpretation of the *Principia* worked out by Dutch scientists, especially by Willem 'sGravesande, to whose works all eighteenth-century epistemology owed a great debt.[59]

During the 1710s and 1720s, when the epistolary relationships between 'sGravesande and Galiani were particularly intense, the Dutch scientist had published his *Physices elementa mathematica . . . sive Introductio ad philosophiam newtonianam* [Mathematical elements of physics . . . or the introduction to Newtonian philosophy], establishing himself as the greatest European interpreter of Newtonian physics. With his *Philosophiae newtonianae institutiones in usus academicos* [Institutions of Newtonian philosophy for school use] (1723), promptly translated into English and published in nearly all European countries, including Italy,[60] 'sGravesande inserted the *Principia*'s gnosiological theories into the great European experimentalist tradition. Starting from the Lockean distinction between truth of reason and truth of fact, he largely overcame the scientific probabilism of the *Essay Concerning Human Understanding* and eventually called into doubt one of the *Principia*'s epistemological foundations, namely the absolute priority that Newton gave to what I. B. Cohen has called "the world of numbers,"[61] the physico-mathematical language, and the Neoplatonic identification of the mathematical point with the physical point, and of matter and its trajectories with straight lines and points. During the years to come, 'sGravesande's criticism of mathematicism became one of the polemical arguments usually used by Diderot and Buffon against the "mathematical imperialism" of d'Alembert and the orthodox Newtonians, faithful interpreters of the *Principia*'s physico-mathematical method.[62] This criticism was connected to the rejection of the necessary relationship that some scientists postulated between God, nature, and humans, a link guaranteed by mathematical language, whose truth, of divine origin, allowed it to penetrate natural secrets, giving scientific legality to research. To 'sGravesande, the Newtonian and Galilean thesis of the substantial continuity between mathematics and the natural world was absolutely untenable. A meticulous analysis of mathematical principles in their foundations brought him to conclude in favor of the complete autonomy of mathematical truth from factual truth. This did not, however, mean a repudiation of mathematical language as a tool necessary for rationalizing and bringing experimental data to fruition, but it did imply simply a square confrontation of the problem of a science based entirely on empirical data.

Thus was born the great issue that would agitate enlightened scientists for the entire eighteenth century, namely the identification of a scientific legality that guaranteed the truthfulness of experimental physics, an issue that even in 1753 induced Diderot to exclaim hopefully: "We have reached a moment of great revolution for the sciences."[63] Having rejected mathematical proof as a valid reference for establishing truth in the real world, 'sGravesande worked out the epistemological bases of the new experimental science, formulating the concept of moral evidence. The moral evidence he conceived had nothing to do with what had been theorized by Descartes and other seventeenth-century scholars. For the French philosopher, this evidence had served merely to regulate human behaviors and led to a secondary, probable knowledge, for example historical knowledge, in which one had to refer to human testimony. In the Dutch scholar's viewpoint, moral evidence assumed a profoundly different meaning. In physics, history, ethics, and economics, and in any aspect of reality—not only human reality—certainties of a mathematical sort were unobtainable, but, most important, they had no meaning and no use for humans, considering the clear-cut separation that 'sGravesande posited between truth of fact and truth of reason. In the human world, certainty was, therefore, to be identified with moral evidence, which was absolutely not a secondary knowledge but simply another type of certainty.[64] According to the Dutch scientist, this moral evidence was based on sensation, testimony, and analogy, and its operative limits coincided with those of reality as a whole. Newtonian physics, the *Regulae*, and universal gravitation ultimately found a new meaning in the realm of the "refoundation of experience" that the Dutch scientist theorized, a meaning more suitable for guaranteeing the *Principia*'s extension into other disciplines, both in methods and results. Through the concept of analogy between single events (valid not only for physics but for all disciplines, from morals to economics), it was in fact possible to obtain the distillation of natural laws that could not be further broken down into simpler principles. The repudiation of Aristotelian substantialism limited any research to rigid phenomenalism.

An essential feature of the epistemological frame that 'sGravesande outlined, which Galiani used in a particularly fruitful way when he wrote his *Scienza morale*, lies in the fact that he posited natural law as the basis of the modern science that he theorized.[65] Who could have guaranteed the validity of the passage that scholars took from particular experiments to laws of universal value by applying the concept of analogy? Galileo and Newton had attributed this privilege to the principle of simplicity and continuity in the natural world. 'sGravesande, instead, had recourse to the concept of natural law guaranteed by God, obligating everything and everyone, and in a Spinozan fashion he had subjected God Himself to the dictates of natural law, just as Galiani had done.[66]

Scholars have long discussed what the correct interpretation of the Dutch scientist's concept of the scientific legality of the universe should be. Some have seen him as Hume's greatest precursor,[67] and Hume has rightly been held to be the theoretician of a gnosiology valid for the human sciences. One fact is, however, certain: through the foundations of modern science on natural law, and thanks to the formulation of the concepts of analogy and moral evidence (not to be confused with that of probability, reserved for the examination of scientific hypotheses), 'sGravesande had finally laid out the foundations of modern scientific knowledge. The Newtonian *Regulae*, reinterpreted experimentally, could in fact be applied to morals and economics as well as to politics. The process aimed at making scientific research completely rational was complete throughout Europe by 1793 when Condorcet published his *Tableau général de la science qui a pour objet l'application du calcul aux sciences politiques et morales* [General picture of the science whose object is applying calculation within political and moral sciences] in the *Journal d'instruction sociale* [Journal of social instruction] and introduced the entire world to "social mathematics," the most interesting and richly meaningful fruit of the scientific Enlightenment.[68] Scholars of economics, morals, and demography, not to mention historians, no longer hesitated to resort to algorithms and methods that at the beginning of the century had been used only in the world of the exact sciences. From the 1750s on and the appearance of the entries "Probability," "Certainty," "Analogy," "Induction" and "Knowledge" in the *Encyclopédie*, Diderot, De Prades, and d'Alembert clarified some features of the scientific Enlightenment and the new meaning of the "Newtonian revolution" set forth by Dutch empiricists, and they repeated entire sections of 'sGravesande's works. In the first volume of the *Histoire naturelle*, Buffon, too, illustrated the new scientific methodology in the field of natural history, drawing it largely from those concepts.[69] The teachings and suggestions of Newton's universe-machine, divided into thousands of small streams and then reinterpreted and inserted into many diverse contexts, had finally allowed scholars throughout Europe to address social sciences with an ever more rational view, self-assured and free from the conditionings of the humanist model.

In Naples the integrated relationship between local scholars and 'sGravesande's experimentalist Newtonianism was no less efficient than in the rest of the Continent. One need only attentively observe the evolution that research had undergone in the field of economics from the early decades of the century through the 1730s, research from which emerged the clear-cut determination shared by Intieri, Galiani, Orlandi, and Rinuccini to obtain a genuine science of economics and its laws. In Intieri's letters to Galiani from 1738 to 1739, the term "science of commerce" indicated a veritable desire to understand social mechanisms rationally as well. Both scientists felt the need to study in depth the causes of the inflationary process in the economy of southern Italy, and they completed their research by carefully evaluating both historical precedents (the weight and value of coins in past periods) and the concrete effects of inflation in the contemporary age, with the goal of rigorously deriving laws and models forecasting the future.[70] A letter by Intieri from December 1738 illustrates in all its efficiency the image (that Ferdinando Galiani will make famous in the *Della moneta*) of monetary flow interpreted just like the circulation of blood in the human body, and the related considerations about the velocity of circulation for determining the quantity of money necessary in a hypothetical monetary circuit. Commenting on the scarcity of money in contemporary Naples, Intieri wrote: "I am astonished that this city can hold itself up without cash money, and if it is true that [money] is similar to blood, this marvel grows even greater."[71] In November 1738 he advised Celestino Galiani: "I have diligently looked for the weight of the ducat at the time of Charles V, and I believe I am sure that its weight at that time was nearly double that of the present ducat." Later in the letter, he explained:

In comparing the present incomes of the princes with those of the people as they were before America inundated Europe with gold and silver, without a doubt one must regard the quantity of those metals back then and [the metals] of today. And in fact, I remember I saw an old document obtained from the archives of the *Camera della Summaria* [Supreme Financial

Court] in which it appeared that a *tomolo* of grain was worth one and a half *carlini*, and it is believed that a *tomolo* had the same capacity as the present one.[72]

One of the most interesting features of the economic debate underway in the 1730s among Intieri, Galiani, Rinuccini, and Orlandi lies in the evaluation of the social costs of the "raisings" (a concept equivalent to modern "devaluations") adopted by the princes to resolve the problem of public debt and inflation. The entire fraternity closed ranks in favor of Melon's theses, which approved similar government interventions and judged that the terrible costs they brought to the poor people were only temporary. Ferdinando Galiani reported the entire issue with ingenious clarity in his *Della moneta* (1751), and the matter was refuted by a majority of Italian scholars.[73] Letters about the matter shed light on Intieri's meticulous examination of the effects the raising had on salaries, grain prices, and existing incomes in the kingdom. On first impression, these are harsh, pitiless statements: "Mr. Melon wisely writes that, considering the issue carefully, abundance is more frightening than famine."[74] Their explanation lies in the logic of prices and the laws of the market that Intieri and his friends were bringing into focus. Calculation was an essential tool in the new economic science, and it allowed Galiani and Intieri to establish, among other things, what the best solution was for developing the Tavoliere. Confronting the problem through a demographic examination of the Kingdom of Naples as well, these two asked whether grain cultivation or sheep raising was more profitable for those lands.

> At my request, one of these parish priests, a friend of mine, has found out the number of deaths and births last year in 1738; I am sending Your Most Illustrious Excellence such notice just as it was given to me. It has not been possible to obtain the names of the thirty-five parishes that are in this great city [Naples], but I have received the number of births and deaths separately. For the entire figure for deaths, we are missing numbers from the hospitals and the convents of monks and nuns. . . . If the information is verified, it seems quite different from what they give us for London and Paris, where the number of deaths either is greater or slightly less than the births, whereas in this city, thanks to God, many more are born than die. And who knows that among the other prizes of Italy there might not also be that of human fertility.[75]

Forecasts on the effects of raisings and terms such as "exchanges," "prices," "salaries," "interest," "luxury," "usury," and "incomes" continually reappear in the letters exchanged between Celestino Galiani's friends in those years, giving us the opportunity to see all the premises of the happy synthesis that Ferdinando Galiani achieved in his *Della moneta*.

Raised in the house of his uncle Celestino and guided through his precocious development by Orlandi and Intieri, Ferdinando Galiani[76] carried to a satisfactory completion that shift of interest from natural sciences to social sciences that Celestino Galiani had theorized since 1730. In fact, the main feature of the *Della moneta* was the rigor of its analysis of the economic situation.[77] The author himself as an old man vindicated his reputation as one of the founders of the new "economic sect" in the face of the counter-claims of northern European *économistes*.[78] In the opening of his work, he made explicit what its epistemological foundations were:

> The readers ought to fix in their minds and be persuaded that the laws of commerce correspond with as great exactness to those of gravity and of liquids as nothing else could. Gravity in physics is the desire in humans to earn or to live happily; that said, all the laws of physics about bodies can be perfectly verified, by whomever knows how to do so, in the morals of our life.[79]

The *Della moneta*'s obstinate, scientifically rigorous research and the effort directed at distilling universal economic laws through analogy from particular cases led the author, then about twenty, to express even paradoxical theses, which his own teacher Intieri rejected as the fruit of exceedingly rationalistic abstractions. This was the case with his search for a constant value of reference for all historical epochs to which he could relate imaginary money. Galiani wrote:

> The physics have come to find the unchanging measure and the marvelous union between time, space, and motion, the three great measures of everything. . . . The price of things, that is to say their proportion to our need, has as yet no fixed measure. Perhaps one shall be found; as for myself, I believe it is man himself.[80]

In reality, in order to understand the philosophical system of the *Della moneta* fully, one would have to return to some sections of Celestino Galiani's *Scienza morale*. Celestino Galiani's utilitarianism had especially struck Ferdinando, for he wrote: "I call utility the aptitude that something has for procuring our happiness. Man is composed of passions that move him with unequal force. Pleasure lies in satisfying them".[81] Other concepts in Celestino's unedited treatise that received a complete treatment in the *Della moneta* included scientific rationalism, phenomenalist empiricism, and the rejection of evangelical morality in favor of an unbiased analysis of human passions. Writing to Toccolino de' Lapi Toccoli, count of Punghino, in 1748 on the matter of nature's uniformity, Ferdinando revealed his wholehearted acceptance of the foundation of modern science on natural law theorized by both Celestino Galiani and 'sGravesande. It was a foundation that, as we have seen, guaranteed objective legality in every area of research, from physics to morals. However, the most interesting aspect of Ferdinando's stance lay in his daring extension of natural law and its precepts to the angels and to God Himself, for whom earthly categories such as solidity and universal gravitation had value.[82]

The youthful author's realism, beyond the ingenious discoveries that it hid in pages rich with erudition, biting wit, and irony (where he examined opinions different from his own), in the end revealed in several points the ultimate sense of the scientific attitude held by Intieri, Celestino Galiani, and the entire group of Neapolitan *novatores*. The *Della moneta*'s rational rigor and economic phenomenalism, that cold, precise calculation of economic variables within his system without any concession to human creativity, to the uniqueness and problematic nature of the human-nature relationship, or to the "cries of the people"—pitilessly labeled a "great enemy of the prince's good works"[83] because of the people's ignorance—in fact did not exhaust the objectives that Intieri and Galiani had entrusted to science for renewing society. The *Della moneta*'s corroboration of the primacy of economics over politics and of natural laws implacable in their factuality had the effect of strongly mitigating the reforming and eudaemonic import, so vital and rich in promises for the future, that was present in Intieri's and Celestino Galiani's Neapolitan Enlightenment.[84] For them, scientific phenomenalism and knowledge of reality had been incentives to challenge human intelligence in order to modify the environment and change people's habits, without resorting to empty ideologies or reassuring but sterile metaphysical systems. Near the end of his life, in what remains the true spiritual testament left by his generation to later Neapolitan *illuministi*, Intieri wrote, with youthful enthusiasm: "Soon our Europe will enjoy a happy golden age, not primitive and sylvan as the poets dream, but cultured and urban, full of arts and study, comforts and life's commodities, and finally as much as the wretched human condition is allowed to obtain."[85] On every occasion, Intieri insisted that the tools for realizing such a society were culture, the development of economic activity, and the advancement of science, the same tools that Bacon in the *New Atlantis* had foretold were capable of redeeming humans and guaranteeing them control over nature. But it was Antonio Genovesi rather than Ferdinando Galiani who executed the enlightened bequests of Galiani's fraternity. We ought not condemn the author of the *Della moneta* for not completely sharing the reformatory passions of his teachers. His intellectual shaping had been quite different from that of Bartolomeo Intieri, who had traversed the entire troubled landscape of Neapolitan culture from the inconclusive metaphysics of the Accademia Palatina to the lively reawakening of the Accademia delle Scienze, where he had given concrete form to the Promethean myth of modern science that had been put forward by Fontenelle and the Abbé of Saint-Pierre, Charles-Irénée Castel, deriving from this an extraordinary faith in progress and human capabilities. Ferdinando's intellectual growth was also quite different from that of his uncle Celestino, perhaps one of the few Italian scientists who had known how to carry out his intellectual life with passion but also with political realism, rejecting any rash utopianism and, therefore (with substantial success), putting into practice Horace's *sapere aude* [dare to know],[86] consciously interpreting the meaning of the enlightened revolution.

5. THE HUMANIST SYNTHESIS AND CHRISTIAN TRADITION: DORIA AND BROGGIA

With his *Difesa della metafisica degli antichi filosofi contro il signor Giovanni Locke ed alcuni altri autori moderni* [Defense of the metaphysics of the ancient philosophers against Mr. Locke and some other modern authors] (1732), Paolo Mattia Doria took up again his struggle against the *novatores* with renewed energy, identifying as his new enemies and targets both the circle of empiricist scientists who met in the newly founded Accademia delle Scienze and the spread of Locke's and Newton's thought. The time of bitter disputes with Neapolitan Cartesians was past,[1] but Doria had rigorously begun to outline a true reform program for the development of the Kingdom of Naples, starting with cognitive and ideological suppositions antithetical to the neomercantilism and Enlightenment of Contegna, Intieri, and Galiani. His radical opposition to Newtonianism and Lockeanism went beyond ingenuous positions dictated by a personality easily angered and given to grudges, and it held considerable importance for the history of contemporary Italian culture because of the immediacy with which he was able to grasp the profound social, economic, and political implications that accepting the *Principia's* celestial dynamics would have for Neapolitan intellectuals. Doria knew Newton's works superficially, and many of the *Principia's* theorems probably remained quite obscure for him; even so, his malice against the English scientist was intractable and even crossed the border into genuine insults in his final works, in which the "material and carnal" Newtonian science was identified as the source of all the evils of modern society.[2] As we have already noted, in reality Doria's offensive against modern thought and his scientific counterrevolution had already begun some time earlier with his writings on synthetic geometry. In the 1730s, with the growing success of his adversaries in Naples and the direct involvement of Intieri and Galiani in the direction of cultural and political life in the kingdom, Doria no longer limited his criticism to technical and philosophical aspects, but he initiated a kind of trial against the moral and ideological consequences of Lockean and Newtonian empiricism. He established an intense and organic bond between the diffusion of the *Principia's* "pernicious sciences" and the affirmation of neomercantile and enlightened choices in Neapolitan culture:

> We shall see how much the modern geometricians have damaged modern geometry, and everyone shall be able to know by himself that, with the modern geometricians having damaged geometry, as a consequence they have damaged logic, philosophy, religion, morals, and politics, and they have made Europe barbaric and a slave.[3]

In the *Ritratto della moderna falsa scienza espressa nella malizia dei seguaci di quella* [Portrait of the false modern science expressed in the evilness of its followers], Doria named modern scientists as a genuine sect that, rather

than educating the young in Christian virtues, had come to exalt materialism, utilitarianism, and Epicurean theories, preaching that the individual
should resort to the senses, scientific objectivity, and critical judgment in
every discipline, and exalting those who sought easy profits or the union of
"the useful with the pleasurable."[4] Doria's hostility towards the Newtonian
universe-machine was not, however, merely a simple rejection of a materialist and Epicurean interpretation of the *Principia*'s theories, as might appear on first glance. Actually he had precociously and intuitively grasped
how much was hidden behind the Newtonian natural theology that was
expounded in the Boyle Lectures, and what serious consequences the
Newtonianism propagandized by enlightened Catholics might have for humanist and Christian tradition. This Newtonianism, gained from the apologetic reading of the *Principia* that followed the lead of Clarke and Derham,
had led Intieri and Galiani to Melon's moral economicism and the enlightened rationalism of the *Scienza morale*.[5]

Doria did not hesitate to denounce all those who, using the image of the
Principia's celestial dynamics *ad maiorem Dei gloriam*, had taken the road of
a rationalist reform of Christianity.[6] He expressed his views with *Lettera
alla signora duchessa d'Erce nella quale l'autore indaga il fine oculto che si può
nascondere in un libro il quale è stato ultimamente pubblicato col titolo la religione
naturale* [A letter to the duchess of Erce, in which the author investigates
the hidden goal that might be hidden in a book recently published with
the title Natural religion], probably a reference to the Neapolitan translation of George Cheyne's *Philosophical Principles of Natural Religion*, which
had been published by the printer Mosca on the initiatives of Galiani, Intieri,
and Grimaldi. His rejection of the natural empiricist theology of the Anglican rationalists of the Low Church and the apologetic model of the Boyle
Lectures was a fundamental aspect of the complex role he attributed to
Christianity in the formation of modern society. Newtonian natural theology, with its cosmological a posteriori proof of the existence of God and
the metahistorical dimension of the divinity, in which revelation ultimately
lost all importance, was for Doria another step towards deism and atheism.
God the watchmaker of the *Principia* was in the end nothing but a further
development of the impious Spinozan and Libertine theories. Rationalizing
and interpreting Christian religion through human categories and proceeding
(as Clarke, Derham, Cheyne, and Newton had done) to confirm the existence
of God based on the examination of natural mechanisms in his eyes meant
nothing more than fulfilling the secularization of religious values, a process
extremely dangerous to Western humanist culture, and a process that reduced
or even canceled the importance and the very role of Christianity. Starting
with the supposition that religion always remained a supernatural affair, not
reducible to attempts at understanding or rational justification (as for example
the Socinians and "followers of Mr. Locke's sect" wished to do), Doria saw
Platonism and Ficino's humanism as the sole philosophical frameworks capable

of consistently interpreting and validating the supernatural message of the Christian religion.[7] Religious innatism, the soul's immortality, miracles, demonology, the angelic hierarchies, revelation, and the utter rejection of materialism and theological empiricism all contributed to outline a Christian Neoplatonism in Doria's thought in which philosophy and religion were interwoven and supported each other reciprocally.

In 1741 the very heated arguments against John Locke's reasonableness of Christianity, interpreted (in mistaken chronological succession) as a further and inevitable development of Newtonian natural theology,[8] finally confirmed Doria's profound aversion for the attempt to rationalize and simplify the evangelical message launched by the best European thinkers, who felt the need to renew Christianity's apologetic dimension itself. He accused Locke of having entirely distorted the Christian religious message—robbing it of any aura of mystery or any evocative force without giving any philosophical illustration of fundamental theological issues such as escatology, Christology, and Trinitarian doctrine, as was, instead, possible through Platonic idealism. Locke "tells us that God is intelligent and provident, and he sends the fools home, content."[9] To affirm that "Jesus Christ is the Messiah" was not sufficient for a true Christian, and to deny religious innatism meant "to deny the soul's immortality."[10] As for Locke's attempt and desire to bring all confessions back to a single natural religion that was limited to recognizing Christ as the Messiah, Doria saw this as being the same as undermining Christianity itself at its foundations, in all its ideological import:

> When the author says that Jesus Christ did nothing other than say that he is the Messiah, and that he did not institute the Holy Church, and that he did not reveal the holy Trinity, we can be Socinians, Muslims, Anti-Trinitarians . . ., we can be Quakers, who deny the institution of the priesthood made by our lord Jesus Christ; and in the end we can be of any sect as long as we confess generally that Jesus Christ was the Messiah.[11]

Doria's negative opinion of Newtonian apologetics and the attempt made by rationalist theologians and English empiricists to interpret Christianity through earthly categories, secularizing supernatural values, did not stem merely from his preconceived hostility towards scientific empiricism; it was also fed by the centrality that religion assumed in his thought. Scholars have insisted too strenuously on the Catholic reformism that supposedly united Doria to Muratori and on Doria's arguments against Jansenists and Jesuits whom he accused of internally undermining the peace and unity of the Catholic Church, leaving aside the ultimate meaning of the task that Doria assigned to religion in human society. Doria, who could in no way be considered a Libertine or a Machiavellian,[12] like Vico had, in fact, always recognized that religion made a fundamental contribution to the formation of human society:

It is not that religion is an invention (as some impious men had said), a device necessary for maintaining the republic. Religion is necessary for the republic because it is true. And far from being able to say that religion is a consequence of the republic, it is manifestly proved that the republic is the necessary consequence of religion.[13]

Arguing vehemently against Bayle, the author of the "licentious critical dictionary," Doria pointed to the innate idea of a God who is a font of justice, rewards, and punishments, as the true coagulating force of society: "And thus it is that Saint Augustine said; 'Religio est coagulum populorum,' knowing that it is that which ignites in the hearts of men the desire to unite themselves in civil society."[14]

Doria's ideas about the importance of religion in human life profoundly marked the project of reform that he formulated for Neapolitan society on the arrival of Charles of Bourbon. Galiani and Intieri had courageously worked out a clear-cut separation, already, of an enlightened character, between the methods for economic and civic development they hoped for and the precepts of the evangelical model, holding the latter to be inadequate for interpreting the rhythms and contradictions of an ever more secularized society, hostile to the moral teachings of the Church. Doria, on the other hand, paradoxically resolved the divisive consequences of the crisis of the European mind and the problems posed by tumultuous economic and social growth, restating traditions and the moral teachings of humanism and the Gospels. Despite the fact that he had before him the historical failure of the religious ideals of a Christianity that was increasingly divided within a Church whose political prestige and moral authority were in deep crisis, Doria pointed out "an immense force still intact in Christianity that would have truly been able to change the relationships between men."[15] Its religiosity, however, should not be confused with the Church's post-Tridentine, Counter-Reformation Catholicism, which had corrupted the ancient, classic virtues of Sparta and Athens through the spread of moral laxity. The Jesuits, the Jansenists, priests, and the Catholic Church in its institutional form were, in fact, always among his preferred targets. He ran into quite a few problems of ecclesiastical censure and from the Neapolitan clergy for his ideas on priestly celibacy, on jurisdictional questions, and on useless, meaningless rites.[16] The Christianity that Doria pondered, far from adapting itself to the Catholic conformism of the eighteenth-century Church, instead found its clear-cut and complex physiognomy in the Christian philosophy of Ficino's Platonism, in the Jewish tradition in which the wise and the virtuous coincided, in the call to the evangelical love of the first Fathers of the Church, and, finally, in the continual exaltation of the virtues of the classical world. The result was a particularly interesting ideological crucible capable of blending its various components in an attractive proposal, a kind of heresy against Italian Catholicism motivated by tensions that, while perhaps contradictory, were cemented and fired by an ironclad certainly about the social role of Christianity in the world. The results of such a choice contrasted sharply with the rapid process of secularization in cultural and social life in this period, but even today they demand discussion because of the apparently contradictory quality of some of the solutions he proposed in the fields of science, politics, and economics. Doria had earlier rejected modern science, criticizing its epistemological foundations, whose empiricism he felt was inadequate to grasp the essence of things. In the 1730s he fully developed his cognitive model in various disciplines, and he came to argue impetuously against "the tyranny of philosophers over the ignorant populace," illustrating the disturbing results of Newtonian natural theology and Lockean empiricism in the fields of morals and politics.[17] In his *Difesa della metafisica* (Defense of metaphysics) (1732), an alternative to the *Thoughts Concerning Education* that circulated in Naples in the Accademia delle Scienze, he had momentarily interrupted his fierce invectives and criticisms of the moderns in order to outline his theories on the education of children. Doria placed Christian love between humans and Platonic innatism at the root of his morals, illustrated with philosophical rigor through axioms and lemmas. The criticisms of the "civil Epicurean society" to which Lockean education would lead were expressed by his refusal to recognize the passions as the empirical foundation of human behavior, as well as his arguments against the thesis of moral relativism that were so dear to Celestino Galiani. Doria wrote:

> [Locke] joins himself perfectly in sentiment to Epicure, Thomas Hobbes, and Nicolò Machiavelli, because in virtue of his entirely sensationalist hypotheses, he removes those ideas of the just and the honest that God has given the soul; and instead he teaches (like Hobbes and Machiavelli) that virtue is generally approved, not because its concept is innate in the soul, but only because it is useful.[18]

For Doria, affirming that the virtues and vices are "opinions of men" and that "justice is a material thing" and not an arcane idea whose foundation derives from the very existence of God meant undermining Christian religion and the social peace of nations.[19] It is not surprising, therefore, that Doria believed that Muratori's *Filosofia morale* (1735), which nevertheless forcefully vindicated evangelical morals against Locke's theories, was weak in its denunciation of Epicureanism and not drastic enough in its rejection of the passions.[20] In his defense of the dogmas of the Christian faith, Muratori had revealed that he was overly empiricist—"the sensists oppose religion in general," Doria thundered[21]—and not nearly philosophical enough, resorting to common sense instead of Platonic philosophy. The far-too-"modern" Muratori had addressed children, evading any presentation of more profound explanations; Doria, on the other hand, spoke to learned men, to adults, showing them and philosophically explaining to them true morals, whose foundation rested on the Gospels and whose final objective lay in

realizing a rigorous life. In his axiom XIX, Doria wrote: "Human virtue consists in the imitation of God, and supernatural Christian virtue revealed to
us by God consists in the imitation of Jesus Christ."[22] From this stems his
continual reference to the love between humans, and not the fear of God
as preached by the detested Jansenists, as the criterion for true social justice in human behavior. Locke had impiously spoken of pleasure and pain,
entrusting the intellectual growth of the young child to an empirical confrontation with the world's reality without ever pointing to the need "to
inspire either love or fear of God" in the child's mind.[23] Doria, on the
other hand, indicated the main road of a rigid education that repressed
from birth the human leaning towards the passions, instilling strength of
mind and love towards one's neighbor in the child.

Nevertheless, when being related to and concretely applied in the life of
a modern state, Christian love, understood as social solidarity, as Doria
theorized, reveals truly obscurantist and intolerant traits. In his second axiom,
Doria wrote: "In humans the will is stronger than is reason";[24] hence it was
necessary to condition the will and repress it from birth in the greatest
number of children possible. Education must be "consistent with the religion and human wisdom that the state follows":[25]

> One must guard one's self from believing, as Mr. Locke has taught us,
> that every religion and all wisdom is good for the state, because there is
> only one religion, and it is our sacred Christian religion, that which all
> must follow; and in my opinion there is also only one human wisdom,
> and it is the Platonic one.[26]

Demolishing any concession to libertas philosophandi, religious tolerance, and
a competitive society rich in intellectual differences (as, for example, Anthony
Collins theorized in the Discourse of Freethinking), Doria hoped for a Christian state capable of imposing its essential characteristic, even by resorting
to the most intolerant authoritarianism in which the denunciation and ironclad
control over intellectual activities by any means might guarantee simultaneously peace, social justice, and love between all.[27] Voluntarism, solidarity, and the imposition of evangelical virtues such as temperance, fortitude,
and prudence in the customs of adults and children were the predominant
features of this utopian Christian society, in which the rights of the individual would otherwise be totally disregarded. With profound conviction,
he briefly synthesized his rigid integralism in axiom XXIII, unhesitatingly
writing very specifically: "One must accustom children to pronounce these
words: I am not, I do not know, I do not have, I am not able, I wish
because I have to, I do not wish because I do not have to."[28]

In the heroic period of neomercantile Bourbon politics, even Doria, like
many other Neapolitan intellectuals, was called upon to express an opinion
about the economic situation in the Kingdom of Naples and what criteria
to follow in order to promote development. His report from 1740, addressed

to Francesco Ventura, president of the Supreme Magistrate of Commerce, represents more than the personal opinion of a scholar of considerable political acumen; it is an important document for the entire Neapolitan cultural sector that in the 1730s was centered around the Accademia degli Oziosi. The profound separation on a scientific, philosophical, moral, and religious level between the Oziosi and the neomercantilist *novatores* gathered around Intieri and Galiani could not have been more obvious, and Doria's text assumes the quality of a programmatic, alternative manifesto, even on the level of political and economic choices.

For Doria, as for Intieri, Galiani, and Contegna, commerce was in effect an element to propel the economic rebirth of the Kingdom of Naples. The issue at hand was the establishment of the forms and directions most apt to the Neapolitan situation. Accordingly, Doria put forward a substantial difference between "internal" commerce, based on exportation of local products, and "external" or "ideal" commerce, based on the buying and selling of merchandise from other countries. He then invited the government to insist on increasing the former by favoring agriculture and artisan craft production and alerting peasant farmers and landowners to the need for putting new lands under cultivation.[29] The preference for "internal" and "real" commerce, shared in great measure by the group following Intieri and Galiani as well, did not stem, however, from merely economic considerations, as it had for Intieri; it again found its prime motivations in the project of a Christian society, to which Doria remained firmly bound until the end. One need only read the definition that he gives to commerce, a restatement of the old scholastic conception, in order to perceive the ideological bases of his reform program: "Commerce is the art of making sure that men united in civic society dedicate themselves to each other in mutual aid, providing each other reciprocally with the merchandise that some lack and others have in abundance."[30] The ultimate goal of commerce was, therefore, not enrichment and individual gain but "mutual aid." The social character and the collective nature of mercantile activity are configured in Doria's work as the dominant motif of all his proposals.[31] Intieri restated Melon, Bayle, and Locke and identified self-interest ("men run to where there is profit") as the motor of society's collective progress. Doria, on the other hand, wrote with conviction, turning Mandeville's paradox on its head: "Civil law teaches us this maxim, namely, 'the public good is preferable to the private good.'"[32] From this came his invitation to "make it such that the peoples place their glory not in enriching their private patrimonies through commerce, but in enriching the public treasury."[33] He continued: "Moral and political virtues are the vital spirit of the republics and kingdoms."[34] Nevertheless, the systems for guaranteeing the realization of a "virtuous commerce" and a kind of "moral economy"[35] were yet again coercive: "The excellent virtue of hard labor and enrichment, only with the goal of maintaining one's country, which is one's mother, is nevertheless difficult to practice; hence there is need of a most virtuous education and an optimal discipline."[36]

The "external" commerce desired by "cabalists" like Intieri and rich Jewish and Neapolitan merchants who made profits on the exchanges with Turks and other Mediterranean peoples could not, in Doria's view, guarantee the development of the Neapolitan region, since it could involve only a few people. His fierce criticisms of the crudest aspects of mercantilism (strangely similar to those of Concina, who was, not surprisingly, connected to Pasquale Cirillo and the group of scholars who met at the Accademia degli Oziosi in the 1730s)[37] addressed monopolies, usurers,[38] and those who dealt in luxury items that were useless to the development of the Kingdom of Naples. "Luxury is by nature a vice and poison of republics," Doria wrote.[39] The impassioned reevaluation of the "Christian agrarianism" of Claude Fleury and Fénelon[40] and the criticism of neomercantilism's most negative sides were illustrated in the framework of a program of social and economic reforms that is even today surprising for the acuity of the political analysis and the destructive import it contained: a palingenetic determination that was anything but inconsistent with the profoundly Christian underpinnings of Doria's thought. The solidaristic utopia that grounded it seemed to restate the evangelical message in its entire revolutionary import, and it was there that its very authoritative and coercive dimension found legitimation. The proposals that Doria put forward included the reform of the land register, direct and progressive taxes ("it is very certain that the poorly ordered proportion among the weights that the citizens bear impedes the perfect circulation of wealth"),[41] the foundation of the Banco di San Gennaro on the model of the Genoan Banco di San Giorgio (in order to finance the kingdom's economic life at comfortable rates of interest, eliminating usury), and the institution of the Court of Commerce with a judiciary reform that streamlined the procedure, reducing appeals and finally giving certainty to the law.[42] However, Doria's great merit lay in having underlined the profoundly political character of the choices to be made in order to guarantee the growth of southern Italy. Unlike Intieri and Galiani, who, by adopting an Anglo-Dutch model of development, aimed only at guaranteeing the accumulation of wealth, Doria, conditioned by his vision of an upright and virtuous Christian society, brought the problem of social justice to the foreground. From this arose his penetrating analysis of the power relationships existing in the Kingdom of Naples between the various social orders in continuous struggle among them, the harsh arguments against baronial and ecclesiastical privileges, and, most important, the radical nature of some of his proposals for Neapolitan society, such as direct and progressive taxation.

The *Politico moderno* (Modern politician), written between 1739 and 1740, marked an important phase in Doria's intellectual experience, almost fully revealing the anti-enlightened nature of his reflections on modern culture.[43] His fierce arguments against Voltaire, Bayle, Locke, and 'sGravesande and his denunciation of the new cultural, moral, and scientific order that was hidden behind the Newtonian universe-machine and the Boyle Lectures' natural theology[44] were in fact extended to an examination of the damage produced by the nascent enlightened culture in political and economic spheres. According to Doria, Locke's utilitarianism, Melon's moral economism, and the negative effects of Newtonian "carnal science" had already completely disrupted the European princes' political actions as well. The merchants' rules of commerce had become the rules of conduct for governments: "The politics that the modern princes follow can be described by the following definition, that is, a mercantile politics, natural and practical, supported by the strength of the army."[45] Restating Fénelon's arguments against Louis XIV's mercantilist and militaristic policies, Doria wrote that the princes had neglected their mission as guarantors of peace, well-being, and social justice for the peoples, and that, with their continual wars of conquest and their commerce, they had reduced "man to the nature of beasts, because in the same way in which the merchants traffic in beasts at a fair, thus we see the princes traffic in men."[46]

Doria's reformism and his intransigent rejection of the utilitarian, anti-Christian, and rational developments of the nascent Enlightenment had quite an impact on Neapolitan culture, as becomes clear from the works of many Neapolitan scholars, in particular those of Carlo Antonio Broggia, in which, to a large degree, reappeared the considerations on the primacy of ethics over economics and the image, so dear to Doria, of a Christian society proudly averse to the neomercantilist and Epicurean theses of Melon, Intieri, and Galiani.[47] Unlike Doria, who had long been prejudicially hostile to any manifestation of modern thought, Broggia worked out his penetrating observations of the political and economic situation in southern Italy, operating in a cultural climate different from the one in which the Genoan Doria had been educated. While firmly rooted in the ideological suppositions of a Christian economics faithful to Vico's and Doria's gnosiological model, Broggia was able to confront some aspects of enlightened culture with open eyes. His work, in fact, although rent by contradictions, becomes logical in light of the dilemma "utopia or reform" that was so typical of the Enlightenment and that continually flourished in the projects of eighteenth-century scholars. Rejecting the thought of those who considered the process of secularization in Western culture to be unstoppable and who trusted merely in the rational capabilities of humans and their vocation for progress, Broggia was inspired by Doria, and he clearly identified Christian voluntarism as a formidable force of transformation in the existing economic, political, and social order. His desire to use the direct intervention of the legislator to transform and reform even the customs and the mentality of the people was based on suppositions quite different from those of Intieri and Galiani, and Broggia's fierce criticisms of the *Della moneta* reflect this. Not only did Broggia reject the Anglo-Dutch model and Melon's theories on inflation, he also showed a straightforward hostility towards the Epicureanism that Galiani displayed in his works—Broggia defined Intieri and his group as "sensists, Sophists, and Epicurean skeptics, deists in appearance and rotten in substance; respected, wise, and learned on the surface and evil, crazy, and as ignorant as possible at the core."[48] Broggia focused on the possible negative consequences of the enlightened scientism professed by Bartolomeo Intieri's circle, whose goal was a radical reformism. According to Broggia, to accept the lesson of the "Newtonian revolution," the Principia's mathematizing rationalism, and 'sGravesande's theories meant to confuse social issues and natural facts and to assimilate the scientific logic that presided over natural laws and the historical and factual logic of the human world. In his opinion, all the admirable analysis of economic mechanisms made in the Della moneta led to an ideological and scientific confirmation of the existing social order, taking strength and courage from those who truly aimed at profound reforms.[49] Luxury was far from being an "economic evil" obedient to immutable natural laws, as Ferdinando Galiani had affirmed; it was a "poison" easily eliminated if only the legislator desired so.

> The age of states depends on a mere and absolute moral action of the will; hence it is that if one wishes, one can very well rejuvenate and thus regain a stronger and more robust state than before. No one takes notice of the fact that the legislator, when he wants to and knows how, is capable of making nature itself change for peoples and destroy it in them, as far as habits and customs are concerned.[50]

The primacy of politics over economics and scientific objectivity could not be more explicitly confirmed. Alongside the concrete economic projects that Broggia formulated, one of the most interesting outlets of his reformism was the energetic work of demystifying the arcana iuris (mysteries of law)[51] and the courageous explanation of the political and not quite divine foundations of Roman law—Vico and Doria would never have dared to go that far. This, however, left room for the shadows of the strictest and most repressive Catholic integralism—obligatory Mass for all, unlimited extension of the ecclesiastical mortmain, fierce hatred towards Jews.[52] However, Broggia's important (even though contradictory) presence in Neapolitan culture allows the demonstration of the existence of two different ways of expressing the enlightened determination to change society. We will encounter the two currents of thought represented by Broggia and Intieri again in various forms and measures throughout the Enlightenment in Italy and, in particular, in Naples, sometimes within a single group of intellectuals or even in the same person.

Antonio Genovesi, universally held to be the leader of the Neapolitan illuministi, accepted Bartolomeo Intieri's scientific rationalism alongside Broggia's and Doria's suggestions of Christian economics, and he achieved an interesting synthesis between the irrepressible call for freedom of thought by the scholars cleaving to the school of Bayle and Locke and the teachings of Catholic tradition. The evocative image of the Newtonian universe-machine, which had been a clear reference point in the cultural debate of the so-called heroic period, assumed a different role in the years to come. No longer an element driving confrontation between and clarification of Neapolitan intellectuals' various positions on modern thought, from the 1750s on the reassuring vision of a planetary order that guaranteed the divine existence slowly became a further guarantee of social and ideological stability within Catholic culture. With the failure of Charles's reforms, the conclusion of the debates over the authentic import that science and modern culture offered for the existing social and political order, and the end of the discussion on the gnosiological and philosophical legitimacy of the transformations that had to occur, an important period for the history of Newtonianism in Italy ended. It was a period destined to leave profound traces on enlightened culture well into the future.

SEVEN

The Development and Exhaustion of the Debate: Towards Newtonian Scholasticism

1. ANTONIO GENOVESI'S NEWTONIANISM

With the publication of Pieter van Musschenbroek's *Elementa physicae conscripta in usus academicos* (Elements of physics written for academic use) (1745) in Naples, annotated and commented on by Giuseppe Orlandi and Antonio Genovesi, the *novatores'* battle to introduce Newtonian science into Neapolitan culture could finally claim a victory. The success of the edition[1] was not, however, limited to the Kingdom of Naples, for the book soon crossed its borders, contributing to the spread of the *Principia's* theories throughout Italy in no less than five editions. In the working relationship established between Orlandi and Genovesi in order to produce the *Elementa*, the former reserved for himself the difficult task of annotating the text and illustrating its scientific significance. Genovesi, on the other hand, had the job of introducing the work, opening it with a historical synthesis of the scientific ideas from antiquity until the current age.[2] The *Disputatio physico-historica de rerum corporearum origine et constitutione* (Physico-historical debate on the origin and constitution of bodily objects) that he produced for the purpose nevertheless wound up assuming the features of an autonomous treatise, substantially extraneous to Newtonian phenomenalism and gnosiologically connected to a Lockean reading of reality, which emerged from Orlandi's annotations and the brief but important *De rebus coelestibus tractatus* (Treatise on heavenly things) that Orlandi had inserted in an appendix to the book.[3] Precisely by virtue of its originality, the *Disputatio* circulated successfully throughout the eighteenth century in numerous editions, both alone and reprinted with other works by Genovesi,[4] long representing one of the most interesting readings of the *Principia* made by an Italian intellectual at mid-century.

Divided into three chapters dedicated respectively to the examination of Eastern philosophies (Jewish, Chaldean, Persian, Indian, Ethiopian, Phoenician, and Egyptian), those of the Greek world (Ionic, Platonic, Aristotelian, and

248

Stoic), and the modern philosophies, the work offered the reader an incisive profile of human knowledge in its historical development. The connecting thread that bound Genovesi's agile and learned synthesis through
diverse worlds and cultures was that it went beyond a specific examination
of the scientific discoveries and gnosiological models; it was a kind of research
of fundamental principles that united a number of doctrines pertaining to
such issues as the structure of the universe, the God–nature relationship,
and the composition of matter.[5] In the part dedicated to English philosophy, Genovesi conducted the exposition of Newtonian theories with the
logical, overall plan of the *Disputatio* in mind, for in it he wished to show
the continuous, dialectic relationship between ancient and modern thought,
almost as if to suggest the ceaseless circularity of human knowledge. After
the great cultural flowering of antiquity, the dark years of the Middle Ages
followed, ended by the Renaissance reawakening in which all the Eastern
and Greek philosophies reappeared, even if in different forms, in Giordano
Bruno's pantheism and heliocentrism, Ficino's Neoplatonism, and Gassendi's
atomism, up until the most recent Cartesian and Newtonian doctrines, themselves reducible in their fundamental principles to metaphysics worked out
in the great crucible of Mediterranean culture. Given such a frame of reference, which was meant to highlight continuity rather than discontinuity,
Genovesi's Newtonianism, expounded in a rather dense section of the
Disputatio, ultimately appeared in a form quite different from the phenomenalist and Lockean form propagated during the 1730s and 1740s in the
Accademia delle Scienze by the Neapolitan *novatores* following the example
of 'sGravesande's and Musschenbroek's mathematical empiricism. After a
very quick nod to the *Regulae*'s experimentalism ("there ought not be admitted
more causes of natural things, than what are true and are enough to explain
their phenomena"),[6] Genovesi deftly illustrated the *Principia*'s metaphysical
consequences, taking his cue from some famous phrases of the *Scholium generale*
and the *Optice*'s *quaestiones* in order to delineate a Newtonianism that was
examined in light of the English Neoplatonism of More, Cudworth, Raphson,
and Clarke and that was unusually tied to the pantheist hypothesis of the
anima mundi (world's soul). God, space, matter, and motion were the essential issues treated in Newtonian cosmogony, as Genovesi defined it. They
allowed him to recompose the major outlines and features of the universe
according to the image proposed by Newton. A number of concepts came
to the fore: space, identified with the divinity (*"sensorium Dei"*—God's sensory
organ), inert matter, and motion preserved in the world by the work of
"active principles" ("therefore, God is life, the soul of all bodies and of
each singular part of matter").[7] The extraordinary importance of the
gnosiological and scientific revolution achieved by the *Principia mathematica*
became secondary, almost disappearing without a trace, allowing the ancient
and spiritualizing thesis of the *anima mundi*, particularly dear to Genovesi,
to prevail.[8] The fundamental character of Newtonianism thus became, above

all, a further confirmation of the existence of active principles in the universe. Although in his Metaphysica (1743) Genovesi had sufficiently clearly explained to the reader the commonality of the theses on the deification of space held by Henry More, Joseph Raphson, and Isaac Newton,[9] in the Disputatio he forgot the Newtonian precautions about the cause of universal gravitation, and he brought all the Principia's doctrines back into the realm of an ancient philosophical tradition that saw the divine spirit present everywhere in the world. The names of Pythagoras, Plato, Cardano, and Campanella occur repeatedly in Genovesi's writings, together with that of Newton. According to Genovesi, Campanella, for example,

> seemed to let himself be drawn, but almost unconsciously, where all the ancients had come who had given the universe some first principle, or where more recently the Newtonians arrived, who introduced (or restated and explained) the reciprocal attractions between all bodies, doubtlessly produced by a principle that governs matter.[10]

Quite a bit more ambiguous was his explicit denunciation of the latent pantheism in the Principia. The heritage of Pythagoras, who was a recognized advocate of pantheism in antiquity, was attributed not only to Spinoza and the Free-Thinkers but also to the English Neoplatonists, including Newton himself:

> But among the dogmas of the Pythagoreans this is justly famous: the world is animated by a certain soul, of which Plato and generally all Platonists were persuaded; and so were many more recent men persuaded, especially Cudworth, More, Clarke, Newton, and others.[11]

In reality, the image of Newtonianism that Genovesi sought to outline in the Disputatio was in no way directed at finding heterodox elements in the work of the English scientist. Not surprisingly, Genovesi firmly countered impious Cartesian physics, with its curious Brunian origins[12] and Spinozan developments, with the famous phrases of the Scholium generale, in which the marvels of the cosmos confirmed God's greatness and presence. His presentation of the figure of Isaac Newton, a universal genius humbly and continually engrossed in his prayers and thoughts of God, was itself artfully extrapolated from Voltaire's remarks in the Métaphysique de Newton, and it only confirmed the importance Genovesi attributed to the Principia as an effective bastion against materialists and Libertines.[13] However, his was nothing like the awareness that Celestino Galiani had shown of these problems, for the latter had found that the attraction and mathematical rigor of the Principia's celestial mechanics could form the basis for a new way of conceiving of the divine presence in the world. Galiani's vision, different from the ancient Neoplatonic stereotype of the anima mundi, was related to the empiricist theology of Limborch and the Anglican rationalists and was ready to con-. front all the dramatic questions posed by the crisis of the European mind and the search for new relationships between reason and religion and between science and Christian tradition.[14] Genovesi was quite familiar with all the great disputes over the interpretations of the *Principia* that had been formulated in England in the preceding decades. He was also well informed about the apologetics of the Boyle Lectures, the materialist vitalism of Toland and the Free-Thinkers, and the great disputes on the origins of the earth that had set Thomas Burnet's mechanistic Cartesianism against the Newtonians Whiston and Keill.[15] He was also equally familiar with the harsh arguments between Clarke and Leibniz on the divine presence in the universe-machine. Even so, only a decade after the discussions held in the heart of Galiani's Accademia delle Scienze over the importance and gnosiological meaning of the *Principia*, only a decade from the time in which Pietro Di Martino had published his manual of Newtonian physics and Doria and Galiani had indissolubly linked Newton's name to Locke's, to Dutch mathematical empiricism, and to the new economic and social order of the great maritime powers, Genovesi confronted these very problems with opposing views. In the *Disputatio*, he offered Neapolitan and Italian scholars a unique version of Newtonian metaphysics, an interpretation that ignored the Locke–Newton connection and the effects of the "Newtonian revolution" in the scientific and philosophical field and that, instead, addressed the past to search for confirmation of the vital principles of Cardano and Campanella and of the Platonic *anima mundi*, in order to exalt the pious and religious character of the new science.

This demands more reflection on the problem of Genovesi's philosophical and cultural background and his relationships with Neapolitan intellectuals. After his arrival in Naples in 1737, in fact, Genovesi for a long time remained outside the discussions and problems that still animated Galiani's fraternity. Although a pupil of Niccolò Di Martino, the recognized head of the Neapolitan Newtonians at the university, Genovesi had contacts especially with intellectuals who identified with the Accademia degli Oziosi. It was Genovesi himself who, in his *Autobiografia*, reconstructed the details of his original connections with the *veteres*. Giuseppe Pasquale Cirillo, with whom he shared a "very close friendship" just after his arrival in Naples, introduced him to Vico's thought and introduced him to some of the Oziosi. He read Locke's works simultaneously—and certainly not by chance—with "all that had been written against him by Doria, a man no less distinguished by birth than by learning."[16] Vico and the *Scienza nuova*, too, had a relevant part in his early cultural education.[17] As soon as he met Genovesi in 1741, Celestino Galiani intuitively saw his talent and entrusted him with teaching metaphysics at the university, and Galiani's friendship was certainly important for Genovesi's intellectual life. Genovesi finally had the opportunity to compare his own philosophical ideas, then oriented towards Neoplatonic and Malebranchian theories, with those of an intellectual follower of Locke such as the *cappellano maggiore*. In his *Autobiografia*, he described his first meeting with Galiani, which occurred during a lecture on metaphysics at the university.

He [Genovesi] spoke is Latin about the true nature of the idea, closely examining the opinion of those who confuse "idea" with "perception," including Mr. Arnauld and Mr. Locke. He concluded that this opinion would only occur in two systems, those of Spinoza and Locke. Because if perceptions are the same as ideas and perceptions are essential to the soul, if they derive from sense as in Locke, the soul [becomes] an affection of the body. If one says they are innate or proceeding from God, the soul [becomes] God itself. The Monsignor [Galiani] listened with pleasure and confessed he was highly pleased, except for certain things said against Mr. Locke, of whom Galiani was inordinately fond.[18]

In reality, after his encounter with Galiani, who probably advised him to read Limborch and some texts of Newtonian natural theology in order to get him to moderate his opinion of Locke's heterodoxy,[19] Genovesi "did not become a pure Lockean, a Condillac ahead of his time, nor a man of wholly Newtonian scientific mentality. The metaphysical and systematic need was deeply rooted within him."[20] The Newtonianism in the *Disputatio*, while maintaining its distance from Doria's antiscientific fanaticism and Vico's rejection of Cartesian rationalism, was still an experience born within the Neoplatonic and humanist philosophical climate typical of the Oziosi, foreign to the mathematical empiricism of Intieri, Serao, Orlandi, and Galiani.

Even the so-called Newtonian polemic between Conti and Genovesi, born from the former's curiosity to see the problem of the nature of ideas clarified, since it had been left in the dark by the latter in the first volume of his *Metaphysica* (1743) on closer scrutiny confirms the distance between Genovesi and Celestino Galiani.[21] Genovesi's public response to Conti, beyond the uncertainties and problematic tone with which his answer developed, left no doubt as to his rejection of Locke's empiricism.[22] In another letter from the same period, probably addressed to Conti, he did not hesitate to write: "We find that Mr. Locke's system is incompatible with our principles, and that it can only be said to be internally logical when one establishes that the mind is the body and the perceptions [are] movements."[23] Conti had no difficulty grasping that the *Disputatio*'s Neoplatonic reading of Newtonianism evidently destroyed his Stratonic conception of matter.[24] Even though both started by criticizing those who defended the phenomenalist conception of attraction from a distance ("the great crowd of Italy that wishes to speak Newtonian, even if it is not such, has gone so far in this field that it should no longer be tolerated," wrote the irritated Genovesi),[25] the solutions they posed to clarify the cause of attraction ultimately diverged quite significantly in their conclusions. Conti restated the complete materiality of the world through the hypothesis of force-matter, while Genovesi argued in favor of the thesis of a divine, vivifying spirit as the dynamic element of inert substances.

While for the *Disputatio* Newtonianism was the high point of Genovesi's reflections on modern science, on the meaning of the *Principia*, and on the

God–nature relationship, a new phase of his intellectual life opened when he began to frequent Intieri's circle around 1748–1749. It was the period in which the tensions with ecclesiastical authorities were most acute over the issue of the chair in theology.[26] These years have been much discussed, for during this time Genovesi passed from "metaphysician to merchant." Some have spoken of a turning point in the great reformer's interests, a sensitivity to economic problems and the Enlightenment, in an apparent break with his past metaphysical and theological experiences.[27] Others have insisted on the elements of continuity in Genovesi's intellectual development, for he would in essence have varied the scope of his studies, preserving intact the metaphysicizing spirit of his youthful works.[28]

Both these hypotheses are partially correct. His meeting with Intieri and his diligence in cultivating Intieri's friendship acquire quite another meaning in the light of the level reached in the debates between the *novatores* and *veteres*. Entering into Intieri's household after cultivating Giuseppe Pasquale Cirillo's friendship and carefully studying the works of Doria and Vico, at the end of the 1740s Genovesi could finally compare himself to a group of intellectuals who had resolved many of the problems posed by the crisis of the European mind through already enlightened choices. These were the men behind the refined debates on the *Principia*'s most important theories that were waged in Galiani's academy in 1735, behind the reflections on the relationship between science and economy, behind the thoughts about the new social, economic, and cultural order that modern society faced. Galileo, Newton, Bayle, Locke, and Melon were, for Intieri and Galiani, scientists who had to be read and studied carefully, worthy of admiration and, most important, to be referred to when addressing a reform of southern society directed at freeing it from the humanist–Catholic model that a scholar such as Doria still envisioned. It should not have been difficult for Genovesi to come to grips with the profound diversity of attitudes, reflections, and solutions between Intieri's group, opposed to the great philosophical syntheses and sterile religious meditations, on the one hand, and the friends of Giuseppe Pasquale Cirillo on the other. Passing from the natural to the social sciences, identifying a new discipline such as economics (which Intieri and Galiani already considered an autonomous science by the late 1730s), and establishing an integrated connection between the mathematical laws of nature and those governing human relations and the working of society—these are only some of the results that Intieri's circle left as their inheritance to Genovesi's "civic economics." Establishing the rhythms and timing through which many aspects of the experiences of Intieri, Galiani, Rinuccini, and Orlandi were assimilated into Genovesi's cultural sphere, overlapping or, in some instances, coexisting with the preceding views, is a task that is not only difficult but perhaps not even as meaningful as has been thought. Certainly the intellectual richness of the Neapolitan reformer and the complexity of his cultural roots risk being lost if we do not consider that his "programmatic eclecticism" probably hides not only philosophical syncretism, common to so many other eighteenth-century scholars, but also the overlaying of diverse ideologies and antithetical cultural choices. In his works after the 1750s, enlightened features, derived mostly from Intieri, coexist with disconcerting moral and religious relapses, clearly more consonant with Doria's views and the views of all those who in the 1730s and 1740s aimed to reform Neapolitan society under the banner of Christian humanism.

Genovesi published the *Discorso sopra il vero fine delle lettere e delle scienze* (Discussion of the true goal of arts and sciences) in 1754, when it appeared as a foreword to Ubaldo Montelatici's *Ragionamento sopra i mezzi più necessari per far rifiorire l'agricoltura* (Arguments about the most necessary ways for making agriculture reflower). The *Discorso* documented an important phase in the identification of new cultural interests and the search for the cognitive tools that most conformed to a realization of Muratori's "public happiness" that became Genovesi's great lifelong dream. The most prominent features of the *Discorso* came from reflections honed by Genovesi's long association with Intieri and his friends.[29] From those conversations, Genovesi was eventually convinced that the new way of understanding culture was a direct expression of the scientific world, the mechanical arts, and fruitful experiences well outside traditional bookish culture.[30] The image of modern science outlined in the *Disputatio*, which had only aimed to place scientists and their theories within a philosophical frame, was now outmoded. Genovesi started by saying that if reason "makes us similar to God,"[31] then it is necessary to begin to delineate its functions and powers, and, above all, to use it profitably for society, without wasting any on the sterile research of philosophers and theologians. A cyclical vision of human affairs, drawn from the *Disputatio*, permeated the framework of the *Discorso*, which claimed that after a phase of great intellectual flowering, dark centuries took over during which "philosophical schools of Europe competed to see which would be the most productive in useless figments of the imagination and abstractions." In this vision, Genovesi ultimately perceived the slow unfolding of a new golden age, in which economic development and civic progress would be able to resist victoriously the forces of evil, always waiting in ambush and ready to drive away all hope.[32] At this point the author was faced with the problem of what tools were available to reinforce this historical process of renewal, which had been initiated by Bacon ("the restorer of philosophy in Europe"), Galileo, and Descartes.[33] The solution that he proposed was the correct use of human reason, a tool that must become ever more pragmatic and adaptable to compete with the concrete problems of society. "Reason is not useful unless it becomes practice and reality," Genovesi wrote in the *Discorso*, sketching the framework within which the Italian Enlightenment would later develop all its propulsive force.[34] Therefore "action" had to replace meditation.[35]

Physics, medicine, agriculture, and natural sciences acquired a very prominent position in the reformer's thought. Without research on seeds or oils, "we would still live in caves, wear coarse animal skins, and eat wild acorns or raw animal meat as the savages of America do."[36] Genovesi attributed a key role in the new golden age to modern science, for he felt that it was finally capable of revolutionizing the very development of human society. Nevertheless, such science was a peculiar expression of knowledge, an aspect connected more to the immediate public usefulness through the creation of technological tools that than to a conscious evaluation of the profound gnosiological meaning implicit in the works of Galileo, Descartes, and Newton. Even though he had understood the importance of Intieri's ideas about human progress and the role of technology and machines—the stove, the aerial ropeway, and all Intieri's useful inventions occupy a prominent place in the *Discorso*[37]—Genovesi demonstrated that he was still quite removed both from Celestino Galiani's moral and economic scientism and from his nephew Ferdinando's attempt to give economics a fully rational character. Genovesi made an impassioned invitation to make unbiased use of these new agricultural technologies and modern machinery, writing: "would a thousand savages without knowledge, skill, and tools be capable of making a machine work that Archimedes had a boy operate?"[38] However, this sentiment was inspired more by Muratori's theses on the public usefulness of science[39] than by the conclusions that the Neapolitan Accademia delle Scienze had reached in the 1730s about the common rational underpinnings of the natural and human worlds suggested by the *Principia mathematica*. All this was confirmed by the metaphysical interpretation of Newtonianism present both in the new edition of the *Elementa metaphysicae* (Elements of metaphysics) (1760) and in the *Disputatio* (1763), from which, except for minor aspects,[40] the *Principia*'s profound ideological implications were still absent.

The exact awareness of the scientific revolution that this work brought entered into Genovesi's intellectual heritage only in the 1760s. Only then did he understand the distance that separated him from Hume's daring observations[41] and from those of the French philosophers with respect to the close interrelationship between the new image of the universe-machine and the problems posed by the growing process aimed at making the human sciences wholly rational. With the publication of yet another manual, entitled *Delle scienze metafisiche per gli giovinetti* (The metaphysical sciences for young people), in 1766, Genovesi abandoned the *Disputatio*'s Neoplatonic Newtonianism and vigorously and competently outlined his cosmological vision for students' use. In the first chapter, "Cosmology," the cornerstones of Newton's scientific thought were explained without reference to metaphysical questions or to the parallelisms (mentioned frequently in the *Disputatio*) between the great English physicist and Cardano and Campanella. After having rejected Cartesian mechanicism and the principle of motion's constant quantity in the universe, which excluded God's permanent activity in the world, Genovesi argued against those who had attempted a naturalist

and deterministic reading of the *Principia*'s celestial dynamics. "Providence
is always what orders the world. Why did Buffon not understand this?"[42] he
wrote with ill-concealed resentment against the philosophe's implicit materialism. Referring to the problem of the diminution of motion in the universe that was forecast by Newton's theories, he did not hesitate to ask
what might cause this continuous renewal of driving forces in the cosmos.
This time, however, the answer did not lie in hylarchic principles or in the
world's soul. According to Genovesi, Newton, too, had maintained that
such causes were a veritable "mystery of nature"[43]—a happy enigma, which
had spurred great scientists to formulate interesting theories such as the
principle of minimal action, outlined in Maupertuis's *Essai de cosmologie*, or
d'Alembert's mathematical theories on force illustrated in the *Traité de
dynamique* (Treatise on dynamics).[44] In short, Genovesi came to prefer Newton
the metaphysicist to Newton the scientist, "a marvelous genius" and dis-
coverer of universal mathematical laws, and the artisan of a genuine
gnosiological revolution. He explicitly reproved the English scientist for
yielding ground to traditional ontology. "It is difficult for the most subtle
philosophers to guard themselves from fantasy and always to remain in the
clear and shining light of reason,"[45] he concluded, as if to emphasize his
definitive separation from those hylarchic principles and the *anima mundi*
about which he himself had written in the *Disputatio*.

In his *Elementi di fisica sperimentale* (Elements of experimental physics),
which appeared posthumously but which presumably was written in the same
years as the *Scienze metafisiche*, Genovesi confirmed such a direction, arguing further that the key to Newtonian thought no longer lay in the affirmations
of the *Scholium generale*, but in the famous *Regulae*, and from these he drew
a confirmation of experimentalism and his critical acceptance of the *Principia*'s
most important theses: "Musschenbroek concludes—rightly so, in my opinion—by saying that the reason for gravity is unknown to all. This should
not create such a stir, since we are ignorant of the nature of matter."[46] The
results of this new reading of Newtonianism appear evident in the *Diceosina
o sia della filosofia del giusto e dell'onesto* (The diceosina or on the philosophy of the just and the honest) (1766), in which the author plotted a moral
system inspired directly by the *Principia*'s suggestions and theories.[47] There
were two linchpins to Genovesi's "moral science": "natural law," which
governed every aspect of life in the universe, and the theory of the "collisions," which was an articulation of natural law in the field of human behavior.
The gnosiological premises of his moral science were clearly illustrated in
the first chapters of the *Diceosina*, in which he completed the process of
extending Newtonian mathematical laws into the social sciences. Stating
that "man is one of the animals of this earth, therefore he is subject to all
the laws of animalness,"[48] he united all human affairs, the motion of the
planets, and vegetable life under a single great universal law, rationally
comprehensible to humans.

The laws of heavenly bodies, the laws of the elements, the laws and forces of each of the things of this earth never vary in their essence, though they appear to us under an infinity of diverse modifications. Now the physical laws of the world are the basis on which moral ones rest.[49]

At the root of human behavior, Genovesi posited a "law of the collision of forces," clearly inspired by Newtonian celestial dynamics.

Here one should consider more carefully two internal motor principles, sympathetic and energetic, that are essential to our nature, and they are self-love and love of the species, that could also be expressed as concentrative force and expansive force.... Those who claim that one of these two forces is born from the other are in error. This would be like someone saying that the force of gravity in planets that keeps them in the centers is the daughter of the projection that separates them. These two forces in us are therefore primary, though they are bound together; nothing is more clear for the physical and political history of mankind.[50]

In Genovesi's formulation, the application of Newtonian mechanicism to physiological behavior arrived at curious parallelisms between the law of universal gravitation and family ties.

It is true that as the attraction between bodies is greatest when they are in contact and weakens in proportion to the distances [between them], thus the reciprocal attraction of men and charity is greatest in the unions of blood, shared residence, and the fatherland, etc., and it languishes progressively at greater distances.[51]

One could long continue to examine Genovesi's charming theories. He sought both the point of "least possible evil" through the "law of the balance of the two forces" and the relationship between education and the theory of collisions; but the true linchpin of his moral science was his concept of natural law:

[a] law born eternally in God's intelligence that, infused in the world through the first creation, distinguishes beings by attributing to each its properties and its limits. Then it chains them and orders the end that the creator has predetermined for them. And being immutable upon its origin, because God could not be anything other than what He is, it is also immutable in its course, and this unchangeable nature fixes the certain and sure principles—neither capricious nor mobile—of justice, virtue, and our happiness.[52]

Starting with a vigorous reaffirmation of the existence of a natural law, rational but ambiguously assimilated to divine providence,[53] Genovesi was able to examine every aspect of reality. Nor did his recognition of a scientific order in the universe (beyond the divine guarantee itself) bring the philosopher close to breaking with Catholic and Christian moral tradition, as Celestino Galiani, with profound distress, did in the *Scienza morale*. One has only to scan the dense pages of the *Diceosina* in order to become aware of the uncertain elements and the repentant backpedaling on central issues in the European debate such as moral relativism, the possible existence of virtuous atheist societies, and the rational and hedonistic foundation of an entirely secular and earthly morality. Despite the scientism and Newtonian rationalism that tinge the entire *Diceosina*, Genovesi decisively rejected the model of a secular, utilitarian society upheld by unchangeable economic laws such as Bayle, Locke, Mandeville, and Melon had outlined in their works. He made no concessions in his harsh arguments confirming the innate source of the ideas of good, evil, justice, and divinity. Referring to these ideas, he wrote that there "were those who attributed them to opinion, and among them was the author of the fable of the bees, Mandeville, little reflecting (I believe) on the order and force of nature."[54] The great theme of the existence of atheist societies in human history was demolished in few words: "I do not remember ever having read of any considerable population that did not have some idea of divinity."[55] Vico's thesis regarding feral wandering fared no better, because of the break that it introduced into biblical chronology and the Catholic apologetic tradition,[56] which Genovesi considered (along with the Gospels' teachings) to be the solid bases on which he would begin to construct his "moral science."

The *Diceosina* is not Genovesi's only work in which daring thoughts mix with professions of faith in evangelical teachings and Christian tradition. It was as if all the reformer's political theory was shaped by his need to identify, through modern scientific tools, the mechanisms of development, economic laws, and moral rules, without, however, ever losing sight of the primary objective of a Christianly more just society.[57] The famous *Lettere accademiche su la questione se sieno più felici gli ignoranti che gli scienziati* (Academic letters on the issue of whether the ignorant or scientists are happier), a true core of Genovesi's civic thought, was written after the terrible famines of 1764. In it, enlightened themes—such as faith in scientific rationalism and a renewed culture as a means for progress—are meaningfully interwoven with the Muratorian and Dorian need to maintain the solidarity and Christian character of modern society. Genovesi argued bitterly with Jean-Jacques Rousseau and those who had criticized the so-called excess of civilization—economic, technological, and scientific progress—in order to repeat the pipedream of a return to the primitive naturalness of humanity, ordinary equality, and the happy state of nature of the American savages, restating the driving role of modern science and culture in the development of nations in order to confirm all its validity.[58] Almost angrily he railed against the theologians who lied, denouncing "the imprint of original sin" in the sciences.[59] He believed the solution to the problem of backwardness in southern Italy came about precisely through the increase in technological and scientific knowledge. In contrast to the prevailing opinion of the mercantilists and all those who had made economicism the key to reality, in Genovesi's opinion the progress of a nation was measured in the overall growth of its civilization, the establishment of effective social stability, and the growth of its cultural level. It would have been a serious error to attribute central importance to gold, money, and economic development alone. "Civilization, not the economy, has always been decisive,"[60] he loved to write. The Spanish example, with all its American gold and endemic underdevelopment, confirmed this theory.

The southern society that Genovesi thought of was directly drawn not as much from the economy-minded vision of Intieri and Celestino Galiani[61] or from Doria's radical hypothesis of a utopian Christian society as from Muratori's thesis of a "public happiness" to be realized through the joint efforts of all, without social conflicts.[62] Muratori also inspired some of his more attractive passages on the role of intellectuals in the renewal of Italian society.[63] Compared to his old master, Genovesi could, however, boast new experiences. The attraction of the *Principia*'s mathematical rationalism, the creation of new social sciences, and the expansion of the European political and philosophical debate had in fact reinforced Muratori's old arguments against the Arcadian "nonsense." Genovesi outlined a far-reaching role for the learned. Contradicting Rousseau, he wrote that the poverty and misery of beggars in modern cities did not depend at all on social costs paid for economic and civic progress. Poverty was a political issue, influenced by the lack of laws, the absence of adequate reforms, and the failure to recognize human rights. "The multitude of vagabonds could better be ascribed to the sloth of certain peoples and to politics, rather than to luxury," or to modern civilization.[64] True, "wise" intellectuals, and not the "false pedants" ("for me a wise man is not the one who studies whatever is incomprehensible and useless to mankind"),[65] occupied a key role in his plan for the development of southern society. In fact, Genovesi entrusted intellectuals with the task of disseminating culture and realizing an untiring and energetic reform activity.[66] Harshly arguing against the disheartened government functionaries and skeptical scholars, Genovesi wrote dryly: "I do not like having anything to do with the Diogenes,"[67] and "Do you like to remain earthworms? Brains, brains... Science, letters, humanity, common sense."[68] He felt that the transformation of a society for the better was not at all an unattainable dream. He wrote enthusiastically that the genius of the intellectuals "only shines when it runs without pause from thought to thought, from form to form, from desire to desire, from hope to hope. Inaction is the death of the body."[69]

These were admonitions that recalled Carlo Antonio Broggia's impassioned pleading in favor of reform against Ferdinando Galiani's skepticism. The reformatory passion was not, however, the only point of similarity between the two. Both shared a conception of economics understood as a tool for initiating the politics of renewal, without, however, granting it a genuine scientific status, with ironclad mathematical or "mechanical" laws, as Intieri said.[70] In the realm of economic studies, the Muratorian and Christian underpinnings of all the philosopher's civic thought eventually acquired a noteworthy impact, to the extent of overshadowing many of the teachings and reflections developed within Intieri's circle. The connection that Genovesi established between politics and economics, expressed at first in a true moralism of Doria's type,[71] was later overcome by a greater consciousness of the economic reality and the pitiless mechanisms of the market, significantly influencing his development projects for southern Italy and his reflections on the new economic theories from northern Europe.[72] The Lombard *illuministi*, who received his work very coldly, did not fail to note regretfully his insistence on evangelical teachings, which came to condition the unfolding of the laws of the market and the very authority of the state. Pietro Verri, for example, reproved the author of the *Diceosina* not only for his lack of scientific rigor in the field of economics, but also for his scanty faith in laws and the strength of the state: "The example of England and Prussia sufficiently proves that merely political institutions are enough for earthly power."[73]

A discussion of the features of Genovesi's civic economics would carry us far from our initial theme. One need only have noted that the *Principia*'s scientific suggestions were not sufficiently effective to condition the moralist and the economist greatly. Genovesi early refused the "mechanical," mathematical aspect of the new economic science in favor of the dimension he labeled "civic," because it was subordinated to the primacy of politics and the determination to change and to progress. Nevertheless, he had a very visible role in working out what we would call Newtonian scholastics, or the attempt to impose a rigid interpretation of the *Principia* on Italian culture in the latter half of the eighteenth century, a view closely related to the version that had been offered in the past by the Boyle Lectures. From his first youthful works and the much-discussed *Theologiae elementa* [Elements of theology] to the posthumous *Elementi di fisica*, Genovesi never forgot to stress the importance and apologetic meaning of Newtonian natural theology. The religious reading of the *Principia* was a firm point for him in the *Metaphysica*, the *Disputatio*, the *Elementa artis logico-criticae* [Elements of logical-critical art] and the *Meditazioni filosofiche sulla religione e sulla morale* [Philosophical meditations on religion and morals].[74] In the chapter "Cosmology" in the *Scienze metafisiche per gli giovinetti*, his explanation of Newtonian theorems concluded: "All this supposes a plan, and every overall plan of the world proves the existence of a ruling intelligence."[75] And in the *Logica per gli giovinetti* [Logic for young people], he addressed an explicit exhortation to scholastic authorities to introduce Newtonian natural theology into programs of study: "Mr. Newton's principles of physics, Derham's theology of physics, Nieuwentijt's work, and others of a similar mold, are worth a hundred thousand volumes of nonsense about transcendentals."[76] The meaning that Genovesi attributed to those principles is also evident from some of his thoughts in the *Elementi di fisica*. In his opinion, "God speaks to us not only through revelation, but also in His works and His deeds. Indeed, the world speaks before prophecy does."[77] All modern science was nothing less than continual testimony to God's existence and power:

> As Cicero says in book one of his *De natura deorum*, can there be something more clear and obvious when we have raised our eyes to the heavens and contemplated celestial things, as the existence of some god gifted with most excellent and highest intelligence that supports and governs them? This is what the noteworthy and widely admired works of Galileo entitled the Dialogues of the World, Newton's Physico-Mathematical Principles, Derham's Theological Astronomy, Nieuwentijt's third book, and nearly an infinite number of others, contemplate.[78]

Genovesi placed Newtonian natural theology at the root of the new Catholic apologetics against the Libertines and the deists, thus ideally concluding the enlightened Catholics' project to disseminate Newtonianism. His interpretation, however, had lost a great deal of those elements novel and dangerous to orthodoxy that had accompanied the publication of the texts of Derham and Cheyne at Florence and Naples in the 1720s and 1730s. Like Celestino Galiani, Genovesi had read Spinoza, Marsham, Spencer, Simon, Le Clerc, Toland, Collins, Tindal, and many other scholars who embodied the crisis of the European mind, but he certainly did not attribute to Newtonian apologetics the same meaning that Galiani did. For Galiani, the *Principia* and the Boyle Lectures had constituted not only a bastion against atheists and Libertines but, most important, the basis of theological empiricism and Locke's rationalism, a new definition of Christianity's historical duties, confined to a spiritual dimension, without trespassing into earthly things, politics, or economics. The *Principia* had led Galiani and Intieri to confront the problems of the Enlightenment with a critical spirit and renewed certainties. For Genovesi, on the other hand, that work came to seal up the new frontier of a Christianity that in Italy had escaped the crisis of the European mind nearly unharmed. This was the conclusion of the work of those like Ludovico Antonio Muratori who had sought to renew the entire tradition of Italian Catholicism internally and without substantial concessions, opening it to the problems of society, politics, and cultural renewal. Christianity always occupied a prominent place in Genovesi's thought. To speak of his heterodoxy because of the ecclesiastical persecutions he underwent does not make any sense.[79] His reading of Spinoza, Simon, and Toland perhaps would have created profound disturbances in the early eighteenth century, when the crisis of European Christianity was more acute, but not in the 1740s and 1750s after Muratori, with his theses about "public happiness," and Vico, with his *Scienza morale*, had responded in original terms to those who denied that religion had any role.

Genovesi loved to present himself as a modern apologist, condemned to fight against both misbelievers and zealots who favored the total closing of

Catholicism to all innovative ferment, almost as if to claim for himself the merit of desiring to follow an arduous and dangerous middle road in difficult times. Newtonian natural theology, always accompanied by revelation and the teachings of Catholic tradition, was a further element of strength in his struggle for a Christianity made of few and simple principles, inspired by the Church Fathers' evangelism.

In Genovesi's manuals, the image of the cosmos presented in the *Principia* received one of the first openly apologetic readings by a Catholic intellectual. Separated from the grand and thorny cosmological and philosophical debates of the early eighteenth century and enclosed in the reassuring Italian tradition that did not leave much room for Anglican rationalism or the empiricist theology of Limborch and Le Clerc, and thanks also to Genovesi's work, some of the results of the Boyle Lectures ultimately defined the fundamental outlines of what we have called Newtonian scholastics in Italy.

2. THE UNIVERSE-MACHINE IN THE *NOVELLE LETTERARIE*

In the 1740s the battle to disseminate Newtonianism in Italy could already be considered won. In addition to Francesco Algarotti's and Benedetto Stay's famous popular works,[1] or the myriad of verses composed to introduce a wider public to Newton's most sensational discoveries,[2] the Englishman's theories began to appear increasingly in university programs, everywhere supplanting both Aristotelian and Cartesian physics. For some time, other universities had accepted the teachings contained in the theories of the *Opticks* and the *Principia*. In the 1720s and 1730s Poleni, Riccati, and Crivelli already taught their pupils using the first elements of Newtonian physics. In Piedmont Father Joseph Roma, a disciple of Celestino Galiani whom government authorities entrusted in 1732 with formulating instructions for the courses in philosophy, invited the teachers to broach the study of the *Principia* through readings of 'sGravesande and Clarke, inserting Newtonian experimentalism into the great Galilean tradition.[3] In the 1740s the definitive victory of Newtonianism in Italy was marked by the publication of numerous manuals "for university use" written by prestigious scholars. In 1738 Pietro Di Martino published his *Philosophiae naturalis institutionum libri tres* [Three books of the institutions of natural philosophy] in Naples, with an ample examination of the *Principia*'s theories.[4] In 1748 and 1749, the Somascan priest Giovanni Maria Della Torre, a professor at the seminary in Naples and a pupil of Celestino Galiani, completed two volumes on the *Scienza della natura generale e particolare* [The Science of nature, general and particular], which, according to the *Novelle letterarie*, placed "the opinion of Newton and his pupils constantly before any other opinion."[5] In 1745 and 1746 Father Fortunato da Brescia (whose lay name was Gerolamo Ferrari) sent to the press his famous *Philosophia sensuum mechanica* [Mechanical philosophy of the senses], which reproduced even the beautiful plates of the *Saggio della filosofia del signor cav. Isaaco Newton esposto con chiarezza dal signor Enrico Pemberton* [Essay on Sir Isaac Newton's philosophy clearly explained by Mr. Henry Pemberton], which had appeared in Venice in 1738.[6] Among the many other examples were the translations of Voltaire's *Métaphysique de Newton* [Newton's metaphysics] (Florence, 1742) and *Eléments de la philosophie de Newton* [Elements of Newton's philosophy] (Venice, 1741), which would enjoy noteworthy success.[7] Even more interesting than these publications is the overall attitude of the Holy See towards the growing favor for Newtonian theories in Italy.

The election of Benedict XIV in 1740 marked the beginning of a period of great hopes and receptivity towards modern science in the very heart of Catholicism.[8] We are already well informed about the renewal of studies at the Sapienza University in Rome at the initiative of the secretary of state, Silvio Valenti Gonzaga, who provided for the creation of the chairs in chemistry, physics, and botany.[9] With the arrival of the Ragusan mathematician Ruggero Boscovich at the Collegio Romano, the entire scientific realm seemed to reawaken from the torpor in which it had fallen after the death of Bianchini and the departure of Celestino Galiani. "Curious advances towards heliocentric astronomy"[10] took shape within the Collegio Romano itself, in which Boscovich came to attack Cartesian vortices fearlessly, challenging his own fellow Jesuits, who, throughout Europe, defended the theories of the French philosopher against universal gravitation. There were other signs of a new and more benevolent attitude within the Holy See towards Newtonianism. For quite some time, the greatest center of research controlled directly by pontifical authorities, namely the Istituto Bolognese founded by Marsili, Davia, Leprotti, and Manfredi, had officially recognized the validity of Newtonian theories from a strictly scientific point of view. The Istituto's *Commentari* [Commentaries] from 1742, for example, broached the problem of gravitational attraction with articles by Boscovich, Beccari, and Riccati, recognizing merits in Newtonianism that went far beyond the specific aspects of the *Principia* that were critically discussed.[11] On the level of popularization, the *Giornale de' Letterati* of Rome, which since 1745 had replaced the *Notizie letterarie oltramontane* [Learned news from north of the Alps], under the direction of Gaetano Cenni and with the protection of Cardinal Silvio Valenti Gonzaga, contributed to introducing Rome to the most current scientific debates on Newtonian theories, through the articles of Boscovich and other Roman scholars.[12]

In other Italian periodicals as well, such as the *Giornale de' Letterati* of Florence, the examination of works inspired by the English scientist's theories occupied a growing prominence, contributing to the widespread dissemination of the cornerstones of his thought through reviews and articles.[13] Alongside the affirmation of the *Principia*'s theories, Genovesi and Giovanni Lami developed an intensive propaganda in favor of the Boyle Lectures.

Lami was the principal channel, through the *Novelle letterarie* which appeared for the first time in Florence in 1740 and which was to become the most important Italian journal of those years.[14]

Lami was an untiring scholar of ecclesiastical history, and he had profound knowledge of the works of the Free-Thinkers, Spinoza, the Anglican apologists of the Low Church, and the Lutherans. He traveled all over Europe as a librarian and companion of Gianluca Pallavicini,[15] and he had been able to refine his apologetic weapons, sensitive as he was to new information but rigid in his defense of orthodoxy. As happened with Genovesi, all his work and thought had been influenced by the fascinating Ludovico Antonio Muratori. However, Lami's temperament was different from Muratori's, and he allowed himself to become involved in many disputes, always conducted bitterly, whether his adversaries were prestigious intellectuals such as Le Clerc or Jesuits, his traditional enemies.

The *Novelle letterarie* was founded to fill the gap left by the disappearance of the *Giornale de' Letterati* of Venice, and it reflected to some extent the intransigent and prickly character of its director. In 1743 the editorial group (originally composed of Lami, the Galilean Giovanni Targioni Tozzetti, and the antiquarian Anton Francesco Gori) was brusquely dissolved by Lami, who wished to assume all responsibility for the direction of the periodical himself.[16] For many years, Lami very attentively followed the affairs of Italian culture through the pages of the *Novelle*. Thus he became the vanguard of Muratori's Catholicism, ready to discuss matters openly without ever renouncing the tenets of orthodoxy. His work of disseminating the Boyle Lectures through the *Novelle* was another chapter in the vast and intelligent operation of containing the most destructive aspects of modern thought, a task carried out by a broad sector of the Catholic world at mid-century.

From the first issues, summoning the prestige of the Galilean experimental tradition as well, the *Novelle* defended Newtonian theories from the attacks of the Jesuits and the French Cartesians, and in 1741 the journal took the side of the "great man" Newton against the Jesuit Louis-Bertrand Castel.[17] Lami called attention to the Italian translation of John Thompson's poem *Le lodi d'Isacco Newton* [The praises of Isaac Newton] made by Andrea Bonducci for Sir Horace Mann, the British agent in Tuscany, and on that occasion he did not fail to renew his shots against the Cartesian Jesuits who claimed "to refute Mr. Newton's system of colors."[18] In all probability, the Florentine edition of Voltaire's *Métaphysique de Newton* was not outside his plans. In fact, he commented positively on its appearance, implying that he approved of its editor's plan to have other translations follow this one.[19]

Nevertheless, Lami quickly clarified his thoughts on Newtonian ideology in the pages of the *Novelle*. He violently attacked the works of English deists, of the Socinians, and of all those who aimed to oppose God to nature, and he identified the theology of Anglican rationalists as an effective barrier against the "impious opinions" of the Free-Thinkers and the Libertines. Commenting on Thomas Morgan's *Physico-Theology, or a Philosophico-Moral Disquisition Concerning Human Nature*, he again called attention to the obstacles faced by Italians maintaining such ideas. With his usual bitterness, he argued against the most reactionary branches of Catholic culture, hostile to any concession to natural theology, seen as a source of heresy. He wrote that those who thoughtlessly gave the "title of atheist to whomever set about demonstrating the existence of God authoritatively"[20] ultimately deprived Christian apologetics of new and efficacious weapons of defense. Taking his cue from the appearance of a series of works in England and Holland that were strongly influenced by the theses of the Boyle lecturers, Lami commented favorably on the publication of a volume from the series, exclaiming; "This is one of those many books that must be read by everyone, if it is true that every person must cultivate the study of natural religion in order to shape his heart and spirit by marveling at the creator's amazing works."[21] In his excitement over the Boyle Lectures, Lami even came to hope that a publisher might finally produce a "many-volumed collection" of the lectures of Clarke, Derham, Cheyne, and Bentley, complemented by the *Scholium generale*.[22] The image of the Newtonian universe with its mathematical laws ("the calculations of the famous Mr. Halley on the quantity of vapors that rise from the Mediterranean alone demonstrate meteorological mechanisms") fascinated him. Using the *Novelle letterarie*, he introduced the new frontier of Christianity in the wake of the crisis of the European mind to a vast audience. Once Spinoza and Toland had called into question the divine inspiration of the Old Testament and once the corrosive writings of the Free-Thinkers had diminished the historical role of Christianity, Newtonianism and the Boyle Lectures slowly refounded the principles of God's existence on more solid bases in Italy as well. Besides, who could deny the attraction and persuasive quality of the *Scholium generale*'s theses? Both Lami and Genovesi could only adapt themselves to the rhythms of European Christianity, Catholicizing and explaining the theses of the Boyle lecturers as much as possible.

During those years, the overall significance of Lami's activities found confirmation in the writings of other Catholics. Even Tommaso Mamachi, an enemy of Antonio Genovesi who succeeded the Newtonian Le Seur in teaching at the Roman college De Propaganda Fide in the 1740s, did not hesitate to attribute an essential role to the Boyle Lectures in the defense of Christianity from atheism's perils.[23] This was an important fact, for the college was designed to shape the ecclesiastics destined to conquer the infidels.

One particular contemporary example of the Catholics' apologetic use of Newtonianism was the appearance of the works of Tommaso Moniglia, a teacher of Church history at Pisa. His *Dissertazione contro i fatalisti* [Dissertation against the fatalists], in fact, was one of the last attempts to connect the affirmation of Newtonianism in Italy to a real process of renewal in Catholic culture, by being receptive to Lockean empiricism. His work is particularly interesting for the intelligence with which he sought to soften the less-orthodox elements of Locke's thought in the wake of the *Essay's* condemnation in 1734. Moniglia began by saying:

> Locke is one writer who cannot be put in the class of Spinoza, Hobbes, Toland, Collins, and other similar.... Look at the words of Clarke: In the writings of Mr. Locke, there are some points that on good grounds can cast doubt on the soul's immortality; but in that he has been followed only by some materialists who are enemies of the mathematical principles of philosophy, and they approve of almost nothing but the errors in Mr. Locke's works.[24]

Skillfully linking Newton and Locke according to Voltaire's scheme from the *Métaphysique de Newton* and the marquise de Châtelet's *Institutiones de physique* [Institutions of physics] (translated and published in Venice in 1743), he produced a reading of the *Principia* that was anti-Spinozan and anti-Hobbesian, designed mainly to save gnosiological empiricism. Locke, Clarke, and Newton were grouped together as the true enemies of Toland, Collins, and Tindal. The attempt to propose a softened image of Locke's thought as achieved by Moniglia was expressed especially by the direct efforts to neutralize his ethical thoughts and by the severe criticisms of hedonism and disturbing affirmations about the role of "will" and human freedom, the so-called moral relativism.[25] Discussing the religious phenomenon in history, Moniglia denied that there was any truth in Bayle's and Locke's thesis about the existence of atheist populations, and he corroborated theological innatism and the validity of the *consensus gentium* as the basis of Christian apologetics. His defense of orthodoxy was not limited only to refuting some of the *Essay's* points; it vigorously confronted and rejected both the Libertine thesis about the political origins of religions and Vico's theory positing the primary elements of human sensibility. Those who "attributed the origin of religion to the fear of men" were to be held "impious"; it was not necessary to assign "the origin of religion to the passions."[26]

In the years in which Lami, Moniglia, and other Catholics disseminated the Boyle Lectures' propaganda with manuals of natural philosophy and influential periodicals like the *Novelle letterarie*, the publication of a book in Tuscany inspired by a deist and Toland-like reading of the *Principia* was to interrupt the process of increasing receptivity to modern thought initiated in the early eighteenth century. The volume appeared anonymously in Lucca with the title *Della esistenza e degli attributi di Dio* [On the existence and attributes of God] in 1745. The author was a teacher at the Pisan university, Giovanni Alberto De Soria, who had long been connected to Tuscan Masonic circles.[27] De Soria's treatise was produced only a few years after the papal bull *In Eminenti* and the troubling affair of Crudeli's trial, both of which had relentlessly stricken all Tuscan Masonry,[28] and it could be considered one of the most interesting outcomes of that experience. It is safe to assume that its publication required the direct intervention of English and Tuscan Masons. However, Toland's theses supported in the treatise were able to circulate only in the Florentine lodge, one of whose members was Baron Philip von Stosch, adventurer, art expert, and Jacobite spy who later worked for the house of Hanover, and an exponent of the Masonic wing tied to Libertine and Tolandist circles in The Hague.[29] In the foreword, De Soria himself attributed the motivation behind the work's publication to his connections with England. The book is, in fact, dedicated to an anonymous English baronet who had invited him on behalf of mutual friends to respond to Clarke's conclusions on the attributes and existence of God.[30] Whether or not De Soria was a Mason, the work aroused great interest and contributed decisively to a real turning point in Italian culture in those years, forcing Catholics like Lami to face openly the most radical theses of European thinkers.

Born in 1707 to humble parents in Pisa, Giovanni Alberto De Soria had completed his early studies at Leghorn in a Jesuit college.[31] This was followed by a period of intensive reading of Cartesian, Galilean, and Newtonian works—which were still banned from the Jesuits' scholastic programs—at the direct request of friends in Leghorn. The most important period of his education was at the Pisan university, where his masters were Guido Grandi and Giuseppe Averani. In 1731, while still very young, he was designated as the reader in logic with all honors at the behest of Gian Gastone de Medici. Then his work as a scholar and master began. With his passage from the chair in logic to that of physics, his crowded lectures, according to the accounts of his biographer and pupil Luca Magnanima,[32] became a meeting place for those who wished to learn the most advanced philosophical and scientific theories without censure or reticence. At the center of his attention were Spinoza, Descartes, Locke, Newton, the great philosophical debates between Leibniz and Clarke, and the depiction of deist theses and the refutation of Protestant apologetics. But in the 1730s hostile voices were raised against De Soria, in particular among the Jesuits, who had nevertheless attempted to convince him to enter their order. The protests of the clergy and the traditionalist professors came to a head in a trial within the academic community. The commission entrusted with "secretly" examining the orthodoxy of his lectures, a group whose members included Guido Grandi and Edoardo Corsini, maintained his innocence, despite the serious pressure to find otherwise.[33] De Soria's reputation as a Free-Thinker nevertheless became even greater.

When in 1745 De Soria anonymously published the brief treatise *Della esistenza e degli attributi di Dio*, destined to provoke reactions throughout Italy, he was well known and appreciated even abroad for his *Rationalis philosophiae institutiones sive de emendanda regendaque mente* [Institutions of rational philosophy, or on improving and governing the mind], which appeared in Amsterdam in 1741[34] and outlined a philosophy based on a radical, gnosiological rationalism. This metaphysics, as he defined it, was in reality a kind of supreme science, capable of bridging reality and thought, guaranteeing mankind its creativity and complete domination over nature. In the metaphysics that De Soria hypothesized, reason was transformed into an enlightened tool without any cognitive limits. "For him, reason was a god that he always respectfully admired and would have defended with his own blood,"[35] his pupil Luca Magnanima wrote, emphasizing the rationalist passion, almost a kind of fanaticism, that pervaded De Soria's every activity.

Starting from these premises, De Soria aimed to create an encyclopedia of human knowledge, and he successfully broached difficult matters such as Newtonian cosmology and the economic and political reform of Italy and laid down the foundations of a science of mankind consonant with the times.[36] From the neomercantilist assumptions that he developed for a profound institutional change of the Republic of Genoa in his unedited *Notti alfee* [Alphean Nights] (1740)[37] to his enthusiastic approval of Beccaria's *Dei delitti e delle pene* [On crimes and punishments][38] and the evocative *Cosmologia*, he maintained the primacy of reason. And if reason adapted poorly to the irrationality of some human behaviors, he did not hesitate to abandon concrete reforms in favor of utopian dreams of better universes.[39]

Between 1743 and 1744 he produced the *Cosmologia o fisica universale* [Cosmology or universal physics], which only appeared posthumously in 1772, although it had circulated earlier in manuscript form in Masonic circles and within the English community in Tuscany.[40] Without any reticence he outlined in this work an image of the world different from that of the Boyle lecturers, 'sGravesande, and Voltaire. De Soria rejected both Clarke's traditional cosmology, centered on the thesis of an inert and passive matter, as well as the prudent vision of Voltaire and d'Alembert, of a phenomenalist and mathematized Newtonianism in which the cause of universal gravitation was a secondary problem. He accused mathematicians like d'Alembert of coming to a halt before the phenomenon without attempting to comprehend its inner essence. "Physical bodies are not imaginary objects like the mathematicians' figures";[41] therefore, it was necessary to explain mechanics in real terms and not merely abstract ones, De Soria wrote. "The proponents of immediate actions at a distance say that, though the way they occur is incomprehensible, this, too, is a law of creation demonstrated by facts."[42] On the other hand, he did have an explanation for the dynamic phenomena of the universe acceptable on a logical level; it was a reversal of Clarke's theses and the *Scholium generale*. In fact, he rejected universal gravitation interpreted as an action at a distance between two bodies, noting "even Sir Newton himself allowed himself to be dazzled inadvertently by such an absurd concept."[43] He also restated Toland's hypothesis of motion inherent to matter (with all its corollaries about the nonexistence of a God the watchmaker) associated with the traditional image of the Newtonian universe-machine. De Soria wrote: "No modification and no attribute of any given subject can exist outside of it; thus the gravity in a body or any of its movements cannot exist outside that body."[44] His philosophical attitude was in certain aspects similar to the rationalism of the French materialists who rejected d'Alembert's mathematical phenomenalism, and De Soria worked out in detail a cosmology quite near to Spinoza's monistic naturalism based on the chain of beings, in which everything was interrelated and endowed with its own vitality:

> Given its circumstances, one cannot take away or change a phenomenon without taking away or changing the physical laws of nature, and without as a natural consequence taking away or changing all the rest in the entire corporeal universe. Herein lies sufficient explanation for the reasons and extension of what is improperly called sympathy and that the ancients called connection or consensus.[45]

It was certainly not by chance that the *Cosmologia* remained unedited during its author's lifetime, but for De Soria's thought it represented an indispensable premise underlying the production of his most famous work, *Della esistenza e degli attributi di Dio*, which appeared in 1745 amid difficulties and which finally provided Italian culture with a deist and Tolandist reading of the *Principia*, an alternative to the Boyle Lectures. From the start, the author's intentions were quite evident. He entitled the first paragraph "Della esistenza di Dio e dei suoi attributi fisici e morali. Ragionamento pe' sapienti prescindente da ogni soprannaturale dottrina" [On the existence of God and his physical and moral attributes. Reasoning for learned men leaving aside any supernatural doctrine], maintaining the thesis of the indisputable primacy of metaphysics, or reason, within every discipline, including theology. Congruent with the premise of leaving aside any reference to supernatural facts in his demonstration of God's existence, De Soria did not consider Sacred Scripture, the apologetic tradition, or revelation itself in his reflections. He rejected the old thesis of the Fathers of the Church about the reduction of man's rational capacities because of original sin, for, as he said, "original sin, the cause of the evils of the human race, is beyond philosophy . . ., therefore it should not be used in these discussions, which are merely philosophical and entirely apart from any revealed doctrine as from any tradition."[46] He also denied any validity to Locke's scheme of the *Reasonableness of Christianity*. Antonio Conti even noted this, for in a letter to Muratori he criticized De Soria's refusal to attribute an intrinsic factual and historical dimension to human reason.[47]

In reality, the attraction of the philosopher's reasoning lay precisely in this unbiased use of a reason stripped of historical encrustations. This was also a novelty for English deist culture itself, which held that historical investigation into the great religions of Eastern and Mediterranean peoples was essential for documenting the existence in that area of a single attitude toward religion, imposed by nature and shared by all nations.

Confirming the scientific premises of a vitalist and Tolandist signature developed in the *Cosmologia*, De Soria used his *Della esistenza e degli attributi di Dio* to fulfil the task assigned to him by English friends of combating Clarke's conclusions, which drew the arguments necessary to repel the ideas of the Libertines and the atheists from Newtonian natural theology. The proofs he adopted to confirm the existence of God had their roots in the asserted contingence of matter and the motion inherent in it. Hence the internal finalism of the chain of beings was closely interwoven with the divine presence in the world. He accomplished a unique overturning of the prospects at the core of Newtonian natural theology, fraught with any determinist and materialist developments. Once he denied any authority to Christian tradition and anchored the proofs of God's existence in an autonomous universe, reason finally reached a position of absolute preeminence for evaluating every aspect of creation and the divinity. His ambiguous considerations on the relationship between God and nature and the corporeality of the human soul only strengthened the image that De Soria was by then irreversibly freed from the interpretative schemes of Catholic and Christian culture.[48] How could one demonstrate the soul's immortality?, he asked the reader in the second part of his work. In his opinion, the only way was to proclaim absolute immateriality a priori; otherwise one would inevitably succumb to the atheists' arguments. Apart from the fragility of his solution, which yet again overlooked any reference to Church doctrine, De Soria started with an indemonstrable hypothesis with the intent of sowing more doubts than certainties. In the end, he gave the reader the impression that he himself disapproved of his conclusions, which were so weak that they seemed provocative and which seemed so much less credible because they were placed at the end of a convincing exposition of the materialists' ideas. All that has been created must sooner or later end, De Soria did not hesitate to write; "therefore any human soul and any product superior to it are by their nature always destructible and in this sense always mortal."[49] And if one accepts the materialists' ideas about the existence of thinking matter, he insisted, then this matter would have to be placed within a space, and it would hence be extended: "Therefore, since some thinking being exists, it follows that every thinking being is extended." From similar premises, a very capable reasoner like De Soria had no difficulties in relentlessly concluding in favor of the soul's mortality. "Therefore since matter is our thinking being, our thinking matter is the same thing as our machine. . . . Therefore every thinking being must be matter, therefore by its nature mortal in resolution."[50] It is not difficult to understand how De Soria's conclusions yielded frankly atheist results.

There was no shortage of reactions throughout Italian culture. In particular Giovanni Lami, under the name of Clemente Bini, harshly railed against him in five concise letters in the *Novelle letterarie*. He showed that he had understood in depth how dangerous the Pisan teacher's treatise was, for within it he had identified an attempt to open the path to the materialist and anti-Christian component of the Enlightenment in Italy as well; his threatening responses were of great import in marking the limits that could not be crossed by those like De Soria who began to pay suspicious attention to the ferment of the Enlightenment from north of the Alps. From the first letter, Lami attacked the very philosophical foundations of De Soria's book, which he called "poorly reasoned and of evil consequence for religion"[51] or, as he wrote in the third letter, "a truly pestiferous little book."[52] Inverting the scholastic thesis about the primacy of theology over philosophy, De Soria had proclaimed the supremacy of reason. In his *Della esistenza e degli attributi di Dio*, the divine presence itself had been the object of a rational analysis. Scandalized by such conclusions, Lami replied by reconfirming Galileo's thesis of the double truth, theological and philosophical, explicitly shared by Muratori and Genovesi.[53] Paraphrasing a famous annotation of Le Clerc's *Ars critica*, he wrote: "Revelation and right reason are two sisters so in accord that one does not suggest anything contrary to the other."[54] As Muratori had written in the *De ingeniorum moderatione*, reason could have no voice in the realm of Christian faith. The negative consequences of the fundamental error De Soria committed became evident. He had come to "destroy the attributes of God in some way." The heavenly nature of religion, dogmas, revelation, the Trinity, and the angelic hierarchies in the end remained secondary, almost condemned to disappear into an entirely rational dimension of divinity. "This doctrine of his tends to destroy the punishments of the afterlife," Lami thundered.[55]

The most disturbing aspect of De Soria's message—the invitation to widen the vitalist and Tolandist reading of the *Principia*—had not escaped Lami's sharp mind. The director of the *Novelle* violently attacked De Soria's overturning of the Boyle Lectures, and he accused him of not knowing how to reason, or even of reasoning like an "impious" man. The thesis of a self-moving substance was demolished in a long, pointedly critical section.[56] That matter "can be and is moved by extrinsic force, I concede; that it is mobile of itself and in essence, I deny."[57] According to Lami, to base the existence of God on the self-moving capacity of bodies hid the underhanded attempt to introduce materialism into Italy. De Soria wished to confuse the simple; his true intention was to "call the existence of God into doubt,"[58] also because "according to the materialists it would be superfluous to admit a God while one finds mutability and movement in matter's essence." In the *Continuazione della seconda lettera* [Continuation of the second letter], Lami showed that he had not allowed himself to be deceived by the capable but fragile apologetic cover with which De Soria had sought to camouflage his materialism, for he exclaimed triumphantly: "See the veil removed; see the scene opened; now we see how well our metaphysicist treats the cause of the divinity."[59] "To attribute essential motion to matter is to make the road to atheism easier."[60]

In his pitiless criticism, Lami did not hesitate to accuse De Soria of having denied the existence of God by affirming that there were only "problematic" proofs in this regard, "subject to a great refutation."[61] The only certain argument for De Soria in fact lay in the "contingence of matter" and its self-moving quality, Lami responded that these were the theses of Vanini, of the Free-Thinkers, and, especially of Toland:

> It is said that motion is essential to matter and in its nature. . . . This is a most absurd proposition, which only the impious impudence of John Toland, a great supporter and modern defender of atheism, has been able to advance recently.[62]

For Lami, the author of *Della esistenza e degli attributi di Dio* had drawn nearly all his argumentation from heterodox authors: the hypothesis of an "intelligent" matter originated in Hobbes's and Epicurus's works, just as the affirmation that "the universe is infinite and immense" derived from "the pestiferous book produced by Giordano Bruno, *De immenso et innumeralibus* [On the immense and the innumerable]." From Anthony Collins's pamphlets, De Soria had, instead, derived a determinist conception of the world, or, rather, the conception of the "not entirely free freedom" of mankind.[63] Yet again Lami indicated that the only correct reading of the *Principia* was that of the Boyle Lectures. "It is an article of faith that beauty, order, and the miraculous complex of the world prove God's existence."[64] By this time, the "immortal Newton," Clarke, Cheyne, Derham, and Bentley definitively represented—even for Catholic intellectuals—the new bastion against the atheists. Lami wrote in the *Novelle*, "it would be desirable if these glorious men were read in a public university."[65]

Actually, behind Lami's threatening arguments were men in the foreground of Italian culture and of the ecclesiastical hierarchy itself. Some Catholic scholars—men who in the first decades of the eighteenth century had activated clandestine channels for prohibited books, mounted free debates, and offered protection to suspect editorial initiatives—did not hesitate to intervene with their full weight in the dispute. Gaspare Cerati, director of the Pisan university, made life difficult for De Soria, who was in his opinion an author of a book of "pure deist thought."[66] Bottari was no less forthcoming in advising the director of the *Novelle letterarie* to fight vigorously against De Soria,[67] and even Muratori agreed on the usefulness of that dispute. On 10 February 1747 he wrote, "it has been quite useful in the past, because it has redirected some of his opinions [that were] poorly thought out or not cautiously expressed."[68] It was no coincidence that De Soria was publicly defended only by the Florentine *Giornale de' Letterati*, founded in 1742 by Ottaviano Bonaccorsi, one of the leaders of Tuscan Masonry, and Father Raimondo Adami, a personal enemy of Giovanni Lami.[69] The protection of Minister Richecourt and English Masonic circles helped him to avert a tempest similar to the one that had overcome his friend

Crudeli.[70] All the conditions were right for a repetition of the Crudeli affair; in the *Novelle* in 1745 Lami had publicly called Crudeli "a great example for teaching [people] to be very moderate and circumspect in their speech."[71] The Inquisition-like tones of the director of the *Novelle* did not bode well for the Pisan De Soria. Warning his enemies that he was not alone in the great battle against the materialists and heretics, Lami refused any request to moderate the tenor of the debate, exclaiming: "We are dealing with the opening of the road to atheism, against which it is too little to call upon the flames of revenge and the inexorable iron, at least for this most pestilential book."[72]

Again in the *Novelle*, Lami made public some letters written to him by influential members of the Roman Curia, from which it became evident that he himself had been entrusted with the task of bringing back into line Italian scholars overly restless and fond of philosophical novelties.[73] In a letter from Rome, an anonymous prelate kept him current on the unrest caused by De Soria's book, advising him that the pope, too, had been disturbed ("the pope has annotated the entire book with his own hand").[74] In another letter, a clergyman close to the circle of Inquisition prelates affirmed: "Soria has written very submissively here, and they will spare him the prohibition of his book because he promised to publish it correctly."[75] Shortly thereafter, the victorious Lami advised his readers that Rome had ordered him not to worry himself over the matter any longer. De Soria had in fact published a new, "expurgated" edition of his book in 1746, and, most important, complying with an unfortunately well-tested routine, he "laudably subjected himself to the infallible judgment of the Holy Roman Church."[76]

3. BETWEEN INNOVATION AND REACTION

With Giovanni Alberto De Soria's recantation, the debate over Newtonianism, which to a great degree had grown in Rome from the reflections of Celestino Galiani at Sant'Eusebio and in the scientific dinners organized by prelates attuned to modern thought, by mid-century had already exhausted its role as a stimulus. A new world and a different attitude towards reality had come to a head after the long travail initiated by the crisis of the European mind. From the early eighteenth century, the *Principia* had been for Italy a precise reference for whomever proposed to face the great problems posed by the progressive bankruptcy of ancient certainties.

On the scientific plane, the *Opticks* and the *Principia* were reconnected to the ancient and still-living Galilean and experimentalist tradition, and they made it possible to overcome both qualitative Aristotelian physics and post-Cartesian mechanicism. Through Newton, Galileo had been finally readmitted into the official circuit of Italian intellectual life. Forgotten themes such as Copernicanism, the relationship between reason and faith, and the importance of technology in human progress were debated again with unexpected energy within a "literary republic" still in turmoil after the trial of the Neapolitan atheists. The Newtonian world had, however, focused Italian scholars' attention most centrally on a new, suggestive image of God. With the Boyle Lectures, natural theology, and the profound and thoughtful words of the *Scholium generale*, a mechanical-mathematical and rational God came to replace the historical God of Moses, the avenging God of the Old Testament, who had been irreparably profaned by Spinozan exegesis and the pamphlets of the Free-Thinkers and the Libertines. The God of nature had replaced the God of revelation. The most enlightened Catholics had based themselves precisely on the solid foundations of the Boyle Lectures in order to prime a process of renewal in Italy as well that responded positively to the crisis of Christianity. However, accepting the Newtonian world brought a number of problems. Whoever had read the *quaestiones* of the *Optice* or between the lines of the *Principia* could understand that a new political, economic, philosophical, and religious order was taking shape. The preoccupation of all European intellectuals was to tie the universe-machine and the discoveries of modern science organically to a redefinition of Christianity in a society that was extremely restless, lively, and now open to new values. Even Italian scholars at the turn of the century could not avoid posing troubling questions about Christianity's historical role, its features, and its truth. Spinoza, Richard Simon, and the Libertines found numerous echoes in Naples, Venice, and Rome as well. The answers were multifaceted and interwoven with specifically national problems such as the Galilean heritage, jurisdictionalism, the vindication of *libertas philosophandi*, and the reform in the heart of the Catholic Church. A process of splintering occurred among the responses to those questions and those problems in the span of three decades, leaving profound traces throughout the entire eighteenth century.

The materialist current inspired by Spinoza, the Free-Thinkers' ideas, and Brunian and Renaissance vitalism, guided by Alberto Radicati di Passerano, Pietro Giannone, and Antonio Conti, gave life to a fascinating chapter of Italian culture. As we know, the voices of these scholars nevertheless had little following, especially because of the prompt ecclesiastical repression. Radicati's exile, Giannone's death in prison, and Conti's trial entirely eradicated any possibility for the dissemination of a materialist ideology. To identify the impossibility of knowing Giannone's *Triregno* and Radicati's works as the factor that deprived the Italian eighteenth century of a radical Enlightenment, somehow comparable to Holbach's coterie, is at best reductive and insufficient.[1] Nor can the Inquisitorial pressures hide the inadequacy of such responses as were furnished by Free-Thinkers in Italy. For example, aside from the conditioning of his imprisonment, the central nucleus of Giannone's thought always remained intrinsically outside the most advanced debates on science, on economy, or on a new political and social order. One ought not underestimate the fact that Giannone had overlooked the destructive republican component of Toland's thought, just as he overlooked the neo-

Harringtonian ideology of common law.[2] In the *Triregno*, demystifying the historical origins of Christianity, Giannone had found a further justification for the fierce struggle against the Church, without, however, offering a new image of the world or an entirely earthly society, freed from the oppression of the clerics. And yet the strength and attraction of the currents of these European Free-Thinkers, from Toland to Meslier (who would arouse their great interest in the radical Enlightenment of the latter half of the French eighteenth century) lay precisely in the proposals, even if more utopian than concrete, for a society revolutionized in its political and economic order and based on ethical models opposed to Christian values. Whether in Giannone's works or in Conti's philosophical synthesis or in the writings of Radicati di Passerano (who in his final years even came to advocate the commonality of goods and sexual freedom),[3] there are few references to such a revolution. This lack ought not to be underestimated when investigating the oblivion into which these victims of ecclesiastical persecution fell in the following generations.

The response of Catholic intellectuals regarding the significance that Christianity had assumed in the eighteenth century was naturally fervid and very rich. Recently a too-long-unsatisfied need has become apparent: a complete study of the origins of the Italian Enlightenment must examine that multifaceted culture of "Catholic renewal"—from Magliabechi to Muratori[4]—that, begun at the dawn of the eighteenth century, was destined to conclude brusquely in mid-century with the condemnation of the *Esprit des lois* and the *Encyclopédie*. In the course of a half-century, Catholic culture had finally begun to experience discussions and confrontations at the highest level and import, as had rarely been seen in its centuries-long history. The activity that brought about the dissemination of Newtonianism, the publication of Galileo's and Gassendi's works, and the discussions on Locke's thought would alone be sufficient to sweep away the traditional and narrow image of an early eighteenth century poor in debate and dominated by Arcadian trifles.

Newtonian natural theology and the scientific theories of the *Principia* had the effect of dividing almost all intellectuals of Catholic persuasion on great issues. Galiani and Niccolini found in the *Principia* the premises necessary for shifting Christianity away from sterile apologetic certainties and opening it to scientific rationalism, the daring thematic of deism, and new political themes. Bottari and Cerati, on the other hand, made the *Principia* and the Boyle Lectures bastions of orthodoxy, confining themselves to eliminating the most obscurantist aspects of the spirit of the Counter-Reformation. The solutions of Vico, Doria, and Muratori were extraordinarily interesting as well. They squarely attacked the essential problems of science, economy, morals, politics, and religion. For all of them, redefining a role for Christianity in society meant confronting the task of reconstructing an image of the world *ex novo*. From this came the complexity of arguments, the novelty, the variety, and the interest in the interpretations that came together in a debate whose intensity and originality had few equals in the eighteenth century. To every new idea of Christianity, they associated a specific philosophical and scientific dimension, completely renewed with respect to the past. Galiani saw the solution to problems posed by his contemporaries as Newtonian natural theology, Locke's rationalist morality, and the wholly earthly world of Mandeville and Bayle. In "public happiness," Galilean experimentalism, and social progress, Muratori intuitively grasped the fundamental elements of a new frontier for Christianity, capable of restating traditional evangelical values without bringing the ecclesiastical institution into the discussion. Through the ingenious reassertion of the humanist synthesis and a new conception of the historical process, Vico guaranteed Christianity (and religion in general) the role of the driving force in the development of nations. And also meaningful was Doria's response, a unique scientific counterrevolution that, beginning with a harsh criticism of the gnosiological foundations of the Newtonian universe-machine, allowed him to arrive at a plan for a Christian utopian society founded on evangelical and Neoplatonic values.

By the middle of the century, the ideological confrontation in the Catholic world had practically ended. The threatening apparition in Europe of the philosophes' anti-Christian offensive further reduced in Italy the already faint glimmers of libertas philosophandi. Genovesi was questioned in the 1740s merely because he had cited some heretical authors, generally to disagree with them. De Soria was forced to yield and to recant his writings. The condemnation of Montesquieu's Esprit des lois in 1751 (to which Giovanni Bottari himself contributed)[5] and the appearance of Sigismondo Gerdil's anti-Newtonian and anti-Lockean works were two of the most evident symptoms of this closure.[6] In the latter eighteenth century, the few prominent figures in the ecclesiastical circles were reactionary Jansenists like Fabio De Vecchi or so-called Jacobins like Andrea Serrao, utterly hostile to modern thought in any of its forms.[7] With his synthesis, of a Muratorian stamp, Genovesi affirmed his status as the sole interpreter of that happy period that had developed in the early decades of the eighteenth century. In order to find evidence of a Galiani-style rationalism based on Locke's Essay, one would have to wait for the hedonist morals theorized in Pietro Verri's Del piacere e del dolore [On pleasure and pain], or Cesare Beccaria's Dei delitti e delle pene [On crimes and punishments], a masterpiece of the Italian Enlightenment written by the "little Newton."

All eighteenth-century Italian culture preserved ample traces of the debates over Newtonianism, and it influenced the very ideological underpinnings of reformism. How could one forget the diversity of the contributions of Doria and Muratori, who aimed to construct a Christian society based on evangelical teachings, compared to the secular and enlightened reformism in which Intieri and Galiani believed?[8] These latter two had known how to take advantage of the cultural disorientatin of a Catholic Church unable to find weapons in its Counter-Reformation arsenal with which to combat its new adversaries—deists, Libertines, and Free-Thinkers. Capitalizing on the latitude that was opened to them, they attempted a daring, overall rethinking of Christianity, its reasons, and its roles, in order to absorb the most advanced results of European culture, including empiricism, utilitarianism, and economicism. But these openings closed quickly. From Catholic culture itself came other responses to these same problems, as well as severe denunciations of the destructive dangers implicit in these daring proposals. Having already appropriated the apologetic dimension of Newtonianism, the Church was able to use it by seamlessly overlapping these apologetics over Church tradition and ideology, and thus restrict Newtonianism within the confines of a fixed paradigm. The Lockean and enlightened reading of Newton had to give way to a kind of edifying, vulgarized pseudo-science. The fecund hints of the *Scienza morale* were allowed to fall, opposed and beaten, as the case of De Soria clearly illustrates. The origins of many of the limits that enlightened Italian culture revealed in the latter eighteenth century, and the very contradictions of its brief age of reform, lay in this defeat.

Notes

One: The First Debates on Newtonian Science

1: THE DAWN OF THE EIGHTEENTH CENTURY

1. On the so-called Galilean school, see *La scuola galileiana*, 1979, in particular C. Vasoli, "Sulle fratture del galileismo nel mondo della Controriforma," pp. 203–213. See also Baldini, 1980; Altieri Biagi and Basile, 1980, with a rich bibliography on this subject.
2. See Galluzzi, "Vecchie e nuove prospettive torricelliane," in *La scuola galileiana*, 1979, p. 23.
3. See Torrini, 1977, pp. 30ff.
4. See Pintard, 1943. On the presence of Libertine circles at Rome, see also Spini, 1950; Costa, 1964, pp. 205–295. Regarding Dal Pozzo, see Lumbroso, 1875, pp. 129–238.
5. See Torrini, 1979b, pp. 16–17. For how atomism fared in Tuscany and the reception accorded Alessandro Marchetti's celebrated translation of the *De rerum natura*, see Saccenti, 1966.
6. See Maugain, 1909, pp. 123–143.
7. On Magalotti's Libertinism and the debates over atheism in late-seventeenth-century Italy, see Spini, 1950, pp. 306–317, 331–343.
8. See Garin, 1970, pp. 110–113. On the great Italian academies of the seventeenth century, see Galluzzi and Torrini, 1981.
9. On the knowledge of Spinozan works and other basic texts of the crisis of the European mind in Naples, see Badaloni, 1961, and particularly Ricuperati, 1970a, pp. 10–30, who explains the importance of Spinoza's *Tractatus* in the biblical studies of Aulisio, Giannone's teacher.
10. On the trial of the atheists see Osbat, 1974; Galasso, 1972, pp. 55–86; Nicolini, 1932, pp. 80ff; De Maio, 1971, pp. 78–79.
11. See Comparato, 1970, p. 199.
12. On the responses of the *novatores*, see D'Andrea, "Apologia in difesa degli atomisti," in Quondam, 1970, pp. 887–916; Comparato, 1970, pp. 231ff; Torrini, 1979a, pp. 143–171.
13. See Osbat, 1974, pp. 113ff.
14. See Comparato, 1970, pp. 143ff.
15. *Ibid*, p. 148.
16. Osbat, 1974, p. 24. Of particular interest are the documents from the trial published by the author in an appendix.
17. See Comparato, 1970, p. 148.
18. Letter cited in Amabile, 1892, pp. 53–54.
19. See Galluzzi, 1974; Maugain, 1909, pp. 33–67.
20. On Fardella's trial, see the documents in De Stefano, 1941, pp. 135–146.
21. Letter cited in Torrini, 1979b, pp. 28–29. The Jesuit Tommaso Fantoni wrote to Vincenzo Viviani from Naples on 19 February 1693: "The news from here is that the atomists were almost all discovered to be atheists. Two recanted and twelve are in prison. . . . I find myself in a country where one does no other experiment than to change skin, hoping that the new skin withstands

279

the sword thrusts of duels" (Florence, Biblioteca nazionale, *Manoscritti galileiani*, 257, cc. 122*v*–123*r*).
22. See Favaro, 1887, p. 155. On increased pressure from the Inquisition at the end of the seventeenth century, see Garin, 1970, pp. 106–107.

2: THE *OPTICKS*, THE *PRINCIPIA MATHEMATICA*, AND ROMAN SCIENTISTS

1. This was the case of the Jesuits of the celebrated Collegio Romano. On the high scientific level of their research in the latter half of the seventeenth century, possible because of their conspicuous means and because of the European network of institutions and scholars, and particularly on the ideological meaning that this research would assume in the Jesuits' cultural activities, see Costantini, 1969.
2. On the *Giornale de' Letterati* of Rome, see Ricuperati, "Giornali e società nell'Italia dell'*Ancien Régime* (1668–1789)," in Castronovo and Tranfaglia, 1976, pp. 79–89, and above all the anticipation of wider research underway regarding Roman culture at the end of the century in Gardair, 1979.
3. On the figure of Ciampini, see Datodi, 1974, pp. 207–220; Datodi, 1976, pp. 9–15; Grassi Fiorentino, 1972. There is useful information (despite a hagiographical tone) on Ciampini in Montalto, 1962, pp. 660ff. On Queen Christina of Sweden and the Roman court that surrounded her, see Gribble, 1913; Neumann, 1935.
4. See Grassi Fiorentino, 1972, p. 139. Ciampini guided Mabillon during his Roman stay and remained in contact with him for many years to come.
5. On the group of Roman scientists, the so-called *virtuosi* [virtuous], who surrounded the Campani brothers then at the vanguard of the construction of optical instruments, see Rotta, 1968, pp. 3–5. On Giuseppe Campani, see Daumas, 1972. There is no specific monograph on the Accademia Fisico-matematica, but see Maylender, 1926–1930, vol. 2, pp. 11–17. On the academy's scientific level, see Middleton, 1975, pp. 138–154.
6. See "Vita di Giovanni Giustino Ciampini," in Crescimbeni, 1710, vol. 2, pp. 217–218.
7. Aside from the discussions of atomism and the motion of comets, one should recall that Borelli's *De motu animalium*, with the materialist mechanism implicit in its *being-machine*, has justly been held out as the direct antecedent of eighteenth-century materialism; see Berthé de Besaucèle, 1920, pp. 32ff; Biaggi and Basile, 1980, pp. 378–379.
8. See Rotta, 1968.
9. The veto cast by the Jesuit Eschinardi against the publication of the academy's acts is one example of the internal conflicts among the various members. See Grassi Fiorentino, 1972, p. 139. On Porzio's abandonment of the academy, see Badaloni, 1961, p. 102.
10. On the anti-Galilean activities of Vanni and especially Eschinardi, see Torrini, "Antonio Monforte: Uno scienziato napoletano tra l'Accademia degli Investiganti e quella Palatina di Medinacoeli," in Zambelli, 1973b; Torrini, 1979b.
11. On the problem of atomism during the seventeenth and early eighteenth centuries in Europe and Epicurus's rehabilitation in the works of numerous contemporary scholars, see Spink, 1960, and Gregory, 1967. For a broad picture of Italian atomist culture in the seventeenth century, see Garin, 1970, in particular the first essay by Baldini; Rotta, 1971, in an appendix, publishes important documents on Montanari's atomism.
12. Michelangelo Ricci and Gaspare Berti repeated the experiments shortly after

Torricelli performed his barometric experiment, as did the Jesuits of the Collegio Romano in 1645. The Jesuits saw a further and dangerous attack on Aristotelian physics in Torricelli's experiment, and therefore sided in favor of the plenum, if with some modifications. See De Waard, 1936; Torrini, 1977, pp. 14–25. The experiments repeated in the Accademia dei Concili resumed an old debate, updating it in light of the most recent research; see Middleton, 1975, pp. 142–148, where he examines the academy's unpublished acts conserved among the papers of Girolamo Toschi, and Eschinardi, 1680.

13. See Rhodes, 1964.

14. On the particular apologetic significance that experimentalism and Boyle's corpuscularism acquired in light of Cartesian theories and mechanism, theories accused of dangerous overtures to the Libertines with their "antifinalism," see Pacchi, 1973, pp. 223–254; Dijksterhuis, 1986.

15. On the implicit metaphysical content of the Investiganti's theories, see Badaloni, 1961.

16. Celestino Galiani to Guido Grandi, Rome, 20 July 1714, B.U.P., Carteggio Grandi, ms. 92, c. 371r. Galiani continues: "Not content to have proscribed almost all of the best books that dealt [with theology and philosophy], most recently they have made a decree that warns that there will be no permission to read the prohibited books given to laymen if they do not have a [profession of] faith de vita et moribus from their bishops, and the religious will have to have the same profession from their superiors. In addition, permission will not be granted except to those who have duties; and only for those books that pertain to their actual duty; in your case, for example, even though you are a learned theologian and have taught, in the future no permission will be given but to the pure philosophers, to the exclusion even of history and literature and any other material whatsoever. See for yourself what narrow confines these are. It is best to be tolerant and let them go as long as God wills."

17. Valesio, "Diario di Roma nell'anno MDCIII," cited in Costa, 1968, p. 427.

18. Ricuperati, "Introduzione" to Dal Muratori al Cesarotti, 1978, p. xvi. See also Quondam, 1968.

19. We are referring to Muratori's project, Primi segni della Repubblica letteraria d'Italia, made public in 1703. See Falco and Forti, 1964, vol. 1, pp. 166–221. Bianchini refused to participate, in part for personal motives (he believed that he had not been advised in time by the author), in part because he did not agree with the prejudicially national dimensions of Muratori's plan. See Bianchini's letter to Muratori, 7 February 1705, in Raccolta di prose, 1830, vol. 2, p. 38. Muratori's project will be more amply examined in chapter 4.

20. We will return to the renewal of Roman culture during the early eighteenth century in chapter 5. Regarding Arcadia's crucial role in the reorganization of Italian intellectual life, see Quondam, "L'Arcadia e la Repubblica delle lettere," in Immagini del Settecento, 1980, pp. 198–211. See also Quondam, 1973.

21. We believe that the work of scientists such as Domenico Quartieroni and Vitale Giordani cannot be compared to the work carried out by Bianchini and Galiani in favor of modern science. Quartieroni and Giordani were exponents of a retrograde culture. Giordani in particular, besides denying any scientific validity in Cartesian analytic geometry, mocked the new infinitesimal analysis. On Giordani, see the biography in Crescimbeni, 1710, vol. 3, pp. 147ff; Torrini, 1979b, pp. 105–122. On Quartieroni, see Praja, 1840; Renazzi, 1805, vols. 3–4, p. 100. Giovanni Maria Lancisi, a friend of Bianchini and Galiani and at the center of the European debate on epidemiology, held a different position and authority. On Lancisi, see chapter 4.

22. See Ristretto della vita di Celestino Galiani, S.N.S.P., XXIX.C.7, c. 23v.

23. Ricuperati, 1968a, p. 67.
24. See Costa, 1968, pp. 371-452.
25. See *ibid.*, p. 414. Significant for documenting the active English presence in Rome (even if not strictly tied to the Jacobite court) was the case of the Pavian patrician Francesco Belisomi, charged with heresy and arrested in June 1701 together with some of his English guests. On the entire affair, see *ibid.*, p. 413. The presence of the Jacobite court in Rome seems also to have favored the birth of a Masonic lodge in the 1720s. See Francovich, 1975, pp. 39-41. See also Lewis, 1961, pp. 21-38.
26. On H. Newton, see *D.N.B.*, vol. 40, p. 370; Foster, 1968, vol. 3, p. 1065. On his Tuscan stay, see Rucellai, 1862, pp. 132-136. Crucial for evaluating the diplomat's work in Italy are the numerous reports preserved in London, Public Record Office, S.P., *General Correspondence*, 98 (22).
27. See Cochrane, 1961, pp. 48ff; Costa, 1959, pp. 12ff.
28. H. Newton, 1710, pp. 121-122. For an early evaluation of the dispute involving Muratori, Salvini, Manfredi, and other celebrated Italian scholars, see *Lettere di diversi autori*, 1707.
29. H. Newton, 1710, pp. 9-11. Cochrane (1961, pp. 109ff) focuses on the bond that local Tuscan scholars soon established between Galileo's and Newton's ideas.
30. See the eight letters of H. Newton preserved in Pisa, B.U.P., *Carteggio Grandi*, ms. 94, cc. 390rff. For a historical chronology of these studies that appeared in the "Philosophical Transactions," see Averani, "Esperienze intorno alla natura e velocità del suono," 1744-1761, vol. 2, pp. 191ff.
31. See the letters of H. Newton and G. Grandi cited in the preceding note. Isaac Newton had already written personally to Guido Grandi in 1704 in order to thank him for sending some of his books, including his *Geometrica demonstratio theorematum Hugeniarum circa logisticam seu logarithmicam lineam* (1701), and informing him that he would return the favor by sending the *Opticks*. See the letter published by Paoli, 1899, pp. xciii-xciv.
32. See Carini, 1891, p. 5.
33. In January 1706 the diplomat wrote to his principal Roman correspondent, Piergerolamo Bargellini, a fellow monk and friend of Celestino Galiani: "Next Saturday I will write to England so that as soon as possible they will get and send to you in Rome the *Principia philosophiae mathematica*," H. Newton, 1710, p. 16. Henry Newton maintained close contacts with the entire Roman community, personally writing to Giusto Fontanini and Domenico Passionei, as well as Bargellini.
34. I. Newton, 1706.
35. Turnbull, 1967, vol. 4, pp. 506-508.
36. As we have already seen (see n. 31), Guido Grandi, in Pisa, soon had at his disposition the original English edition of the *Opticks*, sent to him directly by the author. Rotta, 1971, pp. 94-95, collected and discussed the testimonials regarding the early knowledge of the "New Theory about Light and Colors" (which appeared in 1671 in the *Philosophical Transactions*) that some Italian scholars possessed, in particular the celebrated astronomer Geminiano Montanari. In addition, it is possible that in 1708, at the Paduan university circle, Giovanni Poleni repeated some of the *Opticks*'s experiments, preparing a brief, popularized essay that remained unpublished (Cossali, 1813, p. 30). This hypothesis is not very likely, however, for the debate on Newtonian optics gained ground in the Veneto only during the 1720s and 1730s.
37. Galiani himself confirms this, even if with some imprecision about chronology, in a letter to Guido Grandi in which he referred to the *Optice*, writing that he had read this book "five or six years ago now, and Monsignor Bianchini

and I did some of those experiments, which we found were true" (Rome, 21 April 1714; B.U.P., *Carteggio Grandi*, ms. 92, c. 363r).
38. On the Accademia degli Antiquari Alessandrini, see Fabroni, 1780, vol. 6, p. 319.
39. Galiani to Guido Grandi, Rome, 2 March 1715: B.U.P., *Carteggio Grandi* ms. 92, cc. 377v–378r.
40. A good analysis of the *Optice* and its importance within Newton's comprehensive works is found in Pala, 1969, pp. 182–204, and in Mamiani, 1976.
41. See C. Galiani, *Animadversiones nonnullae circa opticem Isaaci Neutoni*, S.N.S.P., XXX.D5, cc. 13r–17r.
42. Pala, 1969, p. 186; Ronchi, 1939.
43. C. Galiani, *Animadversiones*, c. 15r. The transcription corresponds to the *Definitio* of the *Optice*, pp. 102–103.
44. See C. Galiani, *Differenze tra le scoperte di Newton e l'ipotesi cartesiana*, S.N.S.P., XXX.D.2, c. 395rv.
45. *Ibid.*, c. 395r.
46. See Descartes, 1897–1910, vol. 8, pp. 118ff.
47. Garin, 1966, vol. 2, p. 855.
48. C. Galiani, *Differenze tra le scoperte di Newton e l'ipotesi cartesiana*, c. 396r.
49. On the affair of Algarotti, see chapter 4.
50. Koyré, 1965, p. 33.
51. On Christian Pfaulz, see Comparato, 1970, p. 132.
52. See Ricuperati, 1970a, chapter 5.
53. See Mastellone, 1965, pp. 99ff.
54. The reviews in the *Acta* were particularly coveted by Italian scholars, who saw them as a useful vehicle for becoming known in the European "literary republic." The Florentine Magliabechi and the Neapolitan Giannone distinguished themselves as intermediaries between the journal and Italian scholars.
55. One easily comes to this conclusion from hypotheses five through nine regarding the *systema mundi*. In the *Principia*, in fact, Newton leaves the demonstration of the reality of Copernicus's system to the scientific evidence, explicitly avoiding any expression of his Copernican beliefs.
56. *Acta eruditorum*, 1688, p. 310. Pfaultz repeated entire passages of the *Principia* in this article. Newton, too, strangely disregarded Kepler's claims to the discovery of the laws of the elliptical motion of the planets; see Koyré, 1965. Of Newton's works, the *Acta* reviewed the *Optice* (1706, pp. 59ff), with brief notes that do not, however, fully grasp the importance of the work; the *Arithmetica universalis* (1708, pp. 519ff); the *Principia*, 1713 edition (1714, pp. 131ff), a review that was perhaps the work of Leibniz himself, and that was quite critical of gravitational theory; the *Notanda circa theoriam colorum Newtonianam* (1717, p. 232); and the *Leibnizi, Clarkii, Newtoni et aliorum diversae schedae de philosophia, religione naturali, historia, mathesi* (1721, pp. 88ff). The journal's attitude towards Newtonianism, and in particular gravitational theory, became increasingly more open and friendly from the 1730s, once the first phase of open aversion due to Leibniz's influence was overcome.
57. See Comparato, 1970, pp. 132ff.
58. See Ariani, "Intorno all'utilità della geometria: Lezione prima," in Donzelli, 1970, p. 176. The myth that Ariani was deeply versed in Newton was accepted uncritically by many scholars and had its origin in the blatantly hagiographical work of his son (Ariani, 1778). There are no longer doubts that there was early knowledge of the *Principia*'s theories in northern Italy, even if in very restricted circles. Scientists such as Tommaso Ceva and Stefano Degli Angeli already knew some of its features by the end of the seventeenth century; see Casini, 1978, pp. 85–100. Almost no studies of any merit exist

on early knowledge of the *Principia* in Italy; see, however, Arrighi, 1973, pp. 174–179, who attributes the first attempt in Italy to translate the *Principia* to Guido Grandi's friend, the Luccan scientist Tommaso Narducci.

59. On Leibniz's journey through Italy, see Daville, 1909, and especially Baruzi, 1907, pp. 452ff.

60. See Preti, 1953; Hazard, 1963.

61. See the "Illustratio tentaminis de motuum coelestium causis" in Leibniz, 1860, vol. 6, pp. 255ff. In a letter to Huygens (*ibid.*, p. 189), Leibniz affirms that he, too, saw Newton's work for the first time at Rome: "Le livre de M. Newton, que j'ai vû à Rome pour la première fois."

62. See Koyré, 1965. The second, unedited version of the *Tentamen* is found in Leibniz, 1860, pp. 161ff, with interesting annotations by the editor regarding Leibniz's defense of Copernicanism in Rome, pp. 146–147.

63. See Rotta, 1968, p. 187.

64. Goldbeck, 1897, remains fundamental for celestial mechanics and Borelli's Copernicanism. See also Koyré, 1973; Badaloni, 1961, pp. 81–101; Baldini, "Gli studi su Giovanni Alfonso Borelli," in *La scuola galileiana*, 1979, pp. 112–135.

65. For a broad analysis of Leibniz's *Tentamen* and the harsh arguments against it advanced by David Gregory, Isaac Newton, and Roger Cotes, see Koyré, 1965.

66. Leibniz to Bianchini, Hanover, 18 March 1690, in Feder, 1805, pp. 296–297. The political and cultural meaning of the letter's content is evident if we recall the efforts of the Tuscan Galileans, in particular Vincenzo Viviani, to obtain Galileo's complete rehabilitation. The later letters contain interesting information regarding the relations between Leibniz and the Italian Galileans. In September 1690, the German philosopher wrote to Bianchini from Hanover, updating him on his discussions with Huygens about Newtonian and Cartesian gravitational theory; see *ibid.*, pp. 303–305.

67. On this important achievement, commented on favorably not only by Italians but also by foreigners, see Poja, 1947.

68. It seemed that the complex question of the reform of the Gregorian calendar would be able to move towards a solution under the pontificate of Clement XI. Bianchini's *Solutio problematis paschalis* (1703), which appeared anonymously in Rome, was praised by the *Acta eruditorum* (1705: 305–310) and Jean Le Clerc's *Bibliothèque choisie* (17 [1713]: 195–196). Actually scholars throughout Europe were involved in a widespread debate on this thorny issue, in which delicate scientific, political, and cultural problems intersected. In Italy the debate was particularly heated. In 1703, under the pseudonym "Uranophilus, " Domenico Quartieroni launched a poisonous attack against Bianchini (*Responsiones ad nonnullas assertiones pro reformatione calendarii gregoriani*), to which Manfredi replied in 1704 with his *Responsio ad litteras ab Uranophilo ad amicum datas Vindobonae*. Privately, even Celestino Galiani contributed to the Roman debate on the matter; see the *Dimostrazione dell'errore della pasqua dell'anno 1700* and the *Chronologiae elementa*, S.N.S.P., XXX.D.2, respectively, cc. 85rff and cc. 175rff.

69. On the close relationship between Leibniz, Bianchini, and Noris, see Celani, 1888, pp. 155ff, and the letters between Bianchini and Leibniz published by Feder, 1805, pp. 307ff, where the ideological and cultural import of the calendar reform is evident. On 13 October 1703, Leibniz alerted Bianchini to the need for Italian scientists to obtain (even if with certain limits) the *libertas philosophandi* that was indispensable for bringing Italian astronomers back to the European forefront, allowing them to resolve the technical problems imposed by the calendar reform. Without further delay, the new pope was to have proclaimed the "*indubitatam veritatem*" of the Copernican system (Celani,

1888, p. 182). Harsh reactions to the close collaboration between Catholic and Protestant scholars quickly arose. Giusto Fontanini, a fairly influential figure in cultural and Roman curial circles, wrote to Domenico Quartieroni in 1703, referring to the dangerous collaboration between the Catholics and Leibniz: "Leibniz is one of the most cunning and malicious Lutherans one can find. He published the *Codex diplomaticus iuris gentium* in Hanover in 1693 to attack the popes and let the emperors know that all the Church has and does is usurpation. . . . The same Leibniz published in Hanover a part of the most scandalous *Diario di Burcardo sopra Alessandro VI* three years ago, and he promised to publish the rest, having gotten everything from the infamous copyists of Rome during his stay there to spy on our affairs. . . . If one has to overturn and change the Gregorian calendar like that, a great confusion regarding the past two hundred years would be born" (B.V.R., ms. U.25, c. 128rv).
70. See the Flamsteed's letters to Bianchini regarding astronomical observations, B.C.V., *Fondo Bianchini*, ms. CCCCXXVIII (fasc. 17, 18, 19).
71. See Munby, 1952, pp. 28–39; Macomber, 1950. Munby speaks of more than 300 copies; Macomber of only 250.
72. As we know, Valletta possessed a copy of the first edition of the *Principia*. Francesco Bianchini warmly recommended Galiani to the Neapolitan intellectuals; Bianchini wrote to Matteo Egizio on 21 February 1708 that in Galiani he would "find a compendium of the most choice doctrines that the ancient and modern studies collect" (B.N.N., ms. XIII.C.90, c. 33r).
73. One copy, now lost, of the *Philosophiae naturalis principia mathematica* (1687) was located in Rome in the Libraria segreta del Collegio Romano (Rome: Biblioteca Nazionale, Ant. Catal. 23, [52. f. 13]). Presumably one copy of the *Principia* was also in the possession of Galiani's longtime friend Monsignor Vincenzo Santini, according to a comment in a letter (Rome, 22 January 1707, B.U.P., *Carteggio Grandi* ms. 96, c. 5r). According to my findings, there are numerous copies of the first edition of the *Principia* in Italian libraries: the University of Pisa (E.B.7.17), the Malatestiana in Cesena (103.89), the Oratoriana dei Girolamini in Naples (A.17.4.11), the Nazionale in Naples (XXXIV.E.63), the Palatina in Parma (M.5.12707), the Estense in Modena (XXIX.C.5), the Nazionale in Florence (I.F.5.126), the Comunale in Milan (O.Vet.45), and the Marciana in Venice (180.D.4).
74. See I. Newton, 1726, 3d ed., p. 386.
75. Galiani focused particularly on propositions VI, X, and XI of the *Principia*'s first book. His discussion is striking for the simplicity of his explanations, his very precise diagrams, and the valuable premises of the mathematical demonstrations that simplify his exposition and make clear his didactic intentions. See his *Osservazioni sopra il libro del Newton, intitolato "Principia Mathematica,"* S.N.S.P., XXX.D.2, cc. 113v–114r.
76. See I. Newton, 1726, p. 43.
77. See C. Galiani, *Osservazioni*, cc. 95r–100v. See above, n. 75.
78. On these two basic concepts of dynamics, see Jammer, 1957; Jammer, 1961. Insisting on the aspects of Newtonian theory that we might define as positivistic, Galiani quickly dispensed with the difficult problem of the metaphysical underpinnings of concepts such as absolute space and absolute time. [See the original Italian edition of this book for a more in-depth treatment of this topic— Trans.]
79. Pala, 1969, pp. 137ff.
80. C. Galiani, *Osservazioni*, cc. 111v–112r. See above, n. 75.
81. See *ibid.*, cc. 112v–113r. "Our difficulties with the fourth proposition of Newton's first book were in part resolved most learnedly by Mr. Burnet on the last

day of August 1709," wrote Galiani, reconsidering in a new light the arguments that Newton placed in the fourth proposition, whether geometric or, more correctly, philosophical.
82. See *ibid.*, c. 112*v*.
83. *Ibid.*, c. 118*r*.
84. On Gregory, see Hiscock, 1937. His manual of astronomy contributed significantly to the diffusion of Newtonian cosmology in Europe. From the 1710s on, many copies of the book circulated in Italy. Eustachio Manfredi wrote Guido Grandi (Bologna, 31 March 1705; B.U.P., *Carteggio Grandi*, ms. 93, c. 194*r*), asking him to obtain a copy of Gregory's *Astronomia*. Later Manfredi ordered two copies, one for himself and one for "Marsigli's bookstore" (Manfredi to Grandi, Bologna, 22 December 1705, *ibid.*, c. 195*r*).
85. See Gregory, 1702, in the nonpaginated "Praefatio."
86. Gregory maintained that the ancients knew that gravity works as a function of distance and the size of bodies; see his "Praefatio." On the longevity of the Hermetical tradition within the English scientific community, see Yates, 1972. Any hypothesis that brings modern science back to the realm of the development of Hermetism remains nonetheless quite debatable; see Rossi, 1977, pp. 149–181.
87. I. Newton, 1726, pp. 396ff.
88. For Galiani's complete analysis of Newtonian gravitational theory, see his *Osservazioni*, cc. 105*r*–118*v* (see above, n. 75). The exposition is really quite flat and uncritical, even though especially detailed and accompanied by good drawings.

3: FRANCESCO BIANCHINI'S TRIP TO ENGLAND AND CARDINAL GUALTIERI'S ROMAN ACADEMY

1. On Bianchini, see Rotta, 1968, p. 191.
2. The thesis that Bianchini was the pope's political advisor is hinted at by Celani, 1888, who makes a clear reference to some ciphered letters exchanged between the astronomer and secretary of state Cardinal Fabrizio Paolucci regarding the negotiations between the Holy See and Louis XIV. An analysis of Bianchini's *Diarium itineris gallici* (B.C.V., ms. CCCLXXXVI), as well as of his *Lettere di ragguaglio de' viaggi in Francia* (B.C.V., ms. CCXCII), would greatly illuminate the manifold activities of this Catholic intellectual. One aspect begging for evaluation is his role as an authoritative advisor to the congregation of the Index, especially in light of his opinions on the works of men such as Giannone, Mabillon, and Bayle (see B.C.V., ms. CCCXXX, fasc. 5).
3. Beginning in 1706, Bianchini was one of the eight foreign associates of the Académie des Sciences and had the means of meeting the most celebrated *confrères* at Paris, documenting his work with their scientific research.
4. Bianchini wrote to Cardinal Paolucci detailing the favors he received from English scholars (London, 31 January 1713; B.C.V., ms. CCCLXXXIV, cc. 38*r*–39*v*).
5. Bianchini to Cardinal de Rohan, n.d. [January 1713]; B.C.V., ms. CCCLXXXIV, c. 37*r*.
6. On John Keill, an important figure in Newton's circle, see *D.N.B.*, vol. 30, pp. 310–311. The author of several celebrated compendia on Newtonian science, Keill welcomed Bianchini especially cordially as soon as he arrived in England, gave him letters of presentation for his colleagues in Oxford, and had long discussions with him (see Bianchini's warm letter of thanks to Keill, London, 8 February 1713; B.V.R., ms. U. 21, c. 241*rv*).
7. An exact reconstruction of this episode can be found in the entry for 21 January

in Bianchini's diary *Iter in Britanniam* (autograph B.C.V., ms. CCCLXXIV; copy B.V.R., ms. T.46.B). Bianchini noted Newton's intention to entrust him with some copies of Flamsteed's recent book so that he might bring them to Italy and give them to scientists such as Manfredi, Grandi, Galiani, and Quartieroni, whom Newton said he knew and appreciated.

8. The induction ceremony for the two Italians occurred 9 February.

9. See the detailed description of the experience, which Bianchini will repeat later to Galiani on his return to Rome, in the *Iter in Britanniam*, 2 February.

10. *Ibid.*, 9 February.

11. *Ibid.*, 30 January.

12. The visit to the scientific laboratories of the university (then believed to be a den of Jacobites) and the celebrated Bodleian Library did a great service to the cause of cultural relations between England and Italy, in addition to allowing Bianchini to consult valuable codices. The vice-chancellor of Oxford University, Bernard Gardiner, triumphantly welcomed Bianchini, giving a dinner in his honor that was attended by the greatest teachers of the university, including John Keill (Bianchini to Cardinal Paolucci, London, 31 January 1713; B.C.V., ms. CCCLXXIV, c. 39r). Bianchini formed a close relationship with John Hudson, custodian of the Bodleian, who asked the Italian scholar to intervene and renew the contacts between the Bodleian Library and the Vatican Library, which had terminated with the nomination of Lorenzo Zaccagni as first custodian in 1698. See the draft of Bianchini's letters to Gardiner (London, 8 February 1713) and Hudson (Rome, 15 May 1715), respectively in B.V.R., ms. U.12, c. 246r and c. 243rv.

13. See *Iter in Britanniam*, 9 February.

14. Bianchini's letter to Paolucci, 31 January 1713.

15. Bianchini met Newton three times and had long discussions with him. Two extraordinary notes that they exchanged several days after their first meeting on 2 February at the Royal Society survive, testimony to their reciprocal esteem (*Iter in Britanniam*, 7 February). Newton's undated note (actually 7 February 1713) was full of compliments for his Catholic guest (B.V.R., ms. U. 21, cc. 297rv–298rv). Newton gave Bianchini a small book published by William Jones consisting of a miscellany of old writings on Newtonian infinitesimal analysis, as well as a copy of the *Optice* that still survives today in the Vatican Library (*Racc. Gen. Scienze* IV.29). Bianchini sent a response to Newton the same day (B.V.R., ms. U.21, c. 276r). A somewhat superficial examination of Italian scholars' frequent travels to England in the early 1700s can be found in Graf, 1911, pp. 52ff. Of great interest is the report of the meeting between Newton and the future cardinal Angelo Maria Querini during the latter's trip to England in 1710 (see *ibid.*, pp. 55ff).

16. On the harsh dispute between Newton and Leibniz on infinitesimal calculus, see Cantelli, 1958. Bianchini regularly delivered books to their recipients, inclining them towards Newton's primacy in the invention of infinitesimal calculus; see Guido Grandi's letter to Bianchini, Pisa, 14 August 1713 (B.V.R., ms. U.16, cc. 697r–699v). While in England Bianchini bought many scientific books, including all the works that had so far appeared on Newtonian theories: Gregory's *Astronomiae physicae et geometricae elemente*, a collection of Halley's works where Newton's theory on tides was expounded (*The True Theory of the Tides, Extracted from That Admired Treatise of Mr. Isaac Newton*), several valuable works on De Moivre's infinitesimal analysis, and the renowed *New Theory about Light and Colors*. Halley's work can today be seen in Cohen and Schofield, 1958, pp. 445–455.

17. See Galiani's letter to Guido Grandi, Rome, 22 April 1714 (B.U.P., *Carteggio*

Grandi, ms. 92, c. 363r). Referring to the *Epistola* and to its eventual publication in the *Giornale de' Letterati*, Galiani asked Bargellini to have Grandi comment on whether the *Epistola* should be published.

18. See Brunet, 1931a, pp. 1–78.

19. On this important figure of Neapolitan culture, see Cotugno, 1910; Suppa, 1971; Quondam, 1973, pp. 801–805.

20. On the theme of Newtonianism in Neapolitan culture and the specific role Celestino Galiani played, see chapter 5.

21. On the *Giornale de' Letterati*, see chapter 4.

22. See Brunet, 1931a, pp. 15ff.

23. *Giornale de' Letterati* 2 (1710): 477.

24. *Giornale de' Letterati* 5 (1711): 315.

25. *Ibid.*, p. 435. The dispute between Verzaglia and Hermann had assumed a personal character. On the Verzaglia, see Baldini, "L'attività scientifica nel primo Settecento," 1980, p. 498.

26. See "Soluzione generale del problema inverso intorno ai raggi osculatori" in *Giornale de' Letterati* 9 (1712): 204–210. Riccati aligned himself in favor of the Newtonian solution to the problem of central forces. See Riccati's "Risposta ad alcune opposizioni fatte dal sig. Giovanni Bernoulli alla soluzione del problema inverso delle forze centrali nel voto, in ragione reciproca de' quadrati delle distanze, pubb. dal sig. Jacopo Ermanno ed annotazioni relative del sig. Nic. Bernoulli," *Giornale de' Letterati* 21 (1714): 127–134. The periodical subsequently published other articles on the same subject.

27. While we still lack a comprehensive study on scientific culture in the Veneto— which must be undertaken through an examination of the *Giornale de' Letterati*— the footprint of Cartesian mechanicism is nevertheless evident in it. Also significant in that regard is the affirmation of the iatrophysical theories in the circles of Paduan and Venetian doctors and naturalists, theories brought to a notably refined level by scientists of Continent-wide importance such as Morgagni, Michelotti, Zendrini, and others. On science in the Veneto, see Baldini, 1980, pp. 504–507, which includes a lengthy bibliography on the various individuals cited above.

28. On the interpretation of Newtonianism in cultural circles in the Veneto, with particular reference to the works of Conti, Rizzetti, and Riccati, see chapter 4.

29. On Zendrini, see De Tipaldo, 1835, vol. 2, 1835, p. 152.

30. See Zendrini's commentary, "Tre problemi geometrici e con un sistema sopra la gravità proposti dal sig. Giovanni Ceva e sciolti dal sig. Bernardino Zendrini," *Giornale de' Letterati* 4 (1710): 317, with an interesting consideration of the existence of ether, unfolding a series of calculations on the movements of a pendulum in a vacuum. In his attempt to confirm the plenum, he cited an astonishing assertion made by the Newtonian William Burnet, during his Venetian sojourn in 1709, regarding an experiment contradicting Newtonian theory that was carried out at the Royal Society: "[Burnet] assured me that in that illustrious academy they are familiar with an experiment that absolutely in my opinion removes all doubt that gravity is made through a collision of the fluid matter [ether] that spins about the world" (p. 340). On Giovanni Ceva, see Baldini, 1980, pp. 316–319.

31. *Giornale de' Letterati* 9 (1712): 465. The work *De vorticibus coelestibus dialogus* appeared in the same year in Padua, published by G. B. Conzato.

32. See Brunet, 1931a, pp. 62–66.

33. As noted, the most important of the objections Newton formulated in the *Principia* regarded the contradictions between the motion of vortices and Kepler's laws; the problem caused by the contemporaneous existence in space of sev-

eral vortices liable to disrupt each other; the impossibility of reconciling the hypothesis that posited the constancy of the quantity of motion in the universe with the loss of motion that was the consequence of the vortices' attrition; and the complexity of cometary movement, inexplicable within the hypothesis of vortices.

34. See Galiani's letter to Grandi, Rome, 19 May 1714 (B.U.P., *Carteggio Grandi*, ms. 92, c. 365r): "I read Signor Poleni's book *De vorticibus* months ago, and truthfully, I found it quite superficial."

35. Galiani first restated the theses of Keill (1702), whose *Lectio I: De methodo philosophandi* and *Lectio II: De corporis soliditate et extensione* were both harsh diatribes against Descartes. The *Epistola* then reproduced some of the central paragraphs of Gregory's work (1702), specifically Propositio LXXX (p. 87) and Propositio LXXV (p. 92). Another source Galiani utilized was the second book of the *Principia*, regarding the mechanism of fluids, an aspect of Newtonian work already familiar to and appreciated by Italian scholars of hydrodynamics a few years after the arrival of the *Principia* (see Rotta, 1971, pp. 102–107).

36. See C. Galiani, *Epistola de gravitate et cartesianis vorticibus*, S.N.S.P., XXX.D.2, cc. 51v–52r. The critical edition of this important document for the history of Italian Newtonianism is C. Galiani, 1982. Subsequent citations are taken from this edition.

37. C. Galiani, 1982, c. 57r.

38. Giovambattista Pignatelli's letter to Celestino Galiani, Naples, 26 May 1716 (S.N.S.P., XXXI.A.5, c. 301r).

39. C. Galiani, 1982, cc. 58v–59r.

40. See *ibid.*, c. 61rv.

41. Galiani himself states so in the *Epistola*, and he repeated it in a letter to Grandi (Rome, 21 April 1714 (B.U.P., *Carteggio Grandi*, ms. 92, c. 363r). For more on Gravina's circle, see Quondam, 1968; however, Quondam makes no reference to the scientific interests of Gravina, who, as we have seen, was also among those in Rome who first evaluated the veracity of Newtonian optical theories in 1708.

42. Filippo Antonio Gualtieri, born at Fermo in 1660, was a unique figure. After serving as apostolic nuncio in France in 1700, he became a profound admirer of transalpine culture. A close friend of Mabillon, Malebranche, l'Hôpital, and, particularly, Louis de Rouvroy, the duke of Saint-Simon, Gualtieri had an excellent reputation among his contemporaries for great erudition; see Baschet, 1878; Caracciolo, 1968.

43. Bianchini's letter to Newton, Rome, 15 May 1714 (B.V.R., ms. U. 21, c. 266rv). On Clement XI's nephew Alessandro Albani (1692–1770) and his close ties with Hanover England, see Lewis, 1960, pp. 595–598. The writings Bianchini sent were published by Newton with his personal praises in the *Philosophical Transactions* (XXIX, 1714, pp. 88–90, "Observationes occultationis stellae τ in origine cornu Borei Tauri"). The same letter mentioned above provides significant evidence of the direct and privileged rapport established between Newton and Italian scientists tied to the Holy See. Bianchini made assurances that Newton's merits were widely recognized on the Italian side in the dispute over who had primary claim to having invented infinitesimal calculus.

44. Galiani's letter to Bottari, Rome, 5 May 1714 (B.C.R., ms. 1581, 32.E.2, c. 1r).

45. The atomist hypothesis was evaluated with particular care. Fragmentary testimony of these discussions can be recovered from Galiani's letter to Bottari; see *ibid.*, cc. 1v–2r).

46. Galiani's letter to Grandi, Rome, 22 April 1714 (B.U.P., *Carteggio Grandi*, ms. 92, c. 36r).

47. The works of Gualtieri's academy had repercussions reaching abroad as well. Leibniz became familiar with the new center of Roman research from a letter of Giuseppe Antonio Davanzati, future archbishop of Trani and regular visitor at the academy, attesting to the gathering of worthy men to "discuss with logical rigor the hypotheses of Réne Descartes, Pierre Gassendi, and Newton's Opus physico-mathematicum" (Davanzati's letter to Leibniz, Rome, 4 July 1714; Hanover, Niedersächsische Landesbiblioteck, Leibniz-Briefwechsel 197, cc. 2r–3r). Leibniz's response indicates the esteem in which the German scientist held the new academy, urging that the members also study Huygens and Mariotte (ibid., c. 3v). For an overall impression of the eighteenth-century Italian academies, see Accademie e cultura, 1979; Boehm and Raimondi, 1981. However, there is no reference to Gualtieri's academy even in the classic work of Maylender, 1926–1930.

48. See Galiani's letter to Grandi, Rome, 27 April 1714: B.U.P., Carteggio Grandi, ms. 92, cc. 363rff. Galiani kept Grandi constantly updated on the experiments taking place at the academy. Of noteworthy interest are the results of Hauksbee's experiments on electricity and, especially, on optical problems; he wrote Grandi: "It pleases me to tell you something else, which is that what Mariotte counters to Newton's observations is not at all true" (Galiani to Grandi, Rome, 9 February 1715; B.U.P., Carteggio Grandi, ms. 92, c. 374r).

49. Giacomo Grazini's letter to Galiani, Naples, 11 June 1715 (S.N.S.P., XXXI.A.3, c. 72r). On Grazini, see Ajello, 1976a, pp. 393–394.

50. Grazini's letter to Galiani, Naples, September 1715 (S.N.S.P., XXXI.A.3, c. 76r). Notwithstanding the difficulties that arose, almost a year later Giovambattista Pignatelli announced to Galiani (Naples, 26 May 1716, S.N.S.P., XXXI.A.5, c. 301v) that he would repeat the experiments of the Optice in his house with the intent of proving Cartesians wrong.

51. See Bianchini's letter to Grandi, n.d. (B.U.P., Carteggio Grandi, ms. 85, cc. 82v–83r) and his lengthy report to Eustachio Manfredi of a physics experiment performed in London (Rome, 9 February 1715; B.V.R., ms. U. 20, cc. 106v–107r). In response, Manfredi requested "the instructions specific to the said experiments and their outcomes . . ., since I am dying to propose this famous novelty to our academy of the Istituto di Scienze" (Bologna, 20 February 1715, B.V.R., ms. U.17, c. 1016r). On the Istituto in Bologna, see Cavazza, 1979, pp. 97–146; "Riforme dell'università e nuove accademie nella politica culturale dell'arcidiacono Marsili," in Boehm and Raimondi, 1981, pp. 245–282; Cavazza, 1981.

52. More copies were sent to Naples because Galiani hoped to obtain a greater response to his initiative in that city. Other scholars thought it should be published in the Giornale de' Letterati to combat the Neapolitan philosophers' "blind veneration for Descartes" (Rome, 22 April 1714: B.U.P., Carteggio Grandi, ms. 92, c. 363v). Grazini advised Galiani that there were many in Naples who found the Epistola particularly difficult (Naples, n.d.: S.N.S.P., XXXI.A.3, c. 78r); Giovambattista Pignatelli was of the same opinion. Commenting on the arrival of a copy of the Epistola, Antonio Leprotti wrote from Rimini anxiously awaiting news of the impression it made (Rimini, 29 March 1714; S.N.S.P., XXXI.A.3, c. 333v). It was in Rome, however, that the Epistola caused the greatest commotion; with some pride, Galiani wrote to Bottari that he was heartened by the number of requests for copies, but he noted that most were unable to "sink their teeth into" the heavily diagrammed work (Rome, 16 May 1714: B.C.R., ms. 1581, 32.E.2, c. 4r).

53. See Ricuperati, 1968a, pp. 76–77. Galiani's Epistola was also used by Giannone to understand Newtonian theories; see chapter 5.

54. See Galiani's letter to Guido Grandi, Rome, 7 July 1714 (B.U.P., *Carteggio Grandi*, ms. 92, cc. 367vff). This valuable document is quite worn and illegible in numerous passages (indicated here with spaces within square brackets). In reference to Newtonian gravitational attraction, Galiani wrote: "I have therefore conceived of [   ] showing the thing to be likely [   ]. See the second edition of Newton's *Principia*, for an English friend [William Burnet] wrote me that among the things added is a learned preface from Mr. Cotes, professor of mathematics and philosophy at Cambridge University, where he makes sense of Mr. Newton's method of philosophizing." Galiani asked Grandi for clues to the second edition of the *Principia*, for only in August 1715 did he have a few copies from his friend, the bookseller Thomas Johnson (see the accompanying letter in a chest of books from Johnson to Galiani, The Hague, 19 July 1715; S.N.S.P., XXXI.A.3, cc. 277rff). Galiani immediately afterward sold a copy to Giovambattista Pignatelli in Naples (see Galiani's letter to Pignatelli, Rome, 7 October 1715: S.N.S.P., XXXI.A.1, c. 1v). On 12 January 1715 Galiani informed his friend Vincenzo Santini of his plan to write a series of open letters on Newtonianism to Guido Grandi (S.N.S.P., XXXI.B.1, cc. 291rv).

55. On Grandi (1671–1742), see Carranza, 1955–1956, pp. 200–212; Tenca, 1960; Ferrari, 1906. For an early opinion of Grandi, Ortes, 1744, is still a valuable work.

56. Grandi to Galiani, Pisa, 30 July 1714 (S.N.S.P., XXXI.A.3, c. 131v). Grandi was not a strictly orthodox Cartesian; Ortes (1744, p. 161) wrote of him: "His predominating genius was for geometry, over which he generally believed (according to Proclus) that God Himself presided, and (according to Plato) he used to call it the divine occupation, and he had such a rich imagination so full of geometry that he recognized it in every object." One characteristic element of Grandi's myriad activities was his repudiation of philosophical systems.

57. Grandi personally participated in the struggle against the traditional front of the Aristotelians; see Carranza, 1955–1956. For an initial overall view of this set of problems, quite complex and certainly not resolved by a schematic opposition of ancients and moderns, Cartesians and Aristotelians, see Maugain, 1909, pp. 44–80; Garin, 1966, pp. 864–889.

58. Grandi's letter to Galiani, Pisa, 30 July 1714, (S.N.S.P., XXXI.A.3, c. 135r). Grandi confirmed his negative opinion of Newton's gravitational theory in another letter sent to the Jesuit Tommaso Ceva (see Gronda, 1980, pp. 325–328). Referring to a proposition of the *Principia* and the physico-mathematical abstractions it contains, Grandi wrote: "I take these attractions to be more ideal than real, and thinking that the earth's matter is equally dense everywhere is also arbitrary" (Grandi to Ceva, Pisa, 17 January 1725, Milan, Biblioteca Braidense, AF.XIII.13 [7], let. n. 7). On the subject of the dissemination in Tuscany of the charge of Aristotlelianism, Tommaso Buonaventuri's letter to Grandi from September 1715 is also significant (B.U.P., *Carteggio Grandi*, ms. 85, c. 65v).

59. Galiani to Grandi, Rome, 20 July 1714 (B.U.P., *Carteggio Grandi*, ms. 92, c. 370r).

60. Even Roger Cotes had doubts and perplexities about that problem, and he asked Newton directly for clarification. See Koyré, 1965.

61. Galiani to Grandi, Rome, 20 July 1714 (B.U.P., *Carteggio Grandi*, ms. 92, c. 369v).

62. See Casini, 1969, pp. 112–117.

63. See Hoskin, 1961, pp. 353–363; Dugas, 1958; Koyré, 1965; Casini, 1969, p. 292.

64. Confirmation of Ciccarelli's activity comes from a letter of Giovambattista Caracciolo to Guido Grandi, describing the printer as a nonpracticing lawyer who specialized in producing works "that quite rightly the sacrosanct court of the Inquisition would not allow to be printed.... And as you will have read, in these handsome dedicatory pages he signs himself with the name of Cellenio

Zacclori, an anagram for Lorenzo Ciccarelli" (Florence, 5 January 1725–1726, B.U.P., *Carteggio Grandi*, ms. 88, c. 71*v*). For the press's activities, see Ricuperati, 1965a, pp. 388–417. On the role of Ciccarelli and his press, see chapters 2 and 5.

65. Galiani's letter to Bottari, Rome, 25 August 1714 (B.C.R., ms. 1581, 32.E.2, c. 5*v*).

66. Rohault, 1713, vol. 2, chap. 28, p. 100. Galiani's letter to Grandi dated 7 July 1714 attested that the *Tractatus* was particularly studied in Roman circles (B.U.P., *Carteggio Grandi*, ms. 92, cc. 367r*ff*).

67. Galiani's letter to Vincenzo Santini, Rome, 12 January 1715 (S.N.S.P., XXXI.B.1, cc. 291r–292*v*). When he spoke of a "dissertation," Galiani was certainly not referring to the *Epistola*, which appeared in 1714; the reference is unclear.

68. See *Bibliothèque choisie* 26 (1713): 364–375, and the following volumes.

69. Turning to Guido Grandi regarding the problem of the relationship between matter and gravitation, Galiani proposed two hypotheses, namely: "Either that we have no idea of corporeal substance and for that reason we cannot determine whatever may or may not agree with it, or else that gravity—given that for a material substance we mean nothing other than a thing extended according to Descartes . . . or else according to other ideas that are current among the *filosofanti* [philosophizers], which would not shake me at all—consists of nothing other than a law of God of the same manner precisely as the union between mind and body" (Rome, 7 July 1714: B.U.P., *Carteggio Grandi*, ms. 92, c. 367*v*).

4: THE *PRINCIPIA* AND COPERNICANISM

1. See Pala, 1969, pp. 69–75; Hagen, 1910.

2. On the dispute between Riccioli, Borelli, and Degli Angeli, see Dreyer, 1953. On the underground battle that developed in Italy over Copernicanism at the end of the seventeenth century, see Torrini, 1973; Favaro, 1887, p. 101ff. Geminiano Montanari, an adamant Galilean and Copernican, wrote to Viviani in 1671, commenting bitterly on Riccioli's malicious publication of Galileo's recantation: "Oh, how many times have I detested the malign manner with which Father Riccioli treated Galileo, to the point that sometimes I felt an urge to defend him and to write. . . . I was the first to write against the so-called demonstration by Father Riccioli when he published his *Reformed Astronomy*; and my manuscript gave Father Angeli the impetus to print" (p. 127).

3. Koyré, 1965.

4. In the "Praefatio," Poleni wrote: "O benevolent reader, I wish to advise you that I consider the Copernican system completely false, and that I honor with due veneration the decree with which such a system is justly condemned. Rest assured" (Poleni, 1712, p. 1). However, in the text, discussing the problem of parallax of the fixed stars, he did not hide his true sympathies (see pp. 20–22).

5. On the attitude of the religious orders towards modern science, there are some particularly noteworthy studies, especially regarding the Jesuits: see Baldini, 1980, pp. 513–526. On the Theatines, see Masetti-Zannini, 1967, in particular the section on "Astronomia e moto della terra," pp. 34–37.

6. See De Maio, 1973.

7. Momigliano, 1960, p. 259. Much has been written on the problem of the condition of Italian intellectuals in the dark years of the Counter-Reformation and afterward; see De Maio, 1973, and Rotondó, 1973, pp. 1399–1449. See also *Intellettuali e potere*, 1981.

8. On Eustachio Manfredi (1674–1739), see the *Dictionary of Scientific Biography*, vol. 9, pp. 77–78; Cavazza, 1979, pp. 97ff.

9. See his reflections in Manfredi, 1749, "Prefazione dell'autore," pp. vi–vii. This posthumously published work became one of the manuals most used by Italian scholars during the eighteenth century. Alongside the Copernican hypothesis the manual presented other cosmological hypotheses with equal emphasis, without showing any particular preferences. Of particular interest are his chronological discussions contained in Manfredi, 1744, on biblical and Jewish history. Manfredi also compiled the celebrated *Ephemerides motuum coelestium*.

10. See Popper, 1968. One can easily see how Manfredi's position seemed similar to that theorized by Cardinal Roberto Bellarmino, who, revealing the destructive potential of modern science in the face of Counter-Reformation ideology, outlined in a famous letter to the Carmelite Paolo Antonio Foscarini the limits within which Catholic scientists had to operate. However, Bellarmino's suggestion to "limit one's self to speak from supposition and not through absolute truths" (Galilei, 1890–1909, vol. 21, p. 171) does not seem to me capable of completely clarifying the problem of Manfredi's attitude towards modern science. Actually, as Popper has emphasized, the instrumentalist choice has its own intellectual dignity that, at least in part, lies outside of social context and immediate political judgments.

11. Galiani's letter to Grandi, Rome, 20 July 1714, (B.U.P., *Carteggio Grandi*, ms. 92, c. 369r). Galiani refers to Paolo Francone's Neapolitan translation of Adrien Baillet's celebrated work, which appeared in 1713 with the title *Ristretto della vita di Renato Descartes*.

12. Galiani discussed such problems without reticence in his unpublished *Osservazioni al Discourse de la cause de la pesanteur di Cristiano Hugenio stampato a Leida 1690* (S.N.S.P., XXX.D.2, cc. 127r–130r), as well as, in part, in his notes on gravity as it is understood in the writings of Saurin and Villemot (*De gravitate*, ibid., cc. 298v–303v).

13. Galiani to Grandi, Rome, 20 July 1714 (B.U.P., *Carteggio Grandi*, ms. 92, c. 370r).

14. Galiani to Bottari, Rome, 16 May 1714 (B.C.R., ms. 1581, 32.E.21, cc. 3v–4r). Galiani must have discussed these problems in Rome with his circle of pupils at Sant'Eusebio, for in 1726 one of his most faithful disciples, Bernardo Andrea Lama, wrote him from Turin to ask for clarifications on this matter (Ricuperati, 1968a, p. 75).

15. See Leprotti's letter to Galiani, Rimini, 3 June 1714 (S.N.S.P., XXXI.A.3, cc. 336rv). On Leprotti, the future pontifical physician to Benedict XIV, a very worthy doctor tied to Celestino Galiani and the group of Bolognese scholars who surrounded Eustachio Manfredi and Zanotti, see Setti, 1806. Among Leprotti's papers kept in the Biblioteca Lancisiana of Rome (which have yet to be studied), there is an autograph transcription of the *Decretum S. Congr. contra il sistema della mobilità della terra e immobilità del sole* (*Fondo Leprotti*, ms. 283, cc. 45rff), confirming the doctor's interest in the Copernican issue.

16. See Nicolini, 1951, p. 215.

17. See Galiani's detailed analysis of Hauksbee's experiments in *Experimenta physico-mechanica compendiose excerpta ex libro D. F. Hauksbee Regiae Societatis Anglicae* (B.U.P., *Carteggio Grandi*, ms. 78). On the fundamental importance of Hauksbee's work for Newtonian scientific thought, see Guerlac, 1963.

18. See, for example, Grandi's letter to Galiani, Pisa, 20 May 1715: "We now come to the principal point. The Tuscan translation of those English experiments is now being amended and they are cleaning its language, and they are waiting for the copper plates of the author's figures from England" (S.N.S.P., XXXI.A.3, c. 138r).

19. On Buonaventuri's important activities as a publisher, see chapter 2. Averani's metaphysics of light are of noteworthy interest, for he was quite familiar with

Newtonian optical experiments and shared the corpuscular hypothesis of light. See Averani, 1744–1761, vol. 2, p. 45; Carranza, 1962, pp. 658–660.

20. Hauksbee, 1716, "Prefazione." Through Giacomo Grazini, a regular participant in Valletta's circle, Galiani had informed many of his friends throughout Italy, particularly the Neapolitans, of this planned translation (see Giustiniani, 1788, vol. 3, p. 227).

21. There is little information on this figure, to whom we shall return later. We know that the translation was his work from the *Giornale de' Letterati* 25 (1715): 479: "The translator of this work is Mr. Thomas Dereham, an English knight, one of the baronets of that kingdom, that is to say one of rank immediately below the 'My Lords.' His goods and his estates are in the province of Norfolk, but he has been in Florence for some time, at present in the service of the most serene grand duke, in whose court he has had the opportunity to learn our language perfectly."

Two: Galileo, Newton, and *Libertas Philosophandi*

1: THE GALILEAN HERITAGE

1. "Saggio sul Galileo," in Venturi, 1958, pp. 338–339. An introductory note precedes the collection of the scientist's writings.

2. During the eighteenth century the reevaluation of Galileo's works continued to grow outside Italy as well, thanks to increasing affirmations of his links to Newton. Hume and Voltaire were the greatest protagonists in improving Galileo's fortunes; see Hall, 1979.

3. Bury, 1955.

4. See Algarotti, 1737. Algarotti's work made Newtonianism a kind of genuine vindication of Galilean science in the face of its ecclesiastical persecutors. Addressing the ignorant "monks" in a contemptuous and irreverent tone, Algarotti wrote a dialogue in the Galilean mold in which once again Simplicius appeared, this time with the task of refuting the Cartesian scholastics instead of the Aristotelians.

5. See the *Elogio del cavalier Isacco Newton*, in Venturi, 1958, pp. 345–346, where Frisi wrote: "Galileo was long persecuted; Cavalieri, Cassini, and Grandi were not honored at all by their fatherland. Many other illustrious Italians lived in mediocrity and were generally not honored except in death. Newton was recognized and honored by his entire nation, from his early youth." See also Andres, 1776; Brenna, 1778; Nelli, 1793; Targioni Tozzetti, 1780.

6. Nelli, 1793, pp. 251–252.

7. Among the first to point to the importance of this theme was Torcellan, 1963.

8. On this important dispute, see Caverni, 1859, vol. 4, pp. 238ff (with due caution for this "disputant priest's" preconceived anti-Galileism); Galluzzi, 1979; Torrini, 1979b.

9. Galilei, 1890–1909, vol. 8, p. 205. All Galilean dynamics, generally defined as a "dynamics of the fall," are based on this postulate, which Torricelli later transformed into an axiom (Torricelli, 1644, p. 8).

10. See Torrini, 1979b, pp. 36–37.

11. For a complete technical analysis of the Jesuit's affirmations, not to mention his role in the entire affair, see ibid., pp. 41–77.

12. Ibid., p. 48.

13. As Torrini has clearly demonstrated, a Galilean party existed within the Society of Jesus itself, so that the dispute represented not only a violent attack on Galilean science but simultaneously a stern call to order to those Jesuits who

then began to defend Galileo, even if only timidly (as in the case of Giuseppe Ferroni).

14. Informing Antonio Magliabechi of his intention to attack Galileo's famous *Lettera a Madama Cristina di Lorena* publicly, Vanni wrote spitefully: "Regarding Mr. Galileo's letter, I have as much as I need and less than that little I judge necessary to serve me, at least this early, for not creating the impression that I am an implacable enemy of that great man, while I think I am an enemy only of the falsehoods he long taught" (Torrini, 1979b, p. 80).

2: EPISTEMOLOGICAL MODELS IN COMPARISON

1. The overall new meaning of the dispute at the turn of the eighteenth century has already been perceived by Badaloni, 1958.
2. On Bartolomeo Intieri, see Ajello, 1976a, pp. 397–400; see also chapter 6. Venturi (1969, p. 555) has correctly written that Intieri felt he was "the heir and representative of the Tuscan tradition of Galileo and Torricelli" at Naples.
3. Intieri's letter to Magliabechi, Naples, 11 February 1704, in Quondam and Rak, 1978, vol. 2, p. 709. Intieri's letters in this recent edition were also published by Racioppi, 1871, pp. 335ff.
4. Intieri's letter to Magliabechi, Naples, 8 April 1704, in Quondam and Rak, 1978, vol. 2, p. 711.
5. Fisch, 1968; Torrini, 1981. On the Investiganti tradition, see also De Giovanni, 1958.
6. A basic work for any biography of Porzio is Mosca, 1764.
7. Porzio, *Del sorgimento de' licori*, in Porzio, 1736, vol. 2, pp. 323–370. Porzio's role in Neapolitan culture during the early eighteenth century has generally been overlooked in recent studies. But his *Lettere e discorsi accademici* (1711) certainly did not pass unremarked among Neapolitan intellectuals. Even the *Giornale de' Letterati* (8 [1711]: 472) commented favorably on their appearance, emphasizing their importance.
8. Lenoble (1976, pp. 129ff) is very useful for understanding the profound difference between Baconian qualitative physics, which remained quite alien to modern science based on mathematical mechanicism, and complete geometricization of reality.
9. See Torrini, 1977; Crispini, 1970.
10. See *De motu corporum nonnulla et de nonnullis fontibus naturalibus*, in Porzio, 1736, vol. 2, pp. 106–174.
11. Intieri's letter to Magliabechi, Naples, 25 November 1704, in Quondam and Rak, 1978, vol. 2, p. 713.
12. The first work is found in Doria, 1722, vol. 2, p. 177ff. The second, published at Naples, bore the mark of the Augsburg publisher Daniel Hopper on the title page.
13. For a detailed, lengthy, and laudatory review, see *Giornale de' Letterati* 9 (1712): 309ff.
14. *Considerazioni*, in Doria, 1722.
15. Doria based his mechanics on eight definitions and three postulates, including some commonly used scientific notions, such as the principle of inertia, and the distinction between absolute and relative motion. The solutions Doria proposed were essentially Cartesian and mechanist, obscured, however, by an anachronistic restatement of some metascientific aspects of Galilean thought, such as the circularity of the planets' orbits and Platonic circumpulsion.
16. *Giornale de' Letterati* 9 (1712): 320.
17. The outcry of the dispute is described quite well by the editor of the "Notizie letterarie da Napoli" in the *Giornale de' Letterati* (12 [1712]: 427). Earlier in

the same periodical, one can read that Porzio "is occupied with responding to his strong adversaries, who have recently published some pamphlets against him dealing with the motion of bodies on an inclined plane" (7 [1711]: 472).

18. "Lettera al sig. D. Antonio Monforte," in Doria, 1712, p. 4.
19. *Ibid.*, pp. 11–12.
20. On the importance of the time factor in Galilean dynamics, see Koyré, 1978.
21. "Letter to Giacinto De Cristoforo," in Doria, 1712, pp. 58–59.
22. There is a manuscript copy of the letter in Grandi's codex (B.U.P., ms. 44, cc. 14r–15r), with the title *Opuscula quae in hoc volumine continentur spectant ad controversiam inter Jordanum et Grandium.* The codex contains both the most interesting works that appeared during the dispute and letters addressed to Grandi on this matter. Vitale Giordani (1687) had already entered the diatribe, attacking Vanni with a work also preserved in Grandi's codex.
23. A copy of the pamphlet is found in Grandi's codex cited in n. 22.
24. Torrini advanced the thesis naming Bartolomeo Intieri as "sig. N. N." in still doubtful language (1979b, pp. 222–223); I do not believe there can be any doubts about identifying "sig. N. N." as Intieri. Grandi's codex containing letters between himself and Intieri contains the autograph of Grandi's long letter to Intieri from 29 May 1706 (later published) that proves this claim.
25. Grandi, 1710, p. 33.
26. Much discussion has focused on the controversial problem of the role of mathematical language and experiments in Galileo's gnosiology; see in particular Geymonat, 1969, pp. 259–280; Hall, 1963, pp. 67–116; Boas, 1962; and Koyré, 1978, who examines the Galilean postulate that was the object of a lively debate between Intieri and Porzio and confirms his theses about the essential role that mathematical abstraction played in Galileo.
27. Grandi, 1710, p. 41.
28. *Ibid.*, p. 42.
29. The dispute continued for some time, involving other figures. In response to Grandi's *Considerazioni*, Giordani's pupil Girolamo Tambucci, "a poor priest in a tiny village near Priverno" (Galiani to Piergerolamo Bargellini, Rome, 25 July 1711; B.U.P. *Carteggio Grandi*, ms. 97, c. 321r), wrote a short work entitled *Illustrisimo domino Josepho Davanzati patritio florentino ac thesaurario regalis ecclesiae S. Nicolai barensis. Hieronimus Tambucci S.P.D. Datum Romae Kalendis Aprilis 1711.*
30. See Badaloni, 1961, p. 205.

3: THE EIGHTEENTH-CENTURY EDITIONS OF GALILEO'S WORKS

1. See Favaro, 1888.
2. See *ibid.*
3. There is a reconstruction of Viviani's attempts in *Sulla pubblicazione delle sentenza contro Galileo, e sopra alcuni tentatividel Viviani per far rivocare la condanna dei Dialoghi galileiani*, in Favaro, 1887, pp. 97ff.
4. Favaro, 1888, p. 13.
5. See the letters of Tommaso Buonaventuri and Guido Grandi, in B.U.P., *Carteggio Grandi*, ms. 85, generally full of incitements to work with greater vigor to finish the work and documenting the material difficulties of this difficult undertaking. The unfortunate loss of some important Galilean manuscripts at Leghorn is the subject of grievous letters (see for example one dated Florence, 4 July 1713, c. 45r). The collaboration for the publication of the works involved nearly all the greatest Pisan scholars. In 1717 Buonaventuri glowingly informed Grandi that finally "Galileo is close to being produced" (Florence, June 1717, c. 93v).

6. These trips were essential for obtaining Rome's approval for reprinting. See Buonaventuri's letter to Grandi from June 1717 cited in the preceding note. Tommaso Buonaventuri's letters to Giovanni Bottari (B.C.R., ms. 1894, 44.E.4) provide valuable information on Bottari's crucial work as superintendent of the grand ducal press and the support of such Roman friends as Galiani and Cerati for Galileo's publication. In a letter from 5 September 1713 (c. 8r), Buonaventuri congratulated Bottari for the success of his activities in favor of the publication. In another letter from 15 October 1719 (c. 27r), there is a clear reference to Celestino Galiani and the Roman group, whom those in charge at the grand ducal press relied on. On Buonaventuri, who committed suicide in 1731 and who, because of his personality, was called "Bitter" by the academicians at the Crusca, see Cristofolini, 1972, pp. 182–183.

7. Anonymous letter to Grandi, Rome, n.d., B.U.P., *Carteggio Grandi*, ms. 99, c. 311r. In 1717 Buonaventuri announced to Grandi this important find of letters: "A chest has been discovered in Parma with original letters of Galileo, Father Castelli, and Father Cavalieri; they were in the monastery of the Benedictines of Parma" (Florence, 27 October 1717, c. 93v). The original letters were delayed in reaching Buonaventuri, who complained to Bottari about the problem (B.C.R., ms. 1894, 44.E.4, c. 17r).

8. "General Preface" to Galilei, 1718, vol. 1, p. xi. Among the most interesting texts of the edition was Viviani's famous *Vita di Galileo Galilei*. The work was no longer unedited, for it had been published by Salvini (1717), and it reveals the degree of self-censure imposed on the Galileans by ecclesiastical authorities. In the *Vita* Viviani presents a repentant Galileo, grateful to the Church for having saved his soul by putting him on trial (see Galilei, 1718, vol. 1, p. lxxviii).

9. *Lezioni accademiche*, p. xiv. The principal director of this edition was Giovanni Bottari, who after this first printing of Torricelli's works continued to lobby for the publication of the rest of the manuscripts. See Bottari's letter to Grandi, Florence, 31 August 1723 (B.U.P., *Carteggio Grandi*, ms. 85, c. 201r).

10. This is not the only printing of the *Dialogo* to appear in the first half of the century. Galilei, 1744, holds an important place in the history of eighteenth-century editions of Galilean works. After great vicissitudes and many compromises, this edition's editor, Abbot Giuseppe Toaldo, managed to obtain authorization from the Inquisition to publish the famous *Dialogo* (see Maugain, 1909, pp. 80–83; Favaro, 1883, vol. 2, pp. 439–441). It was the crowning achievement of the efforts of the Italian Galileans, who had always fought to see Galileo rehabilitated. Finally, in 1737, Galileo's remains were reinterred at Santa Croce (in "a room behind the sacristy," however). A few months before the appearance of Toaldo's edition of the *Opere* in 1744, some of the most interesting letters between Fulgenzio Micanzio and Galileo Galilei were published by Baglioni in Venice (*Lettere inedite di uomini illustri*). During Benedict XIV's so-called enlightened papacy, the Inquisition even revoked the condemnation of the books demonstrating the earth's motion. Despite these episodes marking a partial change in the attitude of the ecclesiastical authorities, the effects of the salutary edict of 1616 long continued to make themselves felt. The *Dialogo* reprinted in the fourth volume of Toaldo's edition of the *Opere* was pointedly preceded by the *Sententia cardinalium in Galilaeum* and the *Abiuratio Galilaei*, in which the scientist was forced to confess he was a "convinced delinquent." Toaldo warned readers of the persistence of the effects of the salutary edict and drastically censured Galileo's vehemently Copernican positions contained in the notes to which he referred. In them Galileo not only indicated the truth of Copernicanism and the rights of reason, but he openly derided

the obscurantism and ignorance of his judges; see Favaro, 1880. On the ultimate purpose of these notes Galileo made after his recantation, as if to vindicate disdainfully his own freedom of conscience despite the ordeal of the Inquisition, see De Maio, 1981, pp. 3-11.

11. *Giornale de' Letterati* 4 (1710): 433-434.
12. This network of relationships is attested by a collection of sonnets he gathered in 1724 (Ciccarelli, 1725) whose authors included Pietro Metastasio, Giuseppe Lucina, Nicolò Giovio, Nicola Capasso, and other lesser authors. Ajello focused on Ciccarelli in his "Cartesianismo e cultura oltremontana al tempo dell' 'Istoria civile,'" the introduction to *Pietro Giannone*, 1980, pp. 141-142. For more on Ciccarelli, see Fisch, 1968, p. 58, n. 2, especially on the close relationship between Vico and Ciccarelli. Fisch affirms that Ciccarelli was also the author of the definitive reprint of Leonardo di Capua's works, then on the *Index*.
13. See the letters that Ciccarelli wrote to Bottari in 1726 (B.C.R., ms. 1605, 32.E.26, c. 33rff). Intieri, who was a personal friend of Ciccarelli, played an essential role in the contacts between Florence and Naples; see Intieri's letters to Bottari (B.C.R., ms. 1608, 33.E.29).
14. See Nicolini, 1951, p. 29.
15. The work in question in the *Istoria e dimostrazioni intorno alle macchie solari e loro accidenti comprese in tre lettere scritte a Marco Velseri* (1613). The *Istoria* appeared only after difficulties with censorship in two very similar editions, one after the other. The letter in question, dated Naples, 10 October 1709 (S.N.S.P., XXXI.A.3, cc. 301r-306r), is certainly by De Cristoforo, because the author speaks of his treatise *De constructione*, alluding to a little piece entitled *De constructione aequationum libellus* (1700).
16. See Rohault, 1713.
17. See Ajello, "Cartesianismo e cultural oltremontana," in *Pietro Giannone*, 1980, pp. 142-143. Grazini discussed this short book at length with his friend Galiani, creating great embarrassment for the Celestine monk because of his theories favoring clerical marriage (letter, n.d., S.N.S.P., XXXI.A.3, cc. 68rff).
18. On the attempt to publish Marchetti's translation clandestinely at Naples, Grazini wrote to Galiani in 1716 informing him of the failure of the project, first because the printer was frightened, and then because of the clergy's actions (Nicolini, 1951, p. 158).
19. See Galilei, 1636. Elia Diodati sent the work to Mattia Bernegger without Galileo's knowledge. We do not believe that the edition was taken from the printed work because the differences are quite profound, especially in the final part. To establish the provenience of the manuscript used for the printing, it would be necessary to make an exact comparative analysis of each of the thirty-four codices that form the stemma worked out by Antonio Favaro (Galilei, 1890-1909, vol. 5, pp. 272-275). See also Geymonat, 1969, pp. 75ff; Rossi, 1978.
20. Galilei, 1710b, p. 16.
21. *Ibid.*, p. 18.
22. *Ibid.*, p. 9.
23. To confirm the fluidity of the Neapolitan cultural situation and the continued flourishing of editorial initiatives in favor of modern thought in the city, one need only examine a very important work generally overlooked by historians: B. Varen, 1715. This openly Copernican book (see chapter 6, "De loco Telluris in mundi systemate," pp. 38ff) started with a publication of the *Abiuratio Galilaei*, without a single word of comment, as if to emphasize the merely formal aspect of such a premise. Celestino Galiani was also quite interested in

this reprinting; see Grazini's letter to Galiani, Naples, September 1715 (S.N.S.P., XXXI.A.3., c. 77r).

24. See Raimondi, "La formazione culturale del Muratori," in L. A. *Muratori*, 1975, pp. 22–23. Noting Muratori's references to the *Lettera alla Granduchessa*, Raimondi affirms that the treatise *De ingeniorum moderatione* supports the cause of "Galilean Catholicism."

25. See especially the section "Ragione e autorità" in Falco and Forti, 1964, vol. 1, pp. 235–241. On these aspects of Muratori's thought, see Bertelli, 1960, pp. 384–387.

26. See Comparato, "Ragione e fede nelle discussioni storiche, teologiche e filosofiche di Costantino Grimaldi," in *Saggi e ricerche*, 1968, pp. 78ff; Ricuperati, "Costantino Grimaldi," in *Dal Muratori al Cesarotti*, 1978, pp. 741ff; Grimaldi, 1964.

27. See Ricuperati, "Costantino Grimaldi," in *Dal Muratori al Cesarotti*, 1978, p. 755.

28. On Giannone and Radicati di Passerano, see, respectively, Ricuperati, 1970a, and Venturi, 1954.

4: A MANIFESTO FOR THE RENEWAL OF ITALIAN CULTURE

1. See Garin, "Aspetti e motivi della ricerca sulla scuola galileiana," in *La scuola galileiana*, 1979, pp. 158ff, a restatement of his "Galileo e la cultura del suo tempo," in Garin, 1975b, pp. 109ff.

2. The two theses were the focus of the scholarly conference of Santa Margherita Ligure; see *La scuola galileiana*, 1979.

3. This absence was already noticed by eighteenth-century intellectuals. Andres, for example, in his essay on Galileo, asked, "why has no party of the philosophical school formed in Italy with Galileo at its head, and why has it not resisted France's glory with Descartes, or England's with Newton and Germany's with Leibniz?" (Andres, 1776, p. 329).

4. For an exhaustive picture of Italian and European Cartesianism, see Ajello, "Cartesianismo e cultura oltremontana," in *Pietro Giannone*, 1980, which confirms our conclusions. We believe that the theories of Negri (1970), while interesting, are not historically valid.

5. There are various opinions about the relationship between Cartesianism and modern science. Undoubtedly Descartes fostered a definitive break with the substantially Aristotelian forms of magic and natural animism common to some European philosophical currents in the sixteenth and seventeenth centuries and deepened the rift between science and religion (Lenoble, 1976). Nevertheless, there are legitimate uncertainties and confusions about the subsequent development of Cartesianism in Europe and its positive effects for modern science. In England, however, under Baconian auspices, the repudiation of Cartesianism culminated in Newtonian mathematical empiricism; see Pacchi, 1973; Webster, 1976. Also significant was the Dutch empiricists' anti-Cartesian debate (Gori, 1972; Brunet, 1926; Cassirer, 1951), and the profound difference between Galileo and Descartes on a methodological level (Lenoble, 1943, pp. 603–613; Butterfield, 1969).

6. Regarding eighteenth-century interpretations of Galileism, Nicola Badaloni (1968, pp. 44–46) has advanced a rather general hypothesis linking two different tendencies then underway in Italian culture: one naturalistic with supporters in Padua, Pisa, and Naples, the other based on a privileged relationship between mathematical language and natural reality, with followers everywhere. On the dispute between Grandi and Marchetti about the different ways of integrating Galileo's heritage, see also Badaloni, 1968b. In the absence of in-depth studies on eighteenth-century Galileism, see Paoli, 1899; Rotta, 1971; Natali, 1950;

Baldini, "L'attività scientifica del primo Settecento," in *Le scienze*, 1980.

7. It is not difficult to discern an ideal pursuit of Galileo's initial plan in this project that, during the years in which the Counter-Reformation Church's extraordinary organizational power unfolded, aimed at "converting the Church to the cause of science" (Geymonat, 1969, p. 79). Cozzi ("Galileo Galilei, Paolo Sarpi e la società veneziana," in Cozzi, 1979, pp. 136ff) has demonstrated how Galileo explicitly posed the problem of the choice between the two parties: the Roman Catholic one and the Venetian one of Sarpi, a layman strongly antagonistic towards the other party. Galileo's tragic choice in favor of Rome was criticized at length by Venetian patricians who were not at all involved in the trial.

8. An example of this is Lorenzo Magalotti's "Epicurean apologetics," outlined in the famous *Lettere familiari* (1680–1684). Following Galilean experimentalism and atomism, Magalotti completely repudiated Cartesian metaphysics and the theory of the vortices of ether; see Garin, 1970, pp. 98–99; Casini, 1980a, vol. 1, pp. 232–235.

9. Gassendi, 1727.

10. Carranza, 1962, p. 660. Carranza, however, softens such a judgment by affirming that "the meaning of this edition also remains obscure on many points because it has not been the subject of a detailed study."

11. See Antonio Niccolini's letters to Bottari, B.C.R., ms. 1891, 44.E.11^1, respectively Rome, 1 July 1724 (c. 16r) and Rome, 6 July 1727 (c. 78r). In the subsequent letters it becomes evident that Galiani attempted to entice some of his friends in Naples, in particular Niccolò Di Martino, to associate themselves with the enterprise (cc. 80rff).

12. See Intieri's letters from Naples to Bottari (B.C.R., ms. 1608, 32.E.29).

13. Carranza, 1962, refers to the governmental protections, naming secretary of Royal Law Giulio Rucellai. Also among the collaborators in the enterprise was the still inexperienced Giovanni Lami.

14. Buonaventuri's letter to Bottari, Florence, 24 March 1725 (B.C.R., ms. 1894, 44.E.4, c. 67rv).

15. Buonaventuri's letters document Bottari's stay in Rome. In April 1725, the Holy See's consent arrived through Bottari, who was in Rome. On 21 April 1725 Buonaventuri wrote ironically to congratulate Bottari: "Oh how terrible! They send me approval for Gassendi and don't undersign it, and it says in the approval to do so" (*ibid.*, c. 69r). On the intensive debate underway among Galiani's friends about the risks that publication carried, there is a valuable letter from Galiani to Bottari, lamenting that Inquisitors and bishops had been ordered to prevent "modern philosophy" from being introduced into universities and seminaries (Rome, 28 February 1721, B.C.R., ms. 1581, 32.E.2, cc. 15v–16r).

16. Naples, 2 February 1726, B.C.R., ms. 1608, 32.E.29, c. 1r.

17. The introduction was not signed by the editor of the work, and it explicitly indicated in its title those responsible to the press, Buonaventuri and Bottari. Nicola Averani, the official editor (as is apparent from the letters between Buonaventuri and Bottari), limited himself to a merely technical collaboration. In fact, Buonaventuri and Bottari at one point thought of eliminating him entirely and excluding him from the enterprise; see Buonaventuri's letter to Bottari, Florence, 15 March 1725 (B.C.R., ms. 1894, 44.E.4, c. 65r). The final version of the introduction, whoever its author, nevertheless pleased Bottari and his Roman friends. Even the *Giornale de' Letterati*, which had favorably followed the production of the edition, emphasized the cloud of mystery engulfing the author of the preface (38 [1727]: 401).

18. See *Typographus philosophiae studiosis*, in Gassendi, 1727, pp. ir*v*.
19. *Ibid.*, p. iir.
20. See *ibid.*, p. ii*v*.
21. *Ibid.*, p. iii*v*.
22. "The anonymous continuator of this most elevated text indicated new paths for Catholic culture, weaving his discussion with quotations taken from Lucretius, Hobbes, Newton, Gassendi, Democritus, and Leucippus" (*ibid.*, pp. iii*v*–iv*r*). The conclusion of this preface still bore the imprint of Galileo, whom Gassendi wished to meet in Italy (p. vii*r*).
23. On Gassendi's hostility towards mathematical-deductive language as the gnosiological foundation of modern science, see Gregory, 1961, pp. 158ff. Gassendi anticipated Vico's criticism of mathematical rationalism, saying the "phenomena are recognized in the measure in which we are capable of understanding the *ratio constructionis*" (p. 161).
24. Much room is dedicated to empiricism's validity as the methodology necessary to revitalize medical science in a rapid historical excursus citing some of the Investiganti, in particular Leonardo di Capua, as among the modern founders of empiricism in medicine (*Typographus philosophiae studiosis*, in Gassendi, 1727, p. iv*r*).
25. Bertelli, 1955, pp. 435–456.
26. On the currency of this theme in Europe during this period, see Spink, 1960.
27. Regarding this important issue, see Rosso, 1954; Gregory 1961, pp. 236–249.
28. See Venturi, 1969, pp. 394–410.
29. *Typographus philosophiae studiosis*, in Gassendi, 1727, p. v*r*.
30. See Bertelli, 1965.
31. I refer to the debatable and much-discussed book of Appolis, 1960. Certainly one ought to make a vast distinction between those who have privileged only the theological-religious aspects of Italian Jansenism and those who, instead, have made a considerable contribution to defining its cultural dimensions. For an exhaustive bibliography on these problems, see Rosa, 1974, pp. 50–58.
32. See Carranza, 1974, and also Rosa, 1969, especially regarding the relationship between the Enlightenment and Catholicism.
33. Carranza, 1974, p. 61. The complex question of the role of Italian Catholics in the early eighteenth century is still a source of heated discussion. The works of Merkle (1909) and Plongeron (1970) posed the problem of defining the intensive reform activities of some Catholic intellectuals. See also De Maio, "Pensiero e storia religiosa," in *Immagini*, 1980, pp. 32–40, who says of the term "Catholic Enlightenment": "If the Enlightenment is autonomy of reason, and Catholicism is revealed authority received in faith, there is an essential contradiction between the two terms" (*ibid.*, p. 34). See also Rosa, 1981b, with an extensive bibliography.
34. Venturi, 1969, pp. 22–23.
35. On Bottari's role in the condemnation of the *Esprit des lois*, see Rosa, 1969, pp. 93–94. On Bottari, see Palozzi, 1941; Dammig, 1945, pp. 63–98. None of these works really mentions Bottari's editorial and scientific interests, which, as we have said, were also at the center of his youthful cultural activities. There is some comment on these projects in Pignatelli and Petrucci, 1971, pp. 409–418.
36. Venturi, 1969, pp. 562–563.
37. See Setti, 1806.
38. See Rotta, "Montesquieu nel Settecento italiano: Note e ricerche," in Tarello, 1971, vol. 1, pp. 108–112.

Three: Enlightened Catholics and Newtonian Natural Theology

1: A NEW IMAGE OF GOD

1. On the complex affairs that preceded the publication of these *quaestiones*, see Koyré, 1957.
2. See H. Newton's letter to I. Newton, which repeats long passages of letters sent by the diplomat to Roman scholars (Turnbull, 1967, vol. 4, p. 507).
3. I. Newton, 1706, p. 314.
4. *Ibid.*, p. 346.
5. See Koyré, 1957.
6. I. Newton, 1706, p. 322.
7. *Ibid.*, p. 341.
8. *Ibid.*, p. 343.
9. Regarding the dispute, see Rossi, 1979, pp. 63–71.
10. I. Newton, 1706, p. 345.
11. *Ibid.*, pp. 346–347.
12. *Ibid.*, pp. 345–348.
13. On Jean Le Clerc, see Barnes, 1938; Giuntini, 1979, pp. 33ff; Sina, 1978. On the dissemination of his periodicals in Italy, see Comparato, 1970, pp. 135ff; Mirri, 1963, pp. 294–327.
14. See Jacob, 1976.
15. See Johnson's letter to Galiani, which accompanied the volumes, The Hague, 19 July 1715 (S.N.S.P., XXXI.A.3, c. 270rv). In October 1711 Galiani wrote from Rome to his friend Bargellini that he had gotten a real bargain, acquiring all the issues of the *Bibliothèque choisie* cheaply from a high prelate (B.U.P., *Carteggio Grandi*, ms. 97, c. 226r).
16. For more on the intense and cordial relations between the Roman scholars and Le Clerc, see Caracciolo, 1968.
17. Le Clerc wrote: "Italian books arrive here so rarely and so late that unless one is able to make them arrive express, it is not always possible to give the scholars of that country the honor that is their due" (*Bibliothèque choisie* 27 [1713]: 178).
18. See the positive reviews of the works of Vignolio and Fontanini in the *Bibliothèque choisie* (20 [1710]: 195ff and 211ff, respectively) and of the works of the Tuscan Averani (22 [1711]: 2ff) and, particularly, Le Clerc's enthusiastic commentary on Cardinal Noris's famous *Historia pelagiania* (1 [1703]: 13ff). Especially meaningful was the relationship between Bianchini and Le Clerc, who enthusiastically reviewed the *Solutio problematis Paschalis* and *De calendario et cyclo Caesaris* (*Bibliothèque choisie* 27 [1713]: 177ff). Bianchini personally met Le Clerc during his trip to Europe in 1713 (see Fabroni, 1780, vol. 6, pp. 324–325) and had a financial relationship with him as well, for the Genevan helped him to sell the *Solutio* in Holland and England; see Giovanni Antonio Baldini's letter to Bianchini, Amsterdam, 22 September 1713 (B.V.R., ms. U. 15, cc. 182r–183r). Le Clerc's letter dated 1725 (B.V.R., ms. U. 16, cc. 508rff) confirms the good relations between him and Bianchini.
19. See Le Clerc's review of H. Newton's *Sive de Nova Villa* (*Bibliothèque choisie* 22 [1711]; 51ff) which well documents the capable role the diplomat played connecting Florentine scholars such as Salvini, Magalotti, and Averani, and Le Clerc. Also important are Le Clerc's letters to Henry Newton and Averani published in H. Newton, 1710, pp. 24, 27, 161.
20. See Barnes, 1938, p. 116.
21. See *Bibliothèque choisie* 9 (1706): 245ff.

22. *Ibid.*, 22 (1711): 102.
23. See Galiani's letter to Grandi, Rome, 9 February 1715 (B.U.P., *Carteggio Grandi*, ms. 92, cc. 372rff).
24. On this debate, which had repercussions throughout Europe, see Casini, 1969, pp. 190–192. I do not believe Casini's claim that Le Clerc was "devoid of Newtonian science" or "an improvised Newtonian." He dedicated much time to the European scientific debate and especially the one in English, which argues in favor of his broad knowledge of Newton's works, whatever his dispute with Hartsoeker might suggest. In Italy this debate came to the attention of a wide audience through the *Raccolta d'opuscoli sopra l'opinioni filosofiche di Newton* (1745), which had also appeared two years earlier in Florence.
25. See "Histoire des systèmes des anciens athées, tirée des chapitres II et III du systeme intellectuel de Mr. Cudworth," *Bibliothèque choisie* 2 (1703): 61.
26. *Ibid.*, p. 18.
27. *Ibid.*, pp. 24–25.
28. *Ibid.*, pp. 73–74.
29. *Bibliothèque choisie* 1 (1703): 228ff.
30. The philo-Aristotelianism present in Cudworth's work was particularly irritating to some European and Italian intellectuals. Zambelli (1972, p. 347) rightly called the repercussions in Italy following Le Clerc's review "an unpopular defense."
31. On Dodwell, see *D.N.B.*, vol. 5, pp. 1084–1087. On Samuel Clarke, see Garin, 1934, pp. 106–116, 294–304, 385–462; Garin, 1942; Casini, 1969, pp. 109–148.
32. Among the most interesting, see Dodwell's "An Epistolary Discourse, Proving from the Scriptures and the First Fathers That the Soul Is a Principle Naturally Mortal, but Immortalized Actually by the Pleasure of God to Punishment or to Reward, by His Union with the Baptismal Spirit," *Bibliothèque choisie* 24 (1713): 364–375; and "A Letter to the Learned Mr. Henry Dodwell, Containing Some Remarks on a Pretended Demonstration of the Immateriality and Natural Immortality of the Soul, in Mr. Clarke's Answer to His Late Epistolary Discourse Etc.," *ibid.*, pp. 386–397. The latter is one of the most interesting letters of the intense debate for its evaluation of the relationship between soul and matter that evolves within the framework of a science that analyzes the structure of matter.
33. The commentary on *A Demonstration of the Being and Attributes of God*, *ibid.*, pp. 294–295.
34. *Ibid.*, pp. 302–303. He then emphasized Clarke's harsh charges against Cartesianism, "under whose veil Spinoza was hiding and from which he indeed drew various things" (p. 311).
35. Casini (1969, p. 127) makes a persuasive argument for Clarke's direct collaboration in the production of the last fundamental *quaestiones* that appeared in the Latin edition of the *Opticks*.
36. Commentary on the *Demonstration*, *Bibliothèque choisie* 24 (1713): 314–315.
37. *Ibid.*, p. 308.
38. *Ibid.*, p. 330–331.
39. *Ibid.*, p. 334.

2: THE NEWTONIANS OF LONDON, THE HAGUE, AND ROME

1. On the life and brilliant career of William Burnet, see *D.N.B.*, vol. 3, p. 404. Regarding the close ties between Burnet and the Newtonian circle, see Gori, 1972, pp. 70–72. The English intellectual had studied mathematics and physics at Leyden, and he was part of the commission formed in 1712 by the Royal

Society to resolve the intricate matter of assigning priority to Newton or Leibniz for the discovery of infinitesimal calculus. See Turnbull, 1967, vol. 5, p. xxv.

2. Jacob (1976) has made this passage the crux of her book.

3. See Nicolini, 1951, pp. 150–152.

4. On millenarianism in Augustan England, see Jacob, 1976. Burnet cultivated a considerable interest in religious studies. Again in June 1728, he wrote to Galiani from America (where he had been sent by George II as governor of Massachusetts), updating him on his studies in sacred history, referring explicitly to Newton's analogous studies (see the classic works of Manuel, 1963 and 1959).

5. See the draft of Galiani's letter from Rome to Giovambattista Baroni in Venice, n.d. [1712] (S.N.S.P., XXXI.B.1, c. 205r), actually addressed to Abbot Antonio Conti. The volumes were bound not so much for Galiani, whom Burnet thought was already advanced in his knowledge of Newtonian theories, as for Giovambattista Resta, a Roman engineer in the circle of Crati, Bianchini, and Galiani (London, 6 April 1711, S.N.S.P., XXXI.A.2, c. 74r). On 7 June 1705 Burnet, then in London, invited Galiani to visit England (S.N.S.P., XXXI.A.2, cc. 80v–81r).

6. The *Scholium generale* appears in Burnet's letter to Galiani (S.N.S.P., XXXI.A.2, cc. 76r–77v). It was sent with a letter dated 14 November 1713 from 'sGravesande to Galiani at Burnet's suggestion (S.N.S.P., XXXI.A.3, cc. 94rff). The transcription is scrupulously faithful, even reproducing the italics and marginal notes that appear in the printed version, and, from the manuscript's poor condition, it evidently circulated widely among Galiani's friends. For a detailed study of Newton's *Scholium* and its extraordinary importance for eighteenth-century natural theology, see Casini, 1981, pp. 7–53.

7. For more on 'sGravesande, see Gori, 1972; Ruestow, 1973.

8. See Jacob, 1981.

9. On Baron von Stosch, believed to be one of the heads of the Florentine Masonic lodge, see Francovich, 1975, pp. 75–79, and the thorough work of Lewis, 1961, pp. 65–90, who clearly demonstrates the international contacts, squalid intrigues, and rich antiquarian market in Rome during the early eighteenth century.

10. See *ibid.*, pp. 38–62.

11. For more on this fascinating group, see Ricuperati, 1970a, pp. 395–409; Ricuperati, 1973. For the effects of Libertinism on Habsburg diplomatic circles, see Braubach, 1950, pp. 126–164.

12. On French Libertine circles, see Simon, 1939; Wade, 1938.

13. See Jacob, 1981. (Following paragraph has been edited by M.C.J.)

14. On the Hermetic and Brunian aspects of the Tolandists, see Giuntini, 1979, pp. 291–316, pp. 441–492.

15. See Jacob, 1981, pp. 112ff.

16. *Ibid.*, p. 185.

17. Gori (1972, pp. 73ff) has already pointed out the importance of this "societé de jeunes gens"; Jacob (1981) has identified its Libertine component, represented by the Knights.

18. See for example William Derham's lengthy and favorable exposition in "Physico-Theology: Or a Demonstration of the Being and Attributes of God from His Works of Creation," containing sixteen lectures given by the author as a Boyle lecturer in 1711 and 1712 (*Journal littéraire* 3 [1714]: 364–391).

19. The brief Newtonian notes against Leibniz's comments on the well-known *Commercium epistolicum* appeared in the *Journal littéraire* 7 (1715): 361ff. For an examination of this important periodical, see Hemprich, 1915; Gori, 1972, pp. 73–88.

20. In fact, Johnson wrote to Galiani: "I will not fail to bring up in the *Journal littéraire* the good literary news that you have sent me" (The Hague, 2 March 1717: S.N.S.P., XXXI.A.3, c. 280r).

21. Among the numerous books Thomas Johnson sent to Galiani (see the list of these books in the letter cited in the previous note, c. 280v) was the French translation of the famous *Discourse of Freethinking*, listing London, 1714, on the title page but actually printed in Johnson's workshop in The Hague, according to the publication announcement in the *Journal littéraire* (1 [1713]: 474). On Johnson's part in the translation, see O'Higgins, 1970, pp. 211ff. Along with the *Discourse* was the translation of Toland's very rare *Letter from an Arabian Physician* (1713), which appeared in London (see Carabelli, 1975, pp. 167–168) and which aimed to explain the Islamic religion and the materialism of Arab philosophies. In the same chest of books, Johnson also sent Galiani "two other [books] of the same sort," almost certainly Toland's *Adeisidaemon sive Titus Livius a superstitione vindicatus* and *Origines Iudaicae* (1709), which appeared in The Hague and were overseen by Johnson. Johnson had Baron von Stosch ask Galiani to obtain Marchetti's Italian translation of the *De rerum natura* for him (letter dated 26 March 1716 from The Hague; S.N.S.P., XXXI.A.3, c. 102rv).

22. See Burnet's letter accompanying the *Scholium generale* (S.N.S.P., XXXI.A.2, c. 77v).

23. I. Newton, 1726, p. 527.

24. See, for example, Galiani's letter to Bottari, Rome, 16 May 1714 (B.C.R., ms. 1581, 32.E.2, cc. 3r–4v), in which he stated: "For now I am sending you the letter of my friend from England, and after you have read it, please return it to me."

25. Leprotti's letter to Galiani, Rimini, 20 May 1724; S.N.S.P., XXXI.A.3, c. 335v. At the time Leprotti was undertaking an in-depth analysis of Newtonian theories, as evident from these studies in his papers preserved in Rome, Biblioteca Lancisiana, *Fondo Leprotti*, mss. 269–276. The collection includes eight volumes entitled *Physica*, rich in information about Newtonian physics and the works of Burnet, Whiston, and Keill, in particular ms. 269, commenting on the most important European works on cosmology. In ms. 276 (cc. 99rff), entitled *Elementi di fisica sperimentale*, Leprotti explained Newton's laws of motion, agreeing with him that gravity's cause is unknown. Leprotti's epistolary collection, containing letters from Ludovico Antonio Muratori, Francesco Serao, Giannantonio Davia, and many others, merits a serious study.

26. This is the expression used by Casini, 1969.

3: THE ITALIAN EDITIONS OF THE BOYLE LECTURES

1. On the importance of the natural model as a reference for all eighteenth-century scholars, see the classic work of Willey, 1975; see also Ehrard, 1964; Roger, 1963.

2. The vast literature on this point includes the classic works of Stephen, 1876; Gragg, 1964; Casini, 1969; see the works of Jacob, 1976 and 1981. There is a useful summary of the historiography of English deism in Firpo, 1978.

3. On the role played by Puritan intellectuals in favor of modern science, see the masterful work of Webster, 1976; see also Carabelli, 1974.

4. On the intellectual and personal ties between Locke and Le Clerc, see Barnes, 1938, pp. 157ff. In the same issue of the *Bibliothèque* (8 [1688]: 49ff) in which Le Clerc published the "Extrait d'un livre anglois qui n'est pas encore publié, intitulé Essai philosohique concernant l'entendement . . . communiqué par monsieur Locke," there was also a lengthy and positive review of the *Principia*

mathematica (pp. 436-450). According to Le Clerc, this review was the work of Locke himself, then a collaborator for the Dutch periodical.

5. On Locke's religious thought, see Firpo, 1980. There are Socinian features in the anti-Trinitarianism of Isaac Newton (Manuel, 1974) and Samuel Clarke. Biddle (1976) has revised the view still accepted today of the concrete tie existing between John Toland's *Christianity Not Mysterious* and Locke's *Reasonableness of Christianity*. He documents Locke's awareness of Toland's work before he was able to finish his *Reasonableness* and suggests we discard the common assumption that Toland drew inspiration from Locke's work. That Locke's work was orthodoxly Christian nevertheless seems irrefutable, a fact that allowed Galiani, Bottari, and Cerati unhesitatingly to consider him a "sublime spirit" and "the Archimedes of the best metaphysics" (Carranza, 1974, p. 150).

6. The scant available information on the English baronet Thomas Dereham appeared in the *Giornale de' Letterati* (see above, chapter 1). We know only that he was a fervent Jacobite, well known in diplomatic circles (Lewis, 1961). With close ties to the group of enlightened Catholics, Dereham made himself useful as a translator of many English works; see the list of these translations in his letter to Guido Grandi, Florence, 3 October 1727 (B.U.P., *Carteggio Grandi*, ms. 90, cc. 127r-128r). Thomas Dereham enjoyed the protection of high prelates in Rome, including Cardinal Neri Corsini (see Dereham's letter to Corsini from 6 January 1734, Vatican City, Vatican Library, *Fondo Capponi*, ms. 279, c. 6rv).

7. See Derham, 1719, pp. 381-382. On the active efforts of Senator Buonarroti in Tuscan culture, see Parise, 1972, pp. 145-147.

8. Despite some rough language, the translation was good and was subjected to direct approval of the author, who from England engaged in profuse correspondence with Dereham. See the valuable "Lettere di uomini eruditi di vari paesi intorno le Transazioni filosofiche e diverse altre materie e notizie scientifiche scritte al cavalier Tommaso Dereham" in the fifth volume (pp. 210ff) of the first Italian edition of the *Philosophical Transactions*, which appeared in Naples (Lowthorp, 1729-1734). In these letters, Derham confidingly familiarized his friend with extraordinary success that his *Physico-Theology* enjoyed in France, Holland, and Germany and with the translations of the work all over Europe. The notes that Thomas Dereham added to the Italian translation are distinguished from the author's notes by the symbol ⚕.

9. See Derham, 1719, pp. 35ff.

10. Derham synthesized the best results of research thus far completed in the fields of medicine, biology, and botany, basing his analysis on the works of Boyle, Willis, Ray, Grew, Bellini, Severino, and Descartes. Citing the classic works of Aristotle, Pliny, Cicero, and Epicurus, Derham produced a thesis of natural finalism that, in his opinion, was borne out by modern scientific research.

11. Casini, 1969, p. 173.

12. The suppressed volume is the eleventh and final one. The textual comparison was done in the fourth edition of the *Physico-Theology* (1716). In the preface, Derham confirmed that he had made changes from the previous editions only in a few paragraphs, in particular the first note to chapter 5, regarding the concept of gravity, and a few citations from Seneca.

13. See *Giornale de' Letterati* 32 (1719): 554.

14. See Vallisnieri's many letters to Morgagni and Derham in *Lettere di uomini eruditi* in Lowthorp, vol. 5, 1734, dealing with the theological works translated by the English baronet.

15. Derham's translation, 1728, p. xvii. From the comparison with the second English edition (London, W. Innys, 1715), the only part omitted is the eighth and

final book, *Practical Inferences from the Foregoing Survey*, in which Derham violently attacked religious superstition and the atheists.

16. *Ibid.*, p. xi. Derham continued: "It is not at all necessary to confine those texts to a literal meaning, but they can be taken as pronounced to save the appearance of things and according to the common maxims and opinions of men."

17. Of great importance are the titles of some sections of the work, which asked whether God was responsible for celestial bodies' motions and forms. The entire sixth book was dedicated to the apologetic interpretation of Newtonian universal gravitation, and it confirmed that Newton did not claim "to assign the cause of gravity to anything, because his plan was not to occupy himself forming hypotheses, but to explain the phenomena only via experiments" (Derham, 1728, p. 70).

18. See *ibid.*, pp. xxiii–xxiv. According to Derham, a universe with many inhabited worlds was "a good deal more magnificent than any other and worthy of an infinite creator whose power and wisdom are without limits and measure."

19. In an undated letter (presumably from this period) Dereham wrote Galiani: "Abbot Niccolini made me privy to advisor Grimaldi's letter to Your Reverend Eminence, from which it seems the longed-for publication of my translations took a good turn in Naples, as long as they were sent there to be seen; hence you can send them, on the condition that if they do not please, they should return them and take care not to lose them" (S.N.S.P., XXXI.A.3, c. 1r).

20. See the unpaginated introduction in Derham, 1728.

21. The "Lettere di uomini eruditi" in Lowthorp, vol. 5, 1734, are a wealth of information for documenting Dereham's role as intermediary. Along with letters from high prelates and English scientists such as Derham, Jurin, and Sloane are those of Conti, Bianchini, Manfredi, Beccari, Poleni, Morgagni, and Vallisnieri. These last two confirm the dissemination of Dereham's translations, for they asked that they be sent on more than one occasion in 1728 and 1729.

22. Manfredi's letter to Dereham from Bologna, dated 28 January 1728 (*ibid.*, pp. 254–255) confirms Galiani's role in the new edition. At the end of the operation, neither Galiani nor anyone in his group was particularly satisfied with the results, given the difficulties in understanding the texts and a certain disorder in the presentation of the memoirs; see Galiani's letter to Bottari, Naples, 26 February 1737, B.C.R., ms. 1581, 32.E.w, c. 69rv.

23. See Lowthorp, vol. 3, 1731, pp. 189–193. On the importance of this work in the history of social mathematics, see Todhunter, 1865, pp. 48–51.

24. See Théophile Désaguliers's "Saggio delle Transazioni filosofiche della Società Reale. Dall'anno 1720 a tutto l'anno 1730 tradotte dall'idioma inglese dal cavalier Tommaso Dereham," in Lowthorp, vol. 4, 1734, pp. 42–74. See also the defense Edmund Halley made before the Royal Society in favor of Newton's chronology, attacked in France by the Jesuit Etienne Souciet (*ibid.*, pp. 25ff). On this dispute, see Manuel, 1963, pp. 22–23.

25. See Lowthorp, vol. 4, 1734, p. 241ff. On the value of the astronomical discovery, see Daumas, 1957.

26. "Lettere di uomini eruditi," in Lowthorp, vol. 5, 1734, p. 278.

27. The translation appeared with the title *Principi filosofici di religione naturale, ovvero elementi della filosofia e della religione da essi derivanti: Opera di Giorgio Cheyne M. D. della Società Regia* (Cheyne, 1729). There is an interesting dedication to Count Ferdinando von Daun, son of Viceroy Wierich Philipp Lorenz von Daun, signed by an otherwise unidentified Pietro Palfaligi.

28. See "L'editor a chi legge," in Cheyne, 1729.

29. On occultism and mysticism in Cheyne's thought, see Casini, 1969, pp. 193–202.

30. Cheyne, 1729, p. 1.
31. *Ibid.*, p. 2.
32. *Ibid.*, pp. 1–2.
33. On the lively debates throughout the eighteenth century between the Newtonian geologists, who denied that the creation of the universe had been governed by merely mechanical laws, and the Cartesian advocates of nature's self-sufficiency, see Rossi, 1979.
34. Cheyne, 1729, p. 23.
35. See *ibid.*, pp. 66ff.
36. For example, when referring to Newton's problematic explanation of the equivalence of rest and motion and the experimental difficulties in distinguishing one from the other, Toland affirms: "And tho Mr. Newton be deem'd an advocate for extended incorporeal space, yet he declares that perhaps no one body is in absolute rest, that perhaps no immovable bodily center is to be found in nature; and in one place he expresses himself in these words: 'The vulgar attribute resistance to quiescent and impulse to movent bodys, but motion and rest, as commonly conceiv'd, are only respectively distinguish'd from one another, nor are those things always in true repose, which are vulgarly consider'd as quiescent'" (Toland, 1704, pp. 201–202).
37. *Ibid.*, p. 188.
38. *Ibid.*, p. 191.
39. See *ibid.*, pp. 182–183. Once again Toland brought Newton directly into the picture, interpreting him in his own way.
40. On Toland's interpretation of the *Principia*, see Casini, 1969, pp. 205–238; Giuntini, 1979, pp. 335–381.
41. See Cheyne, 1729, section 3, pp. 67ff.
42. See *ibid.*, section 4, pp. 86ff.
43. The influence of English rationalist theology on the religious crisis of Italian Catholics is a subject that has yet to be studied. An examination of the attraction that some of the tenets of moderate Anglican deism had for the most open of enlightened Italian Catholics could in fact greatly enrich the historiographical debate underway among Italian Catholic reformers of the early eighteenth century. In the latter eighteenth century, at the urging of enlightened culture, interest in some aspects of modern thought seemed to diminish notably among Italian Catholics. The very philo-Jansenist philosophy that had animated the group of enlightened Catholics began to acquire frankly obscurantist connotations, extremely hostile to any concession to the Enlightenment (see Rosa, 1969, especially pp. 101ff). Far from illuminating positive elements or anything new regarding Catholic culture, Prandi (1966), rather, confirms the decadence and backwardness existing there, already standing staunchly on purely defensive positions.
44. On the dissemination of Newtonianism in France, see Brunet, 1931a; Ehrard, 1964, vol. 1, especially pp. 146ff, covering the French anti-Newtonians; Briggs, 1934. On the longevity of Cartesianism in French culture among the philosophes themselves, see Vartanian, 1953.
45. On the relation between Jesuit culture in France and modern science, see the fundamental collection of essays in De Dainville, 1978; Desautels, 1956; and Ehrard, 1964, vol. 1, pp. 155–157, describing the French Jesuits' rearguard battles against modern science.
46. On French culture in the early eighteenth century, see Vernière, 1954, vol. 1; Wade, 1938; Spink, 1960.
47. On these aspects of Voltaire's thought, see Pomeau, 1956; Torrey, 1963. On Voltaire's Newtonianism, see Staum, 1968, pp. 29–56.

48. On these important Italian translations of Voltaire's works, see Rotta, 1970, pp. 387–444. Reconstructing the background of these translations, Rotta documents Italian editors' substantial acceptance of the philosophe's general theses.
49. Niccolini wrote Galiani in a letter from Rome on 19 July 1732, commenting on Voltaire's *Histoire de Charles XII* (1731)—"admirable for its style, opinions, manner of thinking, and freedom of the author"— and urging that he read it (S.N.S.P., XXXI.A.5, c. 20r). Niccolini also approved the *Lettres philosophiques* in a letter to Galiani from Rome dated 19 March 1735 (S.N.S.P., XXXI.A.5, c. 38r), confirming his remarkable attention to Voltaire's works. On Gaspare Cerati's interest in the Frenchman, see Carranza, 1974, pp. 146–148. Commenting on the *Siècle de Louis XIV*, Cerati, who had personally met Voltaire during his trip to France, wrote to Bottari in 1753 that he had read the book twice, despite many unpardonable Libertine sections (*ibid.*, p. 146). Affirming the general admiration for Voltaire's works in those years, the *Novelle letterarie* of Florence (1 [1740]: col. 10) called him "one of the most brilliant spirits of France," a judgment destined to change radically during the latter eighteenth century.
50. In France Voltaire's strategy aimed at defending Newtonianism clashed with Diderot's disciplined materialist wing and Baron d'Holbach's entire coterie. Voltaire's Newtonian cosmos, supported by the infinite wisdom of a geometrician God and by theories of enlightened despotism, were staunchly denounced both by Diderot and d'Holbach, who did not recognize even the epistemological foundations of the Newtonian system. Diderot's harsh accusations against the *Principia*'s abstract mathematicism and his conservative use of the Boyle lecturers' natural theology restated some of Toland's most important theses. Diderot, however, proposed a solid materialism, scientifically based on the new structure of natural reality prominent in Guillaume-François Roulle's chemistry research (Guedon, 1979). Baron d'Holbach's *Système de la nature* contained not only analyses in Diderot's style but also the most organic and articulated attack against Voltaire's plan that was focused on the *Principia*'s cosmology. The baron emphasized the close ties between a fundamentally moderate political project based on enlightened despotism and the "cosmic conservatism" of eighteenth-century English science (see Willey, 1975, chapter 3). On d'Holbach's political and philosophical thought, see Naville, 1976; Tega, 1975, pp. 369–407; Kors, 1977. On the political struggles in France and the internal divisions among the philosophes on these problems as well, see Diaz, 1962, especially pp. 505–521.

Four: Newton and Scientific Traditions in the Veneto

1: ANTI-NEWTONIAN POLEMICS

1. Benzoni, 1978.
2. Only towards the end of the eighteenth century was there a difficult crisis; see Berengo, 1957. There is a comprehensive view of the conflict between the Venetian press and Rome in Grendler, 1977. On the tolerant nature of censorship in the Veneto regarding the press, see Berengo, 1956, pp. 134–151.
3. Useful general histories of the Republic of San Marco include Cessi, 1946, and Lane, 1978. On the specific matter of Venetian culture, see Logan, 1972. On eighteenth-century society in the Veneto, see Annales-school disciple Georgelin, 1978; see also Berengo, 1956; Torcellan, 1969; Venturi, 1969, chapter 4; Brusatin, 1980.
4. There is an explicit evaluation of the political dimension of Muratori's project

in Vecchi, "La nuova Accademia letteraria d'Italia," in *Accademie e cultura*, 1979, pp. 39–70. Extremely useful for framing the cultural environment within which Muratori operated is the collection of the *Atti del Convegno internazionale di studi muratoriani*, held in Modena in 1972. The most important of the four volumes are the first, *Ludovico Antonio Muratori e la cultura contemporanea* (1975), and the fourth, the work of A. Dupront, *Ludovico Antonio Muratori et la société européenne des pré-Lumières: Essai d'inventaire et de typologie d'aprés l' "epistolario"* (1976).

5. On the dispute over the possession of Comacchio and the figure of Muratori the jurisdictionalist, see Bertelli, 1960, pp. 100–174.

6. Nearly all the most important texts of Muratori's project are in Falco and Forti, 1964, vol. 1, pp. 177–202. The editors have rightly included in a single long chapter ("La riforma della cultura italiana") the *Riflessioni sopra il buon gusto*, the *De ingeniorum moderatione*, and the *Primi disegni*, emphasizing that all are part of the same Muratorian plan. For the complex circumstances of the enterprise, besides the editors' introductory notes, see Vecchi in *Accademie e cultura*, 1979, pp. 39ff. On the part played by Bernardo Trevisan and the Roman Circle of the Drum, see Calapaj, "I rapporti tra Lamindo Pritanio e Bernardo Trevisan," in *Accademie e cultura*, 1979, pp. 73–94.

7. For more on the Arcadia's ritualism and the political and cultural plan implicit in it, see Quondam, 1973.

8. On the role of Romans Francesco Bianchini, Giovanni Maria Lancisi, Giusto Fontanini, and Domenico Passionei, see Caracciolo, 1968, pp. 45–49.

9. L. A. Muratori, *Primi disegni della Repubblica letteraria d'Italia esposti al pubblico da Lamindo Pritanio*, in Falco and Forti, 1964, vol. 1, p. 188.

10. There are no particularly good studies on Muratori's scientific and philosophical thought, although see Vecchi, 1951; Raimondi, "La formazione culturale del Muratori: Il magistero del Bacchini," in Muratori, 1975, vol. 1, pp. 3–23; Di Pietro "Riflessi medici e naturalistici nel pensiero di Ludovico Antonio Muratori," *ibid.*, pp. 155–166; Ricuperati, 1975.

11. L. A. Muratori, *Riflessioni sopra il buon gusto*, in Falco and Forti, 1964, vol. 1, pp. 282–283.

12. L. A. Muratori, *Lettera esortatoria ai capi, maestri, lettori ed altri ministri di ordini religiosi d'Italia*, in Falco and Forti, 1964, vol. 1, p. 218.

13. In his mature works, however, Muratori completely repudiated Cartesian physics, calling it fanciful, although in his *Della forza della fantasia umana* (1745) he did not deny the genius behind the theory of vortices (Falco and Forti, 1964, vol. 1, p. 926). Commenting on the Cartesian works of the Sicilian Tommaso Campailla, whom he called a "Christian and Italian Lucretius" (Falco and Forti, 1964, vol. 2, pp. 1899–1902), Muratori lamented the fanaticism of these followers of Descartes who remained faithful to the philosopher's every word, without making critical progress forward. On Campailla and the debate against Newtonian cosmology in favor of Cartesian theories, see Cristofolini, 1974, pp. 324–328.

14. See *Giornale de' Letterati*, 1 (1710): 267ff. The close relationship between Muratori's reform and the overall goals of the journal is the focus of an analysis by Ricuperati, "Giornali nell'Italia dell'Ancien Régime," in Castronovo and Tranfaglia, 1976, pp. 135ff. For more on the *Giornale*, see also Berengo, 1962.

15. See chapter 1 above.

16. On Leibniz's conceptions and the *querelle* over living forces, see Jammer, 1957; Dugas, 1958; Koyré, 1957. Among those who took Leibniz's view were Johann Bernoulli, Willem 'sGravesande, Christian Wolff, Georg Bernhard Bulfinger, and Samuel König; those against included Jean-Simon Mazière, Colin MacLaurin,

James Stirling, and Samuel Clarke. For a scientific analysis of the *querelle*, see also Westfall, 1982, pp. 352ff.

17. See Koyré, 1965, who cites Malebranche as another of those who did not entirely grasp the principle of inertia.

18. While there are no significant works on Poleni, see De Tipaldo, 1845, and, especially, Cossali, 1813, who recounts the background to the debate over living forces, describes Poleni's experiment in great detail, and provides a long list of his published and manuscript works. See the lengthy description of Poleni's papers conserved in the Marciana in *Catalogo dei codici*, 1911, pp. 196–231). On Poleni's importance as a scientist, see the entry in the *Dictionary of Scientific Biography*, vol. 11, 1975, pp. 65–67.

19. According to Antonio Conti, 1756, vol. 2, pp. 6–8. He names some scholars and noble Venetians who were already gathering to carry out these experiments after having together read the *Acta eruditorum* of Leipzig.

20. For the dispute between Pemberton and Poleni, it is useful to refer to their respective writings as compared in the important Italian translation of Pemberton's *View of Sir Isaac Newton's Philosophy* (London, 1732). The translation was titled *Saggio della filosofia del signor cav. Isacco Newton esposto con chiarezza dal signor Enrico Pemberton: Con una dissertazione dello stesso sulla misura della forza de' corpi in moto cavata dagli atti filosofici d'Inghilterra*; it was published in Venice by the Storti Press in 1733, although the authorization from the "Reformatori delle studio di Padova" dates from 9 September 1732. It enjoyed immediate success, as attested by the second Venetian edition (Storti, 1745).

21. A valuable source for reconstructing the *querelle* in the Veneto is Poleni, 1728, which contains Antonio Conti's important letter-treatise "In qua disputatur de viribus vivis motorum corporum ab experimento aestimandis."

22. Real opposition developed over this issue between Galiani's group at the Neapolitan Accademia delle Scienze and scholars in the Veneto. On 27 October 1733, Bartolomeo Intieri wrote Giovanni Bottari from Naples, telling him that experiments had begun at the academy; nevertheless he did not hide his prejudicial aversion to Poleni's thesis (B.C.R., ms. 1582, 32.E.3, c. 155r). On hearing of the Neapolitans' negative opinion (through Niccolò Di Martino), Poleni and Jacopo Riccati reacted badly, questioning whether the experiment had been reproduced exactly; see Riccati, 1761–1764, vol. 4, p. xli.

23. See above, chapter 1.

24. See *Supplemento del Giornale de' Letterati d'Italia* 1 (1721): 223ff. On Giovanni Rizzetti (1675–1751), see Moschini, 1806, vol. 2, pp. 185ff.

25. See the letter in Garibotto, 1955, vol. 2, p. 805. Antonio Vallisnieri, who, with other instructors at the Pavian university, had followed the affair, on his own initiative sent Bourguet in Switzerland a copy of Rizzetti's book; see Kurmann, 1976, pp. 105–106.

26. The *Acta* (8 [1724]: 127ff) reprinted the letter to Martinelli, making it known throughout Europe. The same volume contains Richter's reply (p. 226). The dispute between Richter and Rizzetti was the object of commentaries in the *Journal des savants* (1728). For a scientific analysis of the *querelle*, see Montucla, 1802, vol. 3, pp. 558ff.

27. See the "Epistolae ad socios Societatis Regiae Londini excerpta," *Acta* 8 (1724): 236ff.

28. See James Jurin's letter to Thomas Dereham, London, 20 December 1728, in "Lettere di uomini eruditi," in Lowthorp, 1734, vol. 5, p. 212.

29. "Sperienze ottiche," in Lowthorp, 1729–1734, vol. 4, p. 221.

30. *Ibid.*, p. 214.

31. See Hall, 1963.

32. See "Lettera in difesa del sig. co. Giovanni Rizzetti sopra le affezioni del lume," in Riccati, 1761–1764.
33. See Rizzetti, 1741.
34. See Manfredi's letters to Dereham from October 1728, in which he speaks of the experiments performed by Zanotti and Algarotti in Bologna, and the latter's efforts to write a dissertation against Rizzetti in the "Lettere di uomini eruditi," in Lowthorp, 1734, vol. 5, pp. 271ff.
35. On Francesco Algarotti, see Bonora, 1974, pp. 366–388.
36. Algarotti actually made a report of the rigorous scientific analysis of Newton's experiments refuted by Rizzetti in his *De colorum immutabilitate eorum diversa refrangibilitate dissertatio* (Algarotti, 1791–1794, vol. 2, pp. 366–388). The plan to produce a book to respond to those opposing Newtonianism and to introduce English science everywhere took shape precisely in these years because of Rizzetti's friends' anti-Newtonian campaign, at the direct behest of Zanotti, Manfredi, and the enlightened Catholics. In a letter to Azzolino Malaspina (*ibid.*, vol. 10, p. 196), Algarotti himself confirms the influence that Eustachio Manfredi's Roman friends had.
37. See Crucitti-Ullrich, 1974.
38. On the attribution of the letter to Lama and Roma, see Ricuperati, 1968a, pp. 74–79. The "Estrait" is found in *Bibliothèque italique* 11 (1731): 1–43. The *Bibliothèque* (12 [1731]: 1–44) also devoted considerable attention to the dispute between Pemberton and Poleni over living forces, through a review of Poleni's *Epistolarum mathematicarum fasciculus* sympathetic to his ideas.
39. See "Elogio del P. Giovanni Crivelli cavato dal tomo XXIX della Raccolta d'opuscoli scientifici e filologici," in Crivelli, 2d ed., 1744, vol. 1.
40. *Ibid.*, p. 13.
41. *Ibid.*, p. 19.
42. *Ibid.*, p. 36.
43. This part, which appears in the second volume, centers on the analysis "of the passions," "the imaginations," and meteorological and astronomical phenomena. At the end of the volume, there is a complete overview of the *querelle* on living forces in a letter-treatise entitled "Della estimazione delle forze vive, dissertazione fisico-mathematica" (*ibid.*, pp. 282ff), presumably addressed to Antonio Conti.

2: GALILEAN REASON IN CONTI AND MURATORI

1. *Giornale de' Letterati* 4 (1710): 253ff.
2. Actually Nigrisoli did not refer to Cudworth or Le Clerc in the *Considerazioni* (Nigrisoli, 1712), but in his theories of plastic forces there are clear echoes of the *querelle* between Pierre Bayle and Jean Le Clerc on this matter. On Francesco Maria Nigrisoli (1648–1727), see Ughi, 1804, vol. 2, pp. 89–90.
3. A. Conti, "Lettera sopra le Considerazioni," *Giornale de' Letterati* 12 (1712): 250.
4. *Ibid.*, p. 261.
5. *Ibid.*, p. 298.
6. *Ibid.*, pp. 225–226.
7. *Ibid.*, p. 280.
8. *Ibid.*, p. 251. Among the fathers of his theory of seminal light, Nigrisoli had expressly mentioned Hermes Trismegistus and Marsilio Ficino (see Nigrisoli, 1712, pp. 306–307); this justified Conti's harsh charges; Conti ironically accused Nigrisoli of having failed to mention Cudworth, More, and Robert Fludd (true "prince of the cabalists") among his sources (A. Conti, "Lettera" [see n. 3], p. 300).

9. *Ibid.*, p. 303. Conti finally defended Descartes from Nigrisoli's accusations of irreligiosity.
10. See *Giornale de' Letterati* 16 (1713): 254ff, which contains a new review without any comment on the book. A letter from Vallisnieri (the author of the review) to Conti reveals the spite that the *Giornale*'s editors bore towards Nigrisoli. Vallisnieri wrote that he had wanted even more with this new review to "ruin Mr. Nigrisoli, bringing to light his unordered order, replies, and false ideas" (letter from Padua, 5 August 1713, in A. Conti, 1972, pp. 380–381).
11. Conti's letter to Vallisnieri, Venice, 13 May 1727, in A. Conti, 1972, p. 417. In the *Risposta*, Conti's attitude towards Newton, whom he had personally met during his stay in London, appears profoundly changed with respect to the commentary that had appeared in the *Giornale de' Letterati* (Conti, 1716, p. 16).
12. On Muratori's constant solidarity with Conti in his battle against Nigrisoli, see the letter sent to him from Modena, 4 June 1716, in *Lettere scelte*, 1812, p. 81. The "Lettera" in the *Giornale de' Letterati* had presumably been read before its publication by Muratori as well (see Conti's letter to Vallisnieri, Padua, 9 September 1711, in A. Conti, 1972, p. 355).
13. Muratori became a member of the Royal Society in 1716, thanks to the intervention of Antonio Conti, who attempted to involve him in the debate between Newton and Leibniz on infinitesimal calculus. At the time Muratori was involved in his own disagreement with Leibniz over the problem of the genealogy of the ducal d'Este family of Modena, and while personally thanking Newton for the honor bestowed on him through association with the Royal Society, he nevertheless refused to become involved in their dispute. See Bertelli, 1960, pp. 217–218.
14. See above, chapter 3.
15. This model of Newtonianism was very common in Europe during the early eighteenth century, and the intellectuals had to oppose it rather than the solid but limited apologetic frame of the Boyle Lectures. Hence the basis of the particular image of Newtonianism disseminated in Europe was the complex interweaving between Locke's gnosiology and Newton's science, and Locke's moral thought and politics and the *Principia*'s universe-machine. As we shall see, at least in Italy knowledge of Newton's works paralleled the spread of Locke's philosophy. Jacob (1976) outlines the components of the English ideological and political framework in the age of Restoration but is strangely silent about the role John Locke might have played in giving a concrete philosophical and political reference to the Boyle lecturers. Le Clerc's task of uniting in a single plan Locke's thought and the successive apologetic interpretations of the Newtonian universe-machine provided by the Latitudinarians cannot be completely freed from an attentive analysis of the English cultural situation.
16. Letter cited in Badaloni, 1968a, p. 237, n. 57.
17. On the identification of Socinians in the eighteenth century, see Firpo, 1980.
18. L. A. Muratori, *De ingeniorum moderatione*, in Falco and Forti, 1964, vol. 1, p. 299. Muratori called the Socinians' method foolhardy and claimed it was difficult to establish which were true and false readings of Scripture: "The most famous and sharp philosopher Descartes established above all: God and His works cannot be measured by a human yardstick."
19. On Muratori's religious thought, see Jemolo, 1965; Vecchi, "L'itinerario spirituale del Muratori," in Muratori, 1975, pp. 181–223. A complete analysis of the dispute between Le Clerc and Muratori appears in Vecchi, 1955, pp. 120ff.
20. L. A. Muratori, *Riflessioni sopra il buon gusto*, in Falco and Forti, 1964, vol. 1, p. 236.
21. *Ibid.*, p. 237.

22. Bertelli (1960, pp. 373–378) emphasizes the centrality of Newtonian science and Lockean gnosiology for working out a philosophy of Muratorian history locked in battle with Pierre-Daniel Huet's skepticism and historical Pyhrronism, based on empiricism and the critical-philological analysis of texts.

3: THE LIBERTINE AND NATURALIST HERITAGES: VALLISNIERI AND RICCATI

1. See Ricuperati, 1970, pp. 510–511; Vecchi, 1962, pp. 259–261. On the important seventeenth-century tradition of Libertinism in the Veneto flourishing around Giovan Francesco Loredano in the Accademia Veneziana degli Incogniti, see Spini, 1950, pp. 140–171; see also Spini's "Alcuni appunti sui libertini italiani," in Bertelli, 1980, pp. 117–124.
2. On seventeenth-century Libertinism, see Pintard, 1943; Spink, 1960; Schneider, 1970.
3. There is an effective description of this opposition in Comparato, 1974, pp. 609–619. On the relationship between the Libertine tradition and the Enlightenment, see Venturi, 1971, and 1954, pp. 14ff; Ajello, 1976a, pp. 229ff.
4. See Spini, 1950, pp. 148–149.
5. Ricuperati, 1970a, p. 511.
6. See *ibid.* These include the philosopher Jacopo Stellini. Ricuperati also mentions the trials that took place in Venice against some patricians accused of Libertinism. On Antonio Conti's trial for Libertinism in 1735, see Badaloni, 1968a, pp. 190–193.
7. While there is no real intellectual profile of Vallisnieri, see Fabroni, 1780, vol. 7, pp. 9–81; "Eloge historique de Mr. Antoine Vallisnieri," *Bibliothèque italique* 5 (1729): 46ff; Spallanzani, 1977; Savelli, 1961.
8. A general outline of these problems in eighteenth-century biology appears in Roger, 1963, pp. 370ff. Regarding Vallisnieri's position in these matters, see Solinas, 1967, pp. 60ff; Badaloni, 1968a, pp. 32ff.
9. Vallisnieri, 1721, p. 244.
10. *Ibid.*, pp. 243–244. For an effective explanation of Galileo's theory of the infiniteness of the impact, see Torricelli, 1715, "Lezione prima," pp. 6–8.
11. We refer to the classic work of Lovejoy, 1936. For more on the issue of the chain of beings in Vallisnieri, see Badaloni, 1968a, pp. 32–33 and pp. 220–221.
12. See "Intorno all'ordine della progressione e della connessione che hanno insieme tutte le cose create: A' miei stimatissimi compatrioti e dottissimi colleghi dell'Accademia de' Muti di Reggio," in Vallisnieri, 1721, pp. 421–437.
13. *Ibid.*, p. 436.
14. Letter from Antonio Maria Borromeo, Rome, 21 September 1711, in Vallisnieri, 1726, p. 103.
15. *Ibid.*, pp. 115–116.
16. *Ibid.*, p. 117.
17. Vallisnieri made this affirmation in "Lezione accademica intorno all'ordine della progressione" (Vallisnieri, 1726, p. 436), concluding a further clarification of the Hobbesian character of his chain of beings. On the theological discussions at Padua during Vallisnieri's period of teaching, see Vecchi, 1962, pp. 258–276. On Vallisnieri's intolerance towards the clergy and his sympathy for Giannone, see *ibid.*, pp. 260 and 262.
18. There is an analysis of Vallisnieri's hypothesis on the Flood in Rossi, 1979, pp. 100–104. Rossi does not seem to share the thesis that Vallisnieri did not explicitly deny the Flood. This was, however, the impression of many contemporaries, and Antonio Conti called him "the greatest enemy of the Flood that

I know" (undated letter from Paris to Vallisnieri, in A. Conti, 1972, p. 386).
19. Vallisnieri, 2d ed., 1728, p. 24. This book is composed of a collection of very long letters to various men with some of their responses. Among the most interesting are the anonymous "Annotazioni sopra due lettere del sig. cavaliere Antonio Vallisnieri intorno al diluvio," actually written by Jacopo Riccati.
20. See *ibid.*, pp. 45ff, for the hypothesis that the world changed imperceptibly without unforeseen catastrophes.
21. *Ibid.*, p. 50.
22. *Ibid.*, p. 65.
23. On Giovanni Maria Lancisi, see Bacchini, 1920. The close tie between this important Roman figure and Vallisnieri's circle of the *Giornale de' Letterati* is documented by Lancisi's letters to Vallisnieri, published by Roncetti, 1845, pp. 150ff. Among his papers at the Biblioteca Lancisiana in Rome, there is an unpublished and important Italian translation of Fontenelle's famous work of decidedly Libertine inspiration, the *Trattenimenti sopra la pluralità de' mondi, tradotti in idioma italiano da A.A.P.A. e dedicati a G. M. Lancisi (Fondo Lancisi, ms. 362)*. I have not been able to establish who A.A.P.A. is, but the existence of this elegantly bound translation obviously intended for circulation in Lancisi's circle argues in favor of the papal doctor's open-mindedness in his thought, which merits serious study.
24. On Gimma, see below, chapter 5.
25. Letter from Padua, dated 18 April 1727, published in A. Conti, 1972, pp. 415–418, also cited in Badaloni, 1968a, p. 109.
26. Lacking any recent study on Count Riccati, see Michieli, 1942–1943; for a good biography, one must turn to the eighteenth-century "Vita del conte Jacopo Riccati" by his pupil Cristoforo di Rovero, in Riccati, 1761–1764, vol. 4, pp. i–lx.
27. The Paduan astronomer Stefano Degli Angeli had Riccati study Newton's work, according to the "Vita del conte," *ibid.*, p. vii.
28. On Riccati's considerable scientific importance, see his entry in the *Dictionary of Scientific Biography*, vol. 11, pp. 399–401; Loria, 1950, pp. 659–663.
29. Among Count Riccati's works one should note his repudiation of the system of Malebranchian Chinese boxes accepted by Vallisnieri and Conti (written under the pseudonym Cesare Marangoni), as well as his interesting *Discorsi di argomento ecclesiastico* (1761–1764, vol. 4, pp. 187ff), which show a profound erudition, especially regarding biblical exegesis, and considerable accomplishment as a scholar of ecclesiastical history.
30. "Vita del conte," *ibid.*, vol. 4, p. xxxvi. On Vallisnieri's relationship with Riccati, see the latter's "Lettera al sig. cavaliere A. Vallisnieri . . ." (*ibid*).
31. On the contacts between Conti and Riccati, see the "Lettera al sig. abbate conte Antonio Conti patrizio veneziano sopra le Prose e poesie da lui messe in pubblico e principalmente sopra la Dissertazione dell'aurore boreali," in which Riccati enthusiastically shared Conti's theses (*ibid*). On the interest Conti displayed towards the scientific opinions Riccati expressed, see "Vita del conte," *ibid.*, p. xxxviii.
32. See Brusatin, 1980, pp. 140–176.
33. His numerous articles in the *Giornale de' Letterati* regarding the central forces and disputes with Morgagni and Johann Bernoulli in the "Difesa del corollario II della proposizione XXXVI del libro II dei Principia matematici della filosofia naturale del cavalier Isacco Newton" are in Riccati, 1761–1764, vol. 3, pp. 40–45.
34. *Saggio*, in *ibid.*, vol. 1, p. 17.
35. *Ibid.*, p. 34.
36. *Ibid.*, p. 135.

37. *Ibid.*, p. 136. Riccati affirms that the Spinozan God did not coincide with Cartesian extension but rather with matter, whose properties are not reducible to extension alone. From this came his Tolandist reading of Spinoza, interpreted as a philosopher near to Straton of Lampsacus's thought (*ibid.*, p. 138). For Riccati, the essential contradiction of Spinozism lay in the impossible attempt to reconcile cosmic determinism and mankind's free will.

38. *Ibid.*, p. 137.
39. *Ibid.*, p. 44.
40. *Ibid.*, p. 46.
41. See, for example, the affirmations of Rambaldo degli Azoni Avogaro, Riccati's heir, who in the opening of the "Discorsi di argomento ecclesiastico" underscored the role of revelation in Conti's writings (*ibid.*, vol. 4, p. 187).
42. See *Riflessioni fisiche*, in *ibid.*, p. 124.
43. See *ibid.*, p. 137.
44. *Ibid.*, p. 145.

4: THE MATERIALIST READING OF THE *PRINCIPIA*

1. On Cuenz's Christian Spinozism, see Badaloni, 1970; Cuenz maintained that souls were themselves material and became immaterial following a precise, voluntary act of God, who was Himself material. The soul's materiality was drawn from Lockean considerations. For Cuenz, as for Riccati, the universe was created from an unfolding of force-matter, whose basis lay in the initial divine fiat. On Cuenz's theories and the success that they enjoyed in the eighteenth century, see Ricuperati, "Il problema della corporeità dell'anima dai libertini ai deisti," in Bertelli, 1980, pp. 413–414.
2. On the issue of the neutrality of the ideological plan of modern science, see Colletti, 1980, pp. 51–62.
3. On the problem of the relationship between Toland and Leibniz, see Giuntini, 1979, pp. 160–161; Casini, 1969, pp. 218–219.
4. See Cassirer, 1951.
5. According to Nicola Badaloni (A. Conti, 1972, p. 18), the true inventor of the collection was Conti, to whom were addressed several important letters from Leibniz and Newton which appear in the compilation.
6. Rathegel wrote that Dereham had brought the recently published *Recueil de diverses pièces sur la philosophie, la religion, les mathématiques par Mr. Leibniz, Clarke, Newton* (1720). It included letters from Leibniz attacking Newton's philosophy, with Clarke's responses; Newton's replies about the invention of the infinitesimal; Leibniz's notes on Locke's *Essay*, Malebranche's research; and other works (Florence, 11 November 1720, S.N.S.P., XXXI.A.6, c. 77r).
7. Letter from Naples dated 5 January 1723 (S.N.S.P., XXXI.A.6, c. 111r).
8. When he wrote these letters, Leibniz had in mind Toland's ideas and the debates over deism in England; see Giuntini, 1979, p. 372. See Koyré, 1957, for an excellent analysis of the *Recueil*.
9. Des Maizeaux, 1740, vol. 1, p. 2.
10. Wishing to schematize the respective arguments, Clarke responded harshly, affirming that, far from giving new life to materialism and English deism, the *Principia* was their principal obstacle. The Newtonian theories were in fact "the sole principles that prove that matter is the smallest and least considerable part of the universe" (*ibid.*, p. 4). On the Clarke-Leibniz debate, see Koyré, 1957; Casini, 1969; Jammer, 1954.
11. See *Index*, 1783, p. 288.
12. On the few known exemplars of manuscripts of Toland's works in French, some of which probably passed through Giannone's hands in Vienna, see

Ricuperati, 1970a, pp. 415–416. On the circulation of Toland's manuscripts in the circle of nobles in the Veneto and Lombardy, especially that of Marquis Teodoro Alessandro Trivulzio's friends, see Ricuperati, 1970b; Bertelli, 1968, p. 530. On the diffusion of heterodox works in the Veneto, see also Zambelli, 1972, pp. 621–622.

13. See *Acta eruditorum* 3 (1729): 308–356.
14. On Radicati di Passerano's important political-cultural plan, see Venturi, 1954. The most important text documenting the profound influence that Toland exercised on Radicati is the *Philosophical Dissertation upon Death* (1732), which appeared in London. For a more lengthy discussion of Radicati's work, see the Italian edition.
15. A basic work on Pietro Giannone is Ricuperati, 1970a. Of noteworthy interest are the *Atti del Convegno di studi nel tricentenario della nascita di Pietro Giannone*; see *Pietro Giannone*, 1980.
16. In Giannone's *Agger obiectus Cartesianorum vorticum eluvionibus*, in addition to the internal structure of the brief treatise that recalls Galileo's *Epistola* in its themes and presentation, there is an explicit reference to a work of "the most ingenious Celestino Galiani" that circulated unpublished throughout Italy (Turin, State Archives, *Carte Giannone*, mazzo 1 (Ja. V), n. 19, c. 5r).
17. Giannone, 1971, p. 1005.
18. *Ibid.*, p. 995.
19. See E. Garin in "Galileo e la cultura del suo tempo" (1975b, pp. 117–119), where he sets Galileo against Cremonini and the Libertinism of Paduan Aristotelians. On overcoming the yet Aristotelian and qualitative science professed by the Libertines in opposition to Galileo, see Lenoble, 1976, chapter 2; Spini, 1950, pp. 148–149.
20. See Ricuperati, 1970a, p. 492.

Five: Celestino Galiani: Religious Uneasiness and Crises of the European Mind

1: HIS EARLY TRAINING

1. See Badaloni, 1968a.
2. See Croce, 3d ed., 1972, p. 178.
3. See Sbigoli, 1884, p. 81. Actually, according to Rotta ("Montesquieu," in Tarello, 1971, pp. 108–109), the punitive measures enacted against Niccolini were taken in the 1740s because of the "little measured" discussions he held in 1748 in England and Holland; Rosa (1964, pp. 10–11) agrees. On Niccolini, see Codignola, 1947, pp. 61ff; Dammig, 1945, pp. 130ff.
4. See Venturi, 1969, pp. 54–55, and especially Francovich, 1975, pp. 59–60.
5. On the importance and positive meaning that the concordat of 1741 had for southern jurisdictionalism, see Ajello, 1961, pp. 25–96; Rosa, "Politica concordataria, giurisdizionalismo e organizzazione ecclesiastica nel Regno di Napoli sotto Carlo di Borbone," in Rosa, 1969, pp. 119ff.
6. On this early confrontation with the Inquisition, see Nicolini, 1951, pp. 30–33. The congregation of seven cardinals (Ferdinando Dadda, Giambattista Gabrielli, Ranuccio Pallavicini, Fulvio Astalli, Carlo Agostino Fabroni, Lorenzo Imperiali, and Tommaso Maria Ferrari), instituted in order to judge Galiani's theses, after long meetings between 1710 and 1713, decided on Galiani's innocence, thanks to a last-minute intervention by Clement XI at the request of Imperiali and Cardinal Giannantonio Davia. For some details of this dramatic affair, see the few confidential letters Galiani sent to Piergerolamo Bargellini,

preserved oddly enough among Guido Grandi's papers (B.U.P., *Carteggio Grandi*, ms. 97, cc. 219*v*ff). Until now, the episode has been considered a simple Inquisitorial action limited to Galiani's person; as we shall later see, it was part of a general increase in pressure by the Curia, beginning in 1708, against all those in Rome who began to broach dangerous Spinozan themes of biblical exegesis.

7. Galiani's letter to Bargellini, Rome, 25 July 1711, B.U.P., *Carteggio Grandi*, ms. 97, c. 220*r*.

8. Among Galiani's pupils were cardinal Silvio Valenti Gonzaga, secretary of state for Benedict XIV from 1740; Abbot Giovanni Perlas, son of the marquis of Rialp and prime minister of Charles VI; cardinals Fortunato Tamburini and Giuseppe Spinelli; Count Gianluca Pallavicini, plenipotentiary minister and captain-general of Lombardy in 1746; and Abbot Ernst von Harrach, son of the Neapolitan viceroy. Galiani always devoted much attention to the organization of academies. There has been much discussion about the famous Neapolitan Accademia delle Scienze of 1732; little is known of analogous institutions that also bore Galiani's imprint. The creation in Genoa in 1724 of an academy of study reserved for nobles that aimed to educate the new ruling class (Rotta, 1961) deserves careful research. Galiani's support for the Accademia degli Illuminati of Foggia in 1733 merits similar attention (see some letters on this matter preserved in Naples, S.N.S.P., XXXI.C.8, cc. 78*r*ff).

9. See the *Ristretto della vita di Celestino Galiani*, S.N.S.P., XXIX.C.7, cc. 7*r*ff.

10. *Ibid.*, c. 6*r*. Cited in Ajello, "Cartesianismo e cultura oltremontana," in *Pietro Giannone*, 1980.

11. See above, chapter 2.

12. There is no precise proof documenting this hypothesis; nevertheless, I believe we can fairly certainly place his autobiography in the framework of the important "Progetto ai letterati d'Italia per scrivere la loro vita," made public by Count Giovanni Artico di Porcía in Angelo Calogerà's *Raccolta d'opuscoli scientifici e letterari* (1728). Scholars whose autobiographies were requested include Vico, Doria, Francesco Maria Spinelli, Niccolò Cirillo, and others. On Porcía's project, see Zambelli, 1972, pp. 8–15.

13. See *Ristretto della vita di Celestino Galiani*, S.N.S.P., XXIX.C.7, c. 15*rv*.

14. *Animadversiones physis*, S.N.S.P., XXX.D.5, c. 2*r*.

15. On the importance of the example of the statue to empiricist philosophers in the eighteenth century, who used it to demonstrate the "conquest of objectivity" in the field of gnosiology, see Guerci, 1978, pp. 38–39.

16. Galiani's letter to Antonio Conti, undated [1712], S.N.S.P., XXXI.B.1, c. 296*v*. Although the letters were addressed to the Oratorian Father Giovan Battista Baroni, he was only the intermediary between Conti and Galiani.

17. *Animadversiones physis*, S.N.S.P., XXX.D.5, c. 34*v*.

18. See *ibid.*, cc. 4*r*ff.

19. See C. Galiani, "Osservazioni alla quarta proposizione," in *Osservazioni sopra il libro di Newton*, S.N.S.P., XXX.D.2, cc. 112*v*ff.

20. See *Animadversiones physis*, S.N.S.P., XXX.D.5, c. 3*rv*.

21. *Ibid.*, c. 4*v*.

22. *Ibid.*, c. 9*rv*.

23. *Ibid.*, c. 11*r*.

24. *Ibid.*, c. 12*r*.

25. Confirmation of the enlightened Catholics' favorable attitude towards Gassendi's naturalism exists in one of the few and almost unknown scientific works of Giovanni Bottari, who was closely tied to the Roman group beginning in 1713–1714. In his *Tre lezioni sopra i tremoti dedicate all'E. principe il signor Cardinale Alemanno Salviati legato d'Urbino* (B.C.R., ms. 1884, 44.D.42), written in 1728

and published anonymously in Calogerà's *Raccolta d'opuscoli scientifici e filologici* 7 (1733): 1ff, we find the same basic theses articulated by Galiani.

26. Leprotti's letter to Bianchi, Rome, 23 March 1733, cited in Ajello, "Cartesianismo e cultura oltremontana," in *Pietro Giannone*, 1980, p. 174.

27. There are eleven letters, written between 1709 and 1721, that synthesize an important part of the history of infinitesimal calculus in Italy (S.N.S.P., XXX.D.3).

28. Among the best works for understanding the intricate philosophical and scientific problems generated by the new calculus are those of Castelnuovo, 1962, and Geymonat, 1947.

29. On Burnet's visit to Rome, see above, chapter 3. The letters Burnet and Galiani exchanged on the problem of analysis are extremely interesting for their clarification of the kinematical interpretation that the Newtonian school gave to the meaning of the derivative. See the letter from Venice dated 22 November 1709 (S.N.S.P., XXXI.A.2, cc. 72rff).

30. This brief treatise written in French on infinitesimal calculus can be found among Galiani's papers (S.N.S.P., XXXI.B.1, cc. 299rff). Among Roman scholars, both Domenico Quartieroni and Vitale Giordani, mathematician at the Sapienza University, always remained very hostile to the new algorithm.

31. The letters between Guido Grandi and Antonio Conti (Tenca, 1953–1954, pp. 103ff) are especially interesting for understanding the profound philosophical implications that the analysis brought. Among the issues they dealt with was the relationship between the structure of matter and the reality of the mathematical infinitesimal. The debate between Varignon and Grandi over the interpretation of this latter problem was at the center of Italian scholars' attention, engendering many articles in the *Giornale de' Letterati*.

32. Conti's letter to Hermann from January 1710, with the plea that it be sent along to Galiani as well, published by Croce, 1907, p. 37.

33. *Ibid.*, p. 38. Conti confuses the concept of the differential with that of the derivative, a common occurrence among many scholars puzzled by the divergence between the philosophical underpinnings of the Newtonian and Leibnizian analyses.

34. Galiani's letter to Conti, Rome, undated (but 1712), S.N.S.P., XXXI.B.1, c. 295v.

35. See Badaloni, 1968a, pp. 27–49.

36. Grandi's work is among the most telling examples of that combination of mathematical research and philosophical investigations quite common among scholars of his day. Examining a famous series that took its name from him, namely the sum of infinite terms $a - a + a \ldots$, he came to the erroneous conclusion that it converged on the value $a/2$. Actually, in the absence of any notion about the interval of convergence, Grandi did not notice that this was a typical series oscillating between the null value and the value of a. Through a peculiar interpretation, he claimed to demonstrate the passage from the null to a finite value in the presence of infinite terms, just as the infinite God could create the world from nothing.

37. See Pascal's thoughts on the mathematical infinite in the first chapter of the *Pensées*; on Pascal, see Serini, 1942.

38. Galiani's letter to Conti, Rome, undated [1712], S.N.S.P., XXX.B.1, c. 295v.

2: THE EPISTEMOLOGICAL DEBATE WITH ANTONIO CONTI

1. See above, chapters 1 and 4.

2. Conti, 1716, pp. 135–136.

3. See Badaloni, 1968a, pp. 50–57.

4. On this well-known protagonist of French culture and his relationships with Conti, see Manuel, 1959, pp. 90–100. While Simon (1961) is somewhat de-

batable, see Cantelli, 1974, part one, fasc. III, pp. 264–283; part two, fasc. IV, pp. 386–406.

5. On Fréret's *Lettre*, see Wade, 1938, pp. 187–194; Badaloni, 1968a, pp. 97–99.

6. See Badaloni's analysis of these themes (1968a, pp. 64ff).

7. Montesquieu had met Galiani on his trip to Italy and considered him among the "leading savants of Italy" (Montesquieu, 1950, vol. 2, p. 1213). In 1713 Maffei personally lobbied for Celestino Galiani to obtain the chair in mathematics at the University of Padua. He wrote to Vallisnieri, seeking to convince him to support Galiani's candidacy and praising his qualifications (Garibotto, 1955, p. 65).

8. Conti's letter to Galiani, Padua, 5 May 1712, in Croce, 1907, p. 40.

9. *Ibid.*, pp. 41–42.

10. Galiani's letter to Conti, Rome, undated [1712], S.N.S.P., XXXI.B.1, c. 296r.

11. *Ibid.*, cc. 296v–297r.

12. Baroni's letter to Galiani, Venice, 18 January 1716 (S.N.S.P., ms. XXXI.B.1, c. 301r). Conti's autobiography points to Baroni's importance in his intellectual development. Baroni shared his friend Galiani's sympathies for Locke and discussed the English philosopher's books with Conti in the 1710s (Conti, 1756, vol. 2, p. 14).

13. On these important contacts, see Nicolini, 1951, pp. 65–67. The trips took place 1719–1721 and 1729–1730. Again on the complex question of the regulation of water, in 1717 Galiani (and his pupil Bernardo Andrea Lama) had to oppose Conti's Parisian initiatives, which sought to align the scientists of the Académie des Sciences in favor of the Venetian theses against those of the pope; see Ricuperati, 1968a, p. 22.

14. See Conti, *Il globo di Venere. Sogno*, in Conti, 1739, vol. 1, pp. iii–xxix. The *Sogno* was composed in 1734 and read in an early version at a Venetian academy where Cerati was present.

15. See Badaloni, 1968a, pp. 155–156.

16. See *Dalla dissertazione sulla egizia poesia: Lettera a mons. Galiani*, in A. Conti, 1972, p. 285.

17. Franco Venturi has rightly spoken of the enlightened Catholics' seizing of "power," especially in the realm of cultural institutions during the 1730s in Italy (Venturi, 1969, pp. 22–23).

18. A. Conti, 1972, p. 286.

19. *Ibid.*, p. 285.

20. *Ibid.*, pp. 296–297.

21. *Ibid.*, pp. 288–289.

22. *Ibid.*, p. 290.

23. *Ibid.*, p. 294.

24. See *Riflessioni fisiche intorno l'anima unita al corpo*, in Riccati, 1761–1764, vol. 4, pp. 145ff.

25. There are two autograph codices of the *Scienza morale* preserved in Naples (S.N.S.P., XXXI.B.1, cc. 174r–266r; XXX.C.16, cc. 1r–68r), together with a brief treatise entitled *Schediasmata delle morali scienze* (S.N.S.P., XXX.D.2, cc. 69r–74r) and an autograph dealing with the same subject. Of the two codices, the second incorporates the interlinear corrections Galiani added to the first; it has, therefore, been considered the more authoritative of the two, representing the author's definitive revision. We refer to this latter codex in the following notes, advising the reader of the error in the codex's pagination in folios 34r–43v, which occur twice. To avoid misunderstandings in references to the second set of pages, they will be indicated as cc. 34 bis r–43 bis v. While the text cannot be dated precisely from the indications in the codex, I

am convinced the *Scienza morale* was produced during Galiani's stay in Rome, particularly the years 1720–1730. This is apparently confirmed by some letters between Cerati, Nicolini, and Galiani regarding the debate on Locke's thought. Authors such as Descartes, Newton, Bayle, Pufendorf, and Lafitau, whom we find discussed in the *Scienza morale*, were studied and discussed by Galiani during the Roman years, while during the period he spent in Naples, the *cappellano maggiore*'s interest shifted principally to scientific and economic problems, without overlooking his increased public responsibilities.

26. C. Galiani, *Della scienza morale*, c. 24v.
27. *Ibid.*, c. 26v.
28. On this problem in Locke, see Viano, 1960, pp. 453–461; De Ruggiero, 1972, vol. 1, pp. 74–75; Pala, 1953.
29. C. Galiani, *Della scienza morale*, c. 30v. In order to deal with the complex question of substance, Galiani explicitly follows Locke's *Essay Concerning Human Understanding*, book 2, ch. 12.
30. See Gregory, 1961, pp. 82–92.
31. C. Galiani, *Della scienza morale*, c. 32v. Galiani takes from Locke the criticism, in its entirety of those identifying substance with extension (*Essay*, book 3, ch. 6, para. 21).
32. I. Newton, *Principia mathematica*, 1726, p. 529.
33. On the Dutch scientists' mathematical empiricism, see Gori, 1972; Brunet, 1931b; Cassirer, 1951; Pala, "Lo sperimentalismo francese dal 1650 al 1750," in Solinas, 1973, pp. 225ff.
34. On Conti's gnosiology, see Badaloni, 1968a, pp. 118ff.
35. In Italy even Conti, who was certainly not among the scholars most loyal to Catholic orthodoxy, judged Locke "obscure" and saw a "half-atheism" in his allowing the possibility that God added thought to extension (Conti, 1756, vol. 2, p. 14).
36. Referring to the continual disputes about religious problems in Europe, Nicolini wrote of an encounter, which he described as "a pleasure," wherein he witnessed a debate on mathematical issues between Galiani and a follower of Malebranche (Nicolini's letter to Bottari, Rome, 29 July 1729, B.C.R., ms. 1891, 44.E.1¹, c. 20r).
37. See Locke, *Essay* (book 2, ch. 1, para. 9). Locke's affirmation that it is easier for our minds to attribute to God the power to give "to matter a faculty of thinking, than that He should superimpose on it another substance with a faculty of thinking" (*Essay*, book 4, ch. 3, para. 6) fed the dispute.
38. See Nicolini's letter to Galiani, Rome, 19 March 1735, S.N.S.P., XXXI.A.5, c. 38r. The 2,500 copies of the edition produced by the bookseller Claude François Joré of Rouen had begun to circulate in Paris only a year earlier.
39. Addressing Girolamo Tartarotti in March 1733, Muratori wrote that Locke's assertion that matter could think horrified him, and he affirmed his religious faith (Falco and Forti, 1964, vol. 2, pp. 1916–1917).
40. C. Galiani, *Della scienza morale*, c. 39 bis v.
41. *Ibid.*, c. 35 bis v.
42. *Ibid.*, cc. 37 bis v–38 bis r.
43. See *ibid.*, c. 42 bis rv. Galiani's solution is the same as the one that Genovesi and Lami will give against the Cartesians' automatism and similar to that of the Frenchman Condillac. On this important matter at the center of the European debate in the seventeenth and eighteenth centuries, see Kirkinen, 1960; Rosenfield, 1940. For an analysis of the dispute in Italy, see Garin, 1966, vol. 2, pp. 912–914; Ricuperati, "Il problema della corporeità dell'anima dai libertini ai deisti," in Bertelli, 1980, pp. 369–415.

44. C. Galiani, *Della scienza morale*, cc. 13v–14r.
45. *Ibid.*, c. 56r. On Clarke's analogous stance, see Casini, 1969, p. 142.
46. C. Galiani, *Della scienza morale*, c. 55v.
47. See *ibid.*, c. 55r. On these themes—widely debated in early-eighteenth-century Europe—see Roger, 1963, pp. 370ff. With respect to Italy, see above, chapter 4.

3: FROM THE *TRACTATUS THEOLOGICO-POLITICUS* TO THE *REASONABLENESS* OF CHRISTIANITY

1. See Caravale and Caracciolo, 1978, vol. 14.
2. See *ibid.*, pp. 482ff. Pastor (1941, vols. 33 and 34) insists that Clement XI had a positive role in Roman culture; see also Giuntella, 1971.
3. See above, chapter 4, for more on the political and cultural import of the "Literary Republic" that Muratori proposed to Italian intellectuals in the 1710s.
4. See Quondam, 1973, and Ricuperati's "Introduzione" to Cesarotti, 1978, p. xxxvi.
5. On this academy, see Maylender, 1926–1930, vol. 2, pp. 40–42; Paschini, 1960, pp. 371–382.
6. The new regulations and a lengthy letter to Clement XI regarding the projected restructuring are preserved among Bencini's manuscripts (Bencini, *Scritti sulla gerarchia ecclesiastica*, Turin, Biblioteca Nazionale, ms. O².III.35, respectively cc. 171rff and cc. 7rff).
7. On the importance of the Circle of the Drum in Rome in the early eighteenth century, see Caracciolo, 1968, pp. 10ff.
8. Bencini, "Della maniera e metodo de i Ragionamenti," in *Scritti sulla gerarchia* (see n. 6), cc. 172rff.
9. See Bencini, "Statuti e regole dell'Accademia ecclesiastica sopra i Concili," *ibid.*, cc. 181rff.
10. On Bencini, see Quazza, 1966, pp. 204–207, and Ricuperati, 1968a, pp. 35–36, for more on his teaching stint in Turin beginning in 1718.
11. See the untitled "argument" in Bencini, *Scritti sulla gerarchia* (see n. 6), cc. 219r–222v. On eighteenth-century euhemerism, see the classic work of Manuel, 1959.
12. Bencini, *Scritti sulla gerarchia*, c. 219r.
13. See *ibid.*, c. 221r.
14. Of special interest is the argument that examines those Mediterranean cultures that first attributed "the divine cult to fire," *ibid.*, cc. 311r–317v.
15. The lecture read in Rome in the college De Propaganda Fide was the basis of Bencini's inaugural lecture for the academic year of 1720 in Turin, and it evoked diverse reactions. Although in Rome it elicited no particular comment, in Turin the growing interest in Spinoza in the Piedmont was unhesitatingly attributed to similar teachings. See Ricuperati, 1966b, pp. 354–355.
16. Bencini, *Tractatio historico-polemica* [1720], p. 25. Two copies of the lecture given at De Propaganda Fide and then substantially repeated in the *Tractatio* are found among Bencini's manuscripts, cc. 13r–17v and cc. 30rff, both entitled *Trium impostorum liber*. In all likelihood, Bencini took inspiration for the argument in this work from Chancellor Kortholt, who in 1680 published a severe treatise against Hobbes, Spinoza, and Herbert of Cherbury entitled *De tribus impostoribus magnis*.
17. Bencini [1720], pp. 25–27.
18. *Ibid.*, p. 25.
19. See *ibid.*, p. 26.

20. See *ibid.*, p. 27.
21. There are numerous citations from Spinoza in the *Tractatio*, especially in the part dedicated to examining the *Sacrorum Bibliorum Veteris Testamenti tabulae*. Although the citations are in an argumentative tone, they are pertinent and betray an attentive reading of Spinoza's works.
22. Cited in Venturi, 1954, p. 125.
23. On the importance of chronological matters in these years, see Hazard, 1963; Rossi, 1969, pp. 150–225; Ricuperati, 1965b, pp. 602–638; Dini, 1979. As yet there is no thorough monograph on Bianchini; see, however, Rotta, 1968, pp. 187–194.
24. Bianchini, 1823, vol. 1, p. 11.
25. *Ibid.*, p. 22.
26. *Ibid.*, p. 40. For an overall view of the European historiographical debate in these years, see Ricuperati, 1981.
27. The first scholar to emphasize the influence of Spinoza and Richard Simon in Garofalo's works was Hazard, 1963. Besides being a friend of Galiani and Bianchini, Garofalo played an active part in Giannone's defense (Giannone, 1960, pp. 154–155). Despite regret that Galiani had ultimately been chosen as *cappellano maggiore*, Garofalo assured him of imperial protection from ecclesiastical accusations against the Neapolitan Accademia delle Scienze, inviting him to resist (see below, chapter 6). On Garofalo, see Garms-Cornides, 1977, pp. 77–97.
28. Garofalo, 1707, p. x.
29. See *Index*, 1738, p. 133. The book caused a certain outcry throughout Italy because of the reaction of a Jewish Paduan named Raffaele Rabbegno, who wrote under the pseudonym Bernabò Scacchi (1710). This was followed by Garofalo's reply and the intervention of the *Giornale de' Letterati d'Italia* (2 [1710]: 499). For the entire argument and information on Garofalo, see Ricuperati, 1965b, pp. 618–619. There is an interesting *Memoriale della congregazione dell'Indice rispetto alla censura della opera. Considerazioni intorno alla poesia dell'Ebrei* in Rome, B.C., ms. 891, 41.A.3. The Inquisition's offensive against Galiani, headed by Giacomo Laderchi, was probably related to the atmosphere that had been created through the discussion of Garofalo's work. On Garofalo's participation in the Circle of the Drum, see Caracciolo, 1968, p. 66.
30. See Garofalo, 1707, p. 13. Spinoza expressed a similar opinion in the *Tractatus*, 1924, vol. 3, chapter 7, "De interpretatione Scripturae," pp. 97ff. Garofalo's basic thesis was that Hebrew poetry had to be interpreted from "a certain harmonious cadence expressed in rhyme" (p. ix).
31. Garofalo, 1707, p. 23.
32. *Ibid.*, p. 25. On the origins and history of Hebrew, Garofalo followed the lead of his teacher Domenico Aulisio, who had maintained along with Grotius and Dupin that, over time, Hebrew had been profoundly influenced by the Assyrian language and that of the peoples living around Palestine (on Aulisio's thesis see Ricuperati, 1970a, pp. 54–55). In the posthumous *Delle scuole sacre* (1723), Aulisio, who was also Giannone's teacher, broached Spinozan themes in a new exegesis of the Old Testament, opening the way for the works of men like Giannone and Garofalo. On Spinoza's fortunes in Italy, see Giancotti Boscherini, 1963; Badaloni, 1961.
33. Garofalo, 1707, p. 24. The matter of the interpretation of Masoretic punctuation is one of the crucial issues mentioned by Spinoza (see Spinoza, *Tractatus*, 1924, pp. 107–108).
34. Garofalo, 1707, second part: "Della poesia dei greci," p. 25.

35. In the *Ristretto della vita di Celestino Galiani* (S.N.S.P., XXIX.C.7, c. 12v), Galiani emphasizes the importance of his close contacts with Bencini, Garofalo, Gravina, Fontanini, and others, to his studies of sacred history.

36. See Galiani, 1708, p. 7. There is one copy of this extremely rare pamphlet, perhaps Galiani's only official publication, in the library of S.N.S.P. (XX.B.22).

37. On the import of the debate over the Flood among European intellectuals, see Bligny, 1973, pp. 47–63; Collier, 1934.

38. On the many-sided figure of Huet, in open conflict with Spinoza, see Dupront, 1930; Vernière, 1954, vol. 1, pp. 227–254; Ricuperati, 1970a, pp. 58–60.

39. See C. Galiani, *De Aegyptiorum origine*, S.N.S.P., XXX.D.2, cc. 75r–79r. In addition to Marsham's work, Galiani explicitly refers to Samuel Bochart's *Geographia* (c. 76r), which supported the remote historical origins of Phoenicians, and the works of Pliny, Macrobius, Plutarch, and Diodorus Siculus, as well as Saint Augustine's *De civitate Dei*, which denied the fabled Egyptian historicity. Despite his attempt at impartiality, Galiani betrayed his sympathy and interest in Marsham's affirmations; nevertheless, the *De Aegyptiorum origine* proves his complete mastery of the best European literature on the subject.

40. These two responses by Christian scholars to the dissemination of the myths of extreme antiquity are examined carefully by Rossi, 1969, pp. 182–215.

41. The notes (*Excerpta ex Hugoni Grotii notis*, S.N.S.P., XXX.D.2, cc. 215rff) are in fact ordered according to the same arrangement as Grotius's *Adnotationes ad Vetus Testamentum*; see Grotius, 1732, vol. 1.

42. On Galiani's possession of Spinoza's books, see Nicolini, 1918, pp. 105–132.

43. *Excerpta ex Hugoni Grotii notis*, c. 252v.

44. See the entry "Arabes," *ibid.*, c. 258v. On the problem of the origin of Hebrew and its successive transformations, Galiani followed Jean Le Clerc's theses; see his *Excerpta ex dissertationibus Clerici de lingua hebraica, auctore Pentateuchi et S. Scripturae interprete*, S.N.S.P., XXX.D.2, cc. 230rff.

45. See *Excerpta ex Hugoni Grotii notis* (see n. 41), cc. 236r–243v. The lengthy analysis, conducted with many references to Grotius, is carried out entirely through an examination of the semantic value of some Hebrew terms.

46. See "Urim et Thummin," *ibid.*, c. 222v.

47. See "Serpens," *ibid.*, c. 227v.

48. See *ibid.*, c. 227v. However, Galiani argued against the deist and anti-Christian conclusions that Herbert of Cherbury drew from the analyses of Jewish rites in the Old Testament.

49. Particularly interesting for the discussion that this subject had elicited throughout Europe is Galiani's examination of the historical origins of circumcision; see C. Galiani, *Observationes in Genesim et alias quattuor Moysis libros*, S.N.S.P., XXX.D.2, c. 281r, where, regarding this case and the rites of purification, he clearly accepted the theses of the Egyptian origins behind many of these rites.

50. On the hypothesis of Moses the pantheist in Libertine European culture, see Ricuperati, 1970a, p. 485, and especially his commentary on the first book of the *Triregno* in Giannone, 1971, pp. 602–603; see also Vernière, 1954, vol. 2, pp. 355–360. On Galiani's knowledge of Toland's works, see above, chapter 2.

51. C. Galiani, *Observationes in Genesim*, S.N.S.P., XXX.D.2, c. 275r.

52. Referring to the interpretation of *bārā*, Galiani wrote: "Le Clerc thinks that the ancient Hebrews, when they used such a word, were not at all thinking of the creation from nothing, nor that such a meaning was inherent in the word *bārā* [written in Hebrew characters], from which, in the thought of whomever spoke, the idea of a production from nothing was excluded. Le Clerc instead felt that they thought of the same thing that those who spoke Latin and Greek had in mind when they used the terms χτίζειν and *condere* [both mean 'to

found'].'' According to Galiani, there were also precise confirmations of the pantheist hypothesis in the analysis of Chaldean, Egyptian, and Phoenician cosmological traditions, brought to light by the works of Thomas Stanley, Hugo Grotius, and John Marsham.

53. On Le Clerc's biblical studies, see Barnes, 1938, pp. 110–116; Vernière, 1954, vol. 1, pp. 194ff; Voeltzel, 1968, pp. 30ff. Giuntini has pointed to the influence that Le Clerc's works commenting on sacred text had on Toland's writings (1979, pp. 99–119). In addition to the commentaries on the Pentateuch clearly inspired by Spinoza's method, Le Clerc's research into the myths and fables of ancient cultures proved to be particularly dangerous in the hands of the Free-Thinkers; see Cantelli, 1972, pp. 269–286. On Richard Simon, see Margival, 1900; Auvray, 1968, pp. 201–214.

54. C. Galiani, Excerpta ex dissertationibus Clerici, S.N.S.P., XXX.D.2, c. 230r. He drew Le Clerc's analyses on the authenticity of Moses' authorship of the Pentateuch almost entirely from a single book (Le Clerc, 1710a, vol. 1, pp. xxixff). In other notes, Galiani returned to the question of whether "God had truly revealed to Moses what was written in the sacred texts" (ibid., cc. 202rff); he had, however, concluded by accepting Le Clerc's thesis of Genesis' fundamental historicity as opposed to Richard Simon's thesis that all the biblical books should be considered "inspired."

55. Galiani's examination of other books in the Pentateuch (Observationes in Genesim, S.N.S.P., XXX.D.2, cc. 285r–290v) follows the lead of Le Clerc, 1710b.

56. The theme of de-Christianization from the eighteenth century through the affirmation of Enlightenment values is analyzed in Groethuysen, 1968; Goldmann, 1967; and, especially, Gay, 1966. Of fundamental importance for the historical interpretation of Christianity in the eighteenth century is Giarrizzo, 1954, pp. 301–401.

4: THE SOCINIAN TRADITION: REASON AND TOLERANCE

1. On Le Clerc's following among enlightened Catholics, in particular in Rome in the 1710s and 1720s, see above, chapter 2.

2. We ought not assume that Galiani was uninformed about these issues. In 1711 his English friend William Burnet sent him the works of the Socinians Samuel Crell (1700) and George Bull (1703); see Burnet's letter to Galiani, London, 6 April 1711, S.N.S.P., XXXI.A.2, cc. 74r–75r). Galiani had his pupil Bernardo Andrea Lama buy many books in Geneva of a theological nature such as Calvin's Institutions and the works of the Protestant Jean Daillé (Ricuperati, 1968a, p. 30). On the contribution of Socinian and Arminian thinkers to the growth of the Enlightenment, see Trevor-Roper, 1967.

3. Le Clerc, 1699, vol. 1, p. 356. Thomas Johnson sent the work to Galiani in 1715, according to a list of books that accompanied Johnson's letter from The Hague dated 19 July 1715 (S.N.S.P., XXXI.A.3, c. 277r). Among Le Clerc's other books that reached Galiani on that occasion were the Opera philosophica, with Thomas Stanley's new edition of the Historia philosophiae orientalis; the Traité de l'incredulité (1696), which Toland translated into English in 1697, confirming Le Clerc's noteworthy influence on Toland's development; Le Clerc's edition of Livy's historical works; the Veteris Testamenti libri historici ex translatione J. Clerici (1708); and the Historia ecclesiastica duorum primorum a Christo nato saeculorum e veteris monumentis depromta a Joanne Clerico.

4. On Muratori's bitter disagreement with Le Clerc, see L. A. Muratori, De ingeniorum moderatione, in Falco and Forti, 1964, vol. 1. For more on this dispute, see above, chapter 4.

5. See Excerpta ex dissertationibus Clerici, S.N.S.P., XXX.D.2.

6. There is a penetrating analysis of the dispute in Vernière, 1954, vol. 1, pp. 193–198.
7. See Le Clerc, 1698, vol. 1, pp. 125–130.
8. See *Oratio*, S.N.S.P., XXX.D.2, c. 36ff. One might be able to confirm Le Clerc's profound influence on Galiani from a comparison between the ideas in Galiani's *Oratio* and Le Clerc's *Oratio inauguralis de praestantia et utilitate historiae ecclesiasticae* (1712). On the *Sapienza*, see Di Simone, 1980. In those years Galiani became a well-respected theologian, even among ecclesiastical authorities, as his authoritative presence at the Roman Council of 1725 testifies; see Fiorani, 1978, pp. 76–77.
9. See his *Notizie ricavate dalla storia del Regno d'Italia del Sigonio*, which synthesized entire chapters of the *Historiae de Regno Italiae* (1574) (S.N.S.P., XXX.D.2, cc. 307r–383r), and especially his *Estratto della storia del Guicciardini*, a commentary on several chapters of Guicciardini's *Storia d'Italia*. As a teacher of the history of the Church at the Sapienza University, Galiani carried out an intensive program of study directed at reconstructing the primitive Church and its evolution in relation to political events. He availed himself of the work of almost all the most important scholars of ecclesiastical history, whether Protestant or Catholic: the works of canonist Zeger Bernard van Espen, Noël d'Alexandre (1699), Huguenot pastor Jacques Basnage (1706–1711), and the Anglican Humphrey Prideaux (1722), in addition to the celebrated works of Ellies Dupin, Mabillon, Martène, and Spanheim.
10. See *Chronologiae elementa*, S.N.S.P., XXX.D.2, cc. 177r–184r, where Galiani attempted to rationalize the study of chronology by examining the temporal and astronomical aspect of the subdivision of the year into weeks. On the historiographical debate in the early eighteenth century, see Bertelli, 1955. For an overall picture of the historiographical debate in the modern period, see Bertelli, 1973.
11. See above, chapter 3. O'Higgins (1970, pp. 211ff) has reconstructed the history of this first important French edition of the famous *Discourse of Freethinking* (which listed London on the title page, no publisher, 1714—although it was printed at Johnson's press in The Hague).
12. Collins, 1766, pp. 34ff.
13. *Ibid.*, p. 71.
14. *Ibid.*, p. 150.
15. Niccolini's letter to Galiani, Rome, 28 February 1733 (S.N.S.P., XXXI.A.5, c. 17v). On Niccolini's concept of freedom of thought and his bitter arguments against the degeneration of the Holy See, see his letters to Bottari in Amati, 1867.
16. Letter cited in Rosa, 1969, p. 116. Niccolini's deism also ought to be placed the context of his membership in the Masonic lodge of Florence, founded between 1731 and 1732. On the prevailing presence of Free-Thinkers and deists in this lodge, see Francovich, 1975, pp. 55–63. Galiani always demonstrated a special interest for Masonry as a phenomenon, particularly for the rationalist brand of the Hanover rite. In 1738 he read the anonymous *Rélation apologique* (1738), in which Toland's materialism from the *Letters to Serena* was indicated as the foundation of the Masonic ideology of the London Grand Lodge. See Bartolomeo Corsini's anonymous letters from Palermo to Galiani with pressing requests for this book (S.N.S.P., XXXI.A.7, c. 159r). The author of the *Rélation*, who hid behind the initials J.G.D.M.F.M., was none other than Martin Folkes, a mathematician and member of the Royal Society, and the grand master of the London Grand Lodge (see Francovich, 1975, p. 71). Folkes presented Galiani's candidacy for membership in the Royal Society. On the events during his Roman visit in 1734, see Leprotti's letters to Galiani in Niccolini, 1951, pp. 206–207.

17. Actually Galiani was able to gain useful information on the Libertine ferments that fed the debates of those years not only from Thomas Johnson and many friends throughout Europe but also from his trusted pupil Bernardo Andrea Lama, who had frequented the circles of Boulainvilliers and Fréret in France; see Ricuperati, 1968a. In Rome itself one could not ignore the renewed interest in European Libertine circles in the works of Giordano Bruno, for in 1710 Gianvincenzo Gravina, a man closely tied to Galiani, was forced to respond to pressing requests from Vienna for Bruno's books; see Quondam, 1968, pp. 138–140; Ricuperati, 1970a, pp. 421–422.

18. C. Galiani, *Excerpta ex Hugoni Grotii notis*, S.N.S.P., XXX.D.2, c. 288*v.*

19. See *ibid.*, c. 228*v.* Galiani drew his conclusion from the entirely worldly dimension of the Jewish rites from Simon, 1685, pp. viii, 164.

20. Grotius expressed his approval of such a wholly worldly vision of Mosaic law among the Hebrews, not so much in his *Adnotationes ad Vetus Testamentum* as in his *De veritate religionis christianae*, a work that, as we shall see, was quite important to Galiani. On the discussion of these matters between Toland and Giannone, see Ricuperati, 1970a, pp. 457–461.

21. See C. Galiani, *Excerpta ex Hugoni Grotii notis*, S.N.S.P., XXX.D.2, c. 262*v.* On the problem of the introduction of the idea of resurrection into Jewish religious culture during the Maccabees' persecution, see Bolgiani, 1975, pp. 61–66. While Toland, Giannone, and European Libertines in general preferred to accentuate how foreign to true Hebrew tradition ideas like immortality and resurrection were, Galiani, while accepting the Egyptian and partly Assyrian origins of such ideas, preferred to emphasize the gradual evolution of the Mosaic tradition from the primitive, totally earthly vision, as opposed to the New Testament theses. Therefore he saw no arbitrary break but merely a gradual uncovering of the evangelical truth through the use of reason, as in the spirit of the Socinians and theological rationalists.

22. If the ideological and, especially, the institutional reconstruction of Christianity is a religious problem posed not in political terms but, rather, in terms of individual conscience, Giannone appears to be entirely outside this process; see Ricuperati, 1970a. Despite the title Ricuperati gives chapter 8, "Giannone a Torino: riflusso del deismo e 'cristianesimo ragionevole' nelle opere dal carcere," the Socinian bases of the reasonableness of Christianity, as well as Locke's conclusions, are completely foreign to Giannone's mentality. The attempt to reconstruct Christianity on rational and theologically valid bases was never at the center of Giannone's concerns, for he accepted Newton's universe-machine only superficially, without ever understanding its profound philosophical, political, and theological import.

23. Le Clerc's edition appeared in 1709 and was placed on the *Index* in 1714. On Grotius, see De Michelis, 1967, and, especially, Corsano, 1948.

24. See Corsano, 1948, pp. 196–200.

25. See Grotius, *De veritate religionis christianae*, in Grotius, 1732, vol. 4, pp. 89–91. Emphasizing Grotius's severe observations in the *De veritate* about the wholly worldly ferocity of the Mosaic laws, Corsano (1948, p. 196) ties him to the Toland of the *Origines Iudaicae*, forgetting the fundamental role that Grotius assigned to the New Testament.

26. See Grotius, *De veritate*, 1732, pp. 72–88.

27. For an examination of Locke's work, see Viano, 1960, pp. 369–387; Firpo, 1980.

28. On the matter of Locke's dispute with the deists and his relationship with Socinianism, see Firpo, 1980; Hefelbower, 1918; McLachlan, 1941.

29. See Viano, 1960, pp. 354–358.

30. The scenario is similar to that of Grotius's *De veritate* and common among rationalist theologians, namely a distinction between Old and New Testaments, between Mosaic law and Gospel law. Locke, however, saw no clear-cut break, as Grotius did. While emphasizing the materiality of some Hebrew rites (not to be confused with Mosaic Law itself) directed at interpreting the "law of works" solely in an earthly sense, Locke long insists on the substantial continuity between the Mosaic message and that of Christ.

31. There has been much discussion on the ambiguous role Locke assigned to revelation regarding faith and human reason; see Firpo, 1980, pp. 53-59. For Locke, revelation did more than announce the truths of Christianity, which could also be understood through reason alone; it was a majestic confirmation of Christianity's validity for all humans on earth. He saw Christ's authoritative word as a necessary element for enlightening the peoples, the ignorant, and the great masses of the earth who, in contrast to the few select, intellectually and culturally privileged, would never have reached a knowledge of the truth by themselves. Locke's "Jesus is the Messiah" grew out of the troubled need to reconcile Christianity's absolute truths of an essentially moral type that one could reach through reason with the historical tradition that assigned an essential role to revelation.

32. See Viano, 1960, pp. 155-157.

33. Limborch's *Theologia christiana* appeared in 1686, and Galiani had its editor Johnson send him a copy from Holland in 1715. There are also elements of Locke's "*Reasonableness of Christianity*" in the *Theologia*; see Bourne, 1876, pp. 60-61; Viano, 1960, pp. 378-384. On the diffusion of moderate theological rationalism among some Italian scholars, especially in the Neapolitan environment, where scholars were certainly familiar with Galiani's work, see Zambelli, 1972, pp. 359-362.

34. See C. Galiani, *Della scienza morale*, c. 43r. On Galiani's harsh accusations against innatism and his reference to the *consensus gentium* in Catholic apologetics, see below, p. 170.

35. See C. Galiani, *Della scienza morale*, c. 43 bis *rv*.

36. *Ibid.*, c. 43v.

37. See Pinot, 1932; Etiemble, 1966. For the repercussions in Italy, see Zoli, 1972, pp. 409-467; Venturi, 1954, pp. 47-60.

38. Voltaire's ironic and penetrating affirmation in the *Siècle de Louis XIV* serves as a partial synthesis of the implications of this *querelle*, for the work emphasizes well the breadth of the themes handled and, particularly, the lucid involvement of deist and Libertine arguments in the matter, thanks to the *espris forts* (Voltaire, 1819, vol. 2, p. 391).

39. C. Galiani, *Rappresentazione per la causa delle controversie cinesi*, S.N.S.P., XXXI.B.1, c. 112r. The Biblioteca Corsiniana of Rome contains many writings about the dispute over Chinese rites, confirming the group of the Archetto's noteworthy interest in the matter. See B.C.R., ms. 1450, with some rather rare pamphlets on this issue, and especially ms. 1452, with notes written by Cardinal Neri Corsini.

40. C. Galiani, *Rappresentazione*, c. 113v.

41. *Ibid.*, c. 136r.

42. On the intransigent attitude of the philo-Jansenists in Italy, particularly in the works of Jacques Serry, see Venturi 1954, pp. 53-55. This was perhaps the only time that Galiani sympathized with the Jesuits' positions, to the detriment of his friends Bottari and Cerati. Actually he was anxious only to confirm the essential elements of Christianity, without any consideration of the disputes over rites.

43. Galiani argued bitterly against Bishop Maigrot's radicalism, for the bishop had expected that the discussed definitions of God should be expunged from Confucian texts (C. Galiani, *Rappresentazione*, cc. 133v–134r).
44. The entire affair was a test of Charles's determination for reform; see Venturi, 1969, pp. 75–78; Giura, 1978.
45. In his *Parere teologico* (S.N.S.P., XXXI.B.1, c. 238v), Galiani wrote that only the king's will, and no license from Rome, was necessary to introduce the Jews.
46. C. Galiani, *Parere teologico*, c. 245v. Denying the Church's moral or spiritual jurisdiction over non-Catholics, Galiani greatly limited the Church's mission and the Holy See's proclaimed universal rights over all souls, in particular in Catholic states. Although Galiani's defense of the Jews' rights matured in the realm of southern jurisdictionalism, it certainly found further confirmation in Lockeism and in Le Clerc's and Limborch's Socinian theories about tolerance.
47. C. Galiani, *Parere teologico*, c. 257v.
48. *Ibid.*, c. 252v. On the melancholic end of the entire affair, see Giura, 1978, pp. 73–76. Venturi (1969, p. 77) emphasized the wave of fanaticism and superstition unleashed by local preachers and its efficacy within the royal family as well, concluding: "In some ways, the king was as supersitious as the *lazzari* [Neapolitan mob]."
49. D'Aguirre's letter to Galiani, Turin, 20 April 1718, published by Mandalari, 1907, p. 144; Galiani's response is found in Milan, Biblioteca Trivulziana, ms. 196, c. 12rff.
50. There ought to be a careful investigation of this important aspect of Galiani's life, for there is valuable information in his correspondence. In a letter to the apostolic nuncio in Brussels, his longtime friend Monsignor Vincenzo Santini, Galiani indicated two safe addresses for hiding shipments of books from the Inquisition: the deacon of the cathedral at Leghorn, a certain Franceschi; and Cardinal Antonio Gualtieri in Rome (Rome, 12 January 1715, S.N.S.P., XXXI.B.1, c. 291r). Other occasional collaborators were Galiani's pupil Bernardo Andrea Lama and Abbot Francesco Landi, who, from Paris in 1718, sent him many famous books (see the list of books and their respective prices in Landi's letters to Galiani, S.N.S.P., XXXI.A.1, cc. 146rff). In addition to his dangerous relationship with Thomas Johnson, the editor for Toland, Collins and Radicati di Passerano and the supplier of prohibited works, in 1725 Galiani established business relations with an important Swiss publisher, Marc-Michel Bousquet, acquiring numerous books that he then resold to his Roman and Neapolitan friends (see Bousquet's six letters to Galiani, S.N.S.P., XXXI.A.2, cc. 86rff). On Bousquet's relationships with Italian scholars, see Crucitti-Ullrich (1974), who, however, overlooks Galiani. Other enlightened Catholics—Bottari, Nicolini, and Cerati—established a strong network of relations to guarantee the free circulation of prohibited books in Italy. See Carranza, 1974, pp. 148ff.

5: DELLA SCIENZA MORALE

1. See above, chapter 2.
2. See the chapter "Bonheur mondain et vie chrétienne," in Mauzi, 1960, pp. 180ff.
3. See Ajello, "Cartesianismo e cultura oltremontana," in *Pietro Giannone*, 1980, pp. 88–95.
4. On the internal divisions within the movement of thought that is known as jusnaturalism [the doctrine of natural law], see the works of Bobbio, 1980; Passerin d'Entrèves, 1962. On jusnaturalism's fundamental role in the formation of modern Neapolitan culture, to which Galiani remained tied after his initial visit to the city in 1708, see Mastellone, 1965.

5. Commenting on the second chapter of the first book of *De jure naturae et gentium*, which focuses on the certainty of moral laws, Barbeyrac broached the matter of the objectivity and rationality of moral science, citing Locke's *Essay* as the work that definitively theorized the possibility of arriving at a rigorously demonstrable ethics. See his "Préface du traducteur" in Pufendorf, 1712 (a translation of the 1706 edition), pp. xxii–xxvi. Bobbio (1980, pp. 502–504) has argued for the profound impact of natural sciences on moral, jusnaturalist doctrines.

6. C. Galiani, *Della scienza morale*, c. 1r.

7. On the importance for European culture of acquiring the concepts of cultural and moral relativism, see Landucci, 1972, pp. 23–84. For more on the theme of moral relativism, see Elliott, 1972; Gliozzi, 1977.

8. C. Galiani, *Della scienza morale*, c. 1v. Galiani copies a passage from book 2, chapter 2 ("De l'état de nature") of Pufendorf's *Droit de la nature et des gens*, 1712, p. 149. On Samuel Pufendorf's thought, see Krieger, 1965; Bobbio, "Leibniz e Pufendorf," in Bobbio, 1965, pp. 129–146.

9. See Landucci, 1972, pp. 185–234. Regarding the criticism of the universal consensus within European culture, see also Ajello, 1976a, p. 84; Cantelli, 1969, pp. 15ff.

10. On the especially friendly relations between Galiani and Vico, see Croce, 1948, vol. 1, pp. 227–229. On the dating of the *Scienza morale*, see above, pp. 320–321, n. 25.

11. See Garin, "Per una storia dei rapporti fra Bayle e l'Italia," in Garin, 1970, pp. 179ff; Cantelli, 1971; Landucci, 1972, pp. 273–331.

12. Belgrado (1970) presents a short overview and an ample bibliography of European scholars' various attitudes towards religion, from the old theory of imposture to the theses of Fréret, Bayle, d'Holbach, and Hume.

13. Vico, 1953, section 317. Vico addresses the issue of the ancient peoples' intense religiosity, expressed in fierce and bloody forms, in the *Scienza nuova prima* (1931, sections 132, 426, and 427).

14. C. Galiani, *Della scienza morale*, c. 65r. Galiani wrote explicitly: "See Bayle in the Diction[ary] p. 139." Regarding Bayle, see Labrousse, 1963–1964, 2 vols.; Ricuperati, 1968b, pp. 365–376; Cantelli, 1969; Paganini, 1980.

15. C. Galiani, *Della scienza morale*, cc. 40v–41r. These are quite momentous affirmations, taken, as we can see, from the first book of Locke's *Essay*. Locke was attacked forcefully by Edward Stillingfleet for these affirmations in the *Answer to the Modern Objections of Atheists and Deists* (1701).

16. "Fear made the first gods in the world," Vico repeatedly wrote (1931, section 485).

17. C. Galiani, "Della religione naturale," in *Della scienza morale*, c. 24r. The ideological divergences are nevertheless profound. As we shall see, Galiani was tied to the jusnaturalist tradition and insisted on the universal value of the law of nature. Vico, however, introduced a "natural law" for each nation, completely destroying the rationalist structure of the jusnaturalists. On Vico's criticism of jusnaturalism, see Landucci, 1972, pp. 307–308; Bobbio, 1980, pp. 507–508.

18. C. Galiani, *Della scienza morale*, c. 8rv.

19. On such complex issues as civil and natural society, see Landucci, 1972, pp. 93–177; Bobbio, 1968, pp. 19–36; Bobbio, 1977, pp. 22–30; Guerci, 1979, pp. 246–249. For an analysis of Pufendorf's theses on the state of nature and the various forms of natural society, on which Galiani drew amply, see Krieger, 1965, pp. 107ff.

20. C. Galiani, *Della scienza morale*, c. 18rv. Despite his affirmation (which he based on Aristotle) of mankind's natural sociability, we shall later see the central importance Galiani attributed to pleasure and pain in human social behavior.

21. Vico, 1953, section 13; *Scienza nuova prima*, (Vico, 1931), section 58.
22. On Vico's treatment of problems of chronology, see Rossi, 1969.
23. C. Galiani, *Della scienza morale*, c. 50rv.
24. See *ibid.*, cc. 50v–51r. On the importance in modern culture of the concept of the cumulative quality of knowledge, see Rossi, 1977, pp. 40–42.
25. C. Galiani, *Della scienza morale*, cc. 10v–11r. Just as Locke had done, Galiani took this formulation from Pufendorf, 1712, book 1, ch. 6, "De la règle des actions morales ou de la loi en générale," pp. 87–97. On Locke's concept of natural law, see Viano, 1960, pp. 80–101. Galiani borrowed from Pufendorf's works the subdivision into chapters for the *Scienza morale*, borrowing verbatim some of the chapter titles from Pufendorf 1707, in particular the titles to chapters 1 through 4. On the concept of natural law in the eighteenth century, see Guerci, 1978, pp. 163–188.
26. C. Galiani, *Della scienza morale*, c. 14v.
27. *Ibid.*, c. 20rv, where Galiani begins a lucid insertion of the *Essay's* theories into the general framework of Pufendorf's jusnaturalism. Galiani skillfully integrated Pufendorf's thought with Locke's hedonist theories, Bayle's idea of a primitive society of virtuous atheists, and, above all, Newtonian natural theology, which through its scientific certainties finally guaranteed the existence of a God-the-legislator and a universal natural law. From Locke, Galiani also drew the particularly innovative conviction that moral ideas were far from being (as tradition demanded) direct heirs of reason (Descartes) or direct reflections of man's divinity (Christian apologetics) but derived instead from the senses, as did all other ideas. On the importance of Locke's morality for the maturation of the European Enlightenment, see Koselleck, 1988.
28. Viano, 1960, pp. 140–143.
29. C. Galiani, *Della scienza morale*, c. 63r. It is a faithful translation of Locke's definition of good and evil and pleasure and pain, taken from the second book of the *Essay* (ch. 20, paras. 1–2).
30. See Venturi, 1969, p. 390.
31. C. Galiani, *Della scienza morale*, c. 17v. One of the best Italian scholars of the calculus of probability, Galiani also broached the problem of calculating pleasures and pains, (S.N.S.P., XXXI.B.1, cc. 303r–304v), without, however, reaching particular results. On Italian hedonism and particularly the dissemination of Locke's morality, see Losacco, 1903, pp. 181ff.
32. C. Galiani, *Della scienza morale*, cc. 42 bis v–43 bis r.
33. See Giuseppe Rathegel's letter to Galiani, Florence, 11 November 1720 (S.N.S.P., XXXI.A.6, c. 77r). The *Recueil de diverses pièces sur la philosophie, la religion naturelle, l'histoire, les mathématiques* (1720) from Amsterdam had additions to the English edition of 1717.
34. O'Higgins, 1970, p. 107.
35. *Ibid.*, pp. 101–110.
36. Locke, *Essay*, book 2, ch. 21, para. 31.
37. See *ibid.*
38. A section of codex S.N.S.P., XXX.C.16 (cc. 180rff) contains one of the copies of the *Scienza morale*. Brief notes indicate an outline for later chapters of the *Scienza morale*, entitled "Medicina dell'anima," "Lettera morale," and "Ricordi morali."
39. C. Galiani, *Della scienza morale*, c. 65r.
40. *Ibid.*, c. 15rv. Galiani's reflections on the deterministic nature of natural law are in part drawn from Pufendorf, 1712, book 1, ch. 7, pp. 114–132. Unlike Pufendorf and the rationalist theologians of the Anglican Low Church, Galiani did not accept the subtle distinction between "moral necessity" and "physical

necessity," according to which, on the one hand, God could turn the physical laws of the world on their heads, as Clarke wrote, forcing bodies to rise, yet, on the other, He could not wish for evil, because in that case He would be going against His very nature. For Galiani the basic scientific laws were intangible, and even God had to obey them. Science and human reason were for him unrelinquishable certainties on which one constructed all the other disciplines, from morality to economics. Hence we see the fascination and efficacy that Newtonianism held for eighteenth-century intellectuals; it lies at the basis of their confirmation of human reason's extraordinary creativity and certainty, opening the path to enlightened eudaemonism.

6: THE MANY FACES OF ENLIGHTENED CATHOLICISM

1. See the introduction to the *Filosofia morale* in Falco and Forti, 1964, vol. 1, p. 817.
2. See Badaloni, 1973, pp. 786-790.
3. Muratori, 1964, section 7, p. 162.
4. On Muratori's tolerant attitude towards Cartesianism, see above, chapter 4.
5. See Muratori, 1964, section 21, p. 332.
6. *Ibid.*, section 17, p. 282.
7. *Ibid.*, section 13, p. 255.
8. *Ibid.*, section 9, p. 196.
9. *Ibid.*, section 21, p. 345.
10. *Ibid.*, section 8, pp. 174-181.
11. Articulating a form of good Catholic's social doctrine, Muratori added that the world had long been limping and could not be changed (*ibid.*, section 35, p. 626). On Muratori's political thought, see Salvatorelli, 1975, pp. 20-40, who argues for Muratori's "Christian moralism," since his ideal government was "a paternalistic absolutism, with the accent on the adjective rather than the noun" (p. 24). In reference to the governmental ideal that Muratori expressed in his *Pubblica felicità*, Giorgio Falco has written that Muratori's goal was "a paternalistic regime, that police state, that enlightened despotism, that during the second half of the century would serve as a model for the princes of Europe" ("Introduzione" to Muratori's *Opere* in Falco and Forti, vol. 1, p. xxix).
12. Franco Venturi correctly observes that some of Muratori's writings (*Dei difetti della giurisdizione* and *Della pubblica felicità*) "along with Broggia's work represent the most mature expression of all reformist thought in Italy during the War of Austrian Succession." He affirms that Muratori "had reached the limits of the possibilities for renewal during the period and those of the efforts and determination of the first half of the eighteenth century. In order to go further, it was necessary that he no longer fear Sacred Scriptures and agree to break from them; in the face of this decision he had, instead, retreated" (Venturi, 1969, p. 159). Celestino Galiani was the fearless one, but it was certainly not by chance that his thoughts remained secret in his papers, which, nevertheless, through an underground network of diffusion, became a fundamental point of reference for the Neapolitan Enlightenment. On the cultural climate in which European Catholics' interest in new models of social and political behavior developed, see Rothkrug, 1965, pp. 234-351.
13. See Muratori, 1964, sections 1 and 2.
14. Venturi, 1969, p. 180.
15. On the importance of Galileo's theory of the double truth for Italian intellectuals in the early eighteenth century, see above, chapter 4.
16. There is a complete reconstruction of the affairs connected to the Inquisition's denunciation of the Accademia delle Scienze, which was created by Galiani

in Naples and accused of spreading Lockeism, in Ajello, "Cartesianismo e cultura oltremontana," in Pietro Giannone, 1980, pp. 163-177. See also below, chapter 6.

17. Letter cited in Rotondò, 1973, p. 1488. In a letter to Giovanni Bianchi, Antonio Leprotti, the most prestigious physician frequently cited, gave a lively account of the overall sense of attention that the entire group displayed for Locke's ideas, notwithstanding the danger of some affirmations: "There are some things regarding revelation and the confines of reason and faith which (to tell the truth) I would not know if they concur with our sacrosanct principles, but just since in this field I proposed the Creed as the foundation, I do not worry about what Locke or the other philosophers say" (Letter cited in Ajello, "Cartesianismo e cultura oltremontana," in Pietro Giannone, 1980, pp. 173-174).

18. See, for example, Woolf, 1973, p. 63; Nicolini, 1951, p. 218.

19. Galiani's letter to Santini, Rome, 12 January 1715, S.N.P.S., XXXI.B.1, c. 291r.

20. Ferdinando Galiani's letter to Francesco Sanseverino, Naples, 12 April 1772, published in F. Galiani, 1975, letter 88, p. 1144.

21. Galiani's rich correspondence provides evidence of the close relationships between Galiani and the Catholic hierarchy formed by requests, small favors, and cultural contacts. Especially important are several important cardinals' letters to Galiani, particularly those of Cardinal Neri Corsini (five letters, S.N.S.P., XXXI.A.1, cc. 116rff), Prospero Lambertini (later Pope Benedict XIV—five letters, ibid., cc. 129rff), Angelo Maria Querini (nineteen letters, S.N.S.P., XXXI.A.2, cc. 228rff), and Giuseppe Spinelli, archbishop of Naples (seven letters, ibid., cc. 274rff).

22. For more on Galiani's support of the Neapolitan Enlightenment, see Ajello, 1976a, pp. 391-395; Ajello, "Cartesianismo e cultura oltremontana," in Pietro Giannone, 1980, pp. 163-181. Referring to Galiani's creation of the Neapolitan Accademia delle Scienze in 1732, Franco Venturi states that with this initiative "we truly witness the first attempts at finding a philosophical justification for the new spirit then dawning" (Venturi, 1959b, p. 442).

Six: From the Natural Sciences to the Social Sciences: The Origins of the Neapolitan Enlightenment

1: THE TWILIGHT OF THE INVESTIGANTI'S HERITAGE

1. See Osbat, 1974, pp. 243-244.

2. On the presence of the Investiganti in the political affairs of the kingdom, see De Giovanni, 1970; Galasso, 1976; Villani, 1968; R. Villari, 1967.

3. On the new political consciousness flowering in the Neapolitan ceto civile, see Mastellone, 1965, pp. 13ff. On the formation of the bureaucratic structures of the modern state in Naples, invaluable for evaluating the political autonomy of the ceto civile, see Rovito, 1982.

4. On the importance of Grotius's and Pufendorf's jusnaturalism in eighteenth-century Neapolitan culture, see Mastellone, 1965, ch. 2. On D'Andrea as a philosopher and politician, see De Giovanni, 1958.

5. De Giovanni (1970, pp. 28-30) has argued that there was a progressive impoverishment of political activity among the ceto civile at the end of the century. Rather more problematic in evaluating the political and cultural role of the ceto civile is Quazza's survey (1971, pp. 63-85), which discusses Mastellone, Marini, Colapietra, Ajello, Ricuperati, and others.

6. See above, chapter 2.

7. On the arguments against the history developed by Monforte in the Accademia Palatina del Medinaceli, see Torrini, "Antonio Monforte," in Zambelli, 1973b,

pp. 112–115. I believe, however, that Torrini has overgeneralized the entire Investiganti group's "aversion for history," valid for individuals such as Porzio and Monforte, but certainly not for Giuseppe Valletta, who was also a member of the Accademia Palatina and attuned to developing historical and political themes without renouncing the scientific ideas of Cornelio and Di Capua. On Di Capua's interest in history, see Nicolini, 1932, p. 154. With Mabillon's and Burnet's trips in 1685 (Venturi, 1973), there was a notable increase in attention to Neapolitan history. The great debates on historical Pyrrhonism and Spinozan biblical exegesis (Ricuperati, 1970a, pp. 48–78) well document local scholars' new concern for the study of historical events.

8. See De Giovanni, 1970, pp. 35ff; Badaloni, 1961, p. 272.
9. See Suppa, 1971.
10. Ricuperati, 1972, p. 63. On the *lezioni* at the academy, see Rak, "Le lezioni dell'Accademia Medina Coeli. La tradizione manoscritta," in *Pietro Giannone*, 1980, vol. 2, pp. 659–689.
11. See Ricuperati, 1972, pp. 63–64. Rak (1971) has correctly reevaluated the importance of the late-Investigante Giuseppe Valletta in the academy's internal debate.
12. Salvatore Rotta ("Paolo Mattia Doria," in Cesarotti, 1978, p. 486) has rightly defined the Palatina's scientific culture as "retarded." Their most advanced scientific text was, in fact, the only lecture read by Monforte, entitled "Lezioni matematiche" (Torrini, "Antonio Monforte," in Zambelli, 1973b, pp. 110–114).
13. See Rotta, "Paolo Mattia Doria," in Cesarotti, 1978, p. 846.
14. Vico's *Orazioni inaugurali* (1699–1707), *De nostri temporis studiorum ratione* (1708), and *De antiquissima Italorum sapientia* (1710) are certainly a valuable testimony to Neapolitan scholars' search for new solutions to these problems.
15. See Ajello, 1976a, pp. 169ff, who examines the ultimate meaning of the qualification "Cartesian" in Neapolitan culture during the 1710s and 1720s. He has quite fairly written that the adjective was more often "attributed by the *veteres* than recognized without reservation by the *juvenes*, and it came to designate all the moderns' positions in the dispute, even if they were quite far from those of Descartes."
16. On Ciccarelli and his print shop, see above, chapters 1 and 2. See also Costa, 1980, on the protection Ciccarelli enjoyed from the dukes of Laurenzano. Ciccarelli's frenetic activities as a publisher are also noted in some of Metastasio's letters to d'Aguirre (Milan, Biblioteca Trivulziana, ms. 196, 46rff).
17. Despite the absence of a thorough study of this early, mysterious London edition of 1717, it is well known that the problem of printing the *De rerum natura* was particularly felt in Naples. Ajello ("Cartesianismo e cultura oltremontana," in Pietro Giannone, 1980, p. 142) has pointed out Alessandro Berti's letter to Ludovico Antonio Muratori proving the translation had been printed in Naples in 1717 and not in London, as the title page claimed. There had already been an earlier printing of a few copies in 1713, according to Vallisnieri's letter to Conti (Padua, 21 November 1713, in A. Conti, 1972, p. 383). See also Costa (1979, pp. 140–146), who confirms the suspicions about a Neapolitan edition of the *De rerum natura*.
18. See Comparato, 1970; Rak, 1971.
19. See Rak, 1971, pp. 14–15.
20. *Ibid.*, p. 105.
21. For a complete examination of Valletta's philosophical theses, see Comparato, 1970, pp. 230ff.
22. See Maurodenoja, 1738, pp. 338–427.
23. See Vasoli, 1970, pp. 789–827.

24. See Maylender, 1926–1930, vol. 5, pp. 239–243.
25. See Gimma, 1703. Of particular interest is the presence of many members of the Arcadia in the society, along with prestigious representatives of the Roman Curia such as cardinals Tommaso Maria Ferrari and Fabrizio Paolucci. Gimma was among the few southern scholars to maintain close ties with northern intellectuals, especially the editorial group of the *Giornale de' Letterati;* see Roncetti, 1845, pp. 150ff. Marodenoja (1738, pp. 376ff) insists that Gimma enjoyed great prestige among ecclesiastical authorities.
26. The idea of publishing eulogies of the academicians sprouted within the Investiganti circle, as demonstrated by Monforte's letter to Magliabechi announcing the beginning of a work by Gimma, two years before it would be published (Naples, 19 July 1701, in Quondam and Rak, 1978, vol. 2, p. 799).
27. Cotugno, 1914, is still useful regarding the scientific debate in Naples during the late seventeenth and early eighteenth centuries; see also Nicolini, 1932.
28. See Tremigliozzi, 1700, pp. 27–29. The background to the work is fully reconstructed in the second volume *Memorie storiche della società degli Spensierati di Rossano raccolte da Gaetano Tremigliozzi* (pp. 401ff). Gimma himself actually wrote this short work, and then he had Tremigliozzi get it published in the name of the entire academy (Maurodenoja, 1738, pp. 376–378).
29. Particularly important are Gimma's investigations into the figures of giants who appeared on the earth after the Flood (Gimma, 1714, *Pars secunda, De gigantibus,* pp. 32ff); these investigations were certainly known to Vico, for he was Gimma's friend, as confirmed by Maurodenoja (1738, p. 378). Of particular interest are Gimma's discussions on Mary's virginity. He restated all of these themes in Gimma, 1732.
30. See Gimma, 1730, 2 vols. The citation is from the title page of the work. Until now, the *Fisica sotterranea* has been practically ignored by all historians of science.
31. Gimma, 1730, vol. 1, pp. 65ff. The first chapter on gems is particularly interesting because it presents a kind of history of geology from antiquity to the eighteenth century. The young abbot's ideal of an encyclopedia of all human knowledge is clearly present in the *Fisica sotterranea.* On the Jesuit Kircher, an author much loved by Gimma, see Pastine, 1978.
32. See Gimma, 1730, vol. 1, pp. 170ff. On the importance of Hermetic culture in the modern era, see Evans, 1979.
33. See Gimma, 1730, vol. 2, pp. 261ff.
34. See Gimma, 1723, vol. 2, pp. 636ff. Gimma held that Galileo was the father of modern philosophy and a marvelous astronomer (p. 637). The drama of Galileo's trial and the ecclesiastical stance regarding the Pisan scientist were by then a distant memory for Gimma, and, as he saw it, neither of the two parties in the case had been wrong. Gimma wrote that even in his own day, illustrious prelates affirmed "that Galileo's opinion was not condemned by the men of the Inquisition as heretical, but as reckless" (p. 642).
35. The crudely nationalist tone goes back to the role of the *Idea* in the dispute between Italian scholars and the Frenchman Dominique Bouhours. On this episode, and for a commentary on the *Idea,* which enjoyed great success throughout Italy and echoes abroad as well, see Getto, 1946, pp. 53ff; Ricuperati, 1970a, pp. 155–156; Crucitti-Ullrich, 1974, pp. 69ff.
36. Gimma, 1730, vol. 1, pp. 30–31.
37. Gimma, 1723, vol. 1, p. 11.
38. *Ibid.,* p. 14. Gimma identified Cham with the magician Zoroaster.
39. See *ibid.,* pp. 15–16. On Bruno's Hermetism and his thesis of "Christ the magician," which is part of the new "religion of the world," see Yates, 1964. On

the subject of Renaissance magic and its developments in the following centuries, see Vasoli, 1976. Gimma knew Bruno well and rightly considered him one of the great supporters of Copernicanism (Gimma, 1723, vol. 2, pp. 638ff). He interpreted Bruno's philosophy in a peculiar way (1732, p. 127), developing a hypothesis already present in the *Idea* that anticipated Cartesianism. Gimma's distinction between the acceptable *magia naturalis* and the *magia daemoniaca* to be avoided reflected the influence of Marsilio Ficino's works, with which he was quite familiar; see Vasoli, 1970, pp. 809–810, 822–823.

40. Gimma, 1723, vol. 1, p. 15.
41. See *ibid.*, ch. 4, "Che Giano sia Noè, che nell'Italia fondò le colonie e portò le scienze."
42. On the profound ideological differences between Hermetic philosophy and modern science, see Rossi, 1977, pp. 42–69.
43. The longevity of an underground current of Hermetic naturalism in Neapolitan culture should not be underestimated. Vico's arguments against Athanasius Kircher are an important key in this respect; see Corsano, 1968, pp. 9–24. Pastine (1980, pp. 150ff) has to some extent redefined Vico's arguments against Hermetism, at least regarding the matter of sacred chronology. At the dawn of the age of Enlightenment, Hermetic motives connected to the new Masonic ideology were yet present in the Raimondo di Sangro, prince of Sansevero's works (see Di Sangro, 1750), or in Costantino Grimaldi, 1751, which appeared posthumously in Rome.
44. See Comparato, "Ragione e fede," in *Saggi e ricerche*, 1968, pp. 48ff; Ricuperati, "Costantino Grimaldi," in Cesarotti, 1978, pp. 737–834; Grimaldi, 1964. For jurisdictionalist works, see Lauro, 1974.
45. On his friendship with Bottari, see his letters to Bottari in Sposato, 1960, pp. 72–100.
46. On these matters, see De Maio, 1971, pp. 74–87.
47. Comparato, "Ragione e fede," in *Saggi e ricerche*, 1968, p. 60.
48. These are the Galilean ideas of the double truth that Muratori developed in the *De ingeniorum moderatione* and known in Naples in 1710 through Ciccarelli's clandestine edition of the *Lettera alla Granduchessa di Toscana*. As Ricuperati has emphasized ("Costantino Grimaldi," in Cesarotti, 1978, pp. 756ff), Grimaldi dealt with these matters particularly effectively, above all in his *Risposte*, which remained unpublished and was continually revised and retouched by the author through 1730.
49. See Comparato, "Ragione e fede," in *Saggi e ricerche*, 1968, pp. 79ff. Even more courageously than Muratori, Grimaldi aligned himself openly in favor of Copernicanism.
50. See Ricuperati, "Costantino Grimaldi," in Cesarotti, 1978, p. 757.
51. Giannone, 1960, p. 37.
52. See above, chapter 3.
53. See above, chapter 2.
54. See Intieri, 1703, 1704, and 1706.
55. The sole remaining evidence of Intieri's activity in this period are his letters to Magliabechi; see Quondam and Rak, 1978, vol. 2, pp. 701–717. The attention Neapolitan scholars paid to mathematical problems in the 1710s is particularly evident in the interesting introductory essay to this edition.
56. See Intieri's letter to Galiani, Naples, 6 July 1711 (S.N.S.P., XXXI.B.1, cc. 6rff).
57. Intieri's letter to Bottari, Naples, 2 March 1731 (B.C.R., ms. 1608, 32.E.29, c. 81r). Intieri was also quite familiar with the English baronet Thomas Dereham, the translator of the works of Cheyne and Derham who helped enlightened

Catholics to disseminate Newtonianism in Italy; see Intieri's letter to Celestino Galiani, Naples, 17 October 1739 (S.N.S.P., XXXI.A.7, c. 28r).
58. See Racioppi, 1871, pp. 89ff.
59. Intieri's numerous letters to Magliabechi, in particular that from November 1704 (Quondam and Rak, 1978, vol. 2, p. 713), make clear his admiration for Marchetti and his translation, which, according to Intieri, was brought to Naples for the first time by Serafino Biscardi. I believe there can be no doubts as to Intieri's Gassendist Epicureanism—there is explicit evidence from his pupil Broggia dating to 1726 (Ajello, "Carlo Antonio Broggia," in Cesarotti, 1978, p. 1130).
60. Intieri, 1716, unpaginated preface.
61. See Venturi's commentary on this work (1969, pp. 553–554).
62. A valuable source for reconstructing contemporary events are the numerous letters of Giacomo Grazini and Giovambattista Pignatelli, prince of Marsiconovo, to Celestino Galiani (S.N.S.P., respectively XXXI.A.3, cc. 68rff, and XXXI.A.5, cc. 298rff).
63. See the introductory essay to the *Typographus philosophiae studiosis* in Gassendi, 1727, commented on at length above in chapter 2.

2: THE PARTY OF THE MODERNS AND IDEOLOGICAL REFOUNDATION

1. See Nicolini, 1951, pp. 76–77. Lamenting the burdens that the office of *cappellano maggiore* brought, Galiani wrote in his autobiography that life in Taranto was "more restful and tranquil" than in Naples (*Ristretto della vita di Celestino Galiani*, S.N.S.P., XXIX.C.7, c. 98r).
2. See *ibid.*, cc. 96rff.
3. On the crisis, see Ajello, "Vico e Riccardi nella crisi politica del 1726," in Ajello, 1976a, pp. 149–225; Casella, "Il Consiglio collaterale ed il viceré d'Althann: Dall'esilio di Giannone alla rivincita del ministero togato," in *Pietro Giannone*, 1980, vol. 2, pp. 567–633.
4. There are a number of important works on the period of the Austrian vice regency, including Benedikt, 1927; Colapietra, 1961; Marini, 1953, pp. 3–69; L. Villari, 1964, pp. 46–80; Zangari, 1922. Ricuperati (1975) correctly points out that the Viennese directives oscillated "between reformist attempts and rapacious fiscal politics." Di Vittorio (1969b and 1973) is more attentive to the elements of effective reformism in the Austrian rulers' actions.
5. On the Banco di San Carlo, see Di Vittorio, 1969c, pp. 235–263; Di Vittorio, 1969a, pp. 778–802; Ajello, 1969.
6. See Ricuperati, 1976, pp. 400–414; Casella, "Il Consiglio collaterale e il viceré d'Althann," in *Pietro Giannone*, 1980.
7. On the political significance that this funeral assumed and on Riccardi, see Ricuperati, 1969, pp. 745–777; Ajello, 1976a.
8. Bartolomeo Intieri's opinions regarding von Althann's policies were particularly harsh, for he wrote to Bottari singing hymns of joy for the cardinal's defeat and expulsion (letter dated 1730 cited in Venturi, 1959b, p. 418).
9. See Ajello, 1976a, pp. 159–160.
10. Ricuperati, 1966, pp. 57–87.
11. On the background to the struggle for the nomination of the *cappellano maggiore*, see Ajello, "Cartesianismo e cultura oltremontana," in *Pietro Giannone*, 1980, pp. 165–166; see also Benedikt, 1927, pp. 380–382.
12. Simonetti's report is of great interest for a biography of Garofalo. It continued: "Once back in Naples ... he became familiar with doctrines not always healthy, and he was not at all endeared to our court" (B.N.N., ms. XVI.B.6, 25 November 1732).

13. On the importance of the *Istoria*, see Ricuperati, 1966a, pp. 63–65; see also Grimaldi, 1964, pp. xv–xvi.
14. In his "La storiografia meridionale nel Settecento," (Giarrizzo, 1981, pp. 178–239), the author focuses on the positive role of the antiquarians in southern culture, especially in the struggle to overcome historical Pyhrronism. For more on Matteo Egizio, at the center of a vast network of contacts with all southern antiquarians, see Ussia, 1977; Ussia, "Le lettere di Arrigo Enriques a Matteo Egizio," in *Pietro Giannone*, 1980, pp. 709–762.
15. See Garofalo's letter to Giannone dated 18 January 1732, in Bertelli, 1968, pp. 522–523, where the moderate element is described as the minority position among jurisdictionalists in Naples.
16. Intieri's letter to Bottari dated 15 December 1731, cited in Venturi, 1959b, p. 421.
17. See especially De Giovanni, 1970.
18. On the episode of the "drowning," see Grimaldi, 1964, pp. 94–95.
19. Galiani's letter to Guido Grandi, Rome, 11 October 1726 (B.U.P., ms. 92, c. 381r).
20. See Spinelli, 1753, pp. 507–508.
21. See Origlia Paolino, 1753–1754, vol. 2, pp. 259–260.
22. On Niccolò Cirillo, see Baldini, 1981, pp. 801–805; Serao, 1742, vol. 1, pp. 180ff; Zambelli, 1972, pp. 30–54. On Cirillo's teachings of Newtonian theories in the Neapolitan University, see Capassi, 1728, p. 388.
23. On the longstanding friendship between Galiani and Cirillo, see Francesco Serao's "Vita Nicolai Cyrilli," the foreword to Cirillo, 1741, vol. 1.
24. See Zambelli, 1972, p. 31.
25. See Ettmüller, 1734, vol. 1, pp. 54–55, note (B) by Cirillo. The Neapolitan edition of this work appeared in 1728. On naturalistic Cartesianism in Naples, see Garin, 1950, pp. 385–405. An interesting document attesting to the persistence of mechanistic and naturalistic Cartesianism among Neapolitan physicians is Nicolò Giovio's unpublished *Lettere ad una signora sopra argomenti fisici e morali* (1727). The finely bound manuscript (B.N.N., I.E.19) to a large extent reprises Descartes's *De homine*.
26. See Ettmüller, 1734, vol. 1, pp. 242ff, in which Cirillo examines Newtonian and Cartesian optical theories in a very lengthy note (T).
27. See *ibid.*, vol. 1, pp. 309ff.
28. Capassi, 1728, p. 387.
29. See Spinelli's affirmations above, p. 198. Opposition grew up in Naples between Newtonians and Cartesians at the end of the 1720s, a fact well documented in the writings of Niccolò Di Martino, Niccolò Cirillo, Francesco Serao, and Celestino Galiani. In fact, Neapolitan Newtonianism was not an evolutionary outgrowth of post-Cartesian physics, but developed mainly through the successes of the Gassendist and Galilean traditions, which preserved their own vital space in Naples even during the early eighteenth century. This in no way contradicts the innovative role played by Neapolitan Cartesianism. Starting in 1728–1729, the distinction between Cartesians and Newtonians was already a reality, and the dialectic between the two groups developed along lines quite similar to what was happening in the rest of Europe.
30. Galiani's letter to Guido Grandi, 22 April 1714 (B.U.P., ms. 92, c. 363r).
31. See the "Discorso del sig.ʳ D. Mario Lama recitato nell'accademia in gennaio 1733" [c. 3r] in *Discorsi dell'Accademia De Alteriis*, B.N.N., ms. XV.D.24.
32. There is no detailed study on this figure, but see Amodeo, 1902, pp. 16–34.
33. See N. Di Martino, 1727. Of particular importance is the section in the preface that Di Martino dedicates to Newton's *Principia*, considering it without hesitation (and not without a pointed argument against Descartes) the most important fruit of the great Galileo (pp. xxxii–xxxvii).

34. N. Di Martino, 1728, was a manual used by Neapolitan students, including Antonio Genovesi. An entire chapter of the treatise was dedicated to experimental philosophies; see chapter 4, p. 285ff. There are many unpublished works of Niccolò Di Martino in the B.N.N., *Fondo biblioteca provinciale*. Of particular note are ms. 90 (*Optices elementa*) and ms. 89 (*Hydrostatices elementa*), quite probably the nucleus of the university lectures he gave during his long teaching career at the university.

35. Celestino Galiani followed Pietro Di Martino extremely attentively from his youth, and he sent Di Martino to Bologna to stay with his friend Eustachio Manfredi for a course on astronomy. On Pietro Di Martino, see Amodeo, 1902, pp. 26–32; Napoli-Signorelli, 1786, vol. 5, pp. 475–477.

36. P. Di Martino, 1738, vol. 1, "Prolegomena," p. 2.

37. *Ibid.*, pp. 3–6.

38. P. Di Martino's particularly hostile tone towards Descartes is noteworthy; in his treatise, affirmations such as "Therefore the opinion of the Cartesians is false" (*ibid.*, p. 144) are common.

39. See above, chapter 3.

40. See Bartolomeo Intieri's letter to Giovanni Bottari cited in Venturi, 1959b. p. 421.

41. *Ristretto della vita di Celestino Galiani*, c. 117r.

42. Cited by Nicolini, 1932, p. 187. Galasso (in Doria, 1973, pp. viii–ix) has argued that there was heavy governmental conditioning.

43. See Ajello, "Cartesianismo e cultura oltremontana," in *Pietro Giannone*, 1980, p. 163, citing a manuscript (B.N.N., ms. XVI.B.6) containing copies of reports sent by the nuncio Simonetti to the secretary of state. A source generally overlooked when reconstructing the Holy See's attitude during these years is the unpublished *Memoria e dettaglio del carteggio fra la corte di Roma e il signor cardinale Passionei nunzio di Vienna [. . .] sulle materie appartenenti alla religione e al tribunale del S. Officio del Regno di Napoli e Sicilia* (Vatican City, Secret Archives, *Nunziatura Napoli*, 512). The matter of the academy was debated in Rome, Naples, and Vienna. Simonetti's report was sent to Vienna as well; see *Memoria e dettaglio*, c. 81r.

44. See *ibid.*, c. 80r.

45. Letter dated 23 March 1733 cited in Ajello, "Cartesianismo e cultura oltremontana," in *Pietro Giannone*, 1980, pp. 172–173.

46. See *ibid.*

47. See the letter dated 12 December 1732, in Zambelli, 1977, p. 119.

48. Undated letter (but certainly from 1732), B.C.R., ms. 2027, 32.G.14, c. 40v.

49. See Zambelli, 1977, pp. 118–121. Zambelli states that she found the copy in the *Fondo Gambetti* of the Biblioteca Gambalunghiana di Rimini, among the papers of the physician Giovanni Bianchi, who evidently had had the original from Antonio Leprotti. This latter thesis is also accepted by Ajello, "Cartesianismo e cultura oltremontana," in *Pietro Giannone*, 1980, p. 169. Actually the letter was not sent just to Leprotti but made the rounds of all enlightened Catholics. The original autograph is among Giovanni Bottari's papers (B.C.R., ms. 1581, 32.E.2, cc. 52r–55v).

50. There is an interesting and anonymous letter from 1732 on the Accademia delle Scienza in the codex containing Galiani's letter to Grandi (B.U.P., ms. 92).

51. On the importance of Davia's protection, see the letters in Nicolini, 1951, pp. 192–194. On 22 November Davia wrote that he had heard a rumor that Galiani would introduce the study of Locke in Naples. If it was true, he urged caution. A month later Davia informed Galiani that he had intervened on his behalf

with the pope and claimed to have convinced him of Galiani's integrity (*ibid.*, p. 194).

52. See Biagio Garofalo's letter to Galiani dated 4 April 1733 (S.N.S.P., XXXI.B.1, c. 328r). On the matter of imperial protection for the academy, see Bertelli, 1968, p. 293.

53. See *Memoria o dettaglio*, c. 56. With the help of Leprotti, Davia, and Bottari, Galiani was able to persuade everyone of the complete orthodoxy of the academy's theses. In this regard, see the conciliatory tone towards the new *cappellano maggiore* in Banchieri's instructions to Archbishop Francesco Pignatelli, sent in January 1733 (Osbat, "Il Sant'Ufficio nella Napoli di Giannone. Contributo alla storia della giurisdizione ecclesiastica," in *Pietro Giannone*, 1980, vol. 2, p. 656).

54. Undated letter, B.C.R., ms. 2027, 32.G.14, c. 30r. Intieri confirms the seriousness of the situation that had developed with Galiani's denunciation to the Inquisition in his letter to Cardinal Corsini, whom he begged "to tear up this page, which even if full of truths cannot but bring great prejudice upon me" (*ibid.*, c. 31r).

55. Intieri wrote: "There has been some mention of a little treatise composed by this author [Locke] about the good education of the sons of great lords, but otherwise his metaphysical treatise has never been discussed" (*ibid.*, c. 30v).

56. See *Ristretto della vita di Celestino Galiani* c. 117v.

57. *Ibid.*, cc. 116rff. On the academy, see Napoli-Signorelli, 1786, vol. 5, pp. 401–406, 478–479.

58. Letter from Milan dated 8 April 1733 (S.N.S.P., XXXI.B.1, c. 263r).

59. See Galiani's letter to Bottari from 16 June 1733 (B.C.R., ms. 1581, 32.E.2, c. 62v).

60. See Galiani's letter to Bottari from 13 October 1733 (*ibid.*, c. 68v).

61. See Intieri's letter to Bottari, Naples, 10 February 1733 (B.C.R., ms. 1582, 32.E.3, c. 157r). From the subsequent letters it is apparent that Bottari personally came to Naples for a brief period and attended some sessions at the academy.

62. See Galiani's letter to Bottari, Naples, 12 March 1735 (B.C.R., ms. 1581, 32.E.2, c. 90r).

63. On Serao, see Zambelli, 1973a, pp. 132–146.

64. Serao, 1740, p. 3.

65. There is an accurate examination of this work by Serao in Zambelli, 1973a, pp. 135–139.

66. On the development of "practical medicine" in Europe, see the chapter "Medicine," in Taton, 1964–1966, vol. 2; Gusdorf, 1972, pp. 189–222.

67. Both Zambelli (1973a, p. 137) and Napoli-Signorelli (1786, vol. 5, pp. 471–472) correctly insist on Serao's Gassendism.

69. See *Discorsi dell'Accademia de Alteriis*. On the academy (also called "dei Ruffo"), see Minieri Riccio, 1879, p. 167. The significance of the simultaneous presence of men tied to Galiani (such as Lama and Di Martino) and important members of the *veteres* (including Giuseppe Pasquale Cirillo) within the academy remains a mystery.

69. Intieri's letter to Bottari, Naples, 27 October 1733 (B.C.R., ms. 1582, 32.E.3, c. 155r).

70. On these problems, ever at the center of the discussions in Europe engendered by the *Principia*, see Casini, 1969, pp. 21–54. On Mario Lama, see Origlia Paolino, 1753–1754, p. 283.

71. See "Discorso del sig. D. Mario Lama recitato nell'accademia in gennaio 1733," in *Discorsi dell'Accademia de Alteriis* (c. 1r). The echo of these discussions must have been considerable in Naples, for Napoli-Signorelli (1786, vol. 5, pp. 478–479) and Fasano (1784, pp. 29–31) remember them as one of the most important

cultural events to occur within the Accademia delle Scienze.

72. Two other long discussions on the subject were held by Mario Lama in 1734 and 1735; they appear in the *Discorsi dell'Accademia de Alteriis*.

73. "Discorso del sig. D. Mario Lama recitata nell'accademia in agosto 1734," (c. 2*v*), *ibid.*

74. See Intieri's letter to Bottari, Naples, 18 December 1734 (B.C.R., ms. 1608, 32.E.29, c. 201*v*).

75. On the attempt, see Ricuperati, 1976, pp. 375–381; Schipa, 1924, pp. 435ff; Filippo Caravita's interesting report published in De Blasiis, 1876, pp. 141–166.

76. See Intieri's letter to Bottari, Naples, 28 June 1732 (B.C.R., ms. 1608, 32.E.29, c. 134*r*).

77. The principal source for reconstructing the vicissitudes of Galiani's reform is still Origlia Paolino, 1753–1754, vol. 2, pp. 247–259; see also Guadagno, 1956; Ricuperati, 1976, pp. 420–424. There are valuable documents on Galiani's activities as a reformer in the university in Monti, 1924. The references to the discussion in the Collaterale referred to in the text are taken from the unpublished volume 16 of the *Notamenti del Consiglio Collaterale* preserved in Brindisi, Biblioteca arcivescovile Annibale De Leo, ms. B/48 (cc. 35–40, 21 July 1732).

78. Origlia Paolino, 1753–1754, vol. 2, p. 247. From Vienna, Pio Garelli sent him, for example, the plan of Victor Amadeus II's university reform, which he had evidently obtained through d'Aguirre (see *ibid.*, p. 248). For a comparison with the situation in European universities that points to the importance of the renewal Celestino Galiani desired, see *Les universités*, 1967, in particular Leśnodorski, "Les universités au siècle des lumières," pp. 143–159. On university teaching in Italy during the eighteenth century, see Roggero, 1981a, pp. 1039–1081. On the plans for reform in the Pisan university, see Carranza, 1974, pp. 318–331.

79. This becomes clearly evident from Giannone's *Parere*, published by Guadagno. Guadagno, however, does not allude at all to the different ideological perspectives between Galiani's plan of a great cultural breadth and already receptive to Locke's teachings, and Giannone's counterdeductions, which were all aimed at bringing the reform back into the realm of the most staunch jurisdictionalism, even if at the expense of important proposals such as the reduction of chairs in Roman law and the establishment of those in experimental physics and history of the Church.

80. See Guadagno, 1956, pp. 114–150.

81. See Origlia Paolino, 1753–1754, vol. 2, pp. 260–295.

82. It would be extremely interesting to study the entire background to the renewal of the teaching corps that Galiani carried out through his correspondence. Cusani (see Gisondi, 1979–1980) is a good example of a scholar especially sensitive towards modern thought who was protected by the *cappellano maggiore*.

83. Letter dated 12 December in Zambelli, 1977, p. 119.

3: PAOLO MATTIA DORIA'S SCIENTIFIC COUNTERREVOLUTION

1. On the Accademia degli Oziosi, see Maylender, 1926–1930, vol. 4, pp. 190–193; Minieri Riccio, 1180, pp. 349–351; V. Conti, 1978, pp. 63–65.

2. On Cirillo, entrusted with Charles's attempt at codification, see Ajello, 1976a, pp. 46–50. See also Ajello, 1981, pp. 796–801.

3. The principal source is still G. P. Cirillo, 1734, which he dedicated to Doria, the most prestigious figure at the academy; to this was added another work, Cirillo [1735]. Also particularly useful is *Vari componimenti recitati*, 1735. From its "Introduzione" by Giannantonio Sergio, this work's exaltation of Saint Augustine (p. iii) was interwoven with the determination to renew a strong

defense of orthodoxy in the academy. See also Doria's verses (p. xxvii) and those of Vico contained in the book.

4. The lectures Doria held (some of whose titles we have given above) were in part published in Doria, 1737. Conti (1978, p. 63) and Ricuperati (1979, pp. 261–285) have rightly called attention to the importance of the Accademia degli Oziosi in Doria's intellectual life.

5. See G. P. Cirillo, 1734, p. B$_4$r.

6. In Cirillo, 1735, among the most significant discussions are those of Doria, "Dell'antica polizia di Napoli dopo che fu in Regno costituita" (ibid., p. A$_2$r); Duchess of Marigliano Isabella Mastrilli's "Della tragedia e tragedi napoletani" (ibid., p. A$_3$v); and Ortensio Magnocavallo's "Dell'origine de' feudi nel Regno di Napoli" (ibid., pp. A$_3$r–A$_4$v). In 1734 a great deal of time was set aside in the academy for sacred history; see G. P. Cirillo, 1734, pp. B$_1$r–B$_4$r. Of particular importance for understanding the spirit of the Oziosi, who were still tied to baroque and Arcadian rituals, is the members' assumption of cover names such as "idler," "sleepy," "feeble," "stunned," and "dumbfounded." Doria adopted the name "yawner."

7. See ibid., pp. A$_2$rv.

8. See Minieri Riccio, 1880, p. 350. The author speaks of seventy-eight members in 1738.

9. See the "Discorso del sig. D. Giuseppe Pasquale Cirillo recitato nell'accademia a 25 marzo," in Discorsi dell'Accademia de Alteriis. Quite plain in Cirillo's discussion is his bitter argument with Lama and Di Martino, who were also members of the Accademia de Alteriis but part of Galiani's faction.

10. On this episode, see G. P. Cirillo, 1734, the unpaginated preface that also contains a letter from Vico to Cirillo. The verses Vico recited in the academy are in Vico, 1970, p. 213.

11. Galiani's letter to Bottari, Naples 2 August 1732 (B.C.R., ms. 1581, 32.E.2, cc. 50v–51r). Galiani authorized his Roman friends to guarantee Vico's orthodoxy on his authority "if there was ever any opposition that Vico did not merit such a favor because he wrote doctrines worthy of censure," a particularly interesting action because it all the more confirms Vico's complex position in Neapolitan culture.

12. There is a synthesis of the entire argument in Doria, 1722–1726, which also includes some of the fierce opinions of his contemporaries. Doria's antagonists during the entire affair were Galiani and Intieri, who were not stingy with their criticism. See Grazini's letters to Galiani (S.N.S.P., XXXI.A.3, cc. 68rff).

13. See Rotta, "Paolo Mattia Doria," in Cesarotti, 1978, pp. 849–850.

14. For an examination of the international repercussions sparked by the Vita civile, see Vidal, 1953, pp. 18–20.

15. See Zambelli's thoughts on the Vita civile ("Il rogo postumo di Paolo Mattia Doria," in Zambelli, 1973b, pp. 156–157). On the relationship between Doria and Montesquieu, see Shackleton, 1961, pp. 274–275.

16. On Doria's contemporary political thought, see V. Conti, 1978.

17. See Rotta, "Paolo Mattia Doria," in Cesarotti, 1978, p. 849.

18. See Amodeo, 1902, pp. 19ff, and above all V. Conti, 1981, pp. 185–198.

19. Galiani's letter to Grandi, Rome, 26 October 1722 (B.U.P., ms. 92, c. 448r). Doria had also written to Galiani in 1718, without, however, obtaining any comfort, as suggested by the letter cited here.

20. See Doria, 1724, pp. 81ff, and the ample "Introduzione" to his Opere matematiche (Doria, 1722, vol. 1), in which he stated that he had erred in the way in which he had proposed his epistemological model by opposing Descartes and his followers.

21. On this historical development of the profound distinction between Galileo's mathematizing model and the circumstantial procedure in a discipline such as medicine, see Ginzburg, 1979, pp. 59–106.

22. On Doria's complex philosophical thought, which contains elements from the thought of authors such as Plato, Descartes, Galileo, and Spinoza and, above all, an idealistic and spiritualizing reading of the last, see Badaloni, 1961, pp. 278–286; Badaloni, 1973, pp. 748ff; Garin, 1966, pp. 889–899.

23. See Doria, 1728. The Spinozan results of Doria's philosophy were pitilessly laid bare in the debate between Doria and Spinelli, who accused each other of being Spinozans; see Belgioioso, 1973. Givambattista Lamberti cited many passages from Spinoza (1734), and he accused Doria of having proposed dangerous analogies with the Spinozan "One" in his thesis "of the immaterial One"; see Spinelli, 1733.

24. See Lachterman, 1980.

25. See Alberti, 1977, pp. 155ff.

26. The problem of quantifying the physical phenomenon in its temporal variation (and the elaboration of a mathematical algorithm capable of taking this into account) is at the center of some penetrating observations in Dijksterhuis, 1986.

27. See Doria's "Introduzione" to his *Opere matematiche* (1722). Such concepts are expressed in all Doria's works, especially in the manuscript *Considerazioni geometriche, logiche e metafisiche sopa li Elementi di Euclide* (Doria, 1980). For an examination of the work, see Lachterman, 1980.

28. See above, chapter 2.

29. On the time factor in modern science, see Koyré, 1967. There is a fascinating examination of how, thanks to scientists, the determination of time and space wound up involving all aspects of social, political, and religious life in Le Goff, 1980; see also Gusdorf, 1972, pp. 345–370, 398–400.

30. See Doria, 1724, pp. 142–143.

31. See Doria, 1745, pp. 63–91, where he contested Newton's "arbitrary hypotheses" on universal gravitation, harkening back to his *Meccanica* of 1711. For Doria, nature "is geometry which in its operations would use perfect geometry" (*ibid.*, p. 66). Rejecting the images of the universe-machine and God the watchmaker ("God has produced the universe in Himself"), Doria refuted the *Principia*'s claim to explain the universe with "sensible mechanical geometry," and he believed he explained planetary orbits without having to take recourse in universal attraction (*ibid.*, p. 67). There is also an exmination of the work of Newton in some manuscripts only recently published in Marangio, 1979, vol. 2, pp. 419–432.

32. On Doria's arguments against infinitesimal analysis, which in his opinion had corrupted Bonaventura Cavalieri's "most ingenious method" of indivisibles, see his "Introduzione" (Doria, 1722).

33. For a critical reexamination of the myth of Vico's isolation in Naples, see Costa, 1976, pp. 10–30; Ajello, "Cartesianismo e cultura oltremontana," in *Pietro Giannone*, 1980, pp. 105–121.

34. In particular, in the third and sixth of the *Orazioni inaugurali* there is an open profession of Baconian experimentalism; see Vico, 1971, pp. 733–758, 771–785. On Vico's scientific thought and, especially, the role of mathematics in the cognitive process, see Lachterman, 1980, pp. 19–20, in which he critically discusses the works of Corsano, Berlin, Garin, Croce, and the thesis of Vico as a "fictionalist." See also Torrini, 1978, pp. 104–121.

35. Vico's most penetrating observations against mathematicism are in the *De nostri temporis studiorum ratione* (Vico, 1971, pp. 801–808). De Giovanni (1980, pp. 141–192) drew a parallel between Vico's position and that of Doria. Lachterman

(1980, p. 22) preferred to emphasize not so much the different conclusions reached by Vico and Doria as, rather, their evidently common criticism of analytic geometry, reevaluating the cognitive role of mathematics in Vico's philosophy.

36. Giuseppe Giarrizzo (1981, pp. 55–122) has convincingly illustrated the "substantial political nature of Vico's reflection."

37. On the separation that Vico foresaw between science and humanism, see Berlin, "The Divorce between the Sciences and the Humanities," in Berlin, 1975.

38. Ajello, "Carlo Antonio Broggia," in Cesarotti, 1978, p. 987, with an ample reference bibliography.

39. Venturi (1967, pp. 298–307; 1968, pp. 830–853) has already pointed out the myriad points of contact between Broggia's and Vico's thought.

4: Neomercantilism and the Enlightenment: From Intieri to Ventura

1. On the importance of this event and the expectations that it raised, see Venturi, 1969, pp. 29ff.

2. The best work on this historical period of Neapolitan life is certainly Ajello, 1976b; see also Schipa, 1904.

3. See Ajello, 1982, pp. 3–30.

4. See Schipa, 1898, p. 26.

5. See Ajello, 1976a.

6. On Contegna, see Ajello, 1980, pp. 383–412.

7. See De Rosa, 1958.

8. See Ajello, 1980, pp. 407ff.

9. See the examination provided by Ricuperati, 1966a, pp. 81–87, from which the author's clearly mercantilist vision emerges in his commentary on Jacques Savary's *Dictionnaire du commerce*.

10. On Pallante, see Ajello, 1976a, pp. 89–96.

11. On the political background to the concordat and the role played by Contegna, see, Ajello, 1976b, p. 625ff.

12. See Ajello, "Legislazione e crisi del diritto comune nel Regno di Napoli: il tentativo di codificazione carolina," in Ajello, 1976a, pp. 29–103.

13. See Venturi, 1969, pp. 32–46, 70–98.

14. See *ibid.*, pp. 80–81; Villani, "Il catasto onciario e il sistema tributario," in Villani, 1967, pp. 105–154.

15. See Ajello, 1979. On the stormy developments of this initiative in Sicily, see Sciuti Russi, 1968, pp. 146–168.

16. On the matter of commercial treaties, see Barbagallo, 1971, pp. 264–296; Di Vittorio, 1979.

17. See the political and economic arguments adopted by Galiani above, chapter 5.

18. On the public works at Capodimonte, Caserta, and Naples, see Venturi, 1969, pp. 78–80. On the work on Naples's harbor, see De Rosa, "Navi, merci, nazionalità in un porto dell'età pre-industriale: Il porto di Napoli nel 1760," in *Saggi e ricerche*, 1968, p. 337.

19. See *Civiltà del '700*, 1979; De Seta, 1981.

20. Intieri's letter to Galiani, Naples, 11 October 1738 (S.N.S.P., XXXI.A.7, c. 5r).

21. See the letter to Galiani dated 13 January 1739 (*ibid.*, c. 25rff). Intieri referred to the difficulties raised by an influential member of the *Giunta di commercio* for the treaties with Constantinople as "so empty, even ridiculous."

22. Intieri's letter to Galiani, Naples, 13 January 1739 (*ibid.*, c. 26v).

23. Intieri's letter to Galiani, Naples, 31 January 1739 (*ibid.*, c. 30v).

24. See Villani, 1967, p. 21; Romano, 1976; Macry, 1974. Intieri, and later Doria, Galiani, and Genovesi insisted that an increase in agricultural production rather than commerce would guarantee the economic development of the kingdom; see Aymard, 1978.

25. On the social dynamism during the 1730s primed by mercantilist choices and the emergence of a culture now oriented towards the Enlightenment, see Ajello, "Potere ministeriale e società al tempo di Giannone. Il modello napoletano nella storia del pubblico funzionario," in *Pietro Giannone*, 1980, vol. 1, pp. 451–511, where he discusses the lengthy bibliography on the topic of social hierarchies during the seventeenth and eighteenth centuries.

26. See Venturi, 1969, pp. 77ff; Ajello, 1976b, pp. 681ff.

27. On the development of an economicist ideology in Europe, see Dumont, 1977. On the ever-stimulating ideological aspect of mercantilism, its moral values, and political indications, see Heckscher, 1934, vol. 2, pp. 269–310. For a general evaluation of mercantilism's economic theories, see De Maddalena, 1980.

28. See Melon, 1734, p. 92. This work appeared anonymously in Paris without any indication of editor or place of publication. On Melon and the French neomercantilists, such as Voltaire and Montesquieu, favorably disposed towards luxury and the spread of commerce, see Borghero, 1974; De Labriolle-Rutheford, 1963, pp. 1025–1036; Guerci, 1979a, pp. 18–25. On the affair of the debate over luxury in Naples, see Frascani, 1971, pp. 397ff.

29. See Hirschman, 1977. On the figure of the merchant during the Middle Ages and its gradual rehabilitation thanks to the Church itself, see Le Goff, 1980, especially the good bibliography.

30. On Mandeville's direct influence on Melon, see Borghero, 1974, p. 25.

31. See Melon, 1734, pp. 61–63.

32. On Mandeville's famous paradox—private vices, public virtues—see Goretti, 1958; Dumont, 1977, pp. 83–104; and especially Scribano, 1980, who brings to light the role and originality of Bayle, an author very well known in Naples (see Pii, 1972, pp. 320–342) for illustrating the evident contrast between evangelical morals and human activities. However, he distinguishes between the rationalist direction of Bayle and the English deists (so dear to Galiani and Intieri) aimed at establishing a connection between morality and reason, and the naturalist direction developed by Mandeville, still somewhat anchored in the primacy of passions and human sentiments. For more on Bayle and his penetrating criticism of evangelical morals, see James, 1975, pp. 43–65; Morize, 1909; Labrousse, 1963.

33. On an entire wing of French Catholicism's harsh opposition towards mercantilist ideology, see Rothkrug, 1965, pp. 10–85; Rotta, 1974, pp. 51–89. The emergence of a secular and rationalist morality tied to the study of human passions and freed from the traditional Catholic frame of reference represented quite a trauma to French and European culture; see Groethuysen, 1968.

34. Melon, 1734, p. 130.

35. *Ibid.*, p. 152. In reference to usury, Melon wrote: "The opinions of the causists on usury do not extend to commerce, which knows no other law than public authority" (p. 242).

36. Intieri's letter to Galiani, Naples, 29 November 1738 (S.N.S.P., XXXI.A.7, c. 17r).

37. On Bayle's theses, see Scribano, 1980, pp. 21–46.

38. For an exhaustive analysis of the dispute, see Venturi, 1969, pp. 118–136.

39. *Ibid.*, p. 124.

40. Galiani's letter to Bottari, Naples, 11 December 1745 (B.C.R., ms. 1581, 32.E.2, cc. 117rff). Also interesting is the following letter from 21 December 1745

(*ibid.*, cc. 178ff), in which there are some comments directed against Scipione Maffei, who was guilty of having plagiarized from the famous book of the Jansenist Nicolaus Brodersen, *De usuris licitis et illicitis.*

41. The letters are in part published by Nicolini, 1951, pp. 232–236. Bottari's opinions were less modern than Galiani's on the issue of usury.

42. Galiani's letter to Bottari, Naples, 21 December 1745 (B.C.R., ms. 1581, 32.E.2, c. 178r). Above all, Galiani criticized the traditional scholastic formulation of the problem of usury, already only poorly able to explain the phenomenon, which had acquired a fundamentally economic meaning.

43. See Venturi, 1969, pp. 133–136, who nevertheless ignores Galiani's personal intervention to mitigate Concina's furor. On Concina, see *Dictionnaire de théologie catholique*, vol. 3, pp. 676ff.

44. Galiani's letter to Bottari, Naples, 18 February 1746 (B.C.R., ms. 1581, 32.E.w, c. 181v).

45. Galiani's letter to Bottari, Naples, 26 June 1751 (*ibid.*, c. 223r).

46. Intieri's letter to Galiani, Naples, 31 January 1739 (S.N.S.P., XXXI.A.7, c. 30r).

47. On the emergence of the concept of individual interest in European culture, understood as a useful instrument of control and restraint on human passions with the goal of directing them to a presumed collective good through the constancy and foreseeability of a world governed by interest, see Hirschman, 1977. Intieri wrote that if one wished to guarantee an economic equilibrium and margins of development for all society through the profits of merchants and agrarian entrepreneurs, it was better not to give to "the peasant and to the majority of men, who work only with their bodies, as do horses and asses and the waters and wind, anything but a very restricted diet and a wretched suit, taking also into account his wretched little family" because for the "happiness of a state, this sort of people merit nothing more" (Intieri's letter to Galiani, Naples, 29 November 1738, S.N.S.P., XXXI.A.7, c. 16rv).

48. Intieri's letter to Galiani, Naples, February 1739 (*ibid.*, c. 34v).

49. Intieri's letter to Galiani, Naples, 4 October 1738, *ibid.*, c. 3v. The problem of luxury was at the center of the debate between Intieri and Galiani. In a letter from 30 December 1738 (*ibid.*, cc. 23r–24v) Intieri sent Galiani a diligent transcription of some passages of Melon's chapter on luxury.

50. Intieri's letter to Galiani, Naples, 11 November 1738 (S.N.S.P., XXXI.A.7, cc. 12v–13r).

51. On the myth of Prometheus in the culture of the modern age, see Rossi, 1976, pp. 174–186; Landes, 1969; Merton, 1978.

52. See Rossi, 1976, pp. 134–137; Venturi, 1970, pp. 109–120.

53. On contemporaries' impression that they were living through a genuine scientific revolution, see Cohen, 1980, pp. 40ff.

54. On the relationship between science and the Enlightenment, see Antonio Santucci's "Introduzione" (1979, pp. 56–71), with a rich bibliography on the subject.

55. Among the most significant research on the topic, Jacob (1976) is of considerable importance, particularly the first chapter, "Science and the Philosophical Origins of the Radical Enlightenment," and the third, "The Newtonian Enlightenment and Its Critics," which at last focuses on the role of Newtonianism in the genesis of enlightened thought, if only within the particular framework of the Radical Enlightenment. For more on the relationship between Newtonianism and the Enlightenment, see *Newton and the Enlightenment*, 1979; Hankins, 1970.

56. See Venturi, 1969, p. 359.

57. Galiani's letter to Bottari, Naples, 22 February 1750 (B.C.R., ms. 1581, 33.E.2, c. 217r).

58. Galiani's letter to Bottari, Aquila, 12 August 1730 (ibid., c. 37rv). In a striking counterpoint to Galiani's theses, Antonio Leprotti on 23 September 1730 wrote to Galiani, applying Newtonian terms of attraction and repulsion to a description of moral forces in courtly behavior (letter cited in Nicolini, 1951, pp. 202–203). On Francesco Maria Zanotti's book written in 1747 on the attracting force of ideas that partly restated these impressions, see Badaloni, 1968a, p. 277.

59. On 'sGravesande, see Gori, 1972; Jacob (1976) has argued for the importance of the network of relationships that bound many European scholars to this key figure in Continental Newtonianism.

60. Venice, Remondini, 1749. The two very important volumes of the Introductio ad philosophiam newtonianam (1720–1721) were also published in Venice by Pasquinelli in 1737.

61. Cohen, 1980, p. 17.

62. On d'Alembert's mathematizing Newtonianism, especially in the Traité de dynamique, see Hankins, 1970; Gusdorf, 1972, pp. 388ff; Ferrone, 1980, pp. 46ff; Casini, 1970.

63. Diderot, 1961, p. 180.

64. See Gori, 1972, pp. 202ff.

65. See ibid., pp. 123ff.

66. See ibid., pp. 149ff. We see many points of contact between Galiani and 'sGravesande, if we recall the Scienza morale and Galiani's concept of natural law.

67. See Cassirer, 1951; Cohen, 1956, pp. 237–38. On Hume the Newtonian and theoretician of social sciences, see Dal Pra, 1973.

68. On social mathematics, see Baker, 1975; Moravia, 1967; Gusdorf, 1972.

69. Regarding the debate on social mathematics among the philosophes during the 1750s and 1760s, see Ferrone, 1980. There is an examination of the repercussions of 'sGravesande's theses in the Encyclopédie in Gori, 1972, pp. 277ff.

70. Intieri's letter to Galiani (Naples, 29 November 1738, S.N.S.P., XXXI.A.7, cc. 15r–18r) is an example of this rationalistic determination, for he sought to evaluate quantitatively the effect of inflation on the Neapolitan economy. In 1752 Intieri also explicitly clarified to Antonio Cocchi his thoughts on the new economic science, writing: "Your maxim that physics is the basis of economics, politics, and morals is so true that it seems to me a dishonor to humanity not to have known it" (Venturi, 1959b, p. 436).

71. Intieri's letter to Galiani, Naples, 16 December 1738 (S.N.S.P., XXXI.A.7, c. 19v).

72. Letter dated 29 November 1738 (ibid., c. 15v).

73. The most accurate examination of the debate surrounding coinage in the 1750s in Italy is that of Venturi, 1969, chapter 7.

74. Intieri's letter to Galiani, Naples, 25 January 1739 (S.N.S.P., XXXI.A.7, c. 27v).

75. Intieri's letter to Galiani, Naples, 14 April 1739 (ibid., c. 39rv).

76. A detailed examination of the letters to Intieri, Galiani, and Rinuccini would certainly lead to a breakthrough in the reconstruction of the background of the Della moneta. On Ferdinando Galiani's youth, see Nicolini, 1918.

77. See Einaudi, 1953, pp. 282ff; Kauder, 1953; pp. 638–650.

78. See Ferdinando Galiani's letter to Madame d'Epinay, Naples, 13 December 1770 (F. Galiani, 1975, p. 1056).

79. Della moneta, in F. Galiani, 1975, p. 59. As we see, these were the same ideas that Celestino Galiani had communicated to Bottari when he theorized on the extension of Newtonian natural laws to every aspect of reality. Pompeo Neri, one of the greatest experts on monetary problems of the day, wrote in

his famous *Osservazioni sopra il prezzo legale delle monete* (1751): "The measure of value is regulated by the very same natural laws that regulate the measure of length, the cubic extension, gravity, etc." (cited in Venturi, 1969, p. 477). On the historical development of economic science, see Letwin, 1965.

80. *Della moneta*, in F. Galiani, 1975, pp. 91–92. Intieri criticized a similar concept in a letter to Ferdinando Galiani in October 1751 (S.N.S.P., XXXI.B.18, cc. 51v–53r). Galiani reformulated the entire matter in the following years; see the *Note* to the second edition of the work, in *Della moneta*, p. 285.

81. *Della moneta*, in F. Galiani, 1975, p. 44.

82. See the Count of Punghino's letters to Galiani (S.N.S.P., XXXI.C.12), especially that from 13 October 1748 (c. 19rff), in which the count requested explanations: "I would like to know how it is that the superior beings, the pure spirits, the angels, God, and all that is above human nature, act and govern their passions under your two principles, namely *solidity* and *attraction*."

83. F. Galiani, *Della moneta*, p. 98.

84. Opinions are still divided on the complex Ferdinando Galiani and on the meaning of his work. In his "Introduzione" to the *Opere* (F. Galiani, 1975), Furio Diaz preferred to emphasize Galiani's lack of reforming pathos and a clear acceptance of enlightened culture, highlighting the elements of Machiavellianism. However, the more balanced and convincing image is drawn by Luciano Guerci, the other editor of the *Opere*, who critically discusses the rich bibliography on the man and his early works, identifying, with a great deal of finesse, the reforming and enlightened features present in the work of the youthful Galiani, separating these aspects from the conservative layers of his later years. See Guerci, 1972, pp. 80–110.

85. See the foreword in Intieri, 1754, presumably written by Ferdinando Galiani, who faithfully restated the ideas of his teacher (see Guerci in F. Galiani, 1975, p. 1055). For Genovesi's commentary on the foreword, see Venturi, 1959b, p. 450.

86. See Venturi, 1959a, pp. 118ff. In order better to frame the Enlightenment of Galiani and Intieri in a European context, see Vernière, 1977, pp. 136–137.

5: The Humanist Synthesis and Christian Tradition: Doria and Broggia

1. Doria came to invoke the armed strength of the prince against the Neapolitan Cartesians and *libertas philosophandi* (Doria, 1724, p. 8). Francesco Maria Spinelli's harsh response, accusing Doria of Spinozism and vindicating a possible Neoplatonic reading of Descartes, opened an important debate on the relations between Cartesianism and Spinozism in Neapolitan culture.

2. For Doria's argument against Newton, see Doria, 1745, pp. 71ff. His attack against Willem 'sGravesande, rightly considered the most dangerous of the Newtonian authors studied in Naples, is developed in Doria, 1741, vol. 1, pp. 116–117, and in the *Commento al Filebo* (B.N.N., ms. Branc., V.D.8, c. 49rff). In his work in 1741 Doria also took into account Voltaire's enlightened historiography and the Lockeanism and Newtonianism in the *Lettres anglaises*, which Charles of Bourbon prohibited in Naples; see V. Conti, 1978, pp. 68–74.

3. Doria, 1745, p. 57.

4. See the *Ritratto della moderna falsa scienza*, in De Fabrizio, 1981, pp. 129–205.

5. Bernardo Tanucci, among the most important figures of the Neapolitan political and cultural world, also clearly saw the destructive potential that Newtonian and Lockean empiricism and English culture ("without history, without jurisprudence, without poetry") could have for the social stability still guaranteed by the Christian humanist model, to which Gravina and Muratori had given

impetus in the eighteenth century. See Ajello, 1976a, pp. 248–249.

6. See *Lettera alla signora duchessa d'Erce*, in De Fabrizio, 1981, pp. 7–29, containing an accusation of deism against Newton and all the followers of natural theology.

7. On the features of Ficino's Christianity, see Garin, 1966, vol. 1, pp. 373–436, with a good bibliography, and especially Yates, 1964; Walker, 1958.

8. Apart from the unique but significant chronological reversal by which the early-eighteenth-century Boyle Lectures of Derham and Clarke came to be viewed as the ideological premise of the anonymous *Reasonableness of Christianity* (1695), Doria was not at all convinced that the *Reasonableness* was by Locke, but he felt it was written by "some modern, living follower of Mr. Locke's sect" (Doria, 1745, p. 15).

9. *Ibid.*, p. 24.

10. *Ibid.*, p. 11.

11. *Ibid.*, p. 54.

12. As, for examples, V. Conti (1978, pp. 78–79) and Badaloni (1973, pp. 742–743) maintain. I believe a more likely view is the image of Doria's Christianity as traced by Rotta, "Paolo Mattia Doria," in Cesarotti, 1978.

13. Doria, 1732, vol. 2, p. 284.

14. *Ibid.*, p. 285.

15. Rotta, "Paolo Mattia Doria," in Cesarotti, 1978, p. 863.

16. See Zambelli, "Il rogo postumo di Paolo Mattia Doria," in Zambelli, 1973b, pp. 182ff.

17. See the *Lettera alla signora duchessa d'Erce*, in De Fabrizio, 1981, and particularly Doria, 1741.

18. Doria, 1732, vol. 1, p. 61.

19. See *ibid.*, pp. 61–66.

20. Doria's attack on Muratori's *Filosofia morale* appears in Doria, 1741, pp. ixff; for a commentary, see Vidal, 1953, pp. 70–72.

21. Doria, 1732, vol. 1, p. 61.

22. *Ibid.*, vol. 2, p. 384. In the fundamental axiom of his morals, Doria restated an old theme dear to some Italian apologetics (Genovesi, for example, used it frequently), affirming "the driving force of all human actions is love" (*ibid.*, p. 295).

23. *Ibid.*, p. 322.

24. See *ibid.*, axiom II, p. 327.

25. See *ibid.*, axiom VII, p. 348.

26. *Ibid.*, p. 352.

27. On the repressive character of Christian society as hypothesized by Doria, a society that encouraged delation and denied any value to freedom of conscience, see Rotta, "Paolo Mattia Doria," in Cesarotti, 1973, p. 869, who correctly states: "A theoretician of a limited monarchy, Doria is in no way a supporter of individual rights."

28. Doria, 1732, vol. 2, p. 408.

29. See Doria, "Del commercio del Regno di Napoli," (1740), in Vidal, 1953, pp. 166–167. He wrote: "I do not, however, say that external commerce, the ideal one, ought not be practiced in part in Naples, but rather I say that in order to make the Kingdom of Naples abound in gold and silver, it is necessary to place primary hopes in internal and real commerce in the kingdom" (*ibid.*, p. 168).

30. See *ibid.*, p. 162. This is the definition of commerce always accepted in the social doctrine of the Church from the time of Saint Thomas Aquinas, who was among the first to put it forward; see Le Goff, 1980.

31. Doria complained that in Naples no one practiced "right and just," mutually beneficial commerce; all was reduced to usury ("Del commercio del Regno di Napoli," in Vidal, 1953, pp. 168–169).
32. *Ibid.*, p. 180. Emphasis mine.
33. *Ibid.*, p. 219.
34. *Ibid.*, p. 227, where Doria expounds the traditional thesis of the ruin of great empires due to the spread of vices.
35. On the concept of "moral economy" during the eighteenth century, especially the English view, see Thompson, "L'economia morale delle classi popolari inglesi nel secolo XVIII," in Thompson, 1981, pp. 57–136.
36. See Doria, p. 219.
37. The close tie between Concina and the Oziosi was stated by the author in his *Esposizione* (Concina, 1746, p. 172).
38. Doria wrote: "The usurers are the worms of the state, because in the way that worms feed off the dead flesh of men, the usurers feed and grow fat by eating the meat and blood of poor and needy citizens" (Doria, "Del commercio del Regno di Napoli," in Vidal, 1953, p. 222).
39. *Ibid.*, p. 209.
40. On "Christian agrarianism," see Rothkrug, 1965, pp. 234–286.
41. Doria, "Del commercio del Regno di Napoli," in Vidal, 1953, p. 209.
42. There is a broad analysis of Doria's reforms in V. Conti, 1978, pp. 91ff, and Venturi, 1969, pp. 42–46.
43. The profoundly anti-enlightened nature of Doria's work and its use in Italy to restrain the spread of enlightened culture have been properly emphasized by Ricuperati, 1979, who nevertheless has to a great extent overlooked the interesting reformist outcomes of his radical Christian solidarity.
44. In the light of Doria's considerations, Jacob's (1976, p. 142) conclusions assume a clear significance: "For the present I shall be content to have shown that Newton's philosophy of nature developed within a social context and served as the underpinning of a social and political ideology that attempted to ensure stability and piety and yet allow for the expression of individual self-interest, which in the course of the eighteenth century became increasingly synonymous with capitalistic enterprise." All this was beyond any simplification, historically unacceptable, that placed the Neapolitan circumstances on the same level as those of England, for the two were then quite different.
45. See Doria, "Il politico alla moda di mente adequata e prattico," in the appendix to V. Conti, 1978, p. 132.
46. *Ibid.*, p. 146. On Doria's political thought and the role he attributed to the "notables" (learned intellectuals who in some way had to condition the absolute power of the prince), see Conti's analysis (*ibid.*, pp. 125ff). On the resentment of Intieri and Ferdinando Galiani towards Montesquieu's ideas against enlightened despotism, in favor of mixed regimes, see Berselli Ambri, 1960, pp. 150–152, partially corrected in some philological errors by Venturi, 1969, pp. 565–566, and especially Rotta, "Montesquieu nel Settecento italiano," in Tarello, 1971, pp. 57–209. On the "Machiavellian leaven" present in the political thought of Intieri's group, which will eventually become largely foreign to Genovesi's mentality, see Venturi, 1962, p. 17. On the disputes within Intieri's group against Montesquieu's parliamentarianism, see Venturi, 1969, p. 566.
47. See Venturi, 1969, pp. 89–98, and especially Ajello, "Carlo Antonio Broggia," in Cesarotti, 1980, who rightly underscores Broggia's attitude towards the role of commerce, which was rather more open than Doria's moralist prejudices.
48. See Broggia, "Lettere a Fontanesi," edited in Ajello, "Carlo Antonio Broggia," in Cesarotti, 1980, p. 1128.

49. See *ibid.*, pp. 1023–1025.
50. *Ibid.*, p. 1140.
51. See Ajello, "L'esperienza giuridica di Carlantonio Broggia in tre sue opere ritenute disperse," in Ajello, 1976a, pp. 361–388.
52. See *ibid.*, pp. 365–369, and Ajello, "Carlo Antonio Broggia," in Cesarotti, 1980, p. 1012.

Seven: The Development and Exhaustion of the Debate: Towards Newtonian Scholasticism

1: ANTONIO GENOVESI'S NEWTONIANISM

1. See Garin, "Antonio Genovesi storico della scienza," in Garin, 1970, pp. 223–240; Marcialis, 1969, pp. 301–333. On the importance of the *Disputatio* and its success, see Venturi, 1969, p. 528.
2. There is not much information on the background to this edition. Genovesi speaks briefly of it in his *Autobiografia* (see Genovesi, 1962, pp. 19–20). There is no proof of Galiani's direct intervention, although Giuseppe Orlandi was certainly one of his most faithful pupils. A Celestine like Galiani, Orlandi wrote many works on mathematics and physics, commenting on Newtonian works and serving as a preceptor to Ferdinando and Bernardo Galiani, the *cappellano maggiore*'s nephews; see De Tipaldo, 1835, vol. 3, pp. 427–428. On Orlandi, see Galiani's letters (S.N.S.P., XXXI.A.5, cc. 57rff) and Intieri's to Galiani (S.N.S.P., XXXI.A.7, cc. 1rff).
3. See Genovesi and Orlando, 1745, vol. 2.
4. There is an examination of these reprints and the related variants in Marcialis, 1969, pp. 309–310.
5. See the exhaustive examination of the *Disputatio* in Garin, 1970, pp. 223ff.
6. *Disputatio physico-historica de rerum corporearum origine et constitutione*, in Genovesi and Orlando, 1745, vol. 1, p. 69.
7. *Ibid.*, pp. 70–71.
8. On the importance of the concept of *anima mundi* in Genovesi's early Newtonianism, see Badaloni, 1968a, pp. 204–206.
9. See Genovesi, 1743, pp. 7–8, 108ff.
10. *Disputatio*, in Genovesi and Orlando, 1745, p. 56.
11. *Ibid.*, p. 28.
12. See *ibid.*, pp. 55–56. The theme of the Brunian origin of Cartesianism recurs often in eighteenth-century European culture, after Huet spoke of it in his celebrated *Censura* of Cartesian philosophy. In Naples, Giacinto Gimma, in his *Idea della storia dell'Italia letterata* (1723), also restated a similar thesis.
13. See *Disputatio*, in Genovesi and Orlando, 1745, p. 70.
14. One can glimpse interesting hints of his position in this debate, even if in a substantially orthodox realm, in Genovesi's contemporary *Theologiae elementa*. See Genovesi's posthumous work, 1771, vol. 1, p. 165 and, especially, pp. 216ff, and Zambelli's study of this fundamental text, with all the variants in Genovesi's own handwriting, some regarding the problems of Newtonianism (1972, pp. 437ff).
15. There are ample references to these themes, in particular in the commentaries elicited by the *Telluris theoria sacra di Burnet* in the *Disputatio* in Genovesi and Orlando, 1745, pp. 66–68, and Genovesi, 1771, vol. 1, pp. 180ff.
16. See Genovesi, "La prima autobiografia," in the "Appendice" to Zambelli, 1972, pp. 813–816.
17. *Ibid.*, p. 819. Zambelli's work establishes Vico's and Doria's considerable influence

on Genovesi's early intellectual training, an opinion shared by Galasso, 1977, pp. 336-359.

18. See Genovesi, 1972, pp. 15-17, 21; and the more detailed "Prima autobiografia," in Zambelli, 1972, pp. 828-829.

19. Zambelli, 1972, p. 833.

20. Venturi, 1966, p. 8.

21. At the center of this conflict was not Newtonianism but the problem of the origin of ideas; see Badaloni, 1968a, pp. 204-207; Gentile, 1908, pp. 20ff; Santucci, 1953, pp. 681-710.

22. The "Lettera del signor abate Conti nobile veneto ad Antonio Genovesi: Risposta del Genovesi" appeared in 1746 without indicating place of publication or editor. The author, however, treated it as the premise to his other works. In the "Risposta," Genovesi revealed that he had been in contact with Conti thanks to Giuseppe Orlandi; see Genovesi, 1762, pp. 461ff.

23. Genovesi, "Lettera a N. N.," in Genovesi, 1972, p. 54.

24. There is an explicit reference to the theses of the *Disputatio* in Genovesi's letter to Conti dated 23 March 1746 (see Genovesi, 1972, pp. 56-58).

25. *Ibid.*, p. 57.

26. See Venturi, 1969, pp. 531-532. Somewhat stingily, Genovesi accused Galiani of lacking resolve when defending him from the charges of the Neapolitan clergy. "Galiani had written in my favor in Rome, but he lost his nerve in Naples. The king had been told that he was the main author of my opinions. This terrified him" (Genovesi, 1972, p. 21).

27. This is the basic thesis maintained by Venturi, 1969, pp. 532-533; see also R. Villari, 1970, pp. 26-52.

28. A theory proposed mainly by Zambelli, 1972, pp. 422-425.

29. Venturi (1969, pp. 560ff) rightly insists that the *Discorso* was an expression of "Intieri's group." Genovesi himself, in the *Autobiografia* (1962, p. 32), wrote that "the majority of the discussions in Mr. Intieri's small but brilliant circle centered about the progress of human reason, the arts, commerce, the economy of the state, mechanics, and physics."

30. On the already enlightened aspect of this image of culture, see R. Villari, 1970, pp. 37ff.

31. Genovesi, "Discorso sopra il vero fine delle lettere e delle scienze," in Genovesi, 1972, p. 231.

32. On the problems of the historical eras in modern thought and Italian literature, see "Età buie e rinascita: Un problema di confini," in Garin, 1975a, pp. 7-38; Costa, 1972.

33. See "Discorso," in Genovesi, 1972, p. 243.

34. Genovesi wrote: "One cannot say that reason has reached its maturity in a nation when it still resides in the abstract intellect more than in the hearts and souls. . . . Reason is not useful except when it has become practical and a reality; nor does it become such except if it is so entirely spread in the customs and the arts that we adopt it as our sovereign rule, almost without taking notice. But has knowledge reached this level among us?" (*ibid.*, p. 245).

35. *Ibid.*, p. 262.

36. *Ibid.*, p. 257.

37. See *ibid.*, pp. 261-262.

38. *Ibid.*, p. 253.

39. On the profound influence of Muratori's thought on Genovesi, see Zambelli, 1972, pp. 95-163, especially p. 145. Genovesi certainly found Muratori's *"pubblica felicità"* (an expression that recurs often in his works) to be yet another confirmation of the Baconian dimension of modern science viewed as a useful

tool for human progress. As Zambelli has observed, "what is useful for human-kind" was the basic motivation for the mature Genovesi's "cultural and political program" (ibid., p. 756).

40. See Garin, "Antonio Genovesi storico delle scienza," in Garin, 1970, p. 229.
41. On the importance of the Newtonian model in Hume's thought, see Dal Pra, 1973, pp. 63ff.
42. Genovesi, 1782, p. 17.
43. Ibid., p. 51.
44. Genovesi exhibited a considerable knowledge of the European scientific debate in his Scienze metafisiche. His comments on d'Alembert's Traité, Maupertuis's cosmological theses, and Buffon's theory of organic molecules reveal an extraordinary interest in modern science.
45. Genovesi, 1782, p. 58.
46. Genovesi, 1783, vol. 1, p. 61. For a commentary on Newton's Regulae, see pp. 5ff. The Elementa physicae that Genovesi used for his private school first appeared in Naples in 1779. Later there was a second edition of Fassadoni's translation printed in Naples in 1786 by Di Bisogno.
47. One should never forget that Newton himself in the conclusion of the famous quaestio XXXI of the Optice had suggested that "if natural philosophy in all its parts, by pursuing this method, shall at length be perfected, the bounds of moral philosophy will be also enlarged. For so far as we can know by natural philosophy what is the First Cause, what power He has over us, and what benefits we receive from Him, so far our duty towards Him, as well as that towards one another, will appear to us by the light of Nature" (I. Newton, 1706, p. 348).
48. See Genovesi, 1973, p. 32.
49. Ibid., p. 59.
50. See ibid., pp. 42, 270. There is a complete examination of the foundations of Genovesi's "moral science" in his important "Considerazioni su le scienze" developed in the Logica per giovinetti (see the collection of writings edited by Venturi, 1962, pp. 270–281). Genovesi identified three parts of human nature requiring consideration: the intellect, the heart, and the body, and the heart contained two opposing forces he called "concentrative" and "diffusive" (p. 271). Beginning with such premises, Genovesi concluded that "mankind's happiness is placed in harmony in these two forces." Restating a conviction common among Intieri's group in the 1740s, politics itself was applied to a social mechanics: "Republics have first had a diffusive force, then a concentrative. Montesquieu claims that the diffusive force is not meant for monarchies. This ought to be examined more closely. For now I believe [the claim] false and dangerous" (p. 272).
51. Genovesi, 1973, pp. 42–43.
52. Ibid., p. 26. On the importance of the concept of natural law in the eighteenth century, see above, chapter 6.
53. See Genovesi, 1973, pp. 50ff. Were Genovesi's insistence on natural law—even if cautiously assimilated to divine providence itself—and his self-proclamation as "both priest of nature and of Christ" perhaps not (as his enemy Mamachi wrote) evident proof of his pantheism and heterodoxy? Venturi (1963, p. 602) restated this question in problematic terms.
54. See Genovesi, 1973, p. 72. Genovesi wrote clearly about moral innatism: "There is no one who does not feel there is a natural law for distinguishing right from wrong, and virtue from vice. From this one can demonstrate that there is no people so savage or so corrupt that when interest and the passions are silent, this people does not judge well regarding certain injustices and do not praise

certain acts of virtue . . ., and where could it come from except an innate rule? For a [moral] criterion always comes before judgment" (*ibid.*, p. 50).

55. *Ibid.*, p. 93. Just as Vico and Muratori had done, Genovesi argued harshly in all his writings against Bayle's thesis that virtuous atheists existed.

56. See *ibid.*, pp. 270–271. On the significance of Genovesi's prudent distancing from Vico, see Zambelli, 1972, pp. 279ff.

57. "Genovesi's contradictions" have been noticed also by Venturi, 1969, pp. 602–603, beginning with his examination of the *Diceosina*. On Genovesi's moral thought, see Arata, 1978.

58. See the examination made by Venturi, 1969, pp. 600ff.

59. "Lettere accademiche su la questione se sieno piú felici gli ignoranti che gli scienziati," in Genovesi, 1972, p. 469.

60. See Venturi, 1969, pp. 577ff.

61. For example, referring to the problem of salaries in the economic development of the south, Intieri had identified salary reductions as an effective tool for guaranteeing agrarian entrepreneurs the profits indispensable for new investments. Genovesi radically refused such an economically oriented view of the south's development problem, arguing bitterly with those "nasty animals" inspired by Melon and Mandeville ("Lettere accademiche," in Genovesi, 1972, p. 492).

62. On Genovesi's political and economic thought in relation to the forces that were to guarantee southern development, especially the role of the middling "rank," see R. Villari, 1970, with wide-ranging bibliographic references.

63. On the intellectuals and power in Italy, see Perini, 1981, particularly pp. 831ff.

64. See "Lettere accademiche," in Genovesi, 1972, p. 444.

65. *Ibid.*, p. 377.

66. There has long been discussion of whether Genovesi outlined a kind of programmatic manifesto for Italian intellectuals in the "Lettere accademiche," in view of their direct involvement in the development of the south. While R. Villari (1970, p. 48) has denied it, I am more inclined towards the opinions expressed by Venturi (1969, pp. 560ff) and Galasso (1971, pp. 143ff). Another question entirely is the issue of the existence of a true party of intellectuals headed by Genovesi. For views against the myths surrounding a Genovesian school, see Chiosi, 1981, pp. 133–138; Villani, 1964, pp. 64ff.

67. "Lettere accademiche," in Genovesi, 1972, p. 457.

68. *Ibid.*, p. 463.

69. *Ibid.*, p. 465.

70. On this aspect of Genovesi's thought, see Pii, 1979, pp. 334–343; Galasso, 1977, p. 340. On Genovesi's economic theories, see L. Villari, 1958, pp. 45–66.

71. See Venturi, 1969, pp. 576ff, who identifies an enduring kind of Catholic moralism in the work of the young economist Genovesi, in particular in his rejection of the monetarism of Ferdinando Galiani and David Hume, and the acceptance of the traditional Catholic (and Doria's) conception of money as "pure poison" and the source of corruption.

72. See L. Villari, 1958, pp. 40ff.

73. Pietro Verri's letter to his brother Alessandro, Milan, 3 November 1766, in Greppi and Giolini, 1923, vol. 1, p. 32. On Verri's arguments against Genovesi's religious preoccupations, see Venturi, 1969, p. 635.

74. See, for example, Genovesi, 1773, pp. 155ff.

75. Genovesi, 1782, p. 14.

76. Genovesi, 1775, p. 231, following Nieuwentijt, 1717.

77. Genovesi, 1783, vol. 1, p. vi.

78. *Ibid.*, vol. 2, unpaginated preface.

79. On Genovesi's religious thought and presumed heterodoxy, see Galasso, 1970, pp. 807–808, who emphasizes its essentially evangelical dimension and the "humanitarian and solidaristic" component "strongly tinged by rationalist and social inspirations" (p. 805). Zambelli's examination (1972, particularly pp. 774ff) is more attentive to Genovesi's restlessness. Actually, beyond his intransigent jurisdictionalist and anticlerical battle, his essential orthodoxy appears to be undeniable.

2: THE UNIVERSE-MACHINE IN THE NOVELLE LETTERARIE

1. We refer to the famous *Newtonianismo per le dame* (see above, chapter 4), and the work of Stay (1744); on the latter, see Garin, 1970, pp. 225–226.
2. On the method of disseminating the new Newtonian science through verse, see Graf, 1911, pp. 384ff; Natali, 1950, vol. 2, pp. 687ff.
3. See Roggero, 1981b, pp. 205ff.
4. See above, chapter 6.
5. See *Novelle letterarie* 14 (1752): col. 224. Giovanni Maria Della Torre's work appeared in Naples, issued by the Porsile Press in two dense volumes. On Della Torre, see Napoli-Signorelli, 1786, pp. 485–486.
6. See Fortunato da Brescia, 1745–1746. Examining the problem of universal gravity in the second volume (1746), the friar followed Clarke's explanations as the sole and authentic interpretations of the *Principia* (p. 7ff).
7. See Rotta, 1970, pp. 389–390.
8. See Venturi, 1969, pp. 102ff, and Rosa, 1966, pp. 393–408.
9. See Renazzi, 1971, vol. 2, pp. 273ff.
10. Casini, 1980b, p. 359.
11. See *De Bononiensi scientiarum*, 1742, vol. 2, second part.
12. See Casini, 1980b, pp. 358–359.
13. See, for example, the *Giornale de' Letterati pubblicato in Firenze* 1 (1742): 137–155, in which Newton was defended against the French Cartesians, or the article "Observatoines cometae inaerentes anno 1744 in collegio Anglicano Romae habitae et cum theoria newtoniana comparatae a P. Christoforo Maire S. J.," *ibid.*, 3 (1744): 153ff.
14. For a thorough examination of this periodical and its importance to Italian culture, see Ricuperati, "Giornali e società nell'Italia dell'*Ancien Régime*," in Castronovo and Tranfaglia, 1976, pp. 165–187.
15. On Lami, see Cochrane, "Giovanni Lami," in Cesarotti, 1978, pp. 452–534, and especially Rosa, 1956, pp. 260–333.
16. See Ricuperati, "Giornali e società nell'Italia dell'*Ancien Régime*," in Castronovo and Tranfaglia, 1976, pp. 171–172.
17. See *Novelle letterarie* 39 (1741): cols. 609ff. The defense continued in the following issue. There were many articles in the *Novelle* that dealt with Newtonianism. In the first year of the journal's appearance, there was a discussion of a "Lettera di un fisico sopra la filosofia newtoniana accomodata all'intendimento di tutti dal sig. Voltaire, Venezia, Pasquali, 1739, pp. 38" (18 [1740]: cols. 281ff). Two years later the *Novelle* favorably reviewed the marquise of Châtelet's *Institutions de physique* (34 [1742]: cols. 39ff). In 1744 Newtonian theories were discussed in issues 6 (cols. 33ff), 7 (col. 103), 20 (col. 312), and 28 (col. 432).
18. See *Novelle letterarie* 28 (1741): cols. 436ff.
19. Lami wrote: "At the end of the preface there is a promise of a whole series on metaphysics and dissertations on the best and most interesting issues treated today by the most excellent and esteemed philosophers in this field" (*Novelle letterarie* 11 [1742]: col. 161).

20. *Ibid.*, 36 (1741): cols. 572ff.
21. *Ibid.*, 42 (1741): cols. 667ff.
22. *Ibid.*, col. 670.
23. See Mamachi, 1774, pp. 17–18, and especially pp. 23, 25, where he cited, extremely favorably, Clarke's and Derham's Boyle Lectures and emphasized the apologetic value of Newtonian natural theology. On Mamachi, see Papillon, 1935, pp. 241–260.
24. Moniglia, 1744, "Discorso preliminare sopra l'origine della religione," section 31. On Moniglia, see Carranza, 1974, pp. 140–141.
25. See Moniglia, 1744, pp. 47ff, especially pp. 61, 78.
26. See *ibid.*, "Discorso preliminare sopra l'origine della religione," section 27. There is a blatantly argumentative reference to Vico.
27. On the Florentine lodge, see Venturi, 1969, pp. 55ff; and especially Francovich, 1975, pp. 49–63. Regarding eighteenth-century Masonry one should generally consult the questionable works of the Jesuit Benimeli only as a source of factual information and not for their interpretation; they have been examined by Francovich, 1979, pp. 470–476. There is no doubt about De Soria's close friendship with people in the foreground of the Florentine Masonic world like Cocchi, Crudeli, and Bonaccorsi; see his affectionate profiles of Cocchi and Crudeli outlined in De Soria, 1783, vol. 1, respectively pp. 112ff and pp. 125ff.
28. See Francovich, 1975, pp. 68–85.
29. See above, chapter 3.
30. See "Articolo di lettera scritta dall'autore al cavaliere N. N. baronetto della Gran Bretagna del dì primo marzo 1743," in De Soria, 1745.
31. Magnanima, 1777, p. 8. There is no monograph on De Soria, although he deserves one; see, however, the brief notes in Garin, 1966, vol. 3, pp. 959ff; Badaloni, 1973, pp. 845–847; and especially the nice work of Venturi, 1969, pp. 346–354; Rotta, 1961, pp. 213–224.
32. Magnanima, 1777, pp. 31ff. Magnanima recounts that De Soria had earlier obtained a chair in philosophy at Turin and that he had refused in favor of one at Pisa.
33. See *ibid.*, pp. 34–36. Magnanima wrote: "They [De Soria's enemies] had recourse to the presidents of the university, accusing him of filling his writings with ideas against religion. . . . They decided to collect the writings of our philosopher secretly and, even if they were merely speculative, they entrusted their revision to three illustrious men who had to be theologians" (p. 35).
34. Muratori, for example, had praised him publicly. See Venturi, 1969, p. 348, who emphasizes the positive reactions the work elicited abroad. On the philosophical value of the *Institutiones*, see Gentile's favorable view (1936, pp. 284–302).
35. Magnanima, 1777, p. 33. Commenting on De Soria's concept of metaphysics, Magnanima wrote: "In order to be more certain, it is necessary to think of one's self as within the great empire of metaphysics that uncovers all, dominates, and confronts" (p. 25).
36. On this aspect of his work, see De Soria, 1750.
37. There is a detailed examination of De Soria's political and economic ideas in Rotta, 1961, pp. 222ff.
38. See De Soria's "Giudizio di un celebre professore sopra il libro Dei delitti e delle pene," in Beccaria, 1965, pp. 198–205.
39. On the existence of utopian elements in De Soria's thought, see Venturi, 1969, p. 249. On eighteenth-century utopias, see Baczko, 1978.
40. There is valuable information on the background of De Soria's cosmology in Magnanima, 1777, pp. 79ff.
41. De Soria, 1772, p. 10.

42. *Ibid.*, p. 8.
43. *Ibid.*, pp. 5ff.
44. *Ibid.*, p. 4.
45. See "Ragionamento filosofico della simpatia letto dall'autore nella gran sala dei cavalieri," in De Soria 1766, vol. 2, p. 10.
46. De Soria, 1745, pp. 47–48.
47. There is a brief examination of the contrasts between Conti and De Soria, who both rejected the Boyle Lectures, in Badaloni, 1968a, pp. 198ff. A unique and entirely Lockean reading of De Soria's philosophy has been suggested by his pupil and biographer Magnanima (1777, pp. 50ff). De Soria's philosophical thought nevertheless proves to be very complex and original, and it merits an in-depth analysis.
48. In his *Cosmologia*, De Soria paradoxically came to confirm the accusation of atheism against the Boyle lecturers and Newton (p. 103).
49. De Soria, 1745, p. 50.
50. *Ibid.*, pp. 56–58.
51. *Novelle letterarie* 45 (1745): col. 708.
52. *Novelle letterarie* 58 (1745): col. 787.
53. On Genovesi's acceptance of the so-called Galilean thesis of the double truth, see Zambelli, 1972, pp. 543–545. As we have tried to show in chapter 2, Galileo's reason paradoxically became the new frontier for Italian Catholic intellectuals against the danger of an enlightened reason irreverent towards Christianity's dogmas. Through a complex historical process, Galileo, who had first broken with the hegemony of a scholastic and strongly theologicized reason, then came to assume (against his will) the defense of the Christian citadel, ever more besieged by the Enlightenment.
54. *Novelle letterarie* 45 (1745): cols. 708–709.
55. *Novelle letterarie* 46 (1745): cols. 730ff.
56. See especially Lami's second letter in the *Novelle letterarie* 47 (1745): cols. 739–751.
57. *Ibid.*, col. 741.
58. *Novelle letterarie* 45 (1745): col. 712. In another issue of the *Novelle* (47 [1745]: col. 746) Lami wrote that De Soria "seems to make fun of the divinity and his existence."
59. *Novelle letterarie* 48 (1745): col.s 758ff.
60. *Novelle letterarie* 58 (1745): cols. 787ff. According to Lami, De Soria had maintained that "matter is God, the producer of all."
61. See the "Lettera quarta del signor abate Giuseppe Clemente Bini," in *Novelle letterarie* 1 (1746): cols. 1ff.
62. *Ibid.*, col. 7.
63. See *ibid.*, cols. 7–8.
64. *Novelle letterarie* 2 (1746): cols. 18–19.
65. *Novelle letterarie* 51 (1745): col. 809. Arguing against the Free-Thinkers, Lami concluded: "What a marvel that not even in London they wished to admit these doctrines, and these thinkers have sent them back" (col. 810).
66. Carranza, 1974, p. 278. On 3 January 1746 Cerati wrote to Bottari from Pisa: "I would not at all be surprised if De Soria's book were to be placed in the catalogue of prohibited books. The first exercise is full of opinions that cannot be reconciled with Trinitarian dogmas, and it also contains, in my opinion, considerable errors in the area of pure philosophy. I was not pleased that this book came out, because it cannot spread a good impression of our university, and I am pained by the fear that the author teaches to his many pupils some rather inexact opinions" (B.C.R., ms. 1589, 32.E.10, c. 193*v*).

67. See Carranza, 1974, pp. 278–279. Particularly interesting are the letters between Moniglia and Bottari regarding De Soria's book. Moniglia wrote to Bottari in December of 1745, describing his eagerness to read De Soria and his disappointment after reading it. Moniglia then told Bottari of all the subterfuge carried out by De Soria and his friends to obtain his public approval, which he was always refused despite the heavy pressure from very prestigious people in Tuscan intellectual and public life.

68. See Rotta, 1961, p. 210. On the complete convergence of Muratori's criticisms with those of Lami, see the brief comments in Badaloni, 1968a, p. 198.

69. The *Giornale de' Letterati* was the first periodical to review De Soria's book, giving it an enthusiastic review. The article (4 [1745]: 185–207) stated that the journal's editors had discussed the book personally with the author, who in the end authorized them to reveal his name. Toland's thesis of motion inherent in matter was appropriated by the periodical (p. 189). There are no worthwhile studies on the *Giornale de' Letterati*, although the presence of Masons among the founders of the periodical certainly deserves an attentive investigation. On Father Adami, who intervened in the argument under the name of Gelaste Mastigoforo, see Venturi, 1969, p. 347; Rotta, 1961, p. 210.

70. Regarding the powerful protection on which De Soria could rely, see Carranza, 1974, pp. 279–280.

71. See Francovich, 1975, p. 83.

72. *Novelle letterarie* 58 (1745): col. 792. In order to spare poor De Soria eventual physical persecution and to respond to various entreaties in this matter, Lami later began to maintain that De Soria had probably not correctly understood the significance of his own statements, either because of too little acumen or because of excessive carelessness in expressing himself. See *Novelle letterarie* 2 (1746): cols. 17–26.

73. See *Novelle letterarie* 21 (1746): cols. 324ff. The "command of Rome" appears clear in all the letters.

74. *Ibid.*, col. 332.

75. *Ibid.*, cols. 331–332.

76. *Novelle letterarie* 9 (1746): cols. 140–141.

3: BETWEEN INNOVATION AND REACTION

1. The discussion is still open; see the stimulating reflections in Ricuperati, "Pietro Giannone: Bilancio storiografico e prospettive di ricerca," in *Pietro Giannone*, 1980, vol. 1, pp. 185–249. On the difficulties that Italian materialists encountered in the early eighteenth century, see above, chapter 4.

2. On Toland's political thought, see Venturi, 1971. On Harrington, see Pocock, 1975, vol. 2.

3. See Venturi, 1969, pp. 248ff.

4. Galasso, "Conclusione" in Giannone, 1980, vol. 2, p. 867.

5. "Cattolicesimo e 'lumi': La condanna romana dell'*Esprit des lois*," in Rosa, 1969, pp. 87ff.

6. Rosa justly insists on this change of course in the Catholic Church's cultural policy, *ibid.*, pp. 112ff.

7. On Serrao's preconceived hostility towards modern thought, see the sharp observations in Chiosi, 1981, pp. 19–63.

8. On the matter of reform in Italy, see Sestan, 1955, pp. 20ff; "Illuminismo riformatore in Italia," in Diaz, 1973, pp. 613ff; Capra, 1979, pp. 313–368; Ajello, 1980.

Bibliography

Index of Manuscripts and Archival Documents

Brindisi, Biblioteca, arcivescovile Annibale De Leo
  Notamenti del Consiglio Collaterale, ms. B/48

Florence, Biblioteca Nazionale
  Manoscritti galileiani, ms. 257

Hanover, Niedersächsische Landesbibliothek
  Leibniz-Briefwechsel, 197

London, Public Record Office
  S. P., General Correspondence, 98 (22)

Milan, Biblioteca Braidense
  AF.XIII.13(7)

Naples, Biblioteca Nazionale
  mss. I.E.19, XIII.C.90, XV.D.24, XVI.B.6
  Fondo Biblioteca Brancacciana, ms. V.D.8
  Fondo Biblioteca Provinciale, mss. 89 and 90
  Biblioteca Società Napoletana di Storia Patria
  XX.B.22, XXIX.C.7, XXX.D.2, XXX.D.5, XXXI.A.1, XXXI.A.2, XXXI.A.3,
  XXXI.A.5, XXXI.A.6, XXXI.A.7, XXXI.B.1, XXXI.C.8, XXXI.C.12

Pisa, Biblioteca Universitaria
  Carteggio Grandi, mss. 44, 78, 85, 88, 90, 92–94, 96, 97, 99

Rome, Biblioteca Corsiniana
  mss. 891, 1450, 1452, 1581, 1582, 1605, 1608, 1884, 1891, 1894, 2027
  Biblioteca Lancisiana
  Fondo Lancisi, ms. 362
  Fondo Leprotti, mss. 269–276, 283
  Biblioteca Vallicelliana
  mss. T.46.B, U.15–U.17, U.20, U.21, U.25

Turin, Archivio di Stato
  Carte Giannone, mazzo I (Ja. V)
  Biblioteca Nazionale
  ms. O^2.III.35

Vatican City, Secret Vatican Archives [Archivio Segreto Vaticano]
  Nunziatura Napoli, 512
  Vatican Library [Biblioteca Apostolica Vaticana]
  Fondo Capponi, ms. 279
  Ottob. lat. 3116, tav. IV

Verona, Biblioteca Capitolare
  Fondo Bianchini, mss. CCCLXXIV, CCCLXXXIV, CCCLXXXVI, CCCXCII,
  CCCCXXVIII, CCCCXXX

Bibliography of Printed Seventeenth- and Eighteenth-Century Sources

Algarotti, F. 1737. *Il newtonianesimo per le dame ovvero dialoghi sopra la luce e i colori.* 2d ed. Naples.

———. 1791–94. *Opere.* Venice: Palese.

Andres, G. 1776. *Saggio sulla filosofia del Galileo.* Mantua: Pazzoni.

Ariani, V. 1778. *Memoria della vita e degli scritti di Vincenzo Ariani giureconsulto.* Naples: Stamperia di Castello Longobardo.

Averani, G. 1744–1761. *Lezioni toscane.* Florence: Albizzini.

Basnage, J. 1706–1711. *L'histoire et la religion des Juifs depuis Jesus Christ jusqu'au present.* Rotterdam: R. Leers.

Bayle, P. 1697. *Dictionnaire historique et critique.* Rotterdam: R. Leers.

Bencini, D. [1720]. *Tractatio historico-polemica.* Turin: N.p.

Bochart, S. 1646. *Geographia Sacrae pars prior Phaleg seu de dispersione gentium et terrarum divisione facta in aedificatione turris Babel.* Cadomi: Typis Petri Cardonelli.

———. 1663. *Hierozoicon, sive bipartitum opus De animalibus Sacrae Scripturae.* London: J. Martyn.

Brenna, L. 1778. *Vita di Galileo.* In *Vitae Italorum doctrina excellentium,* ed. A. Fabroni, vol. 1, 1–230. Pisa: Jacobus Gratiolius.

Bull, G. 1703. *Opera omnia quibus duo praecipui catholicae fidei articuli de S. Trinitate et justificatione . . . explorantur . . .* London: Smith.

Capassi, J. B. 1728. *Historiae philosophiae synopsis.* Naples: Mosca.

Cheyne, G. 1729. *Principi filosofici di religione naturale, ovvero elementi della filosofia e della religione da essi derivanti: Opera di George Cheyne M.D. della Società Regia.* Naples: Mosca.

Ciccarelli, L. 1725. *Vari componimenti poetici di più illustri autori in occasione delle nozze degli eccellentissimi signori D. Francesco Gaetano de' Duchi di Laurenzano e D. Giovanni Sanseverina de' Principi di Bisignano, raccolti da Lorenzo Ciccarelli e dedicati agli eccellentissimi sposi.* Piedmont: Parrino.

Cirillo, G. P. 1734. *Brieve ragguaglio dell'Accademia degli Oziosi.* Naples: Vocola.

———. [1735]. *Indice delle materie intorno alle quali ragioneranno gli Accademici Oziosi nell'anno 1735.* Naples: Mosca.

Cirillo, N. 1741. *Consulti medici.* 2 vols. Venice: Pitteri.

Collins, A. 1712. *A Philosophical Inquiry Concerning Human Liberty.* London: Robinson.

———. 1714. *A Discourse of Free-thinking . . .* London: N.p.

———. 1766. *Discours sur la liberté de penser . . .; traduit de l'Anglois et augmenté d'une lettre d'un médecin arabe.* Nouvelle édition. London: N.p.

Concina, D. 1746. *Esposizione del dogma che la chiesa romana propone a credersi intorno l'usura colla confutazione del libro intitolato Dell'impiego del denaro.* Naples: Palumbo.

Conti, A. 1716. *Risposta del signor abate Antonio Conti nobile veneziano alla difesa del libro delle considerazioni intorno alla generazione de' viventi indirizzata al signor marchese Scipione Maffei.* Venice: Tommasini.

———. 1739–1756. *Prose e poesie.* 2 vols. Venice: Pasquali.

Crell, S. 1700. *Cogitationum novarum de primo et secundum Adamo, sive de ratione salutis per illum amissae per hunc recuperatae compendium.* Amsterdam: I. Aspidium.

Crescimbeni, G. M. 1710. *Le vite degli arcadi illustri.* Rome: De Rossi.

Crivelli, G. 1731. *Elementi de fisica.* Venice: Orlandini. 2d ed.: Venice: Simone Occhi, 1744.

De Bononiensi scientiarum et artium instituto atque academia commentari. 1742. Bologna: Della Volpe.

De Cristoforo, F. 1700. *De constuctione aequationibus libellus*. Naples: Roselli.

Derham, W. 1716. *Physico-Theology*. 4th ed. London: W. Innys.

———. 1719. *Dimostrazione dell'essenza e degli attributi di Dio dall'opera della sua creazione*. Florence: Tartini e Franchi.

———. 1728. *Teologia astronomica, overo parte seconda della dimostrazione della essenza e degli attributi d'Iddio dall'esame de' cieli, opera di Guglielmo Derham della Società Regia. Tradotta dall'idioma inglese*. Naples: Mosca.

Des Maizeaux, P., ed. 1720. *Recueil de diverses pièces sur la philosophie, la religion naturelle, l'histoire, les mathématiques par Mrs. Leibniz, Clarke, Newton*. Amsterdam: H. Du Sauzet.

———, ed. 1740. *Recueil de diverses pièces sur la philosophie, la religion naturelle, l'histoire, les mathématiques, etc., par Mrs. Leibniz, Clarke, Newton et autres célèbres auteurs*. 2d ed. Amsterdam: Changuion.

De Soria, G. A. 1741. *Rationalis philosophiae institutiones sive de emendanda regendaque mente*. Amsterdam: N.p.

———. 1745. *Dell'esistenza e degli attributi di Dio e della immaterialità e immortalità dello spirito umano secondo la mera filosofia*. Lucca: Bandini. (The work appeared anonymously.)

———. 1750. *La scienza dell'uomo e la scienza della natura espurgate da tutte le ipotesi e ridotte alla intelligenza comune*. In *Opere filosofiche*. Lucca: Bedini.

———. 1766. *Raccolta di opuscoli filosofici e filologici di Gio. Guadalberto De Soria*. 2 vols. Pisa: Pizzorno.

———. 1772. *Cosmologia o fisica universale del dott. Gio. Guadalberto De Soria*. Florence: Marzi.

———. 1783. *Raccolta di opere inedite: Contenente i caratteri di vari uomini illustri*. 2 vols. Leghorn: Masi.

Di Martino, N. 1727. *Elementa staticae in Tyronum gratiam tumultuorio studio concinnata*. Naples: Mosca.

———. 1728. *Logicae seu artis cogitandi institutiones*. Naples: Mosca.

Di Martino, P. 1738. *Philosophia naturalis institutionum libri tres*. 2 vols. Naples: Mosca.

Di Sangro, R. 1740. *Lettera apologetica dell'esercitato accademico della Crusca contenente la difesa del libro intitolato lettera d'una peruana per rispetto alla supposizione de' quipu . . .* Naples: N.p.

Doria, P. M. 1712. *Giunta di P. M. Doria al suo libro del moto e della meccanica in cui si risponde a varie obiezioni che al medesimo potrebbon farsi per avventura*. Augsburg: Hopper.

———. 1722. *Delle opere matematiche*. 2 vols. Venice: N.p.

———. 1724. *Discorsi critici filosofici intorno alla filosofia di Renato Descartes con un progetto di una metafisica*. Venice: N.p.

———. 1728. *Filosofia di Paolo Mattia Doria colla quale si schiarisce quella di Platone*. Amsterdam: N.p.

———. 1732. *Difesa metafisica degli antichi filosofi contro il signor Giovanni Locke ed alcuni altri autori moderni*. 2 vols. Venice [Naples]: N.p.

———. 1741. *Lettere e ragionamenti vari dedicati ai signori dell'accademia etrusca*. 2 vols. Perugia [Naples]: N.p.

———. 1745. *Narrazione di un libro inedito di Paolo Mattia Doria. Fatto affine di preservare e difendere le numerose sue opere da quell'oblio nel quale tentano di seppellirle i suoi contrari*. Naples: Vocola.

Eschinardi, F. 1680. *Ragguagli . . . sopra alcuni pensieri sperimentabili proposti nell'Accademia Fisico-matematica di Roma*. Rome: N.p.

Ettmüller, M. 1734. *Opera omnia in quinque tomos distributa: Editio novissima veneta . . . accesserunt notae, consilia, etc. Nicolai Cyrilli*. Venice: Herz.

Fabroni, A. 1780. *Franciscus Blanchinus*. In *Vitae Italorum doctrina excellentium qui saeculis XVII et XVIII floruerunt*, ed. A. Fabroni, vol. 6, pp. 280–352. Pisa: Jacobus Gratiolius.

Fasano, T. 1784. *De vita, muniis et scriptis Francisci Serai philosophi et medici neapolitani clarissimi commentarius*. Naples: Typographia Simoniana.

Fortunato da Brescia. 1745–1746. *Philosophia sensuum mechanica methodice tractata atque ad usus academicos accomodata*. 2 vols. Brescia: Rizzardi.

Galiani, C. 1708. *Conclusiones selectae ex historia Veteris Testamenti ab orbe condito ad Abraham in Chananaeam profectionem, quas sub auspiciis eminentiss. et reverendiss. principis Josephi Renati Imperialis S.R.E. cardinalis diaconi Sancti Georgii publico examini exponet in Monasterio Sancti Eusebii Congregationis Coelestinorum Ordinis Sancti Benedicti D. Bonifacius Pepe eiusdem Congregationis alumnus, praeside D. Coelestino Galiano. In praefato monasterio Sacrae Scripturae interprete: anno 1708 mense Januarii die*. Rome: Franciscus Gonzaga.

Galilei, G. 1613. *L'istoria e dimostrazioni intorno alle macchie solari e loro accidenti comprese in tre lettere scritte a Marco Velseri*. Rome: Mascardi.

———. 1636. *Nova-antiqua sanctissimorum patrum et probatorum theologorum doctrina de sacrae scripturae testimoniis in conclusionibus mere naturalibus quae sensata experentia et necessariis demonstrationibus evinci possunt, temere non usurpandis. Nunc vero iuris publici facta, cum latina versione italico textui simul adiuncta*. Augustae Treboc, impensis Elzevirium: Typis Davidis Hautti.

———. 1710a. *Dialogo intorno ai due massimi sistemi*. Naples: N.p.

———. 1710b. *Lettera del signor Galileo Galilei scritta alla granduchessa di Toscana in cui teologicamente e con ragioni saldissime cavate da padri più sentiti si risponde alle calunnie di coloro i quali a tutto potere si sforzarono non solo di sbandirne la sua opinione intorno alla costituzione delle parti dell'universo, ma altresì di addurne una perpetua infamia alla sua persona*. Florence: N.p.

———. 1718. *Opere di Galileo Galilei*. 3 vols. Florence: Stamperia di S.A.R. per Gio. Gaetano Tartini e Santi Franchi.

———. 1744. *Opere di Galileo Galilei divise in quattro tomi . . . accresciut[e] di molte cose inedite*. Padua: Stamperia del Seminario.

Garofalo, B. 1707. *Considerazioni intorno alla poesia degli ebrei e dei greci*. Rome: Gonzaga.

Gassendi, P. 1727. *Petri Gassendi Diniensis ecclesiae praepositi et in academia Parisiensi matheseos regii professoris opera omnia in sex tomos divisa curante Nicolao Averanio advocato florentino*. Florence: Tartini e Franchi.

Genovesi, A. 1743. *Elementa metaphisicae in usum privatorum adolescentium mathematicum in morem adornata ab Antonio Genuensi in Regia Neapolitana Academia philosophiae professore*. Naples: Gessari.

———. 1746. *Lettera del signor abate Conti nobile veneto ad Antonio Genovesi. Risposta del Genovesi*. N.p.

———. 1755. *La logica per gli giovinetti*. Bassano: Remondini.

———. 1762. *Elementorum artis logico-criticae libri v. Editio novissima*. Venice: Occhi.

———. 1771. *Universae christianae theologiae elementa dogmatica, historica, critica*. 2 vols. Venice: Pasquali.

———. 1773. *Elementa metaphysicae mathematicum in morem adornata ab Antonio Genuensi*. Venice: Bettinelli.

———. 1782. *Delle scienze metafisiche per gli giovinetti*. Venice: Bettinelli.

———. 1783. *Elementi di fisica sperimentale ad uso dei giovani principianti di Antonio Genovesi: Trasportati dal latino in italiano dall'abate Marco Fassadoni*. 2 vols. Venice: Pezzana.

Genovesi, A., and G. Orlandi, eds. 1745. *Elementa physicae conscripta in usus academicos a Petro van Musschembroek, quibus nunc primum in gratiam studiosae inventutis accedunt ab alienis manibus ubique auctaria et notae disputatio physico-historica de rerum corporearum origine, ac demum de rebus coelestibus tractatus.* With annotation and commentary. 2 vols. Naples: Palumbo.

Gimma, G. 1703. *Elogi accademici della Società degli spensierati di Rossano descritti dal dottor sign. D. Giacinto Gimma promotor perpetuo della medesima avvocato fedelissimo della città di Napoli ecc. Pubblicato da Gaetano Tremiglizzi consiglier-promotoriale colle memorie storiche della società aggiunte dal medesimo nella seconda parte.* 2 vols. Naples: Carlo Troise.

————. 1714. *Dissertationum academicorum tomus primus.* Naples: Muzio.

————. 1723. *Idea della storia dell'Italia letteraria.* 2 vols. Naples: Mosca.

————. 1730. *Della storia naturale delle gemme, delle pietre e di tutti i minerali ovvero della fisica sotterranea.* 2 vols. Naples: Mosca e Muzio.

————. 1732. *Dissertationum academicorum tomus secundus.* Naples: Mosca.

Giordani, V. 1687. *De componendis gravium momentis dissertatio.* Rome: A. Barnabò.

Giustiniani, L. 1788. *Memorie istoriche degli scrittori legali del Regno di Napoli.* 3 vols. Naples: Stamperia Simoniana.

Grandi, G. 1701. *Geometrica demonstratio theorematum Hugeniarum circa logisticam seu logarithmicam lineam.* Florence: Bigonci.

————. [1710]. *Considerazioni del P. D., Guidone Grandi e del sig. N. N. sopra le scritture del signor Luc'Antonio Porzio circa il moto de' gravi per il piano inclinato.* N.p.

Gregory, D. 1702. *Astronomia physicae et geometricae elementa.* Oxford: Sheldon Theatre.

Grimaldi, C. 1751. *Dissertazione in cui si investiga quali sieno le operazioni che dipendono dalla magia diabolica e quali che derivano dalle magie artificiali e naturali.* Rome: N.p.

Grotius, H. 1732. *Opera omnia theologica in quatuor tomos divisa.* Basil: Thurnisius.

Hauksbee, F. 1716. *Esperienze fisico-meccaniche sopra i vari soggetti contenenti un racconto di diversi stupendi fenomeni intorno la luce e l'elettricità producibile dallo strofinamento de' corpi con molte altre notabili apparenze non mai prima osservate: Colle spiegazioni di tutte le macchine: Opera di F. Hauksbee della Società Regia,* tradotta dall'idioma inglese. Florence: Stamperia di Sua Altezza Reale per Jacopo Guiducci e Santi Franchi.

Horn, G. 1659. *Defensio dissertationis de vera aetate mundi contra castigationes I. Vossii.* Leyden: Johannes Elzevirius.

Huet, P. D. 1679. *Demonstratio evangelica.* Paris: N.p.

Index librorum prohibitorum. 1783. Parma: Philip Carmignano.

Intieri, B. 1703. *Ad nova arcana geometrica detegenda aditus.* Benevento: Typographia archiepiscopalis.

————. 1704. *Apollonius ac Serenus promotus.* Naples: Leonardo Giuseppe Sellitto.

————. 1706. *Facilissimo metodo per la quadratura delle parabole di qualsivoglia grado, colla risposta alla questione posta dal sig. N. N. [Giacinto De Cristoforo]* Naples: N.p.

————. 1716. *Nuova invenzione di fabbricar mulini a vento di B. I. fiorentino dedicata all'eccellentissimo signor D. Wirrigo Daun.* Naples: Mosca.

Lafitau, J. 1724. *Mœurs des sauvages ameriquains.* Paris: Saugrain l'aîné.

Lamberti, G. 1734. *Lettera di N. ad un suo amico nella quale si fanno alcune considerazioni sopra la risposta del signor D. Paolo Mattia Doria al libro del sign. Principe della Scalea.* Lucca: N.p.

Lapeyrère, I. 1655. *Systema theologicum ex praeadamitarum hypotesi.* [Amsterdam]: N.p.

Le Clerc, J. 1698. *Opera philosophica.* Vol. 1. Amsterdam: Gallet.

————. 1699. *Parrahasiana ou pensèe diverses sur de matières de critique, d'histoire, de morale, et de politique.* Vol. 1, Amsterdam: Schelte.

————. 1710a. *Genesis sive Mosis prophetae liber primus ex translatione Joannis Clerici, cum eiusdem paraphrasi perpetua, commentario philologico, dissertationibus criticis quinque et tabulis chronologicis.* 2 vols. 2d ed. Amsterdam: Schelte.

―――. 1710b. *Mosis prophetae libri quatuor.: Exodus, Leviticus, Numeri, et Deuteronomium.* 2d ed. Amsterdam: Schelte. 1st ed.: 1693.

Lettere di diversi autori in proposito delle considerazioni del marchese Giovan Gioseffo Orsi, sopra il famoso libro franzese intitolato La Maniera di Bien Penser. 1707. Bologna: Pisani.

Lettere inedite di uomini illustri. 1744. Venice: Baglioni.

Limborch, P. van. 1686. *Theologia christiana.* Amsterdam: Henricus Wetstenius.

Locke, J. 1690. *An Essay Concerning Human Understanding.* London: Thomas Basset.

―――. 1695. *Reasonableness of Christianity.* London: Awnsham and John Churchil.

Lowthorp, J. 1729–1734. *Saggio delle transazioni filosofiche della Società Regia compediate da Giovanni Lowthorp: Tradotte dall'inglese nell'idioma toscano e dedicate a sua eccellenza la signora Donna Clelia Grilla-Borromeo.* 5 vols. Naples: Mosca.

Magnanima, L. 1777. *Elogio istorico e filosofico di Giovanni Alberto De Soria scritto dall'abate Luca Magnanima.* Leghorn: Giorgi.

Mamachi, T. 1774. *Oratio de ratione tradendae philosophiae designatis orthodoxae religionis propagatoribus.* Rome: Collini.

Manfredi, E. 1744. *Elementi di cronologia con diverse scritture appartenenti al calendario romano.* Bologna: Della Volpe.

―――. 1749. *Istituzioni di astronomia.* Bologna: Della Volpe.

Marsham, J. 1696. *Canon chronicus aegyptiacus, hebraicus, graecus.* London: G. Wells.

Martino, N. 1727. *Elementa staticae in Tyronum gratiam tumultuorio studio concinnata.* Naples: Mosca.

Maurodenoja, D. 1738. "Breve ristretto della vita dell'abate sig. D. Giacinto Gimma." *Raccolta d'opuscoli scientifici e filosofici* 17: 338–427.

Melon, J. F. 1734. *Essai politique sur le commerce.* [Paris]: N.p.

Moniglia, T. 1744. *Dissertazione contro i fatalisti.* Pisa: Ciuffetti e Benedini.

Mosca, G. 1764. *Vita di Luc'Antonio Porzio.* Naples: Manfredi.

Muratori, L. A. 1735. *La filosofia morale esposta e proposta ai giovani.* Verona: Tasca.

Napoli-Signorelli, P. 1786. *Vicende della cultura nelle due Sicilie.* Naples: Flauto.

Nelli, G. C. 1793. *Vita e commercio letterario di Galileo Galilei.* Lausanne: N.p.

Newton, H. 1710. *Sive de Nova Villa Societatis Regiae Londini, Arcadiae Romanae Academiae Florentinae et eius quae vulgo vocatur della Crusca socii epistolae, orationes et carmina.* Lucca: Domenic Ciuffetti.

Newton, I. 1687. *Philosophiae naturais principia mathematica.* London: Royal Society and Joseph Streater. 3d ed.: London: Innys, 1726.

―――. 1704. *Opticks, or a Treatise of the Reflexions, Refractions, Inflexions and Colours of Light.* London: N.p.. 2d ed.: London: W. & J. Innys, 1717.

―――. 1706. *Optice sive de reflexionibus, inflexionibus et coloribus lucis.* London: Smith & Walford.

Nicole, p. 1700. *Essai de morale, contenu en divers traitez sur plusieurs devoir importans.* The Hague: Moetjen.

Nieuwentijdt, B. 1717. *L'existence de Dieu démontrée par les merveilles de la nature.* Paris: J. Vincent.

Nigrisoli, F. M. 1712. *Considerazioni intorno alla generazione de' viventi e particolarmente de' mostri.* Ferrara: Barbieri.

Noël d'Alexandre. 1699. *Historia Ecclesiasticae Veteris et Novis Testamentum.* 8 vols. Paris: Migue.

Origlia Paolino, G. 1753–1754. *Istoria dello Studio di Napoli.* 2 vols. Naples: De Simone.

Ortes, G. 1744. *Vita del padre Guido abate camaldolese matematico dello studio pisano scritta da un suo discepolo.* Venice: Pasquali.

Pemberton, H. 1733. *Saggio della filosofia del cavalier Isacco Newton esposto con chiarezza dal signor Enrico Pemberton: Con una dissertazione dello stesso sulla misura della forza de' corpi in moto cavata dagli atti filosofici d'Inghilterra.* Venice: Storti. 2d ed.: Venice: Storti, 1745.

Pezron, P. 1687. *L'antiquité des temps rétablie et defendue contre les Juifs et les nouveaux chronologistes.* Paris: Edme Martin.

Poleni, G. 1712. *De vorticibus coelestibus dialogus.* Pavia: J. B. Gonzati.

———. 1728. *Epistolarum mathematicarum fasciculus.* Pavia: N.p.

Porzio, L. 1711. *Lettere e discorsi accademici a sua eccellenza il signor D. Marzio Pacecco Caraffa Colonna.* Naples: Muzio.

———. 1736. *Opera omnia.* Naples: Mosca.

Prideaux, H. 1722. *L'histoire des Juifs et des peuples voisins, depuis la décadence des royaumes d'Israël et Juda jusqu'à la mort de Jesus-Christ.* Amsterdam: H. du Sauzet.

Pufendorf, S. 1707. *Devoirs de l'homme et du citoyen, tels qu'ils lui sont prescrits par la loi naturelle.* Ed. and trans. J. Barbeyrac. Amsterdam: Schelte.

———. 1712. *Le droit de la nature et des gens ou système générale des principes les plus importans de la morale, de la jurisprudence et de la politique.* Amsterdam: Decoup.

Raccolta d'opuscoli sopra l'opinioni filosofiche di Newton. 1746. Venice: Recurti.

Rélation apologique [sic] et historique de la société de Francs-Maçons. 1738. Dublin: Odonoko.

Riccati, J. 1761–1764. *Opere.* 4 vols. Lucca: Giusti. (Vol. 4 was published in Lucca by Giuseppe Rocchi.)

Rizzetti, G. 1741. *Saggio dell'antineutonianismo sopra le leggi del moto e dei colori.* Venice: Pasinelli.

Rohault, J. 1713. *Tractatus physicus. Latine vertit, recensuit et uberioribus iam adnotationibus ex illustrissimi Isaaci Newtoni philosophia maximam partem haustis amplificavit et ornavit Samuel Clarke A.M.* 2 vols. Cologne: N.p.

Salvini, A. M. 1717. *Fasti consolari dell'Accademia Florentina.* Florence: Tartini e Franchi.

Scacchi, B. [Raffaele Rabbegno]. 1710. *Squarcio di lettere del dottor Bernabò Scacchi sopra le considerazioni del signor B. G. intorno la poesia degli ebrei.* Padua: N.p.

Selden, J. 1617. *De diis syris syntagmata.* London: G. Stausbeius.

———. 1640. *De iure naturali et gentium iuxta disciplinam hebraeorum libri septem.* London: R. Bishopius.

Serao, F. 1740. *Istoria dell'incendio del Vesuvio.* 2d rev. ed. Naples: Vocola.

———. 1742. *Nicolaus Cyrillus.* In *Memorabilia italorum eruditione praestantium,* ed. G. Lami, vol. 1, 180–94. Florence: Typographia societatis ad insignam centauri.

'sGravesande, W. J. S. van. 1737. *Physices elementa mathematica . . . sive Introductio ad philosophiam newtonianam.* Venice: Pasquinelli.

———. 1749. *Philosophiae newtoniane institutiones in usus academicos.* Venice: Remondini.

Simon, Richard. 1685. *Historia critica Vet. Test.' auctore Riccardo Simonio.* 4th ed. Amsterdam.

Spanheim, F. 1694. *Historia Jobi. Sive de obscuribus historiae commentatio.* Leyden: J. Verbessel.

Spencer, J. 1670. *Dissertatio de Urim et Thummin in Deuteron. . . .* Cambridge: T. Garthwart.

———. 1685. *De legibus hebraeocrum ritualibus et earum rationalibus libri tres.* London: R. Chiswel.

Spinelli, F. M. 1733. *Riflessioni . . . sulle principali materie della prima filosofia fatte ad occasione di esaminare la prima parte d'un libro intitolato Discorsi critici filosofici intorno alla filosofia degli antichi e de' moderni di Paolo Mattia Doria.* Naples: Mosca.

————. 1753. "Vita e studi di Francesco Maria Spinelli principe della Scalea scritta da lui medesimo in una lettera." *Raccolta d'opuscoli scientifici e filologici* 49: 504–23.

Stay, B. 1744. *Philosophia cartesiana versibus tradita.* Venice: N.p.

Stillingfleet, E. 1701. *Answer to the Modern Objections of Atheists and Deists.* London: H. Mortlock.

Targioni Tozzetti, G. 1780. *Notizie degli ingrandimenti delle scienze fisiche accaduti in Toscana nel corso di anni LX del secolo XVII.* Florence: Bouchard.

Toland, J. 1704. *Letters to Serena.* London: Lintot.

Torricelli, E. 1644. *Opera geometrica.* Florence: A. Massae.

————. 1715. *Lezioni accademiche di Evangelista Torricelli mattematico e filosofo del serenissimo Ferdinando II granduca di Toscana.* Florence: Tartini e Santi.

Tremigliozzi, G. 1700. *Nuova staffetta da Parnaso circa gli affari della medicina . . . indirizzata all'illustrissima accademia di medicina.* Frankfurt: N.p.

Vallisnieri, A. 1721. *Istoria della generazione dell'uomo e degli animali se sia da vermicelli spermatici o dalle ouva.* Venice: Herz.

————. 1726. *Nuove osservazioni ed esperienze intorno all'ovaia scoperta ne' vermi tondi dell'uomo e de' vitelli con varie lettere spettanti alla storia medica e naturale.* Padua: Manfré.

————. 1728. *De' corpi marini che su monti si trovano.* 2d ed. Venice: Lovisa.

Varen, B. 1715. *Geographia generalis in qua affectiones generales telluris explicantur, summa cura quam plurimis in loci emendata, et XXXIII schematibus novis, aere incisis, una cum tabb. aliquot quae desiderabantur aucta et illustrata, ab Isaaco Newton Math. Prof. Lucasiano apud Cantabrigienses . . . pluribus fig. adornata a Jacobo Jurin. Editio Quarta.* Naples: Gessari.

Vari componimenti recitati nell'Accademia degli Oziosi in onore di S. Aurelio Agostino protettore della medesima. 1735. Padua [Naples]: N.p.

Vossius, I. 1659. *Dissertatio de vera aetate mundi qua ostenditur Natale mundi tempus annis minimum 1400 vulgarem aeram anticipare.* The Hague: Adrian Vlacq.

Bibliography of Modern Editions and Secondary Sources

Accademie e cultura: Aspetti storici tra sei e settecento. 1979. Florence: Olschki.

Ajello, R. 1961. *Il problema della riforma giudiziaria e legislativa nel regno di Napoli durante la prima metà del secolo XVIII. I: La vita guidiziaria.* Naples: Jovene.

————. 1969. "Il Banco di San Carlo: Organi di governo e opinione pubblica nel Regno di Napoli di fronte al problema della ricompera dei diritti fiscali." *Rivista storica italiana* 81: 812–81.

————. 1976a. *Arcana juris: Diritto e politica nel Settecento italiano.* Naples: Jovene.

————. 1976b. "La vita politica napoletana sotto Carlo di Borbone: 'La fondazione ed il tempo eroico' della dinastia." In *Storia di Napoli*, vol. 4, 461–984. Naples: ESI.

————. 1979. *Le origini della politica mercantilistica nel Regno di Napoli.* Introduction by F. Strazzullo, "Le manifatture d'arte di Carlo di Borbone." Naples: Liguori.

————. 1980. "Dal giurisdizionalismo all'illuminismo nelle Sicilie: Pietro Contegna." *Archivio storico per le provincie napoletane* 48: 383–412.

————. 1981. "Cirillo, Giovanni Pasquale." *D.B.I.*, vol. 25, 796–801.

————. 1982. "Napoli tra Spagna e Francia: problemi politici e culturali." In *Arti e civiltà del Settecento a Napoli*, ed. C. De Seta, 3–30. Bari: Laterza.

Alberti, A. M. 1977. *Empirismo e metafisica alle origini della scienza moderna.* Bologna: Tamari.

Altieri Biaggi, M. L., and B. Basile, eds. 1980. *Scienziati del Seicento.* Milan, Naples: Ricciardi.

Amabile, L. 1892. *Il Santo Officio e l'Inquisizione in Napoli.* 2 vols. Città di Castello: Lapi.

Amati, G., ed. 1867. *Alcune lettere dell'abate Niccolini a Monsignor Giovanni Bottari intorno alla corte di Roma (1724–1761).* Bologna: Romagnoli.

Amodeo, F. 1902. *Dai fratelli Di Martino a Vito Caravelli: Memoria letta all'Accademia Pontaniana.* Naples: Tessitore.

Appolis, E. 1960. *Le "tiers parti" catholique au XVIIIe siècle.* Paris: Picard.

Arata, F. 1978. *Antonio Genovesi: Una proposta di morale illuminista.* Padua: Marsilio.

Arrighi, G. 1973. "La prima traduzione italiana dei *Philosophie naturalis principia mathematica.*" *Bollettino Unione Matematica Italiana* 8: 174–79.

Auvray, P. 1968. "R. Simon et Spinoza." In *Religion, érudition et critique à la fin du XVIIe siècle et au début du XVIIIe siècle,* 201–14. Paris: PUF.

Aymard, M. 1978. "La transizione dal feudalesimo al capitalismo." In *Storia d'Italia, Annali,* vol. 1, ed. Ruggiero Romano and Corrado Vivanti, 1133–92. Turin: Einaudi.

Bacchini, A. 1920. *La vita e le opere di Giovanni Maria Lancisi (1654–1720).* Rome: Stabilimento Sansaiori.

Baczko, B. 1978. *Lumières de l'utopie.* Paris: Payot.

Badaloni, N. 1958. "Una polemica scientifica ai primi del '700 ed uno sconosciuto 'parere' del Vico." *Società* 6: 1149–60.

———. 1961. *Introduzione a G. B. Vico.* Milan: Feltrinelli.

———. 1968a. *Antonio Conti: Un abate libero pensatore tra Newton e Voltaire.* Milan: Feltrinelli.

———. 1968b. "Intorno alla filosofia di Alessandro Marchetti." *Belfagor* 23: 283–316.

———. 1970. "Spinoza e Illuminismo: Note sulla fortuna di Gaspard Cuenz (1676–1756)." In *Studi in onore di Antonio Corsano.* Manduria: Lacaita.

———. 1973. "La cultura." In *Storia d'Italia,* vol. 3, ed. Ruggiero Romano and Corrado Vivanti, 699–984. Turin: Einaudi.

Baker, K. M. 1975. *Condorcet: From Natural Philosophy to Social Mathematics.* Chicago: University of Chicago Press.

Baldini, U. 1980a. "L'attività scientifica nel primo Settecento." In *Storia d'Italia, Annali,* vol. 3, ed. Gianni Micheli, 467–545. Turin: Einaudi.

———. 1980b. "Ceva, Giovanni." *D.B.I.,* vol. 24, 316–19.

———. 1980c. "La scuola galileiana." In *Storia d'Italia, Annali,* vol. 3, ed. Gianni Micheli, 383–463. Turin: Einaudi.

———. 1981. "Cirillo, Niccolò." *D.B.I.,* vol. 25, 801–5.

Barbagallo, F. 1971. "Discussioni e progetti sul commercio tra Napoli e Costantinopoli." *Rivista storica italiana* 83: 264–96.

Barnes, A. 1983. *Jean Le Clerc (1657–1736) et la république des lettres.* Paris: Droz.

Baruzzi, J. 1907. *Leibnitz et l'organisation religeuse de la terre d'après des documents inédits.* Paris: Alcan.

Baschet, A. 1878. *Le duc de Saint-Simon et le card. Gualtiero: Mémoire sur la recherche de leur correspondance (1706–1728).* Paris: N.p.

Beccaria, C. 1965. *Dei delitti e delle pene: Con una raccolta di lettere e documenti relativi alla nascita dell'opera e alla sua fortuna nell'Europa del Settecento.* Ed. F. Venturi. Turin: Einaudi.

Belgioioso, G. 1973. "I discorsi critici filosofici di Paolo Mattia Doria." *Bollettino di storia della filosofia dell'Università degli studi di Lecce* 1: 199–242.

Belgrado, A. M. 1977. *Materialismo e origini della religione nel '700.* Florence: Sansoni.

Benedikt, H. 1927. *Das Königreich Neapel unter Kaiser Karl VI.* Vienna, Leipzig: Manz.

Benzoni, G. 1978. *Gli affanni della cultura: Intellettuali e potere nell'Italia della Controriforma e barocca.* Milan: Feltrinelli.

Berengo, M. 1956. *La società veneziana alla fine del Settecento: Ricerche storiche.* Florence: Sansoni.

———. 1957. "La crisi dell'arte della stampa veneziana alla fine del XVIII secolo." In *Studi in onore di Armando Sapori,* vol. 2, 1321–1338. Milan: Istituto editoriale Cisalpino.

———. 1962. *Giornali veneziani del Settecento.* Milan: Feltrinelli.

Berhté de Besaucèle, L. 1920. *Les cartésiens d'Italie.* Paris: Picard.

Berlin, I. 1975. "The Divorce between the Sciences and the Humanities." In *Giambàttista Vico, Galiani, Joyce, Lévi-Strauss, Piaget,* ed. G. Tagliacozzo, 219–65. Rome: Armando.

Berselli Ambri, P. 1960. *L'ombra di Montesquieu nel Settecento italiano.* Florence: Olschki.

Bertelli, S. 1955. "La crisi dello scetticismo e il rapporto erudizione-scienza agli inizi del secolo XVIII." *Società* 11: 435–56.

———. 1960. *Erudizione e storia in Ludovico Antonio Muratori.* Naples: Istituto italiano per gli studi storici.

———. 1965. Review of the edition of the *Opere di L. A. Muratori,* ed. G. Falco and F. Forti. *Rivista storica italiana* 77: 221–26.

———. 1968. *Giannoniana: Autografi, manoscritti e documenti della fortuna di Pietro Giannone.* Milan, Naples: Ricciardi.

———. 1973. *Ribelli, libertini e ortodossi nella storiografia barocca.* Florence: La Nuova Italia.

———, ed. 1980. *Il libertinismo in Europa.* Naples: Ricciardi.

Bianchini, F. 1823. *La storia universale.* Venice: Battaggia.

Biddle, J. C. 1976. "Locke's Criticism of Innate Principles and Toland's Deism." *Journal of the History of Ideas* 37: 411–22.

Bligny, M. 1973. "Il mito del diluvio universale nella coscienza europea del Settecento." *Rivista storica italiana* 85: 47–63.

Boas, M. 1962. *The Scientific Renaissance, 1450–1630.* New York: Harper & Row, 1962.

Bobbio, N. 1947. *Il diritto naturale nel secolo XVIII.* Turin: Giappichelli.

———. 1965. *Da Hobbes a Marx.* Naples: Morano.

———. 1968. "Sulla nozione di società civile." *De Homine* 25: 19–36.

———. 1977. *Gramsci e la concezione della società civile.* 3d ed. Milan: Feltrinelli.

———. 1980. "Il giusnaturalismo." In *Storia delle idee politiche economiche e sociali,* ed. L. Firpo, vol. 4, 490–551. Turin: UTET.

Boehm, L., and E. Raimondi. 1981. *Università, Accademie e Società scientifiche in Italia e in Germania dal Cinquecento al Settecento.* Bologna: Il Mulino.

Bolgiani, F. 1975. *La formazione del patrimonio d'idee del cristianesimo.* Turin: Giappichelli.

Bonora, E. 1974. "Algarotti, Francesco." *D.B.I.,* vol. 17, 356–60.

Borghero, C., ed. 1974. *La polemica sul lusso nel Settecento francese.* Turin: Einaudi.

Bourne, H. R. F. 1876. *The Life of John Locke.* London: King, 1876. Reprint: Aalen: Scientia-Verlag, 1969.

Braubach, M. 1950. *Geschichte und Abenteuer, Gestalten um den Prinzen Eugen.* Munich: Bruckmann.

Briggs, E. R. 1934. "L'incrédulité et la pensée en France au début du dix-huitième siècle, I. Un magistrat spinoziste et newtonien: M. Pérelle." *Revue d'histoire littéraire de la France* 41: 479–519.

Brunet, P. 1926. *Les physiciens hollandais et la méthode expérimentale en France au XVIIIe siècle.* Paris: Blanchard.

———. 1931a. *L'introduction des théories de Newton en France au XVIIIe siècle avant 1738.* Paris: Blanchard.

————. 1931b. *Les physiciens hollandais et la méthode expérimentale en France au XVIIIᵉ siècle avant 1738.* Paris: Blanchard.

Brusatin, M. 1980. *Venezia nel Settecento: Stato, architettura, territorio.* Turin: Einaudi.

Bury, J. B. 1955. *The Idea of Progress: An Inquiry into Its Origin and Growth.* New York: Dover Publications.

Butterfield, H. 1969. *The Origins of Modern Science, 1300–1800.* New ed. New York: Macmillan.

Cajori, F. 1929. "Sir Isaac Newton's Edition of Varen's Geography." *Mathematic Gazette,* 415–447.

Cantelli, G. 1958. *La disputa Leibniz-Newton sull'analisi.* Turin: Boringhieri.

————. 1969. *Teologia e ateismo: Saggio sul pensiero filosofico e religioso di Pierre Bayle.* Florence: La Nuova Italia.

————. 1971. *Vico e Bayle: Premesse per un confronto.* Naples: Guida.

————. 1972. "Mito e storia in Jean Le Clerc, Tournemine e Fontenelle." *Rivista critica di storia della filosofia* 3: 269–86.

————. 1974. "Nicola Fréret: Tradizione religiosa e allegoria nell'interpretazione dei miti pagani." *Rivista critica di storia della filosofia* 29: part one, fasc. 3, 264–83; part two, fasc. 4, 386–406.

Capra, C. 1979. "Riforme finanziarie e mutamento istituzionale nello Stato di Milano: Gli anni sessanta del secolo XVIII." *Rivista storica italiana* 91: 313–68.

Carabelli, G. 1974. "Comunicazioni." In *Deismo e scienza nell'Inghilterra tra la fine del '600 e l'inizio del '700.* Atti del XXV congresso nazionale di filosofia, vol. 2, 459–65. Rome: S.F.I.

————. 1975. *Tolandiana: Materiali bibliografici per lo studio dell'opera e della' fortuna di John Toland (1670–1722).* Florence: La Nuova Italia.

Caracciolo, A. 1968. *Domenico Passionei tra Roma e la repubblica delle lettere.* Rome: Edizioni di storia e letteratura.

Caravale, M., and A. Caracciolo. 1978. "Lo Stato pontificio da Martino V a Pio IX." In *La storia d'Italia,* ed. G. Galasso, vol. 14. Turin: UTET.

Carini, I. 1891. *L'Arcadia dal 1690 al 1890: Memorie storiche.* Rome: Guggiani.

Carpanetto, D. 1980. *L'Italia del Settecento: Illuminismo e movimento riformatore.* Turin: Loescher.

Carranza, N. 1955–1956. "Prospero Lambertini e Guido Grandi." *Bollettino storico pisano* 24–25, 200–212.

————. 1962. "Averani, Nicola." *D.B.I.,* vol. 4, 658–60.

————. 1974. *Monsignor Gaspare Cerati provveditore dell'università di Pisa nel Settecento delle riforme.* Pisa: Pacini.

Casini, P. 1969. *L'universo-macchina: Origini della filosofia newtoniana.* Bari: Laterza.

————. 1970. "D'Alembert epistemologo." *Rivista critica di storia della filosofia* 1: 26–47.

————. 1978. "Les débuts du newtonianisme en Italie." *Dix-huitième siècle* 10: 85–100.

————. 1980a. *Introduzione all'illuminismo: Scienza miscredenza e politica.* 2 vols. Bari: Laterza.

————. 1980b. "Ottica, astronomia, relatività: Boscovich a Roma. 1738–1748." *Rivista di filosofia* 18: 354–81.

————. 1981. "Newton: Gli scolii classici. Presentazione, testo inedito e note." *Giornale critico della filosofia italiana* 40: 7–53.

Cassirer, E. 1951. *The Philosophy of the Enlightenment.* Trans. F. C. A. Koelin and J. P. Pettegrove. Princeton, NJ: Princeton University Press. Reprint: 1979.

Castelnuovo, G. 1962. *Le origini del calcolo infinitesimale nell'era moderna, con scritti di Newton, Leibniz e Torricelli.* 2d ed. Milan: Feltrinelli.

Castronovo, V., and N. Tranfaglia, eds. 1976. *La stampa italiana dal '500 all '800.* Bari, Rome: Laterza.

Cavazza, M. 1979. "Verso la fondazione dell'Istituto di scienze: filosofia 'libera,' baconismo, religione a Bologna." In Sull'identità del pensiero moderno, 97–147. Florence: La Nuova Italia.

————. 1981. "Accademie scientifiche a Bologna dal 'coro anatomico' agli inquieti (1650–1714)." Quaderni storici 16, no. 48: 894–921.

Caverni, R. 1859. Storia del metodo sperimentale in Italia. Vol. 4, Florence: Civelli.

Cellani, E. 1888. "L'espitolario di monsignor Francesco Bianchini, veronese." Archivio veneto 34: 155–212.

Cessi, R. 1946. Storia della Repubblica di Venezia. Milan, Messina: G. Principato.

Chiosi, E. 1981. Andrea Serrao: Apologia e crisi del regalismo nel Settecento napoletano Naples: Jovene.

Civiltà del '700 a Napoli 1734–1799. 1979. Exhibition Catalogue of Naples. Florence: Centro Di.

Cochrane, E. W. 1961. Tradition and Enlightenment in Tuscan Academies (1690–1800). Rome: Edizioni di Storia e Letteratura.

Codignola, E. 1947. Illuministi, giansenisti e giacobini nell'Italia del Settecento. Florence: La Nuova Italia.

Cohen, I. B. 1956. Franklin and Newton: An Inquiry into Speculative Newtonian Experimental Science and Franklin's Works in Electricity. An Example of Theory. Philadelphia, PA: American Philosophical Society.

————. 1980. The Newtonian Revolution: With Illustrations of the Transformation of Scientific Ideas. Cambridge: Cambridge University Press.

Cohen, I. B., and R. E. Schofield, eds. 1958. Isaac Newton's Papers and Letters on Natural Philosophy and Related Documents. Cambridge, MA: Harvard University Press.

Colapietra, R. 1961. Vita pubblica e classi politiche del viceregno napoletano (1656–1734). Rome: Edizioni di Storia e Letteratura.

Colletti, L. 1980. Tramonto dell'ideologia. Bari: Laterza.

Comparato, V. I. 1970. Giuseppe Valletta. Un intellettuale napoletano alla fine del Seicento. Naples: Istituto italiano per gli studi storici.

————. 1974. "I libertini in Francia e in Europa nel secolo XVII (Florence-Perugia, 23–25 March 1974)." Rivista storica italiana 86: 609–19.

Conti, A. 1972. Scritti filosofici. Ed. N. Badaloni. Naples: Rossi.

Conti, V. 1978. Paolo Mattia Doria: Dalla Repubblica dei togati alla Repubblica dei notabili. Florence: Olschki.

————. 1981. "Le polemiche matematiche di P. M. Doria (con alcune lettere sconosciute)." Bollettino del centro di studi vichiani 11: 185–98.

Corsano, A. 1948. Ugo Grozio: L'umanista, il teologo, il giurista. Bari: Laterza.

————. 1968. "Vico e la tradizione ermetica." In Omaggio a Vico, 9–24. Naples: Morano.

Cossali, P. 1813. Elogio di Giovanni Poleni. Padua: Bellaria.

Costa, G. 1959. La critica omerica di Thomas Blackwell. Florence: Sansoni.

————. 1964. "Un collaboratore del conte di Boulanvilliers: Francesco Maria Pompeo Colonna (1644–1726)." Atti e memorie dell'accademia toscana di scienze e lettere La Colombaria 29: 205–95.

————. 1972. La leggenda dei secoli d'oro nella letteratura italiana. Bari: Laterza.

————. 1976. "Vico e il settecento." Forum italicum 10: 10–30.

————. 1979. "Antonfrancesco Marmi, Claude de Vic e la cultura napoletana." Bollettino del centro di studi vichiani 9: 140–46.

————. 1980. "La cerchia dei duchi di Laurenzano e un collaboratore di Vico." Bollettino del centro di studi vichiani 10: 36–58.

Costantini, C. 1969. Baliani e i gesuiti: Annotazioni in margine alla corrispondenza del Baliani con Gio. Luigi Confalonieri e Orazio Grassi. Florence: Giunti-Barbéra.

Cotugno, R. 1910. Gregorio Caloprese. Trani: Vecchi.

———. 1914. *La sorte di G. B. Vico e le polemiche scientifiche e letterarie dalla fine del XVII secolo alla metà del XVIII secolo.* Bari: Laterza.

Cozzi, G. 1979. *Paolo Sarpi tra Venezia e l'Europa.* Turin: Einaudi.

Crispini, F. 1970. *Metafisica del senso e scienze della vita. Tommaso Cornelio.* Naples: Guida.

Cristofolini, P. 1972 "Buonaventuri, Tommaso." *D.B.I,* vol. 15, 182–83.

———. 1974. "Campailla, Tommaso." *D.B.I.,* vol. 17, 324–28.

Croce, B. 1907. "Per la storia delle matematiche." In *Raccolta di scritti in onore del prof. Giacinto Romano nel suo XXV anno d'insegnamento,* pp. 37ff. Pavia: N.p.

———. 1948. *Bibliografia vichiana accresciuta e rielaborata da F. Nicolini.* Naples: Ricciardi.

———. 1973. *Storia del Regno di Napoli.* 3d ed. Bari: Laterza.

Crucitti-Ullrich, F. B. 1974. *La "Bibliothèque italique," cultura "italianisante" e giornalismo letterario.* Milan, Naples: Ricciardi.

Dal Muratori al Cesarotti: Politici ed economisti del primo Settecento. 1978. Vol. 5. Milan, Naples: Ricciardi.

Dal Pra, M. 1973 *Hume e la scienza della natura umana.* Bari: Laterza.

Dammig, E. 1945. *Il movimento giansenista a Roma nella metà del secolo XVIII.* Vatican City: Biblioteca Apostolica Vaticana.

Danville, L. 1909. *Leibnitz historien.* Paris: Alcan.

Datodi, P. 1974. "G. G. Ciampini e il beato G. M. Tomasi." *Regnum Dei* 30: 207–20.

———. 1976. "Un erudito romano del Seicento: Giovanni Giustino Ciampini." *L'urbe* 2: 9–15.

Daumas, M. 1972. *Scientific Instruments of the Seventeenth and Eighteenth Centuries.* Ed. and trans. M. Holbrook. New York: Praeger Publications.

———, ed. 1957. *Histoire de la science.* Bruges: Libraire Gallimard.

De Blasis, G., ed. 1876. "L'Università di Napoli nel 1714." *Archivio storico per le provincie napoletane* 1: 141–66.

De Daiville, F. 1978. *L'éducation des jésuites (XVIᵉ–XVIIIᵉ siècle): Textes réunis et présentés par Marie Madelaine Compere.* Paris: Editions de Minuit.

De Fabrizio, P., ed. 1981. *Manoscritti napoletani di Paolo Mattia Doria.* Vol. 4, Galatina: Congedo.

De Giovanni, B. 1958. *Filosofia e diritto in F. D'Andrea: Contributo alla storia del previchismo.* Milan: Giuffrè.

———. 1968. "Il *De nostri temporis studiorum ratione* nella cultura napoletana del primo Settecento." In *Omaggio a Vico,* 141–92. Naples: Morano.

———. 1970. "La vita intellettuale a Napoli fra la metà del '600 e la Restaurazione del Regno." In *Storia di Napoli,* vol. 6, tom. 1, 403–42. Naples: ESI.

De Labriole-Rutherford, M. R. 1963. "L'évolution de la notion de luxe depuis Mandeville jusqu'à la Révolution." *Studies on Voltaire* 26: 1025–36.

De Maddalena, A. 1980. "Il mercantilismo." In *Storia delle idee politiche economiche e sociali,* ed. L. Firpo, vol. 4, 637–704. Turin: UTET.

De Maio, R. 1971. *Società e vita religiosa a Napoli nell'età moderna (1656–1799).* Naples: ESI.

———. 1973. *Riforme e miti nella Chiesa del Cinquecento.* Naples: Guida.

———. 1981. "Galileo e la competenza dei teologi." *Il Centauro* 2: 3–11.

De Michelis, F. 1967. *Le origini storiche e culturali del pensiero di Ugo Grozio.* Florence: La Nuova Italia.

De Rosa, L. 1958. *Studi sugli arrendamenti del Regno di Napoli: Aspetti della distribuzione della ricchezza mobiliare nel Mezzogiorno continentale (1649–1806).* Naples: L'Arte tipografica.

De Ruggiero, G. 1972. *L'età dell'Illuminismo.* Bari: Laterza.

Desautels, A. R. 1956. *Les Mémoires de Trévoux et le mouvement des idées au XVIIIᵉ siècle (1701–1734).* Rome: Institutum Historicum S. I.

Descartes, R. 1897–1910. *Oeuvres*. Ed. C. Adam and P. Tannery. Paris: CERF.
De Seta, C. 1981. *Architettura, ambiente e società a Napoli nel '700*. Turin: Einaudi.
De Stefano, A. 1941. "Un processo dell'Inquisizione veneziana contro Michelangelo Fardella." *Siculorum Gymnasium* 1: 135–46.
De Tipaldo, E. 1835. 1845. *Biografia degli italiani illustri*. Vol. 2, 1835, and vol. 10, 1845. Venice: Cecchini.
De Waard, C. 1936. *L'expérience barométrique: Ses antécédents et ses explications. Etude historique*. Thouars: Imp. Nouvelle.
Diaz, F. 1962. *Filosofia e politica nel Settecento francese*. 2d ed. Turin: Einaudi.
———. 1973. *Per una storia illuministica*. Naples: Guida.
Diderot, D. 1961. *De l'interprétation de la nature*. In *Oeuvres philosophiques*, ed. P. Vernière. Paris: Garnier.
Dijksterhuis, E. J. 1986. *The Mechanization of the World Picture: Pythagoras to Newton*. Princeton, NJ: Princeton University Press.
Dini, A. 1979. *Le teorie preadamitiche e il libertinismo di La Peyrère*. Annali dell'Istituto di Filosofia della Facoltà di lettere e filosofia dell'Università di Firenze. Florence: Olschki.
Di Simone, M. R. 1980. *La "Sapienza" romana nel Settecento*. Rome: Edizioni dell'Ateneo.
Di Vittorio, A. 1969a. "L'Austria e il problema monetario e bancario del Viceregno di Napoli (1707–1734)." *Rivista storica italiana* 81: 778–802.
———. 1969b. *Gli austriaci e il Regno di Napoli, 1707–1734. I: Le finanze pubbliche*. Naples: Giannini.
———. 1969c. "Il Banco di San Carlo e il riformismo asburgico." *Rassegna economica* 2: 235–63.
———. 1973. *Gli austriaci e il Regno di Napoli, 1707–1734. II: Ideologia e politica di sviluppo*. Naples: Giannini.
———. 1979. *Il commercio tra Levante ottomano e Napoli nel secolo XVIII*. Naples: Giannini.
Donzelli, M. 1970. *Natura e humanitas nel giovane Vico*. Naples: Istituto italiano per gli studi storici.
Doria, Paolo Mattia. 1973. *Massime generali e particolari con le quali di tempo hanno gli spagnoli governato il Regno di Napoli*. Ed. V. Conti, with an introduction by G. Galasso. Naples: Guida.
———. 1980. *Considerazioni geometriche, logiche e metafisiche sopra li elementi di Euclide*. In *Manoscritti napoletani di Paolo Mattia Doria*, ed. A. Spedicati. Galatina: Congedo.
Dreyer, J. L. E. 1953. *A History of Astronomy from Thales to Kepler*. 2d ed. New York: Dover Publications.
Dugas, R. 1958. *Mechanics in the Seventeenth Century from the Scholastic Antecedents to Classical Thought*. Trans. Freda Jacquot. New York: Central Cook Co.
Dumont, L. 1977. *Homo aequalis: Genèse et épanouissement de l'idéologie économique*. Paris: Gallimard.
Dupront, A. 1930. *Daniel Huet et l'exégèse comparatiste au XVIIIe siècle*. Paris: Beroux.
Ehrard, J. 1964. *L'idée de nature en France dans la première moitié du XIIIe siècle*. 2 vols. Paris: SEVPEN.
Einaudi, L. 1953. "Galiani economista." In *Saggi bibliografici e storici intorno alle dottrine economiche*, 269–305. Rome: Edizioni di storia e letteratura.
Elliot, J. H. 1972. *The Old World and the New, 1492–1650*. Cambridge: Cambridge University Press.
Etiemble, R. 1966. *Les Jésuites et la Chine, la querelle des rites (1552–1773)*. Paris: Juillard.
Evans, R. J. W. 1979. *The Making of the Habsburg Monarchy 1550–1700: An Interpretation*. New York: Oxford University Press.

Falco, G., and F. Forti, eds. *Opere di Ludovico Antonio Muratori*. Milan, Naples: Ricciardi, 1964.

Favaro, A. 1880. *Le aggiunte autografe di Galileo al Dialogo sopra i due massimi sistemi nell'esemplare posseduto dalla biblioteca del seminario di Padova*. Modena: Società tipografica.

——. 1883. *Galileo Galilei e lo studio di Padova*. 2 vols. Florence: Le Monier.

——. 1887. *Miscellanea galileiana inedita: Studi e ricerche*. Venice: Antonelli.

——. 1888. *Per la edizione nazionale delle opere di Galileo Galilei*. Florence: Barbéra.

Feder, J. G. H. 1805. *Commercii epistolici Leibnitiani typis nondum vulgati selecta specimina*. Hanover: Hahn.

Ferrari, L. 1906. "L'epistolario manoscritto del Padre Guido Grandi." *Archivio storico lombardo* 33: 216–42.

Ferrone, V. 1980. "Il dibattito su probabilità e scienze sociali nel secolo XVIII." *Physis* 22: 27–71.

Fiorani, L. 1978. *Il concilio romano del 1725*. Rome: Edizioni di storia e letteratura.

Firpo, M. 1978. "John Toland e il deismo inglese." *Rivista storica italiana* 90: 327–80.

——. 1980. "John Locke e il socinianesimo." *Rivista storica italiana* 92: 34–124.

Fisch, M. H. 1968. "L'Accademia degli Investiganti." *De Homine* 27: 18–78.

Foster, J. 1968. *Alumni Oxonienses*. Liechtenstein: Nelden.

Francovich, C. 1975. *Storia della massoneria italiana dalle origini alla Rivoluzione francese*. 2d ed. Florence: La Nuova Italia. Anastatic reprint, 1989.

——. 1979. "Il problema della massoneria settecentesca." *Rivista storica italiana* 91: 470–76.

Galasso, G. 1970. "Il pensiero religioso di Antonio Genovesi." *Rivista storica italiana* 82: 800–823.

——. 1971. *Dal comune medievale all'unità: Linee di storia meridionale*. Bari: Laterza.

——. 1972. "Il processo agli 'ateisti'." In *Storia di Napoli*, vol. 7, 55–86. Naples: ESI.

——. 1976. "Napoli nel Viceregno spagnolo 1696–1707." In *Storia di Napoli*, vol. 7, 1–346. Naples: ESI.

——. 1977. "Il pensiero economico di Genovesi." In *Nuove idee e nuova arte nel '700 italiano*. Atti dei Convegni Lincei, 336–59. Rome: Accademia nazionale dei Lincei.

Galiani, C. 1982. *Epistola de gravitate et cartesianis vorticibus*. In the appendix to V. Ferrone, "Celestino Galiani e la diffusione del newtonianesimo: Appunti e documenti per una storia della cultura scientifica italiana del primo Settecento." *Giornale critico della filosofia italiana* 61: 1–33.

Galiani, F. 1975. *Opere*. ed. F. Diaz and L. Guerci. Milan-Naples: Ricciardi.

Galilei, G. 1890–1909. *Le opere*. Edizione nazionale, ed. A. Favaro. Florence: Barbèra.

Galluzzi, P. 1974. "Libertà scientifica, educazione e ragion di stato in un polemica pisana del 1670." In *Atti del XXIV congresso nazionale di filosofia, L'Aquila 28 aprile–2 maggio 1973*, vol. 2, 404–12. Rome: S.F.I.

——. 1979. *Momento. Studi galileiani*. Rome: Edizioni dell'Ateneo.

Galluzzi, P., and M. Torrini, eds. 1981. "Accademie scientifiche del '600. Professioni borghesi." *Quaderni storici* 16, no. 48.

Gardair, J. M. 1979. "La naissance des périodiques savants en Italie: Le "Giornale de' Letterati: "de Rome (1668–1681)." *Atti IX Ce.R.D.C.A. 1977–1978*, 317–27. Milan: Cisalpina.

Garibotto, C., ed. 1955. *Epistolario di Scipione Maffei (1700–1750)*. 2 vols. Milan: Giuffrè.

Garin, E. 1934. "Samuel Clarke e il razionalismo inglese del secolo XVII." *Sophia* 2: 106–16, 294–304, 385–462.

——. 1942. *L'illuminismo inglese: I moralisti*. Milan: Bocca.

——. 1950. "Cartesio e l'Italia." *Giornale critico della filosofia italiana* 29: 385–405.

————. 1966. *Storia della filosofia italiana*. 2d ed. Turin: Einaudi.

————. 1970. *Dal rinascimento all'illuminismo*. Pisa: Nistri-Lischi.

————. 1975a. *Rinascite e rivoluzioni: Movimenti culturali dal XIV al XVIII secolo*. Bari: Laterza.

————. 1975b. *Scienza e vita civile nel rinascimento italiano*. Bari: Laterza.

Garms-Cornides, E. 1977. "Zur Geschichte der geistigen Beziehungen zwischen Österreich und Italien im 18. Jahrhundert: Der Abate Biagio Garofalo." *Mitteilungen des Instituts für österreichische Geschichtsforschung* 85: 77–97.

Gay, P. 1966. *The Enlightenment: An Interpretation*. Vol. I: *The Rise of Modern Paganism*. New York: Knopf.

Genovesi, A. 1962. *Autobiografia, lettere e altri scritti*. Ed. G. Savarese. Milan: Feltrinelli.

————. 1973. *Della Diceosina o sia della filosofia del giusto e dell'onesto*. Ed. F. Arata. Milan: Marzorati.

Gentile, G. 1908. *Storia della filosofia italiana dal Genovesi al Galluppi*. Naples: Trani.

Georgelin, J. 1978. *Venise aux siècle des lumières*. Paris: Mouton.

Getto, G. 1946. *La storia delle storie letterarie*. Milan: Bompiani.

Geymonat, L. 1947. *Storia e filosofia dell'analisi infinitesimale*. Turin: Levrotto e Bella.

————. 1969. *Galileo Galilei*. 7th ed. Turin: Einaudi.

Giancotti Boscherini, E. 1963. "Note sulla diffusione della filosofia di Spinoza in Italia." *Giornale critico della filosofia italiana* 42: 339–62.

Giannone, P. 1960. *Vita scritta da lui medesimo*. Ed. S. Bertelli. Milan: Feltrinelli.

————. 1971. *Opere*. Ed. S. Bertelli and G. Ricuperati. Milan, Naples: Ricciardi.

Giarrizzo, G. 1954. *Edward Gibbon e la cultura europea del Settecento*. Naples: Istituto italiano per gli studi storici.

————. 1981. *Vico, la politica e la storia*. Naples: Guida.

Ginzburg, C. 1979. "Spie. Radici di un paradigma indiziario." In *Crisi della ragione*, ed. A. Gargani, 59–106. Turin: Einaudi.

Gisondi, A. 1979–1980. "Marcello Papiniano Cusani (1690–1766): regalismo e riformismo nella sua esperienza civile e pastorale altamurana." *Altamura* 21–22: 88–137.

Giuntella, V. E. 1971. *Roma nel Settecento*. Bologna: Cappelli.

Giuntini, C. 1979. *Panteismo e ideologia repubblicana: John Toland (1670–1722)*. Bologna: Il Mulino.

Giura, V. 1978. *Gli ebrei e la ripresa economica del regno di Napoli 1740–1747*. Geneva: Droz.

Gliozzi, G. 1977. *Adamo e il nuovo mondo: La nascita dell'antropologia come ideologia coloniale: dalle genealogie bibliche alle teorie razziali (1500–1700)*. Florence: La Nuova Italia.

Goldbeck, E. 1897. *Die Gravitationshypothese bei Galilei und Borelli*. Berlin: Gaertner.

Goldman, L. 1967. *L'illuminismo e la società moderna: Storia e funzione attuale dei valori di "libertà," "eguaglianza," "tolleranza."* Turin: Einaudi.

Goretti, M. 1958. *Il paradosso Mandeville: Saggio sulla "favola delle api" col testo inglese a fronte e bibliografia*. Florence: Le Monnier.

Gori, G. 1972. *La fondazione dell'esperienza in 'sGravesande*. Florence: La Nuova Italia.

Graf, A. 1911. *L'anglomania e l'influsso inglese in Italia nel secolo XVIII*. Turin: Loescher.

Gragg, G. R. 1964. *Reason and Authority in the Eighteenth Century*. Cambridge: Cambridge University Press.

Grandler, P. 1977. *The Roman Inquisition and the Venetian Press (1540–1605)*. Princeton, NJ: Princeton University Press.

Grassi Fiorentino, S. 1972. "Ciampini, Giovanni Giustino." *D.B.I.*, vol. 15, 136–43.

Gregory, T. 1961. *Scetticismo ed empirismo: Studio su Gassendi.* Bari: Laterza.

————. 1967. "Studi sull'atomismo nel Seicento." *Giornale critico della filosofia italiana* 46: 528–41.

Greppi, E., and A. Giulini, eds. 1923. *Carteggio di Pietro e Alessandro Verri dal 1766 al 1796.* Vol. 1. Milan: Cogliati.

Gribble, F. 1913. *The Court of Christina of Sweden and the Later Adventures of the Queen in Exile.* London: Nash.

Grimaldi, C. 1964. *Memorie di un anticurialista del Settecento.* Ed. V. I. Comparato. Florence: Olschki.

Groethuysen, B. 1968. *The Bourgeois: Catholicism vs. Capitalism in Eighteenth-Century France.* Trans. M. Ilford. New York: Holt, Rinehart & Winston.

Gronda, G. 1980. "Ceva, Tommaso." *D.B.I.*, vol. 24, 325–28.

Guadagno, V. 1956. *Un illustre avvocato riformatore di Università: Con il parere inedito di Pietro Giannone.* Naples: La Fiaccola.

Guedon, J.-C. 1979. "Chimie et matérialisme: La stratégie anti-newtonienne de Diderot." *Dix-huitième siècle* 11: 185–200.

Guerci, L. 1972. "Aspetti e problemi dell'epistolario di Ferdinando Galiani." *Rivista storica italiana* 84: 80–110.

————. 1978. *Condillac storico: Storia e politica nel "Cours d'études pour l'instruction du Prince de Parme."* Milan, Naples: Ricciardi.

————. 1979a. *Libertà degli antichi e libertà dei moderni: Sparta, Atene e i "philosophes" nella Francia del '700.* Naples: Guida.

————. 1979b. "Note sulla storiografia illuministica." *Il pensiero politico* 12: 246–49.

Guerlac, H. 1963. "Francis Hauksbee: Expérimentateur au profit de Newton." *Archives Internationales d'Histoire des Sciences* 16: 113–28.

Gusdorf, G. 1960. *Introduzione alle scienze.* Bologna: Il Mulino, 1972. French ed.: 1960.

Hagen, J. G. 1910. *La rotation de la terre: Les preuves mécaniques anciennes et nouvelles.* Rome: Tipografia poliglotta Vaticana.

Hall, A. R. 1963. *From Galileo to Newton, 1630–1720.* New York: Harper & Row.

————. 1979. "Galileo nel XVIII secolo." *Rivista di filosofia* 15: 367–90.

Hankins, T. L. 1970. *Jean d'Alembert: Science and Enlightenment.* Oxford: Clarendon Press.

Hazard, P. 1963. *The European Mind, 1680–1715.* Trans. J. L. May. New York: Meridian.

Heckscher, E. F. 1934. *Mercantilism.* London: Allen & Unwin.

Hefelbower, S. G. 1918. *The Relation of John Locke to English Deism.* Chicago: University of Chicago Press.

Hemprich, P. 1915. *Le Journal littéraire de La Haye, 1713–37.* Berlin: Herrman.

Hirschman, A. O. 1977. *The Passions and the Interests: Political Arguments for Capitalism before Its Triumph.* Princeton, NJ: Princeton University Press.

Hiscock, W. G., ed. 1937. *David Gregory, Isaac Newton, and Their Circle: Extract from David Gregory's Memoranda, 1667–1708.* Oxford: Pr. for the editor.

Hoskin, M. A. 1961. "'Mining All Within': Clarke's Notes to Rohault's *Traité de Physique.*" *The Thomist* 24: 353–63.

Immagini del Settecento in Italia. 1980. Bari, Rome: Laterza.

Intellettuali e potere. 1981. In *Storia d'Italia, Annali*, vol. 4, ed. Corrado Vivanti. Turin: Einaudi.

Jacob, M. C. 1976. *The Newtonians and the English Revolution, 1689–1720.* Ithaca, NY: Cornell University Press.

————. 1981. *The Radical Enlightenment: Pantheists, Freemasons, and Republicans.* London: Allen & Unwin.

James, E. D. 1975. "Faith, Sincerity, and Morality: Mandeville and Bayle." In

Mandeville Studies: New Explorations in the Art and Thought of Dr. Bernard Mandeville (1670–1733), ed. I. Primer, 43–65. The Hague: Nijhoff.

Jammer, M. 1957. *Concepts of Force: A Study in the Foundations of Dynamics*. Cambridge, MA: Harvard University Press.

———. 1961. *Concepts of Mass in Classical and Modern Physics*. Cambridge, MA: Harvard University Press.

———. 1969. *Concepts of Space: The History of the Theories of Space in Physics*. 2d ed. Cambridge, MA: Harvard University Press.

Jemolo, A. C. 1965. "Il pensiero religioso di Ludovico Antonio Muratori." In *Scritti vari di storia religiosa e civile*, ed. F. Margiotta Broglio, 139–188. Milan: Giuffrè.

Kauder, E. 1953. "Genesis of the Marginal Utility Theory from Aristotle to the End of the Eighteenth Century." *The Economic Journal* 63: 638–50.

Kirkinen, H. 1960. *Les origines de la conception moderne de l'homme-machine: Le problème de l'âme en France à la fin du règne de Louis XIV (1670–1715)*. Helsinki: N.p.

Kollier, K. B. 1934. *The Cosmogonies of Our Fathers: Some Theories of the 17th and 18th Centuries*. New York: Columbia University Press.

Kors, A. C. 1977. *D'Holbach's Circle: An Enlightenment in Paris*. Princeton, NJ: Princeton University Press.

Koselleck, R. 1988. *Critique and Crisis: Enlightenment and the Pathogenesis of Modern Society*. Cambridge, MA: MIT Press.

Koyré, A. 1957, 1958. *From the Closed World to the Infinite Universe*. Baltimore, MD: Johns Hopkins Press, 1957. New York: Harper, 1958.

———. 1961. *Dal mondo del pressapoco all'universo della precisione. Tecniche, strumenti, e filosofia dal mondo classico alla rivoluzione scientifica*. Turin: Einaudi, 1967. French ed.: 1961.

———. 1965. *Newtonian Studies*. London: Chapman & Hall. Cambridge, MA: Harvard University Press.

———. 1973. *The Astronomical Revolution. Copernicus, Kepler, Borelli*. Trans. R. E. W. Maddison. Paris: Hermann. Ithaca, NY: Cornell University Press.

———. 1978. *Galileo Studies*. Trans. J. Mepham. Hassocks, Eng.: Harvester Press.

Krieger, L. 1965. *The Politics of Discretion: Pufendorf and the Acceptance of Natural Law*. Chicago: University of Chicago Press.

Kurmann, W. 1976. *Presenze italiane nei giornali elvetici del primo Settecento*. Bern: Lang.

L. A. Muratori e la cultura contemporanea. 1975. Atti del convegno internazionale di studi muratoriani (Modena, 1972). 4 vols. Florence: Olschki.

Labrousse, E. 1963. "Obscurantisme et lumière chez Pierre Bayle." *Studies on Voltaire* 26: 1040–81.

———. 1963–1964. *Pierre Bayle*. 2 vols. The Hague: Nijhoff.

Lachterman, D. 1980. "Vico, Doria e la geometria sintetica." *Bollettino del centro di studi vichiano* 10: 10–36.

Landes, D. S. 1969. *The Unbound Prometheus: Technological Change and Industrial Development in Western Europe from 1750 to the Present*. London: Cambridge University Press.

Landucci. S. 1972. *I filosofi e i selvaggi 1580–1780*. Bari: Laterza.

Lane, F. C. 1978. *Storia di Venezia*. Turin: Einaudi.

Lauro, A. 1974. *Il giurisdizionalismo pregiannoniano nel Regno di Napoli: Problemi e bibliografia*. Rome: Edizioni di storia e letteratura.

Le Goff, J. 1980. *Time, Work, and Culture in the Middle Ages*. Trans. A. Goldhammer. Chicago: University of Chicago Press.

Leibniz, G. W. 1860. *Illustratio tentaminis de motuum coelestibus causis*. In *Leibnizens mathematische Schriften*, ed. C. J. Gerhardt, vol. 4, 255–68. The Hague: Schmid.

Lenoble, R. 1943. M. *Mersenne ou la naissance du mécanisme*. Paris: J. Vrin.

———. 1976. *Le origini del pensiero scientifico moderno*. Bari: Laterza, 1976. French ed.: 1976.

Lettere scelte di celebri autori all'abate Antonio Conti pubblicate per le nozze Da Ponte–Di Sergio. 1812. Venice: Fracasso.

Letwin, W. 1965. *The Origins of Scientific Economics*. Garden City, NY: Anchor Books.

Lewis, L. 1960. "Albani, Alessandro." *D.B.I.*, vol. 1, 595–98.

———. 1961. *Connoisseurs and Secret Agents in Eighteenth Century Rome*. London: Chatto & Windus.

Logan, O. 1972. *Culture and Society in Venice, 1470–1790*. London: Tinling & Co.

Loria, G. 1950. *Storia delle matematiche: Dall'alba delle civiltà al secolo XIX*. 2d ed. Milan: Hoepli.

Losacco, M. 1903. "Le dottrine edonistiche italiane del secolo XVIII." *Atti della Reale Accademia di scienze morali e politiche di Napoli* 24: 181–206.

Lovejoy, A. O. 1936. *The Great Chain of Being: A Study of the History of an Idea*. Cambridge, MA: Harvard University Press. Reprint: New York: Harper & Row, 1960.

Lumbroso, G. 1875. "Notizie sulla vita di Cassiano dal Pozzo con alcuni suoi ricordi e una centuria di lettere." *Miscellanea di Storie italiane* 15: 129–238.

Macomber, H. P. 1950. *A Descriptive Catalogue of the Grace K. Babson Collection of the Works of Isaac Newton*. New York: Reichner.

Macry, P. 1974. *Mercato e società nel Regno di Napoli: Commercio del grano e politica economica del '700*. Naples: Guida.

Mamiani, M. 1976. *Isaac Newton filosofo della natura: Le lezioni giovanili di ottica e la genesi del metodo newtoniano*. Florence: La Nuova Italia.

Mandalari, M. 1907. "Quindici lettere del conte Francesco de Aguirre di Salemi." *Archivio storico per la Sicila Orientale* 4: 140–52.

Manuel, F. E. 1959. *The Eighteenth Century Confronts the Gods*. Cambridge, MA: Harvard University Press.

———. 1963. *Isaac Newton, Historian*. Cambridge, MA: Harvard University Press.

———. 1974. *The Religion of Isaac Newton*. Oxford: Clarendon Press.

Marcialis, M. T. 1969. "Note sulla 'Disputatio physico-historica' di Antonio Genovesi." *Annali della facoltà di lettere e filosofia e magistero dell'Università di Cagliari* 32: 301–33.

Margival, H. 1900. *Essai sur Richard Simon et la critique biblique au XVIIᵉ siècle*. Paris: Maillet.

Marini, L. 1953. "Il Mezzogiorno d'Italia di fronte a Vienna e a Roma (1707–1734)." *Annuario dell'Istituto storico italiano per l'età moderna e contemporanea* 5: 3–69.

Marongio, M., ed. 1979. *Manoscritti napoletani di Paolo Mattia Doria*. Vol. 2. Galatina: Congedo.

Masetti-Zanini, G. L. 1967. "I teatini, la nuova scienza e la nuova filosofia in Italia. (Note e ricerche d'archivio)." *Regnum Dei* 23: 3–150.

Mastellone, S. 1965. *Pensiero politico e vita culturale a Napoli nella seconda metà del Seicento*. Messina-Florence: D'Anna.

Maugain, G. 1909. *Etude sur l'évolution intellectuelle de l'Italie de 1657 à 1750 environ*. Paris: Hachette.

Mauzi, R. 1960. *L'idée du bonheur dans la littérature et la pensée françaises au XVIIIᵉ siècle*. Paris: Colin.

Maylender, M. 1926–1930. *Storia delle accademie d'Italia*. Bologna: Cappelli.

McLachlan, H. 1941. *The Religious Opinions of Milton, Locke, and Newton*. Manchester: University of Manchester Press.

Merkle, S. 1909. *Die Katholische Beurteilung des Aufklärungszeitalters*. Berlin: N.p.

Merton, R. K. 1978. *Science, Technology, and Society in Seventeenth-Century England*. Atlantic Highlands, NJ: Humanities Press.

Michieli, A. A. 1942–1943. "Una famiglia di matematici e di poligrafi trevigiani: I Riccati. I. Jacopo Riccati." *Atti del Reale Istituto Veneto di scienze lettere e arti* 102: 535–87.

Middleton, W. E. K. 1975. "Science in Rome, 1675–1700, and the Academia Fisico-matematica of Giovanni Giustino Ciampini." *The British Journal for the History of Science* 8: 138–54.

Minieri Riccio, C. 1979–1980. "Cenno storico sulle accademie fiorite nella città di Napoli." *Archivio storico per le provincie napoletane* 4 (1979): 180–220; and 5 (1980): 349–51.

Mirri, M. 1963. "Considerazioni su moderni e illuministi." *Critica storica* 2: 294–327.

Momigliano, A. 1960. "Gli studi classici di Scipione Maffei." In *Secondo contributo alla storia degli studi classici*, 255–72. Rome: Edizioni di Storia e Letteratura.

Montalto, L. 1962. "Un ateneo internazionale vagheggiato in Roma alla fine del secolo XVII." *Studi romani* 10: 660–72.

Montesquieu, 1950. *Oeuvres complètes*. Vol. 2, Paris: Impr. française de Musique.

Monti, G. M. 1924. *Per la storia dell'Università di Napoli: Ricerche e documenti*. Naples: Perella.

Montucla, J. E. 1802. *Histoire de la mathématique*. Vol. 3. Paris: Agasse.

Moravia, S. 1967. *La scienza della società in Francia alla fine del secolo XVIII*. Florence: Olschki.

Morize, A. 1909. *L'apologie du luxe au XVIIIᵉ siècle et "Le mondain" de Voltaire*. Geneva: Slatkine. Reprint: 1970.

Moschini, G. 1806. *Della letteratura veneziana dal secolo XVIII fino a' nostri giorni*. Vol. 2. Venice: Palese.

Munby, A. N. L. 1952. "The Distribution of the First Edition of Newton's Principia: The Keynes Collection of the Works of Isaac Newton at King's College, Cambridge." *Notes and Records of the Royal Society of London* 10: 28–39.

Muratori, L. A. 1964. *La filosofia morale*. Ed. P. G. Nonis. Rome: Edizioni Paoline.

Natali, G. 1950. *Storia letteraria d'Italia: Il Settecento*. 2 vols. Milan: Vallardi.

Naville, P. 1976. *D'Holbach e la filosofia scientifica del XVIII secolo*. Milan: Feltrinelli.

Negri, A. 1970. *Descartes politico o della ragionevole ideologia*. Milan: Feltrinelli.

Neumann, A. 1935. *The Life of Christina of Sweden*. London: Hutchinson.

Newton and the Enlightenment. 1979. Proceedings of an International Symposium held at Cagliari, 3–5 October 1977. Oxford: Pergamon Press.

Nicolini, F. 1918. "La puerizia e l'adolescenza dell'abate Galiani (1735–1745): Notizie, lettere, versi, documenti." *Archivio storico per le province napoletane* 43: 105–32.

———. 1932. *La giovinezza di G. B. Vico*. Bari: Laterza.

———. 1951. *Un grande educatore italiano, Celestino Galiani*. Naples: Giannini.

O'Higgins, J. 1970. *Anthony Collins: The Man and His Works*. The Hague: Nijhoff.

Osbat, L. 1974. *L'Inquisizione a Napoli: Il processo agli ateisti 1688–1697*, Rome: Edizioni di storia e letteratura.

Pacchi, A. 1973. *Cartesio in Inghilterra: Da More a Boyle*. Bari, Rome: Laterza.

Paganini, G. 1980. *Analisi della fede e critica della ragione nella filosofia di Pierre Bayle*. Florence: La Nuova Italia.

Pala, A. 1953. "Definizione operativa dei concetti di sostanza e di tabula rasa in John Locke." *Annali della facoltà di lettere e filosofia dell'Università di Cagliari* 21, part 2: 221–70.

———. 1969. *Isaac Newton: Scienza e filosofia*. Turin: Einaudi.

Palozzi, R. 1941. "Monsignor Giovanni Bottari e il circolo dei giansenisti romani." *Annali della Scuola Normale Superiore di Pisa* 10: 70–220.

Paoli, A. 1899. "La scuola di Galileo nella storia della filosofia." *Annali università toscane* 22: xciii–xciv.

Papillon, A. M. 1935. "Opera omnia Th. M. Mamachi O.P." *Archivum fratrum praedicatorum* 5: 241–60.

Parise, N. 1972. "Buonarroti, Filippo." *D.B.I.*, vol. 15, 145–47.

Paschini, P. 1960. "La conferenza dei concili a Propaganda Fide." *Rivista di storia della Chiesa in Italia* 14: 371–82.

Passerin d'Antrèves, A. 1962. *La dottrina del diritto naturale.* 2d ed. Milan: Ed. di Comunità.

Pastine, D. 1978. *La nascita dell'idolatria: L'oriente religioso di Athanasius Kircher.* Florence: La Nuova Italia.

———. 1980. "Teocrazia e storia sacra in Kircher e Vico." *Bollettino del centro di studi vichiani* 10: 150–72.

Pastor, L. von. 1941. *The History of the Popes from the Close of the Middle Ages.* Vols. 33 and 34, ed. E. Graf, O.S.B. London: Kegan Paul, Trench, Trubner & Co.

Perini, L. 1981. "Editori e potere dalla fine del secolo XV all'Unità." In *Storia d'Italia*, vol. 4, 810–50. Turin: Einaudi.

Petrucci, A., and G. Pignatelli. 1971. "Bottari, Giovanni." *D.B.I.*, vol. 13, 409–18.

Pietro Giannone e il suo tempo. 1980. Atti del convegno di studi sul tricentenario della nascita. Naples: Jovene.

Pii, E. 1972. "Bayle e la cultura napoletana intorno al 1750." *Il pensiero politico* 5: 320–42.

———. 1979. "Le origini dell'economia 'civile' in Antonio Genovesi." *Il pensiero politico* 12: 334–43.

Pinot, V. 1932. *La Chine et la formation de l'esprit philosophique en France (1640–1740).* Paris: Librairie Orientaliste Paul Gethner.

Pintard, R. 1943. *Le libertinage érudit dans la première moitié du XVII⁰ siècle.* 2 vols. Paris: Boivin. New ed.: Geneva: Slatkine, 1983.

Plongeron, B. 1970. "Question pour L'Aufklärung catholique en Italie." *Il pensiero politico* 3: 30–58.

Pocock, J. G. A. 1975. *The Machiavellian Moment: Florentine Political Thought and the Atlantic Republican Tradition.* 2 vols. Princeton, NJ: Princeton University Press.

Poja, A. [1947]. *La meridiana della chiesa di Santa Maria degli Angeli: Pasqua cristiana e pasqua ebraica.* Rome: N.p.

Pomeau, R. 1956. *La religion de Voltaire.* Paris: Nizet.

Popper, K. R. 1968. *The Logic of Scientific Discovery.* 3d ed., rev. London: Hutchinson.

Praja, S. 1840. *Vita di Domenico Quartieroni.* Rome: N.p.

Prandi, A. 1966. *Religiosità e cultura nel '700 italiano.* Bologna: Il Mulino.

Preti, G. 1935. *Il cristianesimo universale di G. G. Leibniz.* Milan: Bocca.

Quazza, G. 1966. "Bencini, Francesco Domenico." *D.B.I.*, vol. 8, 204–7.

———. 1971. *La decadenza italiana nella storia europea: Saggi sul Sei-Settecento.* 2d ed. Turin: Einaudi.

Quondam, A. 1968. *Cultura e ideologia di Gianvincenzo Gravina.* Milan: Mursia.

———. 1970. "Minima Dandreiana." *Rivista storica italiana* 4: 887–916.

———. 1973a. "Caloprese, Gregorio." *D.B.I.*, vol. 16, 801–5.

———. 1973b. "L'Istituzione Arcadia: Sociologia e ideologia di un'accademia." *Quaderni storici* 8, no. 33: 389–438.

Quondam, A., and M. Rak, eds. 1978. *Lettere dal Regno ad Antonio Magliabecchi.* 2 vols. Naples: Guida.

Raccolta di prose e lettere scritte nel secolo XVIII. 1830. Vol. 2. Milan: Società tipografica dei classici italiani.

Racioppi, G. 1871. *Genovesi Antonio.* Naples: Morano.

Rak, M. 1971. *La parte istorica: Storia della filosofia e libertinismo erudito*. Naples: Guida.

Renazzi, F. M. 1805. *Storia dell'Università degli studi di Roma detta comunemente La Sapienza*. Rome: N.p. Reprint: Bologna: Forni, 1971.

Rhodes, D. E. 1964. "Libri recensiti a Roma, 1668–1681." *Studi Seicenteschi* 5: 151–60.

Ricerche sull'atomismo del Seicento. 1977. Florence: La Nuova Italia.

Ricuperati, G. 1965a. "La difesa dei 'Rerum Italicarum scriptores' di L. A. Muratori in un inedito giannoniano." *Giornale storico della letteratura italiana* 142: 388–417.

———. 1965b. "Alle origini del Triregno: La philosophia adamitico-noetica di A. Costantino." *Rivista storica italiana* 77: 602–38.

———. 1966a. "Giannone e i suoi contemporanei: Lenglet du Fresnoy, Matteo Egizio e Gregorio Grimaldi." In *Miscellanea Walter Maturi*, 55–87. Turin: Giappichelli.

———. 1966b. "L'università di Torino e le polemiche contro i professori in una relazione di parte curialista del 1731." *Bollettino storico-subalpino* 64: 341–74.

———. 1968a. "Bernardo Andrea Lama professore e storiografo nel Piemonte di Vittorio Amedeo II." *Bollettino storico-bibliografico subalpino* 66: 11–101.

———. 1968b. "Studi recenti su Bayle." *Rivista storica italiana* 80: 365–76.

———. 1969. "Alessandro Riccardi e le richieste del 'ceto civile' all'Austria nel 1707." *Rivista storica italiana* 81: 745–77.

———. 1970a. *L'esperienza civile e religiosa di Pietro Giannone*. Milan, Naples: Ricciardi.

———. 1970b. "Studi recenti sul primo '700 italiano: Gianvincenzo Gravina e Antonio Conti." *Rivista storica italiana* 82: 612–42.

———. 1972. "A proposito dell'Accademia Medina Coeli." *Rivista storica italiana* 84: 57–79.

———. 1973. "Pio Nicolò Garelli predecessore del van Swieten nella Hofbibliothek." In *Gerard van Swieten und Seine Zeit*, ed. Erna Lesky and Adam Wandruszka, 137–153. Vienna, Cologne, Graz: Böhlau.

———. 1975. "Ludovico Antonio Muratori e il Piemonte." In *La fortuna di Ludovico Antonio Muratori*, 3–38. Florence: Olschki.

———. 1976. "Napoli e i viceré austriaci (1707–1734)." In *Storia di Napoli*, vol. 4. Naples: ESI.

———. 1979. "A proposito di Paolo Mattia Doria." *Rivista storica italiana*, 91: 261–85.

———. 1981. "Alle origini della storiografia illuminista: Storia sacra e storia profana nell'età della crisi della coscienza europea." In *Il ruolo della storia e degli storici nella civiltà*, Atti del Convegno di Macerata, 11–14 September 1979, 275–386. Messina: La Grafica.

Roger, J. 1963. *Les sciences de la vie dans la pensée française du XVIIIᵉ siècle*. Paris: Colin, 2d ed.: 1971.

Roggero, M. 1981a. "Professori e studenti nelle università tra Cinque e Settecento." In *Storia d'Italia*, Annali, vol. 4, ed. Corrado Vivanti, 1039–81. Turin: Einaudi.

———. 1981b. *Scuole e riforme nello stato sabaudo: L'istruzione secondaria dalla ratio studiorum alle costituzioni del 1772*. Turin: Deputazione subalpina di storia patria.

Romano, R. 1976. *Napoli: Dal Viceregno al Regno. Storia economica*. Turin: Einaudi.

Roncetti, A. 1845. *Lettere inedite scientifico letterarie di Ludovico Antonio Muratori, Vitaliano Donati, Antonio Vallisnieri, e Daniel Le Clerc*. Milan: Silvestri.

Ronchi, V. 1939. *Storia della luce*. Bologna: Zanichelli.

Rosa, M. 1956. "Atteggiamenti culturali e religiosi di Giovanni Lami nelle *Novelle Letterarie*." *Annali della Scuola normale superiore di Pisa* 25: 260–330.

———. 1964. *Dispotismo e libertà nel Settecento: Interpretazioni "repubblicane" di Machiavelli*. Bari: Dedalo.

———. 1966. "Benedetto XIV." *D.B.I.*, vol. 8, 393–408.

———. 1969. *Riformatori e ribelli nel '700 religioso italiano*. Bari: Dedalo.

————. 1974. *Politica e religióne nel '700 europeo*. Florence: Sansoni.

————. ed. 1981a. *Cattolicesimo e lumi nel Settecento italiano*. Rome: Herder.

————. 1981b. "Introduzione all'Aufklärung cattolica in Italia." In *Cattolicesimo e lumi nel Settecento italiano*, ed. M. Rosa, 1–47. Rome: Herder.

Rosenfield, L. C. 1940. *From Beast-Machine to Man-Machine: The Theme of Animal Soul in French Letters from Descartes to La Mettrie*. New York: Oxford University Press.

Rossi, P. 1969. *Le sterminate antichità: Studi vichiani*. Pisa: Nistri-Lischi.

————. 1976. *I filosofi e le macchine (1400–1700)*. 2d ed. Milan: Feltrinelli.

————. 1977. *Immagini della scienza*. Rome: Editori Riuniti.

————. 1978. "Galileo e il libro dei Salmi." *Rivista di filosofia* 69: 45–71.

————. 1979. *I segni del tempo: Storia della terra e storia delle nazioni da Hooke a Vico*. Milan: Feltrinelli.

Rosso, C. 1954. *Moralisti del "Bonheur."* Turin: Edizioni di Filosofia.

Rothkrug, L. 1965. *Opposition to Louis XIV: The Political and Social Origins of the French Enlightenment*. Princeton, NJ: Princeton University Press.

Rotondó, A. 1973. "La censura ecclesiastica e la cultura." In *Storia d'Italia*, vol. 5, ed. Ruggiero Romano and Corrado Vivanti, 1399–1449. Turin: Einaudi.

Rotta, S. 1961. "Idee di riforma nella Genova settecentesca e la diffusione del pensiero di Montesquieu." *Il movimento operaio e socialista in Liguria* 7: 205–84.

————. 1968a. "Bianchini, Francesco." *D.B.I.*, vol. 10, 187–94.

————. 1968b. "Sulla costruzione e diffusione in Italia dei telescopi a riflessione." *Le macchine* 1: 87–90.

————. 1970. "Voltaire in Italia: Note sulle traduzioni settecentesche delle opere voltairiane." *Annali della Scuola normale superiore di Pisa* 39: 387–444.

————. 1971. *Scienza e pubblica felicità in Geminiano Montanari*. In *Miscellanea Seicento*, 65–208. Florence: Le Monnier.

————. 1974. *Il pensiero politico francese da Bayle a Montesquieu*. Pisa: Pacini.

Rovito, P. 1982. *Respublica dei togati. Giuristi e società nella Napoli del Seicento*. Naples: Jovene.

Rucellai, O. 1862. *Saggio di lettere d' Orazio Rucellai e di testimonianze autorevoli in lode e difesa dell'Accademia della Crusca*. Florence: Magheri.

Ruestow, E. G. 1973. *Physics at Seventeenth and Eighteenth Century Leiden*. The Hague: Nijhoff.

Saccenti, M. 1966. *Lucrezio in Toscana: Studio su Alessandro Marchetti*. Florence: Olschki.

Saggi e ricerche sul Settecento. 1968. Naples: Istituto italiano per gli studi storici.

Salvatorelli, L. 1975. *Il pensiero politico italiano dal 1700 al 1870*. 7th ed. Turin: Einaudi.

Santucci, A. 1953. "Il problema della conoscenza nella filosofia dell'abate Antonio Genovesi." *Il Mulino* 25–26: 681–710.

————. ed. 1979. *Interpretazioni dell'Illuminismo*. Bologna: Il Mulino.

Savelli, R. 1961. "L'opera biologica di Antonio Vallisnieri." *Physis* 3: 269–308.

Sbigoli, F. 1884. *Tommaso Crudeli e i primi framassoni in Firenze*. Milan: Battezzati.

Schipa, M. 1898. "Problemi napoletani al principio del secolo XVIII. notizie storiche (1701–1713)." *Atti Accademia pontaniana* 28: 25–32.

————. 1904. *Il Regno di Napoli al tempo di Carlo di Borbone*. Naples: Pierro.

————. 1924. "Il secolo decimottavo." In *Storia dell'università di Napoli*, 22–40. Naples: Ricciardi.

Schneider, G. 1970. *Der Libertin, zur Geistes- und Sozialgeschichte des Bürgertums im 16. und 17. Jahrhundert*. Stuttgart: J. B. Metzler.

Scienza e tecnica nella cultura e nella società dal Rinascimento a oggi. 1980. In *Storia d'Italia, Annali*, vol. 3, ed. Gianni Micheli. Turin: Einaudi.

Scribano, M. 1980. *Natura umana e società competitiva: Studio su Mandeville*. Milan: Feltrinelli.

La scuola galileiana: Prospettive di ricerca. 1979. Atti del convegno di studi di Santa Margherita Ligure (26–28 October 1978). Florence: La Nuova Italia.

Serini, P. 1942. *Pascal*. Turin: Einaudi.

Sestan, E. 1955. "Il riformismo settecentesco in Italia. Orientamenti politici generali." *Rassegna storica toscana* 1: 19–37.

Setti, E. 1806. *Elogio storico di Monsignor Antonio Leprotti*. Carpi: Stamperia municipale.

Shackleton, R. 1961. *Montesquieu: A Critical Biography*. Oxford: Oxford University Press.

Simon, R. [1939]. *Henry de Boulanvilliers: Historien, politique, philosophe, astrologue 1658–1722*. Paris: Boivin.

———. 1961. "Nicolas Fréret académicien." *Studies on Voltaire* 17: 52–64.

Sina, M. 1978. *Vico e Le Clerc fra filosofia e filologia*. Naples: Guida.

Solinas, G. 1967. *Il microscopio e le metafisiche: Epigenesi e preesistenza da Cartesio a Kant*. Milan: Feltrinelli.

———, ed. 1973. *Saggi sull'Illuminismo*. Cagliari: Istituto di filosofia.

Spallanzani, M. F. 1977. "Esperienza e natura in Antonio Vallisnieri." *Contributi* 1: 5–36.

Spini. G. 1950. *Ricerca dei libertini: La teoria dell'impostura delle religioni nel Seicento italiano*. Rome: Universale di Roma.

Spink, J. S. 1960. *French Free-Thought from Gassendi to Voltaire*. London: Athlone Press.

Spinoza, B. 1924. *Tractatus theologico-politicus*. In *Opere*, ed. Carl Gebhardt, vol. 3. Heidelberg: Winter.

Sposato, P. 1960. *Le lettere provinciali di Biagio Pascal e la loro diffusione a Napoli durante la rivoluzione intellettuale della seconda metà del secolo XVII*. Tivoli: Chicca.

Staum, M. 1968. "Newton and Voltaire: Constructive Skceptics." *Studies on Voltaire* 62: 29–56.

Stephen, L. 1876. *History of English Thought in the Eighteenth Century*. London: Elder.

Suppa, S. 1971. *L'Accademia di Medinacoeli: Fra tradizione investigante e nuova scienza civile*. Naples: Istituto italiano per gli studi storici.

Tarello, G., ed. 1971. *Materiali per una storia giuridica*. Vol. 1. Bologna: Il Mulino.

Taton, R., ed. 1964–1966. *History of Science*. 4 vols. Trans. A. J. Pomerans. New York: Basic Books.

Tega, W. 1975. "Il newtonianesimo dei philosophes." *Rivista di Filosofia* 3: 369–407.

Tenca, L. 1953–1954. "Otto lettere inedite dell'abate Antonio Conti." *Atti dell'Istituto veneto di scienze, lettere ed arti* 112: 101–42.

———. 1960. "Guido Grandi matematico e teologo del granduca di Toscana." *Physis* 2, fasc. 1: 84–96.

Thompson, E. P. 1981. *Società patrizia cultura plebea: Otto saggi di antropologia storica sull'Inghilterra del Settecento*. Turin: Einaudi.

Todhunter, I. 1865. *History of the Mathematical Theory of Probability from the Time of Pascal to That of Laplace*. Cambridge, London: Macmillan.

Torcellan, G. 1963. "Un economista settecentesco: Giammaria Ortes." *Rivista storica italiana* 75: 728–77.

———. 1969. *Settecento veneto*. Turin: Ciappichelli.

Torrey, N. L. 1963. *Voltaire and the English Deists*. Oxford: Marston.

Torrini, M. 1973. "Giuseppe Ferroni gesuita e galileiano." *Physis* 15: 411–23.

———. 1977. *Tommaso Cornelio e la ricostruzione della scienza*. Naples: Guida.

———. 1978. "Il problema del rapporto scienza-filosofia nel pensiero del primo Vico." *Physis* 20: 104–21.

————. 1979a. "Cinque lettere di Lucantonio Porzio in difesa della moderna filosofia." *Atti dell'accademia di scienze morali e politiche* 90: 143–71.

————. 1979b. *Dopo Galileo: Una polemica scientifica (1684–1711).* Florence: Olschki.

————. 1981. "L'accademia degli Investiganti: Napoli 1663–1670." *Quaderni storici* 16, no. 48: 845–83.

Trevor-Roper, H. R. 1967. *Religion, the Reformation and Social Change, and Other Essays.* London, Melbourne: Macmillan.

Turnbull, H. W., ed. 1967. *The Correspondence of Isaac Newton.* Vol 4. Cambridge: Royal Society at University Press.

Ughi, L. 1804. *Dizionario storico degli uomini illustri ferraresi.* Vol. 2. Ferrara: Rinaldi.

Les Universités européennes du XIVᵉ au XVIIIᵉ siècle. 1967. Geneva: Droz.

Ussia, S. 1977. *L'epistolario di Matteo Egizio e la cultura napoletana del primo Settecento.* Naples: Liguori.

Vartanian, A. 1953. *Diderot and Descartes: A Study of Scientific Naturalism in the Enlightenment.* Princeton, NJ: Princeton University Press.

Vasoli. C. 1970. "L'abate Gimma e la *Nova encyclopedia* (cabalismo, lullismo, magia e 'nuova scienza' in un testo alla fine del Seicento)." In *Studi in onore di Antonio Corsano,* 789–827. Manduria: Lacaita.

————, ed. 1976. *Magia e scienza nella civiltà umanistica.* Bologna: Il Mulino.

Vecchi, A. 1951. "Il Muratori e la filosofia del suo tempo." In *Miscellanea di studi muratoriani,* 315–332. Modena: Aedes muratoriana.

————. 1955. *L'opera religiosa del Muratori.* Modena: Edizioni Paoline.

————. 1962. *Correnti religiose nel Sei-Settecento veneto.* Venice, Rome: Istituto per la collaborazione culturale.

Venturi, F. 1954. *Saggi sull'Europa illuminista. 1. Alberto Radicati di Passerano.* Turin: Einaudi.

————, ed. 1958. *Illuministi Italiani.* Vol. 3 of *Riformatori lombardi, piemontesi e toscani.* Milan, Naples: Ricciardi.

————. 1959a. "Contributi ad un dizionario storico: Was ist Aufklärung? Sapere aude." *Rivista storica italiana* 71: 118–30.

————. 1959b. "Alle origini dell'illuminismo napoletano: Dal carteggio di Bartolomeo Intieri." *Rivista storica italiana* 71: 416–456.

————. 1962. "Nota introduttiva" to *Illuministi italiani. Riformatori napoletani.* Milan, Naples: Ricciardi.

————. 1966. "Nota introduttiva" to "Antonio Genovesi." In *Illuministi italiani. V. Riformatori napoletani,* ed. Franco Venturi, 3–46. Milan, Naples: Ricciardi.

————. 1967. "Broggia e Vico." In *The Age of Enlightenment: Studies Presented to Theodore Besterman,* ed. W. H. Barber et al., 298–307. Edinburgh: Oliver and Boyd.

————. 1968. "Tre note su Carlantonio Broggia." *Rivista storica italiana* 80: 830–53.

————. 1969. *Settecento riformatore.* Vol. 1 of *Da Muratori a Beccaria.* Turin: Einaudi.

————. 1970. *Le origini dell'Enciclopedia.* 2d ed. Turin: Einaudi.

————. 1971. *Utopia and Reform in the Enlightenment.* Cambridge: Cambridge University Press.

————. 1973. "L'Italia fuori d'Italia." In *Storia d'Italia,* vol. 3, ed. Ruggiero Romano and Corrado Vivanti, 986–97. Turin: Einaudi.

Vernière, P. 1954. *Spinoza et la pensée française avant la Révolution.* 2 vols. Paris: PUF.

————. 1977. *Montesquieu et l'Esprit des lois ou la raison impure.* Paris: Société d'édition d'enseignement supérieur.

Viano, C. A. 1960. *John Locke, Dal razionalismo all'illuminismo.* Turin: Einaudi.

Vico, G. B. 1931. *Scienza nuova prima.* Ed. F. Nicolini. Bari: Laterza.

————. 1953. *Orazioni inaugurali,* (1699–1707); *De nostri temporis studiorum ratione,*

(1708); *De antiquissima Italorum sapientia*, (1710). All in *Opere di Giambattista Vico*, ed. F. Nicolini. Milan, Naples: Ricciardi.

————. 1970. *Autobiografia*. Ed. M. Fubini. Turin: Einaudi.

————. 1971. *Opere filosofiche*. Ed P. Cristofolini, with an Introduction by N. Badaloni. Florence: Sansoni.

Vidal, E. 1953. *Il pensiero civile di Paolo Mattia Doria negli scritti inediti: Con il testo del manoscritto "Del commercio del Regno di Napoli"*. Milan: Giuffrè.

Villani, P. 1964. "Illuminismo e riforme nel Settecento napoletano." *Critica storica* 3: 64–90.

————. 1967. *Mezzogiorno tra riforma e rivoluzione*. 3d ed. Bari: Laterza.

————. 1968. *Feudalità, riforme, capitalismo agrario*. Bari: Laterza.

Villari, L. 1958. *Il pensiero economico di Antonio Genovesi*. Florence: Le Monnier.

————. 1964. "Aspetti e problemi della dominazione asburgica sul Regno di Napoli." *Annali della scuola speciale per archivisti e bibliotecari dell'università di Roma* 4: 46–80.

Villari, R. 1967. *La rivolta antispagnola a Napoli*. Bari: Laterza.

————. 1970. "Antonio Genovesi e la ricerca delle force motrici dello sviluppo sociale." *Studi storici* 11: 26–52.

Voeltzel, R. 1968. "Jean Le Clerc (1657–1736) et la critique biblique." In *Religion, érudition et critique à la fin du XVIIe siècle et au debut du XVIIIe siècle*. 30–45. Paris: PUF.

Voltaire, 1819. *Le siècle de Louis XIV*. In *Oeuvres complètes*, vol. 2. Paris; Renouard.

Wade, I. O. 1938. *The Clandestine Organization and Diffusion of Philosophical Ideas in France from 1700 to 1750*. Princeton, NJ: Princeton University Press.

Walker, D. P. 1958. *Spiritual and Demonic Magic from Ficino to Campanella*. London: Warburg Institute.

Webster, C. 1975. *The Great Insaturation: Science, Medicine, and Reform, 1626–1660*. London: Duckworth. New York: Holmes & Meier Publishers, 1976.

Westfall, R. S. 1971. *Force in Newton's Physics: The Science of Dynamics in the Seventeenth Century*. London: MacDonald and Co. New York: Elsevier.

Willey, B. 1975. *La cultura inglese del Seicento e del Settecento*. Bologna: Il Mulino. A translation of two works in English: *The Seventeenth Century Background: Studies in the Thought of the Age in Relation to Poetry and Religion* (London: Chatto and Windus, 1934); and *The Eighteenth Century Background: Studies on the Idea of Nature in the Thought of the Period* (London: Chatto and Windus, 1940).

Woolf, S. J. 1973. "La storia politica e sociale." In *Dal primo Settecento all'unità*, Vol. 3 of *Storia d'Italia*, ed. Ruggiero Romano and Corrado Vivanti. Turin: Einaudi.

Yates, F. A. 1964. *Giordano Bruno and the Hermetic Tradition*. London: Routledge & Kegan Paul.

————. 1972. *The Rosicrucian Enlightenment*. London: Routledge & Kegan Paul.

Zambelli, P. 1972. *La formazione filosofica di Antonio Genovesi*. Naples: Morano.

————. 1973a. "Un epigono degli investiganti, amico e 'supplente' del Vico: Il medico Serao." *Bollettino del centro di studi vichiani* 3; 132–46.

————, ed. 1973b. *Ricerche sulla cultura dell'Italia moderna*. Bari, Rome: Laterza.

————. 1977. "Prime iniziative di un cappellano maggiore: Una lettera inedita di Celestino Galiani." *Bollettino del centro di studi vichiani* 7: 113–21.

Zangari, D. 1922. *Gaetano Argento: Presidente del Sacro Regio Consiglio (1661–1730)*. Naples: Editrice "La cultura calabrese."

Zoli, S. 1972. "Le polemiche sulla Cina nella cultura storica, filosofica e letteraria italiana della prima metà del Settecento." *Archivio storico italiano* 130: 409–67.

Bibliographic Update

On the occasion of the American edition, it seemed useful to note the publication of new works that have appeared since 1982 pertaining to the themes dealt with in this book.

Biagi, M. L., and B. Basile, eds. 1983. *Scienziati del Settecento.* Milan, Naples: Ricciardi.

Carpanetto, D., and G. Ricuperati. 1987. *Italy in the Age of Reason: 1685–1789.* Trans. C. Higgitt. London, New York: Longman.

Casini, P. 1983. *Newton e la coscienza europea.* Bologna: Il Mulino.

Cremante, R., and W. Tega, eds. 1984. *Scienza e letteratura nella cultura italiana del Settecento.* Bologna: Il Mulino.

Dini, A. 1985. *Filosofia della natura, medicina, religione: L. A. Porzio (1639–1724).* Milan: Angeli.

Dooley, B. 1991. *Science, Politics, and Society in Eighteenth-Century Italy: The Giornali de' letterati d'Italia and its World.* New York, London: Garland Publishing.

Gardair, J.-M. 1984. *Le "Giornale de' letterati" de Rome (1668–1681).* Florence: Olschiki.

Generali, D., and M. De Zan. 1985. "Sulla diffusione del newtonianesimo in Italia: 'Scienza Natura Religione' di Vincenzo Ferrone." *Società e storia* 8: 936–46.

Manzoni, C. 1992. *Il "cattolicesimo illuminato" in Italia tra cartesianismo, leibnizismo e newtonianismo-lockismo nel primo Settecento (1700–1750): Note di ricerca sulla recente storiografia.* Trieste: Edizioni Lint.

Predeval Magrini, M. V., ed. 1990. *Scienza, filosofia e religione tra '600 e '700 in Italia.* Milan: Angeli.

Waquet, F. 1989. *Le modèle française et l'Italie savante: Conscience de soi et perception de l'autre dans la République des lettres (1660–1750).* Rome: Ecole Française de Rome.

Index of Names

Because they are so frequently mentioned in the text, Isaac Newton, and Celestino Galiani are not included in this index.

Abraham, 155, 165
Acquaviva, Francesco (cardinal), 205
Adam, 3, 108, 110, 153, 157, 169, 190–91
Adami, Raimondo, 272
Agrippa, Cornelio, 188
Aguirre, Francesco d', 166, 205, 334n. 16, 341n. 78
Albani, Alessandro (cardinal), 11, 30, 73
Albani, Annibale (cardinal), 147
Aletino. See De Benedictis, Giovanni Battista
Alexander VI (pope), 284n. 69
Algarotti, Francesco, 13, 41, 96–97, 262
Alnano Meleo. See Clement XI (pope)
Althann, Michael Fredrich von (cardinal and viceroy of Naples), 195–197
Anaxagoras, 21
Anaximander, 67
Anaximenes of Miletus, 21
Arbuthnot, John, 23, 82
Archelaus of Athens, 21
Argento, Gaetano, 195, 209, 221
Argeste, Melichio. See Newton, Henry
Ariani, Agostino, 15, 184, 185, 186, 188, 199, 210, 215
Ariani, Vincenzo, 283n. 58
Aristotle, 44, 58, 83, 85, 98, 198, 209, 306n. 10
Aspro. See Buonaventuri, Tommaso
Astalli, Fulvio (cardinal), 317n. 6
Augustine, Saint, 110, 125, 240, 324n. 39, 341n. 3
Aulisio, Domenico, 119, 279n. 9, 323n. 32
Averani, Benedetto, 9, 50, 66
Averani, Giuseppe, 6, 9, 10, 39, 43, 50, 81, 267
Averani, Nicola, 300n. 17
Azoni Avogaro, Rambaldo degli (canon), 316n. 41

Bacchini, Benedetto, 50, 136
Bacon, Francis, 190, 194, 236, 254
Baglivi, Giorgio, 6, 189
Baillet, Adrien, 187, 293n. 11
Baldigiani, Antonio, 4, 49
Baldini, Giovanni Antonio (count), 22, 23, 302n. 18
Banchieri, Antonio (cardinal), 196, 202, 340n. 53
Barberini, Carlo (cardinal), 3
Barbeyrac, Jean, 168
Bargellini, Piergerolamo, 9, 33, 63, 124, 287n. 17, 296n. 29
Baroni, Giovambattista, 134, 135, 282n. 33, 302n. 15, 304n. 5, 316n. 18
Bayle, Pierre, 66–67, 74, 133, 144, 157, 160, 169–70, 175, 191, 228, 240, 243–44, 247, 253, 258, 276, 312n. 2, 321–22n. 25, 345n. 32, 354n. 85
Beccari, Jacopo Bartolomeo, 81, 263
Bellarmino, Roberto (cardinal). See Roberto Bellarmino, Saint
Belli, Filippo, 2
Bellini, Lorenzo, 101, 306n. 10
Bencini, Domenico, 145–49, 151, 322n. 15, n. 16, 324n. 35
Benedict XIV (pope), 226, 263, 293n. 15, 297n. 10, 318n. 8, 333n. 21
Benimeli, José Antonio, 356n. 27
Bentley, Richard, 63, 67, 75, 77, 84, 265, 272
Berkeley, George, 67, 74
Bernegger, Mattia, 298n. 19
Bernoulli, Johann, 94, 98, 111, 112, 288n. 26
Bernoulli, Nicolas, 94, 288n. 26
Berti, Alessandro, 334n. 17
Berti, Gaspare, 280n. 12
Bianchi, Giovanni, 129, 203, 333n. 17
Bianchini, Francesco, 5–6, 8, 10, 12, 14, 16, 17, 18, 22–24, 30–32, 36, 39, 63, 66, 73, 94, 125, 126, 132,